CAMBRIDGE MUSICAL TEXTS AND MONOGRAPHS

General Editors: Howard Mayer Brown, Peter le Huray, John Stevens

THE MAKING OF THE VICTORIAN ORGAN

CAMBRIDGE MUSICAL TEXTS AND MONOGRAPHS

General Editors: Howard Mayer Brown, Peter le Huray, John Stevens

The series Cambridge Musical Texts and Monographs has as its centres of interest the history of performance and the history of instruments. It includes annotated translations of important historical documents, authentic historical texts on music, and monographs on various aspects of historical performance.

Published

Ian Woodfield *The Early History of the Viol*

Rebecca Harris-Warrick (trans. and ed.) *Principles of the Harpsichord by Monsieur de Saint Lambert*

Robin Stowell *Violin Technique and Performance Practice in the Late Eighteenth and Early Nineteenth Centuries*

Vincent J. Panetta (trans. and ed.) *Treatise on Harpsichord Tuning by Jean Denis*

John Butt *Bach Interpretation*

Grant O'Brien *Ruckers. A Harpsichord and Virginal Building Tradition*

Frontispiece, William Hill (1789–1870)

THE MAKING OF THE
VICTORIAN ORGAN

NICHOLAS THISTLETHWAITE

Fellow, Tutor and Chaplain
Gonville and Caius College Cambridge

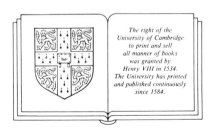

The right of the
University of Cambridge
to print and sell
all manner of books
was granted by
Henry VIII in 1534.
The University has printed
and published continuously
since 1584.

CAMBRIDGE UNIVERSITY PRESS

Cambridge
New York   Port Chester
Melbourne   Sydney

Published by the Press Syndicate of the University of Cambridge
The Pitt Building, Trumpington Street, Cambridge CB2 1RP
40 West 20th Street, New York, NY 10011, USA
10 Stamford Road, Oakleigh, Melbourne 3166, Australia

First published 1990

Printed in Great Britain at the University Press, Cambridge

British Library cataloguing in publication data

Thistlethwaite, N. J.
The making of the Victorian organ. – (Cambridge musical
texts and monographs).
1. Great Britain. Musical instruments: Pipe organs,
history
1. Title
786.6'241

Library of Congress cataloguing in publication data

Thistlethwaite, Nicholas.
The making of the Victorian organ / Nicholas Thistlethwaite.
    p.   cm. – (Cambridge musical texts and monographs)
Includes bibliographical references.
ISBN 0–521–34345–3
1. Organs – England.   2. Organ – Construction.   3. Organ-builders –
England.   4. Organ music – England – 19th century – History and
criticism.   I. Title.   II. Series.
ML578.T5   1990
786.5'1942'09034 – dc20   89-71280   CIP

ISBN 0 521 34345 3

FP

To Tessa and Peter,
without whose understanding
this could not have been written

Contents

Contents

Illustrations

FIGURES

TABLES

Preface

Two publications provided the starting point for the present work. There was, on the one hand, C. W. Pearce's *Notes on English organs* (1912) which, together with the earlier *Notes on old London city churches, their organs, organists, and musical associations* (1909) represented a partial transcription of Henry Leffler's manuscript collection of organ specifications compiled between 1800 and 1819. The instruments he described possessed strong family likenesses. Few had more than twenty stops, the specifications were repetitious and the keyboard compasses invariably began at GG or FF. Pedals were seldom mentioned, pedal pipes almost never. Noting the dates of the various instruments (some of them apparently untouched since the late-seventeenth century) one was left with an impression of deep conservatism, even of stagnation. Subsequent research has modified this view, but the initial reaction was significant. Then, turning to a second volume, the prospect was transformed. Hopkins & Rimbault's *The organ, its history and construction* was published thirty-six years after Leffler's death (1855). Its appendix of specifications is a record of dramatic change. True, there are still many older instruments with long compasses and limited pedal arrangements, still plenty of sesquialteras and cornets, but the catalogue of English organs includes a large number of instruments utterly unlike any noted by Leffler earlier in the century. There is one organ with 100 stops and many with thirty-five or more. Most of the instruments by builders like Hill and Gray & Davison have C-compasses and ambitious Pedal divisions strongly reminiscent of other parts of northern Europe. The variety of stops has increased enormously: novel strings, flutes and reeds abound. Swell divisions have expanded and there are even a few references to the use of pneumatics to assist the organ's action. A transformation has taken place: one that is totally unexpected after the comfortable, slightly musty predictability of Leffler's record.

What follows is an attempt to understand the reasons for this transformation and to describe its character. Some may object that the title is misleading: the period under review (1820–70) is scarcely coterminus with the reign of Queen Victoria (1837–1901). It is, though, the author's belief that just as the adjective 'Victorian' is useful in other spheres to define a distinct school or type (Victorian architecture, the Victorian novel) it may appropriately be attached to a distinct approach to organ design which flourished in the nineteenth century and which had effectively come to maturity by about 1870 when most builders had shed the remaining vestiges of an eighteenth-century technology and tonal ethos, and adopted in their place methods and principles more in keeping with the new era. The intention was not to write a history of the Victorian organ but rather to study the origins of a style.

A further justification for this approach is the fact that the period 1820 to 1870 effectively embraces the working life of the man who probably made the greatest contribution to the transformation of the English organ during the nineteenth century, William Hill (1789–1870). His work will prove to be a thread running through the somewhat diffuse narrative that follows, and will, it is hoped, impart a coherence which it might otherwise be felt to lack.

It is more difficult to put up a defence against a second criticism which might be levelled at this book's title. The 'making' of the Victorian organ is bound to arouse expectations of a detailed technical study of the instrument's manufacture. The text includes much information about the construction of organs during the nineteenth century, as well as diagrams illustrating their layout and tables recording selective (highly selective) scalings, but it would not claim to be a technical study in the sense of, say, David Wickens's excellent monograph on Samuel Green (1987). There are various reasons for this. One is sheer lack of space. In a book endeavouring to give an overview of English organ-building during the most innovative fifty years in its history there simply is no room for definitive technical studies of individual builders or particular instruments. There is, though, another difficulty. Of the 180 British organs whose stop lists are recorded in the appendix to the third edition of Hopkins & Rimbault (1877) only five have survived to the present day without major alteration; another dozen or so remain in an altered but still recognisable state. The rate of destruction has been deplorable. Sometimes the losses were unavoidable: fire, for example, has taken its toll. The advent of new forms of action, at the end of the last century and the beginning of the present one, promoted the reconstruction of existing organs at a time when the Victorian organ was at its most unfashionable. But much of the destruction is more recent. The redundancy of many large Victorian churches has posed the often insuperable difficulty of finding homes for their large Victorian organs. Indifference led first to vandalism and then to the total destruction of Hill's organ of 1841 in the Great George Street Chapel, Liverpool, and although this highlighted the problem, there have been many losses since: Hill organs at St Stephen's, Lambeth (1861) and St Mary's, Hulme (1858), the 4-manual Willis in St Peter's, Blackburn (1872). All too often losses have been the result of ignorance or philistinism.

The re-ordering of churches has not infrequently led to applications to remove organs in order to make way for something useful like a coffee bar. And then, those who should be the organ's protectors are sometimes its worst enemies. Despite the best endeavours of (some) diocesan organ advisers, and the work of bodies such as the British Institute of Organ Studies, there are still organists who are not content to preserve an historic instrument as they find it and organ-builders who are only too ready to indulge their whims. A blight of balanced swell pedals, electro-pneumatic actions, detached consoles and neo-classical upperwork has made deep inroads into the surviving stock of nineteenth-century organs during the last forty years. As a consequence, our heritage is impoverished and the number of organs available for study is sadly depleted. If the present work only succeeds in increasing awareness of the value of these instruments, it will have served some purpose.

In acknowledging the many debts that I have incurred in the course of my research I must first express my thanks to all those organists, clergy and custodians of organs who have responded willingly to my requests for access to the instruments in their charge. In fifteen years I have encountered only one absolute refusal and have generally met with nothing but kindness and cooperation.

Another general acknowledgement is to the staff of the various libraries and record offices in which I have worked; I am grateful for their help, and for permission to quote from the manuscripts in their care. I would like though to record the particular assistance I have received from the British Organ Archive (Birmingham Central Library), Hereford Cathedral Library (Miss P. Morgan), the Royal College of Music, the Royal College of Organists (Mr Barry Lyndon) and the University Library, Cambridge.

This work began life as a doctoral dissertation. I was greatly encouraged at that time by Peter le Huray and Peter Williams (a constant source of inspiration in matters of organ history). My supervisor, George Guest, was tireless in writing to support my requests for access to particular instruments and I remain grateful for his interest and help.

Three special debts must now be acknowledged. The Reverend B. B. Edmonds possesses an apparently inexhaustible fund of knowledge concerning English organs and organ-builders. He has been generous beyond belief in making available the results of his own work on William Hill and in passing on information and hints which have proved of the greatest value. He was probably the first to appreciate the musical importance of the organs built during the Hill–Gauntlett collaboration, and if more of us have now come to recognise their qualities, and if, indeed, there is even a certain fashion for praising and imitating these instruments, it is largely due to him. It is Michael Gillingham whom I have to thank for first giving me access to the working records of an English organ-builder. Having rescued the Gray & Davison archive when the firm ceased to trade in about 1970, he allowed me unrestricted access to these fascinating documents so redolent of the days when John Gray and Frederick Davison embarked on their partnership in the works on the north side of the New Road. He has been equally generous in sharing his profound knowledge of case design, and whilst the errors in the sections dealing with this topic remain my responsibility, there would have been many more had it not been for his guidance. My third special debt is to Stephen Bicknell who kindly agreed to wade through my manuscript, doing his best, as a practising organ-builder and historian of the organ, to alert me to solecisms and inaccuracies. I am deeply grateful for his assistance.

Many organ-builders have contributed directly to my work by allowing me access to their records, by being prepared to spend time answering what were to them elementary questions, and by helping me in my study of individual instruments. Among them, I would wish to mention: Ian Bell, John Budgen, Bill Drake, Frank Fowler, David Frostick, Dominic Gwynn, Peter Hopps, William Johnson, Roger Pulham, Martin Renshaw, John Mander, Noel Mander, Maurice Merrell, Bob Pennells, Eric Shepherd, John Shepherd, Dennis Thurlow, Mark Venning, John Sinclair Willis and Peter Wood.

I am similarly indebted to other writers and players who have been kind enough to help me in a variety of ways: James Berrow, John Bishop, John Bowles, Douglas Carrington, Cecil Clutton, Donald Davison, Laurence Elvin, Paul Hale, Bryan Hughes, Francis Jackson, Malcolm Jones, Christopher Kent, Betty Matthews, Colin Menzies, Timothy Morris, Austin Niland, John Norman, Nicholas Plumley, John Rowntree, Michael Sayer, Gerald Sumner, James Thomas, David Wickens and Donald Wright.

In the nature of things, I must have omitted the names of some people who ought to be included in the two preceding lists: I hope that they will accept my apologies.

My colleagues at Gonville and Caius College, Cambridge, have offered advice on various technical matters outside my immediate province, and I ought particularly to thank the staff of the Tutorial Office, and Michael Prichard, formerly Senior Tutor, for their help in elucidating the mysteries of word-processing and for forbearance when photocopying machines were mysteriously out of order.

I am grateful to Stuart White for advice on the execution of the technical drawings accompanying the text, and to all at Cambridge University Press who have been involved in the production of this book, especially Penny Souster.

My outstanding debt is left until last, and is in any case expressed in the dedication of this volume to two people who probably never again want to see or hear a Victorian organ.

Cambridge   Nicholas Thistlethwaite

Explanatory notes

I TECHNICAL DATA

All the diameters of pipe bodies were taken with callipers around the middle of the body; they may therefore reflect that 'bellying out' of the pipe practised by most pipe-makers. At best, they give a general indication of the scaling patterns. Few of the instruments investigated have been dismantled in recent years and detailed studies must await a future restoration when the pipework can be readily inspected. For the same reason little data relating to reeds can be given. The measurements recorded for wooden ranks are internal; the thickness of the timber sides of the pipe is also noted, but this is, again, indicative rather than definitive: most wooden pipes employ timber of slightly different thicknesses for the front and back panels and the sides.

2 FIGURES

The figures showing the internal layout of organs are drawn to scale. The details of the action and soundboards are simplified for the sake of clarity (e.g. pallet springs are not always shown) and sometimes enlarged (e.g. squares). Some details are conjectural (e.g. the design and arrangement of the pallets inside a chest). The drawings of organs are based on the author's own researches; most of the drawings of action components are taken from other sources which are duly acknowledged.

3 REFERENCES

The author-date system is used in the text for secondary sources; these are then given in the List of References. Manuscript sources are numbered, and are identified in the List of References. In order to reduce congestion in the text, references are not given there for sources of the stop lists of individual instruments nor (usually) for details of their original design or subsequent reconstruction. All instruments mentioned in the text are listed in the third section of the List of References with accompanying notes on sources.

4   SOURCES OF STOP LISTS

The specifications of many of the organs discussed in the earlier part of the text survive only in manuscript. The principal sources are the Leffler notebook (partly transcribed in: Pearce 1909, 1912), the 'G. P. England' notebook (a copy of which belongs to Noel Mander), *Organographia* (RCM MS 1161) and the Sperling notebooks (RCO). These sources, their relationship and reliability are discussed in: Thistlethwaite 1977. The establishing of accurate stop lists for later instruments poses fewer problems on account of the survival of organ-builders' records (though these are by no means an unimpeachable source) and the proliferation of musical journals containing details of organs after the middle of the century.

5   COMPASSES

Much confusion is caused by a diversity of systems for describing compasses. Here, the following scheme is adopted:

$$CC\ (16') - C\ (8') - c\ (4') - c^1\ (2') - c^2\ (1') - c^3\ (\tfrac{1}{2}') - c^4\ (\tfrac{1}{4}')$$

These refer to the keys (or pedals) of the organ, not to the pitch of the registers.

Abbreviations

N.S.	New series (journals)
OOD	*The organs and organists of Doncaster (c.* 1970*)*
PA	*Patents for inventions: Abridgement of specifications* (*see* List of References)
PMA	*Proceedings of the Musical Association*
PMEM	*The Practical Mechanic and Engineer's Magazine*
PC	Parish church
QMMR	*The Quarterly Musical Magazine and Review*
RAM	*The Repertory of Arts and Manufactures*
RCO	Royal College of Organists
VCH	*Victoria County History*
YG	*York Gazette*

2   ABBREVIATIONS IN SPECIFICATIONS AND TABLES

m	metal
n.a.	not available
n.o.	not original
wd	wood
8ve	octave
*	approximate measurement

PART I

I

The English organ in 1820

CONTINUITY AND CHANGE

The English organ of 1820 was a lineal descendant of the instruments built in the latter part of the seventeenth century to make good the depredations of, first, religious fanatics and, then, fire. The type of organ which evolved in these circumstances under the joint (though sometimes conflicting) influence of 'Father' Smith – who learnt his craft in north-west Germany and practised it first in Holland (Freeman & Rowntree 1977: 103–12; Rowntree 1978: 10–20) – and Renatus Harris – heir to the organ-building experience which the Dallam and Harris families acquired during their exile in France (Bicknell 1981: 6–9; Cocheril 1982) – endured with some modification into the early years of the nineteenth century. Its most characteristic feature was the absence, in all but a handful of cases, of pedals, and the related provision of 'long' compasses, usually commencing at G G, for the Great and Choir (or Chair) Organs. In the seventeenth and early-eighteenth centuries these tended to have 'short' octaves in the bass. The lowest note of the keyboard sounded G G, and the next, C. There was no C♯ pipe, but the C♯ key sounded A A. The next note was D and the compass then continued in regular fashion to c^3 or d^3. From the mid-eighteenth century it became increasingly common in church organs to make the bottom octave a 'long' octave (omitting only the G G♯) and the top of the compass crept up, first, to e^3, and then, from the mid-1790s, to f^3.[1] Other modest developments took place. Jordan's 'invention' of the Swell Organ (c. 1712) greatly commended itself to the English with their taste for expressive melody, and the old Echo Organs were gradually converted into Swells (though a short-compass Swell, commencing at middle c, or possibly fiddle g, satisfied organists for long enough) (Sumner 1962: 191–3). To John Snetzler, a Swiss organ-builder who settled in England during the early 1740s, is owed the only tonal novelty to be universally adopted into the English organ during the course of the century: the narrow-scaled, cylindrical dulciana, which first appeared in Snetzler's organ for St Margaret's, King's Lynn (1754) (Sumner 1962: 164, 308).

3

Snetzler seems occasionally to have introduced another novelty into his organs, namely pedals, but as an innovation they made little headway in England during his lifetime (Pearce 1927: 30–6; Williams 1962: 238, 285). Organists and organ builders remained conservative in outlook, disinclined to make innovations, and already, in the mid-eighteenth century, prone to retrospection – the veneration in which the organs of 'Father' Smith were held ('for the fineness of their tone they have never yet been equalled', as Sir John Hawkins put it) (1776, IV: 355) was a symptom of this.

In moving forward to the early-nineteenth century the casual observer could be forgiven for concluding that the design of the English organ had altered little in the seventy or eighty years leading up to 1820. Stop lists remained remarkably similar throughout these years. The large organs of George Pike England (Newark Parish Church, 1804, or Lancaster Parish Church, 1811) closely resemble, on paper, those of Richard Bridge or John Byfield from the mid-eighteenth century, with their two mixtures, a tierce and a mounted cornet on the Great, a small mixture to complete the Choir chorus, and semi-imitative reeds in the Choir and Swell Organs. John Avery's organs for King's College, Cambridge (1803) and St Margaret's, Westminster (1804) display a similarly generous provision of mixtures, cornets and reeds in the (apparently) eighteenth-century manner, as do Hugh Russell's reconstructions of organs by Renatus Harris (St Dunstan, Stepney, 1808) and Richard Bridge (St Anne, Limehouse, 1811). There are some features which distinguish these instruments of the early-nineteenth century from those being built seventy years before. All except the Stepney organ had pedals and some pedal pipes (though there were no pipes at Lancaster), all had 'long' octaves and a compass which ran to f³; the Swell compass, too, had expanded cautiously downwards: to tenor d at Newark and Lancaster, but more conventionally to e or f in other instances. Although each of these innovations suggested lines of development which the later nineteenth-century organ builders would pursue rigorously (and sometimes fruitlessly) it must be remembered that these were among the most ambitious organs of their day; a study of the smaller instruments of the period would underline yet more strongly the conservative, and minimise the innovative tendencies of the organ-builders. Altogether, it is striking that so little seems to have occurred in English organ design between 1750 and 1820. One is bound to ask, is this a true picture?

In general, the English organ of the first two decades of the nineteenth century earns its characterisation as a highly conservative instrument. There were, though, subtle and significant distinctions to be drawn between the conception and construction of the organ at this time and the practice and taste of the previous century.

These may be illustrated by referring to the entry relating to the organ in Rees's *Cyclopaedia* (1819, xxv: n.p.). It is said to have been written by

Burney, but whilst the rambling, structureless character of the first part of the article is compatible with an author whose powers were failing (Burney died at the age of eighty-four in 1814) the second, more technical part of the article suggests that another writer took a hand and added to Burney's work before publication. A couple of sentences which echo a passage from Burney's *History of music* (1789) combine reverence for 'Father' Smith with a claim that his successors genuinely improved upon his work in certain respects:

The organs in our churches, that have been well preserved of father Schmidt's make, such as St. Paul's, the Temple, St. Mary's, Oxford, Trinity College, Cambridge, &c. are far superior in tone to any of more modern construction; but the mechanism has been improved during the last century, by Byfield, Snetzler, Green, Gray, &c. The touch is lighter, the compass extended, and the reed-work admirable.

The (other?) writer takes up the point about an improvement in mechanism and mentions the qualities which organists of his generation expected of a good key action:

The touch of the keys should be free and elastic, and exactly the same pressure should be requisite to put down every key throughout the scale. No better proof can be given of a good touch, than that a turned shake can be executed with equal facility in every part of the scale, except perhaps in the lowest octave, where it is not to be expected or desired. If all these things act without noise, the mechanical parts of the organ may be considered good, and in order.

The implied comparison here with old organs is carried further when the writer turns to consider the tonal structure of the organ. He remarks on the indispensability of a good stopped diapason, 'as that stop is the foundation of the organ', and has little to say of the open diapason, except that it should be 'full, smooth, and articulate'. No eighteenth-century organist would have disagreed with him. He goes on, however, to make the point that the 'relative strength' of the various registers 'is of great importance to the goodness of the chorus':

As a single stop should not be loudest at the top, so the chorus stops should not predominate over the diapasons; a fault very general in the old organs, arising from the bad taste of the times in which they were made. The chorus should be rich, brilliant, and articulate; the twelfth and tierce, and their octaves, should not be heard, except when listened for.

Despite the taste for brilliance, this passage exhibits a concern for unison diapason tone which was to prove characteristic of the nineteenth century. The writer's remarks about reeds also suggest a certain distancing from the work of earlier builders. He approves of the trumpet as adding greatly to the 'majesty as to the strength' of the chorus, and the clarion because it increases the brilliancy of the chorus. He continues:

The goodness of these, and all other reed stops, besides the requisites already mentioned, depends upon their speaking readily and quickly; and being free from the nasal tone, such as is produced by bad players on the clarionet, or hautboy . . .

and, he might have added, by the reeds of older organs. Again, there are the beginnings of a preoccupation which was to possess builders and players alike during the next hundred years: how to get reeds to speak promptly and cleanly, and with a full, regular tone. This preoccupation eventually led to reeds which were very different from those made by Smith, Harris and their immediate successors.

It is illuminating, finally, to turn to an account of the St Paul's Cathedral organ which was published in the *English Musical Gazette* in 1819, for as well as casting light on the cult of Smith, it helps to sharpen the distinction between the musical taste of the early-nineteenth century and that of the previous century, and at the same time to expose the roots of some later-nineteenth-century fashions in organ use and tonality. The author is discussing Smith's diapasons on the Great Organ:

These have always been esteemed the finest that Schmidt ever made. Those at the Temple are very fine in bass, but fall off exceedingly in the treble; these do not, but are regular and uniform, in the quality of tone throughout. We cannot say whether the richness, smoothness and beauty of the treble is more enchanting, than the fine, full, and sonorous tones of the bass. We are speaking of the three diapasons when used together. The effect of them with pedal basses (the right hand being engaged with the melody in the treble, while the left is accompanying it on the swell) is beautiful, and shows the diapasons off to the utmost advantage possible. The style best calculated for the diapasons is adagio, legati, and cantabile movements, which have the most rich effect that can be imagined. Three or four notes, or a chord, held down in the bass on these diapasons, has all the effect of thunder at a distance; and we must say, when comparing these diapasons with any other that Schmidt ever made, or even Harris, or Schreider, Schmidt's principal man, who built the organ at Westminster Abbey; or even Green, that they fall short in respect of the quality as well as body of tone.   (*EMG*, 1 January 1819: 7)

The admiration for smoothness and sonority, the pleasure taken in an effect suggestive of thunder, the taste for gentle melodic movements and legato passages of full harmony place this writer firmly in the nineteenth century. Considered alongside the extracts from Rees, it becomes apparent that the similarity of stop lists over the better part of a century does not tell the full story. To discover what was really happening in English organ-building in the first quarter of the nineteenth century it will be helpful to look in some detail at an extant instrument of the period.

THE THAXTED ORGAN

Few substantial organs have survived from the years around 1820. It was not, perhaps, a distinguished period in the history of English organ-building.

1   Thaxted Parish Church, H. C. Lincoln, 1821.

One era was drawing to its close, another had yet to begin. A later generation found little of value in the organs built during the 1810s, 1820s and 1830s, and either destroyed them or made drastic modifications. No survivor from this period is more important than the organ built by Henry Cephas Lincoln for St John's Chapel, Bedford Row, London, and now standing in Thaxted Parish Church, Essex (Plate 1). Despite its present state of dereliction (or because of it) it survives as the only largely unaltered 3-manual organ to have come down to us from the first four decades of the nineteenth century. It is therefore particularly unfortunate that its history is poorly documented.

There is no maker's plate, but both the Sperling Notebooks (MS 79: 71) and H. C. Lincoln's 1824 circular (MS 78: 322) confirm that Lincoln built an organ for St John's Chapel, Bedford Row.[2] It is known that the Chapel was closed for some months in 1821 whilst the galleries were enlarged to provide additional seating, and it is probable that the organ was installed then (Bateman 1860: 218).

St John's Chapel, Bedford Row, was a proprietary chapel. It became unsafe and was demolished in 1863.[3] The organ had been removed in 1858 to Thaxted, and appears in its present position in the north transept on a plan attached to a faculty application of 1879 (MS 30).[4] The organ was repaired by Alfred Kirkland in 1907 (MS 82). The scope of his work is not known, but it may have included making the present Great roller-board (which is not original), re-leathering the bellows and applying tuning slides to the two open diapasons and the principal on the Great (fortunately, the tops of the pipes were not trimmed). Someone, at some stage, re-made part of the Great stop action, with the result that the stops now have round shanks (the surviving originals are square). An electric blower was installed and some of the rack boards were renewed. The organ has been deteriorating for some years, and the pipes of three registers – the mixture and trumpet (Great), and the bassoon (Choir) – have disappeared since 1913, when a correspondent recorded their existence in a letter to *Musical Opinion* (37, 1913: 33); a few trebles are missing from the surviving mixture.

None of these alterations (with the exception of the incongruous stop shanks) has seriously compromised the character of the organ, and regrettable though the losses of pipework are, they have to be set against the otherwise complete survival of the flue choruses and the three Swell reeds.

The stop list is as follows:

Great Organ (FF, no FF♯, to f³)

Open Diapason Front	8	
Open Diapason (C)	8	
Stopped Diapason	8	
Principal	4	
Twelfth	2 2/3	
Fifteenth	2	
Sesquialtra (FF–b)	IV	
Cornet (c¹–f³)	IV–III	
Mixture	II	[missing]
Trumpet	8	[missing]
Pedals (FF–c)	8	[unison pedal pipes]

Choir Organ (FF, no FF♯, to f³)

Dulciana (FF–e grooved)	8	
Stopped Diapason	8	
Principal	4	
Flute	4	
Fifteenth	2	
Bassoon	8	[missing]

Swell Organ (e to f³)

Open Diapason	8
Stopped Diapason	8
Principal	4
Cremona	8
Hautboy	8
Trumpet	8

Coupler Swell	[Swell to Great]
Pedals Great	[Great to Pedal]
Pedals Choir	[Choir to Pedal]

Swell lever

Pedal board: FF to c (FF♯ coupled to F♯)

The Thaxted organ provides a useful starting point for a consideration of the construction and design of the English organ in 1820. Care must be exercised in treating it as a typical product of the English organ-builder's workshop at that time. It would have been satisfactory to have been able to discuss Lincoln's organ alongside similarly intact survivals from the workshops of, say, William Gray and Hugh Russell, each of whom was regarded as being among the leading builders of the day, but – sadly – no substantial instrument by either builder has survived in a state of completeness comparable to Thaxted. We are in a stronger position in regard to another leading metropolitan builder of the 1810s and 1820s. Thomas Elliot's work (and especially that of his partner and successor, William Hill) is central to the present study, and enough of it survives for us to form a reliable impression of his instruments. Particular reference will be made in what follows to three of these: Scone Palace (1813), Ashridge (1818) and the organ for the Chapel Royal, St James's Palace (1819), which, since 1841, has stood in St Margaret's, Crick. The Scone organ is intact – a remarkable survival, still standing in its handsome Gothic case at one end of the Long Gallery, and so little used over the years that its moving parts have suffered a minimum of wear and tear. Various features distinguish it from Elliot's later instruments, and it may be that it has at least as much in common with organ-building of the late-eighteenth century as it has with that of the 1820s and 1830s; for this reason, a detailed consideration would be out of place in the present study.

Table 1 *Thaxted Parish Church, 1821: scales*

(1)   Diapason choruses

Great Organ		C	c	c¹	c²	c³
Front Open Diapason				49.5	30.5	16.5
Open Diapason		152*	89.25	49	30	16.5
Principal			49	30	17	10
Twelfth		51	32	19.75	12.75	8.25
Fifteenth		49	29.25	17	10	7
Sesquialtra I		42	25.5	26.5	16.5	10.75
II		37	22	19.5	12.5	8.25
III		32	20.25	16	10.75	8.25
IV		25.5	16.5	14	9	

	Composition:			
	FF	17.19.22		
	C	15.17.19.22		
	c¹	8.12.15.17		
	f²	8.12.15		

Choir Organ	C	c	c¹	c²	c³
Dulciana		59.75	35.75	21	12.5
Principal	79	44.5	24.75	16	10.75
Fifteenth	42	24.75	16	11.5	7

Swell Organ	C	c	c¹	c²	c³
Open Diapason			38	24.75	15.25
Principal			25.5	16.5	10

(2)   Flutes

		(a)	(b)
Gt Stopped Diapason	c	63.5 × 54	8
	c¹	48.25	152 × 12.5
	c²	31.25	82.5 × 8.5
	c³	21	47.5 × 5.75
Ch Stopped Diapason	C	127.5 × 101.5	12.5
	c	66.5 × 57	9.5
	c¹	45.5	149 × 12.5
	c²	30.5	76 × 8.5
	c³	21	38 × 6.5
Ch Flute	C	65.5 × 57	9.5
	c	48.25	136.5 × 12.5
	c¹	31.25	76 × 9
	c²	21	38 × 6.5
	c³	14.5	22 × 4.5

(a)   Internal dimensions (wooden pipes) or diameters (metal pipes).
(b)   Thickness of sides (wooden pipes) or length and diameter of chimney (metal pipes).

Ashridge (Appendix 1, p. 444) and Crick (Appendix 1, pp. 444–5) have each suffered indignities in the course of their history (Crick, especially, awaits a sympathetic restoration) and it seems that the latter was not a very good organ to start with.[5] Each, however, offers valuable evidence of Elliot's practice, and proves at various points to present an informative contrast to Lincoln's work at Thaxted.

SPECIFICATION

The stop list of the Thaxted organ is wholly characteristic of the period in which it was conceived. Another builder might have included a clarion on the Great, or preferred a cremona to a bassoon on the Choir, or arranged his mixtures a little differently, but, in all essentials, any one of the metropolitan organ-builders of the day would have produced an almost identical specification for a 3-manual organ of twenty-three stops. Half a century before, the stop list would have been much the same. Yet there had been some innovations in the course of fifty years, and although their full significance would not become apparent until after 1821, a consideration of the Thaxted specification provides an opportunity to study three of them in more detail.

The doubling of the 8' open diapason

In the eighteenth century, a number of schemes for the largest organs had admitted that the only logical way of extending the stylised stop lists of English organs was to resort to duplication. Richard Bridge's organ for Christ Church, Spitalfields (1735), for example, contained two open diapasons and two principals on the Great of what was then the largest organ in England, and Parker's organ for the Foundling Hospital (1768) followed suit. Both organs were single-fronted: the intention therefore differed from that of builders who provided (as English organ-builders had for many years) an open diapason for each front of a double-fronted organ standing on a central screen. The most likely explanation was either a desire to increase the power of the instrument or a wish to reinforce the unison (8') registers within the chorus – perhaps both. Whatever the intention, this innovation was imitated, and during the final quarter of the eighteenth century, a number of 3-manual organs appeared with two open diapasons on the Great. Crang & Hancock may have done it as early as 1772 and 1773 at Chelmsford and Leicester respectively, Holland did it at St George's, Bloomsbury, in 1788, and the 1790s produced a number of examples including Avery's organs at Croydon (1794) and Sevenoaks (1798), and England's at St James's, Clerkenwell (1792). Samuel Green may have been the first to provide a 2-manual organ with a second open diapason (Concert Room, Opera House, Covent Garden, 1794).

After 1800 it became usual to include a second open diapason in 3-manual instruments, unless they were particularly small. G. P. England's work demonstrates this.[6] Avery, oddly, became more conservative towards the end of his career; his large organ for St Margaret's, Westminster (1804), and that for the cathedral at Carlisle (1806) had no doubling. Thomas Elliot, on the other hand, practised duplication widely, and many of his 2-manual organs built after 1807 include two open diapasons on the Great.[7] It may be that to Elliot belongs the distinction (if such it be) of finally establishing this characteristic feature of the nineteenth-century English organ.

The use to which the second diapason was put remains obscure. Avery, at Winchester, seemed to be implying some distinction between the two registers when he named one of them 'Great Open Diapason' (though, as the other was of wood, it must have been unusually important for the organist to know which was which) but for a long time, organ-builders attempted to distinguish between the two registers neither in nomenclature nor in construction; the scaling was commonly identical (as at Thaxted), and where the ear can detect a difference between the two registers it can usually be attributed to the better projection of the register which stands (partly) in the case front, and the fact that (unlike the 'inside' open diapason) it is likely to have a complete and generously scaled bass of metal pipes. The Elliot organ at Ashridge is a modest exception. There, the distinction is noticeable – but, then, Ashridge is, in many respects, atypical. The only other clue as to the use of the second open diapason may lie in the fact that doubling frequently appears in organs that had to accompany large numbers of singers. John Gray's Stock Account (1832) includes 'Large Metal Open for Oratorios' (presumably, a large-scale open diapason which was introduced into organs used to accompany oratorio performances) and it may be that this notion of increasing the power of the instrument by reinforcing the unison registers had been abroad for some time (MS 1). More will be said about this interesting, if misconceived, notion below (pp. 109–11).

Solo registers

The provision of solo registers in the Thaxted organ is slight by comparison with instruments of a similar size built later in the century, but it is significant of an important shift in taste that there is no mounted cornet on the Great, and the customary Swell cornet is displaced by an imitative reed.

The cornet was an early victim of a certain novel earnestness of manner which accompanied, in secular terms, the rise of the romantic movement, and, in religion, the onset of the evangelical movement. It was particularly associated with the English solo voluntary – a genre which was rapidly passing out of favour in the early years of the nineteenth century. Crotch (1812) dismissed this type of voluntary as 'too often vulgar, trifling and ridiculous' (Crotch 1812: 120), Rees (1819) commented upon 'the trifling and vitiated style of performance' which the traditional solo stops (cornets, trumpets and flutes) encouraged (Rees 1819: n.p.), and Marsh (1791) urged the rejection as a Middle Voluntary of 'all such [voluntaries] as are of a thin, light or trivial nature, particularly many of the Cornet or Flute pieces in Major keys, which are fitter for the harpsichord than for the Organ' (Marsh 1791: Preface). The feeling grew that the cornet voluntary offended against 'that decorous gravity of style which should ever characterise church music' (Crotch 1812: 120), and by 1830, a writer could dismiss the cornet with the tart remark, 'the more noise, the more honour to the organ builder and the organist' (*EE* xv: 679). Nor could the cornet's other traditional function (of giving out the psalm tune) save it. It became subsumed into the ranks of the main chorus, from whence, retaining its tierce, and drawing separately as the treble of a 3- or 4-rank chorus mixture, it was able to supply the solo cornet's place in sounding out the tune (Done 1839: 13). Thaxted, with its 'Sesquialtra & Cornet', is typical in this respect of the larger organs of the period.

It may be that the cornet fell out of favour with organists somewhat before organ-builders began to exclude it from their new instruments. As early as 1802, the Swell cornet at St George's, Hanover Square, had been reduced to a single rank – the 4' (Pearce 1912: 105) – and by 1811, all but the 8' rank of the Great cornet in the organ of Gravesend Parish Church had been stopped up (Pearce 1911: 139). The final exclusion of the mounted cornet appears to have come about with a speed unusual in the annals of English organ-building. Avery and G. P. England continued to include a solo cornet in 3-manual organs until the end of their respective careers (1807, 1815).[8] Gray usually included a 4-rank cornet in large organs, the latest probably being that for Huddersfield Parish Church (1812); an organ for Arundel (1816) contained an isolated example of a 3-rank mounted cornet, but, in the following year, an ambitious new organ for St Marylebone Parish Church omitted the cornet altogether, and no later examples by Gray have come to light (MS 81: 71, 8; MS 79: 80). Elliot's organs suggest similar timing: Bromsgrove Church (1808) and Stockport Sunday School (1811) each had a cornet, but large 3-manual instruments of 1815, 1816, and 1817 did not (Buckingham LIII: 79–81).[9]

At Thaxted, the absence of a solo cornet is therefore significant, and added point is given by the omission of the Swell cornet in favour of a third reed – a cremona. This is typical of a trend which will be examined in greater detail below (pp. 90–1). The brasher solo voices were out of fashion, and mild, orchestral registers were taking their place. On the one hand, these tonalities were more suitable for the melodic lines of vocal transcriptions (then popular); on the other, they recalled the orchestral textures of the most approved contemporary composers. In this context, and bearing in mind that the

Swell Organ at this period was still, essentially, an expressive collection of solo voices, a third imitative reed was to be preferred to the vulgarities of the cornet.

Pedal pipes

The Thaxted organ has a short-compass pedal board, controlling an octave and a half of unison (8′) pedal pipes. At the time it was built, there was no apparent consensus among English organ-builders concerning pedal arrangements; it was generally accepted that larger organs should have a few pedals, permanently coupled to one of the keyboards (pull-downs), but, beyond this – in matters of compass, the construction of the pedals, and the provision (or not) of independent pedal pipes – everything depended upon the quirks of the individual builder or organist. The results of this *laissez-faire* approach may appear distinctly peculiar to modern organists with different priorities from their early nineteenth-century forebears, but a study of the introduction of pedals (and pedal pipes) in English organs reveals a certain coherence of approach, even if it also underlines the limited objectives which the builders had within their sights.

   The provision of pedals in English organs seems, initially, to have met two needs. The first was mechanical, and had to do with the weight of touch which was required at the keyboard to draw down the soundboard pallets supplying wind to the basses. As pallets increased in size, and the touch became consequently heavier, pedals allowed the organist to transfer this duty from his fingers to an agency better equipped by nature to exert the necessary force. (It can be no coincidence that two of the first organs in England to be fitted with pull-downs – the instruments in St Paul's Cathedral (1720/1) and St Mary Redcliffe, Bristol (1726) – each had a CC [16′] keyboard compass (Freeman 1922a: 5: Morgan 1912: 7–8).) The second need was musical, the pedals assisting the player in making full use of the extended keyboard compass by placing the lowest notes under the control of the feet, thus freeing the left hand for work in the tenor octave and above; Samuel Wesley saw the point when he commented (disapprovingly) that 'pedals might be of service to those who could not use their fingers' (*MW* XIII, 1840: 315). Kollmann's illustration (1799) of an *obbligato* pedal passage from the first movement of J. S. Bach's *Trio Sonata in Eb* (BWV 525), however interesting it may be to later musicologists, can have meant little to most English organists, who would have expected to play such passages with the left hand – to play them with the feet would have seemed unnecessarily complicated when the fingers could cope much more easily (Kollman 1799: 97).

   Pull-downs were rare in English organs before the 1790s. Towards the end of his life, Samuel Wesley recalled that, in his youth (he was born in 1766) 'the only Organ in London to which Pedals were affixed was that of the German Church in the Savoy, built by Snetzler' (he had evidently over-looked St Paul's Cathedral) (MS 67: 42). It may be that pull-downs were not quite so uncommon as the paucity of evidence implies (regarded as of little account musically, their existence may simply not have been recorded), but it was probably not until around 1800 that an octave of pull-downs became customary in most new organs of the larger class.[10]

By that date, pedal pipes had made their appearance, beginning most probably with Avery's addition of thirteen pedal pipes 'of very large dimen-sions' to the organ of Westminster Abbey in 1793 (Pearce 1911: 59). Table 2 is an attempt to list all the organs which are known to have had pedal pipes before 1821; whilst not definitive, it probably includes the most important examples, and is representative of the prevailing situation.

The earliest pedal pipes were of unison (8') pitch. In a number of instances, they were part of a single-fronted organ with two open diapasons on the Great, of which the second had no pipes available below gamut G; the pedal pipes effectively completed this short-compass register. The pipes were always made of wood (as, often, were the bottom notes of the second open diapason), were nearly always open, and presumably were scaled to match the incomplete open diapason; so, in 1819, Elliot was able to transfer the Pedal Pipes of Avery's Croydon organ (1794) to the Great in order to supply the missing bottom octave of an open diapason, and three years earlier, in his own organ for St James's, Nottingham, the drawstop control-ling the pedal pipes was brought on automatically when the second open diapason was drawn. Similarly, at St Anne's, Limehouse, following Hugh Russell's work in 1811, there were no pedal pipes as such, but the lowest six notes of the second diapason were of wood and playable only from the pedals. Such expedients were not without significance. What may have begun as an economy measure (constructing large basses of wood rather than metal) came to be attractive for other reasons as organists and organ-builders began to desire a greater weight of tone in the bass and detected something of what they were seeking in the ponderous and (relatively) unfocused tone of large wooden pipes. Though the earliest of these manual basses were of modest scale (cf. Croydon) they soon came to be appreciated for their distinctive effect, and experiments were made by increasing the scale. Sometimes, effects which eventually came to be associated properly with the Pedal Organ were tried out on organs without pedals, or in which the pedals were no more than pull-downs. Russell added a (metal) double diapason to the Great of St Saviour's, Southwark, at a time when that instrument had no pedals (1800); it was only an octave in compass (C–c) and was clearly intended to serve the same function as the pedal doubles which were added to English organs in the course of the next four decades. The same is true of the seven (?) doubles which Russell introduced in the

Table 2 *English organs with pedal pipes: to 1820*

Date	Builder	Location	Type	Compass (Pipes)	Compass (Pedals)
1773	Green	*Walsall Parish Church	coupled to Choir Stopped Diapason	?	?
1793	Avery	*Westminster Abbey[a]	Unisons	GG–G (13)	?
1794	Avery	Croydon Parish Church	Unisons	GG–G (?)	1 octave
1798	Avery	Sevenoaks Parish Church	Unisons	GG–G	GG–c
1801	Avery	Cambridge, Trinity College	Unisons	?	?
1803	Avery	Cambridge, King's College	Unisons	(12)	1 octave
1804	Avery	St Margaret, Westminster	Unisons	1 octave	1 octave
1804	Elliot	*Hanover Square Rooms	Unisons (?)	C–f# (19)	?
	England	Newark Parish Church	Unisons (?)	'to A–12'	?
1805	Avery	Cambridge, University Organ	Unisons	1 octave	?
	England	Sheffield Parish Church	Unisons	GG–? (12)	GG–A (14)
1806	Elliot	Hereford Cathedral[b]	Unisons	GG–F (?)	?
1808	Elliot	Derby, All Saints	Doubles (open)	GG–G (13)	GG–G
			Doubles (stopped)	GG–G (13)	
1809	?	Southwark, St George	?	1 octave	1 octave
	Elliot	Stockport Parish Church	?	?	1½ octaves
	Gray	St Swithun, London Stone, London	?	1 octave	?
1810	Gray	St Patrick, Soho (RC)	Doubles (stopped)	GG–F# (11)	GG–F#
1811	Russell	St Anne, Limehouse	Unisons	FF–BB (6)	FF–c (?)
	Russell	Chelmsford Parish Church	Unisons	?	?
	Elliot	Stockport Sunday School	Dwarf	GG–G (12)	GG–G
1812	England	St Nicholas, Great Yarmouth	Doubles	GG–c (17)	GG–c
1813	Elliot	Scone Palace	Unisons (open) / Doubles (stopped)	GG–D / D#–G } GG–G	GG–G
1814	Elliot	Whitehall, Chapel Royal	Dwarf	GG–G (12)	GG–G (12)
1815	Elliot	St John, Hull	Unisons	GG–G (12)	GG–c (17)
	Elliot	Christ Church, Birmingham	Dwarf	GG–G (12)	GG–G (12)
1816	Elliot	St James, Nottingham	Unisons	GG–F# (11)	GG–c (17)
	Elliot	Montreal Cathedral	Dwarf (GG–C#) / Doubles (D–c) }	GG–c (17)	GG–c (17)
1817	Flight & Robson	The Apollonicon[c]	Doubles	3½ octaves [sic]	2 octaves

Year	Builder	Location	Type		
	Gray	St Sepulchre, Holborn, London	Unisons	GG (1 octave)	GG (1 octave)
	Elliot	Waterford Cathedral	Dwarf (GG–BB) Doubles (C–c) }	GG–c (17)	GG–c (17)
1818	Smith	*St Michael, Bristol[d]	Doubles	C–B	?
	Elliot	Ashridge, Chapel	<u>Dwarf</u>	GG–G (12)	GG–c (17)
	Gray	St Mary, Woodbridge	Unisons	1 octave (12)	1 octave
	Davis	St Saviour, Southwark	Doubles	GG–G	1½ octaves
	Gray	St Marylebone Parish Church	'double-Bass Pedal Pipes'	1 octave	?
1819	Elliot	Croydon Parish Church	Unisons	1½ octaves	1½ octaves
1820	Gray	St Dunstan-in-the-East, London	Unisons	GG–G	GG–G
	Gray	St Albans Abbey	?	1 octave	?
	Flight & Robson	*St David, Exeter	?	GG–F	1½ octaves
	Gray	Arundel Parish Church	?	GG (1 octave)	?
	Dobson	*St Mary, Whitechapel, London[e]	?	?	?
Undated	Nicholls	St Mary, Reading[f]	?	?	?

Notes:

[1] Where the 'type' of pedal pipes is underlined, there was a second open diapason on the Great, with a short-compass.

[2] It should be remembered that many of these early pedal arrangements omitted the GG' (as did the manual keyboards) and this explains the apparent disparity in some of the examples above between the compasses, and the number of pipes or notes which are recorded.

[3] A number of instruments which have been recorded in previous writings as having possessed pedal pipes at an early stage have been omitted from the list for lack of adequate supporting evidence. These include:

St Katharine by the Tower, London[g]
St Saviour, Southwark (1800)[h]
Surrey Chapel, Blackfriars Road, London[i]
Durham Cathedral (1815)[j]
St Matthew, Friday Street, London (1790)[k]
St Andrew-by-the-Wardrobe, London (1805)[l]
St Peter, Brighton (1818)[m]

[a] HR3: 227; cf. CR, xv, 1833: 498, according to which the addition took place during Dr Arnold's tenure of the organistship (1793–1802). The Abbey records are tantalisingly unspecific; the Chapter Minutes (vol. xiii) record an order (23 April 1793) to pay Avery £43.7s.0d 'for cleaning, repairing & improving the Organ', and two further orders (23 July 1801, 7 December 1802) authorised payments to him totalling £48.5s.11d for cleaning and repairing the instrument. The pedal pipes could have been introduced on either occasion (or neither), though probability perhaps favours the earlier date in view of the reference to improvement.

[b] MS 38: 163. Shaw's assertion (1976: 30–2) that the pedal pipes of 1806 were doubles is incorrect.

[c] Ord-Hume 1978: 113; the upper octave-and-a-half of the doubles could presumably be played from one of the manual keyboards.

[d] MS 80: 109. The date is Sperling's, and may be on the early side. However, a letter written by Smith to the Dean & Chapter of Bristol Cathedral in 1825 confirms that he had, by then, installed pedal pipes at St Michael's (BRO DC/A/11/2/1). I am indebted to Dr Christopher Kent for this reference.

[e] GPE attributes work to Dobson in both 1817 and 1820, and it is not clear on which occasion the pedal pipes were introduced.

f GPE: 76; it is possible that either the writer or his transcriber have confused this instrument with another.

g Pearce (1909: 193; 1927: 48) has been responsible for this instrument's reputation of being one of the first in England to possess pedal pipes. There is, however, no evidence to support this. Leffler does not include it in his list of organs with pedals (MS 88: 127) and nor does he record the existence of pedals in his account of the specification (in other words, Pearce has amended Leffler's account) (MS 88: 97). There is no mention of pedals in the detailed account of the organ in *Bibliotheca Topographia Britannica* (London, 1790, vol. II, p. 39). GPE states that the organ was repaired by Blyth in 1820, and records the presence of pedals (no pipes) which may therefore have been added by Blyth (35). It seems likely that the pedal pipes referred to by Pearce were added when the organ was moved, during the 1820s, to the new church of St Katherine, Regent's Park, where it still stands.

h Russell added a metal double diapason of twelve notes (curiously said to be of C–c compass, i.e. thirteen notes) to the Great Organ in 1800 (Pearce 1912: 60; GPE: 61). It is not clear whether the organ possessed pedals at that time, but, in any case, there is nothing to suggest that the double diapason could be played other than from the Great keyboard (see also CR, XV, 1833: 683).

i F. G. Edwards (1896: 653) claimed that the Surrey Chapel organ 'was one of the first in England to have separate pedal pipes'. He may have had access to some now lost source, but Leffler (Pearce 1912: 105) makes no mention of either pedals or pipes, and GPE (20) notes only 'Pedals up to D'. The use of this organ for Jacob and Wesley's performances might imply the existence of pedals, but in the absence of corroborative evidence, the existence of pipes at an early date must be doubted.

j According to Buckingham (LII: 7–8) G. P. England added a double diapason, GG–g (24) to the Great Organ; Hopkins (HR2: 526) states that this was in 1815 and that the work was completed by Nicholls upon England's death – he also states that the seventeen (GG–c) pedals noted by Buckingham were added by England at the same time. In view of the disparity between the compass of the double diapason and that of the pedals, it is likely that the register was not available independently on the pedals; even so, it must have been intended to provide the effect of pedal pipes.

k Hopkins (HR3: 227) records a tradition that the organ in St Matthew's was one of the first in England to have pedal pipes; the pedals were said to consist of two octaves from C [*sic*] and to be provided with a complete set of double (stopped) pipes. The date of the addition was 1790 and 'the late Rev. Mr. Latrobe' was said to have been the instigator. Unfortunately, neither the early collections of specifications nor the parish records offer any supporting evidence for this tradition. If such an addition were made, it seems likely that it would have been later than 1790, and, in view of this, and in the absence of other evidence, Friday Street's claim has to be set aside.

l Pearce (1909: 164–5) gives the specification of this organ, including 'Pedal pipes', drawing upon a source dating from 1855; the pedal compass is given as GG–d. In the absence of other evidence, it seems unsafe to assume that these pedal arrangements were necessarily original.

m Sperling (MS 81: 3) states that this organ was built by Nicholls in 1818 and put up in St Peter's by a builder named Bunter in 1825; there were one-and-a-half octaves of pedal pipes commencing at GG. As these may well have been introduced by Bunter, this instrument is not included in the table.

Choir Organ at St Anne's, Limehouse, in 1811, and the more ambitious two octaves of doubles which England added to the Great Organs at the Portuguese Chapel in 1808 and Durham Cathedral in 1815 (though all these instruments had pull-downs). England was of the generation which saw no purpose in placing these generously scaled pipes under the control of the feet unless there were compelling mechanical reasons for doing so; his last organ (St Mary Magdalene's, Islington: 1814) was a large 3-manual in which the lowest octave of the first open diapason consisted of 'large wood pipes resembling pedal pipes' – but the pedals were simple pull-downs.

It is impossible to be certain at what stage a clear distinction came to be drawn between large-scaled manual basses, which were for convenience played from the pedals, and true pedal pipes of a scale, and with a function, quite distinct from that of any manual register. Ambiguities persisted into the 1820s: the physical location of the pedal pipes in the Thaxted organ (alongside the Great, in space which might otherwise have been occupied by basses conveyanced off the soundboard), and the suggestion that some of these early pedal pipes could be played from a keyboard as well as from the pedals, underscore this.[11] Yet, from the first, pedal pipes introduced a novel feature into English organ design. According to Leffler, Avery's pedal pipes at Westminster Abbey were 'of very large dimensions, and though only unisons with the Diapasons, from their increased size have the effect of a Double Diapason' (Pearce 1912: 59). Buckingham made a similar claim for the lowest (wood) octave of the second open diapason in Elliot's Bromsgrove organ (1808): it was, he said, 'of a large scale that answers for a Double Diapason'. Sub-unison (16') registers had been virtually unknown in English organs of the eighteenth century, and hence the gradual appearance of pedal pipes which were either true doubles, or contrived to produce the effect of doubles, was of considerable significance. For a long time, builders and their clients remained unwilling to go to the trouble and expense of full-length doubles – no mean undertaking on a GG-compass organ – and Elliot (and doubtless others) devised scales for pedal pipes which were intended to convey the impression of a 16' register without incurring the cost. Buckingham referred to them as 'common dwarf scale'. A set survives at Ashridge, in which the GG pipe has a speaking length of 8' 5" – Buckingham quotes 8' 6" as the norm (LIII: 81) – and external dimensions of 320 × 278 mm. They are tuned by means of sliding frames which sit inside the tops of the pipes. It seems that these 'dwarf' pipes were occasionally used for the lowest notes (to save on materials and space), and then the rank was completed with open, or, curiously, stopped pipes (at Scone, GG–D are open pipes, dwarf scale, then D♯–G are stopped) (Buckingham LIII: 79–80). There remains doubt as to the first appearance of full-length doubles in England (on the Pedal). Elliot's octave (GG–G) of open doubles at All Saints', Derby (1808) must have been one of the earliest examples, though

James Davis seems to have set a new standard in 1818 when he added an octave of doubles to the organ in St Saviour's, Southwark, which were 'the first ever made upon so large a scale' (*CR* xv, 1833: 683). Wherever the priority lies in certain matters, pedal pipes, whether unisons or doubles, remained rare in 1820.

So, too, did pedal couplers. A study of the organs pre-dating 1820 described by Buckingham indicates that, in nearly all cases where there were pedals, these were permanently coupled to one of the keyboards – usually the Great, but occasionally the Choir, in which case there would usually be a 'Pedals to Great' coupler (St Peter's, Sheffield, 1805; Chapel Royal, White-hall, 1814; Christ Church, Birmingham, 1815). The latter arrangement might imply that the pedals were used to supply a 'Choir Bass' to the short-compass Swell, rather as was described in the *English Musical Gazette* (1 January 1819: 8). The writer remarked upon the variety of colouring and shading which a discriminating player could introduce by a judicious use of the swell, 'especially if he be dexterous at the pedals; as he can then play the bass with his feet, while his hands are engaged alternately at each set of keys.' In most instances, the limited compass of the pedals would pose difficulties, though occasionally there may have been a conscious effort to make the pedals 'meet' the Swell – as at the Portuguese Chapel, following England's work in 1808, with pedals from G G–d, and a Swell from e–f^3. It may be that the permanent coupling of the pedals to the Choir keyboard was a fairly recent innovation designed to facilitate the practice described by the writer cited above; there is hardly any evidence for couplers between Choir and pedals before 1820, and when the pedals were permanently coupled to the Great, such a coupler would have served no purpose.

It may be that some of the earliest pedal pipes were permanently con-nected to the pedals. John Gray's estimate for a reconstruction of the organ in Trinity College, Cambridge (1835) includes a provision that the pedal pipes should be brought on and off by means of a drawstop, and this may imply that Avery's pedal pipes (1801) lacked this facility (MS 27). Buck-ingham sometimes records that pedal pipes were controlled by a separate drawstop – sometimes not: it is impossible to say whether any significance should be read into this. Similarly, he sometimes includes pedal pipes in his list of stops, but on other occasions, only mentions them when calculating the total number of pipes in the instrument; again, there may or may not be significance in this. What can be asserted with some confidence is that if the earliest pedal pipes *were* permanently connected to the pedals, organists must soon have demanded the facility of a drawstop, so as to increase the scope of the pedals.

It is apparent that the design of the pedals themselves did nothing to enhance their usefulness. Dr Hodges (writing in 1827) describes the pedals encountered in English organs at this period:

2   Scone Palace, Thomas Elliot, 1813. Toe pedals.

As usually constructed they are a set of clumsy pieces of wood, measuring from an inch to an inch and a half in width, and varying in length (according to the fancy of different builders) from a few inches to about two feet. In many instruments they are so short that the foot cannot be placed at length upon any one of them. These are called 'toe pedals', to distinguish them from the German pedals, which, affording room for the employment of both toe and heel, are therefore much more convenient to the performer . . .   (*QMMR*, IX, 1827: 4)

Toe pedals, of the sort described by Hodges, survive today in some chamber organs and in Elliot's Scone Palace organ (Plate 2); in the latter, the 'naturals' are 160 mm long, the 'sharps' are 64 mm, and each key is 19.5 mm wide. These were probably the earliest type of pedals employed by English organ-builders (some were even more stunted than those at Scone) and their construction emphasises the restricted rôle which was conceived for them. How soon German pedals made an appearance is not known. Scone reveals that Elliot was content to use toe pedals in an organ with separate pedal pipes in 1813, and G. P. England seems still to have been using them in large organs at the end of his career (Durham Cathedral, 1815). Thaxted, however, is probably reliable evidence that German pedals were in use by 1821 (Plate 3). The pedals are parallel ('straight') and arranged in the same plane ('flat'); they are also widely spaced (51 mm between adjacent naturals) with the result that this pedal board of only twenty notes occupies the same width as the keyboards. This was not always the case. The shortcomings of the

3   Thaxted Parish Church. Pedal board.

early pedals (whether of the toe or German variety) were often compounded by their eccentric location in relation to the keyboards; those at Scone are placed centrally, but others were placed left-of-centre, and this, combined with the frequent closeness of the pedal keys to one another, made their management a matter of some difficulty. Compasses, too, varied considerably, as Table 2 indicates. An octave (GG–G, usually omitting the GG♯) was common, though an octave-and-a-half (GG–c) was becoming established as the norm for the pedals by the end of the 1810s. The number of pipes (where these existed) did not necessarily correspond to the number of pedals. All in all, there is ample evidence to support the claim in Rees (1819)

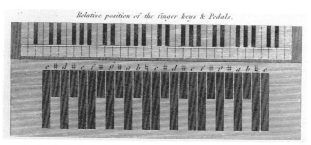

4   St Paul's Cathedral. Detail of engraving (1814) from *Rees's Cyclopaedia* ('Organ', Plate 1) showing relative position of keys and pedals. Foreigners complained of the shortness of the pedals (*EMG* 1 January 1819: 8), from which it may be deduced that they were some sort of toe pedals.

that 'scarcely two organs in the kingdom have their pedals alike . . . so that every performer who comes to an organ (be he ever so skilful in the use of pedals), has the whole of his business to learn again'. Rees's contributor was perhaps the first in a chorus of voices which continued until virtually the end of the century to urge a standardisation of pedal arrangements. He proposed that the placing (and presumably the compass) of the two octaves of pedals (C–c^1) at St Paul's Cathedral should serve as a model, with pedal c's placed directly under keyboard c's so that each pedal octave occupied two keyboard octaves (Plate 4). His plea fell on deaf ears.

WINDING

The Thaxted organ has horizontal bellows with two feeders (Figure 1); the organ in Rees's 'Interior Profile' (Plate 5), drawn only a few years earlier, has the older wedge-shaped bellows. The comparison highlights the fact that the first two decades of the nineteenth century represented a period of

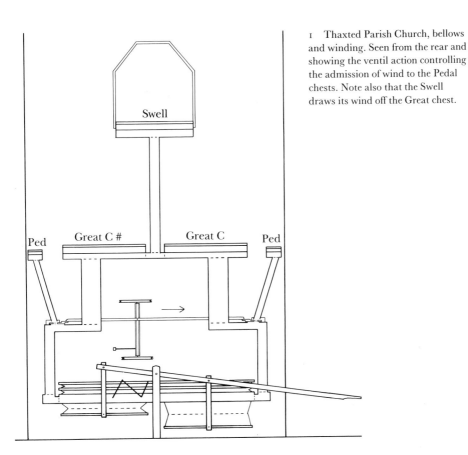

1   Thaxted Parish Church, bellows and winding. Seen from the rear and showing the ventil action controlling the admission of wind to the Pedal chests. Note also that the Swell draws its wind off the Great chest.

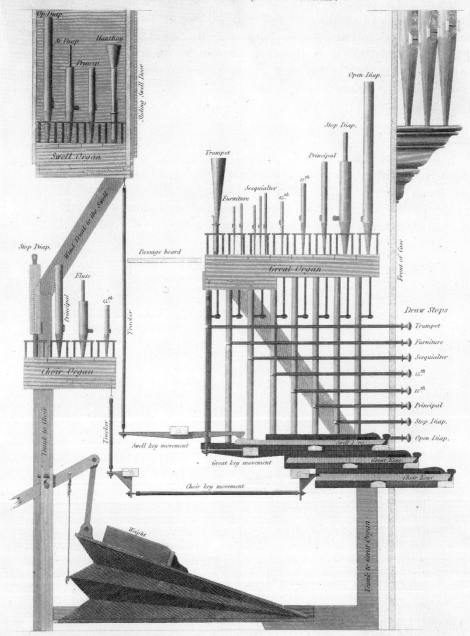

ORGAN.

Interior Profile of an English Church ORGAN.

PLATE II.

Op.Diap.

St.Diap. *Hautboy*

Principl.

Sliding Swell Door

Swell Organ

Open Diap.

Stop Diap.

Trumpet

Principal

12.ᵗʰ

Sesquialter

Furniture *15.ᵗʰ*

Wind Trunk to the Swell

Stop Diap.

Passage board

Front of Case

Flute

Principal

15.ᵗʰ

Great Organ

Tracker

Draw Stops

Trumpet

Furniture

Sesquialter

15.ᵗʰ

12.ᵗʰ

Principal

Stop Diap.

Open Diap.

Choir Organ

Trunk to Choir

Tracker

Swell key movement

Swell Keys

Great key movement

Great Keys

Choir key movement

Choir Keys

Weight

Trunk to Great Organ

Facey Jun. del.

Published as the Act directs, 1816, by Longman, Hurst, Rees, Orme, & Brown, Paternoster Row London.

Lowry sculp.

5 'Interior Profile of an English Church Organ'; engraving dated 1816 from *Rees's Cyclopaedia* ('Organ', Plate II).

transition in the design of wind systems for larger organs. The consequences of the innovations which were made at that time were far-reaching. Mr T. Wooley of Nottingham, writing of Buckingham's additions (1839) to the Snetzler organ in the parish church, commented that the new horizontal bellows 'supply a greater quantity of wind, with less manual labour, and the blasts of wind [are] more regular, in consequence of which the voices of the pipes [are] more steady; they mix and harmonize with each other in a very different manner than when effected with that tremulous pulsation of the wind which is always produced by the old diagonal bellows' (Buckingham LIV: 48). By establishing the means of providing an adequate and (relatively) steady supply of wind, organ-builders paved the way for organs with larger wind-chests, more stops, generously scaled pedal pipes, and more powerful reeds. In fact, the introduction of a reliable form of horizontal bellows in place of the old diagonal bellows was crucial to the development of the English organ in the 1830s and 1840s.

There is extensive evidence of the shortcomings presented by blowing and winding arrangements in the eighteenth century. G. P. England criticised the wind trunks in the old Exeter Cathedral organ as being 'all too small' with the result that 'many of the pipes do not speak well' (MS 37). In Blyth's reconstruction of the York Minster organ (1803) the gutters of the Choir soundboard were so narrow that, if more than two stops were drawn together, 'the whole became intolerably flat' (Gray 1837: 8). A single trunk supplied the Great Organ at Ely, entering the chest at the treble end: the inevitable result was chronic unsteadiness of wind (MS 28). A similar effect could be experienced at St Paul's where Smith's four diagonal bellows gave rise to the 'sad shaking' which was said to be characteristic of that otherwise admirable instrument (*EMG*, 1 January, 1819: 8). In general, English organ-builders were perplexed by the problems of raising sufficient wind and distributing it adequately; unlike the Germans, they commonly maintained the under-board in a horizontal position (thus aggravating the tendency of diagonal bellows to produce an unsteady supply of wind) and attempted an economic distribution of the limited supply of wind obtainable from two or three bellows by constructing narrow trunking, reducing the width of the bass grooves of the soundboard, and reducing the dimensions of the chest by standing the larger pipes off the soundboard (HR3: 13; *EE* xv: 675). The shortcomings of these expedients must have become critical towards the end of the eighteenth century, with the introduction of additional 8' registers, long octaves and (even) pedal pipes.

The circumstances and dating of the invention of horizontal bellows have been discussed elsewhere (Freeman 1945: 109–15; Ord-Hume 1978: 88–94; Wickens 1987: 30–4, 50–1). It seems that the inventor was either Alexander Cumming (1733–1814), a Scottish watch-maker domiciled in London, or Samuel Green (1740–96), the organ-builder. The earliest surviving examples of horizontal bellows are to be found in chamber organs by Green made in the mid-1780s. Although Hopkins claims that Green also used them in two church organs at a similar date (HR3: 14), it may be that these early horizontal bellows were chiefly adopted in smaller organs. Green made the old diagonal form of bellows for Lichfield Cathedral (1789) and St George's Chapel, Windsor (1790), experimenting in the latter instrument with a system of gradually increasing counterpoise to steady the wind as the bellows emptied (HR3: 13–14): this implies that he had serious reservations about the introduction of horizontal bellows in large organs. Yet within a decade of his death few builders were constructing diagonal bellows. Hopkins states that the making of diagonal bellows was abandoned shortly after 1800, and he claims that Avery's organ for St Margaret's, Westminster (1804) was one of the latest to be provided 'with bellows of the single or diagonal kind' (HR3: 10). A survey of the organs described by Buckingham largely supports Hopkins's contention.

The early horizontal bellows were open to improvement. Counter-balances ('square frames') were essential to ensure that the sets of ribs closed at the same rate, and these appeared in the organ which Cumming built for the Earl of Bute in 1787 (Freeman 1945: 112). The earliest ones were constructed of wood (some survive in chamber organs); later, iron was used. A second problem was the design of the feeders. Builders were tempted to make them too large, and the resistance arising from the inertia of the weights on the upper-board as it rose in response to vigorous pumping caused blasts of varying strength to be directed along the wind trunks (HR3: 20). By adjusting the relative capacities of reservoir and feeder this problem was overcome. Builders experimented in the early stages by multiplying the number of feeders. Elliot's large organ for All Saints, Derby (1808) had two pairs of horizontal bellows, one for the bass and one for the treble, and the former was provided with five feeders. Another possibility was the 'cuckoo' feeder (designed on the same principles as the cuckoo toy which was popular in the nineteenth century). Here, the bottom-board rocked on a central pivot, effectively creating two feeders with ribs and folds (HR3: 20–1). The strain on the bottom-board was considerable, and it was the double feeder which finally established itself as the most satisfactory means of feeding the reservoir. This form survives at Thaxted. Two feeders are positioned beside one another and at right-angles to the reservoir above them; the bellows handle is arranged so that, as one feeder closes, the other opens, and a steady supply of wind to the reservoir is assured. A third refinement was the introduction of a waste pallet to prevent further compression of the wind once the reservoir was full. The earliest form resembled the key of a wind instrument and covered an aperture in the top-board; an elementary, but workable, example survives in a chamber organ by G. P. England at Colne, Cambridgeshire (Figure 2). When the top-board has risen to a certain height the arm strikes the building frame causing the valve to open and permit wind to escape; another (rigid) arm keeps this movement in check. Later, builders

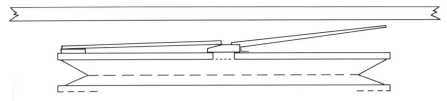

2   Colne Parish Church, waste pallet. When the bellows rise the arm eventually comes into
contact with the frame and thus opens the pallet.

removed the pallet to the underside of the top-board where it was operated
by a rope or leather thong attaching its free end to the middle-board (HR3:
20). This was susceptible to grit, which prevented the pallet closing fully,
and a further application of the basic principle took place, leaving the waste
pallet set in the middle-board and connected internally to the top-board by a
rope; wind could then escape into one or other of the feeders, or outside the
bellows altogether. A fourth feature of the horizontal bellows in their developed form was the use of inverted folds for the two sets of bellows ribs so that
each neutralised the influence of the other upon the compressed air as the
reservoir emptied. Cumming's claim to have originated this idea is better
substantiated than his claim to the horizontal bellows as such (Freeman
1945: 112). What is far from clear is how widely they were used. The
engraving of Flight & Robson's machine organ for the Earl of Kirkwall
(1811) (Ord-Hume 1978: 96–7) shows a bellows with inverted folds, but
some large organs from later years lack them – Elliot's organ at Crick, for
example.

    All these innovations aimed to steady the wind by redesigning the source
of supply itself. A further reform – the introduction of a circular handle and
crank to replace the usual straight handle – was directed at achieving a
steady supply by a uniform and gradual raising of the feeders. It also had the
advantage of easing the physical burden of blowing the organ. It may have
been first applied in domestic organs (at Scone, a servant could stand in the
corridor outside the Gallery turning a handle in order to blow the organ) but
some builders also employed it in large church organs – Elliot at Derby and
Bromsgrove (both 1808); Smith at Bristol Cathedral (1821) and St James's,
Bristol (1824); Flight & Robson at Trinity College, Cambridge (1819).

LAYOUT AND ACTION

The layout of the Thaxted organ is straightforward. The Great Organ stands
to the fore, with most of the basses of the front open diapason conveyanced
off the soundboard and displayed in the case. The Choir stands behind the
Great, the Swell is mounted directly over it (Figure 3). The pedal pipes stand
on chests to either side of the Great soundboard (Figure 4).

    Variations on this standard disposition were possible. The Thaxted organ

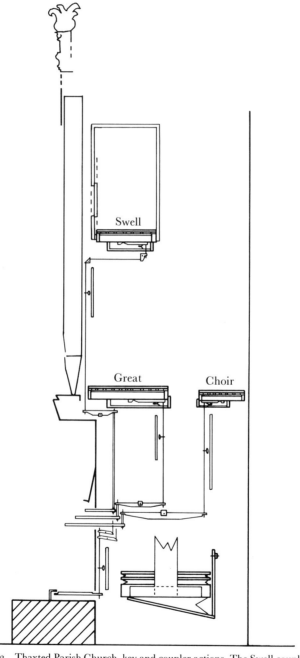

3   Thaxted Parish Church, key and coupler actions. The Swell coupler is omitted for
purposes of clarity.

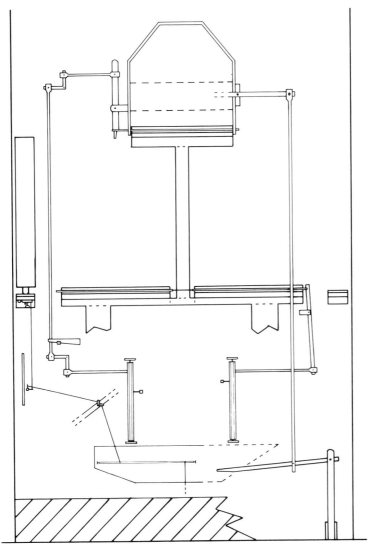

4 Thaxted Parish Church, pedal and stop actions. Seen from the front. The action to the
C♯ Pedal chest is similar to that shown for the C chest. The Swell is virtually inaccessible
and the details of its sliding front cannot be established precisely.

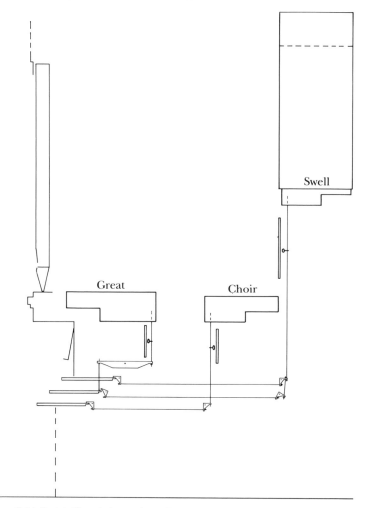

5   Crick Parish Church, key actions. The pedal action, which is not original, and
the manual coupler action, which may not be, are omitted.

enjoys the advantage of ample height, but in different circumstances a
builder might be obliged to adopt another solution. In the Crick organ, Elliot
placed the soundboards one behind the other; the Choir stands between the
Great and the (raised) Swell (Figure 5). This horizontal disposition found
increasing favour with builders as the nineteenth century advanced and they
had to cope with sites in chambers and aisles where height was limited but
depth (sometimes) was not. A Swell placed behind the Great was, in any
case, more accessible than one perched above it (the Thaxted Swell is almost
inaccessible) and this was the arrangement commonly adopted in 2-manual
organs: Scone and Ashridge are examples. It had other advantages besides
accessibility. A stand (building frame) supporting even the compact Swell
boxes of the early nineteenth century in a position over the Great (or Choir)

was a more complicated and expensive affair than one which effectively carried all the soundboards at the same level. The Thaxted building frame is a substantial, two-storied structure which has to support the tall casework as well as soundboards at two levels. The stands at Crick and Ashridge are simple frames, no more than 6′ high, easily set up in the organ-builder's workshop, dismantled and re-erected on site.

Lincoln's siting of the pedal pipes in the Thaxted organ represents one solution to the problem of accommodating these bulky intruders. Where space generally (and height in particular) was at a premium, an organ-builder might tackle the problem differently and stand the pipes across the back of the organ, to either side of the Swell. This is the arrangement employed by Elliot at Ashridge. Occasionally, the pedal pipes were stood apart (though still within the case) as at Scone; there, the two pedal chests stand side by side in an enclosure on one side of the case. All three arrangements are found throughout the period under consideration.

The provision of a separate case for the Choir Organ, whilst far from common in the early nineteenth century, continued to be the custom in certain instances. The Choir was held to be an accompanimental division, and the virtue of the encased Choir Organ in cathedrals and collegiate foundations where organs frequently stood on screens was that it brought the accompanimental registers into closer proximity to the singers. The cathedrals of Carlisle (1806) and Lincoln (1826) acquired new organs in new cases during this period, and each had an encased Choir Organ; Elliot's organs for Montreal Cathedral (1816) and Waterford Cathedral (1817) observed the same convention. The situation was different in parish churches and chapels where singers (if there were any) would usually perform from the gallery in which the organ stood. There were exceptions,[12] but by the 1820s an encased Choir Organ was a rarity in new parochial organs.

Two forms of key action were employed at this period and they were sometimes (frequently?) combined in the same instrument. There was what Rees referred to as 'the *long* movement', and which is applied to the action of the Choir Organ in an accompanying engraving (Plate 5). The movement of the key was conveyed to the pallet by means of squares, trackers and a roller-board. Elliot used it for the Choir, Swell and coupler action of the Crick organ (Figure 5). It was called the long movement because it allowed the keys to be placed some distance in front of the organ and so was useful in oratorio performances;[13] it also gave the organist in town churches an advantage in permitting him to keep the charity children (who might be ranged in tiers on either side of the organ, and expected to lead the singing) under surveillance. Then, there was the backfall action. Lincoln used it (exclusively) in his Thaxted organ in the form which incorporated stickers; Rees's engraving illustrates an (earlier?) form in which the backfall simply sits on the key tail without the intervention of a sticker. Builders employed backfalls for relatively short horizontal runs, squares and trackers for longer

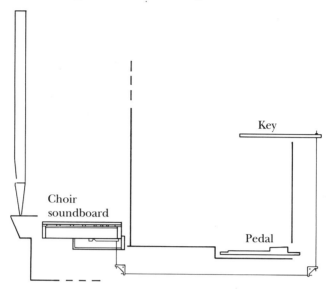

6 Action for a Choir Organ ('Preston', 1842) from Gray & Davison shop books (MS 3: f. 47).

runs. A modification of the latter form was used for pedal chests placed at the sides of the organ. Thaxted illustrates the principle (Figure 4). Three roller-boards were required – one immediately behind the pedal board, one under each of the chests – with three tracker runs assisted by sets of squares to convey the movement to the pallet. A simpler form of the same action (squares resting on the pedal tails, and only one roller-board) was often used for pedal chests at the rear of the organ.

Evidence for the action layout of an encased Choir Organ is elusive. There is, though, a sketch dating from 1842 in an organ-builder's shop book showing the action which was to be applied to an encased Choir Organ in an unidentified Preston organ (Figure 6). In view of the inveterate conservatism of craftsmen this may well have been a standard design for many years.

Three mechanical accessories should, finally, be mentioned: couplers, shifting movements and swells.

Provision of couplers followed no consistent pattern before 1820. Some builders introduced a Swell coupler, but its usefulness was restricted by the short compass of the Swell. More common in the first two decades of the nineteenth century was the Choir coupler (though, again, it can hardly have served much musical purpose); several of the Elliot organs recorded by Buckingham from the 1810s possess this, but none appears to have a Swell coupler (LIII: 79–85). Pedal couplers were of greater utility, and these (to both Great and Choir in some instances) were usually provided in organs with independent pedal pipes (see above, p. 20). At Thaxted, the pedal couplers act by means of two additional sets of (inverted) backfalls connected to stickers, which, when the coupler is drawn, force the tails of the Great or Choir keys to rise, ultimately causing the pallets to descend (Figure

3). The Swell coupler (i.e. Swell to Great) is a form of the tumbler coupler described by Hopkins (HR3: 54–5). Elliot's organ at Crick couples Swell to Great by a different method; the vertical trackers which are connected to the Swell roller-board have a second set of squares and horizontal trackers in addition to those which connect with the Swell keys, and these are brought into motion when the Swell coupler causes one set of squares to descend onto the Great key tails (Figure 5).

In the early 1800s, shifting movements were the sole means available to the organist of supplementing hand registration. By depressing a pedal and holding (or hitching) it down, the player moved the sliders of certain registers and silenced them; when the pedal was released springs caused the sliders to return.[14] It was a device which was useful in domestic instruments – Elliot provided a shifting movement at Scone which reduces the registration to 'diapasons' – and in the smaller church organ where it was sometimes known as a 'choir' pedal (because it reduced the registration to those accompanimental stops which would be placed in the Choir Organ of a larger instrument).[15] Significantly, Lincoln and Elliot found it unnecessary to include shifting movements in their Thaxted and Crick instruments because each had a proper Choir division.

The other mechanical device by means of which the organist could effect sudden changes of volume was the swell box. Most still had sliding fronts, resembling a sash window (cf. Figure 3), and though the construction varied a little their musical usefulness was severely restricted by the difficulty of managing the weight of the panel. By 1820, these nag's-head swells (as they were known: presumably because they imitated the up-and-down motion of a toiling horse's head) were being superseded by the venetian swell.[16] This had a front consisting of a number of horizontal shutters, opening or closing in consonance with one another, and was easier to control than the older device. Buckingham was frequently employed in the 1820s and 1830s in substituting these venetian fronts for the sliding variety, and his notebook serves as an illuminating barometer of change. Hence, in 1823, he replaced a nag's-head swell in the organ of St John's, Hull, which Elliot had built as recently as 1815 (LII: 13). The Hull organ must have been one of the last of Elliot's to be furnished with the older form of swell front. Ashridge (1818) has a venetian front consisting of four shutters. These shutters are not flush with the front when closed, but overlap each other, bedding into felted grooves provided for the purpose. Doubtless this represents just one of a number of possible ways of treating the design of these early venetian fronts.

CASE AND CONSOLE

English organs of the early-nineteenth century were almost invariably encased. The cases tended to be deeper than those of the previous century (to accommodate the more ambitious Swell Organs which were then becoming

6 Crick Parish Church, Thomas Elliot, 1819. Formerly in the Chapel Royal, St James's Palace. (1936)

fashionable, and maybe even a few pedal pipes) and there was a growing willingness to utilise the rear wall of the gallery to serve as the back of the organ, so saving on the cost of wooden panelling. Neither development enhanced the acoustical character of the organ case, which seems to have been largely overlooked or misunderstood in the early years of the century, but in other important respects, organ cases of this period display a clear continuity with those of the eighteenth century.

The Thaxted organ is an example. It is totally encased. The case has an ornamental front composed of towers and flats of gilded pipes (the upper flats consist of wooden dummies) and embellished with carving, fretwork and mouldings. The front and parts of the sides are made of mahogany, and there is a plain (but complete) back made of pine. The scale of the front, as in English organs of the eighteenth century, is dictated by two principal considerations: the height by one of the basses of the open diapason (in this instance the GG pipe, standing in the middle of the centre flat), and the width by the dimensions of the main soundboards. The inclusion of pedal pipes may have led to a marginal increase in the width, and the choice of a 5-pipe flat, rather than a tower, as the central feature of the front is unusual (though not without precedent), but in all essentials the Thaxted case is a direct descendant of those made for English organs during the course of the preceding century. (Crick stands in the same tradition, but there, lack of height meant that E was the longest pipe which could be accommodated in the front, and the remaining basses had to be stood off the soundboard inside the case (Plate 6).)

Ashridge is a different matter. The organ stands in a shallow (6'6") gallery to the 'west' of the antechapel immediately behind an arch which is only 5'6" wide (Plate 7). The keyboards are deeply recessed (so as to permit access to the loft from a nearby stairway) and are framed by Jeffry Wyatt's Gothic case which stands in front of, and above, the arch. In siting the organ in a chamber, and reducing the case to an ornamental front holding a total of seventeen speaking pipes from the tenor octaves of the two open diapasons (the remainder of the displayed pipes are dummies), Elliot and Wyatt adopted a solution which was exceptional for the period, but which presaged important developments of the 1840s and 1850s.

The console arrangements in all three organs are similar (Plates 8 and 9). The keyboards have ivory-covered 'naturals', with 'accidentals' of ebony, or stained wood, and the stop knobs – which have engraved ivory faces and square shanks (Plates 10 and 11) – are set in jambs at right angles to the keys.

The use of ivory for the 'naturals' was still sufficiently novel in the 1810s for Rees to comment upon it:

The long keys of our church organs were made of box or ebony, and the short, or flats and sharps, of ivory. But at present, the long keys, or natural notes, like those in harpsichords and piano-fortes, are of ivory, and the flats and sharps of ebony, or dyed pear-tree wood.   (Rees 1819)

According to Sir John Sutton, it was Samuel Green who first adopted the more modern arrangement for larger organs (by which time it was already extensively used in the construction of chamber instruments) (Sutton 1847: 82–3). No reliable dates can be quoted: Sleaford (Green, 1772) and Rother-ham (Snetzler, 1773) both employ the earlier convention; Lichfield (Green, 1790) was said to have had ivory naturals (Wickens 1987: 141), and Wymondham (Davis, 1793) certainly had them; Sevenoaks (Avery, 1798)

7 Ashridge, the Chapel, Thomas Elliot, 1818.

8 Thaxted Parish Church, keyboards and stop jambs.

9 Ashridge, keyboards and stop jambs (a photograph
taken in 1949 before the replacement of the pedal
board and swell pedal).

10 Thaxted Parish Church, stop faces.

11 Ashridge, stop faces (before re-engraving).

still had black naturals and white sharps (Pearce 1912: 152). Clearly there was no consistency, and different builders altered their practice at different times.

The Thaxted stop knobs are arranged in two columns in each jamb; the Great is to the right, with 'Pedals' (i.e. Pedal Pipes) at the top of the inner column, and 'Pedals to Great' (i.e. Great to Pedal) at the bottom of the outer column. To the left, the Swell stops are in the outer row, with 'Coupler Swell' (i.e. Swell to Great) at the top, and the Choir stops are nearest to the player, forming the inner column, with 'Pedals Choir' (i.e. Choir to Pedal) near the bottom of the jamb. The knobs themselves are small, and quite close together, so that they are easily managed by the organist. There are no department labels, but most of the Swell and Choir knobs are engraved either 'sw.' or 'ch.'.

Thaxted's is a typical console of the early 1800s. The precise arrangement of the stop knobs might vary a little (they might be in single columns, for example, as at Ashridge, or, if there were double columns, the Swell knobs might be grouped in the upper half of the jamb with the Choir below, as at Crick and King's College, Cambridge (MS 83: f22)) but, in general, consoles of this type were used for all but the most ambitious instruments throughout the period studied in this book.

PIPEWORK

In the construction and scaling of pipework the ambitions of the English organ-builder of 1820 were characteristically modest. Bernard Smith's attempts at the end of the seventeenth century to introduce novelties such as hohlflötes, blockflötes, quintadenas and the tapering spitzflöte made little impression on the course of English organ-building, and a similar flirtation with narrow-scaled cylindrical registers in the second half of the eighteenth century bequeathed an anglicised version of the Austrian 'dulciana' to the English organ, but achieved little else (Williams 1966: 88). Rees could confidently assert that the pipes in an English organ 'are of four kinds, stopped, half stopped, (with a funnel or chimney at the top), open and reed pipes' (Plate 12) (Rees 1819), and whilst this is an over-simplification, it is correct in its implication that the English organ of the early-nineteenth century possessed rather limited tonal possibilities by comparison with some, at least, of its European counterparts.

The choruses consisted largely of open metal pipes of cylindrical construction. Pipe metal was an alloy of tin and lead – generally not more than 25 per cent tin, and sometimes much less (in which case antimony might be employed as a hardening agent). According to Hopkins (HR3: 98) Lincoln was in the habit of using spotted metal (an alloy containing 40–50 per cent tin), but there is none in the Thaxted organ and spotted metal is rarely found

PLATE I.

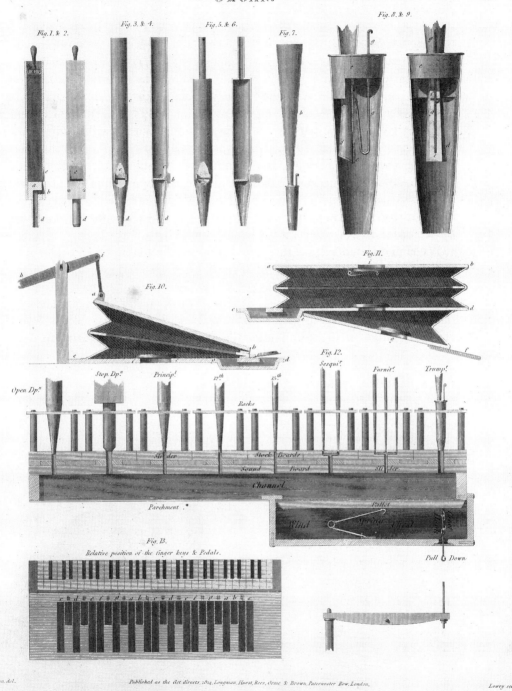

Faren Jun. del.

Published as the Act directs, 1814, Longman, Hurst, Rees, Orme & Brown, Paternoster Row, London.

Lowry sculp.

12 Pipe constructions; engraving dated 1814 from *Rees's Cyclopaedia* (Organ, Plate 1).

at this period. Before 1820, the scaling of the different registers within the chorus did not vary greatly, though a few builders had experimented with increasing the scale of the 8' register(s) and diminishing the scale of the upperwork; Wickens has shown that Samuel Green's organs were particularly innovative in this respect (Wickens 1987: 70–87). The only register of significantly wider scale than the main chorus was the mounted cornet, and this was becoming a rarity by the 1810s (above, pp. 12–13). At the other end of the spectrum, only the dulciana was more narrowly scaled than the chorus registers. Elliot was apparently making dulcianas with beards and narrow mouths in the manner of Snetzler as late as 1813 (Scone Palace); another tradition (to which Samuel Green and G. P. England belonged) treated them as small-scale open diapasons, and this tradition ultimately prevailed (Crick 1819; Bathwick 1820; Thaxted 1821). There was no attempt to distinguish the dulciana from the chorus registers by adopting a narrower mouth or restricting the flue: this would come later.

Wooden registers were of three sorts: stopped, half-stopped and open. The stopped diapason was the basic ingredient of the English organ. When constructed of wood, it might be fully stopped (as are the stopped diapasons on the Great and Choir at Crick) (Table 3) or the treble stoppers might be pierced (half-stopped) to give a little more brightness to the tone (Scone, 1813; Ashridge, 1818). Similar possibilities existed in the treatment of 4'

Table 3 *Crick, 1819: scales of flutes*

	internal		sides
Great Stopped Diapason			
C	127	× 101.5	12.75
c	76	× 60	12.75
c^1	41.25	× 31.75	9.5
c^2	25.25	× 20.5	6.25
c^3	17.25	× 14.25	6.25
Choir Stopped Diapason			
C	101.5	× 82.5	11
c	50.5	× 39.5	11
c^1	31.75	× 25.25	6.25
c^2	20.5	× 15.75	4.75
c^3	13.5	× 11	4.75
Choir Flute			
C	74.5	× 63.5	9.5
c	47.5	× 41.25	7.5
c^1	31.75	× 25.25	6.25
c^2	20.5	× 15.75	4.75
c^3	14.25	× 11	3.5

wooden flutes. Elliot made those at Ashridge (Great) and Crick (Choir) fully stopped, but scaled them very differently. In the former organ the flute is a little smaller in scale than the stopped diapason, whilst at Crick, the treble is of huge scale with very low mouths (Table 3).

Elliot's Scone organ contains another curiosity: a 4′ flute with 'open stoppers' (Buckingham LIII: 37). From tenor c the stoppers have been hollowed out, leaving a hole which is more than two-thirds the width of the stopper. Some of these ovals have wooden bars inserted into them (to strengthen the depleted stopper?) and the pipe bodies have been made about one third longer than would be necessary for fully stopped pipes. The scales are larger, even, than the Crick flute, and the pipes have low mouths (around one-sixth of the mouth width). The scales are as follows:

	c	c^1	c^2	c^3
internal	53 × 45	35 × 26	24.5 × 19.5	17 × 14
sides	9	7	4.5	4

The bodies are of pine, the caps of oak.

Organ builders at this period seem consistently to have used the 'English' block in making wooden pipes (Figure 7). The surface of the front panel was bevelled to create an edge which then formed the upper lip. The block had the same depth as the pipe body, and its face was at right angles to its upper surface. The cap (usually of hard wood, and hollowed out to create the windway) was fixed to the sides of the pipe body and the lower part of the block; its upper edge was set a little lower than the top of the block. Light nicks might be made in the exposed edge of the block.

Wood was also used for pedal pipes, most of which were of open construc-

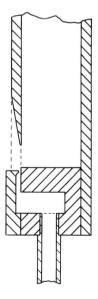

7   Wooden flute: 'English' block.

tion; they frequently had a wooden languid, rather than a block. Otherwise, open flutes were rare at this time.

Wooden flutes had been popular in England since at least the seventeenth century. Some builders, however, favoured metal flutes, and Snetzler adopted the practice he found among some English builders (Jordan, Bridge, Byfield) of making stopped diapasons and flutes with wooden basses and metal trebles, often with chimneys. Thereafter, many builders employed metal flutes (sometimes alongside wooden flutes, sometimes in preference to them), so much so that Elliot's steady adhesion to the wooden variety during the 1810s may have been unusual.

Lincoln's use of metal flutes at Thaxted is typical of the period. The stopped basses are of wood, the trebles (from the 2′ pipe) are metal chimney flutes. The scaling, construction and voicing of all three stopped diapasons and the flute are virtually identical, with slightly curved upper lips and quarter mouths cut up one third. All have large ears. The same arrangement of stopped basses and metal trebles is found in Gray's organ for St Mary, Bathwick (1820), except that the top twelve notes of each of the three stopped diapasons have no chimneys. The Russells also made metal flutes (for example, at Holy Trinity, Southwark, 1824).

Rees lists seven reed stops 'commonly used' by English builders: the trumpet, clarion, bassoon, hautboy, French horn, cremona, and vox humana. The last of these was seldom, if ever, made by the 1810s; the French horn was never common and nothing is known of its construction. The bassoon was increasingly employed as a bass to the Choir cremona which would therefore commence at tenor c or fiddle g (though Lincoln chose to follow an older fashion originated by Snetzler when he provided a full-compass bassoon in the Thaxted organ). The inverted conical resonators of the bassoon were of narrow scale, and might be made of metal or wood. The resonators of the cremona were half-length and cylindrical in construction; it was probably the only fractional-length reed made by English builders at this period. The shanks of the hautboy resonators were of a more generous scale than those of the later Victorian oboe, and the pipes were not capped; as with the oboe, the upper part of the resonator flared more sharply than the lower part, but, in the case of the hautboy, this 'bell' occupied a greater proportion of the total length of the resonator which was also of wider scale than in the later version. Trumpets and clarions had inverted conical resonators which might be mitred to get them into tight corners. Most builders used open shallots for all reeds (in the Thaxted organ, the trumpet, hautboy and cremona on the Swell have shallots of identical design), though Bishop seems to have used closed shallots with unique (?) rectangular openings for the Great reeds in his exceptional organ for St James, Bermondsey (1829). The shallots themselves were made of brass, slightly tapered (as shown in the Rees engraving), and often had 'beak' ends (as in Rees). The

Table 4 *Chaddesley Corbett, 1817: Great trumpet*

| | resonator | | shallot | |
	diameter of top	diameter of base	width of opening	exposed length
C	76	14	7	85
c	63	12	6	63
c^1	51	10	5	44
c^2	44	8	4	25
c^3	35	7	4	17

tongues were of brass. The English practice of cutting reeds to dead length, rather than slotting them, made the reeds more prone to irregularities than the continental variety, and in the period before the weighting of tongues was practised the tone was generally less controlled than would be acceptable later in the century. Table 4 gives details of the Elliot trumpet at Chaddesley Corbett (1817) which have been supplied by Mr John Budgen. These resonator scales are identical with Scone (1813) and with what is left of the trumpets at Ashridge (1818) and Crick (1819). It was usual for the top few notes of the trumpet, and rather more than the top octave of the clarion, to be flues.

Having reviewed the various forms of pipe construction commonly used by organ builders in the second decade of the nineteenth century it will be profitable to return to the scaling and voicing of the main choruses.

We may begin with Thaxted. The overall similarity of scaling throughout the chorus is the most striking feature (Table 1). Not only are the two open diapasons virtually identical with one another, but the principal and fifteenth (certainly from the 2′ pipe) are made to the same scales as the 8′s. The twelfth is rather narrower in the bass than the other ranks (three pipes smaller), but the scale increases as it rises through the compass so that the treble matches the other chorus ranks. This ensures that the quint is not too prominent in the bass but makes a distinctive contribution in the treble. A similar principle is applied to the design of the surviving mixture. The quint ranks there are the same scale as the twelfth, but whilst the unison ranks are kept down in scale in the bass so that they are three or four pipes smaller than the equivalent pipes in the main chorus, they increase in scale to match the chorus ranks in the treble. The tierce is treated similarly, and is, if anything, of a more generous scale in the treble than the corresponding chorus ranks. This seems to show that the potential solo use of the cornet (even when part of the main chorus mixture) was not wholly neglected at this period.

The principal and fifteenth of the Choir Organ are of identical scale for most of their compass (the principal is a little larger in the bass) and approximately three pipes smaller than the Great chorus. The Swell open diapason and principal are of similar scale to the two Choir registers, though the 8' has been kept smaller at the beginning of its compass (possibly for reasons of space) and the scale of the 4' has been slightly increased.

The treatment of all these chorus registers is much the same. The pipes have mouths which are consistently a little less than a quarter of the circumference; the mouths of the unison ranks are cut up by a quarter of their width, whilst the mutation ranks tend to be cut up rather less than a quarter. Languids are on the thin side (approximately 1.5 mm in the 1' pipe), with a steepish angle to the bevel (65°) and light nicking (an average of twenty nicks in the 1' pipe). The flues are unexceptional. The two 8's (now) have slightly wider toes than the other ranks, but, otherwise, there is no attempt to differentiate the registers by this means.

Despite minor variations (larger basses to some ranks, smaller basses to others) Thaxted's scaling is essentially straightline, and, as such, is in conformity with the more conservative builders of the previous century. The most significant departure from their practice is the smaller scaling adopted for the Choir registers, and this anticipates a general tendency which became entrenched as the century progressed.

Certain of Elliot's organs dating from the 1810s suggest a different approach. In the Scone organ (1813) the open diapason is two pipes larger than the principal, which is itself two pipes larger than the remainder of the chorus; the twelfth, the fifteenth and the two mixtures are identical in scale. At Crick (1819) there is evidence of a similar pattern, though the scales are significantly larger than Scone in the bass and halve more rapidly as they ascend the musical scale so that from the 9″ pipe they are much the same as in the earlier organ; Elliot evidently intended the church instrument to have a weightier chorus than the house organ. Ashridge (1818) represents a further variation (Table 5). Here, there is a clear distinction in scaling between the two open diapasons: in the treble, a difference of two pipes. There is also a difference of effect. The smaller of the two appears to be louder, slightly

Table 5 *Ashridge, 1818: Great diapason chorus*

	C	c	c^1	c^2	c^3
Open Diapason			52	30	19
Open Diapason			48	26.75	17
Principal	73	40.5	24.75	15.25	9.5
Twelfth	50.5	30	18.5	11.5	7
Fifteenth	44.5	24.75	16	10.25	6.5
Sesquialtra I	35	24.75	18.5	15.25	9.5
II	30	21	16	11.5	7

Composition:	GG	17.19
	c	15.17
	c^1	12.15
	a♯^{1}	8.12

harder in tone, and speaks more quickly; the larger has the breadth of tone and slow speech which characterise, in many people's minds, the old English diapason. There is little discernible difference in the voicing. The thickness and bevel of the languids are similar to Thaxted, though (and this is characteristic of Elliot's work at this period) the nicking is heavier, with perhaps 18 v-shaped incisions in the languids of the 1′ pipes. The scaling of the rest of the chorus is virtually identical, and is two pipes smaller than the second of the open diapasons (i.e. four pipes smaller than the larger one). It is curious that the principal is so small, especially in the bass, but this may be accounted for by the acute shortage of space within the organ chamber. Mouthing is consistent throughout the chorus: the pipes have quarter mouths, cut up a quarter, with ears up to the 1′ pipe (as at Crick).

Finally, a word should be said about mixture compositions. It is hard to assert anything with confidence on this subject for so few substantial organs have survived with their original mixturework intact. The surviving Thaxted mixture is not above suspicion, but, although it is made up of pipework which seems originally to have been intended for other purposes, it has been consistently re-marked in a hand resembling that found on the other pipework in the organ. The composition (Table 1) resembles Snetzler's for Halifax Parish Church (1766) (HR3: 277), and the 3-rank sesquialtra & cornet in Gray's organ for St Mary's, Bathwick (1820):

Halifax		*Bathwick*	
GG	15.17.19.22	GG	17.19.22
c^1	8.12.15.17	f♯	15.17.19
g^2	1. 8.12.15	c^1	12.15.17

Like Thaxted, the Halifax sesquialtra was originally accompanied by another mixture, but there is nothing to suggest in either case that the design of the sesquialtra would have been very different had this not been so. Each of the three examples highlights a characteristic of many (most?) English mixtures of the eighteenth century, namely, the presence of the tierce throughout all (or most of) the compass, and the two later instruments further testify to the growing practice of treating the treble of the chorus mixture as a substitute for the superseded mounted cornet. The fact that treble and bass drew separately in both instruments is also significant.

Again, Elliot's work departs from the norm. Though he made mixtures of the sesquialtra-and-cornet variety, he also, in the 1810s, made a number of organs with two 2-rank mixtures on the Great. Scone, Ashridge and Crick were among these; so, too, were Stockport Sunday School (1811), Whitehall Chapel (1814), Christ Church, Birmingham (1815) and Montreal Cathedral (1816). Scone has survived unscathed, and, as the unaltered parts of the mixturework at Ashridge and Crick reproduce the Scone compositions exactly, it may be that all the instruments had identical mixtures.

Scone palace (1813)

	Sesquialtra	Mixture
GG	17.19	22.26
c	15.17	19.22
c¹	12.15	19.19
a♯¹	8.12	15

The absence of the tierce (and hence the cornet) in the treble is notable, and also the reduction in the number of ranks towards the top of the compass – a feature of certain organ builders' work later in the century.

Nothing is known with any certainty of the composition of second mixtures, though Thaxted's is said to have had an opening composition of 26.29 'repeating at each octave with no variation' (*MO*, xxxvii, 1913: 33). Some may have included octave tierces (cf. Green's mixtures at St Katherine-by-the-Tower, 1778), some not (cf. Snetzler's work at Halifax) (HR3: 276–7); hard evidence is almost totally lacking.

It has been thought worthwhile to consider the design of the English organ in 1820 at some length because this will establish a useful reference point for what follows in succeeding chapters. The present work is essentially a study of change – and it is therefore fundamental that the point of departure should be clearly perceived at the outset. There is a further consideration. The survival of a handful of substantial instruments (with mechanisms, pipework and winding arrangements) from the period 1813–21 offers an opportunity for detailed commentary upon the design and construction of the English organ at a particular stage in its development that will not recur until we reach the 1850s. The traveller in such a sparsely populated landscape must seize his opportunities as and when they present themselves: hence this extended survey. It is hoped that the observations which have been made have shown that the design of the English organ during the first two decades of the nineteenth century was not static and that innovation (although limited in its nature and application) was not unknown. Over the course of the next two decades various factors would combine to force the pace of change. It was unfortunate that neither the musicians who desired change, nor the organ-builders who were expected to execute it, had much idea of the means by which to attain their objectives, and the results were frequently rather curious. Some of these will be considered below. First, however, it will be appropriate to consider the circumstances in which organs were built, and the ways in which they were used, during the earlier part of the nineteenth century.

2

Organs and organ-building, 1820–40

In January 1829 the Committee of Christ's Hospital approached Thomas Attwood, organist of St Paul's Cathedral, for advice about the purchase of an organ for the school's new Hall, then nearing completion. Attwood responded with stop lists for three organs of differing sizes and the names of four 'of the most eminent Organ Builders' to whom, he suggested, application should be made for tenders. The builders named were J. C. Bishop, John Gray, H. C. Lincoln and Elliot & Hill (Plumley 1981: 24). Other organists might have expressed different preferences. Charles Wesley (organist of St Marylebone) sang the praises of William Allen, who was duly awarded the contract for the new Lincoln Cathedral organ in 1823 (MS 44/k) and Timothy Russell must have been highly regarded by some London organists, to judge by the number of organs that he built for new suburban churches during the 1820s. Other builders will be mentioned in due course, but, for the moment, these six – Bishop, Gray, Lincoln, Elliot & Hill, Allen and Russell – may be taken to constitute a comprehensive list of those judged by their contemporaries to be the leading builders of the day.

All had their workshops in London. England had never developed regional schools of organ-building such as existed in parts of Europe, though a tradition of some independence had established itself in Bristol through the work of the Harrises and the Seedes, and in Manchester and York Richard Parker (*fl.* 1740–80) and John Donaldson (*fl.* 1783–1807) respectively maintained flourishing businesses in major centres away from the capital. Elsewhere, an organ-builder might earn a livelihood by tuning the local organs, undertaking small repairs, even making the occasional chamber or barrel organ, but, in 1820, most churches and private patrons turned to the metropolitan organ-builders when a new organ was required or an old one was to be reconstructed. This was the last generation in which this would be so. The third quarter of the nineteenth century saw the rise of a large number of provincial organ-building firms, of which the most successful could boast

49

workshops and order books to match the London builders, and already, by
the 1820s, the seeds of this significant development were being sown. In
1823, Samuel Renn (1786–1845) and John Boston (1787–1849) set up as
organ-builders in Stockport, removing to Manchester by 1825. Over the
course of the next two decades the firm (from which Boston withdrew around
1836) built over 100 organs for churches and chapels in Manchester, Lancashire, Cheshire and occasionally further afield (Sayer 1974: 3–18; 69–
110). Renn's willingness to utilise machinery and apply principles of
standardisation to the manufacture of organs and organ cases did much to
ensure his success in exploiting the rapidly expanding market for organs in
north-west England, as Sayer has convincingly demonstrated (1976a: 90–
100; 1980: 96–7). Industrialisation, bringing in its train a rapid expansion in
population and the building of new churches, had a similar effect upon the
demand for organs in parts of south and west Yorkshire. Joseph Booth
(c. 1769–1832) established a business in Wakefield in 1824 which passed to
his son Francis upon his death (Booth 1911); Booth senior seems to have
been one of the first to experiment with pneumatic assistance for organ
actions and the large organs for Brunswick Chapel (1828) and St Peter's
Chapel (1838) in Leeds were no less innovative in their design than the most
ambitious contemporary work of the London builders. But Leeds had its
own organ-builders. Thomas Greenwood had established a business there
by 1817, which passed eventually (by 1834) to Joseph and William Greenwood; Matthew Booth (from 1826) and Thomas Robinson (from 1830) are
also recorded as organ-builders in the Leeds directories, and all these are
known to have built organs (*Leeds*: 1817, 1826, 1830, 1834). Further north, in
York, John Ward was in business between about 1814 and 1850 (Gray 1837:
8; White 1851: 500), and in Edinburgh, James Bruce built organs both under
his own name and on commission from the Edinburgh music dealers Muir,
Wood and Company (later, Wood, Small and Company) (Menzies 1986:
82). Bewsher & Fleetwood founded a business in Liverpool in 1821 and
William Wilkinson of Kendal (an early experimenter with the application of
electromagnetism to organ actions) set up in 1829 (*BIOSR*, 5/3: 11; Sumner
1977: 27). In Bristol, John Smith (1772–1847) maintained the city's distinctive tradition of organ-building with some remarkable instruments which
will receive further consideration below. Other names appear in the directories of various towns and cities during the 1820s and 1830s (some of those
called 'organ-builders' were, in reality, music dealers who supplied organs
by commissioning them from an organ-builder, whilst others would devote
most of their energies to the far more lucrative business of selling and tuning
pianos) but, with the possible exceptions of Renn's activities in the Manchester area and Smith's virtual monopoly in Bristol, the metropolitan
builders had little reason to fear serious competition from the provinces
before the 1840s.

Something should now be said concerning these London builders, their establishments and working methods; various matters are still obscure (and will remain so, in the absence of original documentation) but some impression can be gained of the activities of the principal builders in the last two decades before the opening of the Victorian era.

Henry Lincoln and Timothy Russell each worked from premises in the parish of St Andrew, Holborn (a district much inhabited by organ-builders in the eighteenth century). Lincoln was at 196 High Holborn, and Russell at 28 Theobalds Road (*London* 1820: 218, 305). Russell's was the older business. His father, Hugh Russell (*c.* 1738–1825) (Dawe 1983: 140), had been in partnership with John England, but established his own business in *c.* 1784 (MS 75). It is likely that Timothy Russell had charge of the firm's work for some years before his father's death in 1825. Shortly after this, the business moved to 2 Gray's Inn Terrace (by 1830), declining in importance until it finally disappeared from view about 1858 (*BIOSR*, 3/3: 18). The fortunes of the Lincolns followed a similar pattern. Their earliest recorded instrument (for Alfreton Church) was made by John Lincoln in 1789 (Buckingham LIV: 45). It was said that Henry Cephas Lincoln was apprenticed to Flight & Robson before joining his father around 1810 (*MSt* VI, 1867: 203); Buckingham records an organ of 1814 by 'Lincoln and Son' (LII: 178). John Lincoln seems to have retired (or died?) by 1819 (Boeringer 1977: 12). Henry Lincoln collaborated with Dr Gauntlett over a number of instruments in the early-1840s (see below pp. 189, 257) but after his failure to complete the huge organ for St Olave's, Southwark (1844–6) little more is heard of him. It is said that he died in 1864 (Sumner 1962: 233). Russell was the more conservative figure of the two. His larger organs made few advances on the Thaxted model (though his *magnum opus*, the organ for Holy Trinity, Newington (1824) was a little more enterprising) and, if Sperling is to be believed, he was still making tenor-f Swells in 1848 and GG-compass keyboards in 1850 (Woburn Church; St John, Red Hill, Reigate). Lincoln was bolder (not least, in taking on Dr Gauntlett) and, until his loss of nerve over St Olave, Southwark, kept abreast of contemporary developments in organ design. His most ambitious work was in London. The writer in the *Christian Remembrancer* (XVIII, 1836: 108, 175) singled out his organs for the new churches of St George, Camberwell (1824), and St Peter, Walworth (1825), describing the former as 'one of the first class, and inferior to none of this builder's make, in London'; the tone was 'rich and powerful', the reeds blended 'admirably' with the chorus, the latter being 'remarkably brilliant' – so much so, that this neo-Victorian commentator suggested adding another reed to redress the balance. The stop list makes small but significant departures from convention (the inclusion of a double diapason; the unusually extended compass of the Swell; the nine ranks of mixtures) but is curiously conservative in other respects (the absence of pedal couplers; the meeting of the pedal pipes and the keyboard double). Lincoln held the appointment of Organ-Builder to the King, and this may account for the

large number of organs that he built for Brighton churches and chapels. Like
many of his other country organs, most are modest 2-manual instruments of
no obvious distinction. One of his last organs was a 21-stop instrument for St
David's Cathedral (1843); it was a neat German System instrument, with C-
compasses and a fully-developed Great chorus, and suggests that Lincoln
was more resourceful than many in adapting to new ways.

The Allens may be briefly mentioned. William Allen had premises at 11
Sutton Street, Soho, from around 1790. He was succeeded, probably in the
early-1830s, by his son, Charles Allen, who was active in business until
c. 1860. The firm's work tended to be conservative in character; William
Allen's scheme for Peterborough Cathedral (1809) was conventional to the
point of unimaginativeness, and he had little more to offer at Lincoln (1826)
beyond double pedal pipes and a cautiously enlarged Swell stop list.
Twenty-five years later, his son added an absurdly archaic Pedal Organ to
the same instrument (HR2: 531). But the quality of their work was good, as a
number of chamber organs, and the surviving instrument at Everingham
(1837) testify, and, although the business was clearly on a smaller scale than
that of Lincoln or Russell, it seems to have done a steady trade.

James Chapman Bishop (1783–1854), who founded a business at 7 York
Buildings, Marylebone, in 1807 (the business moved to 1 Lisson Grove
South, later re-numbered as 250 Marylebone New Road, in 1829) was one of
the most prolific of the metropolitan builders in the years between 1820 and
1840 (Elvin 1984: 17, 21, 45, 53). The bulk of his work was for London
churches and he had charge of the organ in St Paul's Cathedral from 1826
until his death, undertaking major work there in 1826, 1849 and 1852 (MS 62:
203–4; Elvin 1984: 162–6), but it is a measure of his reputation that he was
also engaged to reconstruct a number of cathedral organs outside the
metropolis: Oxford (1827), Gloucester (1831), Hereford (1832), Norwich
(1833–4) and Durham (1844, 1847) (Elvin 1984: 166–75). At the time of his
death, he could be referred to as 'one of the three great organ-builders of the
metropolis' (MW xxxii, 1854: 836).

Bishop had been apprenticed to Flight & Robson. He first made his mark
with chamber organs, for which there was still a considerable market in the
1810s: according to a contemporary, 'in grace, purity, and a certain unctu-
ous richness of tone, they were altogether unrivalled' (MW xxxii, 1854:
836). Similar characteristics seem to have been admired in Bishop's larger
organs. One of the most enterprising of these stood in St James's, Bermondsey (1829) (Appendix 1, pp. 445–6). This instrument had (exceptionally) a
3-stop Pedal Organ and a large, G-compass Swell. It was much approved by
a writer in the *Examiner*:

The swell is of a very sweet quality; the reeds are very smooth and equal, particularly
the Cremona. The choir organ is silvery in its tone, and the soft stops throughout are
voiced with the utmost delicacy: in a word, Mr. Bishop has eminently succeeded in
the difficult task of combining sweetness and power . . .   (26 April 1829: 264)

Twenty-five years later, taste had moved on. An obituarist commented that, at an early stage in his career, Bishop had arrived at 'a certain *beau idéal* of his own' at which he excelled, but 'from which he never safely departed'. He identified the Bermondsey organ, and organs for St John's, Waterloo Road (1824) and St Edmund's, Lombard Street (1833) as representative of Bishop's best work. The writer was less complimentary about some later instruments, 'wherein Mr. Bishop, unwillingly, as we thought, departed from his settled convictions in search of more modern dimensions and combinations', naming St Giles's, Camberwell (1844) (Appendix 1, pp. 446–7) and St James's, Piccadilly (1852) as examples. The complaint, it seems, was that for all the 'charm and suavity of tone' to be found in his instruments, Bishop had failed to rise to the challenges of the 1840s, and his organs failed to qualify for 'the category of grand instruments' (*MW* xxxii, 1854: 836–7). As another writer (or possibly the same one) put it: Bishop entertained 'certain prejudices, certain adhesions to, not *old*, but *middle-aged* doctrines as to tone, which always interfered with his success in constructing a large organ' (*MW* xxxiii, 1855: 597).

There is a note of condescension in both articles, but it cannot be denied that the writers have a point. That 'full round mellow tone' that Bishop promised the subscribers to the new organ at Kenilworth (1839) (ms 59), and which can be detected in both the Bermondsey organ and the instrument now standing in Kinlet Parish Church (1840), is typical of his work; it did not lend itself to the production of energetic, brilliant choruses of the sort made by Hill or Gray & Davison during the 1840s. By comparison with these, Bishop's work at St Giles's, Camberwell (which, in its conception, is a considerable departure from his usual practice), is tame and a little colourless. A pursuit of delicacy in the voicing of flutes and of smoothness in the regulation of reeds suggests a degree of refinement appropriate to smaller organs but debilitating in larger ones. Both qualities (mellowness and refinement) began to go out of fashion in the mid-1830s, when they were superseded by a taste for massiveness and variety of effect. They persisted, though, in Bishop's work into the 1850s, justifying his identification as a conservative influence in the later part of his career.

Such a judgement could hardly have been made in, say, 1830. Then, Bishop must have appeared to be something of an innovator. He was responsible for the introduction of the claribella stop, and his Pedal Organ at Bermondsey went beyond anything that had been attempted by an English organ-builder at the time. More will be said on both matters below (pp. 102, 112). Equally important were his improvements in the winding and control of the organ.

In the 1820s and 1830s Bishop's estimates frequently stipulated the provision of 'double feeding bellows, inverted folds for evenness of pressure inside waste valves for silence and all my improvements for steadiness of wind' (ms 51: Newark). The 'improvements' included concussion-bellows, applied either to a wind-trunk or the underside of the wind-chest so as to regulate the steadiness of the wind supply when under strain. It has been stated that Bishop first employed concussions in 1826 at St Paul's (Freeman 1922a: 7), but according to Hopkins, they were first introduced in an organ built for the old Covent Garden Theatre 'many years ago' (HR3: 23). Bishop is not known to have built an organ for Covent Garden, but he added a long movement to an existing organ there in 1825 and it may well be then that a concussion-bellows made its first appearance (Elvin 1984: 177). An additional factor which contributed to the steadiness of wind in Bishop's organs was his willingness to provide a separate bellows to supply the pedal pipes in large organs; he first did this in the organ for St John's, Waterloo Road (1824) (MS 51). His work at St Paul's in 1826 included remedying the chronic unsteadiness of wind of which the writer in the *English Musical Gazette* had complained (1 January 1819: 8). As well as the newly-invented concussion-bellows, it was probably on this occasion that Bishop introduced a separate bellows for the pedal pipes. All in all, his improvements were said to have rendered the wind 'perfectly steady; so that there is not, perhaps, an organ in England more complete in this respect' (*CR*, xv, 1833: 431).

The invention of the composition pedal has been consistently attributed to Bishop, on account of the fact that he had to justify his claim against a counter-claim laid by Flight, his former master: the case went before the Society of Arts, and what looked suspiciously like chicanery on Flight's part was exposed (HR3: 88). According to Pole (1851: 58) this was in 1809, though the earliest appearance of composition pedals in Bishop's surviving papers is in an estimate of 1820 for 'Collonell Chichester' for a 7-stop organ (MS 47); it was to be provided with no fewer than five composition pedals. It seems that composition pedals steadily replaced shifting movements as accessories for moving the stops in the work of both Bishop and his contemporaries. They had the advantage of dispensing with springs to operate the sliders (a potential source of irritation to the listener, should the organist release the pedal hastily) and could offer a greater range of pre-set registrations. The earliest composition movements were made of wood (in 1849, Bishop replaced his original composition actions at St Paul's, substituting iron-work for wood 'to make them more firm' (MS 62: 203–4) and it is likely that they were single-action, either drawing stops in or thrusting them out, but not able to effect both operations.

It has been judged worthwhile to spend some time considering the career of J. C. Bishop; he was an important figure in the second quarter of the nineteenth century, but his work was *sui generis*, and his increasing conservatism after 1830 means that he will not be prominent in the following narrative with its central theme of the transformation of English organ design. This can hardly be said of the remaining two organ-builders in the list of leading metropolitan practitioners, and they may therefore be considered more briefly at this stage.

Robert Gray (*c.* 1742–96) established his business in Leigh Street, Red Lion Square, in about 1772 (MS 75). He soon took his brother, William (*c.* 1757–1821), into partnership, and by 1790 the business had moved to 4 New Road ('near the end of Portland Road'). The firm continued to occupy premises in the New Road ('9 New Road, Fitzroy Square') which had, by 1858, become 370 Euston Road (Langwill and Boston 1970: 53–4; Wilson 1968: 71; Dawe 1983: 103). Following Robert Gray's death (1796), William continued the business under his own name, and it duly passed to his son, John, in 1821. John Gray's son, another Robert, accounts for the designation 'Gray & Son' which is occasionally found in the late-1830s, but by 1842, John Gray's son-in-law, Frederick Davison, had become a partner, and the business was known as Gray & Davison. Control finally passed to the Davison family in 1849, upon John Gray's death.

The firm's work enjoyed a high reputation throughout the first half of the nineteenth century. Larger organs of the 1820s and 1830s were on the Thaxted model, with an increase in the size and compass of the Swell, and more frequent provision of pedal pipes (including doubles) as the period progressed; new organs for St Dunstan-in-the-East (1820), St Mark, Kennington (1831) and St Nicholas, Liverpool (1833) illustrate this evolution. There were, though, some exceptional instruments. The large organ for St Marylebone Parish Church (1817) stood in a gallery at the east end of the building; it was divided into two parts, separated by an arch filled with a transparency depicting the angel hailing the shepherds (Smith 1833: 91). The new organ for St Pancras Church (1822) was of similar size; it had a 7-stop Swell Organ, commencing at tenor c, doubles on both Swell and Great, and a 'Violincello' bass to the Choir Cremona (MS 79: 85; MS 1: 26). Gray built an instrument of similar design for Blackburn Parish Church in 1828 (and reconstructed it after a fire in 1832) (Appendix 1, pp. 447–8). Mention should also be made of the organ in St Sepulchre, Holborn. George Cooper (*c.* 1783–1843) was organist there. He was widely consulted for his views on organs and organ builders, and tended to favour Gray (the reason for his antipathy to either the persons, or work, of Elliot & Hill remains obscure).[1] Under his direction, John Gray was responsible for significant alterations to the old Renatus Harris organ in St Sepulchre's, chiefly, the extension of the Swell compass and a revision of the pedal arrangements (below, pp. 102, 114). A reconstruction of the Smith organ in Trinity College, Cambridge, in 1836 – again with Cooper acting as adviser – was equally innovative.

Like Bishop, much of John Gray's work was in London. He had, though, an extensive 'country' connection, especially in the west, building a batch of organs for new churches in Cheltenham, and laying the foundations of the firm's later flourishing business in and around Liverpool. Altogether, Gray was perhaps the most successful and prolific organ builder of the 1820s and 1830s.

The business founded by Thomas Elliot (*c.* 1759–1832) was not far behind in these particular stakes, and might justly, by the late-1830s, claim to be both more experienced in the building of the largest organs and more adventurous in their tonal schemes. Nothing is known of Elliot's background. He is first recorded as an organ-builder in 1790 (Wharton's Court, Holborn) (*Universal British Directory* 1790: 137); by 1794, he was at 10 Sutton Street, Soho Square, and, by 1804, at 12 Tottenham Court (Edmonds and Plumley 1988: 56–9). The business, under its various titles, remained at this address (which had become 261 Euston Road by 1858) (*London*, 1858) until the 1870s. From an early date, the firm claimed a business connection with Snetzler.[2]

For ten years or more, Elliot's foreman was Alexander Buckingham. He had previously worked for John Avery in a similar capacity (Buckingham LII: 6) and it may be that he transferred directly to Elliot upon Avery's death in 1807 and completed the Carlisle Cathedral organ (for which Elliot was paid in 1808). Buckingham's notebook contains details of many Elliot organs; the entries relating to all those built between 1808 and 1818 conclude with a repetitive phrase, claiming that the instrument in question was 'Designed Pland and Built' by A. Buckingham. It is difficult to know how seriously to take this claim, especially when it conflicts with other evidence. The most blatant contradiction concerns William Hill, Elliot's son-in-law, partner and successor. According to an obituary Hill joined Elliot in 1815 (*MSt* XIV, 1871: 4). Shortly afterwards (the account continues) he was responsible for the design of the Ashridge organ, and was given 'the whole credit' for its successful accomplishment by the Earl of Bridgewater. Buckingham's version of the conception and construction of the Ashridge organ differs: according to him, 'the whole was Pland and Built by A. Buckingham' (LIII: 82). The truth is elusive, but it appears that Buckingham left Elliot's employment in 1818, and it is not unreasonable to suggest that friction with Hill may have been a contributory factor.

William Hill (1789–1870) was born at Spilsby, in Lincolnshire. It is not known how he came to be an organ-builder, nor how he occupied himself before joining Elliot's establishment.[3] He entered into partnership with Elliot during the 1820s, possibly during 1825,[4] and the firm was then known as 'Elliot & Hill'. Following his father-in-law's death in 1832, Hill carried the business on alone, entering into a short-lived partnership (1837–8) with Frederick Davison during which the style 'Hill & Davison' was adopted. The firm had become 'Hill & Co.' by the late-1840s, and 'Hill & Son' by 1857.

Much of the firm's work during the 1820s and 1830s was conventional; there was the occasional tenor-c Swell (St George, Kidderminster, 1828), the provision of a choir bass became more common (St Martin, Birmingham, 1822, was an early example), and pedal provision increased slowly. Large organs for Dorking Parish Church and Ely Cathedral (both 1831) had stop lists which were very similar to that of the Thaxted organ, and small organs for St Peter, Saffron Hill (1836) and Holy Trinity, Gray's Inn Road (1840) differed little from the instruments being built twenty years earlier. Despite the (curious) absence of major commissions in London, the business seems to have flourished; it is notable that there was a steady flow of work from Birmingham and the surrounding counties, and, to a lesser extent, from Yorkshire, the East Midlands, Cambridge, and the Manchester area (despite Renn's activities). Elliot was not averse to innovation, and nor, it seems, was Hill. Beginning in 1829, the firm was responsible for a series of organs which, for size, mechanical ingenuity and tonal novelty, were wholly unprecedented in the English experience. More will be said of these remarkable instruments in due course, but they ought, at least, to be listed here: Christ's Hospital (1830), Oldham Parish Church (1830), York Minster (1829–33), Birmingham Town Hall (1834), Christchurch, Newgate Street (1831, 1834), Chapel Royal, St James's Place (1837), and St John's College, Cambridge (1838). The ultimate success of any one of these organs might, rightly, be disputed, but they established William Hill as the leading builder of the day: a position from which he had scarcely been dislodged at the time of his death, in 1870.

Where substantial new organs were required, or else an extensive reconstruction of an old one, there was a good chance, during the 1820s and 1830s, that one or other of the six firms mentioned above would be employed. But for smaller organs – particularly, barrel organs, barrel-and-finger organs, and chamber organs – this was not so. Whereas Gray or Elliot might be occupied building several large organs during the course of a year, other builders, of more modest ambitions, found that there was an excellent trade for mechanical organs and small church organs with a handful of registers and standardised cases. Some of these builders undertook more demanding work when the opportunity presented itself, and some were able to expand their businesses and move into the first division of builders.

Joseph William Walker (1802–70) falls into this last category. He is said to have been a 'parlour apprentice' of G. P. England (though as England died in 1815, this can hardly have been for any extended period) and established his own business in about 1827 at 5 Bentinck Street, Soho, eventually settling at 27 Francis Street (Langwill and Boston 1970: 65). His early reputation was established through the building of barrel organs and small barrel-and-finger organs, but by the late-1830s, he was moving into a different league, as the commission to build a large new organ for the Exeter Hall in 1839 proved (Appendix 1, pp. 448–9). Thereafter, the firm's reputation increased steadily. Contracts for Jamaica Cathedral and Antigua Cathedral came Walker's way in 1847, and during the 1850s and 1860s the firm was responsible for building a large number of substantial instruments, Highfield Chapel, Huddersfield (1854), Romsey Abbey (1857), St Audeon,

Dublin (1861), and a 43-stop instrument for the 1862 Exhibition among them.

George Maydwell Holdich (1816–96) was another metropolitan builder who managed to establish himself as rather more than a manufacturer of barrel organs. He had been apprenticed to Bishop, and set up his own business in 1837. His ambitions were more modest than those of Walker and his most typical (and best) work remains the small village church organs of the 1840s and 1850s, but he built a cathedral organ (Lichfield, 1861) and was responsible for a number of other large instruments in the third quarter of the century. He was in business at 12 Greek Street in 1837, moving to 4 Judd Place East c. 1850 (it became 42 Euston Road), and finally to Liverpool Road, Islington, in the 1860s (Edmonds 1960: 42–3).

Holdich's premises in Greek Street had once been occupied by Henry Bevington. Bevington worked with Robert Gray before establishing his own business in Greek Street in about 1794; he soon moved into Snetzler's former workshop in Rose Yard, Manette Street, retaining the other address as his private residence and later taking a lease on 48 Greek Street (Cardwell, Freeman and Wilton 1898: 220–1; Ord-Hume 1978: 134). The firm was active in building barrel organs and smaller church organs, though it was also responsible for a number of large instruments: Catholic Chapel, Moorfields (c. 1830), Mechanics' Institute, Nottingham (1849), St Martin-in-the-Fields (1854), and the Foundling Hospital (1855). The firm passed to Henry Bevington's four sons, and continued into the present century.

Both Henry Bryceson (who founded his business c. 1796) and T. C. Bates (c. 1812) (Langwill and Boston 1970: 46, 44) were prolific builders of barrel organs; both built finger organs as well, but their importance in the evolution of organ design during the period under consideration was minimal.

Mention should be made, finally, of Flight & Robson. The Flights seem to have been responsible for setting the manufacture of barrel organs onto a commercial footing, and it is said that Benjamin Flight, senior, pioneered the introduction of the barrel organ into churches (1772) (Ord-Hume 1978: 33). Flight (possibly Benjamin, junior, 1767–1846) was joined by Joseph Robson in c. 1806, and the firm established a reputation for ingenuity in the construction of mechanical organs which was demonstrated in a machine organ for the Earl of Kirkwall (1811) and the famous 'Apollonicon' organ (1817). The latter was a huge entertainment organ, designed to be played either by barrels (three of them) or by organists (up to six at separate keyboards), and was, for a time, daily exhibited in Flight & Robson's premises in St Martin's Lane (Ord-Hume 1978: 100–27). It may have inspired an instrument with five keyboards, arranged for three players, which Sir Richard Vyvyan commissioned from the builders for the music room at Trelowarren, near Helston, in 1829 (*Harmonicon* VII, 1829: 253). Flight & Robson built a good number of smaller church (finger) organs, and also some larger ones, but the business got into difficulties and was declared bankrupt in 1832 (Ord-Hume 1978: 121–2). With the partnership dissolved, Robson was able to acquire many of the former business's effects and establish himself on his own account in the old premises at 101 St Martin's Lane; he was eventually succeeded by a son, T. J. F. Robson (Edmonds 1960: 53). The Robsons were responsible for a number of substantial new organs of progressive design, including St Dunstan-in-the-West (1834), St Michael, Chester Square (1845), and Buxton Road Chapel, Huddersfield (late-1840s), and the firm's work seems to have been well-regarded in the 1840s and 1850s. T. J. F. Robson died in 1876, and the business soon disappeared. The Flights also continued on their own account following the dissolution of the partnership, first in King William Street, and then (from 1848) at 36 St Martin's Lane (Langwill and Boston 1970: 51). John Flight (d. 1890) benefited from the patronage of Ouseley, for whom he built the organ in St Barnabas, Pimlico (1849), and the organ for Tenbury (1854), but the firm's work was of no particular distinction and little is heard of it after the Tenbury episode (though the business survived until the 1880s).

BUSINESS AND WORKSHOP

At the end of the eighteenth century, many of the London organ-builders had workshops in the parish of Holborn, especially in the vicinity of Red Lion Square, between Theobalds Road and High Holborn. There, they were unencumbered by the restrictive practices enforced by the livery companies in the City itself, and were still sufficiently close to the northern perimeter of London to have relatively easy access to the network of toll-roads and canals along which organs could be transported to all parts of the kingdom. As the expansion of the metropolis continued, gobbling up former villages and spawning new suburbs, this advantage was lost. From about 1800, organ-builders began to settle, instead, in the more northerly parishes of St Pancras and St Marylebone. The New Road (created, by Act of Parliament, in 1756) ran through these parishes, easing the traffic of goods and people from one side of London to the other, and the Grand Junction Canal reached the northern perimeter of London in 1796. By the 1830s, many of the metropolitan organ-builders had established themselves in this area. Furniture makers proliferated in Tottenham Court Road, and, given the affinities between the two trades, it is not surprising to find that a number of organ-builders had premises near the junction of Tottenham Court Road and the New Road (Hill, Bryceson, Gray, later Walker). Bishop was further west, in Lisson Grove, St Marylebone. All were to find themselves ideally placed when the railway companies built their London terminuses: with Euston, St Pancras and King's Cross just down the road, the organ-builders could convey their instruments to the churches and chapels of the Midlands and North with the minimum of difficulty.

Comparatively little is known about the premises occupied by the various metropolitan organ-builders in the early years of the nineteenth century. Like other tradesmen, they frequently lived and worked in the same building: 12 Tottenham Court (the premises of Elliot, and, later Hill) and 7 York Buildings (J. C. Bishop) were each part of a terrace, built, in the first instance, for domestic occupation. The builders lived there with their families, but some of the rooms in the houses, and outbuildings in the yards or gardens to the rear, must have been turned into workshops and offices.

The fullest description of an organ-builder's premises to have survived from this period is to be found in the catalogues prepared for the auction of Flight & Robson's stock-in-trade following the firm's bankruptcy in 1832. This was discovered by Ord-Hume, and is reproduced as an appendix to his book, *Barrel Organ* (1978: 494–503). The various rooms in the establishment in St Martin's Lane are listed, together with their contents, and suggest a business run on a considerable scale. The catalogue names nine distinct workshops, a yard (where timber was kept), 'piazzas and warehouses' (more timber), a gallery and a counting house. There was also the 'Great Room', containing the Apollonicon and fifteen other instruments, chiefly barrel organs and self-performing pianofortes, to which the public was admitted. The workshops included an assembly room, a turner's shop, a metal shop, a metal pipe shop, and a brass shop. The necessity for such extensive premises is demonstrated by the fact that there were no fewer than thirty completed barrel, or barrel-and-finger organs in stock (and several more incomplete), three chamber organs, thirteen pianofortes, a cabinet organ, a church finger organ, and two incomplete 3-manual church organs. Both the manufacture and the housing of these instruments meant that extensive premises were essential. Builders who were less dependent upon the market for mechanical organs needed less capacity. These builders did not, on the whole, build any quantity of organs for stock (though most had one or two chamber organs available for hire) but built in response to individual orders. John Gray ran a flourishing business during these years, but his stock account for 1832 (MS 1: rear: n.p.) records the existence of only four workshops and a wareroom in Fitzroy Terrace, New Road. One of these workshops was an erecting room, where organs were assembled before being conveyed to their permanent site. It seems that this room was spacious enough for large organs to be completely assembled (and, interestingly, voiced and tuned) before leaving the workshop, and this enabled Gray to arrange for his more ambitious instruments to be demonstrated to the metropolitan organists before they were taken down into the country. So, for example, Thomas Adams was engaged to play a new organ for St George's, Wolverhampton, in 1837, and in the following year, he performed on the organ for Holy Trinity, Clifton, again in

Gray's workshop (*MW* VI, 1837: 76; IX 1838: 264). These semi-public demonstrations of new organs were a valuable advertisement for organ-builders (Gray & Davison eventually built an 'Exhibition Hall' for this purpose, employing no less a person than G. G. Scott as architect) (*MW* XXXI, 1853: 539) but, in the 1830s, not all builders could accommodate them as readily as Gray. Hill's premises may have permitted the erection of some larger organs (the organ for St John's, Chester, was said to be standing in the factory in 1838) (*MW* IX, 1838: 44) but he was obliged to hire the Music Hall, Store Street, in 1837, so that Adams, Pittman and Gauntlett could display the qualities of his new organ for Oxford Place Wesleyan Chapel, Leeds, and some years before, in 1830, he had made use of the Hanover Square Rooms to erect the frame and bellows of the York organ (*MW* VII, 1837: 78; Gray 1837: 18–19). Clearly, his workshops were less spacious than Gray's.

Information concerning the equipment of organ-builders' workshops in the 1820s and 1830s is hard to come by. One intriguing question concerns mechanisation: were machines used at all in the manufacture of organs at this time? Sayer has suggested that Samuel Renn, influenced by the proximity of the most highly mechanised factories in Europe, introduced machinery and the methods of the machine age into the manufacture of organs in his Manchester workshop (Sayer 1976a: 90–1; 1980: 95–7) but comparable evidence for the metropolitan workshops is almost totally lacking. Probably Sayer's suggestion that the London builders would be markedly more conservative than a builder in daily contact with the advanced manufacturing technologies of the North is generally correct (1976a: 91–2), but the Flight & Robson catalogue indicates that one of the London workshops (though probably atypical) was aware of the potential of machinery, at least to a limited extent. The presence of two voicing machines and a casting bench comes as no surprise, and the two machines for marking barrels must have been essential to a business founded upon the manufacture of barrel organs. More interesting are the three turning lathes, the sawing machine, screw machine, and a machine for cutting brass. It is not known how sophisticated these machines were (though the auctioneer thought it worth recording that two of the lathes were manufactured by Holtzapffel), nor how extensively they were employed by Flight & Robson, but their presence is indicative of a small step towards that mechanisation of organ-building which was finally accomplished in the last quarter of the nineteenth century.

Machinery may have penetrated the organ-builder's workshop to a limited extent, speeding up the initial preparation of timber and metal, but most of the operations involved in the making of organs were still undertaken by hand, using simple tools. After serving a formal apprenticeship, an aspiring organ-builder became a journeyman, and was thus qualified for work in any reputable organ-building manufactory. How strictly the rules concerning apprenticeships were enforced is not known (though derogatory remarks were later made about Henry Willis's failure to serve out his 'time' with John Gray: *MG* ii, 1857: 443) and nor is it known whether the qualification of a completed apprenticeship was essential to secure employment. The size of workforce varied from one workshop to another and in response to the state of the order book. In January 1826, J. C. Bishop recorded payments to fourteen men in his account book, and the number seems to have been fairly constant for the next few years (Elvin 1984: 52). Gray's workforce must, if anything, have been a little smaller: his average weekly disbursement on wages during 1826 and 1827 was lower than Bishop's (MS 1, rear: n.p.). Hill was paying wages to eleven men in January 1835 (MS 11, rear: ff. 1–9). It is not clear whether these figures include apprentices. Most interesting of all was Joseph Walker, who, in January 1838, paid wages to fourteen men; later that year, the workforce had risen to twenty-five, including three apprentices (MS 18). Thereafter, the figure fluctuates somewhat, but it seldom dips below twenty, and indicates that Walker's was a flourishing business with a considerable output of new work.

As demand for new organs increased, organ-builders were bound to consider methods by which, correspondingly, production could be increased. One method was to standardise components which could then be manufactured in quantity and put by until needed. The most obvious application of this particular expedient was in the production of small church and chamber organs, both barrel and finger; the similarity, both in appearance and construction, of many such instruments dating from this period is irrefutable testimony that this was done. Builders were, though, more cautious about extending the principle to the construction of large and prestigious instruments. John Gray's stock-lists (dating from the late-1820s) are useful evidence as to how far one of the leading metropolitan organ-builders had gone down that particular road. The list compiled on 1 January 1827 (MS 1, rear: n.p.) reveals that Gray kept extensive stocks of pipes, made to standard scales. The tally was considerable: open diapasons (15), stopped diapasons (10), principals (7), twelfths (6), fifteenths (8), sesquialteras (7), trumpets (6), flutes (2), and a single dulciana, cremona and hautboy. On the other hand, the stock-lists also show that Gray did not extend the principle of standardisation to the mechanical parts of his organs, nor to their cases. In the list of January 1827, there were three church organs and a barrel-and-finger organ under way in the workshop, and another church organ just begun, but there is no evidence that soundboards, bellows, frames, swell boxes, roller-boards or any other major components were made to standard dimensions and put into stock. Smaller components – rack pins, roller arms, iron squares, stop knobs, shallots, tongues – were kept in stock (they may have been bought in from trade suppliers) but it is clear that the structure, casework, soundboards and action of Gray's organs were not, at this period, made until required. When the time came, Gray had ample stocks of timber to hand for the purpose: 3,699 feet of mahogany (worth £232), 5,624 feet of oak (£240), and an unspecified quantity of pine (£107) were stored in his premises at the beginning of 1827.

All in all, Gray reckoned that on 1 January 1827 his stock, work in progress, and shop fixtures together were worth £3,020 15s. 5d. (MS 1, rear: n.p.). He thus had considerable capital tied up in the business. But the profits were not negligible. In 1826, he recorded a profit of £995; in 1825, it had been £1,516 (MS 1, rear: n.p.). Table 6 shows the value of work entered in Gray's ledger for each of the years 1822–37.[5] It indicates that the volume of work was reasonably consistent throughout this period. As the Table also gives an impression of the type of work undertaken by the firm, some further explanation of the details recorded there should be offered.

Barrel organs (1) might be for either church or domestic use. They could be bought quite cheaply, but Gray catered for the upper end of the market and (for example) the average cost of the six barrel organs which he made in

Table 6 *John Gray: analysis of work, 1822–37*

	New organs						Rebuilds, repairs, etc.					
	1	2	3	4	5	6	7	8	9	10	11	
				Church			Rebuild					
Year	Barrel	Chamber	Other	Under £200	Under £600	Over £600	Under £50	Over £50	Clean or repair	Other	Secondhand	Value of work (£s)
1822					3	2	1	1	5	7		3,190
1823	1		2	1			2	1	6	9		553
1824	1	2			6	2	1	1	2			3,868
1825		1			2	1	2		10	6	3	2,513
1826	1	1		1	2	2	3	4	9	4	4	3,759
1827	1	1		3	2			1	6	6		2,321
1828	3				1	2	1	1	9	3	1	2,723
1829	1			2	7		1	2	6	4	1	3,311
1830	4	1			5		1		6	5		2,172
1831	2	1		2	5	2	4	2	7	6	1	4,428
1832					1		3	1	5	4	3	1,166
1833	4	1		1	4		3	1	13	4	3	2,905
1834	2	1			2		5	2	3	2	2	1,610
1835	4				1		4	4	7		3	2,113
1836	7				3	2	2	1	6	1	2	3,844
1837	3			1	3	1			3		1	3,686

Source: MS 1.

1836 was £82. Chamber organs (2) were still popular, and Gray kept a number in stock which were hired out to customers. They were more expensive than barrel organs, usually between £100 and £150, though, in 1837, Gray built one with two manuals (£260) and one with three (£485); these larger examples would more appropriately be designated 'house organs'. Other organs (3) includes the hybrid 'pianoforte organ', and might, in the case of other builders, have embraced such peculiarities as bird organs, flute organs, flageolet organs, and various sorts of mechanical organ designed to amuse or provide music for dancing. Church organs have been divided into three categories. Some of the smaller ones costing less than £200 (4) were barrel-and-finger organs; most had a single keyboard, and six or seven stops. Virtually all the instruments in the second category, costing between £200 and £600 (5) had two keyboards and at least rudimentary pedals, though, among them, Liverpool Parish Church somehow secured a large 3-manual for £540 (perhaps Gray was anxious to establish a connection in the district). At least one of the organs costing more than £600 (Philanthropic Chapel) had only two keyboards, but most of the instruments in this category (6) were substantial 3-manual organs with pedal pipes. Apart from one that went to Boston, USA, in 1837, the most costly of these instruments was that built for St Pancras Church in 1822; the price was £1,050, and the organ had twenty-three stops (MS 1: 26). The reconstruction of existing organs formed a much less significant part of an organ-builder's trade at this time than had come to be the case by the end of the century. Additions or reconstructions costing less than £50 (7) might include conversion of bellows, introduction of unison pedal pipes, re-making of Swell fronts, or replacement of unfashionable reeds. Those costing more than £50 (8) might be more radical (and a few were), but most simply furthered the process of limited mechanical improvement and trifling tonal innovation. Though a relatively large number of jobs under the description of cleaning or repairing organs were undertaken each year (9), the value of the work was seldom great. Other work (10) is mostly trivial: supplying pipework, moving chamber organs, making a barrel. There was a steady market in secondhand organs (11), both for church and domestic use, most of them taken in part exchange for a new instrument; unfortunately, Gray's accounts do not record the origins of these re-located organs, and some survive in unexpected places to puzzle the historian.

John Gray has been taken as an example because his is the only complete set of accounts to survive from the 1820s and 1830s. His prices seem to have been typical of the best class of work (though Bishop's were, if anything, higher) and his business was sufficiently well-established for him to have no need to resort to a detrimental paring of estimates in deference to the iniquitous (and widespread) custom of inviting tenders from several builders accompanied by an undertaking that the lowest tender would be accepted.

Others were less resolute. Elliot confided to Dr Camidge in 1829: 'I am confident the organ we have in hand for Christ's Hospital, will not pay us as it ought; Hill being so very desirous of obtaining business at a very little profit, sooner than lose it' (Gray 1837: 37). A comparison of Elliot & Hill's estimate for the Christ's Hospital organ (£800) with that of Bishop (£1,200) (Plumley 1981: 24) suggests that Elliot's fears were far from groundless, and a number of the firm's contract prices for large organs at this period are distinctly on the low side.[6] It was not only cheese-paring churchwardens who threatened the organ-builder's profit margins, though. The practice of paying commission to organists and music-sellers on orders received was almost universal. Hill responded to an enquiry in 1838 with the information that 'Ten per cent is what I allow to Professional Gentlemen who favour me with orders' (MS 12: 34), and it requires little imagination to see how such an arrangement (from which the client was, of course, excluded) could be abused. Having trimmed his price to please the client, and having signed away a further substantial sum to satisfy the agent, the organ-builder was left to do the best he could with what remained. This circumstance acted as a drag on attempts to improve the quality of English organs for many years.

CHURCHES AND ORGANS

'Most certainly an organ is not necessary in a parish for the decent perform-ance of divine worship . . . But though it is not necessary, it is extremely decent, proper, and even customary in a parish . . . of extent and opulence' (Haggard 1832: 12). Those remarks, made, in 1795, by Sir John Nicholl when he gave judgement in a case concerning the obligation of a parish to maintain its organ, represent a useful, but hardly definitive statement as to the frequency with which organs might be encountered in parish churches during the early 1800s. Just as there were still parishes 'of extent and opulence' that lacked organs, so there were many churches in small towns and villages which had acquired them. By the third decade of the century, a surge in demand for church barrel organs meant that the day was not too far off when a majority of English churches would possess a pipe organ of some sort.

There were various reasons why a parish might, or might not, have an organ. The attitude of the incumbent was crucial, but the existence of the faculty jurisdiction (whereby a parish had to apply to the bishop of the diocese for permission to add to, or alter, the permanent fittings of the church) ensured that the parishioners had an opportunity to object to the introduction of an organ if they so wished. Many of the parochial clergy would have endorsed Latrobe's contention that it was impossible 'for a man of observation to flatter himself, that our church-music is in a healthful and vigorous condition' (Latrobe 1831: 1), and a first step towards its improvement would often be the introduction of an organ of some sort. By this means, psalmody might be rescued from the tyranny of the parish clerk or the excesses of the church band (that, at least, is how reforming clergy saw the matter) and restored to the congregation. It might also be the means (especially in the hands of evangelicals) of varying the character of the church service by introducing hymns to supplement the existing psalmody (Temperley 1979a: 207–23). Not all congregations appreciated such innovations. Some who objected to the installation of organs were motivated by simple conservatism: they had no wish to see the existing pattern of worship changed. Others professed Protestant scruples (the organ had never quite lived down its popish past). But, in most instances, the objection was a more mundane one: the objectors feared that the organ would become a charge upon the parish, to be paid for, or, at least, maintained, out of the church rate. The most common way round this difficulty was the opening of a subscription list, whereby the expense of erecting and, sometimes, maintaining an organ was met by those who most favoured its introduction. Another way was by means of an individual benefaction. Wealthy parishioners not infrequently donated organs to their parish churches, and the desperation of the clergy to improve parochial music is demonstrated by the number of incumbents who themselves gave organs (usually, barrel organs) to their churches. Recourse to individual acts of generosity was not necessary everywhere. In London, many parishes were governed by select vestries, the members of which enjoyed the twin advantages of membership of the Established Church and (in many instances) relative affluence: here, organ and organist might well be supported on the rates, and the proliferation of church organs in the London parishes was doubtless, in part, due to this. The reverse was true in districts where nonconformity was powerful, and general vestries (unaffected by religious qualifications) ran the affairs of the parish. There, the chances of the vestry agreeing to raise a rate for the purchase of an organ were slight, as, indeed, they were in poorer parishes, however loyal the parishioners to the Church.

A selective survey of the provision of organs in parish churches during the 1820s and 1830s confirms that the picture was far from uniform. Most of the larger market-towns with a single parish church had an organ by 1800 (those, at least, in the south of England), but towns and cities with a number of parishes might not find it so easy to raise support for an organ. Temperley (1979a: 108, 112) has drawn attention to the sparsity of organs in the numerous parish churches of York and Norwich at the end of the eighteenth century, and has compiled statistics showing that only ten of York's twenty-eight ancient parishes within the walls had acquired organs by 1840 (Temperley 1979b: 93). By contrast, ten of Cambridge's twelve mediaeval churches possessed organs by the same date (Table 7), and other prosperous

Table 7 *Date of the introduction of organs in Cambridge churches*

All Saints	1790/1830	finger/finger
Holy Sepulchre	c. 1840	barrel (?)
Holy Trinity	1796	finger
St Andrew-the-Great	1810/1844	finger/finger
St Bene't	1827	finger
St Botolph	1833	finger
St Clement	–	
St Edward	1838	barrel-and-finger
St Giles	–	
St Mary-the-Great[a]	1698	finger
St Mary-the-Less	c. 1830/1839	barrel/finger
St Michael	?/1838	?/finger

[a] The organ (built originally by Bernard Smith) was the property of the University, though it had, from the first, been used by the parish, which appointed its own organist.

towns with a number of churches (Colchester, Shrewsbury, Stamford) were equipping them with organs during the same period. It is true (as Nicholl had implied) that organs were in many instances an index of prosperity. The great ports (London, Bristol, Newcastle-upon-Tyne) had a long tradition of placing organs in their parish churches; the visual splendour of these richly encased instruments was quite as important as their musical quality, for it left the least musical in no doubt as to the affluence (and the liberality) of the parochial, civic, or mercantile institution that had provided it. The later town hall organ was to have a similar significance. By comparison, agricultural prosperity fluctuated unpredictably, and this, together with the innate conservatism of the agricultural districts and the frequent non-residence of parson and landowner, meant that organs found their way into country churches much more slowly than into town ones. The general impression of market towns with organs, and village churches largely without, is sustained by a gazetteer of Herefordshire (*Lascelles* 1851), supplemented by other material.[7] By 1851, all four parish churches in Hereford itself, and those in the market towns of Bromyard, Kington, Ledbury, Leominster, and Ross-on-Wye, had organs. Only seventeen of the remaining villages and small towns in the county can be shown to have had organs at this date, and, when allowance has been made for barrel organs which escaped mention and organists who were overlooked, it is apparent that a relatively small proportion of the county's 200 and more churches possessed organs in 1851.

Attention has so far been directed at existing parishes and their churches. Yet it was at this same period that churchmen first seriously addressed themselves to the inadequacies of church accommodation, and inaugurated an era of church-building that was to continue into the early years of the present century. In 1818 and 1824, Parliament voted grants of £1,500,000 for the building of new churches to meet the needs of those parishes (chiefly in London and the new manufacturing districts) in which a rapidly expanding population had outstripped church accommodation, leaving the Established Church ill-equipped to meet the challenge of nonconformity, radicalism and apathy (Chadwick 1970: 84). But individual munificence was not lacking. The Church Building Society was founded in 1818 (Clarke 1938: 23), and in the years which followed, numerous associations sprang up to promote church building at national, diocesan, or parochial level.

The new churches were free from the constraints of established custom. Many were in towns, where the prevalent view was that churches should have organs, and many, especially in the metropolis, were in affluent suburbs where the resources existed to acquire an organ. The church-building movement therefore administered an unprecedented stimulus to organ-building in two respects. First, there was the scale of demand. No fewer than 200 new churches were consecrated in the diocese of London during Bishop Blomfield's episcopate (1828–56) (Clarke 1938: 24). It is not known how many of these possessed an organ, but a figure can be offered for an earlier period, which is almost certainly indicative of the period as a whole. Of seventy-two London churches built between 1818 and 1838, at least fifty-eight (80 per cent) had organs, either at the consecration or shortly afterwards. To take a smaller sample, six new churches were built in Cheltenham between 1819 and 1840 and of these five are known to have possessed organs *ab initio*. It is clear from this that, by the 1830s, the affluent classes in the towns of southern England expected their worship to be accompanied by an organ. And just as they expected the church building to reflect the importance of the district, so they expected the organ to match it in scale. The second significant aspect of the demand for new organs in the 1820s and 1830s was that it was a demand for the *largest* organs. The Ecclesiastical Commissioners, in distributing the Parliamentary grant, sought value for money, and this meant the accommodation of the largest number of people in a single building. By expanding the model offered by Wren's auditory churches and introducing capacious galleries (including a west gallery for organ and, possibly, charity children) architects found themselves able to seat upwards of 1,800 worshippers. A powerful organ was essential, and in appearance it had to complement the architectural pretensions of the building (which were, in some instances, considerable). The novel demands of these huge buildings stimulated organ-builders to produce some of the more innovative schemes of the period: Gray's organ for St Pancras (1822), Nicholls's for St Luke, Chelsea (1824), Lincoln's for St George, Camberwell (1824), and Bishop's for St James, Bermondsey (1829), are notable examples. Innovation by the architects obliged the organ-builders to be innovative, too.

But not all the new churches were in London. A rather different picture emerges in the North, where the churches tended to be more cheaply built, and where the communities which they were designed to serve had neither the same propensity for opening subscription lists, nor comparable resources for supporting them, as had the inhabitants of Cheltenham Spa. A Leeds directory of 1826 (Parson 1826: 252) lists eight Anglican churches (three of them, recently built Commissioners' churches) of which only three possessed organs, and it is significant that the leading London organ-builders made hardly any organs for the industrial districts of Yorkshire during the 1820s and 1830s – at least, for the Established Church. This is an important qualification. Affluence, in these areas, flowed more frequently in the direction of the Chapel than the Church, and once the nonconformists had reconciled themselves to the use of organs in their worship, it was they who purchased the most ambitious instruments. In 1826, only one of the twenty-four nonconformist chapels in Leeds (a Baptist Chapel) seems to have had an organ (Parson 1826: 252–3), and nine years later, it could still be asserted that the organ was an instrument 'rarely found among Dissenters' (Heaton 1835: 18). But a remarkable change was under way. A Leeds directory of 1838 noted:

ORGANS are now to be found in most of the churches in the towns, and in many of the populous villages, as well as in some of the Dissenting Chapels; but it was not till about ten years ago that they were adopted by the *Wesleyan Methodists*, who have now several costly instruments in their extensive and handsome new chapels at Leeds, Sheffield, &c. . . . The organ at *St. Peter's Methodist Chapel, in Leeds*, was built by Booth, of Wakefield, in 1837–8, and is *larger* than any other in the kingdom, except that of York Minster, and another at Birmingham.   (White 1838: II, 118)

Some, at least, thought it a proud day for nonconformity when it could lay claim to an organ which was superior in size to anything the Church had to offer (except York), but the opportunity to make such claims was not won without a struggle. Leeds was the battle-ground, and the provision of an organ for Brunswick Chapel (1828) the principal source of contention. A glance at the pamphlets provoked by the controversy makes it clear that the organ was something of a stalking-horse for both sides in an acrimonious debate touching a variety of contentious issues, but this is not to deny that the acquisition of organs was a difficult step for Methodists to take in view of the instrument's association with the Church and a set liturgy. However, take it they did, and by 1840, not only Brunswick, but Oxford Place (1837) and St Peter's Chapel (1838) could boast organs of a magnitude surpassing that of most cathedral organs.[8] Wesleyans were particularly willing to admit organs, but it was the Independents who commissioned the most important (and grandest) of all nonconformist organs: Hill's instrument for Great George Street Chapel, Liverpool (1841). After this, the wealthier sects (Wesleyans, Independents, Unitarians) gradually introduced organs, at least in their principal places of worship, but it is likely that organs remained a rarity in nonconformist worship generally, at least until the 1860s.

The Catholic community, emerging from more than two centuries of persecution, had no qualms about the use of organs in worship, but neither poverty of resources, nor the restrained style of worship to which Catholics had become accustomed during penal times, encouraged much musical elaboration of the mass in the years between the Relief Act (1791) and Emancipation (1829). There were exceptions. When Thomas Weld built a free-standing chapel in the grounds of Lulworth Castle (1786) he installed an organ there, and this was used both to accompany singers and to provide voluntaries between movements of the mass (Rowntree 1987: 26–8). In London, Catholic and Protestant alike could imbibe the spirit of Tridentine Catholicism by attending mass at one of the embassy chapels. Some maintained music of a high standard. At the Portuguese Chapel, for instance, in the early-1800s, Novello performed arrangements of masses by Haydn and Mozart, and the organ there was an ambitious instrument rebuilt by G. P. England in 1808 (Temperley 1981: 210). As time went by, Catholics became less dependent upon these foreign embassies for a dignified, enriched liturgy. The building of the new Moorfields church (1817–20), with its classical facade and spacious sanctuary, marked a growth in confidence that would eventually bear fruit in the form of dozens of handsome classical and (later) Gothic churches up and down the country; significantly, it had one of the largest organs in the metropolis, and, by the 1830s, its music rivalled the best that the embassy chapels could offer (Temperley 1981: 212). Elsewhere, the picture is less clear. Printed mass settings were readily available, and by the 1830s, many provincial chapels housed a small organ, but the extent to which music played a part in Catholic worship outside London remains obscure. A generation later, with the revival well under way, and numbers of large churches being built, the Catholics began to commission organs which rivalled the grandest instruments of the Established Church and the nonconformists. Gray & Davison's organ for St Francis Xavier, Liverpool (1849), Hill's for St Walburgh's, Preston (1853), and Bishop & Starr's for Brompton Oratory (1857), were as much symbols of the triumph of a resurgent Catholicism as the fine buildings in which they stood. From then onwards, the Catholics would compete with the more-favoured churches on their own terms.

In concluding this section, something should be said as to the use of the organ in the Anglican service at this time. It may be considered under two headings: the cathedral service, and the parochial service.

The principal use of the organ in the cathedral service was to accompany the choir. There was little call for congregational accompaniment (though Jebb records – and deplores – a practice which had grown up in some cathedrals of singing 'a Psalm or Hymn' at the beginning of the service, as

soon as clergy and congregation were in their places) (Jebb 1843: 232) and
the solo use of the organ was severely curtailed. In a few cathedrals, it was
the custom for choir and clergy to process to their places on greater festivals
with the organ playing – though, in most establishments, the organ was
silent and the members of the foundation made their way independently to
their stalls before (or even after) the commencement of the service – and
(again, in a handful of places) the organist played a short voluntary before
the first lesson (Jebb 1843: 229, 317); it may have been customary for the
organist to play a voluntary at the end of Evensong in some cathedrals (on
Sundays and festivals?), but Jebb is silent on the subject. In most cathedrals,
the organ was first heard giving out the chant for the Venite (Mattins) or the
psalms (Evensong). The organist then accompanied the chanting (with
some difficulty, presumably, in view of the rarity of pointed psalters in
cathedrals at this time) (Temperley 1981: 176–9) avoiding – if he took Jebb's
advice – 'the noisy stops, such as trumpet, cornet and sesquialtera' and
relying chiefly upon the stopped diapasons and principals of Great and
Choir (though Jebb did not rule out judicious changes of registration, and
even commended the use of the Swell to give 'life and expression' to the
chant) (Jebb 1843: 270, 310). Thereafter, the organist was largely concerned
with the accompaniment of canticle and anthem settings: more will be said
below (pp. 341–2, 348–9) of their evolving character. On Sundays, Mattins
was succeeded by the chanting of the Litany, after which the choir introduced the Communion Service by singing the Sanctus (which might be
accompanied) and then, in their due place, the responses to the Command-
ments, and the Creed. Few cathedrals performed a fully choral Communion
Service in the early-nineteenth century, and choir and organist usually made
their exit following the Prayer for the Church Militant, whether or not the
officiating minister was to go on to celebrate the Sacrament.

Paradoxically, the organ's solo role was marginally more extensive in the
parochial service. When, in 1833, Lancelot Sharpe was elected organist of St
Katherine Coleman, London, the vestry meeting took the precaution of
setting down an account of his duties. They were as follows:

1. the Sentence when the Minister enters the Desk
2. the Gloria Patri
3. the first Voluntary
4. the first Psalm Tune
5. the Glory be to thee O Lord
6. the Second Psalm Tune
7. the last Voluntary
8. to practice [*sic*] the Children at the least one Hour for the Sunday on the Saturday
    morning.
9. That the Candidate elected should perform the duty in person on all occasions
    unless the Church Wardens give permission at any time for a Substitute.

(MS 70: 21 May 1833)

This list largely reflects what is known, from organists' handbooks such as *Hamilton's Catechism* (Warren 1838, 1842) and Done's *Treatise* (*c.* 1839), of the practice of parochial worship. The first item refers to the chanting of one of the introductory sentences to Mattins and Evensong. In some churches, it had become the custom to sing one of the metrical versions of the psalms at this point (a correspondent in the *Gentleman's Magazine* describes such a practice at Wanstead) (LXXX, 1810: 619) but more orthodox churchmen disapproved of this as a deviation from the form prescribed in the Prayer Book. More usual (though not, evidently, acceptable to the parishioners of St Katherine Coleman) was the performance of a brief introductory voluntary, which, according to Warren, began as the minister entered the church, and ended as he took his place at the desk; it should, he wrote, 'be in a grave and solemn style, abounding in full, close-wrought harmony, and inspiring a feeling of reverential awe' (1842: 50–1). It seems that the psalms and canticles were said at St Katherine Coleman, concluding with the *Gloria*, sung (in a metrical version or to chant) to organ accompaniment. Done (1839) proposes using Full Organ, with or without the reeds, for this. Elsewhere, canticles, and even psalms, might be chanted by the whole congregation, with the organ accompanying. Temperley has marshalled the evidence for the introduction of this practice in York (1977: 17–28; 1979a: 219–23), and a parallel will be found in Bristol (below, pp. 152–3). The 'first Voluntary' mentioned in the St Katherine Coleman schedule was also known as the 'middle voluntary'. It intervened between psalms and first lesson, and, according to Warren (1842: 51) customarily lasted eight or ten minutes. Latrobe describes its character in more detail (1831: 371–2), suggesting that the organist should aim 'by a few soft and solemn chords to win the mind to meditation, and then to carry it forward by the regular, though intricate movements of a short fugue, flowing uninterruptedly with the tide of thought, and sustaining it unimpaired'. Warren (more practically) suggests that the organist should choose a devotional piece from the vocal works of Handel, Haydn, Mozart or Beethoven, for use at this point in the service. Not all organists were as sensitive to the mood of the service as Latrobe hoped, nor as aware of their own limitations as Warren's advice suggests they ought to have been, and there was a good deal of complaint about fanciful, showy and pianistic pieces being intruded by wilful organists; this no doubt accounts for the rapid disappearance of the middle voluntary from the 1840s onwards.

The accompaniment of metrical psalmody was also open to abuse. It was customary in parish churches for a psalm to be sung after the Litany, and another before the Sermon (at the end of the Ante-Communion). The organist would play a prelude, introducing the psalm tune, and would then accompany the congregation's singing. It had been the custom to play very brief interludes between each line of the verse, but, by the 1830s, it appears that these 'musical excrescences' (as Latrobe called them) had been pruned, and only the short extempore interludes between verses remained (1831: 360). They, too, were largely unappreciated by the discerning, and disappeared after the middle of the century. In any case, psalmody was giving place to hymnody. A ruling by the Chancellor of the diocese of York (when a group of parishioners from St Paul's, Sheffield, brought an action against their incumbent, Thomas Cotterill, for using hymns in divine worship) stated that hymns had precisely the same status as metrical psalms, and were authorised for use before and after divine service (Temperley 1979: 208). This was in 1820, and it opened the way for the universal adoption of hymnody in churches during the course of the century.

According to Warren, the concluding voluntary offered the organist an opportunity to display 'the full power and effects of the instrument he presides over'. He recommended the choice of one of the 'masterly fugues' of 'Handel, Sebastian Bach, Graun, Albrechtsberger, Eberlein, Rinck, [or] Hesse' as calculated to evoke 'that feeling of awe, that sense of holiness, which all that have a soul for music must feel, while listening to the voluntary' (1842: 52). Latrobe took a more prosaic view of the final voluntary: the organist, he wrote, 'is unsparing in the use of his pedals, he gives voice to every stop, and puts every finger in requisition to fill up his chords' (1831: 373–4).

A set liturgy imposed (as had been intended) a certain uniformity of character upon divine worship, but, as Temperley has shown in his impressive study of English parish church music (1979a), the contribution made by music was one way of varying that character. Since the early-seventeenth century, the organ had been a necessary component of the cathedral service; by the mid-nineteenth century, it was widely regarded as an essential adjunct of the parochial service – at least, in towns (and, it would soon be maintained, in villages, too). The power exercised by the organist was considerable; Latrobe insisted that, 'according to the tenor of his performance, [the congregation's] minds may be solemnized or dissipated, their devotion elevated or repressed, their thoughts sublimed or secularized' (1831: 366). His stern words suggest that he would almost have preferred to do without an organist, so considerable were the risks entailed. Many others, however, saw not the dangers, but the opportunities. With these firmly in their sights, they set out along the path leading to that multiplication of parochial organists and that proliferation of church organs, which were part and parcel of the Victorian revolution in parish worship.

ORGAN CASES

The early-nineteenth century was not a distinguished period in the history of case design. Though Sutton's judgement that the organ cases made during the preceding hundred years were 'so tasteless in their design, as to become an eye-sore in every Church in which they have been placed' (1847: 95) invites serious qualification by those not disposed to take their stand on the commanding heights of ecclesiological propriety, it is clear that the diversity of style to be found in architecture and ornament during the period 1790–1840, together with the physical expansion of the organ to take account of swell boxes, pedal pipes, and internal choir organs, led to an unsettling of case design which was not to its advantage.

Stylistically, the organ cases of this period fall broadly into three categories: Gothic revival, Grecian, and English classical. The latter category includes those cases in which conventional groupings of towers and flats give rise to a formal structure which has obvious eighteenth-century antecedents, and which retains features such as pipe-shades and toe-boards, carved brackets under the towers, and moulded tower caps, that identify the

13 Everingham, Catholic Chapel, Charles Allen, 1837.

conception as being essentially conservative in spirit. The 4-tower case in St Mary Magdalen, Islington (England, 1814) is an example, as is the case of Charles Allen's organ in the Catholic Chapel at Everingham (1837) (Plate 13). Dissenters would find the style congenial (it had none of the ecclesiastical overtones which rendered Gothic suspect) and the organs in both Brunswick Chapel (1828) and Oxford Place Chapel (1837) in Leeds had cases that should be included in this category.[9] Classical forms were deemed appropriate, too, for secular instruments; though some of the decorative detail of the cases in Birmingham Town Hall (1834) (Plates 14 and 15) and the Exeter Hall, London (1839) was Grecian, the form of these cases owed nothing to that movement, harking back, respectively, to conventional 3- and 4-tower forms. But despite the persistence of English classical cases, it is apparent that the style was largely eclipsed during the 1810s and 1820s by the popularity of the two revival movements.

A majority of the new churches in London (and most of the grandest ones) were in the fashionable Greek revival style, and the new organs for these churches were housed in cases to match. The formal and structural simplicity of the classical portico surmounted by a pediment offered a temptation which few architects could resist. The result was a square, box-like case such as that in St George's, Camberwell (1824) (Plate 16) in which a shallow pediment and over-large acroteria can do little to compensate the eye for the absence of towers and pipe-shades, and the uniform length of the display pipes. This case may have been designed by Francis Bedford. St John's, Waterloo Road (1824) (Plate 17), also by Bedford, was originally rather better on account of the retention of pipe-shades, but John Nash's case in All Souls's, Langham Place (1824), was infinitely worse. Despite the retention of towers, this is the neo-classical pipe-rack *par excellence*, in which a mean pediment and thin little tower caps can do nothing to relieve a relentless expanse of front pipes of almost identical length. All told, neo-classicism in Grecian guise turned its back on too many of the traditional elements of case design (subtle groupings of towers and flats; pipe-shades; varied alignment of pipe mouths) to be capable of producing good organ cases. Even an architect with the imaginative powers of James Savage (1779–1852) failed to think beyond a square box with a flat facade (rendered dangerously top-heavy by a monumental pediment) when he came to design a case for his new church of St James, Bermondsey (1829) (Plate 18), though it must be admitted that the severity of the design is in keeping with the architectural character of this fine church. He fared rather better across the river at St Luke's, Chelsea (1824), in Gothic (though there is, again, an excess of woodwork above the central flat), and it is possible to find other Gothic cases of this period that, for all their archaeological shortcomings, have a strength lacking in the Grecian cases.

Clutton and Niland (1963: 233–41) provide an admirable summary of the

121

Printed & Published at Thos Underwood's   Lithographic Establishment

THE GRAND ORGAN IN THE TOWN HALL BIRMINGHAM.

This gigantic Instrument was built by Mr W Hill of London in 1834, & has cost upwards of £4000. The height of the case is 45 feet, it is 40 feet wide and 17 feet deep. The largest metal pipe in front of the case is 35 ft. 3 in. long & 5 ft. 4 in. in circumference, the total weight of the Instrument is at least 45 Tons ... The Bellows are very large, they contain 300 Square feet of surface, & upwards of 1½ Tons weight are required to give the necessary pressure; there are 4 separate pairs of Bellows & feeders, two for the Grand Organ, Choir Organ & Swell Organ, one for the Pedal Organ & one for the Great Ophicleide; while the Bellows of the Grand Organ has also what are termed Reservoir Bellows, Wind Trunks &c... The number of stops in this magnificent Instrument is about 4070. It is considered equal to, & in some points surpasses every other Organ in existence. (Vide Simpson's Description of the Grand Organ in the Town Hall Birmingham.)

14 Birmingham Town Hall, William Hill, 1834. A print of c. 1850.

15 Birmingham Town Hall. (1984)

16 St George, Camberwell, H. C. Lincoln, 1824. (1913)

influence which the burgeoning Gothic revival had upon case design, and
Wilson (1968: 15–20) traces the origins of a Gothic style for chamber organs
to the drawings of cabinet-makers such as Thomas Chippendale and John
Linnell. The choice of idiom for a domestic organ was largely a matter of
taste: rococo, neo-classical and oriental models were available for imitation,
in addition to Gothic, and the discerning patron of the late-eighteenth
century might choose among them. But it was increasingly felt that no such
liberty could be assumed by those providing organs for churches, especially
the grandest churches of all, the mediaeval cathedrals. Antiquarianism and

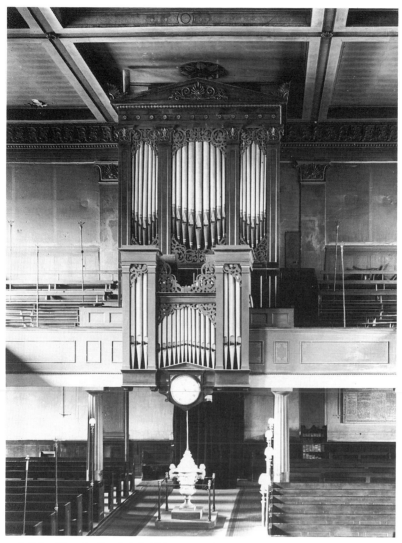

17 St John, Waterloo Road, J. C. Bishop, 1824. (1913)

Romanticism combined to reject the eclecticism of previous generations, which had tolerated Renaissance and Baroque furnishings in mediaeval buildings, and urge the adoption of Gothic as the only proper style for fittings. Among those fittings was to be numbered the organ case, and hence, from the 1780s onwards, the more exuberant cases of the English Baroque fell into disfavour, and were replaced with cases in the Gothic taste when the opportunity presented itself.

The consequences of this were first apparent on an extensive scale in the work of the organ-builder Samuel Green. Sutton described how Green had

18 St James, Bermondsey, J. C. Bishop, 1829. (1912)

conformed to the new taste by grafting 'innumerable pinnacles and incorrect Gothic details upon his tasteless boxes' (1847: 99), and it is true that by the standards of the ecclesiologists, the Gothic cases of the late-eighteenth century demonstrate a lamentable failure of both understanding and execution. One of the earliest of Green's attempts at a Gothic case was that for St Katherine-by-the-Tower (1778); it possesses a certain vapid charm, as do some of the other, smaller examples of the 'Georgian' Gothic organ case. The cathedral cases, though, are more difficult to defend. Green himself can be largely exonerated: they were all designed by someone else, the worst probably being Wyatt's cases for Lichfield and Salisbury Cathedrals (1790, 1792). Some were painted a stone colour to harmonise with their surround-ings (though there was some floral decoration on the front pipes at Lichfield, and the Salisbury case was oak-grained) but in practice this must simply have emphasised the flatness of the entire composition: 'tasteless boxes' is an apt description.

One of the principal weaknesses of Wyatt's cases was their formal ba-nality.[10] Other, wiser practitioners, adhered to more conventional forms. James Davis's case for Wymondham Abbey (1793), for example, is really a 4-tower classical one, skimpily disguised in Gothic, and two of G. P. England's larger Gothic cases (Newark, 1804; Sheffield, 1805) made use of the 3-tower form and flats sub-divided into three compartments to lend strength and interest to the composition. Other cases of the period 1800–25 followed suit. But no compositional ingenuity could hide the poverty of the detailing in practically all the cases of that era. Ignorant of any authentic Gothic organ case to which reference might be made, architects were obliged to look elsewhere for inspiration. As Sutton remarked acidly: 'Every part of a Church has been copied for the Organ Case, and attempts have been made

19 Lincoln Cathedral, case by Willson, 1826.

at one time, to make the Organ look like a tomb, at another like a screen, at another the canopies of the stalls have been placed on the top of the Organ . . .' (1847: 99–100). The latter may be a pardonable exaggeration, and perhaps refers to Edward Blore's case for Winchester Cathedral (1824). S. S. Wesley had a low opinion of it; it was, he commented, 'a sorry affair of some common sort of wood to match the old stall work: the details are of the shallowest and poorest description' (*Musical News*, XXVII, 1904: 426). In fact, Blore's Winchester case is arguably the best of his three cathedral cases, being spared the overlength display pipes which appear in the east front of his Peterborough case (1832), and avoiding the squareness of the case for Westminster Abbey (1833). It should also be noted that Blore was a reputable antiquarian (he began his career as an antiquarian draughtsman) (Colvin 1978: 115), and the detailing of his cases is at least a modest improvement on those of the previous generation. Another antiquarian-architect, Edward James Willson, designed one of the best large cases of the period for Lincoln Cathedral (1826) (Plate 19). Willson (a collaborator of both John Britton and the elder Pugin in their antiquarian publications) was a Lincoln man whose knowledge of Gothic had been deepened by the opportunity that this afforded him of studying the Cathedral and its architecture. As a result, his handling of the detailing of the Lincoln case (for example, the tabernacles over the towers) is markedly more accomplished than is commonly found in work of the period, though the composition displays many of the familiar flaws. By comparison, Robert Smirke's case for York Minster (1833) (Plate 20) is unenterprising and cumbersome. It is not without a certain nobility, but this is in part due to the diapering of the front pipes in 1859 (they were originally bronzed) (*YG* 12 November 1859: 4; Gray 1837: 36) and the monumental scale of both organ case and setting. The squareness of the construction shows little imaginative advance upon Wyatt's attempts, and the filling of both fronts with pipes of similar length makes it an altogether dull affair.

Despite the obvious affinities which the York case bears to the 'tasteless boxes' of an earlier stage in the Gothic revival, the construction is more substantial and the detailing (for all its stylistic infelicities) more confident than in those first, flimsy attempts to create a Gothic organ case. This is generally true of the better cases of the 1830s and 1840s. They have left behind that fancifulness which renders some 'Georgian' Gothic cases attractive, without having gained the justification of archaeological correctness. They may be described as 'worthy', but scarcely as 'distinguished'. John Shaw's cases for Christ's Hospital (1830) and St Dunstan-in-the-West (1834) exemplify this point. They are early products of the Perpendicular phase through which the Gothic revival went in the 1830s and 1840s, and can lay claim a certain grandeur, owing perhaps to the retention of towers, capped with large ogee-sectioned domes terminating in finials. But the lack

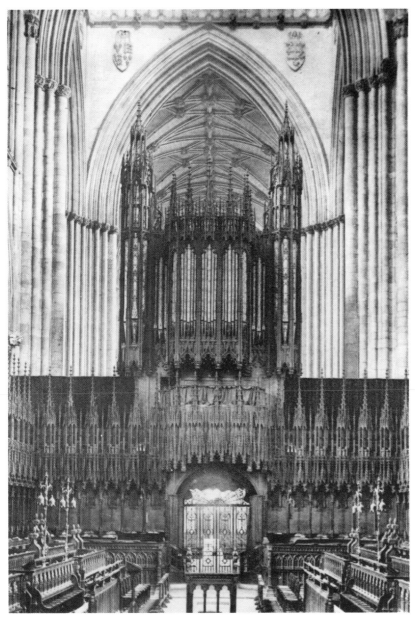

20 York Minster, Elliot & Hill, 1833. The east front.

of refinement in the details, and the effect of scaling-up a 3-tower composition which might have served better for a smaller instrument, renders them intrinsically boring.

Most of the cases mentioned were designed by architects. Yet it has to be remembered that the majority of organ cases were designed by the organ-builder. In most instances, the builder sought to reduce the chosen architectural style to basic elements which could be standardised, easily manufactured, and then applied to various shapes and sizes of organ. Samuel Renn's cases illustrate this approach in a fairly crude form (Sayer 1974: *passim*), but a number of organ-builders had pattern books in which various standard cases for small organs were depicted. Joseph Walker's organ at Bromyard (1839) (Plate 21) has a typical, standardised case, in which architectural

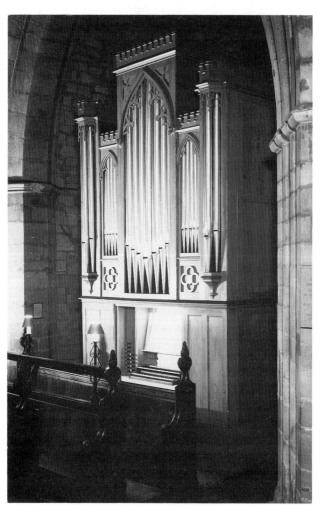

21 Bromyard Parish Church, J. W. Walker, 1839.

22 Ombersley Parish Church, John Gray, 1829. (1935)

devices (the Gothic arch, tracery motifs, crenellations) have been reduced to
the simplest possible form. John Gray's case for Ombersley (1829) (Plate 22)
is a little more ambitious, but is again essentially a routine assemblage of
familiar elements. Such cases were seemly, cheap to manufacture, and
satisfied the view that Gothic churches should have Gothic organ cases.
Perhaps few in the 1830s suspected that the next phase of the Gothic revival
would see an influential movement not only ridiculing the idea that these
cases were in any true sense Gothic, but actually questioning the propriety of
providing an organ case at all.

3

The Insular Movement

INTRODUCTION

A study of English organ design during the 1820s and 1830s reveals a fundamental paradox. For alongside the (apparently) stereotyped stop lists and the persistence of features such as long-compasses and truncated pedal divisions which would, within a few years, seem absurdly archaic, stands the widely substantiated conviction of contemporaries that a radical change was taking place. In 1838, a review in the *Musical World* testified:

> The character of our instruments is changed – the taste of the public has changed. The light and brilliant tones of a Snetzler have receded before the massive diapasons and reeds of an Elliott [*sic*] and Hill; and to these builders, and the Grays, our amateurs owe an acquaintance with the might and omnipotence of the pedal organ. But, in proportion as the powers and capabilities of the organ have been extended, so have the difficulties of a masterly performance been increased. The small palates [sc. pallets] have become large and enormous – hence a weighty and less effective touch; the tone has become thick and massive – hence the necessity of clear part playing; the pedale has erected unto itself an independent kingdom – hence a new system of divided harmony for the hands. (*MW* IX, 1838: 208)

An earlier contributor to the same journal claimed that, in the new organ for York Minster (1829–33), Elliot & Hill had succeeded in completely over-throwing 'the balance of tone adopted by Schmidt, Silbermann, Schnither [*sic*], Burkard, Casparini, Gabler, Hildebrand, Röder, Engler, Wagner, Migent, Schnetzler, and Marx' (*MW* IV, 1836–7: 133). Musical travellers equipped to make such statements with authority were rare in the 1830s, and the writer may be presumed to have reached for his cyclopaedia before putting pen to paper, but this need not obscure the fact that organists believed the character of the English organ to have changed significantly in the years preceding the reforms associated with Dr Gauntlett and William Hill. This leads inevitably to the conclusion that there was not one 'revolution' in English organ design at this period, but two. Under the stimulus of changing circumstances, organ-builders and organists struggled to meet new demands by developing the existing resources of the organ: extending compasses, duplicating registers, expanding the Swell. Their efforts had sufficient coherence to merit identification as a distinct movement. In marked contrast to the reforms of the 1840s, the movement made no serious attempt to seek inspiration beyond the shores of the British Isles, and hence may suitably be dubbed the 'Insular Movement'.

Despite its initial popularity, the Insular Movement led inevitably to a dead end. The reasons are not far to seek. Henry Willis's organ for St George's Hall, Liverpool (1851–5) was the largest instrument built according to the principles of the Insular Movement, and some criticisms of the scheme voiced when it was made public may be applied with equal validity to all the larger essays of this school:

> What does it exhibit beyond a mere magnification of the arrangement of any one out of a hundred smaller instruments? ... Magnitude is attained, and effect, we presume, sought, by simple re-duplications of old and known qualities.
>
> (*MW* xxxii, 1854: 566–7)

Another contemporary expressed the matter more succinctly: the Liverpool organ, he wrote, amounted to 'little else than 2 or 3 large church organs, of ordinary and similar capacity, rolled into one' (*MW* xxxiii, 1855: 361). The writer was inspired by hostility to Willis, but it was undoubtedly true that magnification of scales and duplication of registers were, at best, inefficient means of increasing the power of the organ. It was to be the German System of the 1840s, with its correct understanding of chorus structure, which pointed the way forward, not the Insular Movement. Yet the latter was extremely influential. The York and Liverpool organs, and that for Birmingham Town Hall (1834), captured the imagination of contemporaries, and the success which Henry Willis and Edmund Schulze enjoyed in the third quarter of the nineteenth century was in part due to an ability to satisfy (albeit, in very different ways) the demands that had earlier given rise to the Insular Movement.

The history of the Insular Movement is obscure and dating is elusive. Samuel Green's decision to increase the scale of his basses (cf. *CR* xvi, 1834: 46–7) or Blyth's introduction of a third open diapason in the Great of the York Minster organ (1803) (below, p. 119) are possible starting points, though it was not until the mid-1820s that experiments in duplication, increased scales and the introduction of large-scaled pedal pipes became at all common. Having constructed two of the largest instruments of the genre (York and Birmingham) William Hill abandoned experiment along these lines in the late-1830s in order to pursue a different approach to the problem; other organ-builders followed suit. Yet large organs were still being built during the 1850s standing essentially within the Insular, rather than the Hill and Gauntlett, tradition: Willis's Liverpool organ and Flight's instrument for St Michael's College, Tenbury (1856) are two examples. The later

Victorian organ, with its pedal division frequently limited to one or two 16′ basses, its extensive provision of couplers, its large-scaled open diapason (usually with a second, smaller colleague), and its taste for orchestral colour and expressive contrasts, is as much the child of the Insular Movement as of the German System.

THE BACKGROUND

The emergence of the Insular Movement during the 1820s was, in part, a response to factors described in the previous chapter: the building of new churches and the rise of congregational hymnody being the most significant. In this sense, its preoccupations were functional. No less influential, however, was the decisive shift in musical taste that took place in the early years of the century, and that put pressure on organ-builders to find ways of turning the organ into a more expressive instrument. These aesthetic considerations deserve to be studied in greater detail.

The challenges of the adolescent Romantic spirit in art and literature, and of revolution (or, in muted English terms, of radicalism) in politics, philosophy, and science were changing the face of European civilisation, and, with it, Western culture. Music took its place in the general picture. Composers sought ways of expressing the poetic in music, and investigated orchestral sonorities, the use of contrasting dynamics, and the possibilities suggested by a physical expansion in the scale of music-making. Romanticism ('the apparent domination of feeling over order' (*NG* 16: 141)) was a pervasive influence which enlisted the power of music to stir the emotions. Even a highly conservative figure like William Crotch (1775–1847) was bound to acknowledge this. In a series of lectures delivered at Oxford during the 1820s he asserted:

Music can awaken the affections by her magic influence, producing at her will, and that instantly, serenity, complacency, pleasure, delight, ecstasy, melancholy, woe, pain, terror, and distraction.   (Crotch 1831: 64)

Here, Crotch was articulating a belief which was central to musical endeavour during the Romantic period: music was seen as able to engage the senses, as capable of suggesting pictorial images, as possessing orphic ('magic') qualities. When, however, he sought to categorise music neatly into the 'sublime', the 'beautiful', and the 'ornamental' (Crotch 1831: 26–43) he was advocating a musical aesthetic which had already been swept away by the rising tide of Romanticism, and an orderliness which was wholly out of place in the new era.

At a popular level, the distinctive qualities of the new musical aesthetic were in danger of being reduced to caricatures. A craving for sensation led to the cultivation of extremes of tonality, pitch, and dynamic – most approved

when two extremes could be contrasted. The organ, because of its prominence in church and (later) concert hall, could not escape these debilitating
influences. The design of the Swell box in Gray & Davison's reconstruction
of the Windsor organ (1843) was commended because it enabled the organist, 'from a scarcely audible sound, to arrive at the full swell by the most
gradual increase' (Willemant 1844: 50) and Willis commented in later life of
his Swell Organ at Gloucester (1847) that 'the *pianissimo* was simply
astounding' (Edwards 1898: 298). At the other end of the scale, one audience
was so affected by the massive choral effect produced in the course of a
performance of Handel's *Messiah* that 'some persons could not conceal their
emotions and shed tears, others laughed hysterically, whilst the uninitiated
absolutely jumped from their seats as if electrified at the mass of sound' (*MP*,
16 April 1836), and it may be taken as an indication of popular taste that a
writer reporting Mendelssohn's performance of Bach at Birmingham in
1837 felt that only the climax of the Fugue in E flat (BWV 552), 'employing
the entire capacity of the organ, which is quite overpowering', could possibly
appeal to the public (*ABG*, 25 September 1837). The reporter doubtless
failed to detect a poetical quality in Bach's counterpoint. At the popular
level, 'poetical' was usually translated into 'pictorial': the early-nineteenth
century pianoforte repertoire included large numbers of descriptive pieces
(battles, storms, pastoral scenes, carnivals, state occasions) and organists
were not insensible to the organ's powers of suggestion and description. A
Nottingham organist, for example, visited Haarlem to hear the organ, and
reported: 'I was so overwhelmed by the astounding masses of sound rolling
through the vast space, that I pictured to myself a most dreadful storm in the
Bay of Biscay' (Buckingham LIV: 48). Organists followed the general musical trend, and the repertoire of the early-nineteenth century organist would
include arrangements of movements from the masses and motets of foreign
composers (admired for their 'sublime' qualities), arrangements of Handel
oratorios and overtures (especially those that lent themselves to dramatic
interpretation) and improvised fantasias such as that performed 'with the
imitation of thunder' by Sigismund Neukomm at the opening of the Birmingham Town Hall organ (*MP*, 11 October 1834). Composition for the
organ, too, began slowly to exploit the instrument's ability to stir the senses
with dramatic statement, limpid melody, and ingenuity of registration.
William Russell (1777–1813) through his contacts with theatre music and
the mainstream of European musical composition represented by Haydn
and Mozart offers an early example of this, and in the sinuous melodies of
Samuel Wesley (1766–1837), the dramatic gestures of Thomas Adams
(1785–1858) and the unconventional registrations employed by Samuel
Sebastian Wesley (1810–76) in the accompaniments to his anthems, it is
possible to sense a new spirit reflecting, in a modest way, the whole movement of art and culture in their day.[1]

S. S. Wesley's precise, and sometimes ingenious, registrations reflect a preoccupation with instrumental colour and the deployment of orchestral resources that was altogether characteristic of the period, and that was to have a powerful influence upon the development of the organ throughout the nineteenth century. So marked was this influence that some have been tempted to refer disparagingly to the Victorian organ as a 'one-man-band'. But this is hardly fair. The organ had always been regarded as, in part, a substitute for a band of instrumentalists, and its powers of imitation had been recognised (and appreciated) for long enough: it was simply that the nineteenth century had the technology (and the taste) to be more thorough-going in the pursuit of these objectives. Jonas Blewitt, for instance, in his *Complete treatise on the organ* (*c.* 1790), claimed that 'every stop is in some degree the representation of some single instrument [of which] the style, or manner, should be correspondingly adopted' (5). The open diapason was commended because, if brilliantly voiced, it 'greatly resembles the German Flute', whilst in the lower range it was reminiscent of the 'tenor fiddle', and, with the stopped diapason added, imitations of the horn were possible. The cremona bore a similarity to the violoncello. Most telling of all, the Full Great should be regarded as 'the representation of a Full Band' (7).

There were those who objected to the imitative use of the organ,[2] but, in general, the contemporary taste encouraged it – the success of Flight & Robson's Apollonicon organ (Ord-Hume 1978: 100–27) testified to the public appreciation of the organ as an imitation band. The leading performer of his generation, Thomas Adams, was said to be unrivalled in pieces of an orchestral character and always played from a full score (BM Add. MS. 11730); according to a report of a performance of the overture to Mozart's *Zauberflöte* given by Adams in 1839, 'the orchestral effects he produced could only be equalled, certainly not surpassed, by a large band' (*MW* XII, 1839: 362). On a critical level, the comment is worthless, but it testifies to that combination of ingenuity on the part of the player, and orchestral allusion on the part of the instrument, which the nineteenth century found so acceptable.

In the past, the design of the organ had reflected – however modestly – current orchestral taste. The refinement of woodwind and brass instruments during the first half of the nineteenth century, and the increasingly complex notions of orchestration with which composers experimented, were bound to have repercussions in the design of the organ. The popularity of the clarinet in the decades succeeding 1800, and its extensive employment by Mozart, Spohr and Weber, among others, explains the establishment of the Cremona as the conventional Choir reed during those years; it rapidly displaced the vox humana and the bassoon, though the latter survived until the 1840s as a bass to the short-compass cremona, and often drew separately. In a similar manner, Weber's music, with its frequent and demanding use of the French horn, reflected a taste which led to the reappearance of that register in English organs during the three decades following 1810: Bishop provided one in the Swell at Bermondsey (1829) and Newark (1835), for instance. Earlier, the Grays had attempted an imitation of the violoncello. A register of that name appeared in organs for St Paul's, Covent Garden (1798), and St Martin-in-the-Fields (1800), and then in a number of other instruments including St Marylebone (1817) and St Pancras (1822). It is possible that this was actually a reed of the cremona variety, and Gray was simply playing on the supposed similarity between that register and the violoncello (in each case, it appears to have superseded the customary Choir reed). The established imitative stops (trumpet, flute, hautboy) were evocations of eighteenth-century orchestral instruments; when the development of key mechanisms for woodwind and the valve system for brass led to a sophistication and refinement of orchestral tone, organ-builders naturally sought to follow, and the character of these stops changed as the century progressed. A little ingenuity could produce novelties. Joshua Done observed that 'the modern Cremona, when blended with the Stopt Diapason, is an excellent imitation of the Clarionet' (1839: 16); not content with this, Gray & Davison included a register in the Choir Organ at Chester Cathedral (1844) which was unabashedly called 'Clarionet', and, further, was enclosed in its own swell box.

The older nomenclature survived into the 1850s: 'Clarionet' and 'Oboe' were not unknown by the mid-1840s, but Hill (of all people) was still regularly submitting estimates containing a cremona (treble) and bassoon (bass) at the end of the 1850s.[3] Despite this, the 1850s were crucial in strengthening the existing fashion for imitative stops. The Great Exhibition (1851), with its display of modern orchestral instruments, may have acted as a stimulus. But the principal reason for this exercise of ingenuity in imitating the effects and voices of the modern orchestra was the emergence of a new breed of concert organ, which, in conception and scale, was wholly different from the theatre and assembly room organs of the Georgian era. The formative influence that led to the building of the halls in which these instruments stood and that dictated their tonal development was the oratorio.

The Handel Commemoration of 1784 has been described as 'in some ways the most important single event in the history of English music during the eighteenth century' (Mackerness 1964: 127). It is not proposed to argue the point here, but it is indisputable that the Commemoration both symbolised and stimulated the English enthusiasm for oratorio, and veneration of its chief exponent. The popularity of oratorio reached its zenith in the Victorian years, notably in the Handel Festivals held regularly at the Crystal Palace from 1857. In that year, 2,500 performers gathered to pay homage to the composer of the *Messiah*, easily eclipsing the 525 who took part in the 1784 Commemoration.

Oratorio commended itself to nineteenth-century Englishmen because it was associated with morality and religion. The 'music meetings' at which it was performed were commonly held to raise funds for some philanthropic purpose – hospitals, public charities, orphan asylums, clergy widows (Crosse 1825: *passim*) – and the character of oratorio complemented what Nettel has identified as 'the trend of popular taste ... away from highly-elaborate vocalism towards music with a meaning' (1946: 67). On a more worldly plane, oratorio performances could satisfy the contemporary taste for sensational effects by providing scope for monumental displays by massed vocalists and instrumentalists. Burney remarked that the 1784 performances 'produced not only new and exquisite sensations in judges and lovers of the art, but [also such as] were felt by those who never received pleasure from Music before' (Nettel 1946: 90). To a later generation, the suggestion that large-scale oratorio performances possessed the power to edify the unmusical was irresistible; as a means of promoting religion and improving taste the oratorio had few, if any, rivals during the Victorian era, and performances of oratorios and (by extension) sacred music of all sorts proliferated.

The fashion for oratorio helped to promote the construction of public halls equipped to accommodate large musical forces. At Birmingham, for instance, the scope of the triennial musical festivals was restricted by the limited capacity of St Philip's Church, and this was one of several factors which led to the building of the Town Hall (Thistlethwaite 1984: 5). Where Birmingham led, others followed. A grand organ soon came to be regarded as an essential feature of the more ambitious of these public halls, and in supplying it, the organ-builder was expected to provide an instrument upon which an orchestral score might be realised and that would impress the eye as well as the ear. The challenge was unprecedented, and so were many of the solutions.

Oratorio proved to be the most acceptable outlet for the Romantic spirit in a society which entertained serious reservations about the propriety of opera and lacked native composers capable of establishing a tradition of extended orchestral composition. It was religious in subject, provided scope for musical performances of a sensational character, and its greatest exponent was an honorary Englishman: for all these reasons, it was attractive to the Victorians. It was to be of significance for the development of the organ that oratorio assumed such a prominent place in the nineteenth-century musical landscape. By supplying the basic elements of a popular repertoire of transcriptions, and by creating a demand for a novel type of organ capable of sustaining large-scale choral performances, oratorio lent a new importance to the organ's traditional role as substitute for an orchestral band. This influence was not restricted to organs in town halls and concert rooms. The popularity of transcriptions from oratorios and sacred works led to the publication of numerous arrangements (of varying degrees of difficulty) which were widely used as voluntaries, strengthening the case for the inclusion of imitative registers in the church organ.[4] All told, the orchestral features of the Victorian organ owe as much to the popular taste for oratorio as to the desire on the part of organists to perform transcriptions of purely orchestral pieces.

CHARACTERISTIC FEATURES

In attempting to adapt the English organ to the demands made by player and public in the years succeeding 1820, organ-builders chose the path of reform rather than revolution. This produced a handful of exceptional instruments in which scale, construction and tonal character combined to give the impression of a more radical reform than had actually taken place. The disguise is easily penetrated, and it soon becomes clear that the realisation of the objectives which inspired these schemes was fatally hampered by an inability to set aside the inherited canons of English organ design in favour of a more appropriate model. Three of the instruments in this category will be considered in the next chapter. Generally, though, the effects of the reform were less striking. Bishop's reconstruction (1836) of G. P. England's organ in Newark Parish Church (1804) is an interesting barometer of the changes that had taken place in thirty years. New bellows were provided and the winding arrangements refined; the Swell compass was carried down from d to F; new pedal pipes, pedal keys, couplers and composition pedals were introduced; the two cornets were displaced by a

Table 8 *Everingham, 1837: Great and Swell choruses*

	C	c	c¹	c²	c³
Open Diapason	n.a.	n.a.	52.5	28.25	16.25
Principal	n.a.	52.5	28.25	16. 5	10.75
Twelfth	67*	36	20.25	12.5	9
Fifteenth	52	28.25	16.25	11	7
Sesquialtra & Cornet ı	42	23.5	28.5	15.5	n.o.
ıı	35.75	19.5	20	12.5	10.25
ııı	28.5	16.25	16	11	8
Open Diapason [Sw]			50.5	26.5	15.5
Principal [Sw]			26.5	15.5	10
Fifteenth [Sw]			15.5	10.25	7.25

Sesquialtra & Cornet:	GG	17.19.22
	f♯	12.15.17
	c¹	8.12.15.[17]
	f♯²	1. 8.12.[15]

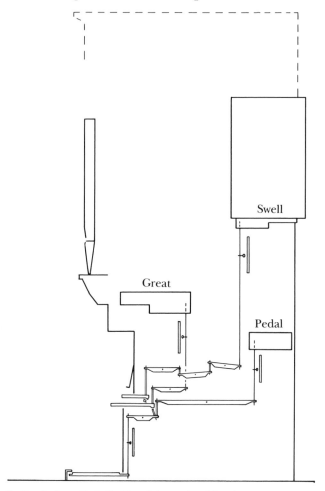

8   Everingham, Catholic Chapel: key and pedal actions.

claribella (Great) and a French horn (Swell), the bassoon treble (Choir) made way for a cremona and the nason for a clarion (MS 58). The changes were significant, but this was hardly a radical reconstruction of an organ deemed hopelessly out-of-date. There was no guarantee that new organs would be any more adventurous, despite the wind of change. Charles Allen's organ for the Catholic chapel at Everingham (1837) is a highly conservative instrument which shows little advance on Lincoln's Thaxted organ of sixteen years earlier. Only the inclusion of a dulciana in the Great and a fifteenth in the Swell (Appendix 1, pp. 449–50) indicate that this instrument post-dates 1820. The composition of the mixturework is curious (and may not be original) and the exclusive use of a backfall action (Figure 8) is a hint of what was to come, but the employment of straightline scaling for the main chorus registers is an expression of deep conservatism in view of the inno-

vations made by Green and Elliot (Table 8). The Everingham organ was by
no means exceptional, and the changes discussed below can only be evalu-
ated once this is understood.

What follows is a summary, under six headings, of the characteristic
features of the Insular Movement. Occasionally, all six could be found in the
same instrument; more usually, two or three can be identified. Some (long
compasses, huge scaling) were short-lived; others were to become permanent features of the nineteenth-century organ.

Long compasses

Hill's instruments at York and Birmingham had manual compasses commencing at CC, and Walmisley proposed that the Liverpool organ should
follow suit (below, pp. 141–2). In general, the effects offered by a keyboard
descending below C continued to be admired. The performer could convince
himself that, by 'grasping at as many notes as he could possibly hold down
with both hands (not forgetting a full chord or two in the bass)' the power of
the instrument was materially increased (*PMEM* ii, 2nd Series, 1846: 25).
On a more immediately practical level, a long compass was regarded as
useful in the accompaniment of singers; it was noted of Gray & Davison's
new organ for Chester Cathedral (1844) that 'attention has been paid ... to
the extended compass of that part of the instrument used more particularly
for the accompaniment of the Choir in our cathedrals' (Hicklin 1846: 80)
with the result that, though the Great Organ commenced at the newly
fashionable C, the Choir still began at GG (Appendix 1, pp. 450–1).

A keyboard compass commencing at GG remained the norm until the
1840s. However, the breaches of this convention were sufficiently numerous

Table 9 *CC-compasses in English organs, 1829–56*

Location	Builder	Date	Gt	Ch	Sw
York Minster	Elliot	1829	$CC-c^4$	$CC-c^4$	$C-c^4$
Christ's Hospital	Elliot	1829	$CC-f^3$	$CC-f^3$	$G-f^3$
Bristol , Mayor's Chapel	Smith	1830	$CC-f^3$	$CC-f^3$	none
Birmingham Town Hall	Hill	1833	$CC-f^3$	$CC-f^3$	$C-f^3$
Bath Abbey	Smith	1836	$CC-c^4$	$CC-c^4$	$C-c^4$
Cambridge, Trinity College	Gray	1836	$CC-f^3$	$GG-f^3$	$G-f^3$
Leeds, Oxford Place Chapel	Hill	1837	$CC-?$	$CC-?$	$c-?$
Leeds, St Peter's Chapel	Booth	1838	$CC-f^3$	$GG-f^3$	$C-f^3$
Gloucester Cathedral	Willis	1847	$CC-f^3$	$GG-f^3$	$C-f^3$
Westminster Abbey	Hill	1848	$CC-f^3$	$FF-f^3$	$C-f^3$
Pimlico, St Barnabas	Flight	1849	$CC-f^3$	$CC-f^3$	$c-f^3$
Chesterfield Parish Church	Jones	1851	$CC-f^3$	$CC-f^3$	$C-f^3$
Tenbury, St Michael's College	Flight	1856	$CC-g^3$	$CC-g^3$	$C-g^3$

to amount to a trend. Both Green and G. P. England had occasionally begun their keyboards at FF, and in the two decades following 1820 it became increasingly common to adopt this practice in large organs.[5] EE was used occasionally,[6] but more significant was the rash of CC-compasses that appeared in the first half of the nineteenth century (Table 9). Indicative at once of an awareness of the limitations of the existing English organ and of an incapacity to propose a radical alternative, they posed formidable difficulties for both builder and player, and were rendered obsolete by the innovations of the 1840s.

Pedals and pedal pipes

In attempting to substantiate his opinion that the English organ had, during the 1830s, become 'almost a new instrument', Wooley claimed that this was demonstrably true 'in one grand and important particular, viz. in the application of pedal pipes of large dimensions . . . played on by the feet of the organist' (Buckingham LIV: 47). Wooley's remarks are useful in establishing that the introduction of pedal pipes is not to be connected exclusively with the innovations of the German System (scarcely under way by 1839), but was an important feature of the Insular Movement in the two decades before 1840.

The introduction of pedals in the years preceding 1820 has already been discussed (above pp. 14–23); at the end of that period, neither pedals nor pedal pipes featured in the description of a typical cathedral organ in Rees's *Cyclopaedia* (1819), and nor were they listed as being among 'the requisites of a good organ' in the Rees article. A few years later, another publication was more informative:

Till within these [last] few years, pedals were scarcely known in England, and even now are generally what are termed 'sham'; i.e. they are only a range of sticks for the feet, connected with the keys of the great Organ. Even these are of such use, that a person accustomed to them, can scarcely endure the emptiness of the performance, which is manifest when they are wanting. They enable the Performer to double his *bass*, without being under the necessity of deserting the *tenor*, to which the left hand should be almost exclusively devoted. Indeed, an organ played with pedals, is as much superior to an organ played without them . . . as the modern Grand Piano-Forte is, to the Spinett of our Great Grandmothers.   (*Edinburgh Gazetteer c.* 1825)

The view that pedals were principally useful in doubling the bass and releasing the left hand to thicken the harmonies is supported by another Edinburgh publication; organs, according to the *Edinburgh Encyclopaedia* (1830: 677–8), 'have often . . . pedal stops, consisting of two octaves, doubling the bass in the octave below'. Not only did pedal keys allow the organist to hold down the bass notes of the keyboard, but pedal pipes (if they were doubles) created the effect of a bass line played in octaves. Pedal pipes were also valued at this period because they lent gravity to the chorus. A critic of the 1830s complained that Bridge's organ at St Anne, Limehouse, lacked 'sufficient weight or ponderosity in the bass' to match 'the brilliancy of the treble' (*CR* xvi, 1834: 568). Making a similar criticism of Avery's instrument in Croydon Church he offered a solution:

the great brilliancy in the upper or acute part of the instrument, requires a ponderous and weighty quality in the bass, or grave part of the instrument. It still wants a real double open diapason, as pedal pipes, to render the full organ what it should be – majestic.   (*CR* xvi, 1834: 698)

It is interesting to observe that a brilliant Great chorus was still admired in the 1830s, though the taste for 'ponderosity' was ultimately to prove more significant.

The development of pedals and pedal pipes by the Insular Movement was thus a response to a movement of taste away from the light, brilliant keyboard textures of the previous century, towards an effect which possessed a certain majestic grandeur. The pedal was still viewed by most players and organ-builders as an adjunct to the manual. Despite the reputation enjoyed by a handful of 'pedalists' during the 1830s (Thomas Adams and Samuel Sebastian Wesley among them), and despite the appearance by the mid-1830s of organ tutors which gave instruction in the use and management of the pedals,[7] few organists acquired a proficient pedal technique or a real understanding of the possibilities of an independent pedal division before the end of that decade. Dr Camidge's taste for long compasses persisted because he 'was not very brilliant on the pedals, but very brilliant with the left hand' (*PMA*, 1906–7: 129), and many other organists must have had a similar reason for being unenthusiastic about changes that would have made excessive demands on their technique. As late as 1856, it was proposed in all seriousness that the adoption of CC-compass (16′) for the keyboards, would, 'in a great measure, if not altogether, do away with the necessity for a pedal organ' (*MG* i, 1856: 44).

Table 10 illustrates the bewildering diversity of pedal arrangements in English organs between 1821 and 1840, and concludes with some examples demonstrating the tenacity of this insular tradition in the years which followed the introduction of the German System. The instruments cited are taken as representative of the period; they are chosen because the details of their design can be established with some certainty, and because, taken together, they offer a fair indication of the pace of change. The importance of this curious catalogue should not be underestimated. During the 1820s and 1830s, the provision of a single set of pedal pipes to reinforce the bass became established custom in English organ-building and remained the convention (for the majority of organs) well into the twentieth century: this particular feature of English organ design is a legacy of the Insular Movement, not of the German System, and it had considerable influence upon repertoire and playing styles throughout the period.

Table 10 *English organs with pedal pipes: 1821–56*

Year	Builder	Location	Pedal specification	Pedal board compass
1821	Smith	Bristol Cathedral	none	GG–c (PDs)
	Buckingham	Southwell Minster	none pedals permanently coupled to Choir, but with Pedals to Great coupler	GG–c (PDs)
	Lincoln	St John's Chapel, Bedford Row	Unisons	FF–c (GPs)
1822	Gray	St Pancras PC	Unisons, FF–c (?)	?
1823	Buckingham	Doncaster PC	none	? (TPs)
	Davis	Stockport PC	none double diapasons on Great and Choir; 17-note open diapason bass on Great	GG–B
	Blyth	Salisbury Cathedral	Pedal Pipes, FF–G: FF–BB dwarf } with helpers C–G doubles }	FF–c
	Ward	York Minster	[see below, p. 121]	
1824	Bishop	St John, Waterloo Road	Doubles: GG–BB unisons C–g doubles	GG–g (?)
	Bishop	All Souls, St Marylebone	pedals coupled to bass of Great open diapason by independent coupler labelled 'Pedal Pipes'	GG–c (GPs)
	Smith	Bristol, St James	[see below, p. 458]	
	Nicholls/Gray	Chelsea, St Luke	Doubles (GG–BB Unisons)	GG–c
	Lincoln	Camberwell, St George	Doubles (GG–BB returns)	GG–g
1825	Lincoln	Walworth, St Peter	Doubles (GG–BB Unisons)	GG–c
1826	Gray	St Stephen Walbrook	Unisons: 1 8ve, GG–G (?)	GG–c
	Bishop	St Paul's Cathedral	Doubles, C–c	C–c¹ (GPs)
	Buckingham	Nottingham, St Peter	none	GG–c (PDs)
	Gray	St Sepulchre, Holborn	Doubles, C–g: C–F♯ stopped G–g open wood	C–c¹
1827	Elliot & Hill	Christ Church, Newgate Street	Doubles, GG–c	?
	Bishop	Holy Trinity, St Marylebone	Doubles (GG–BB returns?)	GG–c
1828	Elliot & Hill	Westminster Abbey	Doubles Unisons (1793)	GG–G (?)
	Gray	St John, Hackney	Doubles, C–c	GG–c
1829	Bishop	St James, Bermondsey	Double Pedal Pipes [16] Unison Pedal Pipes [8]	GG–g
		manual keyboard	Trombone [8]	
	Pilcher	Chichester Cathedral	Unisons	GG–c
	Elliot & Hill	Christ's Hospital *manual keyboard*	Doubles	C–c¹
	Elliot & Hill	York Minster	[see below, p. 124]	

Year	Builder	Location	Pedal specification	Pedal board compass
1830	Smith	Bristol, Lord Mayor's Chapel (manual C C)	Open Diapason 16 Stopped Diapason 16 Principal 8 Trumpet 16 Octave coupler	?
1831	Bishop	Gloucester Cathedral	Unisons	G G–c (?)
1832	Bishop	St Philip, Waterloo Place	Doubles (D–?) (G G–C♯ Unisons)	G G–?
1833	Bishop	St Edmund, Lombard Street *manual keyboard*	Doubles	G G–c
1834	Hill	Birmingham Town Hall	[see below, pp. 129–30]	
	Hill	Cambridge, King's College	Doubles, C–c Unisons (1803)	G G–c (G Ps)
	Gray	St Sepulchre, Holborn	Doubles	C–c¹
	Robson	St Dunstan-in-the-West	Doubles	G G–c
1835	Butler	St Mary Woolnoth	Unisons	G G–c
	Bishop	Newark P C	Doubles, C–c Unisons (1804) 'to D'	F F–d (?)
	?	Windsor, St George's Chapel (stood at one side of loft, with own clavier and bellows: required second player)	Doubles	F F–c
	Smith	Bristol, St Stephen (keyboards to C C, with lowest 8ve acting *only* on pedals)	Doubles, C–b 'Pedals octave to Great'	C–b (?)
1836	Smith	Bath Abbey (keyboards C C)	Doubles	C–b
	Gray	Cambridge, Trinity College	Double Open Diapason (metal?) 'Melody Coupler' [Choir to Pedal 2′]	C–c¹
1837	Allen	Everingham, Catholic Chapel	Unisons	G G–c
	Lincoln	Spitalfields, Christ Church	Doubles, G G–g 'canto-firmo-copula' [Swell octave to Pedal]	G G–e¹ (?)
	Hill & Davison	Christ Church, Newgate Street	Doubles, G G–c 'canto-firmo-copula' [Swell octave to Pedal]	C–g¹ [sic]
	Hill & Davison	St James's Palace, Chapel Royal	Unisons	G G–c
	Hill & Davison	Leeds, Oxford Place Chapel	Doubles	G G–g
	Smith	Bristol, Christ Church	Open Diapason 16 Open Diapason 16 [sic] Stopped Diapason ? Principal ? Pedals to Great Octave	C–f♯

Table 10 – *cont.*

Year	Builder	Location	Pedal specification	Pedal board compass
1838	Booth	Leeds, St Peter's Chapel	Double Open Diapason, C–g (?) Open Diapason ⎱ C–c¹ Principal ⎰	C–c¹
	Telford	Dublin, Trinity College	Open Diapason Principal Twelfth Fifteenth Trumpet	GG–c
	Hill	Cambridge, St John's College (proposed)	Unisons, FF–c Octave Trumpet, FF–E, (to meet Swell)	?
		Cambridge, St John's College (as built)	'Double Stop Diapason 16ft giving 32ft note'	FF–f
1839	Walker	Exeter Hall, London	Open Double Diapason (w) 16 Open Double Diapason (m) 16 Principal 8 Fifteenth 4 Mixture III Posaune 16 Trumpet 8 (?) ⎱ C–e (to meet Swell?)	C–e¹
	Buckingham	Nottingham PC	Doubles (GG–BB Unisons)	GG–e
1841	Gray & Davison	Eton College Chapel	Doubles, C–c	GG–c
	Gray & Davison	Cork	Double Open Diapason 16 (GG–BB returns) Open Diapason 8	GG–c
1842	Gray & Davison	St John's Wood Chapel	Unisons	GG–d
1843	Bishop	Temple Church	Doubles (FF–BB returns)	FF–c
	Gray & Davison	Windsor, St George's Chapel	Double Open Diapason 16 Open Diapason 8	FF–?
1844	Bishop	Camberwell, St Giles	Double Open Diapason 16 Open Diapason 8 Open Diapason 8 (from Great) Trombone 16	C–d¹
1845	Walker	Nottingham, Holy Trinity	Doubles *manuals GG*	C–c¹ (GPs)
	Allen	Walthamstow PC	Double Stopped Diapason 16 (FF–BB Unisons, open)	FF–f
	Bewsher	Everton, St George	Doubles (wd) Unisons (m)	EE–e
1846	Bevington	Cashel Cathedral	Doubles	FF–c
	Walker	St Olave Jewry	Unisons, GG–G	2 octaves
	Bishop	Paddington, Holy Trinity	Doubles, C–c	GG–c
	Bevington	Battle Abbey	Bourdon, C–c Unisons, FF–c	FF–d [*sic*]

Year	Builder	Location	Pedal specification	Pedal board compass
1847	Walker	Jamaica Cathedral	Doubles *manuals to FF*	C–c¹
	Gray & Davison	Oxford, Christ Church Cathedral	Double Open Diapason 16 (GG–BB returns)	GG–g
1849	Flight	Pimlico, St Barnabas	Open Diapason 16 *manuals to CC*	C–f¹
	Walker	Clifton, Christ Church	Double Open Diapason 16 Bourdon 16 Principal (m) 8 *manuals to FF*	C–e¹
	Hill	Canterbury Cathedral	Open Diapason (wd) 16 ⎫ Bourdon (wd) 16 ⎬ C–c Principal (m) 8 Open Flute (wd) 8 ⎭	GG–g
1851	Jones	Chesterfield PC	Grand Pedal Pipes 16 — C–d¹ Bourdon 16 Open Diapason 8 — to provide bass Stopped Diapason 8 — to short-compass Principal 4 — Swell, hence C–f♯ Sesquialtra v	C–d¹
	Allen	Lincoln Cathedral	Sub-Bourdon 32 ⎫ C–g¹ Open Diapason 16 ⎬ C–g¹ Principal 8 Twelfth 5⅓ Fifteenth 4 ⎫ C–F♯ Sesquialtera ⎬ Trombone 16 ⎭ *manuals to GG*	C–g¹
1852	Gray & Davison	Eton College Chapel	Grand Open Diapason, C–c¹ *manuals to GG*	GG–c¹
	Bryceson	Amersham PC	Double Stopped Diapason 16 Trumpet 8	GG–g
1855	Willis	Liverpool, St George's Hall	[see below, pp. 145–6]	
1856	Flight	Tenbury, St Michael's College	Pyramydon 32 Open Diapason (wd) 16 Quint 12 Principal 8 *manuals to CC*	C–f¹

Abbreviations
P Ds Pull-downs
T Ps Toe pedals
G Ps German pedals

NB Where the compass of the registers is not recorded separately, it is understood to be the same as the pedal board.

Despite the inconsistencies highlighted in Table 10, certain generalisations may be tentatively advanced. At the beginning of the period, substantial organs were still being built without any independent pedal pipes, though few, by then, lacked rudimentary pedal pull-downs. Davis's large 3-manual organ for Stockport Parish Church (1823) was unusually conservative in conception, having no pedal pipes at all, but the absence of doubles from Gray's ambitious instrument (1822) for St Pancras underlines the rarity of this register at the time. J. C. Bishop tacitly acknowledged one of the major drawbacks of pedal pipes when he provided 'Extra Bellows' to wind the doubles ('of Very Large Scale') in his new organ for St John's, Waterloo Road (1824), and by the close of the 1820s, doubles were becoming more common. There were even some instruments with full-length doubles to GG (Christ Church, Newgate Street; Westminster Abbey; Christ's Hospital), though most registers broke back to unison pitch at BB, or 'returned' (that is, the pedals were permanently coupled to the octave above and sounded its notes).

Wholly exceptional during the 1820s were reconstructions of the organs in York Minster (Ward, 1823) and St James's, Bristol (Smith, 1824); these will be discussed in their proper place (below, pp. 119–22 and 155–9). More indicative of what would follow was Bishop's organ in St James's, Bermondsey (Appendix 1, pp. 445–6). With three registers, a 2-octave pedal board, and full-length doubles, this can claim to be the largest GG-compass Pedal Organ ever made. During the 1830s, organ-builders gradually expanded the compass of the pedals, occasionally provided more than a single set of pipes, and became more willing to manufacture the large pipes which a GG-compass Pedal Organ required. As late as 1837, Hill & Davison could build a 3-manual organ for no less a place than the Chapel Royal, St James's Palace, with only an octave-and-a-half of unisons; four years later, Gray & Davison made two substantial 2-manual organs with no pedal pipes at all (St Mary Magdalene, Peckham; St George's Cathedral, Demerara) and in 1848, Walker built a 14-stop, GG-compass instrument with just two octaves of pull-downs (Trinity New Church, Brompton). Generally, though, pedals and pedal pipes were an accepted part of the English organ by 1840.

The part played by organists in the development of pedals is obscure. In Bristol, Dr Hodges exercised considerable influence, and more will be said of this below (pp. 156–7). In London, George Cooper, senior (c. 1783–1843), Organist of St Sepulchre, Holborn, and Assistant Organist at St Paul's Cathedral, was influential; he was certainly responsible for the provision of a C-compass, 2-octave pedal board at St Sepulchre's in 1827, and for the installation of double pedal pipes there in 1834. He was, of necessity, closely acquainted with the C-compass pedal board at St Paul's, but whether it was this, or a theoretical belief in the virtues of that compass which led him to propose C-compass boards at St Sepulchre's and Trinity College, Cambridge (1837), and possibly at Christ's Hospital (1829) and Christ Church,

Newgate Street (1837) (Gray 1837: 33) is not known. Whatever the reason, this innovation anticipated a practice which would become almost universal by the end of the 1850s. Another London organist, Josiah Pittman (1816–86), was probably responsible for the extensive compass of the pedal board at Christ Church, Spitalfields (1837). Like Cooper, Pittman belonged to the first generation of English Bach players (*MW* xii, 1839: 186) and this may well explain the unusually extensive compass at Spitalfields. Other innovations were less enduring. A few instruments were built in which the pedal pipes could be played from a manual keyboard (the first seems to have been St James's, Bristol, in 1824). This was mechanically cumbersome – the weight of touch must have been prodigious – and the necessity for such expedients evaporated as the players developed an adequate pedal technique. The provision of this facility at St James's, Bermondsey, permitted a trio of organists to perform Bach's 'St Anne' Fugue and an arrangement of a chorus from *Israel in Egypt* at the opening of the organ (*Examiner*, 26 April 1829: 263); the keyboard survives, though long disconnected (Plate 23). Equally short-lived was the 'Melody Coupler'. It may have been another of

23 St James, Bermondsey. Console, showing separate keyboard for Pedal stops. (1912)

Cooper's innovations, though it is said that the example in the organ at Trinity College, Cambridge, was provided so that Walmisley could solo the melody of the National Anthem in the introduction to Attwood's *I was glad* (*MO* XVI, 1893: 398). The Cambridge specimen took the form of a Choir to Pedal 2' coupler. Similar devices were provided at about the same time in the organs of Christ Church, Spitalfields, and Christ Church, Newgate Street; these were Swell to Pedal 4' (2' at Spitalfields?) couplers.

The organ music of the period remained, for the most part, singularly unadventurous in its use of the pedals. As early as 1804, William Russell, in his first set of *Twelve Voluntaries*, had demonstrated the use of the pedals for sustaining a pedal point or a slow-moving bass (VII.iv; XII.v; etc.), and had written a rudimentary trio in which the pedals, coupled to the Great stopped diapason, played a simple bass line, whilst the right hand was occupied with the Choir cremona and the left with the Swell hautboy (VIII.ii). Composers seldom strayed beyond the bounds indicated by Russell in the course of the next thirty years: Thomas Adams, for example, despite Samuel Wesley's acknowledgement of his 'great skill and ability in the management of the pedals' (MS 66: f.54) makes only modest use of the pedals in his organ compositions, though the second movement of no. 2 of the *Six Organ Pieces* is set out on three staves. Wesley himself was even less enterprising: his organ works were a final (and distinguished) statement of the musical possibilities offered by the long-compass, pedal-less English organ, and it was not to be expected that he would rise to the challenges of a (potentially) radical departure in conception. The next generation, however, was not so constrained. By the time of Samuel Wesley's death (1837), a sluggish trickle of compositions in which the Pedal Organ was given a distinctive musical role had begun. A reviewer in the *Harmonicon* (IX, 1831: 196) commented upon 'the uncommon use of the pedals' in S. S. Wesley's *Variations* on the National Anthem (1829), and questioned whether 'the author will meet with a player, himself excepted, to play the pedal part of the third variation' ('not in England, we surmise', came the rhetorical answer). Wesley sustained his reputation with the publication, five years later, of the first number of a projected *Studio for the Organ*. This was the *Introduction and Fugue in C Sharp Minor*, of which a critic remarked, 'before attacking it, a course of gymnastics is recommended' (*MW* I, 1836: 143) – presumably, on account of the complexity of the pedal part; the accompaniment to the bass solo ('Say to them') in *The Wilderness* (autograph 1834) is equally demanding (MS 40). In the following year, Egerton Webbe's *Prelude and Fugue in A major* appeared (*MW* VIII, 1838: 100–3). It was an isolated publication by a composer who died young (in 1840, at the age of thirty) but the *Prelude*, especially, shows that some English musicians were beginning to grasp the possibilities of texture and effect which the introduction of the Pedal Organ opened up. In 1839, Thomas Attwood Walmisley published a *Prelude and Fugue in E minor* which demonstrated an equally ambitious use of the pedals within a more conventional harmonic framework. By then, another influence was coming to bear that would prove a powerful advocate for pedals and Pedal Organs. More will be said of the recovery of Bach's organ music below (pp. 163–75). It had, in any case, influenced some of the compositions which have been mentioned. Bach's organ works demonstrated conclusively the Pedal's potential contribution to a musical structure with the result that, by the early-1840s, compositions and transcriptions embodying an independent pedal line (and maybe printed on three staves) were becoming more common.

For the same reason, it was, by this time, becoming more difficult to distinguish pedal schemes belonging to the Insular tradition from those influenced by the embryonic German System – many schemes exhibit an ambiguity, with C-compass pedal boards and long-compass keyboards. These ambiguities persisted into the mid-1850s. Walker's organ for the Exeter Hall (1839) is a case in point (Appendix 1, pp. 448–9). It is not known who designed it, and, until one looks closely, the Pedal appears to be an early and brave example of the German System. But then it is noticed that the compass was restricted to seventeen notes, that it terminated at tenor e and the keyboards commenced at FF or F, and, once again, it seems that the pedal division is conceived as a manual bass. Similarly confusing schemes were to be found at Chesterfield Parish Church and Lincoln Cathedral (both 1851). The Insular tradition never came to terms with the North European concept of an independent pedal division, and even in schemes powerfully influenced by the principles of the burgeoning German System there is evidence of a failure to grasp this fundamental point. Ouseley's organ for St Michael's College, Tenbury, is a spectacular instance of this; built in 1856 (by Flight), with CC-compasses to Great and Choir, and a Pedal consisting of four wooden basses, it was probably the last large long-compass organ to be built in England. Despite the persistence of short-compass pedal boards, and single octaves of pedal pipes, in smaller organs for many years after this, the C-compasses of the German System and the open wood basses of the Insular Movement had, by the late-1850s, united to produce the standard Victorian Pedal Organ, with its two octaves or more of pedals, and a 16′ register running throughout the compass.

Manual doubles

Registers of 16′ pitch, playable from a keyboard, were a rarity in English organs before 1820. Loosemore's famous double diapason at Exeter Cathedral (1665: it was extended throughout the compass by Jordan c. 1741) was wholly exceptional for the period, and the other isolated examples which appeared before 1800 – in Snetzler's organ at King's Lynn (1754), for example, or Parker's at the Foundling Hospital (1768) – aroused little enthusiasm and had no obvious musical function.

It is significant that a modest increase in the incidence of manual doubles occurred during the early 1800s, when organ-builders were also experimenting with pedal pipes. As has been noted above (pp. 15, 19), these doubles were intended to serve the same function as early pedal pipes, and for many years they were regarded as being interchangeable; as late as 1830, the *Edinburgh Encyclopaedia* specified the stop list of a typical cathedral organ, and included 'one double diapason of two octaves from GGG (24 feet) to 6 feet G, played by finger or pedals' (xv: 679). In common with pedal pipes, manual doubles added weight to the chorus. They also reinforced the bass by introducing sub-unison tone: an effect similar to playing in octaves. In this latter function, the manual double was particularly useful when it appeared in the Swell. The Swell compass being short (it seldom ventured below tenor c during this period), sub-unison tone was regarded as, in some way, making up for the missing bottom octave or more, by doubling the bass. This may well be the origin of the Victorian convention of including a double diapason in the Swell, even though there was none in the Great Organ.

Whatever its virtues in the bass, the effect of the double in the treble was not universally admired. A correspondent, writing to the *Bristol Mirror* in 1820, endorsed Burney's view that a manual double had the same effect 'as if the treble part in a concert were played by doubles bases [*sic*]' (*QMMR* IV, 1822: 33), and Samuel Wesley, when he heard a double diapason for the first time (possibly in Lincoln's organ at St George's, Camberwell) is said to have enquired, ' "pray who is that person who takes the liberty of humming behind my back all I do?" ' (*MW* VII, 1837: 9n). It was doubtless on account of its comparative discretion in the treble that the double dulciana became popular as a manual (usually, Swell) sub-unison. This register was first employed by J. C. Bishop about 1828 in an organ 'for a new church in Acre Lane, Clapham' (*CR* xv, 1833: 743), and, thereafter, it made regular appearances in his instruments (and, to a lesser extent, in those of Hill and Gray) until the mid-1840s.

Little can now be recovered concerning the scaling of these early doubles. Fortunately, however, the doubles in one of the first instruments to possess a sub-unison register on both Great and Swell have survived: the Elliot & Hill organ in Oldham Parish Church (1830). The double diapason on the Great is of open metal construction from g, stopped wood below. It originally drew in halves, bass and treble (HR2: 512). The Swell double diapason also has a stopped wood bass (below c¹) and both stops are substantially smaller than the open diapasons of the Great (Table 11): the Great register is four pipes smaller, the Swell, six or seven. In mouthing and voicing, neither is distinguished from the rest of the chorus.

With the advent of the German System in the late-1830s the chorus

Table 11 *Oldham Parish Church, 1830: Great chorus & Swell 16′ scales*

	C	c	c¹	c²	c³
Double Open Diapason			n.a.	44	24.5
Open Diapason I			50	29.5	19
Open Diapason II			50	30	19
Principal	81	47	n.o.	17.5	9.5
Twelfth	50.5	28.5	17.5	11	7
Fifteenth	44.5	n.o.	15.5	9.5	n.o.
Sesquialtra I	37	27.5	21.5	17.5	11
II	32	23.5	17.5	n.o.	n.o.
III	27.5	21.5	14	10.5	7
IV	23.5	17.5	13	–	–
Composition:	GG	17.19.22.24			
	c	15.17.19.22			
	c¹	12.15.17.19			
	a¹	8.12.15			
Double Diapason [Sw]			76	38	20.5

function of manual doubles became gradually better understood, and it was realised that the advantages of a 16′ register were not limited to compensating for the absence of a complete compass or freeing the performer from the necessity of tackling the pedals. In 1837, an organist put his finger on a major distinction between the Birmingham and York organs when he wrote:

> The absence of a double diapason on the York organ is much to be deplored; and the advantage which that at Birmingham derives from its two double diapasons is surprising, and will ever place it far above the York organ in grandeur and sublimity of tone.   (*MW* VII, 1837: 179)

In the same year, it was noted that S. S. Wesley, who, as organist of Exeter Cathedral (1835–42) had at his command one of the few doubles in an English cathedral organ, generally used it in the chorus 'throughout the service' (*MW* VII, 1837: 9n). This was a novelty for the 1830s, but it anticipated a practice which was to become common later in the century.

Table 12 gives a representative list of English organs of the Insular tradition which, between 1820 and 1840, had a manual double. The organs

Table 12 *Manual doubles, 1820–1840*

Date	Location	Builder	Details
1820	Waterloo Place, St Philip	Davis	D.D. [Sw]
	Boston PC	Nicholls	D.D. [Gt]
1822	St Pancras PC	Gray	D.D. [Gt]
			D.D. [Sw]
1823	Stockport PC	Davis	D.D. [Gt]
			D.D. [Ch] *stopped*

Table 12 – *cont.*

Date	Location	Builder	Details
1824	Macclesfield, St George	Renn & Boston	D.S.D. [Gt]
	Camberwell, St George	Lincoln	D.D. [Gt] *stopped*
	Newington, Holy Trinity	Russell	D.D. [Sw]
1825	Gateshead, St Mary	Wood & Small	D.D. [Gt]
	Selby Abbey	Renn & Boston	D.S.D. [Gt] *GG–g*
			D.S.D. [Sw]
	Walworth, St Peter	Lincoln	D.D. [Sw]
1826	Pershore Abbey	Russell	D.S.D. [Gt]
1827	Wrexham PC	Bewsher & Fleetwood	D.S.D. [Gt]
			D.S.D. [Sw]
	Plymouth, St Andrew	Lincoln	D.S.D. [Gt]
1828	Leeds, Brunswick Chapel	Booth	D.D. [Gt] *open metal*
	Blackburn PC	Gray	D.S.D. [Sw]
	Clapham, Acre Lane Church	Bishop	D.Dul. [Sw?]
	Clerkenwell, St Mark	Gray	D.Dul. [Sw]
1830	Oldham, St James	Nicholson	D.S.D. [Gt]
	Christ's Hospital	Elliot & Hill	D.Dul. [Sw]
	Moorfields, St Mary (RC)	Bevington	D.D. [Sw]
	Oldham PC	Elliot & Hill	D.D. [Gt]
			D.D. [Sw]
1831	Newgate Street, Christ Church	Elliot & Hill	D.Dul. [Sw]
	Newcastle-upon-Tyne, St Thomas	Elliot & Hill	D.S.D. [Gt] *FF–g*
1832	Clapham, St James	Bishop	D.Dul. [Gt]
1833	Liverpool, St Nicholas	Gray	D.S.D. [Sw]
1834	Birmingham Town Hall	Hill	D.O.D. [Gt] *(c)*
			D.D. [Sw]
	St Dunstan-in-the-West	Robson	D.D. [Sw]
	Stockport, St Thomas	Renn	D.D. [Gt] *st bass and open treble*
1836	Cambridge, Trinity College	Gray	D.S.D. [Sw]
	Newcastle-upon-Tyne, St Andrew	Gray	D.S.D. [Sw]
1837	Spitalfields, Christ Church	Lincoln	D.D. [Sw]
1838	Chester, St John	Hill & Davison	D. Stopped Bass [Ch] *to meet* D.D. [Sw]
	Leeds, St Peter's Chapel	Booth	D.O.D. [Gt] Bourdon + D.O.D. [Sw]
1839	Cambridge, St John's College	Hill	Sub-Bass and D.Dul. [Gt]
	London, Exeter Hall	Walker	Bourdon and Tenoroon Dulciana [Sw]
1840	Belfast, St Patrick	Gray	D.D. [Sw]

Abbreviations

D.O.D.   Double Open Diapason
D.S.D.   Double Stopped Diapason
D.D.   Double Diapason
D.Dul.   Double Dulciana

Unless indicated otherwise, all these registers ran throughout the compass of the keyboard.

were (mainly) large by the standards of the day. It will be noted that 16′ registers on the Great (which were costly to make and bulky to accommodate) remained a rarity throughout this period.

Duplication

A further measure adopted by organ-builders in their quest for ways in which the power of the organ might be increased was the duplication of individual registers within the chorus. Belief in the legitimacy of this approach was widespread. Like the introduction of pedal pipes and doubles, it was thought to possess the twin virtues of lending dignity to the chorus and correcting a potential imbalance between treble and bass. In 1834, the author of *Organo-Historica* noted that John Gray had added a second open diapason and an octave of unison pedal pipes to the George England organ in St Stephen, Walbrook (1826). He went on: 'These additions have considerably enriched the chorus of the great organ, by thickening the foundation-stops; but owing to the scale of the furniture and mixture – the voicing of which is so very brilliant – the instrument would still bear another open diapason, and pedal pipes of greater calibre' (*CR* XVI, 1834: 111).

Something has already been said about the growing practice of including a second open diapason in the main chorus (above, pp. 11–12); during the 1820s, it spread to the other divisions, an open diapason and a dulciana being commonly included in the Choir Organ, and two open diapasons sometimes appearing in the Swell (St James, Bermondsey, 1829; Bath Abbey, 1836; Chapel Royal, St James's Palace, 1837), and it became more usual for the Great open diapasons to be made to different scales with one 'voic'd more powerfully' than the other (MS 56). But, this apart, the 1820s and 1830s saw the building of a number of organs in which duplication was employed upon a wholly novel scale with principals and fifteenths, reeds and dulcianas, all being duplicated. The failure of these instruments was conspicuous. Although examples can be found well into the 1850s, and although the largest of them – Wesley's scheme for St George's Hall, Liverpool – was not completed until 1855, enthusiasm had waned by the 1840s. Even so, as late as 1847, William Hill found it necessary to condemn what he termed 'the prevalent opinion in England' that 'there cannot be too great a proportion of the unison in the great organ', pointing out that 'too many diapasons of the same tone destroy one another' (MS 45: 28 September 1847). Despite Hill's warning, and despite the vocal advocacy of his, and other instruments built on the German System, duplication remained a feature of English organ-building for a century or more, whether in the two open diapasons of the typical Victorian church organ, or in the more extensive schemes of Henry Willis and Arthur Harrison.

Camidge's scheme for the reconstruction of the York Minster organ in

1823 (below, pp. 120–1) is one of the earliest examples of duplication carried beyond the open diapasons. The Nave division, though complete in itself, was intended to reinforce the existing Great Organ by placing two, three, or even four registers of the same pitch under the player's control. The 1829 scheme (below, pp. 123–4) was a logical extension of this. The two divisions of the Great had identical stop lists, and in each the 8', 4', and 2' registers, and the trumpets, were duplicated. The same principle was applied (though on a less spectacular scale) to the other departments. The failure of all this duplication to secure the massive grandeur of effect which he had expected was met by Camidge with blank incomprehension, and to his dying day he blamed Hill for it.

The case of York Minster was exceptional. More significant (because it demonstrated how a conventional stop list could be transformed by duplication) was the organ erected in St Luke's, Chelsea, in 1824 (Appendix 1, pp. 451–2).[8] The Great had three open diapasons and two stopped diapasons, two principals and two fifteenths. The Swell had two open diapasons, two principals, and (of all things) two dulcianas. Such thoroughgoing duplication was to remain unusual (though Bevington's huge organ for St Mary, Moorfields, had a similar Great to Chelsea, with, in addition, two trumpets) but the basic principles continued to find favour throughout the 1830s.

At the beginning of that decade, the *Edinburgh Encyclopaedia* (1830) noted that the Great of a large cathedral organ might be expected to possess 'two, and sometimes three open diapasons ... one, or two principals' (679). Elliot & Hill's organs for Christ's Hospital and Oldham Parish Church (1830), Smith's organ for Bath Abbey (1836), and Booth's for St Peter's Chapel, Leeds (1838), were none of them cathedral organs, but they were conceived on a similar scale and each had two open diapasons and two principals on the Great. Despite the failure of the York organ, Hill continued to employ duplication in his largest instruments throughout the 1830s. The repetitive character of the Birmingham stop list (below, pp. 128–30) was, in practice, relieved by making one of the registers at each pitch of wood. A similar policy was adopted at the Chapel Royal, St James's Palace (1837): one principal and one fifteenth were of wood. In the following year there appeared a curious piece of duplication in Walmisley's scheme for St John's College, Cambridge (Appendix 1, pp. 452–3). There were to be two fifteenths (of metal), one described as 'large scale', the other to draw in permanent combination with the twelfth.

After 1840, with the German System rapidly gaining ground, duplication came to appear increasingly eccentric. J. C. Bishop (a conservative builder by the standards of the 1840s) built two large organs during that decade which retained duplication – St Giles, Camberwell (1844) and the Catholic Cathedral, St George's Fields (1848). Each organ had two principals on the Great, and at Camberwell the eight ranks of mixtures served to provide yet more duplication (Appendix 1, pp. 446–7). It is, though, interesting that the organ-builder who retained the use of duplication longest in large organs was Henry Willis. His first major work, the rebuilding of the Gloucester Cathedral organ (1847), left the Swell with two open diapasons and a dulciana; his organ for the Great Exhibition of 1851 (Appendix 1, pp. 453–5) included duplication at 8′, 4′, and 2′ pitches on both Great and Swell; the St George's Hall scheme (below, pp. 144–6) was subject to emendation at Willis's hands yet it still (1855) retained extensive duplication; two years later, the 13-stop Great of the new Wells Cathedral organ had two open diapasons and two principals (Appendix 1, pp. 455–6). All this was to prove of great significance for the future of English organ-building.

Tonal innovations

Unlike the era which succeeded it, the period 1820–40 was not remarkable for the introduction of new registers or tonal novelties. By and large, attention was concentrated upon adjusting the scale and refining the voicing of existing registers. The only area in which there was genuine experiment (and largely by one man – William Hill) was in the development of reeds, and little evidence of this survives.

Following the work of Samuel Green (Wickens 1987: 59), the organ-builders of the early-nineteenth century steadily extended the use of the dulciana. The pattern was not uniform. G. P. England favoured the dulciana, Thomas Elliot (in the years before 1820) did not. J. C. Bishop was one of the first regularly to include a dulciana on the Great of 2-manual organs (St Mary, Abchurch, 1822; St Peter, Dorchester, 1823; St Mary, Leicester, 1824) and also pioneered the use of the double dulciana 16′ (above, p. 106). The dulciana principal made occasional appearances (Christ Church, Bristol, 1837). By the late-1830s, a degree of consistency had emerged, and most builders included a dulciana in 2-manual organs of any size, usually on the Great.

There were other ways of distinguishing the main and secondary choruses. The celestina 4′ might be an open wood register 'of small scale, producing a delicate and subdued tone' (HR2: 140) or it might be a dulciana principal of metal (Buckingham described an example at Lowther Castle). It made an appearance in two Bewsher & Fleetwood instruments (St George, Everton, 1845; St Paul, Toxteth Park, Liverpool, 1847) and possibly in the Elliot & Hill organ at St Thomas, Newcastle (1831). In the Toxteth Park instrument it was found on the Great; at Everton it was one of three Swell 4′ flues – principal, dulcet (wood), celestina (tin). During this period, it was, however, the harmonica which most regularly appeared as a secondary 4′. It probably developed from the open wood chorus registers which had been known in English organs since the seventeenth century. Buckingham referred to 'the Harmonica (or wood Principal)' (LII: 13), though Camidge seemed to distinguish between a harmonica and a wood principal when he complained (in reference to the York organ) that 'the wood principals are not harmonicas, as they were to have been' (Gray 1837: 36). Perhaps the scaling was larger than that of a wood principal: elsewhere, Buckingham refers to one of Ward's harmonicas as 'a Principal of wood a large scale' (LIII: 120). The register appears in organs by Elliot & Hill during the 1830s as a second 4' on both Great and Swell, and was evidently a favourite of Dr Camidge's, and, through him, of Ward of York. The 'Flute-Principal' in the Elliot & Hill organ for Christ's Hospital (1830) was probably an early harmonica.

The era added little to the stock of solo flutes in the English organ, though an important and enduring exception was the clarabella or claribella. Buckingham's description was straightforward: the clarabella was 'a wood open diapason kept soft' (LIII: 19). Joshua Done referred to it as 'a modern stop of peculiar sweetness; its pipes are metallic [sic], and their sound mellow and brilliant' ([1839]: 15). By the 1850s, Hopkins was sounding a rather different note when he described the 'thick and powerful fluty tone' of the clarabella (HR2: 1837): a change of taste in favour of more opaque sounds was already under way. According to Hopkins and all the early sources the clarabella was introduced by Bishop; the earliest reference to it in the Bishop papers is found in an estimate of 1820 (Wickens 1975: 33). Hamilton noted that it was a half-stop, from middle c, 'and, in general, is accompanied with the stop-diapason bass. Bishop, the organ builder, sometimes combines them both in one, under the name *Stop-diapason*' (Warren 1842: 33). The organ at Kinlet (1840) is an example. Bishop was also given to substituting a clarabella for a disused cornet. This had the advantage of leaving the stopped diapason intact, and, in the case of a mounted cornet, of not crowding the soundboard with bulky wooden pipes. Hereford Cathedral (1832), Norwich Cathedral (1834), and Newark Parish Church (1836) are examples. Bishop made the most extensive use of the clarabella, but it was not unknown in the work of other builders at this period. Hill proposed an 'Octave Claribella' for the Swell at Halifax Parish Church in 1838 and frequently included a short-compass 'Claribella' in his instruments at the end of the 1830s. It later appeared in his early German System instruments, sometimes as 'Claribel Flute' (Wickens 1975: 35–6). A clarabella regularly appeared in the Great or Choir of Gray & Davison's organs until they developed the 'Clarionet Flute'. This was a stopped wood register with large perforations in the stoppers, and it rapidly displaced the clarabella after 1848.

Two other novel flutes appeared during the period, though neither was widely employed. The first was the 'German Flute'. The example at St John's College, Cambridge, was of 4' pitch, 'stopped diapason scale – voiced very softly and smoothly' (MS 25); that at York seems to have been more of a clarabella (HRI: 527). Then there was the flageolet – possibly another name for an open wood fifteenth. Ward added an Octave Flute (wood) 2′ to the Choir Organ at York in 1823, and the Oldham organ is said to have had both a flageolet and a fifteenth on the Choir. It later found a place in Hill's organs of the 1840s.

The study of Hill's organ for Birmingham Town Hall (below, pp. 127–35) includes a discussion of his experiments with reed tone during the 1830s. As so often, Hill seems to have been first in the field, and, apart from his work, no significant innovations appear before the 1840s. The wooden pedal reeds in Ward's 1823 reconstruction of the York organ seem to have had no successors, and the trombone 8′ at Bermondsey (1829) was an ordinary trumpet. Vincent Novello specified both a trumpet and a 'Trombone – voiced very powerfully' for the Great of a proposed organ for Crosby Hall (1834) and submitted his scheme to Bishop for an estimate, but there is no evidence that Bishop experimented with reeds – in view of Novello's involvement in the Birmingham scheme, it may be that this trombone was inspired by Hill's posaune.[9] As well as developing the posaune during the 1830s, Hill refined the Swell reed, yielding eventually the cornopean. This may have been a development of the 'Horn' that appears sometimes in Hill's Swell specifications during the 1830s.[10] What is not clear is whether these horns were themselves modifications of the old French horn.[11] The earliest reference to a cornopean is found in January 1840 when the *Musical Journal* (1: 58–9) included it in a list of novelties to be found in the organ which Hill was building for St Peter's, Cornhill.[12]

Cornopean was the name of an early form of valved cornet, which appeared during the 1830s. The first mouthpieces differed from later ones, producing a 'rounder and more velvet sound' (Baines 1976: 228), and this may offer a clue to the tone quality which Hill was trying to capture. According to Hopkins, it was 'more sonorous than the Trumpet; and smoother, though scarcely so powerful, as that of the Horn'. The latter (which is evidently not identical with either cornopean or posaune) was 'fuller and smoother' than the trumpet, and 'without the clang peculiar and necessary to that Stop' (HR2: 144). Smoothness and sonority seem to have been the principal objectives of all Hill's innovations among the reeds; when it was suggested that he might include an additional open diapason in his organ for the Great George Street Chapel, Liverpool (1840), he replied that it was scarcely necessary because the Great reeds (of the posaune or trombone variety) were 'fine & smooth & full tone like Op. Diaps. that may almost be used as Diaps.' (MS 12: 92).

The style of Hill's reed voicing, with the careful deployment of trumpets, posaunes, cornopeans and horns, was established by the early-1840s. It changed little for the remainder of his career. His most original contribution to the reed family (the high-pressure reed) also dates from this period, and is considered below (pp. 132–3).

The Swell Organ

In considering the evolution of the Swell Organ during the 1820s and 1830s it is instructive to compare the organ built in 1819 for the Chapel Royal, St James's Palace, with its successor, installed in 1837. The Swell in the earlier instrument was a modest affair (Appendix 1, pp. 444–5). Both its 3-octave compass, and a stop list which was, if anything, less enterprising than those found at the end of the previous century, imposed severe restrictions on its musical usefulness. By 1837, it was a different story (Appendix 1, pp. 456–7). Hill & Davison's instrument had a 10-stop Swell with a compass of G–f^3: not yet full-compass, it is true, but offering significantly more musical scope than its predecessor. There was a rudimentary flue chorus, and the appearance of a claribella, a horn, and a wood fifteenth emphasised that the possibilities of the Swell had not been overlooked by the innovators.

Broadly speaking, the Chapel Royal organs illustrate admirably the principal developments in Swell design during the period. There was, first, the matter of compass. James Davis extended the Swell at St Saviour, Southwark, to tenor c in 1818, and four years later, John Gray built a new organ for St Pancras with the same compass. Such generous provision was rare before the mid-1830s.[13] Nicholls's instrument at St Luke, Chelsea (1824), had probably the largest Swell division in England when it was built, but the compass descended no lower than tenor f. Ten years later, there was less excuse for such conservatism, and the appearance of an f-compass Swell in a large new metropolitan organ (Robson's, for St Dunstan-in-the-West) had a distinctly old-fashioned feel about it. By then, at least four metropolitan organs had compasses which descended below tenor c. In 1826, George Cooper had the Swell keys at St Sepulchre, Holborn, carried down to C. The compass of the registers followed in two stages: to G (1828) and C (1834). Something similar happened down the road at Christ Church, Newgate Street, also under Cooper's influence: the Swell was extended to G in 1831 and to C in 1834. Other G-compasses appeared at St James, Bermondsey (1829) and Christ's Hospital (1830), an F-compass at St Mary, Moorfields (c. 1830), and a curious E-compass at St Edmund, Lombard Street (1833). Both York (1833) and Birmingham (1834) had C-compasses, as did Booth's instrument for St Peter's Chapel, Leeds (1838). The last years of the long-compass organ saw a flurry of F- and G-compass Swells,[14] but by the mid-1840s, the c-compass Swell had established itself as the norm; only the largest organs had a full-compass Swell, and only the smallest organs were, for a few years more, restricted to f or g.

These short-compass Swells were not necessarily as limited as they appear

on paper. Although the soundboards were of a short compass, it was usual by
the 1840s to make the Swell keyboard the same compass as the Great, with
the lower notes permanently coupled to a 'Choir bass'. This was usually a
stopped diapason (sometimes a principal as well) which might be borrowed
from the Choir or the Great, or might be provided specially for the purpose.
On other occasions, the need was met simply by coupling the bass keys of the
Swell to one of the other keyboards. It is not certain when the Choir bass first
appeared, but it was found in large organs by the end of the 1820s and was
widely employed over the next four decades.[15]

The increased compass of the Swell was matched by a gradual development of the tonal scheme. The trumpets, hautboys, and cornets of the
eighteenth century gave way to horns, cremonas, and claribellas, but the
Swell retained its traditional rôle as an expressive solo division. A radical
departure occurred, though, when organists and builders began to explore
the possibility of developing a complete flue chorus on the Swell. It had been
rare to find more than two diapasons, a principal, and a cornet representing
the flue chorus in an eighteenth-century Swell, and their usefulness was
restricted to composing an echo cornet or sustaining a short expressive
interlude in the upper reaches of the keyboard. Paradoxically, Nicholls's 12-
stop Swell at St Luke, Chelsea, did little more than duplicate a typical late-
eighteenth-century Swell: in multiplying the same registers, and retaining
the restricted compass, it did nothing to overcome the inherent limitations of
this model. But by 1830, a more enlightened approach was emerging. Elliot
& Hill's organ for Christ's Hospital had a double diapason in the Swell, with
a complete flue chorus (8.8.4.3.2.III) and four reeds. In the following year,
the same builders reconstructed the organ in Christ Church, Newgate
Street, along similar lines. George Cooper may have been the inspiration in
each case, and both instruments anticipate the design of the Swell in the C-
compass organs which Hill and Davison (at first in partnership, later
independently) were building by the late-1830s. Meanwhile, the York and
Birmingham organs included Swells of unprecedented size and scope.

Although Elliot & Hill were the boldest, they were not the only builders to
move in this direction. Gray's c-compass Swells for the parish churches of
Blackburn (1828) and Liverpool (1833) included doubles and a chorus
running up to a fifteenth, and the same builder was responsible for the
gradual expansion of the Swell at St Sepulchre's, Holborn. Bevington's
organ for St Mary, Moorfields, had a double, a mixture, and four reeds.
Later in the decade, Lincoln reconstructed the organ in Christ Church,
Spitalfields (1837), leaving the Swell with eleven stops, and two years later,
Joseph Walker provided a Swell of similar size in his organ for Exeter Hall.
In the provinces, Booth went one stop better at St Peter's Chapel, Leeds, in
1837. Although many organ-builders (including the leading ones) were still
making short-compass Swells with three or four stops, it is clear that the

revolution in the design of the Swell Organ, which was to have such momentous consequences in the next decade, was already well under way by the end of the 1830s.

It was during this period that an interest in the possibilities of enclosure first led to a second manual division being placed in a swell box. Gray seems to have been something of a pioneer. In 1824, his organ for the Philanthropic Chapel had a Choir Organ sited in its own case and enclosed in a venetian swell: this may have contributed to the description of the organ as 'a pretty, and delicately-toned instrument' (MS 78: 326). In the same year, he proposed an enclosed Choir for Blackburn Parish Church, though this was not built until 1828 (Wickens 1977: 162). The enclosure of the clarionet in Gray & Davison's organ for Chester Cathedral has already been mentioned (above, p. 91).

All these innovations had important consequences for the construction of swell boxes. As the boxes got bigger, and the area of the walls increased in proportion to the area of the shutters, the effectiveness of the crescendo and diminuendo declined. At the same time, the growing taste for extremes of volume led organists to desire an effective *pianissimo* when the shutters were closed. As early as 1824, Dr Hodges had tackled these problems in the reconstruction of the organ in St James, Bristol (below, pp. 157–9). Gray made a 'Double Box' for the Swell which he added to the organ in Windsor Castle, Music Room, in 1841 (Warren 1842: 92), and, later, the organs for both St George's Hall, Liverpool (1855) and Leeds Town Hall (1857) had double-panelled boxes packed (respectively) with sawdust and felt wadding (MS 46: 25 October 1851; MS 41). The other problem concerned the swell shutters and their control. Hodges, again, made an early attempt at improvement with his 'Triple Venetian Swell' (below, p. 158), and, later, Gray & Davison followed his example by providing triple sets of shutters at Holy Trinity, Clifton (1838), and in their Exhibition organ (1851). Hill must have experimented with the design of swell boxes, but beyond the fact that he provided sets of vertical shutters in the sides of the swell box at York in addition to the horizontal shutters in the (east?) front (HR2: 93), neither documentary nor physical evidence has survived to illuminate this.

In conclusion, this phase in the evolution of the Swell Organ is nicely illustrated by some remarks about the organ of St George's Chapel, Windsor, following Gray & Davison's work in 1843. The compass had been extended to F, the flue chorus completed by the addition of a double diapason, fifteenth and sesquialtra, and the reed chorus had been expanded by the introduction of a cornopean, a clarion and a new hautboy. According to a contemporary, this left the Swell as 'probably the most perfect in the kingdom. The unusual thickness of the box, and the improved principle of the shutters, enable the organist, from a scarcely audible sound, to arrive at the full swell by the most gradual increase; an effect not to be attained by the swell as usually constructed' (Willemant 1844: 50). The note is authentic: a reminder of the importance which contemporary musicians attached to making the organ a genuinely expressive instrument.

4

Three case studies

The leading characteristics of the Insular Movement can be illustrated by a study of the organs of York Minster during the first half of the nineteenth century. Attempts 'to fill that spacious edifice with a volume of sound' (Gray 1837: 6) cast light on both the preoccupations and the inherent shortcomings of the movement.

The organ was reconstructed by Benjamin Blyth, foreman to Sarah Green (Samuel Green's widow) in 1802–3. The estimate embraced the following work:

To make new Sound Boards, New Keys, new Key movements, new Draw Stop movements to Great Organ, Choir Organ, & Swell, to make three new Pair of Horrizontal [sic] Bellows, Bellows movements, &c. To consist of the following Stops.

Great Organ		Choir Organ		Swell	
Stop Diapason		Stop Diapason		Stop Diapason	
1st Open Diapason	New	Dulciana	New	Open Diapason	
2nd Open Diapason		Principal		Principil	New
3rd Open Diapason		Flute		Dulciana	New
Principil [sic]		Fifteenth		Dulciana Pr.	New
Great Twelfth		Bassoon	New	Cornet	3 Ranks
Fifteenth				Trumpet	New
Sexquialtra 3 ranks				Hautboy	New
Furniture 2 ranks		New Swell Box, Swell Movts &c			
Cornet 5 ranks					
Trumpet treble new					
Trumpet bass new					

New Pedal Key for feet, to 17 notes at Bass, the present Case to be made deeper, to have more room for pipes to speak & more convenient to tune, the present pipes to be us'd such as are good, new ones where they are not. Compass GG. AA. BB. BB♮. &c. to e in alt to great [and] Choir Organ; Swell to F below middle C to e in alt.

The whole to be compleated in a workman like manner for the Sum of Five Hundred Guineas, Exclusive of Carriage and Package. (MS 36)

A clarion and nason were later added to the Great stop list (Pearce 1912: 76).

The most significant feature of the design in the context of the present discussion was the inclusion of a third open diapason on the Great. This is the sole innovation in an otherwise typical School-of-Green scheme which might be said to have addressed the demand for 'an increased body of sound' – one object of the reconstruction, according to Gray (1837: 7). At the time, Blyth's work in this area met with approval. According to Dr Camidge,

Blyth's three great organ diapasons were an honour to him, for they were upon a very large and efficient scale, and were placed by Ward of York in 1823, on the full force of wind which they would bear; they might well be said to be 'unrivalled'; indeed, all who remember their plump and mellow tone, have never ceased to regret their destruction.   (Gray 1837: 49)

In general, however, the Blyth organ was regarded as a failure. Whilst complimenting the 'sweetness and mellowness of tone', and admitting the beauty of many of the softer registers, Gray expressed disappointment that, though there were twice the number of stops, 'the full organ is scarcely more powerful than before'. He also found the balance deficient. The treble of the Great Organ ('being feeble and thin') was drowned by the bass, and there was 'a muddy breathing inarticulation in most of the stops, which, though not easily described, is perceived and felt by the ear' (1837: 6–7).

Gray's views were evidently shared by others, and, most importantly, by John Camidge. Camidge (he became Dr Camidge in 1819) was the son of Matthew Camidge, the Minster organist (1799–1842). He assisted his father as 'the daily officiating organist at the Minster' (Gray 1837: 8), succeeding to the organistship upon the elder Camidge's death. He himself was struck down by paralysis in 1848, and was then assisted by his son (Thomas Simpson Camidge) until forced to resign in 1858. John Camidge's name is inseparable from the history of the Minster organs during the first half of the nineteenth century. Between 1815 and 1829 he directed a reconstruction of Blyth's organ; between 1829 and 1853 he first designed, and then attempted to re-design, a vast instrument built by Elliot & Hill. His objective throughout was to match the power of the organ to the volume and grandeur of the building in which it stood.

Camidge's first attempts were modest by comparison with what was to come later. In 1815, John Ward raised the wind-pressure from 2½ to 3 inches, and revoiced the pipes 'so as to give them more power and brilliancy'. He also supplied a new Choir soundboard to improve the supply of wind to the pipes (above, p. 25). The results were evidently encouraging, though Gray's claim that these measures doubled the power of the instrument is implausible (1837: 8).

Six years later, Camidge secured a major reconstruction. Ward was again the contractor, and over the course of three years (1821–3) he rebuilt the organ to a scheme which was a remarkable conception for the date. There are minor discrepancies in the accounts of this instrument, but the stop list was probably as follows.[1]

Great Organ (FF to f³)

Open Diapason	8
Open Diapason	8
Open Diapason	8
Stop Diapason	8
Principal	4
Nason	4
Twelfth	2⅔
Fifteenth	2
Sesquialtra	III
Cymbal	III
Cornet	V
Trumpet	8
Clarion	4

Choir Organ (FF to f³)

Open Diapason (wood)	8+
Stop Diapason (metal)	8+
Stop Diapason (wood)	8
Dulciana	8
Principal	4
Flute	4
Octave Flute (wood)	2+
Sesquialtra (17.19.22)	III+

Nave Organ (FF to f³)

Open Diapason	8+
Stop Diapason	8+
Principal	4+
Harmonica (wood)	4+
Twelfth	2⅔+
Fifteenth	2+
Flageolet (wood)	2+
Mixture	IV+
Bassoon (ex-Choir)	8
Clarino (a trumpet)	8+

Swell Organ (F to f³)

Open Diapason	8
Stop Diapason (metal)	8
Dulciana	8
Dulciana (wood)	8+
Principal	4
Cornet	III
Trumpet	8
Hautboy	8

Pedal Organ, right side (FF to c)

Double Stop Diapason (wood)	16+
Double Open Diapason (wood)	8+
German Stop Diapason	[8]+
German Principal	[4]+
Sackbut (wood)	16+
Trombone (wood)	8+
Shawm (wood)	4+

Pedal Organ, left side (FF to c)

Double Stop Diapason (wood)	16+
Double Open Diapason (wood)	8+
German Stop Diapason	[8]+
German Principal	[4]+
Sackbut (wood)	16+
Trombone (wood)	8+

+ new registers (1821–3)

The significance of this scheme lies chiefly with the Pedal and Nave divisions.

The Nave Organ was originally situated beneath the Great and enclosed in a venetian swell; in 1827, it was moved to a more favourable position west of the Great, and the case was deepened to accommodate it (*YG*, 20 October 1827). Camidge referred to its registers as 'ten large scale stops' and seems to have thought of them as additions to the Great Organ, rather than as an independent division (Gray 1837: 49–50). The source of his inspiration is obscure, but it may be relevant to point to Jonathan Gray's visit to Haarlem in 1824, when he reported hearing the 'choir organ' (rückpositiv) coupled to the 'great organ' (hauptwerk), 'which filled the church in an astonishing manner, as loud as the most tremendous thunder' (1837: 42). There is some evidence that Camidge visited the continent around 1820, and he may have had a similar experience to Gray's. Slight supporting testimony might be found in Camidge's reference to the 'Large German mixture' in the 1823 Nave Organ (Gray 1837: 50). But however respectable the antecedents, in practice, Camidge justified the Nave division as duplication on a grand scale: a view emphasised by the fact that it was playable from the Great keys.

The Pedal Organ was without precedent. The stops were separated into two almost identical divisions, each housed within the mediaeval pulpitum (which was mercilessly hacked about to accommodate them), one to the right, and one to the left of the central archway, in such a way as to create formidable difficulties for the layout of the action. It is not clear whether there was any difference in function between the two divisions. One account states that the registers in the right hand chamber were played 'by the pedals only' (*YG*, 5 July 1823). There is no similar reference to the registers in the other chamber, prompting the thought that they may have been playable from one of the keyboards (or an independent keyboard?). Assuming, though, that stops from both divisions could be played simultaneously by the pedals, the only explanation for the scheme is (once again) a belief in duplication as a means of achieving power. The scales were generous, suggesting that breadth of tone was an important objective,[2] and the indirect influence of the large pedal organs of Northern Europe (acknowledged in the nomenclature) need not imply any reliable grasp of the principles which lay behind them.

The real success of this instrument is questionable. Ten years later, in the midst of the controversies surrounding the Elliot & Hill organ, Camidge was moved to write in laudatory terms of the former instrument, but at the time, praise for Ward's ingenuity was tempered with disappointment at the effect of the organ. A sympathetic commentator tried to make a virtue out of necessity by contrasting the 'harsh and noisy' organs of the continent with the refinement of York, but was forced to admit that York was 'so smooth and soft in its tone that those who expect an extraordinary loudness are disappointed. The size of the organ is barely in proportion to the immense space of the building which it is required to fill' (*YG*, 5 July 1823). That 'immense space' was the real source of the organ-builders' troubles. Ward voiced the new pipes in his workshop, and 'they sounded sufficiently power-ful, as he thought, for any organ; but being brought into the Minster they were so feeble and soft in their tone, that every pipe required to be voiced a second time, on the spot, in order to make it sufficiently audible' (Gray 1837: 9). It was a problem that would recur.

The fire of 1829 gave Camidge an opportunity to apply his principles to the design of a new organ for the Minster. In doing so, he attempted to give definitive expression to ideas which had inspired aspects of Ward's recon-struction of the old organ: duplication, large scales, extensive compasses. The ultimate failure of the organ which Elliot & Hill built should not obscure the significance of what was attempted. On the one hand, it gave William Hill the experience of designing and constructing a vast instrument, with pedal pipes, soundboards, and action all conceived on the largest scale. On the other hand, it whetted the appetite of organists for large organs, and when they eventually encountered the organs of Northern Europe, they found a source of ideas which led to a flood of successful large organs in the 1840s and 1850s.

It is impossible to establish the original stop list which Camidge drew up in 1829. Four years later, with the organ pronounced complete, the specifica-tion remains elusive, and so soon did Camidge initiate alterations to the finished instrument that none of the various stop lists which appeared over the next two decades agree. The specification which follows is based upon a number of these early sources, principally an account said to have appeared in a York newspaper towards the end of 1833.[3]

Great Organ, West division (CC to c⁴)

Open Diapason	8
Open Diapason	8
Stopped Diapason (metal)	8
Principal	4
Harmonica (wood)	4
Twelfth	2⅔
Fifteenth	2
Flageolet (wood)	2
Sesquialtera	III
Cymbal	IV
Bassoon	8
Horn	8

Great Organ, East division (CC to c⁴)

Open Diapason	8
Open Diapason	8
Stopped Diapason (wood)	8
Principal	4
German Flute (wood)	4
Twelfth	2⅔
Fifteenth	2
Piccolo (wood)	2
Mixture	III
Cornet	IV
Clarino	8
Shawm	8

Choir Organ (CC to c⁴)

Open Diapason	8
Stopped Diapason	8
Dulciana	8
Principal	4
Principal (wood)	4
Flute (stopped)	4[?]
Fifteenth	2
Octave Flute	2
Bassoon[4]	8
Clarionet	4[?]

Swell Organ (C to c⁴)

Open Diapason	8
Stopped Diapason	8
Dulciana	8
Dulciana (wood)	8
Celestina[5]	8

Principal	4
Dulcet	4
Claribella	4
Cornet	v
Trumpet	8
Oboe	8
Clarion [Clarino?]	8

Pedal Organ (C to c^1)^6

Double Open Diapason	32
Double Open Diapason (wood)	32
Sub-bass [wood]	32
Double Principal	16
Double Principal (wood)	16
Double-bass Diapason	16
Sackbut (wood)	32
Trombone	16

Hill's original frame survives. It is a massive affair, constructed of 9″ × 9″ timbers, and having sturdy cross-beams of 12″ × 4″. On this stood the soundboards of the East and West Great, occupying the entire width of the case, though with the largest pipes standing in the case or on blocks. The Swell was sited above the Great, and the Choir soundboard stood immediately behind the east front of the case, bracketed out above the organist's head. The location of the Pedal is something of a mystery. The large pipes certainly stood in the choir aisles (Gray 1837: 43): the remainder were presumably within the screen. It is likely that the bellows were also housed in the much-abused screen.

The construction of the York organ presented Hill with peculiar difficulties. Among these was the manufacture of the large pipes required for the Pedal Organ and for the 16′ octaves of the Great and Choir. Hill resorted to zinc (being both cheaper and more stable than the usual compound of tin and lead) but found that it, too, had its problems. It needed to be heated before it could be manipulated, and there was then the question of *how* to manipulate it. To overcome these difficulties, he 'conceived the plan of bending into shape the sections of the cylinders designed to form the tubes by means of triple rollers. These were so placed that the sheet of metal passing between two of them was caught by a third, the axis of which was depressed at will, so that it was forced out of the horizontal and curved so accurately that no farther manipulation was needed'. By this means, short cylinders were manufactured (each about 3′ long) which were then joined together to form the pipe bodies of the 32′ register.[7] The mouths were formed of plain metal. Hill's machine was widely used in the manufacture of iron tubes and boilers (*MSt*, xiv, 1871: 4).

A further mechanical difficulty was presented by the need to supply these huge pipes with wind. To overcome this, Hill made use of his 'box pallet'. The pallets were located in their own wind-chest which was attached to the side of the Pedal chest. The action of the organist drew up a shield covering an aperture, through which wind passed to the pipe. When the key was released, a spring caused the shield to return (Figure 9). Despite a claim that it was the construction of the York organ that led to the invention of the box pallet (*MSt*, XIV, 1871: 4), the prototype served to wind the double pedal pipes added by Elliot & Hill to the Westminster Abbey organ in 1828 (*Times*, 10 November 1828).[8]

Hill's box pallets at least ensured that wind got to the largest Pedal pipes, but the complexity of the layout, and the size of the conventional pallets in the main soundboards, meant that the keys presented considerable resistance to the player. Camidge informed C. S. Barker that 'Such a difficult touch as that of York Cathedral Organ is doubtless sufficient to paralyse the efforts of most men ... I, with all the energy I can rally about me, am sometimes inclined to make a full stop from actual fatigue in a very short time after the commencement of a full piece' (Audsley 1905: II, 246). This was in 1833 when Barker's experiments with pneumatic levers were in their early stages (below, p. 354); it was not until 1859 that the weight of the York keys was alleviated by pneumatic assistance.

The York organ of 1833 amply demonstrates those features of the Insular Movement discussed in the previous chapter. It could claim to be the most characteristic product of that movement, and its undoubted failure signals the failure of the whole tendency which it represents. Despite the use of

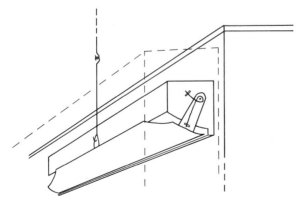

9 William Hill's box pallet. The pallet is contained in its own wind chest which is attached to the side of a Pedal chest. The action of the player causes the pallet wire to draw up the shield, thus allowing compressed air to pass into the main chest. When the player releases the pedal the spring ensures that the shield returns rapidly to obstruct the flow of wind. (*Transactions of the Society of Arts* vol. LIV, 1841–2: 98; HRI: 31)

fanciful stop names, Camidge had put his faith in duplication. When he was criticised for this, he retorted that the writer was 'apparently utterly ignorant of even a *notion* of the solemn grandeur which a great power of diapasons (unmixed with other stops) produces in such a magnificent and spacious building as York Minster; and how particularly suited to a vast portion of our anthems, &c. is that full and heavy quality of sound which cannot be obtained in a sufficient degree in any other way, than by multiplying both them and the principals' (Gray 1837: 53–4). It was the fatal argument of 'Cathedral musical effects', united with a taste for the sublime which is entirely of its period. Nor was Camidge repentant in the face of comparisons with the great continental organs. It was, he wrote, 'very easy for anyone to be able to judge of the effect of the Continental organs ... by drawing out only 2 or 3 of the York 16 feet manual diapasons and trumpets, with 8 or 10 principals and the mixtures, &c.' (Gray 1837: 52). And as a statement of the misconceived principles of the Insular Movement, Camidge's reply to criticism of the retention of long-compasses and the absence of manual doubles, could hardly be bettered:

> If a 16 feet scale be desirable, is it not then much the best and most complete plan to extend the manual compass of the keys to the 16 feet C (by which extension, the diapasons become double diapasons, and the principals, diapasons, according to Continental rating), carrying every stop down to the [C C] key, as I have done in the York organ; thereby giving sufficient scope and a clear range for both hands and feet (as our pedals draw down the two lowest octaves of the manual keys, as well as play their own proper stops) and enabling the organist to work the middle or tenor part of the organ with his left hand, and so produce a much richer and more varied and perfect effect than can be given by a performer (who may be an indifferent or no pedalist) grumbling with his left hand, and squeaking with his right, with so great a distance between them as if they were afraid of each other.   (Gray 1837: 52)

If it is true that Dr Camidge had visited 'most of the great organs on the continent' before designing the York organ (below, p. 175), he had evidently received little enlightenment from the organists whom he encountered there.

The organ as completed by Hill in September 1833 failed to meet Camidge's expectations in many respects. This was especially so in regard to its 'power or loudness contrasted with the late organ' (Gray 1837: 40). Having experimented with large scales for the stops in the 1823 Nave Organ, Camidge had apparently specified unusually large scales for the new organ, and he could only attribute the failure of this measure to negligence on the part of the builder. Writing of the 32′ metal, he commented indignantly to Hill that it was 'a burlesque and absurdity for such pipes to give out such a mere whisper; and most foolish to suppose I can sanction their being left, and the organ said to be complete in such an *infirm* state' (Gray 1837: 40).

The building of the York organ ended in recriminations and a law suit

(*MW*, iv, 1837: 65–8; 103–4). Once Hill had departed, Camidge turned to John Ward, and set about a programme of reconstruction which, it was hoped, would vindicate his original scheme. At first, they concentrated upon increasing the scales by transposition. The manual chorus stops were transposed four notes, the metal 32′ two notes (wooden pipes had to be used for C and C♯) (Allerston & Pickwell 1844). When this failed to achieve the transformation Camidge sought he began to add further stops – reeds, mixtures, mutations – and to increase the wind-pressures (*MW*, xx, 1845: 54, 258). Two high-pressure reeds were crammed into the Swell box (1846) (*YG*, 27 June 1846), and as late as 1850, Forster & Andrews were engaged in adding more diapasons and a cornet to the Choir Organ (ms 43: f.96). By the time Camidge resigned, there were eighty stops (hri: 527–9). Dr Monk, who inherited this curious instrument, summarised his predecessor's follies concisely:

These remedial measures . . . were still based upon the false assumption that a further accession of unison and octave tone was necessary, to secure that density and volume so much needed, and which had not hitherto been obtained. Subsequent additions of stops were therefore made, while the scales of existing ones were enlarged to an enormous extent, upon the erroneous supposition that the originals were too small to emit a vigorous tone suitable to so large a building.

(Purey-Cust 1899: 22)

The picture of Camidge vainly trying to increase the power of the York organ by an extended series of additions and increases in scale over the course of twenty years or so is a graphic representation of the misdirection of the Insular Movement.

BIRMINGHAM TOWN HALL, 1834–40

The plan for the Birmingham Town Hall organ must have been drawn up before the York organ was completed (September, 1833). Claims have been made for both Sigismund Neukomm (1778–1858) and Vincent Novello (1781–1861) as its author. Gauntlett (?) stated that they collaborated: 'The design was by Novello and Neukomm – one had never played a large organ, and the other had adopted the exploded notions of Vogler, who built a large organ at Munich on a plan which has been universally decried' (*MP*, 25 September 1843). The Birmingham scheme reveals no very obvious application of Vogler's 'simplification' system, but Neukomm was certainly involved in some way. This widely-travelled Austrian composer, pianist, and scholar was greatly fêted in Birmingham in the early-1830s, and it is unlikely to be mere coincidence that a letter addressed to him, bearing the date 1832, survives at Birmingham giving details of five large organs in Hamburg (MS 16). The local press attributed the design to Neukomm at an early date (*ABG*, 23 August 1833). Novello's involvement is more elusive, but in an advertisement of 1836, J. Alfred Novello stated that his father had superintended the building of 'the grandest instrument in the world – the new organ in the Town Hall, Birmingham' (*MW*, I, 1836: 19). He may also have been concerned in the work which was done in 1837 (Hurd 1981: 34–5). A third name associated with the commissioning of the organ is that of Joseph Moore. Moore effectively ran the Festivals at this period and was closely concerned with the building of the Town Hall; he is said to have visited a number of continental organs (in Amsterdam, Haarlem, Hamburg and Berlin) before the contract was signed (Gill 1952: I, 400). Possibly all three had a hand in the final scheme.

The 1834 stop list is difficult to establish. No reliable contemporary source has come to light, and the sources usually cited include modifications made in 1837, 1840 or 1843. The specification that follows is an attempt to correlate these sources and produce a likely version of the original scheme.[9]

Great Organ (CC to f³)

Double Open Diapason (c)[10]	16
Open Diapason	8
Open Diapason	8
Open Diapason (wood)	8
Dulciana[11]	8
Stopped Diapason (wood)	8
Principal	4
Principal	4
Principal (wood)	4
Twelfth	2⅔
Fifteenth	2
Fifteenth (wood)	2
Sesquialtra	V
Mixture	III
Trumpet	8
Posaune	8
Clarion	4
Octave Clarion	2

Swell Organ (C to f³, with Choir bass from CC)

Double Diapason	16
Open Diapason	8
Stopped Diapason	8
Principal	4
Harmonica (wood)	4
Fifteenth	2
Horn	8

Trumpet	8
Oboe	8
Clarion	4
Carillon (Bells)[12]	

Choir Organ (CC to f³)

Open Diapason (wood & metal)	8
Open Diapason (c) (wood)	8
Dulciana (G)	8
Stopped Diapason (wood)	8
Principal	4
Principal (wood)	4
Stopped Flute	4
Fifteenth	2
Cremona & Bassoon (GG)	8

Combination Organ (fourth manual)

From Choir:

Open Diapason	8
Dulciana	8
Stopped Diapason	8
Harmonica	4
Stopped Flute	4

From Swell:

Open Diapason	8
Stopped Diapason	8
Principal	4
Harmonica	4
Fifteenth	2
Horn	8
Trumpet	8
Oboe	8
Clarion	4

Pedal Organ (C to c¹)

Double Open Diapason	32
Double Open Diapason (wood)	32
Trumpet (wood)	16

Swell to Great
Choir to Great
Pedals to Great [Great to Pedal]
Pedals to Choir [Choir to Pedal]

The Birmingham organ was designed to provide choral accompaniment. Though it came to be used for other purposes and on other occasions, its original *raison d'être* was to sustain 'those great choral effects, which have hitherto rendered the Birmingham Festivals so attractive' (*Mechanics' Magazine* xx, 1834: 403). It is significant that at both the official opening (29

August 1834) and the ensuing Festival (October 1834) the organ was heard exclusively as an accompanimental instrument; the exception was Neukomm's 'fantasia upon the organ with the imitation of thunder', a performance which was described by a critic (surprisingly, in view of the prevailing taste) as 'unfortunate' (*MP*, 11 October 1834). By the 1840s, the original Birmingham organ could be dismissed (by Gauntlett?) as nothing but 'a large, lumbering, *vocal* accompaniment' (*MP*, 25 September 1843).

The Birmingham scheme was more compact than York's, and must have benefited from the inclusion of doubles and the development of the reed choruses. Yet it exhibited similar weaknesses, most obviously in the resort to duplication and long-compasses, and the Pedal was no more than a down-ward extension of the Great with a 2-octave (finger) keyboard for faint-hearted pedalists (Hamel 1849: I, cxxvi). The appearance of a Combination Organ emphasised the instrument's use as a substitute for orchestral accompaniment. By means of a series of duplicate grooves and slides, registers from the Swell and Choir were made available on a fourth set of keys. The mechanical arrangements are described by Perkins (1905: 6–7), but as this probably reflects what he found when he became City Organist in 1888, it may not be a reliable account of the original design. It can only be assumed that the object of this complicated exercise was to enable a solo stop to be accompanied by a register from the same division, each being played from a different set of keys.[13]

The use of the organ as a choral accompaniment lent a particular relevance to the demand for increased power. Hill attempted to meet the demand in three ways. First, there was duplication. Secondly, the pipes were made to large scales. According to a contemporary, 'the scale of the pipes in the great organ is larger than that of any other instrument' (*MW* vi, 1837: 204). The instrument has been drastically altered over the years (Thistlethwaite 1984: *passim*), and although much of the 1834 pipework survives, it is difficult to collect reliable evidence for the original scalings. What can be gleaned is summarised in Table 13, and if this is compared with Table 11 (the Oldham scales) it becomes apparent that Hill at Birmingham went well beyond the scales of his largest previous organs. The Pedal registers, too, were huge, the zinc 32′ having a scale of 22″ at C. Cavaillé-Coll, when he visited the organ in 1844, deplored the appearance of these zinc front pipes ('just like rainspouts'), but admitted that they produced 'a rather nice tone' (Douglass 1980: I, 205). The 32′ wood was a different matter. The eight lowest pipes were constructed of framed panelling, C having internal dimensions of 3′4″ by 2′10½″, and the French builder described them as sounding 'like wet drums' (Douglass 1980: I, 208). In general, this experimentation with scales failed to achieve its object. Although a writer of the 1830s could refer to the power of the three open

Table 13 *Birmingham Town Hall, 1834: original scales*

	4'	2'	1'	½'	¼'	⅛'
Gt Open Diapason I	94	58	34			
Open Diapason II	90	52.5				
Principal	92	53.5	32			
Twelfth		54	31.5	22		
Fifteenth I	90	51				
Fifteenth II		49				
Sw Double Dulciana	76	42				
Open Diapason		48.5				
Principal	80	48	27	18	11	
Fifteenth		46	27	17.5	10.5	6.75

diapasons as 'finer than any ever built' (*MP*, 31 August 1837), a later description of the tone of the original Birmingham organ as being 'poor and characterless' carries greater conviction (*MW* XLI, 1863: 733).

Hill's third method of increasing the power of the instrument (and much the most successful) was to experiment with the reed choruses. The Great included an octave clarion (which must have consisted largely of flue pipes in the treble), and there was a posaune 8'.

Whatever the limitations of the 2' reed, the posaune certainly made its presence felt. According to the *Penny Magazine* (8 November 1834):

In this organ [sc. Birmingham] there is a reed stop called the *Posaune* or Trombone, which all who are acquainted with the organs of the continent consider to be the most powerful and richest in tone of any existing. The powerful volume of sound proceeding from this stop is mingled with a mellowness which corrects the unpleasant impression which loudness occasionally produces ... It may be fairly stated that while the *Posaune* renders the most effectual aid in blending the voices into one mass, it adds at least fifty per cent to their power.

Unambiguous evidence is lacking, but it seems that Hill's eventual development of the high-pressure reed was the culmination of a series of experiments carried out during the 1830s into the means of amplifying reed tone, and, through it, the power of the whole organ (Edmonds & Thistlethwaite 1976: *passim*). Virtually nothing can now be recovered of these experiments. If Hill's reeds of the 1840s and 1850s are assumed to be lineal descendants of the posaunes, trombones and horns of the 1830s, then his experiments included increasing the scale of resonators and shallots, and attempting to improve regularity and promptness of speech. Power, allied to smoothness and breadth of tone, would seem to have been the objectives Hill was pursuing.

His most sensational achievement in this field received its stimulus from an unexpected quarter. In 1837, the *Musical World* reported:

Mr. Hill has designed ... for the use of the newly-formed railroads at Birmingham ... an instrument which is constructed altogether without the introduction of either wood, leather, or any of the ordinary materials of an organ. The whole is of iron or brass. The bellows, wholly iron, blown by steam; the wind chests, also iron, and the pipes brass, so that the power of tone is rendered (by the force of wind and quality of the metal) extremely penetrating.   (VI, 1837: 76)

This instrument was intended to serve as a signalling device, and Hill's experiments had been undertaken at the suggestion of Mr Ledsam, a Birmingham manufacturer who was active on the committee promoting the construction of the Grand Junction Railway to link the town with Liverpool (Stimpson [1880]: 2). Robson made a similar device for the railways around St Petersburg at about the same time (*MW* VI, 1837: 76). Whether Hill's experiments with organ reeds suggested the possibility of the signalling device, or whether the signalling device was the inspiration for the 'Grand Ophicleide' will never be known. One story attempts to establish an intimate connection:

The son of one of the principal railway directors is a very musical man, and he, imagining that some other and more musical mode of warning people of the approach of a train, than the horrible whistle, might be adopted, had two octaves of these large trumpet pipes made, and acted upon by steam power, but their sound proved to be so beautiful and grand, that instead of people getting out of the way, it was more likely that the reverse would be the effect. The consequence of the experiment was, that they were dispensed with, and the pipes presented to the great organ in the Town Hall, Birmingham and afterwards completed through the extent of the organ keys, by Mr. Hill ...[14]

This has all the marks of a conflation of fact and fiction, but whatever the truth, it can be asserted with confidence that the development of the high-pressure reed was closely bound up with Hill's work on railway signalling devices – an association of art and industry of which early-Victorian Birmingham could be proud.

It seems that the ophicleide was installed in the Town Hall organ early in 1840. The *Musical Journal* for January 1840 reported:

Mr. Hill has just finished the last octave of a set of magnificent reeds for this organ. They are voiced on about 15 inches of wind – (from two-and-a-half to three inches being the usual weight for church organs) and approach as near to the effect of a brass band as anything we have ever heard. They are to be placed in their situation immediately ...   (59)

The reed was in position by April, when the *Mechanics' Magazine* commented that the Birmingham organ 'has lately received a most effective addition, which has nearly doubled its power' (XXXII: 676).

The reed was at first known as the 'Grand' (or 'Great') 'Ophicleide', only later becoming the 'Tuba Mirabilis'. Early accounts state that it was played from the Great keyboard, but it seems much more likely (mechanically) that it would have been attached to the Swell (Thistlethwaite 1984: 12–13). One of the earliest references to its use occurs in an account of Wesley's improvisation on 'Oh! Ruddier than the Cherry' at the 1843 Festival. He commenced 'with an adagio movement in the bass, gradually ascending through the tenor into the treble, with rich and somewhat novel modulations, manifesting the quality and power of each scale of sound, and escaped in a movement in which the grand "Ophicleide" stop uttered with colossal voice the sentiment of the performer' (*A B G*, 25 September 1843). It is impossible now to know what the original ophicleide sounded like, for although much of the pipework survives, it has been considerably altered over the years. The writer who commented upon Wesley's performance referred to the 'clear, smooth, fluty tone of this mighty stop'. That suggests tone more akin to a horn than a trumpet, and, indeed, many of the original resonators are marked 'Horn'. Cavaillé-Coll, on his visit in 1844, thought the ophicleide was the 'most outstanding feature' of the organ and noted that it dominated the whole instrument, 'because of its intensity' (Douglass 1980: I, 205).

The importance of Hill's development of the high-pressure reed is that it made a valid contribution to the expansion of the English organ. It was a genuine innovation (technological and musical) which became an established feature of the largest organs,[15] and, in its employment of a greatly increased wind-pressure, suggested lines of enquiry which organ-builders would pursue in the future. That some of these enquiries produced musically indefensible results need not obscure Hill's original achievement.

The physical layout of the Birmingham organ was straightforward (Figure 10). The frame (18′ wide and 30′ high) carried the soundboards at three levels. The Great occupied the first level with two CC soundboards, each about 17′ long, and divided into C and C# sides. The Choir soundboard (again, divided into halves) occupied the next floor, and the Swell, with an undivided soundboard (were the basses in the middle?) was above. In 1840, the 'Grand Ophicleide' was installed on its own chest, and with its own bellows nearby, in front of the Swell and immediately behind the central tower. The original location of the Pedal registers is less certain. The 32′ metal stood in the case front, and was winded by means of box pallets placed in a wind trunk running round the inside of the case. The 32′ wood stood across the back of the organ, but the position of the Pedal reed is unknown. The console stood 18′ in front of the central tower, and at a lower level than the organ structure. It had a 'long movement'. Squares rested on the key-tails, attached to horizontal trackers, which then conveyed the action by way of roller-boards to the pallets. These huge tracker runs inevitably made for problems. Mendelssohn played the organ on several occasions, but when he

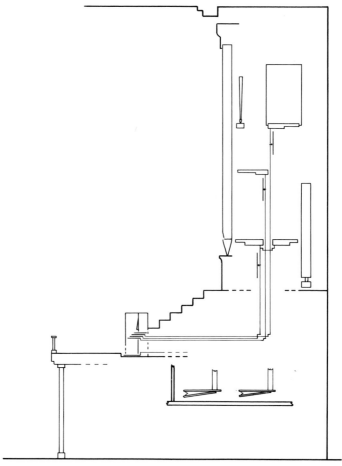

10 Birmingham Town Hall, conjectural layout, c. 1840. The two Great soundboards are at the lowest level, with the Choir above and the Swell above that. The tuba or ophicleide stands in front of the Swell with the large pedal pipes in the case front (metal) and at the rear (wood). The console stands some 18′ in front of the organ and at a lower level. The position of the feeders for the bellows is indicated very approximately. The action layout is largely conjectural and no attempt is made to show the Pedal or Combination Organ actions. Based on drawings by Charles Edge (plans 132 and 134 in *A Collection of 549 plans and drawings* in Birmingham City Library, Reference Division) and information in contemporary sources.

was asked to play at the 1846 Festival replied that he would only consent if something could be done to lighten the touch: ' . . . as for the heavy touch, I am sure that I admired your organist very much who was able to play a Fugue on [the pedals]. I am afraid that I would not have strength enough to do so . . .' (Polko 1869: 235). Cavaillé-Coll was less tactful: he described the Birmingham action as being 'as stiff as those made for carillons' (Douglass 1980: I, 208).

The 1834 organ had five bellows (*Penny Magazine*, 8 November 1834). By 1845, there were three bellows inside the organ case, and the two largest of these (supplying, respectively, the pedal and manual divisions) were fed with wind by feeders located in the blowing room, under the organ. The third bellows supplied the ophicleide; the feeders seem to have been attached to the underside of the bellows, but were worked by levers from the blowing room, 48' below (Stimpson 1845: 5–6; 1846: 8). The two main bellows may be those which survive in the present organ, each being approximately 15' by 6'.

Technologically, Birmingham was an advance on York, but it was not to be William Hill who finally solved the (mechanical) problems of building the largest organs. That distinction fell to Henry Willis.

ST GEORGE'S HALL, LIVERPOOL (1843–55)

Every so often in the history of organ-building, an instrument appears which effectively straddles two epochs, transcending the limitations of the one, and heralding the achievements of the other. Cavaillé-Coll's organ for St Denis (1841) is an example. So, too, is Henry Willis's organ for St George's Hall, Liverpool (1855). It is tempting to draw further parallels. Each builder was in his youth when he received the commission (Willis was thirty, Cavaillé-Coll only twenty-two), and in both instances, the award of a prestigious contract to so youthful a builder provoked ill-natured comment. Both schemes juxtapose old and new. At St Denis, Cavaillé-Coll introduced harmonic registers, strings, the pneumatic lever, higher pressures. At Liverpool, Willis introduced pneumatic thumb pistons, steam power and an improved form of the pneumatic lever, besides taking several hints from Cavaillé-Coll's practice. Yet the St Denis organ, with its cornets and mutations, its Bombarde division and truncated Pedale, was still a traditional French organ, and, as such, should be distinguished from its builder's later work, whilst Willis's instrument, with its G G-compasses, unequal temperament and extensive duplication, could claim to be (almost) the last and (certainly) the largest long-compass organ built in England. Willis would never build anything like it again, and he took full advantage of the opportunities presented in 1867 and 1897 to modernise the instrument.

More will be said below (pp. 349–57, 365–71) about Willis's innovations; for the moment, it is the conservative tendencies of the 1855 scheme which must concern us. Though most of these originated in a conservatism amounting, at times, to eccentricity on the part of the Corporation's chosen adviser, Dr S. S. Wesley, it is important to realise that in turning an unpromising paper scheme into a highly successful musical instrument,

Willis applied his own particular genius to the achievement of those objectives which had inspired the Insular Movement, and created an alternative to the German System organs of the 1840s and 1850s.

Wesley was consulted about an organ for the new Hall as early as 1843 (MS 45: 6 April 1844) but it was not until 1845 that he was formally appointed to give his 'professional assistance' in the matter (MS 45: 10 January 1845). The scheme that he prepared is transcribed below (MS 45: 1 May 1846).

Four sets of Keys.
> Great
> Choir
> Swell
> &
> Combination Keys

All of which are to extend from double G in the bass to A above the usual F in the treble. [63 notes]
> Pedal organ to extend from Double C to F. [30 notes]
> Nine Composition Pedals to the Great Choir and Swell Organs, and three *or four* to the Pedal Organ.

Also, coupling stops to be acted upon by Foot Pedals for connecting the Swell and Great Organ Keys, and for uniting the Pedal Organ with the Swell, Great and Choir Keys, as may hereafter be resolved upon.

List of Stops.

Great Organ

1.	Open Diapason. Double. Metal. The five lowest notes wood			63
2.	Stopt Diapason			63
3.	Open Diapason. Metal. CC. not less than 8 inches			63
4.	ditto	do. CC " 7 "		63
5.	ditto	do. CC " 6 "		63
6.	Claribella	large scale		63
7.	Principal	wood		63
8.	ditto	metal		63
9.	ditto 2 ranks, metal, the upper Stop to draw the 3 principals			126
10.	Fifteenth	metal		63
11.	ditto	ditto the upper to draw both		126
12.	Piccolo	hard wood		63
13.	Quint			
14.	Tenth	the upper to draw the three metal		189
15.	Twelfth			
16.	Doublette	2 ranks	metal	126
17.	Sesquialtera	5 ranks	metal	*about* 315
18.	Mixture	5 ranks	metal	about 315
19.	Fourniture	5 ranks	metal	about 315
20.	Grand Compound 7 ranks		metal	about 461
21.	Double Trumpet	metal		63
22.	Trumpet	metal		63

23.	Horn	metal	63
24.	Clarion	metal	63
25.	8ve Clarion	metal	63
			2918

Swell Organ

1.	Double Diapason	Stopt wood	63
2.	Open ditto	metal	63
3.	Open ditto	ditto	63
4.	Claribella	large scale	63
5.	Stopt Diapn	wood or metal	63
6.	Principal	metal	63
7.	Principal	metal the upper to draw both	126
8.	Fifteenth	metal	63
9.	Fifteenth	metal	63
10.	Quint ⎫		
11.	Tenth ⎬ metal the upper to draw the three		189
12.	Twelfth ⎭		
13.	Picollo [*sic*]	Hard wood [or] metal	63
14.	Doublette 2 ranks	metal	126
15.	Sesquialtera 5 ranks	metal	315
16.	Mixture 5 ranks	metal	315
17.	Trumpet	metal	63
18.	Hautboy	metal	63
19.	Cornopean	metal	63
20.	Cremona-Bassoon	metal	63
21.	Clarion	metal	63
22.	8ve Clarion	metal	63
23.	Open Flute	Hard wood	63
			2079

Choir Organ

1.	Stopt Diapason Double wood	63
2.	Open Diapason (CC not less than 8 inches metal)	63
3.	Dulciana	metal	63
4.	Claribella	large scale	63
5.	Stop Diapason	wood or metal	63
6.	Principal	metal	63
7.	Flute Open	Hard wood Powerfully voiced	63
8.	Flute Stopt		63
9.	Flageolet		63
10.	Picollo [*sic*]	Hard wood	63
11.	Clarionet. tenor c.	Hard wood [*sic*]	46
12.	Bassoon. 8 foot pipe on 4 foot C carried upward. Hard wood.		46
13.	Fifteenth	metal	63
14.	Doublette 2 ranks	metal	126
15.	Mixture 5 ranks	metal	about 315
16.	Hautboy	metal	63
17.	Clarion	metal	63

18.	Cremona	4 foot C	46
19.	Cornopean		63
20.	Echo Cornet. A compound of Double Stopt Diapⁿ. Stopt unison Diapason. Principal. Fifteenth. and 4 rank't Sesquialtera. to be enclosed in a box. Fiddle G upward – about		316
21.	Ophicleide. or Great Solo Reed		63
			1933

Pedal Organ

1.	C.C.C.C. Open Metal. Double Double Diapason Zinc. C.C.C.C. 8 lb: to the square foot. same thickness throughout from which the scale of the whole stop must be deduced. CCCC 30 inches diameter. Metal.	30
2.	C.C.C.C. Open Wood. Double Double Diapason C.C.C.C. 3 feet by 2 ft + 8 [inches]. To be made without joints and of the material and substance most conducive to the best possible effect.	30
3.	C.C.C. Metal Double Diapason. C.C.C. not less than 16 inches Gray's metal, the metal to be of such weight as may ensure the best quality of tone.	30
4.	8 feet Metal. Stop [sc. spot] metal CC. 9 inches	30
5.	4 feet Metal. Stop [sc. spot] metal	30
6.	2 feet Metal. Ditto	30
7.	Mixture. from 6 to 10 ranks as may be found best. Spot metal.	300
8.	Trumpet 16 feet Spot. metal	30
9.	Horn 16 feet Spot. metal	30
10.	Clarion 8 feet Spot. metal	30
11.	8^{ve} Clarion 4 feet Spot. metal	30
12.	C.C.C. 16 feet Double. Wood. CCC. 22 by 24 inches, if made of the best wood ordinary [*sic*] used, C.C.C. to be 2 inches in thickness when finished	30
13.	C.C.C. 16 feet Double, Open Wood, smaller scale	30
14.	Stopt C.C.	30
15.	Stopt 4 feet Spot. metal	30
16.	Stopt 4 feet wood	30
17.	CC. 8 feet. wood CC. 11 by 9.	30
		750

Combination Organ

To give a Selection of Stops from the Choir and Swell Organs, in number from 15 to 20.

The Reed Stops numbered 21.22.23.24.25 in the Great Organ, 11.12.16.17.19.21 in the Choir and 8.9.10. & 11 in the Pedal Organ to be all placed on winds of high pressure, to such an extent as may hereafter be determined upon.

The whole of the metal used in the Great, Choir and Swell Organs to be of the best Spot Metal. and the weight of each and every pipe to be such as may ensure its very best quality of tone.

The Keys of the Organ to be made of the very best wood and ivory. the fillings about the keys to be executed in a perfectly handsome manner by a superior Cabinet

Maker and either in Spanish Mahogany, Maple, Rose Wood or such other Wood as may be selected, and finished in the very best style of Cabinet work. the keys to be brought as near together and as much under the command of the performer as may be, and the Draw Stops arranged by improved Mechanism, in the manner most convenient for use.

Every part of the Mechanism to be constructed of the best and most durable material and to work *without any noise* being observed by the performer and any improvements to be met with in any of the Continental Organs to be introduced in this one, either as regards mechanism or voicing of the pipes . . .

[steam power to be applied to the blowing, but provision to be made for manual blowing as well]

The Composition Pedals to be formed on the Original principle, and act immediately upon the slides themselves and not upon either of the intermediate movements.

All the pipes of the Organ to be voiced in St. George's Hall, or in some building of equal space and magnitude, approved by Dr. Wesley.

A Month's Notice to be given Dr. Wesley previous to the casting of any portion of the Metal . . .

[swell box to be constructed of two-sided panels with sawdust in between]

The experiments respecting the large Pedal pipes to be open to general observation . . .

[the builders to replace any unsatisfactory pipes at their own expense]

[all soundboards to be leathered]

The touch of the four manuals, and the Pedal action, to be perfectly light and elastic, as far as any possibility exists of their being made so in such an instrument . . .

[stops to draw without difficulty in all weathers, and to be perfectly level when drawn]

[all to be subject to Dr Wesley's approval]

The scheme is strikingly incoherent for the mid-1840s. It is essentially an inflated version of the Birmingham Town Hall organ of ten years earlier, with scant regard for the far-reaching innovations made by the leading organ-builders since then. Massive duplication, a preoccupation with large scales, extensive use of open wood registers, the inclusion of 2′ reeds, the lack of a fully-fledged reed chorus on the Swell and provision for a Combination Organ all recall Birmingham's errors, but whilst these were excusable in 1834, their reiteration in a design for a major concert organ in the mid-1840s was remarkable. Odd features of the scheme were obviously inspired by recent developments, but Wesley consistently misunderstood their purpose: the multi-ranked mixtures, the arrangements for drawing the mutations together (as a kind of 16′ mixture) and the curious echo cornet are examples. The novel flutes and strings which Hill had been making for some years, and which were beginning to appear in the work of other builders, were totally absent.

Willis was able to make some improvements, but Wesley's 1845 scheme was largely intact when the organ was completed in 1855 (Plate 24). Critics were not slow to comment upon its peculiarities. 'Dr Camidge's old blunder of attempting to obtain power by means of duplicate stops appears to have

24 St George's Hall, Liverpool, Henry Willis, 1855.

been in danger of being revived at Liverpool' (*MG* 11, 1857: 114) wrote one correspondent, and a hostile notice in the *Musical World* maintained that 'magnitude is attained, and effect, we presume, sought, by simple re-duplication of old and known qualities' (xxxii, 1854: 566–7). Willis could only mitigate the worst effects of the duplication, leading a later commentator to refer to the 'monotonous repetition of stops of the same tonal character', and to compare the power of the full organ unfavourably with that of the smaller, but better-designed instrument in Leeds Town Hall (*Eccl* xxv, 1864: 360).

Wesley's insistence upon particular scales for the pipes is reminiscent of Camidge, and it seems that they shared the same misapprehension concerning the relationship of pipe scales to volume. In this context, Wesley's attempt to explain the rationale behind his Pedal department is relevant:

... although not remarkably extensive, as regards the number of stops, [it] somewhat exceeds, in point of *scale*, the finest organs yet built. But it has not been with the mere object of surpassing the large organs of Rotterdam, Weingarten, Haarlem, and York Minster and Birmingham that I have specified a more costly scale. Had the scale adopted in these instruments been satisfactory, had the pipes so built *spoken their notes well*, I would have had no wish to depart from their scale, but this part of these celebrated organs is notoriously defective, and without entering upon the cause of such defects I beg to say that in the instrument now in question I have adopted a scale, which seems reasonable, and calculated to answer every purpose, but it happens to be, as I have observed, considerably larger and more costly than those referred to –

The C.C.C.C. at Weingarten is exactly 19 inches and a ½ in Diameter. The Haarlem scale, as I am informed ... is still less. The York C.C.C.C. is but 21 inches ... and the Birmingham only a degree larger, the pipes being of very thin metal –

The Liverpool scale not only exceeds them all in diameter, the C.C.C.C. being 30 inches, but the substance of the pipe is intended to be twice that of Birmingham, or larger even. Should the experiment prove it necessary to obtaining *the best possible effect* then the scale of the large pedal pipes will be one third larger than those at York, and nearly half as large again as those at Haarlem. (MS 45: 23 October 1845)

The impracticality of such scales was apparent to many, and although Wesley claimed support from Bishop and Davison, Hill was blunt: the proposed scales were 'preposterous'. His comments are worth reporting, for they illustrate the way in which his own ideas had changed since the 1830s:

The Pedal pipes are much too large in scale. The dimensions of the wood CCCC are taken from some pipes made by me some years ago [Birmingham?], but experience has proved that a much less scale is more effective. I am quite convinced that to increase the scale of large pipes beyond a certain point would disappoint the projector. I have experimented upon some of the largest scale pipes ever made and the conclusion I arrived at was that any diameter beyond 24 inches for the 32 ft. C was perfectly useless and objectionable.   (MS 45: 28 September 1847)

This, as may be imagined, was not the only criticism that Wesley had to endure in an uncharacteristically acerbic letter from Hill, culminating in a description of the scheme as 'quite beyond the science of organ building [at] the present day ... It does not contain a single new invention either in stops or mechanism but on the contrary appears crowded with duplicate and large-scale stops, the only use of which appears to be to swell the number' (MS 45: 28 September 1847).

The question of keyboard compass and its bearing upon the design of the Pedal Organ aroused considerable controversy, reflecting the diversity of opinions to be found at the time. The 'professors' to whom (much to his indignation) Wesley's scheme was referred were greatly exercised on this matter. Hardly surprisingly, they were critical of his proposals.

Wesley had specified a compass of G G–a^3 for the keyboards, and C–f^1 for the pedals, with pedal C coupling to keyboard C. His 17–stop Pedal scheme, together with his undoubted reputation as a 'pedalist' and Bach player, indicate that Wesley was not without some understanding of the principles underlying an independent Pedal Organ. In this, he was more enlightened than Walmisley, who wrote to the Committee to the effect that, if the keyboard compasses were extended to CC, the greater part of the proposed Pedal division would be available by coupling, and the Pedal

Organ itself need only include the stops numbered 1, 2, and 12 in Wesley's scheme, plus a posaune 32′ and a trombone 16′. He proposed in addition that a single octave (CC–BB) of the Great Organ stops numbered 3, 4, 7, 20, 21, and 23, and of Pedal stop 3 be placed upon the Pedal soundboard to be acted upon by separate drawstops: a contribution of magisterial irrelevance emanating from Cambridge's Professor of Music (MS 45: 21 November 1846). The other professors (Turle, Novello, Hopkins) acted in concert, and differed from both Wesley and Walmisley. They suggested that if C coupled to C the lowest 5 notes of the keyboards would be 'comparatively useless' and the Pedal would be deprived of the 'weight of tone' which their associated pipes could provide. If, alternatively, GG of the keyboards were to be coupled to G of the pedals it would be necessary to supply the bottom 5 notes of the pedal by having them permanently coupled to their octaves – an 'unartistic' procedure, 'derogatory to the high character which it is intended that the Liverpool organ shall possess'. They therefore recommended that the keyboard registers should commence at C, but that a further octave of keys be provided below this to act upon the Pedal registers. They also proposed that the keyboards should be carried up to c⁴ – 'which would give scope for the performance of all the full Orchestral Music of every School' (MS 45: 12 October 1846).

Then, and later, Wesley defended his insistence upon GG-compass by reference to the organ's accompanimental role. He wished to facilitate 'the accompaniment of every vocal effort which could possibly occur in [the] building' from a single voice to 'the vast choral force of Lancashire'. For this, C compass was 'so inefficient that almost every passage the player attempts in octaves with his left hand has to be transposed; to be constantly buzzing with pedal scales would be intolerable' (MG II, 1857: 76). Wesley was unwise to be so precise in describing his mode of accompaniment. The use of octaves in the bass was denounced as 'a style of organ playing in vogue with pianoforte players ... one which is not now ... adopted by first-rate performers', and Wesley's position was further undermined by a claim that, when he was Organist of Leeds Parish Church (1842–9), 'the dust on the half-dozen lowest keys on the GG manuals remained undisturbed for months' (MG II, 1857: 114, 89). Yet Wesley's accompanimental practice has an authentic flavour: whatever his abilities as a solo performer, and however radical his ideas on cathedral musical establishments, he was, in other ways, an extremely conservative cathedral musician, and neither the instruments he was obliged to play, nor his tutelage in the older tradition would permit him easily to change his ways. It is likely that, for church musicians of Wesley's generation, the accompaniment of singers remained largely a manual art.

This conservatism dictated Wesley's attitude to another contentious matter: temperament. It is well known that Wesley insisted upon using the old unequal temperament at Liverpool; it is less well known that he claimed Willis's support in this. As late as 1857, Wesley stated that Willis 'had never at any time thought proper to tune his organs by what is called equal temperament'.[16] He [Wesley] had heard the French organs and Hill's organ in the Royal Panopticon, and judged these instruments 'greatly injured by the tuning, as all organs must be having nothing in bearable tune'. However, *both* systems of tuning had been tried at Liverpool, with stops tuned in each temperament for comparison, and the result was 'most convincing as to the great error of the equal temperament system' (*MG* II, 1857: 77). Characteristically, Wesley overstated his case and left himself open to attack; his statement that 'we may fairly question the accuracy of any man's *ear* who can endure equal temperament in the tuning of an organ' elicited the not unreasonable response that 'Dr. Wesley's accuracy of ear may not only be doubted but denied, after writing such passages as constantly occur in his service and anthems, knowing and advocating the ordinary mode of tuning organs in England' (*MG* II, 1857: 114). Wesley was not a man to give way. W. T. Best had the St George's Hall organ tuned to equal temperament in 1867 (HR2: 502), but several years later, Wesley had the satisfaction of putting Hill's Panopticon organ (one of the earliest to be tuned to equal temperament from its inception) into unequal temperament when it was transferred to the Victoria Rooms, Clifton.[17]

Although serious discussions concerning the provision of an organ for the Hall had begun as early as 1843, it was not until 1851 that progress on the building justified the Corporation in entering into a contract. From the start, Wesley had manoeuvred to secure the job for Gray & Davison, and in February 1846 the committee actually resolved to appoint them (MS 45: 17 February 1846). However, further delays in building work, widespread criticism of Wesley's scheme and possibly some doubts about the probity of Wesley's dealings with Davison then intervened, and the decision was never announced. There is a suggestion that the commission was later offered to Hill, who refused it, not being prepared to execute Wesley's scheme (*MG* II, 1857: 114).[18] In the event, Willis secured the contract, but through Walmisley's agency, not Wesley's (MS 46: 8, 24 September 1851; 14 July 1852). The story of the early-morning visit to the Great Exhibition, and the impression which Willis's large organ made upon the Liverpool committee, is well known (Edwards 1898: 299–300), and the resolution to employ Willis is recorded in the minutes of 24 September 1851. The organ was opened in May 1855, though it was not until October of that year that Wesley confirmed that Willis had completed the contract to his full satisfaction: 'the tone is pure, novel, and powerful ... [the organ is] without rival in the facilities afforded the performer for producing the most rapid and various effects' (MS 46: 17 October 1855).

There remain doubts concerning the original specification. One version (apparently issued by Wesley and Willis) differs in some details from the contract scheme (MS 46: 25 October 1851; cf. *MW* xxxII, 1854: 565). In the transcription of the contract below, variations found in the 1854 publication are noted in the right-hand column.

Great Organ (GG – a in alt)

1.	Double Open Diapason	16	
2.	Open Diapason	8	
3.	Open Diapason	8	
4.	Open Diapason	8	
5.	Stopped Diapason	8	
6.	Claribella	8	*Open Diapason (wood) 8*
7.	Principal	4	
8.	Principal	4	
9.	Flute	4	
10.	Quint	6	*Principal 4*
11.	Fifteenth	2	
12.	Fifteenth	2	
13.	Tenth	3	*Twelfth 3*
14.	Twelfth	3	
15.	Doublette	2 & 1	
16.	Sesquialtera	IV	
17.	Mixture	IV	
18.	Fournette [*sic*]	V	
19.	Cymbale	V	
20.	Posaune	16	
21.	Ophicleide	8	
22.	Trombone	8	
23.	Trumpet	8	
24.	Clarion	4	
25.	Octave Clarion	2	*Clarion 4*

Choir Organ (GG – a in alt)

1.	Double Diapason (closed)	16	
2.	Open Diapason	8	
3.	Dulciana	8	
4.	Viol Di Gamba	8	
5.	Claribella	8	
6.	Stopped Diapason	8	
7.	Octave Viol di Gamba	4	*Dulcimer 4*
8.	Principal	4	
9.	Flute	4	
10.	Celestina	4	
11.	Flagolet [*sic*]	2	
12.	Fifteenth	2	
13.	Mixture	III	
14.	Twelfth	3	
15.	Cremona	8	
16.	Trumpet	8	
17.	Orchestra Oboe (c)	8	
18.	Clarion	4	

Swell Organ (GG – a in alt)

1.	Double Diapason (closed wood bass)	16	
2.	Open Diapason	8	
3.	Open Diapason	8	
4.	Stopped Diapason	8	
5.	Gamba	8	*Dulciana 8*
6.	Principal	4	
7.	Principal	4	
8.	Twelfth	3	
9.	Fifteenth	2	
10.	Fifteenth	2	
11.	Doublette 15 & 22	2 & 1	
12.	Flute (open wood)	4	
13.	Flute (closed wood)	4	
14.	Mixture	III	
15.	Fourniture	IV	
16.	Sesquialtera	III	
17.	Piccolo	2	
18.	Trombone	16	
19.	Contra Oboe	16	
20.	Horn	8	
21.	Trumpet	8	
22.	Oboe	8	
23.	Ophicleide	8	
24.	Clarion	4	
25.	Clarion	4	

Solo Organ (GG – a in alt)

1.	Double Diapason	16	
2.	Open Diapason (wood) large scale	8	
3.	Stopped Diapason	8	
4.	Flute Orchestra Flute [*sic*]	8	
5.	Orchestral Oboe (c)	8	
6.	Flageolet	2	
7.	Clarinet (c) wood or metal	8	
8.	Corno di Bassetto	8	
9.	Horn	8	*Harmonic Flute 4*
10.	Ophicleide	8	
11.	Trombone	8	
12.	Harmonic Trumpet	4	*Trumpet (Harmonic) 8*
13.	Cornet Reed	8	*Vox Humana 8*
14.	Bassoon	8	
15.	Contra Fagotta	16	

Pedal Organ (CCC to F, 30)

1.	Double Double Diapason (wood)	32	
2.	Double Double Diapason (metal)	32	
3.	Open Diapason (wood)	16	
4.	Open Diapason (metal)	16	
5.	Salicional (metal)	16	
6.	Bourdon (closed 8 ft)	16	
7.	Principal (metal)	8	

8.	Principal (wood)	8	
9.	Quint	6	
10.	Fifteenth	4	
11.	Mixture	III	
12.	Sesquialtera	V	
13.	Contra Posaune	32	
14.	Posaune	16	
15.	Ophicleide	16	
16.	Trumpet	8	*Trumpet 16*
17.	Clarion	4	*Clarion 8*

The Couplers or Mechanical combinations to be
1.   Swell Organ to Great Organ
2.   Choir   ,,   to Great   ,,
3.   Solo   ,,   to Great   ,,
4.   Great   ,,   to Swell   ,,
5.   Choir   ,,   to Pedals
6.   Great   ,,   to Pedals
7.   Swell   ,,   to Pedals
8.   Solo   ,,   to Choir
9.   Solo   ,,   to Pedals

The metal used in this organ to be for pipes from G.G. (12 feet) to C.C. (8 feet) Lead. a small portion of antimony and ⅙th tin.
From C.C# (8 feet) to Gamut G. ⅕ Tin
From Gamut G# to Tenor C (4 feet) ¼ Tin
All pipes above 4 feet and under 2 feet C in pitch to be ⅓rd Tin.
All pipes from 2 to 1 ft. in pitch ⅖ths tin
All pipes from 1 foot to the highest notes to be half tin. The above is for Flute [*sic*] stops only.
The great Ophicleide in the Swell organ to have brass tubes. All other reed work to be composed of ⅓rd tin and further hardened with antimony.
All pipes standing in front of the Organ to be composed of a hard durable metal composed of Tin, Bismuth, antimony, and Lead, and the whole of the pipes to be planed on both sides and polished.
The improvements contained in a patent granted to Mr. Henry Willis in February and specified on the 28th of August 1851 to be adopted in the construction of the present Instrument namely a Cylindrical or rolling Pedal Valve. Valves for the Manuals. An improved exhausting Valve for the Pneumatic Lever. Threaded centres for the Mechanical connections, the pneumatic combination movement and the drawing of Air from the Swell Box in the same ratio as that supplied to the pipes from the Bellows.
Pneumatic levers to be applied to the whole of the Manuals if considered desirable, and to the Pedals. Those couplers numbered 1.2.3.8 to be brought into action without adding in the least degree to the weight of the touch.
The pneumatic combination movement to be applied as follows –
   Six central changes for the Great Organ
   Six ditto   ,,   ,, ,, Choir   ,,
   Six ditto   ,,   ,, ,, Solo   ,,
   Six ditto   ,,   ,, ,, Swell   ,,
   Six ditto   ,,   ,, ,, Pedal   ,,   through the medium of the Great
Organ Knobs. The last six to be 'ad libitum' by means of a pedal.

On either side of the Great Organ Knobs, there are to be placed three others to act simultaneously upon the whole Instrument, producing by one process of action the required effect.

The couplers to be brought into action by means of pedals placed in the usual position of composition pedals, and if space be available, other pedals to be employed in connection with the combination movements to such extent as may prove advisable.

An improved method of bringing the drawstops and Pedal Board conveniently under the command of the performer to be adopted.

The whole of the movements within this Grand Organ to be consistent with true mechanical principles and completed in the highly finished style of the best French Instrument.

The various bellows supplying this Instrument with wind to be constructed upon the improved method of the celebrated French Organ Builder Cavaillé Coll and to be twelve in number – these to be arranged as near their services as possible and to draw their contents from reservoirs placed in the Vaults of the Hall. The reservoirs to have each three feeders moved by steam power to be supplied by the Corporation for that purpose.

The chamber appointed to contain the Reservoirs of Wind to be hermetically sealed (excepting by a valve) from the rarified air generated for the purposes of ventilation. This together with the formation of Apertures for the passage of the trunks to the Organ and the construction of a suitable foundation for the Instrument to be provided at the expence [sic] of the Corporation.

The Swell Box to be of ample thickness, *Double*, with an intervening space of about 4 inches filled with Sawdust. The front to be a double set of Venetian Shutters with centres working in brass bearings and every other contrivance which may render their action as easy as possible.

The key fittings to be of the handsomest design, and beautiful woods, as well as the best Ivory to be obtained. The metallic plate through which the pneumatic combination movement passes to be electro-plated with Gold: the knobs to be electro-plated and turned.

The whole of the foregoing specified work to be executed in the highest style of excellence possible. The materials to be sound, well seasoned and the best fitted for their respective purposes, and the tone of the Instrument to be in all respects as fine and impressive as skill and labor can make it, and the whole Organ completely erected in St. George's Hall, Liverpool, and guaranteed to give entire satisfaction to competent judges under pain of forfeiture of half the purchase money for the sum of Six Thousand two hundred pounds which sum includes every expense (except the actual carriage from London to Liverpool).

Henry Willis
18, Manchester Street
Grays Inn Road, London
October 22 1851

The organ of 1855 underwent major reconstructions in 1897 and 1931, with further extensive revisions in 1867 and 1957. Little physical evidence survives of Willis's mechanical innovations, and drastic re-scaling and replacement of pipework means that it is now impossible to form a reliable impression of what the instrument sounded like in 1855.

More will be said below (pp. 357, 365–6) about two features of Willis's organ: the pneumatic lever and the combination action. Both were vital to the successful construction and management of large organs, and their employment at Liverpool was of great significance in establishing the course of English organ-building in the second half of the century. Another innovation (Willis's answer to Hill's box pallet) was the cylindrical pedal valve. The valve openings were fitted with covers of leather or vulcanised rubber which, when the wire connected to the tracker began to move, rolled back to allow the passage of compressed air into the groove. Springs caused the cover to return when the key or pedal was released. It was first employed in the Exhibition organ, and was patented in the same year (*LJA* XL, 1851:1–3). Willis described two modes of construction, and one or other was used to wind the large 32′ and 16′ Pedal pipes at Liverpool.

Two large bellows were located in a vault below the floor of the Hall. Each had three feeders. They were driven by an eight horse-power steam engine and supplied twelve reservoirs distributed around the instrument. The high pressure reeds were supplied by a separate bellows, hand-blown, and placed inside the organ. Nothing can be asserted with confidence about the original wind pressures. According to one source, the highest pressure used in the 1855 organ was 'nine inches, and that only in the swell box; nothing outside ever reaches more than six inches' (*Eccl* XXVI, 1865: 116). To this day, the Swell ophicleide and a clarion are mounted on a chest at the back of the box, and it seems likely that these stops spoke on 9″ in 1855. Everything else is

Table 14 *St George's Hall, Liverpool, 1855: original scales*

	4′	2′	1′	½′	¼′	⅛′
Gt Double Open Diapason	n.o	51	30.5			
Open Diapason I	100*	56	33	20		
Open Diapson II	92*	52.5	32	19.25		
Open Diapason III	91*	50.5	31	18.5		
Quint	62	37.5	23	14	9	
Principal I	n.a.	50.5	31	18.5	12	
Principal II	n.a.	48	29.5	18	11	
Tenth		34.5	21	12.5	8	5.5
Twelfth		38	23	14	9	7
Fifteenth		n.a.	27	16.5	11	8
Sw Double Open Diapason	88*	51	30.5			
Open Diapason I	100*	55.5	33	20		
Open Diapason II	n.a.	52.5	32	19.5		
Principal	90*	50.5	31	18.5	12	
Twelfth		n.a.	n.o.	14	9	6
Fifteenth		n.a.	27	16.5	11	7.5
Ch Open Diapason	n.a.	49	30	18		
Principal	n.a.	n.a.	27	17	11	
Fifteenth		n.a.	n.a.	15.5	10.5	5.5

obscure. Presumably some of the Solo reeds were placed on 6″,[19] but it may be that Willis differentiated wind pressures of reeds and fluework elsewhere in the instrument; certainly, he had the opportunity to do so, with twelve reservoirs at his disposal.

The pipework has been so altered over the years that any statements concerning its original scaling and voicing must be of questionable value. Much has been transposed (to facilitate re-scaling or slotting) and much replaced. The scales recorded in Table 14 may give at least an indication of the state of things in 1855, but it would be unwise to make them the basis for any firm conclusions.

5

The Bristol reformation

Although the innovations made in the design and construction of organs during the 1820s and 1830s have been discussed in analytical terms and described as consequences of a general movement of musical taste, and although their application brought about a significant change in the character of the organ, they cannot legitimately be represented as the products of a clearly established set of principles for the reform of the English organ. Innovation was largely piecemeal, and it was not until the end of the 1830s that figures appeared who were able, through a series of fruitful collaborations between players and builders, to exert sufficient influence to bring about a wholesale reformation of the organ. There is an exception. One provincial city had, in the previous generation, experienced a conscious reform movement that in some respects anticipated the reforms later initiated among the metropolitan builders. This was Bristol. Between 1821 and 1837, the John Smiths (father and son) built a number of highly idiosyncratic instruments under the influence of Edward Hodges (1796–1867), organist of both St James's (from 1819) and St Nicholas's Church, Bristol (from 1821) until he emigrated to North America in 1838. In aspiring to make the organ more expressive and more powerful, Hodges and Smith shared the ambitions of progressive organists and organ-builders in London. By employing C-compasses, proper pedal divisions, and large Swell Organs, they anticipated some of the principal features of the organs built under Gauntlett's direction in the 1840s. A discussion of their work therefore effectively concludes our consideration of the Insular Movement and prepares the way for the account of the German System which follows.

Edward Hodges (Plate 25) was a strange, albeit remarkable, man. His mind ranged freely (often wildly) over the mechanical sciences, music, and theology; a list of his inventions would include a mowing machine, a screw propeller for ships, roller skates, designs for the division of ships' hulls into compartments, improvements in musical instruments, and a flying machine. Some, at least, merited practical application. The darker side of this vigorous intellectual activity is represented by the bouts of depression and

25 Edward Hodges (1796–1867).

nervous disorder to which he was subject throughout his life. Brought up an Independent, his wife the daughter of a Moravian, Hodges became a member of the Established Church and served as organist at St James's during the ministry of the Revd Thomas Biddulph, the leading Evangelical in Bristol. Hodges's diaries are evidence that his own outlook was profoundly influenced by Biddulph's brand of churchmanship. As a musician he was largely self-taught, and having extricated himself from the family business music became his chief preoccupation. He earned a high reputation as a player, composed (his 'exercise' for the degree of Doctor of Music was successfully performed at Cambridge in 1825), and wrote on musical matters with characteristic pedantry in both the local, and the London, press. Cathedral posts constantly evaded him, giving rise to wearisome self-questioning and grotesque attempts to discover portents of imminent success (he was comforted by the appearance of a one-legged crow in his Bristol garden after the failure of a bid for the Exeter organistship in 1835), and it was this that finally persuaded him to emigrate in 1838. He went first to Toronto, having been appointed organist of St James's Cathedral, but, finding Canada not to his taste, he promptly moved south to New York and was appointed Director of Music to Trinity parish early in 1839. There, he found adequate scope for his energies and at last felt himself to be appreciated; he remained until a major breakdown in his health obliged him to retire. He returned to Bristol in 1863, and died four year later (Hodges 1896: *passim*).

In attempting to reform organ design, Hodges was motivated by two main concerns. First, was his wish to promote congregational singing. Temperley has drawn attention to the importance attached by many Evangelical clergy to a revival of congregational participation in the musical portions of the church service (Temperley 1979a: 1, 207–23). Sometimes, this was encouraged by the establishment of a choir. At St James's, Bristol, a small choir had been recruited in 1817 'to assist in the Vocal Service of the Church' (MS 21: 382) and when Hodges became organist two years later he made the retention of this choir, and the desire for an improvement in congregational music, principal planks in his appeal for a reconstruction of the organ:

... at no small pains, some little progress has been made towards a restoration of *congregational* music. Respectable individuals have come forward & for a considerable time lent very valuable vocal assistance. Now should the idea of the improvement of the organ be abandoned ... all that has been done would be but lost labour; our little choir would be instantly broken up, & the service of the church would suffer a relapse ...   (MS 23)

The Vestry took the hint, and when the reconstructed organ was opened on 2 May 1824 the choir was in attendance to sing a setting of the full 'Cathedral Service' composed for the occasion by Hodges. His views as to parish church music remain obscure. Despite a commitment to the revival of congregational music, there always seems to have been something of the frustrated cathedral organist about Hodges, and he certainly maintained a quasi-cathedral tradition of anthems and settings at Trinity Church, New York. But in other respects his preferences were surprising. If a report of the opening of the St James's organ is to be believed, Hodges in some measure anticipated the work of Oakeley and Helmore in the 1840s by reintroducing Gregorian chant – though in what garbled form it is impossible to say. According to the *Bristol Mirror*, the Venite and morning psalm were sung on this occasion 'to the ancient Gregorian canto fermo, or plain chaunt, all the voices joining in unison, while the accompaniment was varied according to the Organist's feeling of the Royal Musician's conception' (8 May 1824). In the light of this, it is possible that the use of Gregorian tones at St Nicholas's,

Bristol, noted by Rainbow (1970: 111–12), may have begun in Hodges's day. Whatever the details, it is clear that Hodges was determined to promote the revival of parochial music, and that the provision of an adequate organ, modified in some respects so as to facilitate the accompaniment of both choir and congregation, was central to his strategy.

The second influence which shaped Hodges's ideas about organ design is much more elusive. In his diary, there was an entry for 15 June 1823 in which he recorded that he was 'nearly all the morning practising Bach', and there were apparently further entries in which he referred to playing Bach's fugues and the overtures of Handel on the organ (Hodges 1896: 14–15). This raises the interesting question of whether Hodges had any knowledge of Bach's organ works, and, if so, whether his views on organ design were affected by it. A related question concerns his acquaintance with continental organs. The prominence of C-compasses and developed Pedal divisions in his schemes might imply a North European influence, though it may be significant that there are no detailed references to continental practice in Hodges's writings about the organ. The likelihood is that his veneration of Bach (Hodges's third son was christened John Sebastian Bach) grew from familiarity with the *Well-tempered Clavier*, probably in the Wesley–Horn edition (1811–13); he does not seem to have been a member of Samuel Wesley's circle, and when he played 'Bach's splendid Organ Pedal Fugue in G minor' at the opening of the organ in St Stephen's, Bristol (1836), it was in the (by then) old-fashioned mode of a duet (Hodges 1896: 88). The most that can be said is that a limited acquaintance with the schemes of a few of the great continental organs, and some musical understanding of the place of pedals in Bach's contrapuntal structures, may have exerted some influence upon Hodges's ideas.

A series of letters which appeared first in the *Bristol Mirror* above the signature 'Minimus' and later in the *Quarterly Musical Magazine and Review* (IV, 1822: 33–44, 172–88) indicates where, in Hodges's opinion, the short-comings of the conventional English organ lay.[1] The writer's first complaint concerned depth of tone: 'The common defect of organs is a want of bass. The majesty of the organ lies in the lower notes of the diapason. If these be defective the want cannot be compensated' (*QMMR* IV, 1822: 34). There is an echo here of Hodges's comments (1821) on the old organ in St Nicholas's Church, of which he complained that 'the scale of the diapasons is much too small to support the superincumbent Harmonies' (MS 24: 271). Secondly, the writer found it necessary to define the function and character of the Choir Organ. It was 'intended to be used for the accompaniment of the singers; and is therefore but small, and voiced very soft . . . It is very essential to the light and shade of music . . . a church organ, destitute of it, is like a coat without sleeves, or dinner without salt' (36). Again, the old St Nicholas's organ found little favour with Hodges because it lacked a separate Choir Organ. The

Choir was borrowed from the Great, and hence the distinctive character of each division was compromised, the instrument lacking 'the fulness of tone which for some purposes is requisite, or the delicacy which is necessary on other occasions' (MS 24: 272). Thirdly, 'Minimus' objected to the inconsistencies of English compasses: 'It is much to be wished that some definite standard of compass were adopted, and that all organs should be constructed to terminate at a particular note, varying one from another only by complete octaves; for this purpose C seems the most proper, never omitting the C sharp above it' (36). A fourth proposal concerned a characteristic feature of organs built or rebuilt under Hodges's direction, namely, the reform of the upperwork. He explained that the higher-pitched registers were in effect harmonics of the unison:

... these, when well proportioned ... add a vast richness and brilliancy to the sound; but when predominant, as is too often the case, they tend only to insufferable noise and ear-rending confusion. Three, four or even five of these harmonics, are bundled up commonly into one stop, (as the sesquialtera, mixture, and cornet for instance,) whereby of course the performer is compelled to use all or none. Were every rank made to draw separately, there would be much more room for the exercise of taste and ingenuity on the part of an intelligent organist than the present arrangement affords, and a bungler might draw them altogether, as at present.   (36)

Other points made by 'Minimus' were the necessity of pedals and the desirability of more imitative stops in modern organs.

With one important exception (enclosure) these letters of 1822 summarise the objectives of Hodges's reforms. For the 1820s, his ideas were novel, but they changed little over the years, and his specification for the organ built by Henry Erben at Trinity Church, New York, in 1846 (Ochse 1975: 159–60) includes no significant features that could not have been found in one of the Bristol organs of the 1820s. By English standards, Erben's organ was distinctly anachronistic.

During the 1820s and 1830s Hodges found himself presented with a number of opportunities to direct the construction or reconstruction of Bristol organs, and it is in these instruments that the application of his ideas can be studied. The organs in question were:

    1821   St Nicholas
    1822   St Andrew, Clifton
    1824   St James
    1830   The Lord Mayor's Chapel
    1836   St Stephen
    1837   Christ Church

Little can now be discovered of the Clifton organ, and Hodges was probably not directly involved at Christ Church (though some of his improvements were employed). In the other four instances, the schemes were Hodges's own.

All the organs were built by John Smith, senior, with the certain exception of St Stephen's, and the possible exception of Christ Church. Like Hodges, Smith was an inventor. He was credited with building the first steamboat in Bristol (the claim is difficult to substantiate) and with devising a rocket apparatus which was widely used in coastguard stations (*Work in Bristol*: 163). This curiosity about mechanics and engineering must have been invaluable in his dealings with Hodges. He set up as an organ-builder in Bath, but moved to Bristol in 1814; upon his death in 1847 the business passed to his step-son, Joseph Monday (*Work in Bristol*: 162–4). John Smith, junior, seems not to have been in business with his father, but to have worked on his own account from various Bristol addresses (1827–59); it was he who built the St Stephen's organ, and possibly that for Christ Church. Left to his own devices, the organs built by Smith, senior, were typical of their date. There were some exceptions – Yeovil Church (1840) had divided upperwork in the Swell – but Smith's *magnum opus*, the new organ for Bath Abbey (1836), was surprisingly unadventurous by Hodges's standards; apart from CC-compasses to Great and Choir, and modest duplication, it was a wholly conventional design.

The same could not be said of the reconstruction of the organ in St James's, Bristol, which Smith carried out in 1823–4 under Hodges's direction (Appendix 1, pp. 457–8). The scheme had evolved from a simple proposal to repair the instrument and make a separate soundboard for the Choir Organ at a cost of £120 (MS 22) into a grandiose design for a 4-manual organ, with developed Pedal and Swell divisions, at a cost of around £500 (MSS 22, 23; MS 21: 487, 530, 540, &c.). Although most of the old instrument built by Renatus and John Harris (1717, 1726) was retained, the additions and alterations made by Hodges and Smith were of great significance, and the completed organ must be reckoned a striking achievement in the climate of the 1820s. Hodges would carry further his proposals for making the organ more expressive in the instruments for the Lord Mayor's Chapel and St Stephen's, but, otherwise, the St James's organ effectively summarises the principles behind the 'Bristol reformation'.

These reforms may be discussed under four main headings.

COMPASSES

Hodges advocated regularising compasses so that all began on the note 'c'. Unlike Gauntlett, in the late-1830s, he seems not to have had strong views as to which 'c' and at both the Lord Mayor's Chapel and St Stephen's the lowest note of the keyboards was CC, though, in the latter case, the lowest octave of each played the Pedal registers only (this may have been the arrangement in the former organ, too) (MS 80: 108).

UPPERWORK

Hodges's views on compound stops have already been mentioned (above, p. 154). How his reforms worked in practice may be seen from the St James's specification. The tierce, larigot and twenty-second of the Great could be drawn independently, or else together to form a sesquialtera (17.19.22). Similarly, on the Swell, the cornet drew out the twelfth, fifteenth and tierce to yield a mixture with a starting composition of 12.15.17. Whether the upper two ranks of the sesquialtera broke back at some point is not recorded; if not, it must have justified all Hodge's animadversions on compound stops. At St James's, the mixture was suffered to remain on the Great, but there were no compound stops at all in the instruments for the Lord Mayor's Chapel, St Stephen's or Christ Church, and, with the exception of the mixture, all three have the same arrangement of upperwork as at St James's. Nothing is known about the scaling of these registers, but the likelihood is that they were scaled as part of the diapason chorus. Most probably, this innovation was inspired by Hodges's interest in the theory of sound (a common preoccupation of amateur scientists at the time) rather than any acquaintance with the practice of Italian organ-builders in making the upperwork of their instruments draw in individual ranks.

PEDAL ORGAN AND PEDALS

In 1827, Hodges wrote that, among the essentials of a good organ 'we must include one stop at *least* of good pedal pipes (if two, three, or more, so much the better,) and a convenient set of pedals, of not less than two octaves in compass' (*QMMR* IX, 1827: 4). He turned his attention first to the 'convenient set of pedals', and so came up with one of his most distinctive contributions to Bristol organ design: brass pedals. The origin of this was a desire to reduce the width of individual pedals so that the pedal board as a whole might be more compact and the notes at the upper and lower ends of the compass more accessible. Concluding that wooden pedals could not be made less than one inch wide if they were to retain the necessary strength, Hodges decided to experiment with other materials. The result was a set of iron pedals, two octaves in compass, constructed for St Nicholas's in 1821. Each pedal was just one-eighth of an inch wide. However, in pedal playing, 'it is usual sometimes to make a run by drawing the foot rapidly across several keys. In every such instance, the St Nicholas pedals, being entirely of iron, produce an effect which cannot be considered as musical' (*QMMR* IX, 1827: 6). So, at Clifton, in the following year, Hodges had pedals made of wood, but with a piece of brass about an eighth of an inch in thickness, and an inch-and-a-half in depth, set into each. He claimed to have overcome the problem of noise without having lost the advantage of space, and, hence-forth, all organs built under his superintendance (and others built by Smith) were fitted with these pedals (*QMMR* ix, 1827: 4–7).

The provision of five Pedal registers at St James's in 1824 is remarkable. Hodges was never again able to be so ambitious. The Lord Mayor's Chapel included four Pedal stops (open diapason [16], stopped diapason [16], principal [8], trumpet [16?]) but St Stephen's had only one. However, despite the abundance of Pedal registers in the St James's organ, Hodges's specification for Trinity Church, New York, raises doubts as to how firm a grasp he had on the principles behind independent Pedal divisions. In a large organ, of thirty stops, Hodges provided only one Pedal register: open diapason 32′. There was a Pedal octave coupler, but, more significantly, both Choir and Great had compasses commencing at CC, and the Swell had a 2-stop, two-octave 'swell bass' also beginning at CC (Ochse 1975: 160). The implication is that Hodges viewed the Pedal as supplying that 'want of bass' of which he had complained, but that he did not think of the Pedal Organ as a division independent of the manuals. If the manuals possessed a long compass and pipes capable of producing an impressive depth of tone, there was no necessity for the Pedal to be provided with its own chorus. So, what at first sight looks like a radical innovation anticipating the reforms of the 1840s, may prove to be no more than further evidence of the English preoccupation with 'bass' and manual technique. The finger keyboard for the Pedal stops at St James's, and the bottom octaves of the keyboards acting on the pedal pipes at St Stephen's, would seem to confirm this.

One additional curiosity should be mentioned. In 1825, Hodges and Smith installed a pipe temporarily in the organ of St Mary Redcliffe capable of sounding four notes – CC, CC#, DD, DD#. The principle was similar to the flute. By making apertures on the side of this (wooden) pipe, which were then covered with pallets or stoppers controlled by the pedals, the means were provided of adjusting the speaking length of the pipe to give the required note. At least, this is what Hodges claimed, though the effect was perhaps only tolerable to those accustomed to the imprecise tones of English pedal pipes (*QMMR* ix, 1827: 150–2). This appears to have been the sole application of the idea under Hodges's auspices.

SWELLS

Writing in 1826, Hodges bemoaned the fact that the organ had undergone 'no material change for about two centuries'; where, he asked, 'has there been in organ-building any thing parallel to that grand improvement upon the harpsichord, whereby it became a piano-forte? [*sic*] The organ retains yet its old *harpsichord* character. It wants that capacity for *expression* which the piano-forte possesses' (*QMMR* VIII, 1826: 392–3). The significant term is 'expression'. An important part of Hodges's reform was an attempt to make the organ more expressive, and he sought to achieve this both by improving the construction of the swell box and by placing a larger proportion of the organ under expression.

Unfortunately, the extent and compass of the Swell Organ at St James's prior to Hodges's work cannot be established,[2] but, as left by Smith, it was an impressive 9-stop division with a more or less complete flue chorus and a compass commencing at tenor c. The provision of an octave coupler under- lines the importance attached to this department, and it was probably intended to make a significant contribution to the Full Organ. Hodges had also redesigned the Swell box. The old box was enclosed in a 'case' at the top, bottom and sides, and the interstices between the old and new boxes (a space of 5″) were packed with wood shavings. There were three sets of venetian shutters in the front, one behind the other, all operated by the same pedal, but so contrived that although they began to open in sequence (rather than in parallel) all three reached their extreme open position at the same moment. Each shutter was covered with sound-absorbing material. This was Hodges's 'Triple Slat Venetian Swell' which he later introduced in organs built under his direction in New York. According to the inventor, the shutters in the St James's organ were so effective that, when closed, Full Swell could be used to accompany a single voice. Summing up its virtues, he wrote that the '*varieties* of effect, from the heaving crescendo of the Aeolian harp to the flashing sforzando of an immense orchestra … are brought under the immediate command of a single performer' (*QMMR* VIII, 1826: 399). This sounds an authentic note.

The comparison with an orchestra recurs in the *Bristol Mirror*'s account of the organ in St Stephen's, Bristol. There, Hodges carried the expressive principle to its furthest extent, enclosing nine of the twelve manual stops in a large ('Triple Slat') swell box (Appendix 1, pp. 458–9). He had proceeded along similar lines at the Lord Mayor's Chapel with an enclosed Great Organ of eleven stops, an unenclosed Choir Organ of seven stops, and a 4- stop Pedal division. In its report of the opening of the St Stephen's organ, the *Mirror* commented that, having once been regarded as the instrument most deficient in musical expression, the organ had recently been transformed to become 'the most susceptible of the impress of feeling'. Then came the reference to the orchestra. In the St Stephen's organ, there was a 'rich grandeur' which arose from the imagined remoteness of sounds emanating from a swell box; it was 'a similar effect to that which arises from a large orchestra heard at a distance, which to a chastened ear is much more delightful than the being exposed to the immediate din of contending instruments. In a metaphorical sense, easily understood, this may be termed hearing music in *perspective*' (23 April 1836). If Hodges did not write the passage himself, the reporter had at least been well briefed.

The principal features of Hodges's reform have been described, but there were other, less crucial, innovations. The St James's organ was the first in England to boast a 32′ register; it was stopped, and said to be 'decidedly *fifthy* throughout' (Hodges 1896: 292). The same instrument was claimed to be the first in England to boast a manual octave coupler (HR2: 553).[3] This may be a contrivance that should be ascribed to Smith rather than Hodges: it appeared extensively in his new organs. The coupler united one keyboard with the octave of another, though, if Sperling's account of the organ in the Lord Mayor's Chapel is correct (MS 80: 106), it was sometimes employed as an octave coupler on the same manual, and on the pedals. The provision of an extra eight notes (pipes, but no keys) in the treble of the Swell at St James's for use with this coupler anticipated Holdich's Diaocton. A further improvement was in the blowing arrangements; by the application of a revolving handle and crank, it was said that a small boy could operate the five feeders of the St James's organ (*Harmonicon* III, 1825: 29). Should cyphering occur, the provision of ventils enabled the player to shut off the troublesome division whilst continuing to use the remainder of the instrument. Two other of Hodges's notions seem not to have received practical application. One of his earliest 'improvements' was a 'typhus pedal' about which he wrote to Samuel Wesley in 1819. It was apparently a contrivance to hold down a number of keys for an indefinite length of time, but whether it was merely a 'thunder pedal', or something more harmonious, is not clear (Hodges 1896: 199–200). His second notion was to use zinc in the making of organ pipes. He and Smith looked into this in 1825 (a year or two before William Hill first used zinc for pipes) and apparently conducted some experiments; perhaps they proved unpromising, for there is no record of Smith employing zinc in his organs (Hodges 1896: 41).

   Hodges's departure for North America in 1838 closed an interesting chapter in the history of English organ design. Although many of the paths which he pursued proved to lead to dead ends, and although his influence seems not to have penetrated far beyond the boundaries of the City of Bristol, Hodges deserves more than a footnote in the history of the organ for mounting the only consistent and thorough attempt at reform before the late-1830s. By the time he departed for North America, a more influential and effective reform was underway, at the hands of Hill, Gauntlett and Davison, and it is to this that we must now turn.

PART II

6

Bach, Mendelssohn and the English organ, 1810–45

INTRODUCTION

It is notorious that Burney had found little to commend in the organs encountered on his European travels, summing up his impressions of the Dutch and German organs with the dismissive reflection that 'all these enormous machines seem loaded with useless stops, or such as only contribute to augment noise, and to stiffen the touch' (Burney 1775: II, 210). Despite Camidge's muddle-headed gesture of respect to the North European organ in his two schemes for York Minster, Burney's view was very largely endorsed by English organists and organ-builders until the 1830s, when an influential school of thought emerged maintaining that the deficiencies of the English organ were not to be made good by multiplying existing features of the design (as implied by the innovations of the 1820s and early-1830s), but through a radical reconstitution of organ design upon the principles observed in the organs of Holland and Germany. With Gauntlett as its leading apologist, and Hill its chief practitioner, the 'German System' represented the progressive movement in English organ design throughout the 1840s. The title was one of several that contemporaries employed: 'the German scale', 'the German Plan', and other more exotic titles invented by Gauntlett (below, pp. 189–90) were also in currency. German *System* is, however, particularly appropriate because of the implication lying behind the word 'system'. The movement was primarily concerned with the disposition (system) of the organ – compasses, chorus structure, pedal division – not with reforming the tonal characteristics of the English organ. Hill's scaling and voicing were not radically affected by the adoption of the German System, and although he incorporated his new styles of chorus reed, introduced narrow-scaled and tapering registers, and developed an extensive range of novel flutes for these organs of the 1840s, the similarities with earlier practice are at least as important as the points of departure. This comparative conservatism failed to satisfy the most radical reformers, and during the 1850s, another builder tackled the problem from a different angle. With

Henry Smart as his Gauntlett, Frederick Davison built a series of important organs which drew selectively upon the tonal and mechanical design of the instruments being built by the modern French builders. Like Hill, he failed ultimately to meet the demand for more power, more orchestral effects, more mechanical sophistication, and by the end of the 1850s, it was apparent that neither builder was willing to provide what the most iconoclastic spirits wanted.

This, however, was in the future when in the years around 1840 the English discovery of Bach acted as a catalyst to bring about a transformation in the approach of organist and organ-builder to organ design. The availability of Bach's scores was not, in itself, enough to achieve this. What was needed was the powerful advocacy of a performer who understood the nature of the instrument for which they were originally conceived. Such a person was Felix Mendelssohn Bartholdy.

MENDELSSOHN'S ADVOCACY OF BACH

Mendelssohn first performed publicly on the organ in England at the Birmingham Festival of 1837, and over the course of the next ten years his occasional organ performances, promotion of Bach publications and extensive contact with English musicians proved a stimulus to organ-playing in general and the cause of Bach's compositions in particular. Mendelssohn did little to influence English organ design directly; he requested broader pedal keys at Birmingham, adding that a compass of C–d^1 would be 'quite enough' (Polko 1869: 235), and complained of the absence of chorus registers on the English Choir Organ.[1] These, though, are only details. It was, rather, the organists whom he influenced, and by cultivating their taste for Bach, he predisposed them to favour the German System. In the person of Mendelssohn, the little world of the English organist was brought into contact with a European tradition of organ-playing which observed disciplines and conventions directly related to those of Bach's day.

It was in 1829 that Mendelssohn first visited England, and he returned on nine subsequent occasions before his death in 1847 (Radcliffe 1967: *passim*). The earliest visits were the most protracted, but nearly all extended over a period of weeks. Though he received considerable public exposure as both conductor and performer, was taken up by the Royal family and was received with an acclamation which, until then, the English had reserved for Handel, it may well be that Mendelssohn's greatest influence came about through a growing intimacy with a number of English musicians and musical families. The details are hazy, but his friendship with Thomas Attwood, Organist of St Paul's, probably explains how he came to be playing 'fugue music . . . to the amazement of all the listeners' on the Cathedral organ in 1832 (Lampadius 1876: 18); 'fugue music' included the *Fugue in E minor* (BWV 533) and other pieces by Bach, and it was almost certainly on this, and similar private or semi-private occasions that a privileged band of English musicians first heard authoritative performances from Mendelssohn of major Bach works. The organ works were not unknown in England before the 1830s (below, pp. 168–70), but it is clear from a remark of Gauntlett's, that organists had only the slightest notions of how to perform them. Writing many years later to Elizabeth Mounsey, Gauntlett recalled:

We knew the six Grand Fugues and the Exercises. But what Mendelssohn did was this: He brought out what Marx called the 'not well-known' Pedal organ music. He was the first to play the G minor, the D major, the E major, and the short E minor, of which he gave a copy to Novello, who printed it with a note. And he taught us how to play the *slow* fugue, for [Thomas] Adams had played all fugues fast. I recollect Mendelssohn's saying: 'Your organists think Bach did not write a slow fugue for the organ'.[2]   (*MT* xxxvii, 1896: 724)

Gauntlett's statement rings true (and is supported by Miss Mounsey's own recollections).[3] English organists, accustomed to the old voluntaries in which lethargy distinguished the tempo of the opening movement, and volatility that of the fugue, had little more perception of the style demanded by Bach's great contrapuntal fabrics than they had of the organs for which the compositions were conceived. Mendelssohn showed them how these works should be played, and his influence upon the rising generation of metropolitan organists was profound. Among them should probably be numbered Edward Holmes (All Saints, Poplar, 1833–9), Elizabeth Stirling (All Saints, Poplar, 1839–58; St Andrew Undershaft, 1858–80), Josiah Pittman (Christ Church, Spitalfields, 1835–47; Lincoln's Inn Chapel, 1852–64), Edmund Chipp (St Olave, Southwark, 1847–52; St Mary-at-Hill, 1852–6), Elizabeth Mounsey (St Peter, Cornhill, 1834–82), Ann Mounsey (St Vedast, Foster Lane, 1837–91), William Rea (St Andrew Undershaft, 1847–58), E. J. Hopkins (Temple Church, 1843–98) and the two George Coopers (St Sepulchre, Holborn, 1799–1843, and 1843–76).[4] Most important of all, however, was Gauntlett. According to Elizabeth Mounsey, it was Gauntlett who brought Mendelssohn to St Peter's, Cornhill, to play Bach on one of the first German System organs in the country, built by Hill to Gauntlett's design (1840) (MS 68: ff. 10–11). Their regard was mutual. Mendelssohn chose Gauntlett to play the organ part in the first performance of *Elijah*, at Birmingham in 1846, and testified to his own belief in Gauntlett's crucial part in reforming the English organ with the words, 'but for him – Dr. Gauntlett – I should have had no organ to play upon. He ought to have a statue' (*MSt* x, N.S., 1876: 134).

Mendelssohn's detailed influence upon the technique and interpretation of the first generation of English Bach players is obscure, but first-hand reports shed a little light on the subject. One contemporary remarked on

Mendelssohn's 'wiry, crisp, energetic character of delivery' and contrasted this with the technique of one of the leading English players of the previous generation, Benjamin Jacob (1778–1827), who 'played in the *legato* manner, and therefore never satisfied us in Bach's organ music'. The writer concluded with the reflection that 'freedom of touch is an essential requisite to a tale-telling enunciation of Bach's outline, counterpoints, episodes, and countless modes of diversifying his *motifs*' (*MW* IX, 1838: 210). Three other sources cast fragments of light upon Mendelssohn's registration practice. At St Peter, Cornhill, in 1842, Mendelssohn improvised on the theme of 'God save the Emperor', for half an hour, 'relying altogether upon the internal resources of the art and not upon any change of trumpets into flutes, or flutes into oboes' (*MP*, 20 June 1842) – a comment which illuminates the approach of contemporary English organists to improvisation quite as much as it does Mendelssohn's. It would evidently be mistaken to conclude from this that Mendelssohn eschewed changes of registration on all occasions. In the 'Prefatory Remarks' to his *Six Grand Sonatas for the Organ* (1845) he noted: 'Much depends in these Sonatas on the right choice of the Stops'; and each sonata offers opportunities for changes of registration, indicated by the composer's own directions as to dynamics and changes of keyboard. Miss Mounsey, too, recalled that on both Mendelssohn's visits to Cornhill, Gauntlett and she were in attendance to change the stops. She particularly remembered that he wished to have 'the swell stops varied as he proceeded – giving varied shades of tone without any striking change' (MS 68: f. 10). This, however, was in Mendelssohn's own *Fugue in F minor*, and there is nothing to indicate how he registered Bach or whether he caused the registration to be changed in the course of a piece. The only record to survive is the merest detail, and comes from Dr Hopkins, who was present at Christ Church, Newgate Street, in 1837 when Mendelssohn played the *Fugue in A minor* (BWV 543). Mendelssohn, Hopkins observed, 'took the long episode, beginning in E minor (at the end of the first pedal entry) on the Swell, returning to the Great organ when the pedal re-enters with the subject in its original key, but transferring the inverted pedal note E (in the treble part) to the Great organ, a bar before the other parts, with fine effect' (Pearce [1910]: 24).

The impression created by these sketchy accounts is that as both organ player and organ composer Mendelssohn's inspiration had its roots in the previous century. His veneration of Bach, the contrapuntal character of his own works, and a manual technique which (as far as one can tell) was schooled to encourage clarity of phrasing within a complex musical texture all imply this, and even the interest in registration evidenced by the introduction to the sonatas is carefully qualified to ensure that a good balance is preserved and 'too violent a contrast between . . . distinct qualities of tone' avoided (*Six Grand Sonatas* 1845: Prefatory Remarks). Mendelssohn's influence would not endure; the second half of the century saw the rise of a pianistic technique accompanied by increasing dependence upon console accessories and stop knobs, and this ultimately transformed the style in which Bach was played. But, for a time, Mendelssohn's approach had its imitators. Early editions of Bach by George Cooper and James Stimpson (*c.* 1845) lack the dynamics and registrations that both included in their orchestral transcriptions (below, p. 169), and the sheer intractability of the large C-compass organs built during the 1840s and 1850s must have discouraged players from making frequent changes of registration when tackling Bach's demanding scores.

Mendelssohn's influence was fundamental in securing the acceptance of Bach's organ works by English organists; his enduring influence upon the public as an advocate of Bach is more difficult to assess, though contemporaries had few doubts. He played major Bach pieces before massive audiences at Birmingham Town Hall (1837, 1840), Christ Church, Newgate Street (1837, 1842), St Peter, Cornhill (1840, possibly 1842), and probably at Exeter Hall (1842); on the latter occasion he reported playing 'before three thousand people, who shouted hurrahs and waved their handkerchiefs, and stamped with their feet till the hall resounded with the uproar' (Wallace 1863: 281). A writer in the *Musical World* reflected upon the reasons for this response, and enquired rhetorically why it should be that such a 'sensation' was evoked. Noting that 'the instruments he performed on seemed to assume a new character; the *pedale* appeared with a more grand and imposing tone, and the manuals more brilliant and harmonious', the writer went on to offer an explanation:

Mendelssohn introduced Bach to the English, as an organ composer. Our native artists had known and appreciated him, as a writer for the clavichord, the forty-eight studios [*sic*] had developed his genius, as a profound adept in the strict school of composition; but we had yet to venerate him as the inventor of a set of totally new effects upon the organ. It was not, that [Samuel] Wesley was unacquainted with his Fantasias, Passacaglias, Preludes, and Codas [*sic*], that he did not introduce them to the English: but never having heard a German organ, with its ponderous pedale, he could not realise the inventions of the author; and he was too cautious, and too prudent, to risk the reputation of his favourite, by the performance of passages, which on the squalling organ (which in his day prevailed in our churches) must have sounded absurd and ridiculous . . .   (VIII, 1838: 101–2)

The phrase, 'a set of totally new effects', is surely the key to Mendelssohn's rapturous reception. The dramatic, almost pictorial qualities of pieces such as the preludes and fugues in E minor and A minor when realised on organs with powerful reeds, complete choruses and an independent Pedal division, by a celebrity with an unheard-of facility in the use of keys and pedals created an irresistible sensation. Mendelssohn himself recognised this when he chose to play the *Prelude and Fugue in E flat* (BWV 552) at Birmingham in 1837; it would, he predicted, prove 'peculiarly acceptable' to the English, for 'you can play both prelude and fugue "piano" and "pianissimo", and also bring out the full power of the organ' (Wallace 1863: 128–9). By giving legitimate performances of Bach, Mendelssohn persuaded organists of the worth of the organ compositions; he also had the good fortune to satisfy the popular craving for novelty and sensation. No English organist could have achieved so much so quickly, and it is no exaggeration to describe Mendelssohn's contribution to the acceptance of Bach's music in England as unique.

THE PUBLICATION OF BACH'S ORGAN WORKS IN ENGLAND

A consideration of the influence of Bach's organ music on organ design cannot be divorced from the question of the availability of Bach's scores in England. A definitive study of this subject has yet to appear, though articles by Edwards (1896), Redlich (1952), Williams (1963) and Temperley (1979) are helpful, and indicate some of the problems. Table 15 attempts to present the evidence which is to hand for the publication of the organ music in England before 1850. This is, however, only a partial view, for it takes no account of the availability of continental editions of Bach during the crucial 1820s and 1830s. Certainly, German music in general was readily available in London at this time (Williams 1963: 142–3), and a review which appeared in *Musical World* in 1838 encompassed no fewer than thirty Bach publications, most of them from continental publishing houses (VIII: 260–3). There is, though, evidence that foreign editions of Bach's organ music were known in England before this. In 1816, Samuel Wesley reported having the loan of 'six curious and grand Preludes and Fugues, with an additional base [*sic*] line entirely for the pedals' (Edwards 1896: 657). This must have been Riedl's print of the *Sechs Präludien und sechs Fugen für Orgel oder Pianoforte mit Pedal* which appeared at about that time; it was later published by Steiner *c.* 1824, and then reissued in a corrected version by Haslinger *c.* 1830. Adolph Marx's edition of *Johann Sebastian Bach's noch wenig bekannte Orgelcompositionen*, published by Breitkopf & Härtel (Leipzig, *c.* 1833), was known to Gauntlett, possibly through the agency of Mendelssohn (Edwards 1896: 724). Most illuminating of all, however, is the programme of a recital by Elizabeth Stirling at St Katherine, Regent's Park, in 1837 (Appendix 2, p. 507). The ten Bach pieces were drawn from *Clavierübung III* (of which there was no English edition at the time), the *Sechs Präludien und sechs Fugen* and Haslinger's edition of the *Canonic Variations*, 'Vom Himmel hoch da komm' ich her' (Vienna, 1831). A similar recital in the following year included the *Toccata in D minor* (BWV 565) in the Breitkopf & Härtel edition (Appendix 2, pp. 507–8). To this list of continental Bach editions should be added several more which may have been known to English organists. Peters issued the toccatas and fugues in F major (BWV 540) and D minor (BWV

Table 15 *The publication of Bach's organ music in England, and works arranged for the organ, 1799–1845*

1799	*An Essay on Practical Musical Composition*, by A. F. C. Kollman (London). First movement of Trio Sonata in E flat (вwv 525), pp. 58–67.
1807	*A set of twelve Fugues, composed for the organ by Sebastian Bach, arranged as Quartettos for two violins, tenor, and bass, with the addition of a Piano-forte part, or Thorough Bass . . . by C. F. Horn, Music Master to the Royal Family*. Mostly from the *Well-tempered Clavier*, but including the *Fugue in D minor (Dorian)*.
1809–10	*A Trio, Composed originally for the Organ. By John Sebastian Bach, and now Adapted for Three Hands upon the Piano Forte* (Birchall). The Wesley–Horn edition of the six trio sonatas.
1827	*A Grand Fugue by John Sebastian Bach, in three movements and on three subjects, the principal theme being the first four bars of St Ann's Psalm Tune, Arranged for Two Performers on the Organ or Pianoforte . . . by B. Jacob, Organist of St John's Church, Waterloo Bridge Road* (Clementi & Co.). The *Prelude in E flat* (вwv 552i) was reduced to thirty-six bars to form an introduction to the fugue.
1833	*Select Organ Pieces from the Masses, Motetts, and other Sacred Works of . . . classical composers of the German & Italian Schools, arranged . . . by Vincent Novello* (Novello). No. 42 included a 2-stave version of the 'little' *Prelude and Fugue in E minor* (вwv 533), transmitted to Novello by Mendelssohn.
1836	*John Sebastian Bach's Grand Studies for the Organ Consisting of Preludes, Fugues, Toccatas, and Fantasias, Never before Published in this Country. These Studies may be played on the Piano Forte by one or two performers. A separate Part for the Double Bass or Violoncello Arranged from the Pedale by Signor Dragonetti is added to this Edition* (Coventry & Hollier). 17 (19) numbers.
1838	*Choral and Instrumental Fugues of John Sebastian Bach in continuation of the English Edition of his Forty-Eight Preludes and Fugues arranged from his Masses, Litanies, Oratorios and Exercises . . . by Henry John Gauntlett* (Lonsdale). 54 numbers.
1838?	*A Pastoral Symphony, by John Sebastian Bach, edited by Henry John Gauntlett* (Cramer). For two manuals and pedal obligato.
c. 1840	*Prelude and Fugue in C Sharp Minor for the Organ with Obligato pedals by James Stimpson* (Cocks). From the *Well-tempered Clavier*.
1845–6	*John Sebastian Bach's Organ Compositions on Corales (Psalm Tunes), Edited from the Original Manuscripts by Felix Mendelssohn Bartholdy* (Coventry & Hollier, Breitkopf & Härtel). 4 books.
c. 1845	*The Organist's Standard Library, being Selections from the Works of the Great Masters . . . Arranged and performed at the Town Hall, Birmingham, by James Stimpson, Organist of the Town Hall, St Paul's, &c. &c.* (D'Almaine & Co.). Included: *Fugue in G minor*, вwv 542ii (55); *Fugue in D major*, вwv 532ii (82); *Prelude and Fugue in C major*, вwv 545 (100); *Fugue in E flat*, вwv 552ii (118).
c. 1845	*John Sebastian Bach's Fugue on a Chorale in D minor . . . The Giant Fugue . . . edited by George Cooper* (Addison & Hollier). вwv 680.

538) as numbers 2 and 3 of *Toccata et Fugue pour l'Orgue ou le Piano-Forte* (Leipzig, *c.* 1835),[5] and the first number of Haslinger's *Sämmtliche Werke von J. S. Bach* (the *Canonic Variations* was the second) was the *Fugue in C minor* 'on a theme of Legrenzi' (вwv 574). Dunst of Frankfurt issued the *Passacaglia von J. S. Bach* (вwv 582) *c.* 1830. It is possible that Breitkopf & Härtel's edition of *J. S. Bachs [sic] Choral-Vorspiele* (Leipzig, 1806) was known; a remark in one of Samuel Wesley's letters to Benjamin Jacob (1809) implies that Jacob possessed a copy (Wesley 1957: 25–6) but the absence of any reference to the

preludes before the mid-1830s suggests that the *Choral-Vorspiele* had not circulated widely.

Edwards (1896) and Redlich (1952) discuss the publication of the organ works in the context of the wider discovery of Bach by English musicians, and it is not intended to repeat the details here. It is sufficient to observe that publication of reliable editions was hampered until the 1840s by the necessity of adapting the scores to the peculiarities of the long-compass English organ, and it was probably only when continental editions (which had no need to resort to such subterfuge) became more widely known that the true implications of Bach's music for the design of organs became manifest. The earliest publication of a Bach organ piece in England (setting aside the critical question of whether or not it is really organ music at all) was in Kollman's theoretical work, *An Essay on Practical Musical Composition* (1799). This was the first movement of the *Trio Sonata in E flat* (BWV 525), correctly laid out on three staves. A complete edition of the trio sonatas appeared in 1809–10, prepared by Samuel Wesley from a manuscript in the possession of C. F. Horn (MS 66: f. 46). Though it, too, was laid out on three staves, the sonatas were described as being 'adapted for Three Hands upon the Piano Forte'; the editors advised that one player should take the lower two parts at pitch, whilst the second played the upper part an octave higher than written.

Such expedients were necessary in the early-1800s if the works were to be performed at all. Neither the organs nor the repertoire familiar to English organists had prepared them to think it possible for one player to perform such pieces on an organ with pedals. The incredulity with which the first generation of Bach's English disciples gazed upon his pedal parts is nicely captured in Wesley's introductory 'Advertisement' in his edition of the trio sonatas:

The following Trio was designed for the Organ, and performed by the matchless Author in a very extraordinary Manner: the first and second Treble Parts he played with both Hands on two sets of Keys, and the Base [*sic*] (wonderful as it appears) he executed entirely upon the Pedals, without assistance.

In time, this would seem less 'extraordinary' to English organists, and Elizabeth Stirling used Wesley's edition when she included no fewer than three of the trio sonatas in her 1838 recital (Appendix 2, pp. 507–8).

Jacob published his bowdlerised version of the 'St Ann' Fugue (preceded by a 36-bar version of the prelude) in 1827: again, it was intended to be performed as a duet. In 1833, Vincent Novello secured a copy of the *Prelude and Fugue in E minor* (BWV 533) from Mendelssohn and it was included, set out on three staves, in number 42 of his *Select Organ Pieces* – a series which formed the staple of many a mid-Victorian organist's repertoire. It was not, however, Novello, but a neighbouring publishing house, Coventry & Hollier, of 71 Dean Street, Soho, which made the most significant contribution to the spread of Bach's organ music in England.

In 1836, Coventry & Hollier began to issue *John Sebastian Bach's Grand Studies for the Organ*. Although it was announced that these pieces ('never before published in this country') could be played as duets, and although Coventry took the novel step of issuing simultaneously a separate part for the double bass or violoncello arranged from the original pedal parts by Domenico Dragonetti,[6] this was the first English edition of Bach's organ music laid out on three staves and seriously intended for performance on an organ with a proper pedal division. There were, initially, seventeen numbers issued in eight books. The sources are easily identified. The first nine numbers (1–9) were taken from Marx's edition of the 'noch wenig bekannte' organ compositions;[7] the next six (10–15) from the Haslinger edition of the *Sechs Präludien und Fugen*;[8] the remaining two (16–17) from Peter's *Toccata et Fugue*.[9] Two numbers were subsequently added (18–19): the *Fugue in E flat (St Ann)* (BWV 552ii) and the *Prelude and Fugue in G major* (BWV 541). Mendelssohn wrote to Coventry in 1845 with corrections to a copy of the latter (Polko 1869: 247), perhaps in anticipation of its publication. At some stage, it seems that he also offered corrections to nos. 2, 4 and 15 (Edwards 1896: 724–5; *Grand Studies*: 22), and in view of this, it is at least possible that Mendelssohn was involved in the publication from the start. J. Alfred Novello acquired the plates of the edition from Coventry in 1849 or 1851 (Humphries & Smith 1970: 119) and it then appeared under his imprint.

Mendelssohn and Coventry collaborated over another important Bach project in the 1840s. On 29 August 1844, Mendelssohn wrote to Coventry from Frankfort:

According to yr wishes, I send you a copy of the whole of my collection of organ-pieces by Seb. Bach, wh I have carefully looked over and corrected. (1) 15 grand choral Preludes; (2) 44 little choral Preludes; (3) 6 Variations; (4) 11 Variations; (5) 4 Preludes and Fugues. Of the last I think several (if not all) have already been published in Germany or England. Both the Variations, I believe, have never been published, as also the greatest part of the 44 and the 15 Preludes. Perhaps 9 out of these 59 are known; all the rest are not.   (Wallace 1869: 245)

Coventry agreed to publish the first four items[10] and they appeared in 1845–6 as *John Sebastian Bach's Organ Compositions on Corales (Psalm Tunes)*. The edition (which Mendelssohn had prepared 'from the original manuscripts') was published simultaneously by Coventry & Hollier in London, and Breitkopf & Härtel in Leipzig. In addition to the fifty-nine chorale preludes, there were the variations on 'Christ, der du bist der helle Tag' (BWV 766) and 'Sei gegrüsset, Jesu gütig' (BWV 768). The parochialism of the allusion to 'psalm tunes' ought not to disguise the significance of the publication: altogether, it represented a major expansion in the repertoire of Bach's organ music available in England.

Mendelssohn's edition of the *Compositions on Corales* coincided with the inauguration of the Griepenkerl and Roitzsch complete edition of the organ works, published by Peters in Leipzig (1844–52). This was available in England through Ewer & Company, and finally provided English organists with working scores of virtually all Bach's organ music.

The remaining publications in Table 15 need little comment. Gauntlett's *Choral and Instrumental Fugues* (1838) consists largely of arrangements, but includes the *Passacaglia in C minor* (BWV 582), the fugues in *G minor* (BWV 578), *D minor* (BWV 680) and *E flat* (BWV 552) each laid out on two staves, and also a 3-stave version of 'Schmücke dich, o liebe Seele' (BWV 654) with the right-hand part registered for Choir Cremona. The Cooper and Stimpson editions are largely uninformative on matters of registration and dynamics, though Stimpson suggested Full Great and Pedal fluework for the opening section of the 'St Ann', Choir stopped diapason and principal for the middle section, and then Full Great and Pedal with reeds for the concluding section. No doubt that was how he played it at Birmingham Town Hall (of which he was Organist, 1842–86); it may even be how Mendelssohn played it.

PUBLIC PERFORMANCES OF BACH'S ORGAN MUSIC, 1810–45

Until the 1830s, English organists thought of Bach chiefly as the composer of the *Well-tempered Clavier*. It was through the '48' (recommended by George Frederick Pinto) that Samuel Wesley first became acquainted with Bach's 'matchless compositions' (MS 66: f. 42), and he and Horn prepared a 'new and correct edition' which was issued by Birchall in four books between 1810 and 1813.[11] For the next two decades, English organists remained content with this one specimen of Bach's composition; the demands made by the English church service were modest, and, as Williams comments, 'the *Well-tempered Clavier* was a sufficient repertory for most organists' (1963: 145). Wesley's edition of the trio sonatas seems seldom to have found its way into the organ loft, and mention of Bach preludes and fugues in the 1810s and 1820s can be confidently taken to refer, in almost every case, to the '48'.

This is certainly true of a number of organ 'performances' which took place in the years around 1810 under the inspiration of Wesley. The earliest was probably that given in the New Rooms, Hanover Square, in June 1808, when Wesley announced that he would perform 'several admired compositions of the celebrated Sebastian Bach' (Edwards 1896: 654). On that occasion, and subsequently at the Surrey Chapel and the Portuguese Chapel, Wesley, assisted by Jacob or Novello, gave performances of the '48', the trio sonatas, violin sonatas and choral pieces. It was at one of these concerts that a piece of genuine organ music was first placed before the English musical public. Vincent Novello arranged the *Prelude in E flat* from *Clavier-übung III* as an 'Overture' scored for full orchestra and solo organ, and it was performed at Hanover Square on 5 June 1812 with Novello and Wesley playing the organ part as a duet (Edwards 1896: 655). According to Gauntlett, Dr Crotch was the first to give a public performance of the related *Fugue in E flat* ('St Ann') when he gave an account of it on the piano during a lecture at the Surrey Institution in 1816 (Edwards 1896: 723), but there is some evidence that Wesley played it (publicly?) at St Nicholas, Great Yarmouth, in the previous year.[12]

A succeeding generation, characteristically dismissive of the achievements of its forebears, thought little of these pioneering efforts. According to a writer of the 1860s, the credit for introducing Bach's organ music in public performance lay elsewhere: 'the present Dr. Wesley was the first English organist who introduced Bach's fugues to us, and Mr. Gauntlett, his contemporary, followed in his steps' (*Eccl* 26, 1865: 19). Gauntlett himself declined to cede the priority to Wesley. Writing in 1838, he claimed that the introduction 'of Bach's pedal fugues, and their public performance in the metropolis, took its rise about ten or twelve years ago', adding that he and Wesley were the first to give solo performances of the 'St Ann' fugue when each chose to play it at the audition for the organistship of St Stephen, Coleman Street, in 1827 (*MW* IX, 1838: 208). No earlier reference has been traced to a public (organ) performance of organ music by Bach. In the following year, S. S. Wesley performed the preludes in B minor and E minor at Christ Church, Newgate Street (*MW* IX, 1838: 208), and then in 1829, the appearance of an embryonic pedal department in the new organ at St James, Bermondsey, inspired performances of Bach pedal compositions on two separate occasions. The first occurred at the opening of the organ on 23 April, when a trio of players performed (inevitably, one begins to feel) the 'St Ann' fugue – taking advantage of the finger keyboard provided by Bishop to play the pedal registers (*Examiner*, 26 April 1829). The second occasion was the competition for the post of Organist. Of fourteen candidates, five played pieces by Bach. Two, or possibly three of these were fugues from the *Well-tempered Clavier* (Turle, the successful candidate, played the *Prelude and Fugue in F sharp minor*, no. 38), but Gauntlett performed the B minor fugue, the final movement of the C minor trio sonata and (probably) the *Prelude in E flat* from *Clavierübung III* (*MW* IX, 1838: 208; cf. *MT* L, 1909: 518). An unidentified competitor played the 'St Ann'.

Hodges performed the *Fugue in G minor* as a duet at the opening of the new organ in St Stephen's, Bristol, in 1836 (Hodges 1896: 88), but, otherwise, no further public performances of the organ compositions can be traced before 1837 (though Mendelssohn's rendition of various Bach pieces from manuscripts and from memory at St Paul's in 1832 may have been semi-public) (Edwards 1896: 724). 1837, however, proved an *annus mirabilis*. Mendelssohn's two organ performances (at the Birmingham Festival, and Christ Church, Newgate Street) were anticipated by the first of Elizabeth Stirling's remarkable recitals (Appendix 2, p. 507). Even if Miss Stirling's execution left something to be desired (*MW* ix, 1838: 208–11), it is striking that such a programme was being attempted *before* the reception of Mendelssohn's performance at Birmingham gave decisive momentum to the cause of Bach's music in England. Certainly, it confirms the view that the organ works (or some of them) were already known in progressive circles – and not only in London: in June 1837 (again, before Mendelssohn's appearance at Birmingham), another young player, Jeremiah Rogers, included the *Fugue in E major* (BWV 566ii) in his performance at the opening of a new organ in a Sheffield Methodist Chapel (*MW* vi, 1837: 15).

Mendelssohn's public performances of Bach were inaugurated at Birmingham in September 1837. A contemporary report indicates why presentation was so important, if mid-nineteenth-century Englishmen were to become admirers of Bach:

We are not so infatuated as not to know that the complexity of Bach's fugues is not for the public. Their merits are only appreciated by those who have the power of analysing their construction and estimating the skill of working a number of subjects together. Subjects for fugues are often selected by those whose learning is in advance of their genius, not always of the most melodious form, but for their convenience in *inversions*. In this there is little to awaken the attention of the unsophisticated amateur until the climax, when the *pedales*, and figurative counterpoint, employing the entire grasp of the player, produce a mass of rich and effective combination with the entire capacity of the organ which is quite overpowering.

(*ABG*, 25 September 1837)

Evidently, it needed the sensational qualities of the Town Hall organ and the commendation of a public celebrity to convince some people of the merits of Bach; the note sounded by this reviewer of 1837 already explains why exponents of Bach later in the century felt obliged to paint with a rather broad brush, and in bright colours.

Performance and publication complemented one another, and together furthered the introduction of Bach's organ works in England. By 1842, it was possible for the *Fugue in G minor* to appear as a prescribed piece in the competition for the Organistship of Birmingham Town Hall.[13] In a similar competition for the post of Organist at Highgate Parish Church in 1844, it was stipulated that all candidates should perform a Bach fugue; three played the 'St Ann', three the *G minor*, two the *B minor*, and a contemporary commented, 'it is doubtful whether so many of Bach's pedal fugues were ever before played on one day by a collection of English artists' (*MW* xix, 1844: 37).

Table 16 attempts to summarise the evidence for public performances of Bach's organ music between 1810 and 1845. It is by no means definitive. In the early years, details have not been entered if it seems probable that the pieces concerned were from the *Well-tempered Clavier*. By the end of the period, the stimulus of Mendelssohn, and the availability of many of the organ compositions in print, must have meant that there were many more public performances than are recorded here; by the mid-1840s, the performance of a Bach work had ceased to be the novelty that it was reckoned even five years earlier.

FOREIGN TRAVEL

Just as the English attitude to Bach was undergoing a change during the 1830s and 1840s, so, too, the conventional view of continental organs was being scrutinised and questioned in some quarters. The earlier orthodoxy is represented by Burney's complacent reflections (above, p. 163). Burney did not (then) know Bach, and a later generation (which did) took a different view. The experience of playing or hearing any large organ with C-compasses and a proper pedal division was informative for those who had come to an appreciation of Bach's genius, and as communications improved and travel became both cheaper and less arduous a significant number of them ventured abroad. Many were profoundly affected by what they saw and heard. They returned convinced reformers, and through them the influence of, first, Northern and Central Europe, and then France, was brought to bear on English organ design during the decades succeeding 1840.

Camidge was an early musical tourist. It is said that before designing the York organ, he had done 'what probably no other cathedral organist of his time had accomplished – viz. visited most of the great organs on the continent – Haarlem, Rotterdam, Hamburgh, Freyburgh, etc.' (*Organ* III, 1923: 105). The implication is that this expedition took place before plans were laid for the instrument of 1829–33, but Camidge's reconstruction of the old organ six years earlier already reflected an acquaintance with the continental organs and it seems unlikely that this was simply the result of an armchair perusal of Burney's version of the Haarlem specification (Burney 1775: II, 306–7). Haarlem appears to have been the most visited of the continental instruments, at least in the early years before the rival claims of easy travel and Cavaillé-Coll led to a preference for Paris, and Burney's report may have been the reason. A Nottingham organist's impressions have already been reported (above, p. 89), but he was only one among many who made the pilgrimage in the 1820s, 1830s and 1840s. Jonathan Gray was there in 1824 (with Camidge?) on an extended tour which also took in Antwerp, Rotterdam and a number of unspecified organs in France, Germany and Switzerland (Gray 1837: 42); Vincent Novello's diaries reveal evidence of visits to a number of European organs in 1829 (Hughes 1955: *passim*); Cramer undertook a similar tour sometime before 1831 (*MW* IV, 1836–7: 67); and in about 1836, Gauntlett made what may have been his first trip

Table 16 Public performances of Bach's organ compositions: 1810–45

Year	Performer(s)	Items performed	Location	Source
1810	S. Wesley and 'Major'	'Organ Trio' (duet)	Hanover Square Rooms	Edwards 1896: 655
1812	S. Wesley and V. Novello	Prelude in E flat (552ii); arr. by Novello for orchestra and organ duet	Hanover Square Rooms	Edwards 1896: 655
1815	S. Wesley	'the triple fugues in E' (BWV 552ii?)	St Nicholas, Great Yarmouth	MS 64
1816	Dr Crotch	Fugue in E flat (pianoforte arrangement)	Surrey Institution	Edwards 1896: 723
1827	H. J. Gauntlett and S. S. Wesley (severally)	Fugue in E flat (552ii)	St Stephen, Coleman Street	MW ix, 1838: 208; MT L, 1909: 518
1828	S. S. Wesley	Preludes in B minor and E minor	Christ Church, Newgate Street	MW ix, 1838: 208
1829	Blackburn, Sale and McMurdie	Fugue in E flat (trio)	St James, Bermondsey	Examiner 26 April 1829: 263
1829	H. J. Gauntlett	Fugue in B minor, Trio Sonata in C minor (3rd movement), Prelude in E flat	St James, Bermondsey	MW ix, 1838: 208; MT L, 1909: 518
	Unnamed	Fugue in E flat	ditto	ditto
1832	Mendelssohn	'some Manuscripts of Sebastian Bach', and (from memory) the 'little' Fugue in E minor	St Paul's Cathedral	Lampadius 1876: 18; Edwards 1896: 724
1836	E. Hodges and T. H. Crook	Fugue in G minor (duet)	St Stephen, Bristol	Hodges 1896: 88
1837	Jeremiah Rogers	Fugue in E major	Wesleyan Church, Sheffield	MW vi, 1837: 15
	Elizabeth Stirling	See: Appendix 2, p. 507	St Katherine, Regent's Park	MW ix, 1838: 209
	Mendelssohn	Prelude and Fugue in A minor	St Paul's Cathedral	MW vii, 1837: 9
	Mendelssohn	Fugue in A minor	Christ Church, Newgate Street	MP 12 September 1837
	Mendelssohn	Prelude and Fugue in E flat	Birmingham Town Hall	Wallace 1863: 128; ABG 25 September 1837
1838	Elizabeth Stirling	See: Appendix 2, p. 507	St Sepulchre, Holborn	MW ix, 1838: 209
	Elizabeth Stirling	See: Appendix 2, pp. 507–8	ditto	ditto
1839	Josiah Pittman	Prelude in E flat, Prelude and Fugue in E minor	Christ Church, Spitalfields	MW xii, 1839: 186
1840	Mendelssohn	Prelude and Fugue in E minor, Passacaglia in C minor	St Peter, Cornhill	Pearce 1909: 71
1841	Mendelssohn	'something of Sebastian Bach's'	Birmingham Town Hall	Wallace 1869: 232
	H. J. Gauntlett	Fugue in E flat, Fugue in G minor	Great George Street Chapel, Liverpool	GJ 18 December 1841
	candidates for organistship	Fugue in G minor	Birmingham Town Hall	unidentified cutting[a]
1842	Mendelssohn	?	Exeter Hall, Strand	Wallace 1863: 281
	Mendelssohn	?	Christ Church, Newgate Street	MP 20 June 1842; Wallace 1863: 281

1843	Mendelssohn	?	St Peter, Cornhill	MS 68: f. 85
	H. J. Gauntlett	'Toccata and Fugue in A minor' [*sic*]	Edinburgh Music Hall	*MP* 17 October 1843
	George Cooper	*Fugues in E major and D minor*, part of a fantasia	Crosby Hall	*MW* xviii, 1843: 383
1844	candidates for organistship			
	Frederick Gunton	*Fugues in E flat, G minor and B minor*	Highgate Church	*MW* xix, 1844: 37
		Fugue in E flat	Chester Cathedral	*MW* xix, 1844: 10
1845	James Stimpson	*Fugue in D major*	Birmingham Town Hall	*MW* xx, 1845: 103

a Information from an unidentified newspaper cutting in the collection of the Revd B. B. Edmonds.

abroad to hear the same instrument (*DNB* xxi: 74–5). Birmingham's Joseph Moore seems to have followed Camidge's example, and visited a number of continental organs before the contract was placed for the Town Hall organ (Gill 1952: 1, 400). J. W. Fraser (who was later involved in the design of one of the first German System organs, for St Luke, Cheetham Hill, Manchester) was abroad during the 1830s; a letter to Vincent Novello refers to time spent in Italy (MS 65), and at some stage he visited Spain, sending details of the organ in Seville Cathedral to Hill (HR3: 435).

In 1839, Josiah Pittman (Christ Church, Spitalfields) departed for a stay of six months in Germany (*MW* xii, 1839: 186). He may have joined the small band of English organists who studied abroad, and who must, therefore, have had experience of the continental organs. William Rea spent three years on the continent as a pupil of Moscheles, presumably in the early-1840s (*BMB*: 336); George French Flowers was a pupil of Rinck (*MW* x, 1838: 212); Adam Hamilton, brother of David Hamilton the Edinburgh organ-builder, spent four years as a pupil of Schneider (*MW* xvii, 1842: 38). It is not an extensive tally, but there were probably others, and the ready availability of German organ tutors (Williams 1963: 142–3) would have further influenced the climate of opinion towards continental modes of thought and practice.

With the advent of the 1840s, the tours became more extended. E. J. Hopkins made expeditions to inspect organs, and 'he kept diaries of every tour he made, whether at home or abroad' (Pearce 1926: 138).[14] In 1844, he visited France, calling at Amiens, Rouen and finally Paris, where he met Cavaillé-Coll. Eight years later, in 1852, his destination was Germany and his companion Jeremiah Rogers, Organist of Doncaster Parish Church. They played organs in Cologne and Hamburg, and were then met by Edmund Schulze who accompanied them to Lübeck, Wismar and Bremen. The following years saw them in Paris, where they played a number of organs and called on both Cavaillé-Coll and Ducroquet, before proceeding to Strasburg, Frankfurt, Eisenach, Gotha, Weimar, Cologne and Liège. In 1858, they were abroad again, this time in company with Hopkins's brother (John Hopkins, Organist of Rochester Cathedral) and visited Schulze's workshops at Paulinzelle and Walcker's at Ludwigsburg (Pearce 1910: 54–70). Rogers was one of the most enterprising musical tourists of his day. As early as 1843, it was reported that 'he has visited Paris, and all the principal towns in the Netherlands, possessing celebrated organs' (*MW* xviii, 1843: 388), and by the 1860s, in the course of an article discussing the reasons which had led Rogers to commission Schulze to build the new organ for Doncaster Parish Church, a reviewer could write that 'his [sc. Rogers's] organ-mania had, at various times, led him into most corners of Europe, where grand and choice instruments were to be found, and what, between the rival fascination of France and Germany, he had brought home with him a goodly store of intentions to be carried out when time favoured' (*MW* XLI, 1863: 734).

There were others who travelled abroad at this period, and who returned with a 'goodly store of intentions'. Gauntlett made a further trip to the continent in 1842 (*MW* XVII, 1842: 279) when he visited Germany and, it seems probable, France – he had certainly heard St Denis by 1846 (Gauntlett 1846). S. S. Wesley, not noted for breadth of mind in organ matters, expressed the intention of visiting the continent in connection with the plans for the Liverpool organ, and a later reference confirms that he at least got to France (*MG* II, 1857: 77). Henry Smart visited Cavaillé-Coll in 1852, and most probably on other occasions, too (Spark 1881: 288). Charles McKorkell, who was responsible for the setting up of Schulze's Great Exhibition organ in the Northampton Exchange Rooms, was another traveller (*MW* XXXIV, 1856: 471; XXXVIII, 1860: 168). Few, though, could compete with Sir Frederick Arthur Gore Ouseley. He returned to England in the spring of 1848 following a continental tour in the course of which he had played 190 organs (Alden 1944: 98); he made a further extended tour in 1850–1, and it comes as no surprise to learn that Hopkins drew many of the foreign specifications for his book from Ouseley's notebooks (Pearce 1926: 140).

Few organ-builders had time or inclination to venture abroad. David Hamilton, the Scottish builder, was more adventurous than his English counterparts; his *Remarks on organ building* (1851) recorded that 'Mr. Hamilton originally studied Organ-building in Germany, where he resided for a number of years; and he has now been established in this country for upwards of a quarter of a century' – which would imply that Hamilton was working in Germany in the early-1820s. No other British organ-builders are known to have worked abroad. Hill visited the continent at least twice, sometime between 1834 and 1843, and then in the spring of 1847; Cavaillé-Coll wrote a letter of introduction for him on the latter occasion, and it is likely that Hill visited Cavaillé in Paris (*MP* 25 September 1843; Douglass 1980: 1, 225–6). It would be strange if Frederick Davison had not followed Hill to Paris at some stage, but evidence is lacking. Telford of Dublin visited Cavaillé-Coll sometime before 1848, and was greatly impressed by the organ in La Madeleine (1846); it apparently influenced the conception of the Telford organ for Radley College (Alden 1944: 98). Others felt differently. The *Musical World* carried a story of two (unnamed) English organ-builders who, having heard the fame of the instrument in La Madeleine, determined to hear it: they were unimpressed, pronouncing the organ to be 'altogether beastly' and 'a big brass band and nothing more' (XXXI, 1853: 594). Such a response was probably more characteristic of those (the majority) who had not troubled to make the necessary journey in order to confirm their prejudices, but, in general, both organists and organ-builders found these continental outings enlightening. Consequently, it is no exaggeration to suggest that, between 1840 and 1870, English organ-building was more directly influenced by the continent than at any other time between the 1660s and the 1950s.

7

The German System

Enough has now been said to justify the contention that, almost without exception, those organs of the Insular tradition which seem at first glance to be influenced by Dutch or German instruments, reveal upon further enquiry that their authors had only the haziest notion of the fundamental principles of continental organ design. By the late-1830s, the situation was, however, changing. A few English organists, stimulated by the discovery of Bach's organ music and inspired by Mendelssohn, had acquired a more thorough-going appreciation of the continental organs, and it was their influence which led to the rapid emergence during the 1840s of the C-compass organ, with its Pedal division, fully-developed choruses and tonal novelties, and the consequent disappearance within a single generation of the English long-compass organ. The first indications of impending change appeared as early as 1836. Ten years later, many of the most characterisic instruments of this phase of English organ-building had made their appearance, and principles had been laid down from which the more conservative builders would scarcely depart before the 1890s. It was a remarkable achievement.

The credit for this lies chiefly with three men: the organ-builders Frederick Davison and William Hill, and the organist H. J. Gauntlett. It remains uncertain, though, whether any one of these three was responsible for the first appearance of a genuine German System organ in England. In April 1836, a report appeared in the *Morning Post* concerning the instrument built for the forthcoming Exeter Hall Festival:

It has been constructed by Messrs GRAY and SON according to the German mode. It consists of two parts – the chorus or finger organ, containing twelve stops, and the Pedal Organ, which is perfectly independent of the other, containing six stops, viz. four double diapasons and two trombones or double trumpets. The compass of the pedals is the same usually adopted by the Continental Organ Builders, being two octaves from C the four-feet pipe, to C the sixteen feet.   (12 April 1836)

The passage is clear enough, as far as it goes. There is no obvious explanation for the curious duplication in the Pedal Organ, though it was reported that the pedal pipes added 'a breadth and solidity to the base [*sic*] which no number of *contrabassi* performers could equal' (*MP* 12 April 1836): an asset in the accompaniment of large-scale choral performances. The organ was hired from Gray, and was apparently removed and broken up after the Festival. Three years later, on the eve of the emergence of the mature German System movement in England, 'the magnificent pedal organ' of 1836 was recalled wistfully (*MW* XII, 1839: 410).

It is possible (though unlikely) that Gauntlett was behind the construction of the Festival organ. According to an obituary notice, it was in 1836 that he first turned his attention to 'the improvement of the English organ' (*MSt* XIV, 1876: 134); certainly, at the end of that year he gave testimony on behalf of the plaintiffs in the suit over the York Minster organ, and Camidge's correspondence suggests that Gauntlett was by then drawing attention to the superiority of a properly developed chorus over mere duplication as a means of attaining power (Gray 1837: 51).

Against Gauntlett's claim to have introduced the German System to England can be urged that of Frederick Davison. Introducing a set of organ arrangements, George Cooper noted:

> These arrangements will be particularly adapted to organs built on the German Scale, the Manuals of which extend to CC 8 feet, and the Pedals to CCC 16 feet, first introduced in this country by Mr. Davison, and from its evident superiority now becoming generally adopted by the English organ-builders.
> (*Organist's Manual*, 1853: Preface)

Davison was a pupil of Samuel Wesley, through whom he would have made the acquaintance of Bach's organ works, and this may have been the beginning of an interest in the German organ (*MW* VI, 1837: 76). However, he was only twenty-one years old in 1836, and an involvement in the commissioning of the Festival organ seems, in the absence of other evidence, improbable. We are, though, on much more solid ground in turning to the organs built by Davison during his short-lived partnership with Hill (1837–8). Among them are three instruments which may legitimately be identified as forerunners of the German System organs of the following decade, though (perhaps significantly) having more in common with Gray & Davison's output than with Hill's.

In March 1838, the *Musical World* contained an announcement that 'Messrs. Hill and Davison have just completed a small pedal organ, built under the direction of Mr. Gauntlett, on the German scale, for the parish church of Turvey, Beds.' (VIII: 185). A later notice reported that the organ had been opened by Gauntlett at the end of March and gave a little more detail: it had C-compass manuals, a separate set of pedal pipes, and was the gift of Miss Ann Maria Higgins of Turvey House (VIII: 221). Nothing more is known about the instrument. Gauntlett had been brought up at Olney, a few miles from Turvey, and this must explain his involvement; a 'small' organ would offer no real scope for radical tonal innovations, and it is probable that at this early stage in his career, Gauntlett's efforts were concentrated upon establishing the C-compass and a modest degree of Pedal independence.

More is known about the second of these C-compass organs. This was for St John's, Chester. A report in the *Musical World* spoke enthusiastically of the instrument and of the principles upon which it was built:

In accordance with the feeling so universally prevalent for the adoption of the compass and scale of the German organ, and with a desire to afford every facility for the easy as well as just performance of the organ music of Bach and Mendelssohn, Mr. Davison has drawn out a plan for the building a complete instrument, having the manuals to C the 8 feet pipe, and a separate pedal organ of two octaves, extending to C the 16 feet.   (IX, 1838: 249)

It was blatantly untrue that there was a widespread (let alone universal) preference for C-compasses and Pedal Organs, but the Chester instrument was undeniably a landmark (Appendix 1, pp. 459–60). The tonal scheme of the three manual divisions can hardly be distinguished from that of any other large organ of the 1830s, but the adoption of C-compasses and the provision of an independent Pedal Organ are highly significant, associated as they must be with the remarks about Bach and Mendelssohn. True, there were still compromises. The independence of the Pedal was curtailed by an exclusive reliance upon 16' registers, and the provision of an octave coupler (which was necessarily only of use in the lowest octave) seems to hark back to the fashion for a ponderous bass, but each of the Pedal registers had its full complement of pipes (cf. Exeter Hall, 1840) and the two octaves of pedals enabled the player, with a little ingenuity, to make sense of at least some of Bach's pedal compositions. The *Musical World* was guilty of only slight exaggeration when it claimed that the Chester organ held out 'advantages superior to any other instrument in this country' (*MW* x, 1838: 44).

The relationship of the Chester organ to the organ which Hill & Davison provided for Victoria's Coronation in June 1838 is obsure. In order to accommodate a large band of singers and instrumentalists, the Abbey organ was dismantled and a temporary 'orchestra' erected over and above the screen. The Coronation organ stood at the top of this tiered staging, technically in the nave, and because Sir George Smart who was in charge of the musical arrangements was also to be the organist (a cause of ill-natured comment in the *Musical World*) it was necessary that a long movement be provided. The parallel with a festival organ is inescapable, and is sustained by the fact that the specification included 'three metal open diapasons of large scale, the largest being a similar one to the enormous pipes in the Birmingham organ' (*MW* IX, 1838: 171). However, in other respects, the organ was progressive in design, as a description makes clear:

There are twenty ranks of pipes to each note on the manuals which extend to CC, the 8-foot pipe, and six ranks to each pedal which includes two octaves from CCC, the 16-feet pipe, to C the 4-feet. The compass of the manuals is the same as that adopted by the German organ builders, and the pedal board runs throughout two octaves. The trombone or posaune stop in the pedal is of very fine quality of tone and immense power. The diapasons are rich and massive, the mixtures sparkling and brilliant.

(*MW* IX, 1838: 155)

The 6-stop Pedal is puzzling: *were* there six independent stops, or were there three and an octave coupler? Another obscurity is the number of manuals. With twenty stops, there may have been three, but in view of the evident desire to develop a chorus organ, two is perhaps more probable.

The Coronation Organ incorporated parts of the Chester organ: precisely which, is not known, but quite likely action, frame and soundboards were utilised.[1] Following the service at the Abbey, the Dean and Chapter laid claim to the instrument on the grounds that it stood outside the Choir and so remained within their jurisdiction and not the Earl Marshal's; the matter was eventually resolved by the Government making a payment of £500 to redeem it (*MW* IX, 1838: 201, 217), but not before Davison had been obliged to write to Chester, confessing the reason for the delay in delivering the new organ (MS 12: 21). The motives for the original decision to make use of the Chester organ can easily be imagined. The instrument was already under construction when the order was given for the Coronation Organ, only six weeks before the service. It seems that the builders decided to make a virtue of necessity (solving their difficulties and at the same time publicising the new mode of organ) by 'borrowing' the half-finished Chester organ to form the basis of a temporary organ 'upon the German plan' for the Abbey. With a shrewd business sense, they could pay Chester the compliment of supplying an organ which had been used at the Coronation and still sell off the remaining parts as 'The Coronation Organ' (*MW* IX, 1838: 171).

Davison's partnership with Hill came to an end before the Chester organ was completed; it was Hill who erected the organ, and Gauntlett ('the Pedallist of London') who gave an 'organ performance' on 29 October 1838 (Mathew 1952: 174). Whether or not the dissolution of the partnership is simply to be explained by Davison's marriage to John Gray's daughter is unclear; at times, in the future, there would be an asperity in the relations of Hill and Gray & Davison which hints at something over and above healthy commercial rivalry. It may be that this impression is deceptive, and that the apparent animosity has more to do with the partisans of each firm. Gray had a close association with George Cooper, and Hill with Dr Gauntlett: everything suggests that these two strong-minded men detested one another, and perhaps, as influential London musicians, they managed to involve others in their feud, including the organ-builders whom they patronised. To some extent, this must be true, for Hill's organs of the 1840s are radically different

from the handful of C-compass instruments built during the partnership
with Davison and bear Gauntlett's unmistakable stamp. These instruments
(like their author) provoked decisive reactions, and we must now consider
them in detail.

GAUNTLETT

When Gauntlett died in 1876, an obituary notice described him as one of 'the
old type of British worthies, full of learning, common sense, vehemence, and
dogmatism' (*MSt* x, N.S., 1876: 134). Gauntlett's writings, scattered
throughout the musical and artistic publications of the day, bear ample
witness to the two latter characteristics, and his articles on Beethoven and
lectures on ecclesiastical music composed during the 1830s laid the foundation of a deserved reputation for learning: common sense is more elusive. It is
inescapable that in an age of strong characters and decided opinions,
Gauntlett expressed his views with an ardour and conviction deeply resent-
ful of (but quite impervious to) criticism. The man 'morally elbowed his way
through adverse criticism, utterly unconscious that in pressing a strong
opinion he was offending delicate susceptibilities' (*ibid.*). He was a vigorous
upholder of Protestantism (not, probably, Victorian Evangelicalism, with
its tendency to sentimentalism, but a manly Christianity rooted in Luther's
protest against a decadent Catholicism) and was profoundly suspicious of
any symptoms of aestheticism in worship:

> He had a natural aversion to . . . artificial forms of feeling . . . He was intolerant of the
> ecstatic, and barely tolerant of fancy in natures more delicate and effeminate than
> his own. The sorrows of Hagar would move him too deeply to allow his attention to
> be divided by the scenery of the wilderness. In that respect he at once parted from
> the poetical and picturesque aspirations of the newer generation of musicians. The
> intense Protestant feeling, rather than the realistic poetry, of Sebastian Bach was the
> attraction which led him early to the study of that master, the fibre of whose choral
> songs he worked up in his own psalmody.   (*ibid.*)

This fusion of the impregnable assurance of John Bull with the evangelical
zeal of an Old Testament prophet made Gauntlett as formidable as it made
him (in some quarters) unpopular.

   Gauntlett (Plate 26) received no formal musical education, having originally been intended for the legal profession by his father. This exposed him
to a variety of slighting remarks in the course of his numerous literary
controversies, and probably aggravated a naturally combative nature. He
was born in 1805, son of the Reverend Henry Gauntlett, and learnt to play
the organ at the age of nine when his father required an organist to play in his
church at Olney, Buckinghamshire. Despite the encouragement of Attwood
and Crotch, the father declined to permit the son to pursue a musical career,

26 H. J. Gauntlett (1805–76). A portrait of *c.* 1840, reproduced by kind permission of the Royal College of Organists.

and in 1826, young Gauntlett was articled to a London solicitor. He duly qualified in 1834 (Bishop 1968: 10) but, in the meantime, kept up his playing, and made a name as one of the leading organists in the metropolis. He became Organist of St Olave, Southwark (1827), had lessons with Samuel Wesley, met Mendelssohn, and embarked on a career in musical journalism. For a brief time (1837–8?) he was editor of the *Musical World*, but either his trenchant criticisms or a disagreement with the proprietor (perhaps both) led to his removal; for some years thereafter, the journal indulged in occasional vituperative attacks on its former editor.[2] In 1843 (Bishop 1968: 23) Gauntlett became one of the first musicians since the Reformation to receive a Lambeth Mus.D., and if this is unexpected in view of the ease with which Gauntlett aroused the enmity of the musical establishment, it warns the modern reader, bemused by Gauntlett's literary pedantry and repelled by his sarcasms, against underrating the man. Perhaps feeling that the award of a doctorate finally established his credentials as a musician, he gave up the practice of the law at about this time, and henceforth devoted himself to performance, composition, musical journalism and the compilation of books of psalmody and hymnody. He resigned his posts at St Olave and Christ Church, Newgate Street, in 1846, and thereafter only held organistships sporadically: Union Chapel, Islington (1853–61), All Saints, Notting Hill (1861–3), St Bartholomew the Less (1872–6) (*MSt* x, N.S., 1876: 134; *DNB* xxi: 74–6; Dawe 1983: 100). Gauntlett's close association with Mendelssohn has already been mentioned (above, p. 165). The German's tribute to Gauntlett's multifarious achievements should be weighed carefully against the less favourable impression created by the literary effusions of an eccentric and complex character: 'His literary attainments, his knowledge of the history of music, his acquaintance with acoustical law, his marvellous memory, his philosophical turn of mind as well as practical experience – *these* render him one of the most remarkable professors of the age' (*Athenaeum*, no. 2522, 26 February 1876: 306).

Among those achievements, none has proved more enduring than Gauntlett's contribution to the reform of the English organ. Indeed, to describe it as a 'contribution' is an injustice to Gauntlett. For a few crucial years in the early-1840s he supplied the imagination and the driving force needed to supplant the inherited models with something radically different. By insisting on C-compasses, developing the Pedal division, extending the principal manual choruses, greatly expanding the expressive powers of the instrument, deploying a wide selection of novel flutes, strings and reeds, and experimenting with wind pressures, Gauntlett (in collaboration chiefly with Hill) may be said to have delineated the principal features of the mature Victorian organ. Not content with this, he took out a patent in 1852 for the application of electricity to organ actions (*LJA* xlii, 1853: 169–73), and so anticipated a leading preoccupation of organ-builders in the first half of the present century, too.

Gauntlett's crusade was inaugurated in 1838 with the building of the small organ 'on the German scale' for Turvey and the much more ambitious reconstruction of the instrument in Christ Church, Newgate Street (Plate 27). Gauntlett had been appointed evening organist at Christ Church in 1836, and although the organ was regarded as one of the best in London (not least, in having recently been extensively reconstructed) it may have been the deficiencies of this instrument, in both the accompaniment of a congregation and the performance of Bach's organ music, which led Gauntlett to commence his agitation for reform. The speed with which he accomplished his object was remarkable. By his own account, he 'set to work with the

27 Christ Church, Newgate Street, William Hill, 1838. (1911)

Table 17 *Organs designed by Gauntlett, 1838–49*

1838	Turvey Parish Church	Hill & Davison
	Christ Church, Newgate Street [rebuild]	Hill
1840	St Luke, Cheetham Hill, Manchester	Hill
	St Peter-upon-Cornhill	Hill
	Ewelme Parish Church	Hill
1841	Great George Street Chapel, Liverpool	Hill
	Stanwix Parish Church	Hill
	Stratford-upon-Avon Parish Church	Hill
1842	Crosby Hall, London	Lincoln
	Wivenhoe Parish Church	Flight
	St Thomas the Rolls Chapel, London	Lincoln
1843	Liverpool, Mechanics' Institute (?)	Hill
	St Petersburg, British Embassy Chapel	Hill
	Edinburgh Music Hall	Hill
	Birmingham Town Hall [rebuild]	Hill
	St Paul, Withington, Manchester	Lincoln
1844	Calcutta, St John (?)	Hill
1845	Ashton-under-Lyne	Hill
1846	St Olave, Southwark	Lincoln/Hill
1849	Mechanics' Institute, Nottingham	Bevington

organ and was for some years daily in the organ manufactory' (Grace 1934: 199); 'some years' embraced, at most, a decade (1836–46), by the end of which the character of the English organ as made by its leading builder (and, increasingly, by others) had been radically altered. During those ten years, Gauntlett is known to have been responsible for the design of eighteen (probably twenty) organs, most of them built by Hill, but including others by Flight, Lincoln and Bevington (Table 17). One was a barrel organ (Ewelme), another was a small one-manual (Wivenhoe), but most were ambitious instruments of great originality, incorporating tonal and mechanical novelties which at once set them apart from anything attempted by English organ-builders in the past. All had C-compasses and all (with the possible exception of the three small organs built in 1842) had at least two octaves of pedals. It may be that other organs should be added to this list. Hill's instruments for Sheffield (1840), Worcester (1842), Stalybridge (1844) and Bradford (1845), bear all Gauntlett's hallmarks: whether direct or indirect, the influence is undeniable.

Gauntlett's fertile imagination was responsible for a bewildering variety of innovations and his schemes at times approached perilously close to the boundary between the practical and the impractical. But for all their diversity, Gauntlett's organs may be catalogued under two headings which he himself suggested. The first is found in an unidentified newspaper cutting, probably of 1843, in which Gauntlett advertised the merits of 'The Anglo-Lutheran or Protestant Organ' (MS 86). The second is 'The Concerto Organ', Gauntlett's own term for the Edinburgh Music Hall organ (1843).

The grandiloquent phrases are wholly characteristic; they describe, respectively, the church organ and the concert organ.

Gauntlett's promotion of the 'Protestant Organ' complemented his passionate commitment to the reform of congregational psalmody. Like Hodges, he deplored the state of congregational music in the Established Church, and its improvement was a life-long preoccupation. He compiled a number of extensive and influential collections of music for congregational use (hymns, psalms and plainsong), composed many hundreds of hymn tunes, and earned a high reputation for his conduct of the weekly congregational singing classes whilst Organist of Union Chapel (*MT* xvii, 1876: 396; Bishop 1971: 3). The singing of a large congregation required adequate musical support from the organ: as Gauntlett put it, 'where is heard the voice of "the great congregation", there must be also heard what Maister [*sic*] Mace has styled "the great congregational chorus" of the organ to lead and support it'. This was not to be provided by 'the light accompaniment organ' normally found in English parish churches. Rather, it was necessary to look abroad: 'the great psalmodic organ of Germany will be found the only genuine auxillary to a noble and heart-stirring hymnology' (Gauntlett 1846). Hill's *Circular* of 1841 indicates that he and Gauntlett understood the effectiveness of the German organ to derive from its amalgamation of 'the weight of tone necessary to form the foundation of a Grand Organ' with 'those brilliant and silvery qualities of tone which give life and animation to the *ensemble*'. The provision of an adequate Pedal division was a further vital component. Hill had 'increased the extent of the pedal board, which now embraces two octaves and two notes (from CCC to D), a compass which is required in the execution of the music of Sebastian Bach' (*Circular*). It was not, though, solely a matter of compass. The Pedal in the German organ was, as another writer (possibly Henry Smart) commented, to be 'a third and independent source of power, whereby to accomplish clear and otherwise impracticable combinations of parts, and extended and powerful forms of harmony' (*MW* xiii, 1840: 315). By imitating the chorus structure and disposition of 'the great psalmodic organ of Germany', Hill and Gauntlett's Protestant Organ strove to meet the needs alike of Protestant congregations and of Protestantism's greatest composer.

Beginning with Christ Church, Newgate Street (1838), all the church organs built or rebuilt under Gauntlett's influence illustrate these principles; manual choruses with mixtures, mutations and sub-unisons, and Pedal divisions of varying degrees of independence but mostly with weighty 16′ registers of their own, consistently appear in the organs of the early-1840s. The most ambitious of Gauntlett's realised schemes was that begun by H. C. Lincoln and completed by Hill for St Olave's, Southwark (1844–6) (Appendix 2, pp. 508–10). Constrained by limited funds (£500 'for the musical portion of the instrument') and considering 'the requirements of a large school, and numerous congregation', Gauntlett determined to throw the available resources into the development of 'the great, or chorus organ'. There is a hint of controversy in his further explanation for this decision:

It is a generally received opinion that the erection in England of the congregational organ of Holland and Germany was impossible, owing to its great cost, and Dr Gauntlett was anxious to demonstrate that by confining the attention of the builders to one prominent detail of the great German organ, its more important features might be developed in this country at comparatively a small expense.

(Gauntlett 1846)

The result was a vast 27-stop Great Organ, with a short-compass, 10-stop Swell, and Pedal Organ of three stops. Gauntlett intended that the main chorus 'should excel anything that had yet been attempted in the metropolis', and (on paper at least) he succeeded. The Great included a 32' 'Untersatz', the chorus consisted of no fewer than seventeen ranks, and, should this prove deficient, there was the 'Corno par premier force' (a posaune) to add its 'extraordinary breadth' to the general effect. Gauntlett professed himself satisfied with the result, declaring that 'a more magnificent chorus organ does not exist in any metropolitan or suburban church' (Gauntlett 1846).

An unexecuted scheme for the Surrey Chapel (1841?) represents a full working out of the principles partially realised in the St Olave's organ (Warren 1842: 82–3); the Great is similar, though it includes the 16' reed that Gauntlett was obliged to omit at St Olave's, but there is also a 12-stop Pedal, and a full-compass, 23-stop Swell, with an 11-stop flue chorus and a battery of six chorus reeds. Gauntlett had achieved 'the union of the equally-sized swell and grand organs' at Cornhill (Gauntlett 1846), and it was a standard feature of instruments designed by him when funds permitted; what is not clear is whether he viewed a complete but enclosed 'chorus organ' as an essential requirement for congregational accompaniment, or whether its provision was more with an eye to the use of the organ as an orchestral substitute. The design for the organ at Stanwix (a large, one-manual organ in a swell box) and Hill's construction of at least twelve other totally enclosed organs for churches (below, pp. 208–9), implies that Gauntlett had no objection to a congregational organ being enclosed in a swell box, and may have seen positive advantages in this arrangement. He may have been responsible for the 2-manual, totally enclosed organ which Hill built for All Saints, Gordon Square (1846), and in the following year, he certainly asked Hill for further estimates for organs of this sort (MS 12: 221). To a later generation, it seems sheer perversity to design a complete flue chorus with the intention of accompanying a congregation, and then enclose it in a swell box, but the progressive organist of the mid-nineteenth century had no such difficulty in reconciling his new-found belief in the importance of a complete flue chorus with an enthusiasm for expressive effects.

These principles were taken a stage further in the development of the

'Concerto Organ'. The term was used to describe Hill's instrument for the Edinburgh Music Hall (1843) (*MW* xviii, 1843: 390). In view of Gauntlett's employment elsewhere of the phrase 'concerted music' (*MP* 1 January 1842), and his reference to an organ recital as a 'concerto organ perform-ance' (*MW* ix, 1838: 208), it seems that the Concerto Organ was simply a concert organ, the term usefully serving to distinguish it from the Protestant Organ intended for church use. Just as the peculiar quality of the Protestant Organ was its ability to accompany congregational singing, so the most distinctive feature of the Concerto Organ was its facility for orchestral effect.

Gauntlett clearly felt that the performance of orchestral and vocal pieces on the organ was not only a legitimate branch of the organist's art, but one which grew naturally out of the character of the organ as a musical instru-ment. In the *Advertisement* appended to his *Choral and Instrumental Fugues of Handel* (an edition issued *c*. 1845) he stated his view that it was to a large extent the innovations of the German System that had made it possible to realise the organ's potential in this respect by making it a more flexible and diverse instrument, and in support of his opinion he drew attention to four features of contemporary design:

. . . the great improvements which have taken place in the mechanical construction of this instrument within these few years; the increased volume of tone given to the unison stops; the facilities afforded by numerous contrivances for the production of grand Orchestral effects; and above all the use of the Pedal Organ which now happily so universally obtains amongst the rising members of the profession.

It is interesting that Gauntlett refers to the pieces as being arranged for the organ 'with a view to obtain as great an orchestral effect as is consistent with the character of that Instrument' (title page), but it remains unclear pre-cisely what opportunities and limitations he understood this 'character' to imply. He suggests that the performer should indulge in double pedalling wherever possible ('more particularly in those phrases which abound in rich and massive harmonies') and states that the player who enjoys the use of a 'venetian swell throughout the great organ' (a reference to the totally enclosed organs of the 1840s) or finds himself with a Swell to Great coupler will experience 'little or no difficulty . . . in the due expression of each movement' (*Advertisement*), but otherwise he leaves matters largely to the taste and imagination of individual organists; most of the arrangements are disposed on two staves and there are few detailed registrations.

A comparison of the Edinburgh organ and the instrument built by Hill for Worcester Cathedral in the previous year (1842) will throw further light on Gauntlett's ideas (Appendix 1, pp. 461–2 and 460–1). The organs were of much the same size, but one was for church use, the other for concert performance. The similarities are considerable, and this makes the differ-ences all the more significant. The Great and Swell divisions are virtually identical; Edinburgh had no need of a second open diapason to sit in the west front of the case, and the Swell dulciana (which had a function in the accompaniment of a small cathedral choir) was also dispensed with. The most striking differences between the two schemes lie in the Choir and Pedal divisions. With the exception of the oboe flute and the claribella treble to the stopped diapason, the 7-stop Worcester Choir Organ remains the conventional English model, appropriated to the accompaniment of singers. The Edinburgh Choir is entirely modern in conception – an 11-stop palette of 'fancy stops' designed to simulate orchestral effects. The two Pedal Organs offer a similarly telling contrast. By analogy with the 'Bach, or Lutheran Plan' (Hill's own description of the principles underlying the development of the Worcester scheme) (MS 86: unidentified cutting) the cathedral organ was equipped with a complete Pedal chorus to sustain an independent bass line; in the Concerto Organ, with its primary functions of choral accompaniment and the performance of transcriptions, the principal task of the Pedal was to lend weight to the bass – hence, three 16' registers sufficed.

Two other schemes for large Concerto Organs survive to cast light on Gauntlett's thinking. The first is the original proposal for Edinburgh (Warren 1842: 87–9) – a huge affair, with seventy-five stops. Both Great and Swell have complete flue and reed choruses, accompanied by a generous provision of flute novelties; the Pedal choruses match them in scope. There is, however, no conventional Choir Organ. In its place, Gauntlett specified a 9-stop 'Chamber Organ', of similar design to an 1840s Choir, and presumably intended to serve as a continuo division for the accompaniment of solo voices. There was, in addition, a 13-stop Solo Organ: aptly named, for it is an unashamedly orchestral division, with the majority of stops at unison pitch and no evidence of any attempt to provide a chorus. It was to include a 'Regal, or Violin Reed', an 'Ophicleide (on a separate sound-board)', a glockenspiel, gemshorn, rohr-flute and vox humana. The second proposal was for Birmingham Town Hall, and was drawn up in 1842 (Thistlethwaite 1984: 14–15). It is a little larger than the Edinburgh scheme (eighty stops), but rather more orderly. Great and Pedal are classic Hill divisions, with (probably) thirteen ranks of mixtures on the Great and a complete 32' reed chorus on the Pedal. The Swell is unusual in that Gauntlett intended the upperwork of the flue chorus (which is not as extensive as in the Edinburgh scheme) to draw in separate ranks up to the twenty-ninth: probably an interest in acoustical theory accounts for this, rather than any desire to imitate Hodges. There is a particularly extensive Choir Organ, in which the conventional scheme of the period is expanded to incorporate fancy stops, two mixtures and mutation reeds ('Twelfth Trumpet' and 'Tierce Trumpet'). The Solo division resembles that intended for Edinburgh.

Neither scheme was realised, and in each instance a smaller and less expensive proposal was accepted. But there was one other Concerto Organ built: not by Hill, but by Bevington. This was the organ for the Mechanics' Hall, Nottingham, completed in 1849 (Appendix 1, pp. 462–3).

The specification bears a family likeness to the other schemes that have been discussed, with large Great and Swell divisions, liberally furnished with mutations, mixtures and reeds. These take priority over the development of the Pedal Organ, which has just three stops. Despite its description as the 'Solo or Choir Organ', the third manual division was really the former: a Solo Organ with no metal diapasons and no attempt at chorus structure. The high-pressure reed was played from the Great. There are precedents for all these features in Gauntlett's earlier work. There was, though, an innovation of some importance. According to a contemporary newspaper report,

> . . . the Swell organ . . . is of great weight of tone, of great brilliancy, and of more power than many very large organs. It is, we hear, constructed on a design of Dr. Gauntlett's, and blown by an unusual pressure of wind, nearly three times the force of an ordinary church organ. Notwithstanding it is as delicate and as pure in tone as if of the ordinary force of wind, and it is only when the shutters of the box are opened that the great power is observable.   (*Nottingham Review*, 19 October 1849)

This is further evidence of Gauntlett's preoccupation with the expressive possibilities of the organ, and has to be set alongside his equal insistence upon the importance of chorus work. He had proposed placing the Swell at St Olave's on 'a strong weight of wind', and providing 'a large wooden tube to convey the sound into the belfry . . . [the] swell when open would cause a very distant effect, and when closed bring an extraordinary column [*sic*] of sound into the church', but was prevented by lack of funds (Gauntlett 1846). This fascination with expression is characteristic of the period, just as it is characteristic of Gauntlett to have carried the principle further than anyone else; in experimenting with the placing of a complete division of the organ on a substantially higher pressure of wind than the others, he anticipated the work of Willis (and ultimately Hope-Jones) later in the century.

The essentially classical inspiration of the Protestant Organ and the avowedly orchestral character of the Concerto Organ must always have been at odds with one another (the distinction between the two could not always be drawn) and it seems that as the years passed the tension became more marked. Gauntlett's last recorded submission to Hill (1853) is an eccentric scheme for a large 2-manual organ of twenty-three stops (destination unspecified) in which the flue chorus of the Swell has disintegrated and each division is to be enclosed in a swell box. Novelties – a vox angelica, harmonic flute and tuba mirabilis (Great); contra bourdon 32′ and (16′) cornet v (Swell) – make their appearance, but there are no Pedal stops (ms 12: 311). Together with his contemporary interest in electric actions, this curious scheme identifies Gauntlett as a typical Victorian: a radical spirit, with a firm belief, not only in the possibility, but in the moral rightness of progress; if this makes him a less congenial figure to a generation which has lost such assurances, and which views the orchestral aspirations of the

Concerto Organ with suspicion, it places him correctly in his historical context.

The little that can be recovered of Gauntlett's performance practice bears out his conviction of the legitimacy of orchestral effects on the organ. It is, however, important to recall his qualification that such effects should only be carried to an extent 'consistent with the character of the instrument'. It is not clear what Gauntlett meant by this, and a contemporary account of his performance at the opening of the Great George Street Chapel organ suggests that a comparison between Gauntlett's use of the solo stops and the orchestral use of the instruments themselves left something to be desired (*GJ* 18 December 1841). An account in the *Morning Post* of the opening perform-ances at Edinburgh testifies to Gauntlett's orchestral approach in the play-ing of variations and transcribed vocal pieces. It was reported that 'there are some beautiful tones in the softer stops, and they told well in some Scotch airs played by Dr. Gauntlett'; in the final concert, 'Dr. Gauntlett played with great effect, commencing with an introduction, and then gliding into Han-dell's [*sic*] *Harmonious Blacksmith* which he varied on all the soft stops, the corno-flute of which was much admired' (*MP* 17 October 1843). Others were less impressed. The *Musical World* no doubt took great pleasure in publishing a satirical letter concerning the same Edinburgh performances. The writer criticised Gauntlett's irregular tempo in a Bach fugue, and continued:

A chorus, an overture, or a symphony, was performed with equal freedom from the fetters of time and of score, and in these instances the incessant changes of stops were marvellous. Sometimes the Tierce would pipe its shrill solo, or would be coupled with a Diapason Stop; anon, some grotesque combination of the mixture stops would follow, making the graceful music of Haydn or Mozart wear very motley garb. Indeed 'motley is the only wear' for the 'Concerto Organ'. One accessary [*sic*] alone was wanting to render the performance perfect, and which the incessant jerkings of the performer's head to this side or that, sufficiently indicated his habit of using, viz. a cap and bells.   (XVIII, 1843: 412)

Despite its hostility, this passage is evidence that Gauntlett's registration practice represented a novelty in its day. Aided by Hill's realisation of his intentions, Gauntlett not only succeeded in transforming the design of the English organ, but also paved the way for the 'literalistic' orchestral per-formances of the next generation of players. As both player and designer, Gauntlett has the strongest claim to be considered the 'father' of the Victorian organ.

HILL

We are fortunate in possessing William Hill's own account of the introduc-tion of the German System. Written in 1841, whilst Hill was working on the organ for the Great George Street Chapel, Liverpool, it forms the preface to a business circular issued in August of that year; as a succinct account of the general principles which lay behind the German System and of Hill's particular contribution to its development in the early stages, it could hardly be bettered (Appendix 2, pp. 510–11). Some matters, though, remain obscure. Gauntlett is mentioned as the designer of the organs for Newgate Street, Cornhill and Liverpool, but the real extent of his influence is only hinted at, when Hill acknowledges the assistance of 'eminent professors and amateurs' in the development of his recent organs; it is, he assures the reader, 'only by the union of musical with mechanical skill, that this most noble and commanding of instruments can be brought to perfection'. The distinction is difficult to draw: it is certain that Gauntlett's influence went beyond the purely musical to embrace all aspects of the organ's construction, and equally certain that Hill himself soon formed clear ideas about the tonal design of this new breed of instrument – ideas that distinguish those organs built independently of Gauntlett from those built in collaboration. That Hill was a restraining influence may perhaps be deduced from the fact that Gauntlett seldom succeeded in imposing his idiosyncratic nomenclature in its entirety on a Hill organ; though 'Unison open' (open diapason), 'Unison closed' (stopped diapason) and 'Duodecima' (twelfth) found their way into the Edinburgh Music Hall organ, it is necessary to turn to H. C. Lincoln's organ at St Olave's to see where Gauntlett's flights of fancy might lead: 'Diapente' (quint), 'Quintadecima' (fifteenth), 'Corno du Chant' (corno-pean) and 'Larigot and Sedecima' (mixture) appear to bewilder the unsus-pecting organist.[3] Hill usually managed to retain conventional nomencla-ture (for conventional registers), and in so doing illuminated the true nature of his collaboration with Gauntlett: Gauntlett's ideas were stimulating; he succeeded in provoking the most radical change in English organ-building for two centuries; his musical knowledge and his experience of foreign organs were of immense value. But it was Hill who gave practical shape to Gaunt-lett's proposals, and who, in the organs built after Gauntlett had largely withdrawn from an active part in organ design, gave expression to stylistic principles which would govern his own work, and that of his son and grandson, into the early-1900s.[4]

The practical consequences of Hill's claim to have taken up 'the principles adopted by the celebrated Organ Builders of Germany, in the compass of the manuals, and the mode of the blending of the stops' (Circular 1841) may be quickly grasped by studying synoptic specifications of the most important instruments built by the firm between 1838 and 1860 (Table 18). With the single exception of St Philip, Sheffield, all these organs had two complete choruses, one unenclosed and one enclosed, with sub-unisons and mixtures. The unenclosed chorus frequently incorporated mutations as well: a twelfth and (in some early examples) a tierce, but also the 16' mutations ($5\frac{1}{3}'$, $3\frac{1}{5}'$)

Table 18 *Synoptic specifications of Hill organs, 1838–60*

		Great	Swell	Choir	Pedal
1838	Christ Church, Newgate Street	16.8.8.8.4.2⅔.2.V.V.II.8.8.4	16.8.8.4.4.2.V.8.8.4	8.8.4.4.2	16.16.16.8.5⅓.4.V.V.16.8
1840	St Luke, Cheetham Hill	16/16.8.8.8.4.2⅔.2.I.III.II.8	16/16.8.8.4.II.8.8	8.8.8.8.4.4.4.2.2.8	16.16.16
	St Peter-upon-Cornhill	16/16.8.8/8.8.8.4.4.4.4.2⅔.2.1⅗.II.II.II.8.4.8	16/16.8.8/8.8.4.4.4.2⅔.2.2.III.II.V.8.8.8.4		16.16
	St Philip, Sheffield	16/16.8.8.5⅓.4.2⅔.2.I.III.II.8	8.8.4.II.8.8	8.8.4.4.4.2.2.8	16.8.16
1841	Stratford-upon-Avon	16/16.8.8/8.8.5⅓.4.4.4.2⅔.2.I.III.II.8.4.8	16/16.8.8/8.4.4.2.II.V.8.8		16.16.8.4.V.16
	Great George Street Chapel, Liverpool	16/16.8.8.8/8.5⅓.4.4.2⅔.2.1⅗.II.II.II.8.4.2	16/16.8.8/8.8.4.4.2⅔.2.2.III.II.V.16.8.8.8.4.8.8	8.8.8.4.4.2.8.8	(32.)16.16.16
1842	Worcester Cathedral	16/16.8.8.8.5⅓.4.4.2⅔.2.III.II.II.8	16.8.8.8.4.4.2.II.V.8.8	8/8.8.4.4.4.2.8	16.16.8.4.V.16
1843	Mechanics' Institute, Liverpool	16/16.8.8.8/8.8.5⅓.4.4.3⅕.2⅔.2.III.II.8.8	16.8.8/8.8.4.4.2.2.I.V.8.8.4		16.16
	Birmingham Town Hall	16.8.8.8.8.5⅓.4.4.2⅔.2.II.V.III.V.16.8.4.2.8	16.8.8.4.2.V.8.8.4	8.8.8.4.4.4.4.2.8	32.32.16.16.16.16.8.8.5⅓.4.V.V.32.16.8.4
1844	Calcutta	16/16.8.8/8.8.8.5⅓.4.4.4.3⅕.2⅔.2.2.III.II.II.8.4.8	16/16.8.8/8.8.5⅓.4.4.2⅔.2.2.III.II.V.8.8.8.4.2		16.16.16
1845	Ashton-under-Lyne	16/16.8.8.8/8.5⅓.4.4.3⅕.2⅔.2.1⅗.III.III.II.16/16.8.4.2	16/16.8.8/8.8.4.4.2⅔.2.2.III.II.V.16.8.8.4	8.8.8.8.4.4.4.2.2.8	16.16.8.4.V.16
	Eastbrook Chapel, Bradford	16/16.8.8.8.5⅓.4.4.3⅕.2⅔.2.V.III.8.4	16/16.8.8.8.4.4.2⅔.2.2.III.8.8.4	8.8.8.4.4.2.8/8	32.16.8.5⅓.4.V.16
1848	St Mary-at-Hill	16.8.8.8.5⅓.4.4.2⅔.2.2.III.III.8.4.8	16.8.8/8.8.4.4.2⅔.2.III.8.8.4		16.8.16
	Poplar Wesleyan Chapel	16.8.8.8.5⅓.4.2⅔.2.III.II.III.16.8.4	16.8.8.8.4.4.2⅔.2.III.8.8.4	8/8.8.8.4.4.2.2.8/8	16.16.8.5⅓.4.16
1851	Ely Cathedral	16.8.8.8.5⅓.4.2⅔.2.III.III.8.8.4	16.8.8.4.8.8	8.8.8.4.4.2.8	16.16.8.4.III.16
1852	St George's Hall, Windsor	16/16.8.8.8.5⅓.4.4.2⅔.2.III.8.4	16.8.8.4.2.II.8.8.	8.8/8.8.4.4.8	16.8.16
1853	Royal Panopticon	16.8.8.8.5⅓.4.4.2⅔.2.III.III.III.16.8.8.4	16.8.8.8.4.4.2⅔.2.IV–V.8.8.8.4	16.8.8.8.4.4.2⅔.2.2.II.8/8.8	32.16.16.16.8.5⅓.4.V.16.8
	Solo omitted: see p. 213				
1855	Kidderminster Town Hall	16.8.8.8.4.4.2⅔.2.III.8	16.8.8.8.4.2.8.8	8.8.4.4.2.8	16.16.8.16
1856	Lincoln's Inn Chapel	16.8.8.8.4.4.2⅔.2.III.8	16.8.8.4.2.III.8.8.8	8.8.8.4.2.8	16.16.8
1858	Waterford Cathedral	16.8.8.8.8.5⅓.4.4.2⅔.2.III.III.16.8.8.4	16.8.8.8.4.4.2⅔.2.III.8.8.4.8	8/8.8.8.4.4.2.8	32.16.16.8.4.III.16
1860	King's College, Cambridge	16.8.8.8.8.5⅓.4.4.2⅔.2.III.II.16.8.8.4	16.8.8.8.4.2⅔.2.III.16.8.8.4	8.8.8.8.4.4.2.8	32.16.16.10⅔.8.4.16

hitherto unknown in England. Some of the Swells were of short compass (Cheetham Hill, Worcester), but this was contrary to the spirit of the German System, and, wherever possible, Hill provided a full-compass Swell so that it might, as nearly as possible, be a match for the Great in all respects (Cornhill, Stratford and Liverpool are conspicuous early examples). When circumstances allowed, Hill built a Pedal Organ to reflect the chorus structure of the two main manual divisions, with a mixture, (occasionally) a mutation, and a reed. Birmingham and the Panopticon demonstrate what could be done. Other examples are more modest, but 16.16.8.4.M.16 and 16.8.16 (or 16.16.16) were fairly standard. Large-scaled open wood pipes were invariably retained, whatever else had to go: a reminder that weight of tone remained a principal objective. Complete reed choruses were rare. Birmingham Town Hall acquired a Great 16′ reed during the 1843 reconstruction, and similar registers appeared in the Ashton-under-Lyne, Northampton and Poplar organs, but it was not until the late-1850s that a double reed began to appear with any frequency in this department, and then only in the very largest organs.[5] Much the same was true of the Swell. The Liverpool organ (1841) seems to offer the earliest example of a 16′ reed chorus, though its contra-fagotto was probably intended to serve primarily as an imitative solo stop rather than a chorus reed;[6] this may have been the case, too, with the similarly named stop at Northampton. At both Ashton-under-Lyne (1845) and Westminster Abbey (1848) the Swell double reeds were genuine trumpets, not bassoons, but perhaps for reasons of cost and space, they were of short compass. The lack of a 16′ reed in the Birmingham and Panopticon organs is ample evidence that it had yet to establish itself as an indispensable component of the English Full Swell, and it remained a rarity in Hill's work until the 1860s.

Having gained 'purity, power, and grandeur of tone' by developing the flue and reed choruses, Hill turned his attention to increasing the tonal variety of the instrument. His innovations here fall into four categories: reeds, flutes, strings and mixtures. Their occurrence in the larger organs of the 1840s and 1850s is summarised in Table 19.

Something has already been said of the reeds (above, pp. 113–14). In his *Circular*, Hill claimed to have 'invented' seven reed stops. The 'Grand Ophicleide' was the high-pressure reed, whilst 'Trombone' was the name given by Hill (or Gauntlett) to the Great chorus reed in a number of early German System organs; it, and its accompanying Clarion, were a type of posaune. The 'Contra-fagotto' and 'Clarionet or Chalemeau' were imitative stops. More interesting were the 'Cromorne-flute' and 'Corno-flute'. Despite their names, they were reed stops, 'flute' probably implying no more than an attempt to produce a rounded, even tone. The cromorne-flute was simply a refined cremona; the 'flute' element soon disappeared and there seems to have been little difference between the cromornes, cormornes, krum horns

Table 19 *Registers introduced by Hill into his organs, 1840–55*

		Flutes									Strings					Reeds				Others	
		Clarabel 8	Wald-flute 4	Oboe-flute 4	Suabe-flute 4	Gemshorn 4	Flageolet 4	Harmonic Flute 4	Piccolo 2	Flageolet 2	Salcional 8	Cone Gamba 8	Viol di Gamba 8	Hohl-flute 8	Vox Angelica 8	Swiss Cromorne-flute 8	Corno-flute 8	Cromorne-flute 8	Cromorne/Krum Horn 8	Echo Dulciana Cornet	Glockenspiel
1840	St Luke, Cheetham Hill	Ch	Ch	Ch						Ch											
	St Peter-upon-Cornhill	Gt	Gt	Gt			Sw											Gt	Gt	Sw	
	St Philip, Sheffield		Ch	Ch	Sw				Sw								Ch	Ch	Ch		Ch
1841	Great George Street Chapel, Liverpool	Ch	Ch	Ch	Sw				Ch	Sw						Sw		Ch	Ch	Sw	
	Stratford-upon-Avon		Gt	Gt	Sw		Sw											Gt	Gt	Sw	
1842	Worcester Cathedral	Ch	Gt	Ch	Sw					Sw								Gt	Gt	Sw	
1843	Mechanics' Hall, Liverpool	Sw,Gt	Gt	Ch	Sw				Ch	Sw	Gt		Gt				Ch			Sw	
	Edinburgh Music Hall	Ch	Gt	Ch	Sw				Ch	Ch	Ch		Ch							Sw	Gt
1845	Ashton-under-Lyne	Ch	Gt		Ec					Sw											
1847	St Andrew, Wells Street	Gt	Gt		Sw					Ec		Gt	Ec	Gt					Gt		
1848	St Mary-at-Hill		Gt		Sw			So		Gt		Gt		Sw							
1853	Poplar Wesleyan Chapel	Ch	Ch		Sw	Ch			Ch		Sw		Ch	Ch							
	Royal Panopticon	So	Gt			Ch		So	Ch	So			Ch		So				So		
1855	Kidderminster Town Hall	Gt				Ch			Ch		Ch		Sw						Ch		

and cremonas made by Hill during the 1840s and 1850s. The corno-flute is more puzzling. Only two are known to have been made during the 1840s and neither survives. The specimen at the Great George Street Chapel was said to have 'wood tube, Horn reed' (MS 12: 82), and so was presumably a soft reed with wooden resonators. If so, it was closely related to another stop at Liverpool: the 'Swiss Cromorne-flute', of which nothing is known, except that it had wooden resonators (but why 'Swiss'?). It is safest to conclude that both stops (cromorne-flute and corno-flute) were cremonas, one with metal resonators, the other with wooden ones.

It is a fascinating reflection on the reception of German influences during this phase of the German movement that most of Hill's novelty flutes were wooden registers, and that few of them bore any resemblance to the prototypes implied by their nomenclature (see also below, p. 245). The wald-flute and suabe-flute were open flutes with inverted mouths, i.e. the block was made to project as far as the *outer* surface of the pipe, and the bevelled upper lip was cut on the *inner* surface of the front of the pipe. The oboe-flute was of similar construction, but its small scale and the low cut-up of the mouth ensured that it had a quiet, slightly reedy tone (Figure 11). The flageolet was open, with a conventional English mouth, whilst the piccolo

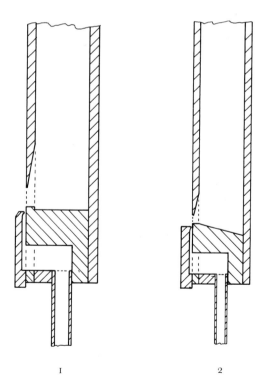

1   2

11 Hill's wald-flute and oboe-flute (1) St Peter-upon-Cornhill, wald-flute; (2) St Peter-upon-Cornhill, oboe-flute.

came in two forms: an open (?) metal register (Edinburgh, Calcutta), and a wooden one, with pierced stoppers. Each of these registers first appeared in 1840, in the organs for Cheetham Hill or Cornhill.

String-toned stops were unknown in Hill's organs before 1843. In that year, a 'Salcional' and 'Viol di Gamba' appeared in the organs for Liverpool and Edinburgh. The salcional was probably the narrow-scaled cylindrical stop which is found under a similar name ('Salicional') in the Swell Organs of many later instruments by the Hill firm, though at this stage in its career it was more commonly found in the Choir; the viol di gamba (plain 'Gamba' in some other stop lists) may have been of similar construction, or it may have had tapering pipe bodies. In the latter form, it was usually designated 'Cone Gamba'. It is frequently found in Hill organs of the 1850s, 1860s and 1870s, sometimes as a broad-toned string in the Choir Organ, sometimes as a substitute for a second open diapason in the Great. The earliest known example is St Mary-at-Hill (1848).[7] William Hill also made a tapering register of 4' pitch called 'Gemshorn'. Unsurprisingly, it appeared at about the same time as the cone gamba, and rapidly established itself in the Choir Organ. Finally, there was the 'Hohl-flute'. Not a flute at all but a cylindrical string, it had two large circular holes in a slide at the top of the pipe, and was said to resemble the keraulophon in tone (hohl-flute = holed flute?). It is first found in 1847.

More will be said about Hill's mixturework below (pp. 243–4); for the moment, it is only necessary to notice two solo compound stops. The first is the echo dulciana cornet, usually of five ranks but occasionally of four. It was probably one of Gauntlett's innovations (it is not found in Hill's work after 1845), was enclosed in its own box within the Swell box, and was normally of tenor-c compass. Then there was the doublette. It is not clear whether this was intended to be a solo stop or a chorus mixture. There were two ranks, fifteenth and twenty-second, though, if the evidence at Cornhill is reliable, the second rank broke back to 4' pitch in the top octave. The scaling was conventional. The 'Glockenspiel' in the Sheffield and Liverpool (Mechanics) specifications may have had a similar character. A stop of this name was added to the Great Organ at York Minster during the reconstruction of 1859. It was of short compass, consisted of a twelfth and tierce, and was intended for use with the stopped diapason (MS 84: f. 2).

Enough has been said to substantiate Hill's claim (voiced in the 1841 circular) to have erected organs 'on a scale of grandeur and magnificence altogether new, and before unattempted in this country'. By re-structuring the choruses, developing the Pedal and expanding the Swell, Hill equipped the English organ to meet the demand for greater power and weight of tone. His innovations among the flutes, strings and reeds transformed the organ's tonal resources, making it, at one and the same time, a more flexible accompanimental tool and a more convincing substitute for an orchestra.

Though some of the more exotic experiments were short-lived, and though the innovations of the 1840s would not satisfy organists for long, Hill's work effectively sounded the death knell of the long-compass organ with its stereotyped specification.

The evolution of Hill's style may best be considered by looking in more detail at some of the schemes summarised in Table 18.

The earliest of these dates from 1838: the reconstruction of the Newgate Street organ (Plate 27). A plaque on the organ recorded that

This organ was extended, 1838. The case was enlarged, and the pedal stops to CCC were added . . . The arrangement of the pedal stops was suggested by Mr. Henry John Gauntlett who also presented a new set of German pedals.

Gauntlett's design included the most enterprising Pedal Organ yet to be introduced into an English organ, and, with the exception of Birmingham Town Hall (1843) and St Sepulchre, Holborn (1849), it was not surpassed before the mid-1850s; the fact that it remained bereft of many of its pipes until 1867[8] need not obscure the significance of the 1838 scheme, with its 32-note compass. In addition, the keyboard compasses were reduced to C, one of the three Great open diapasons was transposed into a double diapason, a doublette of two ranks replaced a tierce, and the existing Great mixtures were recast and augmented. The completed stop list (Appendix 1, pp. 463–4) was remarkable for its date: the earliest example of Gauntlett's character-istic preoccupation with a fully developed Great chorus with adequate upperwork and a sub-unison. Even more remarkable if it, too, dates from 1838 (it cannot be later than 1841) is a 63-stop scheme for a further reconstruction of the Christ Church organ (Appendix 1, pp. 464–6). An early date might be argued for on the grounds that it is the Choir Organ (sixteen stops) rather than the Swell (eleven stops) which is developed as the second manual chorus; in Gauntlett's later work, the secondary chorus was always under expression, and hence in the Swell.

Gauntlett designed a Swell Organ along these lines for Halifax Parish Church in December 1838; it was to have twelve stops, and was to be C-compass (MS 12: 35–6). It was never built. There was a pause, and then in 1840, the mature products of Hill and Gauntlett's collaboration began to emerge from the workshop.

The first to be completed was a 3-manual organ for the new church of St Luke, Cheetham Hill, Manchester; it was given by J. W. Fraser, a wealthy Mancunian and musical amateur who had firsthand experience of foreign organs (above, p. 178), and was opened by Gauntlett in April (Appendix 1, pp. 466–7). Gauntlett's involvement began late in the day after a scheme had been agreed and work begun. A comparison of the completed instru-ment and the original stop list is therefore illuminating. The first proposal was for a substantially smaller version of the Chester organ, with C-compasses and a single Pedal stop (MS 12: 42). Gauntlett drew up a new specification, introducing a 16' flue, a powerful modern reed and additional upperwork to the Great, transforming the Choir by the addition of five 'solo stops', and adding a Pedal Organ of three stops and twenty-seven notes (MS 12: 74). There are certain ambiguities. The Pedal stops in the completed organ had only an octave of pipes, and this, together with Gauntlett's original intention of carrying the Great keys down to CC so that the Pedal stops might be played manually, suggests that he had yet to renounce some of the curious expedients of the Insular Movement.[9]

A similar feature is to be found in the second of the organs of 1840: that built for St Peter, Cornhill, and completed in July. According to Hill's agreement with the parish, the two Pedal stops were to have a compass of fifteen notes, C–d, though C–d¹ was to be the compass of the pedal board. This instrument will be considered in more detail below (pp. 215–22), but its originality, both in general conception and detailed design, should not be overlooked now. Rather than spread the available resources over three manuals, Gauntlett drew up a scheme for a huge 2-manual instrument, with a Swell of full compass and equal in size to the Great. The picture was filled out with the new flute stops, modern reeds and an echo dulciana cornet (the first) to yield an instrument unlike any other in the metropolis.

The third of this trio of 1840 was less striking, though it contained the novelties of the quint (Great) and glockenspiel (Choir). This was the organ for St Philip's, Sheffield, opened in the autumn, and, in reality, a smaller version of Cheetham Hill. It is possible that it was the first German System organ to have Pedal stops of full compass, but it seems more likely that the compasses were curtailed as in the other two organs.

A truly independent Pedal Organ appeared for the first time in the following year. This was in the organ for Stratford-upon-Avon. With its chorus registers, mixture and reed, it held out the possibility of sustaining the pedal line in a contrapuntal piece without recourse to couplers. The scheme was said to have been drawn up by Frederick Marshall of Leamington (was this the man to whom Samuel Wesley dedicated his *Grand Duet for organ*?)[10] but Gauntlett's claim to be its author (Gauntlett 1846) need not be disputed. Hill's records show that an early proposal (1839) for a large GG-compass organ of three manuals (MS 12: 63–4) gave way to a huge German System 2-manual with sub-unisons, mixtures, mutations and a 6-stop Pedal to the same specification as the slightly later Worcester organ. With the exception of the Pedal, it was similar to Cornhill. The other large organ of 1841 also underwent considerable changes at the planning stage (and, indeed, beyond). In July 1840, Hill (was Gauntlett directly involved at this stage?) submitted proposals for a new organ for the Great George Street Chapel, Liverpool (MS 12: 81–5). It was, he informed the committee, 'laid out in a manner that I conceive best adapted for the purposes of congregational worship & at the same time I have had reference to variety and sweetness in the combination of the Stops' (81). The plan for the two manual divisions was not unlike Cornhill. The Great had nineteen stops, with both a cromorne and the mysterious corno-flute in addition to the now customary novelty flutes. It seems that, in this instance, the Swell was not intended to equal the power of the Great, for Hill specified dulciana scales for the upperwork (though the chorus was otherwise complete); a 'small' bassoon (8') and a wood cromorne were among the solo stops. In the light of the progress made at Stratford, the pedal arrangements appear perverse. As at Cornhill, each of the Pedal stops was to have only fifteen pipes (C–d) though the pedal board would have twenty-seven notes. To add to the confusion, Hill proposed that by means of an octave (surely, sub-octave?) coupler, the pedal registers would repeat in the upper octave, and commented ingenuously that 'the large Reeds and the Double Diapasons in the lower Octave of the Great and Swell organs will prevent the repetition of the Pedal pipes from being noticed' (84). The Pedal registers – two 16' flues, a metal quint and a reed – amounted to little more than a manual bass, and, as if to emphasise this, they were to be playable from the lowest octave of the Great, which was to be extended to CC for the purpose. By the time that Gauntlett gave 'an exhibition of the organ's powers' in December 1841 the specification had been considerably altered (Appendix 1, pp. 467–8).[11] The six 'solo' stops originally allotted to the Great had joined a stopped diapason and a piccolo to form a Choir Organ with its own set of keys. This released space for a quint and doublette, and for a more adventurous development of the Great reed chorus. The Swell reed chorus had also been expanded, with the addition of a trumpet and clarion, and the transposition of the bassoon to 16' pitch. For the first time, a high-pressure reed was introduced into an English church organ; despite claims in Hill's 1841 circular that it was played from a fourth keyboard, *Gawthrop's* statement that it was played from the Swell seems likely to be correct (*GJ*: 18 December 1841). Tantalisingly, it is not known whether the Pedal registers were of full compass or not. In the course of the scheme's evolution the Quint had disappeared, and as the Great keyboard in 1841 was of C-compass it may be that the original proposals for the Pedal had been thoroughly revised. This remained the most disappointing feature of the instrument, but, as has been seen, Hill and Gauntlett's views on Pedal divisions were not as clear-cut in these early years as has sometimes been assumed. Despite this deficiency, the organ excited widespread approval. It was (and remained) one of the most important of the German System instruments, and it is worth quoting *Gawthrop's* report of Gauntlett's opening performance to illustrate the impression that these organs of the early-1840s made upon Hill's contemporaries.

The great Organ is of surpassing power and grandeur, with that brilliancy without harshness, for which Mr. Hill is so famous. The Solo stops are as perfect as imitations can possibly be, the reeds being exceedingly clear, rich, and well voiced, the flutes, of which it will be seen there is a great variety, particularly sweet and sparkling. The pedal Organ has great weight and dignity, and the combinations by the copulas gives [*sic*] a variety almost infinite. The Tuba Mirabilis or Ophicleide is a most extraordinary stop: its blasts are almost terrific, yet it has a purity of tone, filling the whole extensive space, with a freedom from what may be emphatically called *noise*, seldom attained by common builders in the ordinary trumpet stop or clarion.   (*GJ*: 18 December 1841)

The passage leaves little doubt that Hill's reputation was built upon solid achievement, triumphantly sustained by an ability to satisfy contemporary taste.

The Great George Street organ was the most adventurous of the early C-compass instruments; like Cheetham Hill and Stratford, the scheme was constantly revised, long after construction had begun. But with the completion of the Liverpool organ this initial experimental phase drew to a close. The Worcester Cathedral organ of 1842 may be seen as a distillation of various ideas tried out in the previous few years; the archaisms of Cheetham Hill and the hyperbole of George Street have disappeared, and the result is a balanced scheme achieving versatility, not by excess, but by discriminating between essentials and inessentials.

The organs of 1840–2 established the principles of Hill's style for the remainder of the decade and well into the 1850s. Design and execution would be refined, novelties would appear from time to time, and there would be a general simplification of the schemes once Gauntlett's direct influence was removed, but the patterns were in place. The Cornhill and Stratford organs were succeeded by St Mary-at-Hill (1848) and St Walburgh's, Preston (1853); Great George Street fathered the organs for Ashton-under-Lyne and Northampton (1845); Worcester provided a model for a whole succession of 3-manual instruments including Poplar (1848), Kidderminster (1855) and Lincoln's Inn (1856). Temperamentally, Hill was a more conservative figure than Gauntlett, and the specifications he evolved himself show a greater concern for proportion, less interest in imitative stops and expression, and a more consistent desire to provide an independent Pedal division than those drawn up by his mentor. The classic example of this is Hill's *magnum opus*, the organ for the Royal Panopticon (1853).

The Royal Panopticon of Science and Art was a quintessentially Victorian project for uniting popular instruction and unexceptionable entertainment under one roof. The building (which stood in Leicester Square, on the site of the Odeon Cinema) was part exhibition gallery, part lecture theatre and part concert hall. No expense was spared in fitting up the premises. The central rotunda was decorated in a Moorish style, and it was here that the 'dissolving views' depicting battles, storms and other stirring events were shown. In order to provide a musical accompaniment to this harmless entertainment a 'Grand Organ' was commissioned from Hill. It was located in a gallery on one side of the rotunda, behind the temporary screen onto which the 'views' were projected. By some quirk, the projection apparatus was installed at the rear of the gallery; the 'views' had therefore to be projected *through* the organ, and so a space had to be left in the middle of the instrument. This is clearly visible in contemporary illustrations (Plate 28). A further curiosity was the provision of three consoles. Only one of these was complete, controlling the entire organ; the others duplicated the Swell, Solo and Choir, and their use was perhaps confined to supplementing the orches-

28 The Royal Panopticon of Science and Art, Leicester Square, Hill, 1853.

tral effects of which a single player, seated at the main console, was capable. There were other mechanical novelties, including the application of the pneumatic lever to the Great and Pedal key actions, and to the coupler, drawstop and combination actions, and the main members of the building frame were made hollow, so as to serve as wind trunks.

The juxtaposition of mechanical gimmickry and optical illusion is apt to suggest that the Panopticon organ was little more than an ancestor of the cinema organ. Some have taken this view (Elvin 1971: 33). Had Gauntlett been involved this might indeed have been the case; we might postulate the inclusion of huge expressive divisions, a plethora of orchestral voices and dangerously fragmented choruses; Gauntlett might even have been tempted by the unusual construction forced upon the builder by the projectionist's requirements to urge the merits of his newly-patented electric action. In Hill's hands, however, the outcome was very different. His scheme was a magisterial summing up of the work of the previous decade in which all the principal features of his (by now) established practice could be found (below, pp. 212–14). Great, Swell and Choir each had a developed flue chorus; the Pedal was independent; all the principal reeds, flutes and strings pioneered by Hill were included; and Hill did not neglect the obligation which the spirit of the age imposed upon the Victorian manufacturer to introduce novelties in any major work. Only the provision of drums, tremulants, a crescendo pedal and a Solo Organ distinguish the organ from Hill's church instruments.[12] Henry Smart, whose own preference was for the work of Hill's main rivals, Gray & Davison, wrote an extended review of the organ in the *Musical World* (XXXII, 1854: 475–7; 533–5). It was, he claimed, 'without equal in this country', and its mechanical arrangements were 'much in advance of everything that [Hill] or any of his countrymen had previously completed' (475–6). The implied comparison with continental organ-building was made explicit in a number of criticisms: the execution of the key actions lacked the finish to be found in the best French instruments and the plan failed to show that mastery of detail which distinguished Cavaillé-Coll's work; but the organ was still 'the most perfect thing of the kind in England' (476). In commenting on the Great Organ, Smart singled out Hill's treatment of the mixtures for commendation:

. . . the compound stops are perfect models in their class . . . The harmonic arrangement of their intervals is skilfully planned, and their *breaks* are so contrived to balance each other, as to create no patchy stops of either thinness or abundance. Their scales increase enormously, as they ascend through the upper octaves of their compass, and this increase of size is variously distributed as this or that rank is intended to act conspicuously in the general chorus. These arrangements yield a vast increase of power by the addition of each three ranks, while the force of the united nine, great as it is, is still tone, genuine tone. The whole flue-work, nine ranks of mixture and all, is grand, strong, brilliant, musical. There is not a whistle or scream in it from first to last.   (534)

The reeds of the Great Organ also met with approval. Smart first gave forceful expression to his own view that reeds and flues 'should march on parallel lines of importance – volume for volume, force for force', condemning a rival view that reeds should be tamed so that they could be absorbed by the fluework to serve as no more than a 'thickening' agent in the full chorus. It is not clear who was the object of this attack, but it was certainly not Hill. Smart commended the Panopticon chorus reeds for 'the splendid service they render to the general volume of tone', and particularly approved of the fact that Hill had here for the first time applied Cavaillé-Coll's increasing pressure system by placing the trebles on a higher pressure than the basses (534). This taste for French inventions inspired Smart's criticisms of Hill's Solo Organ: the harmonic flute was too small in scale, the two ranks of the vox angelica were tuned too far apart, and the vox humana was too refined and should have been enclosed. The tubas – here disposed horizontally for the first time in England – were, however, 'magnificent' (534–5).

The organ for the Panopticon was the largest new instrument built by William Hill after the adoption of C-compasses. This survey of his work would, though, be incomplete if it omitted to mention a notable series of smaller organs which emerged from Hill's workshop during this productive period. These were *multum-in-parvo* instruments, intended to express the ideals of the German System, but using the minimum of resources. Significantly, they were totally enclosed, with an additional swell box for the little Echo Organs. The main division (Great) had a complete chorus, with reeds and solo stops, but the short-compass Echo had (usually) only three or four registers. It was St Olave's, Southwark, in miniature.

Hill is known to have built thirteen of these totally enclosed organs, and his Letter Book includes estimates for many more. Synoptic specifications are set out in Table 20. The earliest was designed by Gauntlett for Stanwix. It had a single manual and no pedal pipes. The solo stops included a wald-flute, oboe-flute, piccolo and cremona, and there may have been a dulciana cornet. The enclosure of the pipework in a swell box inspired the choice of a cornopean rather than a trumpet as the chorus reed, and this rapidly became a standard feature of these instruments. In the second of the series, Staly-bridge, the short-compass Echo made its appearance. Here, it consisted of dulciana, principal and oboe; later examples included a stopped diapason, hohl-flute, claribel or gemshorn, but there were seldom more than four stops. An exception was St Andrew's, Wells Street. The organ installed in 1847 was one of the most modest in the series; in line with the preference of the first incumbent for plainsong this was emphatically not a congregational organ but served to give unobtrusive support to the trained singers whose task it was to lead the congregation. Such restraint was not congenial to the second organist of the church, John Foster, who had ambitions to develop a cathedral-type of musical service (Rainbow 1970: 169–73), and the com-

Table 20 *Synoptic stop lists of Hill's totally enclosed organs, 1841–54*

		Great	Echo	Pedal
1841	Stanwix	16/16.8.8/8.8.4.4.4.2⅔.2.2.III.8.8.(v)		no pipes
1844	St Paul, Stalybridge	16/16.8.8.5⅓.4.4.4.2⅔.2.III.8.8	8.4.8	no pipes (?)
1846	All Saints, Gordon			
	Square	16/16.8.8.5⅓.4.4.4.2⅔.2.2.III.8	8.4.8	no pipes (?)
1847	Portland Chapel	16/16.8.8/8.4.4.2⅔.2.III.8/8	8.4.8	no pipes
	Zion Chapel, Hulme	16/16.8.8.8.4.4.2⅔.2.III.8.8	8.8.4.8	16
	St Andrew, Wells Street			
	(*1849*)	16/16.8.8/8.8.4.4.2⅔.2.III.8.8	16.8.8.8.4.2.8.8	16
	Wanstead Church	16/16.8.8.4.4.2⅔.2.III.8	8.8/8.4.4	no pipes
	St Stephen, Hull	16/16.8.8.8.4.4.2⅔.2.2.III.8	8.8.4.8	no pipes
1850	Cheadle Church	16/16.8.8/8.4.4.2⅔.2.(III.)8/8	8.8.4.8	no pipes
	St Barnabas, Stockwell	16/16.8.8.4.4.2⅔.2.III.8	8.8.4.8	16
	Radnor Street Chapel,			
	Manchester	16/16.8.8.8.4.4.2⅔.2.III.8.8	8.8.4.8	16
1851	Great Exhibition	16.8.8.4.4.2⅔.2.III.8.8	8.8.4.8.8	16
1854	St Stephen, Islington	16/16.8.8.8.4.4.2⅔.2.III.8	8.8.4.8	(16)

pletion of the Great chorus and provision of a new 8-stop Swell (though still short-compass) followed in 1849. Other organists may also have been frustrated by the limitations of these instruments. Though pedals were always provided, pedal pipes frequently were not. This unexpected reversion to an early view of the relationship between keyboard and pedals left the organist with an instrument of which it might be said that the ability to manage a swell pedal was probably more crucial than competence at the other sort of pedalling. (Hill devised a ratchet-type pedal to give the player a greater degree of control over the shutters than was customary (Pole 1851: 65).) Why this should be is a mystery. Had the organs been intended for country areas where organists were scarce, the absence of pedal pipes might have been explained, but most were commissioned by urban churches.

Whatever may have been the merits of these instruments none survives today for us to judge. They were products of a particular phase in the evolution of the nineteenth-century organ and may soon have come to wear an old-fashioned look. The mechanical difficulties of managing the swell pedals must, in any case, have been against them, and it is difficult to believe that they were very effective as a congregational accompaniment. In time, they were either discarded or broken up for their parts to be re-used in more conventional schemes.[13] Hill, though, seems to have believed in them. He chose to exhibit one at the Crystal Palace in 1851. It may be significant (it is certainly in tune with the times) that the official description is a panegyric on mechanical and tonal ingenuity with only the scantiest reference to their musical application (Appendix 2, pp. 511–13).

INSPIRATION

It is apparent that continental traditions of organ design were of fundamental importance in the evolution of the English organ during the middle years of the nineteenth century. In concluding this chapter, we shall try to establish the nature of this influence and identify the selective ways in which organists and organ-builders drew upon it to justify their innovations.

It is not unusual in this period to find the inspiration of the continent acknowledged in general terms in notices of new organs – the Panopticon instrument, for example, was said to embrace 'all the novelties of the continental organs' (*MW* xxxii, 1854: 352). Sometimes the allusion was more specific. This was most common in the early-1840s. With the German System relatively untried, apologists for the new movement evidently found that it strengthened their case to refer to a famous foreign organ. The model most frequently cited was Haarlem. According to the *Musical World*, the Great George Street instrument should be termed 'the English Haarlem organ, for it was built on the same principles' (xviii, 1843: 9), and in 1840, the new organ for St Peter's, Cornhill, was described as 'a remarkably fine one, with a rich, full, imposing tone and power, and with a brilliancy not unlike that of the famous Haarlem' (*MP*, 18 July 1840). In many ways, Haarlem was emblematic of foreign organs in general, but more precise citations are occasionally found. Gauntlett himself (who ought to have known) wrote that George Street was 'erected on the model of the celebrated *chef d'oeuvre* of Silbermann, in the magnificent cathedral of Strasburgh' (*MP*, 1 January 1842), though a comparison of the stop lists of Andreas Silbermann's organ at Strasburg (1714–16) and William Hill's organ in Liverpool leaves the exact nature of the debt obscure. The echo cornet at Cornhill was said to be upon a plan 'borrowed from that of the organ of Cologne cathedral' (*MP*, 18 July 1840) – probably a reference to the 'Cornet, iv ranks' located on the 'Choir' of the Cologne organ, following the rebuild (1817–21) by Maas (hr2: 353–4). Such precise attributions are, however, rare. More common are brief lists of continental organs which seem, to their authors, to place the work of Hill and Gauntlett in context. In Gauntlett's own review of Great George Street, 'the noble instruments of Haarlem, Dresden, Strasburgh, Hamburg, and other large continental towns' are offered as models for large organs; in the same article it is reported that those who had the means of judging believed that the Liverpool organ was not excelled 'in grandeur, variety, purity, and delicacy of tone' by the organs of 'Haarlem, Strasburgh, Seville, Mafra, Freyburgh, Amsterdam, Rotterdam, Malaga, and St. Sulpice, Paris' (*MP*, 1 January 1842). The interest of such an eclectic body of instruments lies less in what it tells of Great George Street, more in the clues it offers to the travels of English organists. A decade

later, the committee appointed to advise the Directors of the Crystal Palace
Company upon the provision of a permanent organ addressed themselves to
the problem of securing a sufficiently powerful instrument for that vast
auditorium. They, too, turned to the continental organs, referring to
Haarlem and Rotterdam, Lucerne and Berne as proof that 32′ tone greatly
augmented the power of an organ and commending the reeds at St Denis and
La Madeleine as lending exceptional power to those instruments (Ouseley,
Willis & Donaldson 1853).

This approbatory allusion to modern French organs should not be
allowed to obscure the chief characteristic of the instruments most commonly identified as exemplars by the reformers of the 1840s – a characteristic
encapsulated in Hill's statement that in making innovations in the construction of the choruses, he had 'acted in the spirit of the old and most celebrated
builders of Holland and Germany' (*Circular*, 1841). The point was reiterated
by Gauntlett when he qualified his claim that the Liverpool organ was built
on a 'new' plan by adding, 'the term *new* is perhaps out of place when applied
to a plan which has been in constant use for upwards of a century in Holland,
France, and Germany' (*MP*, 1 January 1842). In general, it was the organs
of the eighteenth century – rather than the most modern instruments – that
inspired progressive English organists of Gauntlett's generation. This was
not mere antiquarianism, for the English were selective in their taste for the
historical. Schnitger's organs, for instance, are seldom if ever cited in this
early period as models to be imitated: English travellers in Hamburg
commented not upon the Schnitger instruments in the Jacobikirche (1688–
93) or the Nikolaikirche (1682–7), but upon Hildebrandt's organ (1762–7)
in the Michaeliskirche. Similarly, it was to Haarlem and not Alkmaar that
they went: there appears to be no mention of the Alkmaar organ in contemporary English literature. Gauntlett's reference to the organs of Haarlem,
Dresden, Strasburg and Hamburg as 'noble instruments' stands in the same
tradition (*MP*, 1 January 1842); again, the interest is in Müller, the Silber-
manns and (in the context of other remarks in the passage) Hildebrandt,
rather than an earlier (or, for that matter, a later) generation of builders. The
refinements of the former group would be more congenial to English ears
than the drier and, they would say, harsher qualities of the Schnitgers'
organs, and there was also, no doubt, a tendency to think of Bach as an
eighteenth-century figure, overlooking his roots in a seventeenth-century
tradition of organ composition and performance.

The German System was much more than an English attempt to imitate
the great continental organs of the eighteenth century; the many references
to contemporary foreign organs – Cavaillé-Coll's St Denis (1841); Walcker's
organ at St Paul, Frankfurt (1833); Moser's at Fribourg Cathedral (1834) –
together with Hill's claim that, as well as matching the old builders in chorus
structure, he had made improvements in the variety of tone which he

thought had never been surpassed by any builder, ancient or modern (*Circular*, 1841), demonstrate this and prepare the ground for the 1850s. Yet in tonal construction, Hill's German System organs had a closer affinity to the practice of the eighteenth century than to the work of his leading German and French contemporaries, and the Dutch and German organs of the previous century remain the fundamental inspiration of the work of Hill and Gauntlett during this period.

By way of illustration, an English version of the Haarlem specification is given below, set alongside the stop list of Hill's Panopticon organ; the account of Haarlem[14] was published at the end of Hill's 1841 *Circular* (significant enough in itself), and as the two organs have almost the same number of registers, the comparison is valid. Though there are, of course, many points of difference, the similarities are conspicuous, and go a long way to explaining the readiness with which Hill's contemporaries referred to the continental organs when describing his own work.

HAARLEM (1735–8)		PANOPTICON (1853)	
The Grand Organ		**Great Organ**	
Contra Bourdon	32		
Tenoroon Diapason	16	Double Open Diapason	16
Open Diapason	8	Open Diapason	8
		Open Diapason (wd)	8
Viol di Gamba	8		
Stopped Diapason	8	Stopped Diapason (wd)	8
Quint	6	Quint	5⅓
Principal	4	Octave	4
Flute	4	Wald Flute (wd)	4
Twelfth	3	Octave Quint	2⅔
		Super Octave	2
Tierce [*Terzian*]	1¾		
Piccolo	2		
Mixture	x	Sesquialtra	III
		Furniture	III
		Mixture	III
Contra Trumpet	16	Trumpet	16
Trumpet	8	Trumpet	8
		Posaune	8
Oboe	8		
Clarion	4	Clarion	4
The Solo Organ [sic]		**Swell Organ**	
Bourdon	16	Bourdon & Double Diapason	16
Open Diapason	8	Open Diapason	8
Horn Diapason	8		
		Salcional	8
Flute Diapason	8	Stopped Diapason (wd)	8
Principal	4	Octave	4
Flute	4	Suabe Flute (wd)	4

Flute Twelfth	$2\frac{2}{3}$			
		Octave Quint		$2\frac{2}{3}$
Flute Fifteenth	2			
		Super Octave		2
Piccolo	2			
Sesquialtra	II			
Carillons [*Zimbel?*]	IV			
Mixture	IV–VI	Sesquialtra		IV–V
Echo Trumpet	8	Trumpet		8
Fagotto	8	Cornopean		8
Vox Humana	8			
		Hautboy		8
		Clarion		4

The Choir Organ		**Choir Organ**	
		Double Stopped Diapason	16
		Gamba	8
		Dulciana	8
Open Diapason	8		
Stopped Diapason	8	Stopped Diapason (wd/m)	8
Quint [*Quintadena*]	8		
Principal	4		
		Gemshorn	4
Flute	4	Stopped Flute	4
Stopped Twelfth	$2\frac{2}{3}$		
		Octave Quint	$2\frac{2}{3}$
Fifteenth	2	Super Octave	2
		Piccolo (wd)	2
Sesquialtra	II–IV		
Mixture	VI–VIII		
Cornet	V		
Cymballe	II	Cymbal	II
Contra Fagotto	16		
Trumpet	8	Trumpet	8
Regal, or Violin Reed	8		
		Bassoon (wd) & Clarionet	8

Solo Organ	
Grand Tuba Mirabilis	8
Grand Clarion	4
Claribel (wd)	8
Harmonic Flute	4
Flageolet	2
Doublette	II
Vox Angelica (2 ranks)	8
Krum Horn	8
Vox Humana	8

The Pedal Organ		**Pedal Organ**	
Grand Open Diapason	32	Double Open Diapason (wd)	32
Contra Bourdon	32		

Open Diapason	16	Open Diapason	16
		Open Diapason (wd)	16
Bourdon	16	Bourdon (wd)	16
Quint	12		
Principal	8	Octave	8
Twelfth	6	Octave Quint	$5\frac{1}{3}$
Fifteenth	4	Super Octave	4
Stopped Fifteenth	4		
Larigot	3		
Mixture	III	Sesquialtra	v
Contra Posaune	32		
Trumpet	16	Trombone	16
Clarion	8	Octave Trombone	8
		Drums (C–c)	

Swell to Great
Choir to Great
Solo to Great
Pedal to Great [*sic*]
Pedal to Swell [*sic*]
Pedal to Choir [*sic*]
Pedal to Solo [*sic*]

9 composition pedals
2 tremulants (Swell & Solo?]
crescendo pedal

manuals: C–g³
pedals: C–f¹

8

The work of William Hill, 1839–55

INTRODUCTION

Any attempt to provide a technical study of William Hill's work in the era of his greatest influence confronts an insurmountable obstacle. Thanks to the destruction or mutilation of almost all the larger organs of the 1840s and 1850s only partial descriptions and tentative conclusions are possible; in most instances, the task demands the skills of an archaeologist rather than a musical critic. What follows reflects the limitations of the material. Three organs are described in some detail. The Cornhill organ has been much altered, but the unusually complete documentation of its conception and construction, the survival of most of the original pipework, and the fact that this proves to be in many respects a transitional instrument linking Hill's early and middle phases justify its inclusion. Until both church and organ were seriously damaged by fire in 1988, the instrument in St Mary-at-Hill was (tonally) the least altered of Hill's German System organs. How far this claim can be maintained in the aftermath of the fire remains to be seen. The third of the trio, the organ at Kidderminster, is particularly valuable because (unlike the other two) it retains most of its original mechanism, not indeed unaltered, but of great importance nonetheless for those obliged to clutch at straws. The history, design and construction of each of these instruments is considered in turn and there then follows a more general survey of the technical character of Hill's contemporary work drawing upon the evidence of other (even) less complete survivals. At best, it is a preliminary sketch of a frustratingly evasive subject.

ST PETER-UPON-CORNHILL, 1839–40

William Hill's Letter Book contains no references to the commissioning of the Cornhill organ; fortunately, the parish records are more informative.

   The old organ contained work by Smith and Crang. Following the

215

discovery that 'many of the pipes were out of their places lying on the ground and the whole Instrument appeared in a most dilapidated and imperfect state', a 'Special General Vestry' met on 28 August 1839 to consider 'the most expedient plan whereby the Parish Organ may be put into a proper state of Repair' (MS 72: 198). Estimates for essential repairs were received from Hill and Bishop and it was resolved to open a subscription; a leaflet was duly printed, appealing for £300, and noting that 'the decorum and solemnity of public worship have been greatly impaired, since the organ has fallen into its present state'.[1] By early November, the *Musical World* was able to report that 'the inhabitants of St Peter's, Cornhill, are about to erect an organ on the German scale, in their parish church... We believe there is not any instrument on this plan in any of the metropolitan churches...' (XII, 1839: 410). The decision to build what was virtually a new organ rather than simply to repair the existing one was explained at a second Special General Vestry on 18 December 1839, when the organ committee reported that its members had consulted a gentleman 'of high professional reputation' who had (judiciously, we might think) confirmed their 'preconceived opinion, that originally the Organ of St Peter's had been possessed of very fine qualities'. He had confirmed the attribution to 'Father Schmidt', and reported that the organ 'was found to contain many wooden pipes of his constructing, which the mellowing hand of time had rendered of more than ordinary value'. In drawing up their proposals, the members of the committee had decided that, with the exception of these wooden pipes, 'the internal arrangement and mechanism of the organ will be entirely new, the whole being greatly enlarged, and its compass much extended'. A 'new feature of dignity and beauty' would be introduced by inserting a large central tower into the existing organ case in order to increase the height of the front (Plate 29). The professional gentleman previously alluded to was eventually identified as Gauntlett, who had been retained to advise the committee. A specification had been prepared to permit additions, should funds allow, and estimates had been taken in from various 'of the most respectable organ builders in the City and Neighbourhood'. The appeal had succeeded to such an extent that the committee reported £476.15s.0d to have been raised, including £100 from the Corporation of the City, and further donations from the Mercers and the East India Company. This seemed to the committee 'to warrant their adoption of an enlarged Specification comprehending details of so superior a character, as to be descriptive, when completed, of one of the finest organs of which the metropolis can boast'. A contract had been entered into with Mr Hill, and the committee permitted itself a splendid, flowery peroration to its Report, reflecting on the success of the Subscription:

Not only will it allow them to erect an organ in every way worthy the sublime harmonies to which it will be devoted, but the kindred associations of differing

29 St Peter-upon-Cornhill, London. Case of 1681–2, widened by William Hill in 1840.

parties in the work has awakened a moral influence on the side of just and
enlightened principles such as may eventually prove of more value than the most
perfect Musical Instrument. These emotions heighten the enjoyment with which
your committee refer again to their proposed new organ, with its 2090 pipes – its vast
accumulation of scientific mechanism – its every modification of tone – speaking a
language, either grand or solemn, or pathetic or soft, or sweet, as the skill of an able

organist shall guide, and all consecrated as a melodious accompaniment to the praises of the Great Jehovah.   (MS 72: 212–15)

The Vestry voted thanks to the various parties, ordered the committee's Report to be printed and circulated, and gave the churchwarden discretion to enter relevant documents in the Vestry Book. Fortunately, the warden entered Hill's contract; it is transcribed below.

Specification and Estimate for the rebuilding and enlargement of the organ in the Church of St Peter upon Cornhill in the City of London.

I contract to remove the front pipes and the entire [sic] of the interior of the Organ. To make a new Great Organ complete the Manual sound boards to be made of the best seasoned material & to extend from CC the 8 feet pipe to F in alt, the six last notes in the base to have double pallets if necessary. New Keys   Roller Boards   and all the action complete & perfect for and with the following Stops of which all the pipes are to be new ——————————————

1.	Double Diapason Bass	10.	Sesquialtra 2 ranks
2.	Double Open Diapason Treble	11.	Mixture Two ranks
3.	Large Open Diapason	12.	Doublette Two ranks
4.	Stopped Diapason Bass	13.	Large Horn
5.	Stopped Diapason Treble	14.	Octave Horn
6.	Principal	15.	Cremona to Tenor C
7.	Twelfth	16.	Claribel to Do.
8.	Fifteenth	17.	Dulciana to Do.
9.	Tierce	18.	Solo Flute to Do.

I contract also to make a new Swell Sound Board from CC the 8 feet pipe to F in alt.   swell box   New Keys   my newly invented Swell action   draw Stop movements   roller boards   &c   and every part complete and perfect for the following stops ——————————————

1.	Dulciana Treble	11.	Sesquialtra 3 ranks
2.	Double Dulciana Bass	12.	Mixture two ranks
3.	Open Diapason	13.	Oboe
4.	Stopped Diapason Treble	14.	Trumpet
5.	Stopped Diapason bass	15.	French Horn
6.	Principal	16.	Clarion
7.	Flageolet or open flute	17.	Echo Dulciana Cornet to
8.	Twelfth		Tenor C 5 ranks
9.	Fifteenth		enclosed in an inner box
10.	Piccolo		

I contract to supply all the pipes for these Stops either new or from the Pipes in the Old organ if I consider them sound of good preservation and capable of doing justice to myself and the Parishioners – I contract also to put in at all events all the Wood pipes (which appear in excellent preservation) but not to put in any one of the Reed Stops which I cannot consider right to replace and shall therefore make an entire set of new Reed Stops ——————————————

I contract also to make two pedal stops
1.   Double open wood Diapason Pedal Pipes – 15 notes from CCC to CCC♯ and D
2.   Double Trumpet large scale from CCC to D, also 15 notes   these stops to draw
separate in the usual manner acting on the Pedal keys —————————————

I contract also to make four Copula stops
1.   Great Organ Keys to Pedal Board, two, Swell Organ keys to Pedal Board, three,
Great Organ Keys to Swell Organ keys, 4. Ped Organ Copula 8ve [?] (a coupling
rollerboard for the Pedal Pipes whereby each Pedal key has a pedal pipe attached to
it —————————————

I contract also to make a new Pedal Board of two Octaves and two notes from CCC
the 16 feet to D the second Note above the C the four feet pipe. Also to make a new
bellows of ample dimensions horizontal with my improved pallets and action
complete and perfect —————————————

Also to enlarge the case of the organ in such a way as to contain the new organ and to
alter the design in front by adding a middle tower in the place of the present – the
front pipes however I engage to make new as the old ones are past service. The new
pipes to be gilt and if I can consistently with my own interest & for the money
allowed me, paint or diaper the pipes in the same manner & style as those in the
organ of Westminster abbey [sic] & many of the Cathedrals of England, I will do so,
the whole of the case I contract also to paint —————————————

I contract also to make the draw Stop Knobs of Ebony (as Mr Gauntlett may
choose) according to the size and design of those in St Paul's Organ that is of a large
and massive description the names of the different stops to be engraved on little ivory
plates of different colours inlaid opposite their several draw stop knobs. I contract
also to make the keys of ivory – naturals – and white and black sharps or if with
justice to myself and I can afford to do so, I will make the naturals of mother of pearl,
and the sharps of tortoise shell. —————————————

I further contract to execute the whole of the movements with care and accuracy of
mechanical arrangement, of the best seasoned materials, and to complete and
perfect the organ in an artistlike manner – To prepare its situation in the gallery of
St Peter's Church, fix up and erect the whole complete and perfect for performance
by Saturday the 8th day of March, 1840.
I am to have all the old materials and such of the pipes as are not used in the new
organ –
Before payment the instrument to be approved of by Mr Henry Gauntlett Organist
of Christchurch London and St Olave's Southwark, I contract also to keep the organ
in good tune for six months after its erection –
All this I contract to do for the sum of Four hundred and sixty five pounds Sterling
which if no part of it be advanced me during the progress of the Work is to be paid me
on the said Saturday the eighth day of March 1840 provided the Organ meets with
the approval of Mr Gauntlett –
Dated this 4th day of December 1839   (sigd) Wm Hill   (MS 72: 253–5)

In January 1840, the *Musical Journal* carried details of the new organ,
especially noting the presence of six registers which represented 'a new

quality of tone in this country'; these were (on the Great) 'Clear-Flute, Oboe-Flute, Corno-Flute', and (on the Swell) 'Suabe-Flute, Cornopean, Echo Dulciana Corner à v' (1: 58). Of these, only the last was named in the contract, and they are presumably the additional registers which the committee sanctioned upon the advice of Gauntlett: 'such is the sweetness and brilliancy of their tones ... that the Committee expect an ungrudging acquiescence in the extra expense' (MS 72: 244). There was neither a 'Clear-Flute' nor a 'Corno-Flute' in the completed organ, but it is likely that the intention was realised in the wald-flute and cromorne of the Great Organ.

It seems that Hill failed to meet the completion date, and the organ was not finished until July 1840, for gratuities were voted to the Beadle and Sexton for constant attendance at the church between February and July of that year. The final report of the organ committee was presented to a Special General Vestry on 12 August when it was observed that the organ had already been heard at a charitable function and at a performance of sacred music. The committee concluded its labours with the following reflections:

To those who have had opportunities of hearing the New Organ ... it may appear superfluous to advert to its peculiar excellencies; but as some of the qualities of its tones are of a novel character, time must elapse, even to those most frequently hearing it, ere its varied beauties can be fairly appreciated. Few persons need to be informed that an instrument possessing so many Stops, is capable of yielding almost an infinite variety of harmonious sounds. The Committee, however, now leave the organ to tell its own tale; feeling themselves amply rewarded for all their exertions, if it satisfy those who have so generously contributed towards its erection; and if it be found to aid the devotional solemnity of that divine worship it is intended to assist. (MS 72: 244)

The meeting voted a gratuity of 25 guineas to Gauntlett, whose certificate of approval is entered later in the Vestry Book:

Mr. Hill has completed the Organ in your Church, and I feel extreme pleasure in certifying that he has performed his contract perfectly to my satisfaction, and in a manner worthy of his name and character. I know of no instrument that has been erected for a similar sum that can approach the St. Peter's Organ in weight, brilliancy, and variety of tone, or in that ensemble which is so essentially requisite to constitute the character of a fine organ. (MS 72: 245)

This document completes an unusually intact record of the installation of a mid-nineteenth century church organ.

The performance of sacred music mentioned in the Vestry minutes took place on 16 July and prompted the first public review of the instrument. Gauntlett had contrived a programme 'intended to bring out the effects of the new organ', and he himself presided. The 'selections' were exclusively vocal, but this did not inhibit the *Morning Post* (briefed no doubt by Gauntlett) from passing comment on Hill's work:

The organ itself is a remarkably fine one, with a rich, full, imposing tone and power, and with a brilliancy not unlike that of the famous Haarlem. The trumpets and horns struck us as remarkably fine. The design of the instrument is upon a plan adopted upon the continent, each manual (of the same compass) having a double-open, balanced by an unison-open, large reed stop, and several ranks of mixtures. The swell organ is upon a most comprehensive plan, and the reed and flute stops upon new scales. The plan of the echo-cornet is borrowed from that of the organ of Cologne Cathedral. The compass of the Pedal Board is two octaves and two notes, from CCC to D. Four composition pedal movements. The stops are of ebony, inlaid with mother o' pearl, and the keys of tortoiseshell, ebony, and ivory. Having thus passed the technicalities of description, we have only to add that the structure of the instrument does as much credit to Mr. Hill, the builder, as do the design and development of its effects to Mr. Gauntlett, who impressed its full grandeur upon a brilliant and delighted audience, in some very fine performances. The result seemed to give great satisfaction to – as the occasion had certainly created much interest among – the subscribers.   (18 July 1840)

The specification of the completed organ is appended to Hill's *Circular* of 1841 and copied from it into *Hamilton's catechism*.[2] It is as follows.

Great Organ

Compass, 54 Notes, CC

1.	Bourdon, CCC	11.	Mixture, 2 ranks
2.	Tenoroon Diapason, CC	12.	Doublette, 2 ranks
3.	Stopped Diapason, Bass	13.	Corno-trombone
4.	Stopped Diapason, treble	14.	Corno-clarion
5.	Open Diapason	15.	Claribel-flute
6.	Principal	16.	Oboe-flute
7.	Twelfth	17.	Wald-flute
8.	Fifteenth	18.	Stopped-flute
9.	Tierce	19.	Dulciana
10.	Sesquialtera, 2 ranks	20.	Cromorne

Swell Organ

Same Compass as the Great

1.	Bourdon, CCC	11.	Piccolo
2.	Tenoroon Dulciana, CC	12.	Sesquialtera, 3 ranks
3.	Stopped Diapason, bass	13.	Mixture, 2 ranks
4.	Stopped Diapason, treble	14.	Cornopean
5.	Open Diapason	15.	Tromba
6.	Principal	16.	Oboe
7.	Suabe-flute	17.	Clarion
8.	Flageolet	18.	Echo Dulciana Cornet,
9.	Twelfth		5 ranks
10.	Fifteenth	19.	Dulciana

Pedal Organ

1.	Principal Diapason	16 feet CCC
2.	Contra-Trombone	16 feet CCC

Copula Stops

1.	Swell to Great	3.	Swell to Pedal
2.	Great to Pedal	4.	Octave Pedal

Compass of the Pedal Board, two octaves and two notes, from CCC to D. Four composition Pedal Movements. The Stops of ebony inlaid with mother-o'-pearl shell. The keys inlaid with tortoiseshell, ivory, and ebony.   (Warren 1842: 72–3)

The 1840 organ survived with only minor modifications (1867, 1882) until 1891. In that year, Hill & Son converted the action to tubular-pneumatic, added a Choir Organ and several new stops, and provided a new console; the old keyboards and stop jambs were preserved in the vestry where they may still be seen, together with a few bars of the *Passacaglia in C minor* (BWV 582) and a signature scribbled by Mendelssohn after he played at Cornhill in September 1840. The organ was again extensively rebuilt in 1959–60 by Rushworth & Dreaper.

ST MARY-AT-HILL, 1848

The Vestry Minutes of St Mary-at-Hill, Eastcheap, record that at a meeting held on 1 February 1848, a committee was set up to enquire into the necessary repair of the church and to 'report the state of the Organ' (MS 71). This instrument had been built by Samuel Green in 1788, and possibly incorporated some materials from an earlier organ by Smith (Pearce 1909: 83–4). When the committee met on 14 March, it had before it a letter from the organist, John Burrowes, which read as follows:

As I understand that you wish for some Report as to the state of the Organ, and as to whether it would be advisable to spend money in endeavouring to improve it, I should say that the inefficiency of the instrument does not arise from its being out of repair; on the contrary, it is in very good preservation but it appears to have been originally bad and defective – there are no Stops in it which can be made useful for accompanying the Psalmody or for Voluntaries – another great defect is the absence of pedals and of pedal pipes which renders it difficult to play even a Psalm Tune smoothly to say nothing of the fine effect of a good pedal organ.

   With regard to the method of remedying these defects I should certainly not recommend any outlay on the present instrument as it would be impossible by any additions or alterations to make it a good organ, there being no good foundation or materials to work upon: so that, I think any attempt of the kind, however costly, would but result in disappointment and would never repay the money expended on it.   (MS 71: 14 March 1848)

Hill was in attendance and supported Burrowes's assessment. He had good reason to do so, for the committee had before it his own estimate for a new organ, and this it was resolved to recommend the Vestry to accept. The Vestry in turn authorised the committee to enter into a contract with Hill (16 March) which they did on 21 March. Two months later, the committee voted a further £20 'for additional ornamental work on the front of the

Organ' (26 May). There is no reference in the parish records to the completion of the instrument, but if Hill adhered to his original proposal it would have been finished by the end of September 1848.

Hill's estimate formed the basis of his agreement with the organ committee and is entered in the Vestry Book. It is transcribed below.

March 9th 1848
A Specification and Estimate for a New Organ to be erected in St. Mary at Hill Church London.
To contain two manuals compass of each Manual CC to F in alt 54 notes   Also an independent Pedal Organ compass CCC to E, 2 octaves and 4 notes.
To have a Venetian Swell Box and Shutters.
The bellows to be constructed on the improved plan and to have double action feeders.
To have three composition pedals to the great Organ.
To be enclosed in a handsome case deal painted and grained with gilt speaking pipes in front.

List of Stops

	Great Organ			Feet
1.	Double Open Diapason	metal – lowest 7 notes wood open		16
2.	Open Diapason	metal		8
3.	Viol di Gamba	do		8
4.	Stopt Diapason	wood		8
5.	Quint	metal		6
6.	Octave	metal		4
7.	Octave Quint	do		3
8.	Super Octave	do		2
9.	Wald Flute	wood		4
10.	Piccolo	wood		2
11.	Sesquialtra	metal	3 ranks	–
12.	Mixture	do	2 ranks	–
13.	Posaune	do		8
14.	Clarion	do		4
15.	Krum Horn	do	throughout	8
	Pedal Organ			
1.	Open Wood Diapason			16
2.	Principal	metal		8
3.	Posaune	wood		[16]
	Swell Organ			
1.	Double Diapason	lower octave stopt pipes		16
2.	Open Diapason	metal		8
3.	Stopt Diapason	wood		8
4.	Hohl Flute	metal	(tenor c)	8
5.	Octave	do		4
6.	Octave Quint	do		3

7.	Super Octave	do		2
8.	Suabe Flute	do	[sic]	4
9.	Sesquialtra		3 ranks	–
10.	Cornopean	do		8
11.	Hautboy	do		8
12.	Clarion	do		4

Couplers		**Total Number of Stops**	
1.	Swell to Great	Great	15
2.	Pedal to Great [sic]	Swell	12
3.	Pedal to Swell [sic]	Pedal	3
		Couplers	3
			33

The whole Organ to be constructed of the best materials and in the most substantial and workmanlike manner – The action to work perfectly easy and without any noise – The instrument to be erected complete in the Church for the Sum of £600 net and the old organ for which we allow 100 guineas.

Should an oak case be desired in accordance to the interior of the church it will occasion an additional cost of £20 – We also agree to keep the organ in tune for 6 months free of cost – To be completed within 6 months from the date of the agreement.   (MS 71: 14 March 1848)

When, on the morning after his meeting with the organ committee, Hill entered the scheme in his Letter Book (MS 12: 231), the Great mixture had gained a third rank and the Swell stopt diapason was to be 'cut' (i.e. to draw in halves); otherwise, the completed instrument differed from the original estimate only in minor matters of nomenclature.[3]

The organ (Plate 30) seems always to have been regarded as one of Hill's best. In 1855, it was spoken of as one of 'the two most magnificent organs in London' (the other being St Sepulchre, Holborn), and in an obituary of Hill in the *Musical Standard* it was remarked that 'the tone of St. Mary's organ has, in many respects, seldom, if ever, been surpassed' (*MW* XXXIII, 1855: 441; *MSt* XIV, 1871: 4). The only alterations made to the instrument during Hill's lifetime occurred in 1857, when it was put into equal temperament, additional composition pedals were provided, and 'new radiating peds' were introduced (MS 12: 362).

Thomas Hill added a Choir Organ and two Pedal stops in 1880.[4] New keyboards with reversed colours (black naturals, white sharps) were provided – testimony certainly to Hill's conservatism, but possibly also to the spirit in which he knew his father to have conceived the original organ. New stop knobs were made to match those of 1848, and, in general, Hill's scrupulous respect for the existing instrument gave evidence of the regard in which it was held by the firm. A further reconstruction took place in 1971.

Hill, Norman & Beard replaced the 1880 Choir Organ, introduced Pedal upperwork, and added a mounted cornet to the Great Organ. The old actions were replaced with new ones, using modern materials, and some of the panels in the base of the case were pierced to allow the new Pedal stops to be heard to advantage.[5] This was the state of the organ when the church was engulfed in flames on 10 May 1988. Whilst it seems that most of the pipework and much of the organ's structure have survived, the damage has yet to be fully assessed at the time of writing.

30 St Mary-at-Hill, London, William Hill, 1848.

31 Kidderminster Town Hall, Hill, 1855.

KIDDERMINSTER TOWN HALL, 1855

On 8 November 1854, William Hill recorded an estimate sent to a Mr Pardoe in Kidderminster for an organ to stand in the town's new Music Hall (MS 12: 325). The Hall was to be managed by a private company, funded by public subscription, and had as its object 'the establishment of cheap concerts for all classes' (*MW* XXXIII, 1855: 679). Hill's estimate was accepted, and the organ was ordered on 22 November. It was completed by October 1855 with only minor changes to the original stop list: the cone gamba (Choir) and the salicional (Great) changed places, and the Pedal bourdon made way for a violon. The cost was £826, which included the case (Plate 31) and gilding the front pipes.

The *Musical World* published an account of the organ upon its completion, with the following specification.

Great Organ (C to g³)

Double Diapason	16
Open Diapason	8
Stopped Diapason	8
Cone Gamba	8
Octave	4
Wald Flute	4
Octave Quint	2⅔
Super Octave	2
Sesquialtra	III
Posaune	8

Swell Organ (C to g³)

Double Diapason	16
Open Diapason	8
Stopped Diapason	8
Viol di Gamba	8
Octave	4
Super Octave	2
Cornopean	8
Hautboy	8

Choir Organ (C to g³)

Stopped Diapason	8
Salicional	8
Gemshorn	4
Flute	4
Piccolo	2
Cormorne [*sic*]	8

Pedal Organ (C to e¹)

Open Diapason	16
Violon	16
Octave	8
Trombone	16

Swell to Great
Great to Pedal
Swell to Pedal

Tremulant (Swell)
3 composition pedals

Though certain features of the scheme (56-note compass, strings, a tremulant) hint at future lines of development, both the tone of the instrument and the details of its construction ally it firmly with the Cornhill and Eastcheap organs. A contemporary critic confirms this impression:

The great and deserved reputation of the Messrs. Hill's work renders it unnecessary to say more of the tone of the Kidderminster organ than that it amply sustains the position of its builders. Whether its stops be taken singly or in combination, it is a truly admirable specimen of the voicer's art.   (*MW* xxxiii, 1855: 659)

But if the writer found it unnecessary to descend to generalities he commented interestingly on specific points of the scheme. Hill was praised for his inclusion of 'that absolute necessity', a 16′ metal double on the Great, and for being responsible for the first full-compass string in an English Swell Organ. The soundboards, too, met with approval; unlike most English builders, who crowded their pipes together on small soundboards in a 'careless and ignorant' manner, Hill had here provided spacious soundboards affording the pipes room to speak. Finally, the commentator drew attention to a novelty – the violon 16′:

a wood-stop of exceedingly small scale ... its tone [is] delicate yet prompt in a high degree, [and] bears a strong resemblance to that of a metal stop of the same pitch. It replaces, with excellent effect, the bourdon usually found in the same situation, and as a soft bass, for supporting the lighter qualities of the swell and choir, is superior to anything we have elsewhere met with.   (*MW* xxxiii, 1855: 659)

This was probably the first example of a register which soon established itself as a characteristic and useful member of a Hill Pedal Organ.[6]

Although the organ has not been subject to major alterations since its installation, it has suffered periods of neglect, and has, throughout its life, been more vulnerable to casual damage than many church organs. A public hall houses a variety of activities, and the inevitable changes of temperature, variations in humidity, and circulation of dust and dirt have done the organ no good. The Hall was acquired by the Corporation in 1876. Various complaints about the condition of the organ are recorded and in 1902–3 Hill & Son thoroughly repaired and cleaned it, making some alterations at the same time. The only additions to the specification were three couplers and a Swell voix celeste.[7] Shortly after this another (unnamed) firm added a viol d'orchestre and vox humana to the Swell, and in 1924, Hill, Norman & Beard remodelled the posaune, using harmonic trebles and weighting the tongues (Frampton 1960: 39). In 1950, the same firm substituted a balanced

Swell pedal for the original lever, replaced the vox humana with a quartane and placed a clarion on a vacant slide in the Great soundboard; the pedal compass was extended by one note to f'. The organ was again overhauled in 1973 and 1981. On the latter occasion, electro-magnetic assistance was provided for the Swell to Great coupling actions and the Swell double diapason was made available on the Pedal.

LAYOUT AND ACTION

The construction of the organs of the 1840s presented problems of physical disposition which Hill tackled by adapting the conventional layout of the English organ to accommodate full-compass Swells, 16' Pedal divisions and the more resourceful winding arrangements demanded by enlarged tonal schemes. Cases increased in size (extra height, especially, being provided to conceal Swell boxes) and the building frames necessarily became more complex and of sturdier construction than in the previous era. The multiplication of keyboards and registers impressed the eye as well as the ear; the growing preference for stop-knobs 'of a large and massive description' (Cornhill), together with the attention that was increasingly paid to the details of the console (music desk, key cheeks, engraving, builder's plate), offered a visual complement to the weighty Pedal Organs, sonorous reeds and (undeniably) heavy actions of Hill's most ambitious instruments.

The layout at Cornhill follows what seems to have been Hill's usual pattern for large 2-manual organs, and is a clear development of earlier practice (Lincoln's Thaxted organ, for example). The Great soundboard is at impost level with the (single) bellows beneath it in the base of the organ (Figures 12 and 13). As at Thaxted, the Swell stands above the Great, but is of monumental proportions and occupies almost the entire depth of the case. The rear half of the box incorporates a curious 'attic' (Figure 12); if original (and there is no subsequent explanation for it) it may have housed the echo dulciana cornet. In other respects, the box is a forerunner of the 'cottage' swell boxes which were characteristic of the firm's work later in the century (the Kidderminster box, as shown in Figure 14, is a further variation). By placing the basses in the middle of the soundboard, and causing the ends of the roof to slope down to meet the sides (giving the appearance of a blunted gable) Hill managed to combine the tonal advantages of a tightly packed box with a reasonable degree of access for the tuner. Cornhill demonstrates that he was already thinking along these lines in 1840. The original 15-note Pedal Organ stood on two chests to either side of the Great: much the same arrangement as at Thaxted, except that here, with the need to accommodate two registers of 16' pitch, the chests are placed well below the level of the manual soundboard.[8] The layout of St Mary-at-Hill is essentially the same, though the two Pedal soundboards are at a similar level to the Great and between them accommodate three registers of 29-note compass. A blowing apparatus, splendidly evocative of the labours of Victorian organ-blowers in City churches, survives in the tower space behind the organ; it was, however, probably added in 1880 to supply the enlarged Pedal Organ, and supplemented the original bellows in the base of the organ.

One consequence of the enlarged Swell divisions of the 1840s becomes apparent when one considers a 3-manual instrument such as Kidderminster (Figures 14 and 15).[9] Here (and in any number of later Victorian organs) the

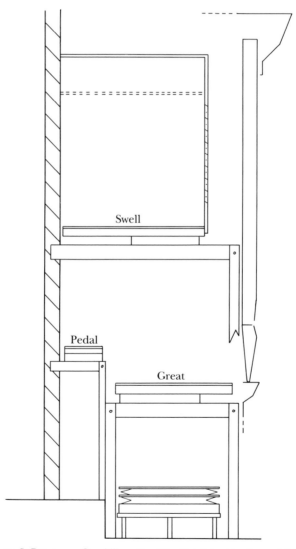

12 St Peter-upon-Cornhill: section. The Pedal chest is a later addition but may be by Hill.

Choir retains its earlier location to the rear of the Great, but in order to
accommodate the full-compass Swell its soundboard is now well below the
level of the Great and its pipework is obscured by roller-boards, passage
boards, action and casework. This situation accurately reflects the relative
importance of Swell and Choir following the reforms of the 1840s (though
some of Hill's schemes suggest that he envisaged a more enterprising role for
the Choir than this might imply) but the masking of what was in any case a
lightly voiced department can hardly have been regarded as satisfactory by
anyone. Later, Henry Willis was to prefer a horizontal layout of the manual
soundboards (an arrangement earlier adopted by Gray & Davison in the

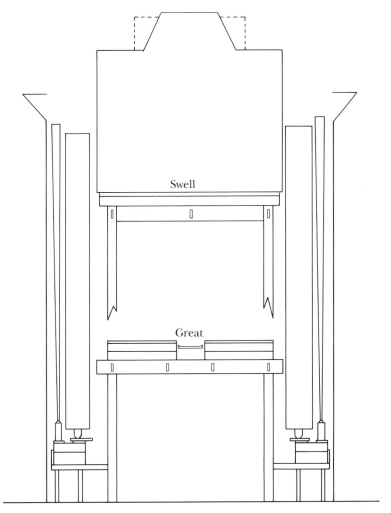

13 St Peter-upon-Cornhill: section. Showing the 1840 Pedal chests that stood on either side
of the main frame.

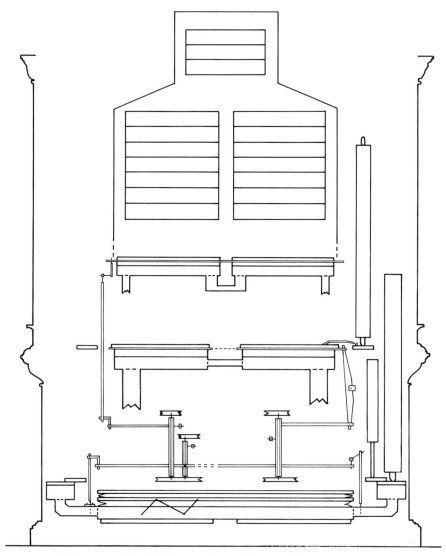

14 Kidderminster Town Hall: stop action and winding of Pedal.

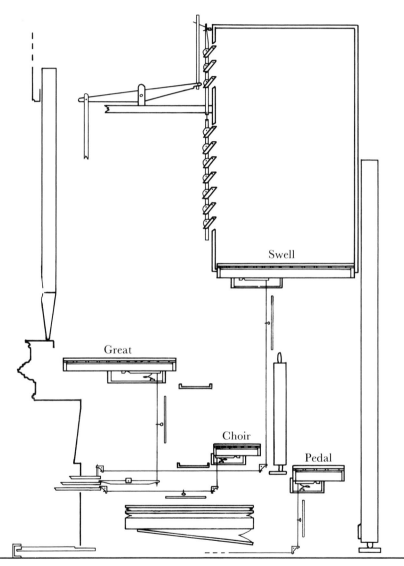

15 Kidderminster Town Hall: key and swell actions. Coupling actions are omitted. The design of the Swell action is curious. It appears that access to the pallets is by means of removing the panel on the underside of the chest [*sic*]. The position of the Swell pallets is conjectural but the position of the pallet wire is accurate.

Exhibition organ of 1851) but this brought other troubles in its train. The truth was that clients were as yet unwilling to provide the space required by enlarged tonal schemes, and builders remained wary of excessively long tracker runs to remote Swell soundboards (a caution amply justified by the results at Kidderminster). These were among a number of factors which gave rise to constant complaints from reformers such as Henry Smart that English builders overcrowded their instruments. Another was the need to find space for the Pedal Organ. At Kidderminster, three of the Pedal registers stand on a slider soundboard at the back of the organ; although this does nothing to ensure clarity, it at least promises a straightforward action layout. But because the open diapason could only be squeezed in down the sides of the case, a complicated action layout had to be adopted whereby the Pedal action travels first to the main soundboard before proceeding, by way of a second roller-board, to the open diapason chests (Figure 16). Such expedients go some way to explaining the enthusiasm with which, first, the pneumatic lever, and then tubular-pneumatic action were greeted.

The action layout at Kidderminster is largely original, though some wooden squares were replaced with metal ones (probably in 1903) and the

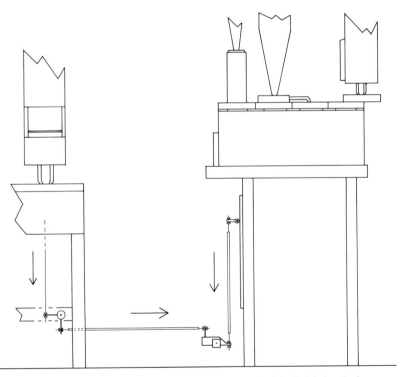

16 Kidderminster Town Hall: detail of pedal action. The end of the Pedal chest is shown on the right; the end of the C♯ Pedal open diapason chest on the left. As well as drawing down the pallet wires in the main Pedal soundboard the rollers connect with a further set of trackers and squares (as shown) attached to trundles beneath the pallet wires of the open diapason chests.

Choir roller-board may have been renewed. It is interesting that the particular combination of backfall action to the Great, and squares and horizontal trackers to Choir and Swell is precisely the same as in Elliot's Crick organ (1819). This meagre evidence is all that survives to give an indication of how Hill designed the action layouts of his larger organs of the 1840s and 1850s. The sparsity of survivals is unfortunate but scarcely surprising. The Victorrian organ, with its soundboards disposed in a horizontal rather than a vertical relationship, perpetuated the use of actions constructed with squares and long tracker runs and these tended to produce a spongy, imprecise touch. Backfall actions offered little improvement, and in all layouts the size of the pallets (especially their excessive width) produced a heavy and frequently deep touch. In the circumstances, we need look no further for an explanation of the fact that a majority of the larger organs of the mid-Victorian years had been pneumaticised by the early-1900s; only neglect (Kidderminster) or poverty (Limehouse) intervened to save a handful from alteration.

   The size of Hill's soundboards made it unnecessary for pipes other than the lowest few notes of a stopped bass or a full-length 8′ register to be stood off. Smart commented on this when reviewing the Panopticon organ:

The sound-boards are of excellent workmanship and unusually large dimensions. In this last particular we recognise an unvarying and important feature of Mr. Hill's practice. He, more than any of our builders, seems to appreciate the fact, that, without ample room round all the pipes on the sound-boards, it is impossible to produce the quality of a grand organ.   (*MW* xxxii, 1854: 476)

In all but the smallest instruments, Hill made the Great soundboard in halves, with basses to either side and trebles in the middle. Some typical dimensions follow (these represent each half of a divided soundboard).

	Length in mm	Width in mm
St Peter, Cornhill (20 slides)	1118	1880
Holy Trinity, Taunton (10 slides)	1219	1372
Eastbrook Chapel, Bradford (14 slides)	1219	1956
St Mary-at-Hill (15 slides)	1270	1829
Kidderminster (11 slides)	1219	1473

The Swell soundboards, which, in a number of instances, had to carry departments of much the same size as the Great, were, if anything, larger than their counterparts, a fact explained by the difficulty of standing any of the pipes off the soundboard. These extensive soundboards presented particular difficulties when it came to winding the pipes. The (comparatively) great width of soundboards with more than a dozen slides meant that the organ-builder had to choose between under-winding the pipes by making the pallet openings (and hence the pallets) too small, and producing a heavy action by enlarging the pallets to admit an adequate flow of wind to the long grooves. Despite developing the box pallet to mitigate the problems of winding large Pedal pipes (above, p. 125) Hill seems not to have tackled the related problem of the manual soundboards. That he was aware of it is clear enough from the provision in the contract for St Peter, Cornhill, that the six lowest notes of the Great Organ should have double pallets 'if necessary' (above, p. 218). In the event, both at Cornhill and in other large organs of this era, they proved very necessary. Wind supply was a further problem when dealing with divisions of the size of the Great at Cornhill. Though the wind-chest is not especially deep internally (111 mm) its width is two-thirds that of the soundboard. With a similar object in mind, Hill provided two chests on the underside of the Great soundboard at Eastbrook Chapel, Bradford (and two sets of pallets), though as this has been altered it is impossible to be sure of the original dimensions. Both were unusually large organs. Kidderminster may be more typical; the wind-chest is half the width of the Great soundboard and the Swell chest is only one-third of its sound-board's width.

Large swell boxes had become such a commonplace of English organ-building by the end of the nineteenth century that it is hard to realise what a novelty Hill's huge Swell divisions represented in the 1840s. By comparison with the boxes which housed the short-compass Swells of earlier years, Hill's mid-century swell boxes were substantial affairs of solid timber, painted on the outside and lined within, provided with doors and removable panels for tuning access, sometimes, even, with internal passage boards. The fronts consisted of sets of horizontal shutters carefully pivoted so that a consider-able weight of timber could be moved with the maximum of ease by the organist. Kidderminster is a typical design, with two main sets of shutters and a subsidiary one in the 'gable' of the box (Figure 14). In the smaller 'cottage' swell boxes which had become common by the 1860s a single set of shutters was usual. It was still unusual to find any means of arresting the movement of the shutters at an intermediate point (above, p. 209), but despite this inconvenience, the mechanical sophistication of the Swell Organs in instruments such as Cornhill and Liverpool united with their extensive tonal resources to inaugurate a new era in English organ-playing.

PIPEWORK

The almost total lack of unaltered Hill organs from the 1840s and 1850s makes it difficult to be sure of the original wind pressures. Although the Hill firm continued to prefer relatively low pressures for both flues and reeds until amalgamation with Norman & Beard (1916) brought about a fundamental change of style, it is probable that wind pressures were slightly increased when the firm reconstructed William Hill's earlier organs, bringing the quality of reeds and foundation work a little more into line with later Victorian and Edwardian taste; it is likely that this was done at Cornhill and

Taunton, where, though most of the original pipework survives without rescaling, and though there are no indications of extensive revoicing, the quality of tone and promptness of speech differ significantly from less altered instruments of the period such as St Mary-at-Hill and Kidderminster. The following wind pressures, recorded recently in organs originally built by William Hill, should therefore be treated with caution.

St Peter, Cornhill (1840)	3″
Holy Trinity, Taunton (1845)	3″
St Mary-at-Hill (1848)	2¾″
Arundel Cathedral (c. 1850)[10]	2⅞″
Kidderminster Town Hall (1855)	3″
St Mary, Hulme (1858)	2¾″

The pressures most likely to be original are those of St Mary-at-Hill and Kidderminster; Arundel and Hulme are less certain, as both organs were extensively reconstructed in the present century (the Hulme organ has now been destroyed). Such slender evidence cannot bear firm conclusions, but we may suggest very tentatively that it was Hill's practice in this period to use a pressure of 3″ for concert organs (Kidderminster) and rather less for church organs. Only in the largest of concert organs (e.g. Panopticon) were chorus reeds placed on a higher pressure than the fluework.

The pipework of the 1840s differs little in construction or style from that of the 1820s and 1830s. Harbouring an ambition to build large organs at (necessarily) low prices, Hill had little incentive to improve the quality of his pipe metal. He continued to use a soft metal with a high lead content, little tin and a portion of antimony, and continued to cast this metal in thin sheets which, when turned into pipe bodies, bruise and dent easily. Things changed after 1855. In the following year, Henry Smart, reviewing the new organ in Lincoln's Inn Chapel, noted thankfully that Hill & Son 'have put aside that nauseous abomination and reproach to English organ-builders in general, "antimony metal", and have made the Lincoln's-Inn pipes of the old-fashioned compound of tin and lead, mingled in pretty nearly the old-fashioned proportions' (*MW* xxxiv, 1856: 788). This appears to mark a new departure. The organ in St Mary's, Hulme (1858), illustrated the change of style; the pipework was of greater substance and weight than that of the preceding decade, and was more resilient to the touch, though in other respects it was very similar.

There is little to distinguish Hill pipework of the early-1840s from that of other English builders. However, in about 1847, Hill began to use a distinctive form of mouthing for his metal pipes, probably best described as an indented French mouth (i.e. the flatting above the mouth bears the impression of two verticals set at right-angles to the upper lip and joined across the top by a semi-circular arch). It is intriguing to speculate why Hill adopted this characteristic feature. It is not unlike the mouthing used by 'Father' Smith 150 years earlier, though lacking the clarity which the stronger and thicker metal of Smith permitted: could this be a conscious allusion? The dating is a little uncertain. The mouthing is not found in the Taunton (1845) or Small Heath (1846) organs, but appears in the chamber organ now in Armitage Mission Church (1847) and in subsequent instruments. It was still found at Hulme (1858) but had changed significantly by the time Hill built the Ulster Hall organ (1861).

All the evidence indicates that it was Hill's practice during these years to design his diapasons with quarter mouths cut up slightly less than a quarter. St John's, Chester (1838), St Peter-upon-Cornhill (1840), Eastbrook Chapel, Bradford (1845), St Mary-at-Hill (1848), Kidderminster Town Hall (1855) and St Mary, Hulme (1858) all bear this out. Languids were thinner than in later practice (between 1 and 1.5 mm at Cornhill, 1.5 to 2 mm at Kidderminster, at the 1' pipe in each case) with a bevel of between 15° and 30° out of the vertical and fairly generous flues. The flatting of the lower lip was not dubbed (i.e. it was not curved in towards the languid) and Hill did not distinguish between unison and mutation ranks in his treatment of either the toes or the flues of his pipes.

Nicking seems to have followed a consistent pattern. There was a distinct change of character between bass and treble, as illustrated in Figure 17. Sketch 1 shows the languid of the 1' pipe of the Great Principal at St Mary-at-Hill; the nicks are lightly made in a 30° languid. Smaller pipes have fewer nicks (4 or 5 in the top octave) and this style of nicking is the one most extensively found in Hill's organs of the 1840s and 1850s. Sketches 2 and 3 illustrate typical nicking in the bass; 2 shows the 2' pipe of the Principal in the Eastcheap organ, and 3 is a type of nicking found in the Taunton (1845) and Ewelme (1840) organs. In the latter, the nicks are quite lightly made: more lightly, in fact, than in some earlier organs by Elliot or Hill (Ashridge, Crick), to which in other respects this style of nicking closely approximates.

A word should be said concerning registers which were not part of the diapason chorus. Hill evidently relied upon scaling, rather than mouthing or voicing, to determine the character of his dulcianas; they have quarter mouths, cut up a quarter, with languids, flues and toes treated identically with the chorus ranks. His practice with cylindrical strings seems to have varied. The hohl-flute in the Swell of St Mary-at-Hill is of the 'holed-flute' type; the upper part of the pipe is a cylindrical slide, made of the same metal as the body, and pierced just below its top edge with two large circular holes located opposite one another; the mouth is narrow (one-fifth), cut up

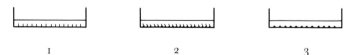

1   2   3

17 Nicking of Hill pipes, 1840s. (1) St Mary-at-Hill, Great principal: 1' pipe; (2) St Mary-at-Hill, Great principal: 2' pipe; (3) Holy Trinity, Taunton: typical nicking.

between a quarter and a third, and the steeply bevelled languids are nicked very lightly. At Kidderminster, however, the Choir salicional is slotted, as is the former Choir viol di gamba (now the Swell salicional) in the Taunton organ. The latter rank exhibits extremely narrow flues, (now) small toes, and little nicking. The mouthing of Hill's other type of string register – the tapering cone gamba – seems to have varied. The scaling of the bodies changed little during the twenty-five years that William Hill made this peculiarly versatile register, and the pipes were voiced much as the diapason ranks apart from a tendency to constrict the windways more than was customary for chorus registers; the mouth widths, however, vary between one-fifth (St Mary-at-Hill) and one quarter (Kidderminster), though the cut-up is consistently a quarter. The tapered gemshorn at Kidderminster has quarter mouths, cut up a quarter.

In turning to matters of scaling it has once again to be stressed that the pipe scales recorded here are highly selective and provide no foundation for definitive conclusions. Reliable studies of all these instruments and their relationship to one another will only become possible when dismantling permits a thorough investigation to be undertaken. Yet even such scanty data as is at present available encourages us to make three general deductions about the design of Hill's German System organs: first, that the scales he employed were not radically different from those of his earlier instruments; secondly, that within a year or two of building the pioneering C-compass organs he had established a scaling practice which, though doubtless varied in special circumstances, then endured for the remainder of the period; and thirdly, that the actual scales used in these organs of the 1840s and 1850s were remarkably similar.

A comparison of the Oldham (Table 11) and Cornhill (Table 21) scales will bear out the first contention. The unusually large scale of the Oldham 4' confuses the issue slightly, but if this is set on one side it will be seen that the scales of the 8's, 2's and mixtures in each case are very similar. Ashridge and Crick reveal a different scaling pattern, but in each case there is an open diapason of virtually identical scale to the example at Cornhill. Despite a limited amount of experimentation with the relationship of ranks within the chorus, there was significant continuity in Hill's scalings before and after the otherwise far-reaching innovations of the 1840s, and a Hill open diapason of the 1850s was made to much the same scale as one of Elliot's from the 1810s or 1820s.

Examples taken from organs of the 1840s and 1850s reveal how rapidly standard scales and scaling practice became established. In general, Hill adopted the same scale for mutations and unisons (including the mixtures) apart from the 16' and 8' registers. This was already the case at Chester (1838) and Cornhill (1840), is largely supported by the surviving details of the Great George Street organ (Renshaw 1968: 90–1), and is demonstrably

Table 21 *St Peter-upon-Cornhill, 1840: scales*

GREAT ORGAN: METAL FLUEWORK

	c	c^1	c^2	c^3
Double Diapason	n.a.	n.a.	40.5	24.25
Open Diapason	n.a.	52	30	19
Dulciana	64*	36	22.5	14
Principal	44	26	16.25	10.5
Twelfth	32	21	14.5	8
Fifteenth	27	17	10.5	n.o.
Tierce	23	15.5	8	7
Sesquialtera I	20.5	18.5	13	10.5
II	16.5	13	12	10

GREAT ORGAN: OPEN WOOD FLUTES (1840)

		Internal	*Sides*
Claribel			
	c^1	36.0 × 45.0	6
	c^2	23.5 × 30.0	5
	c^3	17.0 × 20.0	4
Wald-flute			
	c	36.0 × 46.0	6
	c^1	23.5 × 30.0	5
	c^2	17.5 × 23.0	4
	c^3	12.0 × 18.5	3
Oboe-flute			
	c	28.5 × 39.0	6
	c^1	17.5 × 24.0	4
	c^2	12.0 × 17.0	3
	c^3	6.0 × 10.5	3

true of St Mary-at-Hill (Table 22), Kidderminster (Table 23) and Hulme. In all these instruments the open diapason is three or four pipes larger than the 4′ and the upperwork, and the double diapason (where there is one) is one or two pipes larger. An exception to the latter was Cornhill. There, the double was actually smaller than the 4′, though this may have been due to inexperience (the scaling at Oldham was similar); by the time Hill built the Great George Street organ in the following year the 16′ was larger than the 4′. Evidence is elusive, but this characteristic scaling pattern evolved by Hill during the early-1840s probably differed from his earlier usage. At Crick (1819) and Oldham (1830) the 4′ was of larger scale than the remainder of the upperwork; this gives a distinct breadth to the chorus, in deference to which, perhaps, the twelfth in the Oldham organ is made to a singularly small scale. Influenced by a keener understanding of the purpose of mixturework and mutations, and having in any case increased the massiveness of his choruses by introducing sub-unisons, Hill scaled down his 4′s and kept

Table 22 *St Mary-at-Hill, 1848: scales*

GREAT ORGAN: METAL FLUEWORK

	C	c	c^1	c^2	c^3
Double Open Diapason	n.a.	n.a.	84	48.5	27
Open Diapason	n.a.	n.a.	53	30.5	19
Cone Gamba (top)	n.a.	n.a.	27.5	17	11
(mouth)	n.a.	n.a.	48	26.5	16.5
Quint	91	55	30.5	19.5	11.5
Octave	n.a.	45*	26	17	11.25
Octave Quint	57	32	20.5	12.5	8
Super Octave	46	26.5	17	10.75	6.5

SWELL ORGAN: METAL FLUEWORK

Double Diapason	wd	wd	84	47	27.5
Open Diapason	wd	89*	52	30	18.5
Hohl Flute (a)	n.a.	66	37	24	16
Octave	n.a.	47	26	17.5	11.5
Octave Quint	57	33	20.75	n.o.	8
Super Octave	45	26.5	17.5	12	8

WOODEN FLUTES

	Internal	Sides		Internal	Sides
Gt Stopped Diapason 8' (b)			Sw Stopped Diapason 8' (e)		
c	57 × 69	9.5	c^1	32 × 41	9.5
c^1	33 × 40	7.5	c^2	22 × 29	6.5
c^2	22 × 29	6.5	c^3	16 × 19	5
c^3	16 × 19	5			
			Sw Suabe Flute 4' (f)		
Gt Wald Flute 4' (c)			c	29 × 38	5
c	32 × 44	6.5	c^1	18 × 26	5
c^1	22 × 30	5	c^2	11 × 16	5
c^2	16 × 19	5	c^3	6 × 9	5
c^3	10 × 13	5			
Gt Flageolet 2' (d)					
C	27 × 35	5			
c	18 × 22	5			
c^1	12 × 16	5			
c^2	7 × 10	3.5			
c^3	6.5 (metal)				

(a) Now re-named 'Viola di Gamba' (above, pp. 238–9).
(b) No boring of stoppers.
(c) Open throughout with metal flaps at the tops of the pipes.
(d) Called 'Piccolo' in original specification. Open throughout with metal flaps at the tops of the pipes; the top six notes are metal.
(e) No boring of stoppers.
(f) Open throughout: bottom octave not 1848.

up the scale of his mutations in the 1840s in the interests of a brilliant but still substantial *pleno*. For the same reason, the Swell chorus, conceived as an enclosed Great and quite equal to it in power, was usually scaled in exactly

Table 23 *Kidderminster Town Hall, 1855: scales*

GREAT ORGAN: METAL FLUEWORK

	C	c	c¹	c²	c³
Double Diapason	n.a.	n.a.	n.a.	48.5	27.5
Open Diapason	150*	n.a.	53	30	19.5
Octave	n.a.	45.5	26	16.75	11
Octave Quint	57	33.25	20.5	12.5	9
Super Octave	46	26	n.o.	11	8
Sesquialtra I	38	23	14.25	9.75	11.5
II	32	20.5	13	9	9
III	26	16.5	11.5	11.25	8

SWELL ORGAN: METAL FLUEWORK

	C	c	c¹	c²	c³
Double Diapason		n.a.	n.a.	46	26
Open Diapason		90*	52.5	29.5	19
Octave		46	26.5	16.5	11
Super Octave		26	16.75	11	7.75

CONICAL REGISTERS

		c	c¹	c²	c³
Gt Cone Gamba	top	n.a.	28	17	11
	mouth	n.a.	49	28	17.5
Ch Gemshorn	top	18	14	8	n.a.
	mouth	49	28	17	n.a.

WOODEN FLUTES

	Internal	Sides		Internal	Sides
Gt Stopped Diapason (a)			Ch Stopped Diapason (a)		
c	57 × 68*	10	c¹	32 × 40	6
c¹	33 × 41	7	c²	20 × 27	6
c²	20 × 27	6	c³	15 × 18	4
c³	15 × 18	5	Ch Flute (d)		
Gt Wald Flute (b)			c¹	18 × 26	4.5
c	35 × 45	7	c²	12 × 16	4
c¹	23 × 30	6	c³	8 × 12	2.5
c²	16 × 20	4	Ch Piccolo (e)		
c³	11 × 14	4	C	30 × 38	6
Sw Stopped Diapason (c)			c	18 × 22	4.5
c¹	32 × 40	6	c¹	14 × 17	4
c²	20 × 25	4	c²	10 × 13	3
c³	14 × 18	3.5	c³	n.a.	n.a.

(a) The stoppers are pierced from g♯.
(b) The bottom octave is stopped (and pierced).
(c) The stoppers are pierced from c¹.
(d) The bottom octave is stopped, the remainder open.
(e) A stopped register, with pierced stoppers; the top twelve notes are metal (open).

the same way as the Great Organ; indeed, at St Mary-at-Hill, the Swell scales are if anything slightly larger than those of the main division. Chorus registers on the Pedal seem to have been made to the same scales as Great and Swell (though little material evidence survives). The dismantling of the

Choir Organ's traditional chorus structure, and the disappearance of all the larger Hill Choir Organs of the period, make it impossible to be sure how these divisions were scaled. Original Choir 4's survive at Chester and Taunton (in the latter, as the Swell twelfth); they are much the same scale as the Great 4's in the bass and a little smaller in the treble.

Few of the mixtures in Hill's organs have survived without alteration, and in all but a handful of cases it is impossible to recover their original compositions. Cornhill is a partial exception, and such details as can now be recovered of the original mixture scheme on the Great are set out below.

	Tierce	Sesquialtera	Mixture	Doublette
C	17	19.22	26.29 [?]	15.22
C♯	17	15.19	?	
C♯^{1}	17	12.15	?	
C♯^{2}	17	8.12	?	
g^2				8.15

There are obvious affinities here with earlier instruments. The presence of two 2-rank chorus mixtures is reminiscent of some of Elliot's instruments of the 1810s and 1820s (above, p. 47), and the composition of the lower-pitched mixture allows it to combine with the tierce to make a cornet in the treble octave. The other mixture has not survived but it is likely that its composition was the same as its counterpart in the Great George Street organ; Renshaw suggests that this had had a starting composition of 26.29 (1968: 85–6). The innovation, both at Cornhill and Liverpool, was the doublette. The rack boards survive in the former instrument, and these show clearly that the two ranks were of similar scale to the rest of the upperwork, and that one of them broke back at g^2. This compass suggests that the doublette was intended to serve principally as a solo register.

The independent tierces in the Cornhill and Liverpool organs are atypical (though it is not apparent whether they should be seen as anachronisms or as innovations that failed to command enthusiasm). Hill's standard Great mixture had three ranks, with a starting composition of 17.19.22, and retained the tierce for most of the compass. The earlier examples may have been designed to break back to a cornet composition of 12.15.17 at c^1 or thereabouts (this may still have been the case at St Mary-at-Hill in 1848 – it is now impossible to be certain); by the mid-1850s this was no longer a consideration of any importance, and a rather different pattern was employed at Kidderminster (1855) and Hulme (1858):

C	17.19.22
a^1	15.17.19
c♯^{2}	8.12.15

Tierces were frequently included in second mixtures, too. Though they have otherwise been substantially recast, these mixtures in the Eastbrook Hall and St Mary-at-Hill organs confirm that the starting composition in each case included the octave tierce; it is not known for how much of the compass the tierce was retained, but, by analogy with the other mixture, it is not inconceivable that it remained for most of it.

In the absence of intact survivals an otherwise dubious exercise can, perhaps, be justified. The following mixture compositions are based on information drawn from Hopkins's appendix of specifications and inevitably rely upon the accuracy of the mixture pitches given there. With that qualification, they probably give a reliable account of the starting compositions of the Great mixtures in a number of Hill's larger German System organs.

	Sesquialtra	Mixture
Worcester Cathedral	17.19.22	26.29
Edinburgh Music Hall	17.19.22	26.29
Eastbrook Chapel	17.19.22.26.29	24.26.29
Ashton-under-Lyne	17.19.22	24.26.29
St Mary-at-Hill	17.19.22	24.26.29

Elsewhere (HR1: 258), Hopkins records the starting compositions of the Great mixtures in the Panopticon organ: one of Hill's few opportunities to include three chorus mixtures in a single division. They were:

Furniture III	15.19.22
Sesquialtera III	17.19.22
Mixture III	24.26.29

It may be significant that Hill included a tierce-less mixture in one of the earliest organs to be tuned to equal temperament. It was the abandonment of the old unequal temperament which led many builders also to abandon tierce mixtures in the mistaken belief that the disparity between the tuning of the tierce and the tuning of the thirds would give rise to unacceptable dissonances (cf. HR2: 274–5), though Hill only responded slowly to this view and never altogether discontinued the use of tierces in chorus mixtures.

The Swell mixturework in Hill's organs seems to have followed the same pattern as the Great in as much as the often more limited scope of the choruses would allow. The Swell mixture at Cornhill is probably original and has a starting composition of 17.19.22; it then breaks back in exactly the same way as the Great sesquialtera, with the tierce disappearing at the last break. The initial composition of the sesquialtera at St Mary-at-Hill is the same as at Cornhill and is also original. Even less is known of Hill's Pedal mixtures. They seem usually to have had tierces; if Hopkins is to be believed, Great George Street Chapel, Eastbrook Chapel and Ashton-under-Lyne all had 5-rank Pedal mixtures commencing with the seventeenth, though the largest rank in the Stratford organ was a fifteenth. The only recognisable survivor from the period – in the organ now standing in Arundel Cathedral – commences with a composition of 15.19.22, but it is evident that the pitch of the lowest rank has been altered, possibly when Thomas Hill rebuilt the organ in 1873.

In Hill's organs of the 1840s the wooden stopped diapason retained its traditional place as the foundation of the flute chorus in each division. The construction and scaling were very similar to examples from the previous era (Crick, for instance), though Hill chose to make no distinction between Great, Swell and Choir in the scaling of the pipes (Kidderminster). Cornhill suggests that the earliest wald-flutes were of similar scale to a claribel. Later, the treble was reduced, and a standard scale emerged which is represented by the surviving examples at St Mary-at-Hill and Kidderminster (Figure 11). The suabe-flute and oboe-flute were of virtually identical scale and rather smaller than the wald-flute. The former was really a softer version of the wald-flute, but the tiny cut-up of the oboe-flute (less than one-twelfth), together with the use of a German block rather than an English one, served to produce the quiet reedy timbre which distinguished it from the other novelty flutes with inverted mouths. The flageolet (St Mary-at-Hill) and piccolo (Kidderminster) were open registers of conventional construction; their scaling was similar (though the piccolo is bigger in the treble) and, like all these flutes apart from the oboe-flute, they had lightly nicked blocks and mouths cut up by a quarter of their width.

Hill's chorus reeds (posaunes and trumpets on the Great, cornopeans and horns on the Swell) have suffered alteration even in instruments which are reputed to be tonally unaltered. This is true of both St Mary-at-Hill and Kidderminster. It is therefore impossible to do more than indicate in the most general terms how Hill constructed and scaled these registers.

Most chorus reeds had open brass shallots with flat ends and tongues of soft brass. The shallots sometimes taper, almost imperceptibly, but so as scarcely to reduce the width of the opening. Cornopeans seem to have been constructed with open shallots earlier in the period, but the horn, which gradually established itself as an alternative Swell chorus reed from the mid-1850s onwards, required a closed shallot. Posaunes were of larger scale than trumpets (perhaps as much as twelve notes), as were cornopeans. Some scales (which may or may not be typical) appear in Table 24. They are from an organ which formerly stood in St Mary, Whitechapel (now in St Luke, Cambridge), for which Hill provided new reeds in 1855.

Hill's Pedal reed was nearly always a wooden trombone, though an early example (St Luke, Cheetham Hill) had resonators made of zinc (HR2: 144). The sides of the wood resonators are thin (8 mm at C, in St Mary-at-Hill) and the scales vary a little: Eastcheap and Kidderminster are much the same, the early Cornhill example is rather smaller (165 mm square at the top of the pipe compared with 190 mm). Shallots are of brass, and open, and wood boots are common in the bottom octave.

Little survives of Hill's solo reeds. The present Choir cremona at Cornhill

Table 24 *Hill reeds: St Mary Whitechapel, 1855 (now in St Luke, Chesterton, Cambridge)*

Great Trumpet					
	(1)	(2)	(3)	(4)	(5)
C	105	16	90	16	6
c	80	12	55	11	5
c¹	60	10	38	9	4
c²	48	7	25	8	3
c³	42	6	16	6	2.5
Swell Horn (a)					
c	100	15	66	13	4
c¹	80	12	44	10	3.5
c²	60	10	28	8	3
c³	45	7	19	7	2.5

1 Diameter of resonator (top).
2 Diameter of resonator (neck).
3 Exposed length of shallot.
4 Diameter of shallot at end.
5 Width of shallot opening at widest point.

(a) The horn has closed shallots from C to e².

is the former Great cromorne; it (now) has closed brass shallots, and is in all respects an unexceptional cremona. At Taunton, Hill reverted to earlier custom and provided a bassoon bass (thirteen notes) with wooden resonators to his Choir reed; otherwise, the rank is exactly like the Cornhill stop. The Hautboy at Kidderminster has thin flared resonators in the bottom octave, and above this develops long bells. A similar register in the little organ of 1846, now at St Gregory, Small Heath, Birmingham, has open shallots in which the openings taper markedly (more than the body of the shallot), no doubt to yield a closer tone.

CONSOLES AND CASES

The transformation of the English organ brought about by the German System found an inevitable reflection in the increased physical scale of the organ console and the organ case. Just as the conventional tonal schemes of the English long-compass organ were inadequate to meet the demands of the 1830s and 1840s, so the cases which had served those (largely) modest instruments did not provide wholly satisfactory models for their ambitious successors. The largest German System organs had complete Pedal divisions, and where these were accommodated on divided slider soundboards located on either side of the Great soundboard (Liverpool and Bradford;

probably also Newgate Street, Stratford-upon-Avon and Ashton-under-Lyne) a case of significantly greater width than that necessitated by even the grandest long-compass organ was required. Height was a further important consideration. A number of organs of the 1820s and 1830s had already shown that the enlargement of the Swell Organ would have consequences for case design (above, p. 216). With the advent in the 1840s of Swells competing in size and compass with the Great, the provision of adequate cover for the huge swell boxes became crucial. In some instances a particularly massive central tower was provided (Great George Street had nine pipes, Eastbrook Chapel had seven); in others a wide central flat met the need (Ashton-under-Lyne, Kidderminster); generally, front pipes were made overlength (Great George Street, Kidderminster), and the necessity of contriving a screen to conceal the top-heavy structure which lay behind limited the builder's (or architect's) scope for that subtle interplay of towers and flats, pipe mouths and pipe shades, which is one of the most distinctive features of the best English organ cases of the eighteenth century. Some of the resulting cases impress by sheer grandeur of scale, but there is usually something slightly ungainly about the composition, and it is seldom that the detailing can bear comparison with earlier work.

Sometimes Hill was obliged to retain an existing case, and where this was so, the reconstruction of the old case offers a convincing illustration of the difference in scale between old and new. Organs on screens were generally more easily managed in this respect than those sited on galleries. At Worcester Cathedral (1842) and King's College, Cambridge (1860), Hill simply deepened the main case to accommodate the new organ (in neither instance was this wholly satisfactory: the short-compass Swell at Worcester was probably dictated by lack of space, and at King's, Hill only acquired sufficient space for the enlarged organ by moving the east front of the case so far forward that the keys had to be placed at the side). By contrast, the cases at Christ Church, Newgate Street (by Harris) and St Peter Cornhill (by Smith) had to be completely reconstructed. At Cornhill, the case (Plate 29) was heightened by the introduction of a large central tower, and at Christ Church, greater width was attained by turning a 3-tower case into one with four towers, and introducing a broad central flat of nine pipes (Plate 27). The Newgate Street case was probably deepened at the same time by bracketing the upper part out above the keyboards and supporting it on four Corinthian columns; the original double flats were converted into single ones, no doubt to emphasise the massiveness of the composition (the case before and after Hill's work is illustrated in Plumley 1981: 46, 57). No doubt conservatism dictated the retention, as far as possible, of existing fittings in City churches, and in a similar spirit, the (new) case of Hill's organ for St Mary-at-Hill was, for its day, a brilliant exercise in antiquarianism (Plate 30). It is modelled on 'Father' Smith's 4-tower cases, and, with its double flats, resembles most closely his case in St Clement Danes, now destroyed (Freeman and Rown-tree 1977: 33). With the exception of the rather narrow central flats and the similar lengths of all the pipes in the pairs of outer flats, upper and lower, occasioned by the use of a rising, rather than a horizontal division between these double flats, it is closely attentive to Smith's style and wholly appropriate to its setting. Presumably James Savage (who restored the church at this time following a fire) and W. G. Rogers, who executed much of the magnificent woodwork for the church in a thoroughly antiquarian spirit, had a hand in it, but the idea, and the correctness of the proportions and details, may have been due to Hill.

Outside London, the trend already noted (above, p. 79) continued and Gothic was more and more regarded as the only proper style for church organ cases. Ashton-under-Lyne is a particularly striking example, in which a large west gallery organ case forms part of an integrated scheme of refurbishment in pre-ecclesiological Gothic (Plate 32); this is the organ case as screen at its most unapologetic. Altogether more satisfactory (because its proportions are better and towers have been retained) is the contemporary case for Holy Trinity, Taunton, though its appearance is not improved by the vertical posts which separate the pipes in four of the five towers, nor by the overlength of many of the front pipes (Plate 33). Of a completely different order, both of scale and inspiration, was Scott's case for Ely Cathedral (1851). Like the Great George Street case, it was based on a continental model (in this instance, the Strasburg Cathedral organ) and so offers an informative commentary on the influences shaping the musical character of these German System instruments. Scott's work at Ely represents a new departure in English case design and will be discussed further below (p. 332). At the other end of the spectrum, small church organs of the 1840s and 1850s seem invariably to have had cases in the Gothic style. Hill's organs at Ewelme (1840), Small Heath (built in 1846 for West Bromwich) and Cottenham (1847) are examples.

Gothic still had unhappy associations for nonconformists, and so it was that several of Hill's most ambitious German System organs were clothed in cases of broadly classical inspiration. The most remarkable was Great George Street Chapel, Liverpool (Plate 34). Hill sent a design for a case 'in the Corinthian style' with his original estimate (MS 12: 81, 84), but later correspondence (97–8) implies that the committee was considering opting for another, more expensive design, possibly by a Liverpool architect (Joseph Franklin, the architect of the Chapel, is the most likely candidate). Whoever was finally responsible, and despite the intrusion of a huge central tower, partially masking the Swell box, it is likely that the inspiration for the design was the Chalgrin case of 1776–81 in St-Sulpice, Paris. Like its Parisian prototype, the Liverpool case is spoilt by the uniform length of its front pipes, and the fact that most of them are also overlength contributes to

32 Ashton-under-Lyne Parish Church, Hill, 1845.

33 Holy Trinity, Taunton, Hill, 1845.

the design's failure to attain that monumentality which is one of the strengths of St-Sulpice. It is also much cruder in detail than Chalgrin's case. But an ultimate lack of refinement should not be allowed to detract from the true significance of the Great George Street case. Its appearance in a Lancashire nonconformist chapel of the early-1840s is wholly unexpected, and the testimony which it offers to the broadening vision of at least one English organ-builder is decisive. (Presumably neither Hill nor Gauntlett enlightened the Congregationalists of Liverpool as to the inspiration of the design.)

By comparison with Great George Street, the other large nonconformist

34 Great George Street Chapel, Liverpool, Hill, 1841.

organ case of the 1840s (Eastbrook Chapel, Bradford) harks back to an earlier English tradition. It is massively constructed of Spanish mahogany. The tower caps have a Grecian feel about them, the pipe shades and the flats finished with little ogee-shaped arches allude discreetly to Gothic, and the brackets supporting the two outer towers are similar to those found in so many English cases of the eighteenth and early-nineteenth centuries (Plate 35).

Such an eclectic approach was equally acceptable in concert organs. The Edinburgh Music Hall organ (1843) had a 4-tower case in a plain classical style. Twelve years later, Kidderminster was more enterprising (Plate 31).

35 Eastbrook Hall (formerly Eastbrook Chapel), Bradford, Hill, 1845. (1987)

The style of the case, as of the Hall, is aptly described as 'motley classicism' (Cunningham 1981: 130); the juxtaposition of elements from various classical vocabularies, together with the disarmingly naïve over-scaling of some features, give the case an exuberance wholly appropriate to a place of public entertainment. Whether the design was supplied by Hill or by the architects of the Hall (Bidlake & Lovatt) is not known.

The ambitious tonal schemes which led to the construction of organ cases of a monumental scale also had implications for the console. Pedal boards had to be introduced; a greater number of stop knobs had to be accommodated; a few accessories (in the case of the largest organs) had to be found a place. If the resulting consoles appear to us to be cumbersome and difficult to manage, even by comparison with those which were being constructed fifteen or twenty years later, then it must be remembered, first, that the mechanical arrangement of these vast instruments presented a novel challenge to builders of William Hill's generation, and secondly, that until the 1850s and 1860s few organists had much idea of how the latent resources of these instruments might be effectively exploited if a more perfect mechanism and more sophisticated stop controls were available.

Few of Hill's original consoles survive. The most interesting is that at Cornhill, now preserved as a museum-piece in the vestry (Plate 36). The stops are of ebony, inlaid with mother-of-pearl, and the stop names are engraved on plates set into the jamb above each knob. The stylistic affinity with eighteenth-century consoles in north-west and central Europe is striking, and provides a visual commentary on the inspiration behind Hill and Gauntlett's innovations at the beginning of the crucial decade. But handsome though it is in appearance, this cannot have been the easiest of consoles to manage. The knobs are certainly 'large and massive', as stipulated in Hill's contract, and this, together with the generous spacing between them and the long action runs (to the Swell especially) which would have contributed to a stiff movement, must have militated against smooth stop changing. It is doubtless significant that Mendelssohn required two assistants to change the stops when he played at Cornhill in 1840 (MS 68: f. 10). An additional difficulty for anyone unfamiliar with the console would have been the layout of the knobs. Though there is a rudimentary system behind it (Great to the right, Swell to the left; Pedal below the Great and couplers below the Swell), the detailed arrangement of the stops within each division seems not to have been planned with the slightest regard for their likely use by an organist – a curious omission on Gauntlett's part. By spreading the stops of a single division over three columns Hill introduced an unnecessary complication. Later, in the St Mary-at-Hill organ, the stops were arranged in a more conventional fashion, with Great and Swell each in two columns, reeds at the top and sub-unisons at the bottom (this is assuming that the original arrangement was preserved in 1880, as seems likely). In the largest organs, however, multiple columns could not be avoided. Birmingham Town Hall was an example. A photograph of the organ (c. 1880) shows Hill's 1849 console, with the stops arranged in five columns to the left and four to the right of the player (Thistlethwaite 1984: 20).

The situation was not made any easier by the size of the knobs. Hill continued to use knobs similar to those of the 1820s and 1830s for his smaller instruments (Small Heath, for example), but the knobs employed in his more ambitious organs were distinctly large by both earlier and later standards. Those at Birmingham had a diameter of 51 mm.[11] St Mary-at-Hill's were not as large (45 mm), and by the mid-1850s, Kidderminster (37 mm) represents a norm which endured for a good many years in the firm's work.

36 St Peter-upon-Cornhill. The console of 1840, now preserved behind glass in the organ gallery.

By the time Kidderminster was built, Hill had also adopted a standard disposition for the different departments at the console; there, and at Turvey (1855), Great (above) and Choir (below) occupied the right-hand jamb, and Swell and Pedal the left. Things may have been more flexible in the previous decade; both Small Heath and St Mary-at-Hill have Great and Swell to left and right respectively.

Nothing is known about the dimensions or alignment of pedal boards in Hill's organs at this period, though Mendelssohn evidently found the pedal keys at Birmingham defective and requested broader ones (Polko 1869: 235). Nor is anything known about the accessories provided by Hill in a few of his largest instruments. The Birmingham organ had more than most. There were nine composition pedals acting upon different departments of the instrument, but their real usefulness has to be questioned in the light of Stimpson's reference to his 'huge pedal organ of fifteen stops, to throw out which requires the force of a steam engine, while to draw them in is worse still' (*MO* xiii, 1890: 470). Whatever the constructional strengths of Hill's German System organs, and whatever his skill in developing their tonal resources so as to bring about a radical transformation in the character of the English organ, it cannot be denied that they were, for the most part, mechanically unsophisticated instruments, poorly equipped to meet the demand for greater musical flexibility which the rising generation of organists was voicing.

9

The Transition

Throughout the 1840s, Dr Gauntlett as leading proponent, and William Hill as chief practitioner of the German System, went largely unchallenged. None wrote so comprehensively of the merits of the new system and the demerits of the old as did Gauntlett in his various articles and reviews, and with a succession of the largest organs to his credit, Hill had, by the middle of the decade, an experience and reputation which no other builder could equal. The destruction of these instruments denies us the opportunity of judging for ourselves, but Hill's Letter Book (MS 12) yields evidence of a surge of enquiries about new C-compass organs in the wake of Stratford and Great George Street, and these would hardly have been forthcoming had not the early German System organs excited approval. Another token of success was the gradual adoption by other builders of the principles upon which these organs were designed. The stop lists in the appendix to the 1855 edition of Hopkins & Rimbault (HRI: 145–297) offer the classic illustration of this. They show that metropolitan and country builders alike had chosen or been obliged to take up C-compasses, extensive Swell divisions, manual sub-unisons, Pedal Organs and a whole range of tonal and mechanical novelties. Beside these examples of modern organ-building, the surviving long-compass instruments – a category which still, in 1855, included most of the cathedral and collegiate organs – begin to look distinctly old-fashioned. In adopting the principles first demonstrated by Hill and Gauntlett, most builders had been selective: few had the courage (or the opportunity) to develop schemes as ambitious as the largest of Hill's instruments. Some found themselves defeated by the technical demands, both tonal and mechanical, of the new style, and contemporary reviews make it clear that then, as now, an impressive paper scheme did not guarantee an impressive musical instrument. But whatever their shortcomings, these instruments are irrefutable evidence that the principal reforms of the 1840s had come to stay. By 1855, it took the obduracy of a Wesley to defend long compasses, and he was widely ridiculed for his pains.

The only builder other than Hill to work with Gauntlett on a series of organs was H. C. Lincoln (above, p. 189). All but one were small, and offered limited scope for expressing the principles of the German System. Yet Lincoln's *New organ circular for 1843*, whilst heavily indebted to both Gauntlett and Hill, contains a succinct account of the System which Gauntlett's verbose outpourings never matched, and which was uncomplicated by some of the more bizarre experiments attempted by Hill. The advantages of the new mode of construction over the old are summarised in nine points. First, the introduction of sub-unisons and the quint gives the chorus 'a more weighty and solemn character of tone', neatly complementing the 'brilliant and silvery character' conferred by 'the new mode of arranging the Sesquialteras, Mixtures, and by the use of a new Stop, called the Doublette'. Then, the new organs have 'a more soft and varied character, from the circumstance, that instead of the Instrument only possessing one Flute, it has three, four, or even six, all of which combine with the new Stops in producing an entirely new quality of tone to the Organ'. New reeds also reinforce the 'breadth and body of tone', combining 'the weight of a Diapason with the fullest tone which it is possible to give a Reed Pipe', whilst, at the other end of the spectrum, Lincoln commends the 'distant, subdued, and piano effect, combined with brilliancy' of the tenoroon dulciana and the echo dulciana cornet. Having run through the musical advantages of the new system, he turns to value for money. There are more pipes to each key ('and at a less expense') than hitherto; the soundboards contain 'nearly double' the quantity of pipework in ordinary organs; no money is 'thrown away upon useless mechanism, but the greatest attention is paid to create music in every possible variety and combination'. All in all, the improved organ combines 'the breadth and variety which distinguish the Continental Organ, with the universally recognised sweet and silvery tones produced by the English mode of voicing and finishing the pipes'. As a concise summary of the intentions of progressive builders during the 1840s, this could scarcely be bettered. Given the opportunity to turn theory into practice, Lincoln acquitted himself creditably at St David's Cathedral (1843), building a substantial 2-manual organ with quint, double and wald flute on the Great, and a piccolo and doublette on the tenor-c Swell. But he was defeated by Gauntlett's monster organ at St Olave's, Southwark; Lincoln began its construction in 1844, but had eventually to make way for the more experienced Hill who completed it in 1846.[1]

Other London builders were more successful than Lincoln in coping with the mechanical demands of large organs. Bevington survived the experience of working with Gauntlett at Nottingham (1849) and went on to build two large organs in the metropolis in the mid-1850s. The first was for St Martin-in-the-Fields (1854); it had fforty-nine stops, and with sub-unisons and mixtures in all divisions and a 16′ reed chorus in the Swell, it was one of the largest organs in London. Henry Smart (a forthright critic) wrote approvingly of the design and finish of the mechanical portions of this instrument: they were, he judged, 'considerably better than is usually seen'. The keys were 'at once noiseless and agreeable to the finger', and their actions were 'simply planned, and very carefully executed'. He also commended the stop action, the leverage of the Swell shutters and the blowing action, all of which made extensive use of wrought-iron in their construction, and thereby gained in strength and silence. But turning to the tonal qualities of the instrument, Smart was scathing. Delivering a short lecture on the formidable difficulties of scaling and voicing large organs, he illustrated his remarks with reference to Bevington's failures at St Martin's. The scales were 'injudiciously selected', the voicing 'timid and irresolute'. In the Great Organ, 'the diapasons are strong, horny, and rather fierce in tone, whence, through all the series of quint, principal, tenth, twelfth, and fifteenth, there is a continual abatement of strength, until we arrive at the ten ranks of mixture which suddenly break out with a crash, that startles us the more from the want of all proper middle-support'. A similar 'thinness and want of balance' characterised all the choruses, and the reeds were so poor (according to Smart) that Bevington would be well-advised to replace them forthwith. Despite the 'charming effect' of individual registers, the instrument as a whole was a 'failure' (MW xxxII, 1854: 803; 835–6). Smart's criticisms of Bevington's organ for the Foundling Hospital (1855) were only marginally less damning. Though admitting that the tone was 'a manifest improvement' on St Martin's, he still found the diapason work 'fierce and cutting', and complained that the reeds lacked 'breadth and richness of effect' (MW xxxIII, 1855: 677). Anyone acquainted with Bevington's surviving organ in St Paul's, Covent Garden (1862) may feel that Smart had a point.

Bevington's large organs were not the only examples of achievement failing to match ambition. Robson produced a number of impressive schemes during this period, in which the principles of the German System were fully developed. The organ for St Michael's, Chester Square (1847) was designed 'with especial reference to . . . the accompaniment and support of congregational singing' (HR2: 479); it had complete flue choruses on all three manuals, a 16' reed chorus in the Swell and claimed to be the first London organ in which the 30-note compass of the pedal board was matched by the compass of the (three) Pedal registers. St Michael's, Cornhill (1849), was only a little smaller, and it was followed (probably: the date is elusive) by a 40-stop organ for Buxton Road Chapel, Huddersfield. The Great had a complete chorus in the Hill manner and the Swell had a 16' reed. Each of the Pedal stops was provided with an additional octave of pipes for use with an octave coupler: an unnecessary, if eye-catching, feature for a Pedal Organ that boasted nine independent registers. Equally striking were the three 10-rank [sic] mixtures to be found on the Great of Robson's next large organ: that for St John's Cathedral, Newfoundland (1853). Confronted with such novelties, it is important to set Robson's achievements into perspective, and, with this in mind, Smart's comments on the organ for the Victoria Hall, Belfast (1855) are instructive. He found it 'a marked improvement' on Robson's previous work; the mechanical side was executed 'with great neatness and efficiency', and there was evidence that Robson was 'struggling hard for advancement' in the tonal finish of his instruments. Once again, though, the complaint was 'that his style of voicing . . . has not been at all adapted to the larger class of instruments' (*MW* xxxiii, 1855: 84). Smart's view receives some support from the fact that Walker was called in to carry out a complete revoicing of the Chester Square organ in 1862, softening the loud stops and rearranging the mixtures (ms 20: 35). Robson's large organs were clearly not unqualified successes.

Bevington and Robson must be numbered amongst those builders who, in the wake of the successes of Hill and Gray & Davison in the early-1840s, took up the German System with enthusiasm, if not total assurance. Others relinquished their existing practice less willingly. Joseph Walker for long remained 'an unflinching advocate of that unsymmetrical, inconvenient, and, indeed, absurd arrangement in which the compass of the manuals is G G or F F F, and that of the Pedals C C C' (*MW* xxxii, 1854: 559). Personal conviction had to give way to commercial necessity, and Walker began to make C-compass organs during the 1840s. He was still, though, building large F F-compass organs at the end of the decade, including a 30-stop instrument for Christ Church, Clifton (1849), and persisted in making small organs to the old compass into the early-1850s. But even Walker could not resist the tide indefinitely. By 1850, the Shop Book reveals that C-compass organs had begun to outnumber those with long compasses, and in 1853, a large 2-manual organ for St Vedast, Foster Lane (where Ann Mounsey, one of the Mendelssohn–Gauntlett circle, was organist) marked a new departure. Despite the conventionality of the nomenclature (though 'Tenoroon' and 'Corno Trombone' appear in the original version of the stop list) this was not unlike a smaller version of Hill's instrument at St Mary-at-Hill, with a full-compass Swell and three Pedal stops. In the following year, Walker completed a large 3-manual organ for Highfield Chapel, Huddersfield, which, it was noted, went 'further in the direction of modern completeness than has hitherto been its builder's custom' (*MW* xxxii, 1854: 559); the thirty-four stops included a quint and two 2's on the Great, a viol di gamba on the Choir and a keraulophon on the full-compass Swell. Other substantial C-compass organs followed: among them, Epsom Parish Church and St Barnabas, Kensington (both 1856), and Romsey Abbey (1858); but it was not until the late 1850s that the firm's organs finally discarded the conservative image lent them by old-fashioned nomenclature and an unwillingness to explore the repertoire of modern strings, flutes and reeds. As late as 1860, Walker built an organ with F F compass (ms 17: 324).

Holdich was another reluctant convert. His *métier* remained the small church organ, with one or two manuals and a dozen stops, and he succeeded in adapting his practice to include C-compasses and a sub-unison without much difficulty. The surviving organ at Easton-on-the-Hill, dating from the mid-1850s, is a good example (Appendix 1, pp. 468–9). Tonally, he remained a conservative. The 3-manual organ for St Neots (1855) is little more than an expanded version of Easton-on-the-Hill; each department has a sub-unison, but, otherwise, only a cornopean distinguishes the nomenclature from that of the 1830s. Henley-on-Thames (also 1855) was a little more adventurous: the Choir had a piccolo, and the Swell a viol di gamba and a double trumpet; the tone, though, was said to be coarse, and the reeds 'deficient in quality and finish' (*MW* xxxii, 1854: 756). Holdich's *magnum opus*, the organ for Lichfield Cathedral (1861), exhibited a similar juxtaposition of old and new elements. It was a curious scheme (Appendix 1, pp. 469–70). The Choir Organ was a complete anachronism and might have been designed half a century earlier. The Great and Swell, with their divided registers, short-compass stops and small mixtures, recalled one of Hill's early German System schemes. The surprise was the 10-stop Pedal Organ. With its metal 32', montre 16', two mixtures and two reeds it was more ambitious than any Pedal division provided by Hill for an organ of comparable size. Despite having its good points, neither the incoherence of the scheme, nor the unfortunate siting (it was placed in the chapels on the eastern side of the north transept) augured well for the success of the instrument, and most of Holdich's work was replaced when Hill rebuilt the organ in 1884.

Provincial builders, like their metropolitan counterparts, responded with differing degrees of enthusiasm and competence to the German System. John Banfield, a Birmingham organ-builder, reconstructed the organ in St Mary's, Warwick, in 1842, leaving it with a 16-stop Swell in the Hill manner (though the compass was only from tenor c); in 1853, he built a 3-manual and pedal organ for St Paul's, Liverpool, which, although something of a hybrid, was notable for its 7-stop Pedal and C-compass Swell Organ. John Nicholson of Worcester (established 1841) built a large 3-manual for Gloucester Shire Hall in 1849: the scheme was reminiscent of Hill's work, with its wald- and suabe-flutes, cornopean and trombone, and included strings on Choir and Swell and a 6-stop Pedal division.[2] Five years later (1854), he built an extraordinary instrument for Worcester Music Hall[3] in which extensive enclosure (both Choir and Swell were enclosed, the latter in a vast chamber to one side of the organ) and a thoroughgoing deployment of recent novelties (including some of Nicholson's own contrivance: the dulciana 16' in the Pedal is a significant refinement) produced one of the most advanced orchestral organs of the day (Appendix 1, pp. 471–2). Further north, Kirtland & Jardine, successors to Renn, were making their mark with ambitious organs for Holy Trinity, Hulme (1852) and St Peter's, Manchester (1856); more will be said of both these instruments below (pp. 303–4).

Other builders (Holt of Bradford, Dicker of Exeter, Jones of Sheffield, and the Nicholsons of Bradford and Newcastle) sought to imitate their London counterparts but little has survived of their work. The 1850s and 1860s were crucial years for provincial organ-building. New businesses (some of which would come to rival the metropolitan builders in output and quality) were establishing themselves, and new influences, which would cause the emergence of distinct 'schools' of organ-building outside London, were beginning to make themselves felt. An account of this belongs to a later chapter. There are, though, two metropolitan builders whose work has yet to be considered. Henry Willis's achievement will be discussed below (pp. 412–41). His instruments for Winchester (1854), Carlisle (1856) and Wells (1857) already reveal a characteristic blend of insular tradition, German System and Willis's own highly individual creative imagination, and it seems legitimate to consider his work of the 1850s as a prelude to the mature successes of the following decade. It must be remembered, though, that for contemporaries, the ascendancy of the builder of the St George's Hall organ lay in the future. It was not Willis, but Gray & Davison who mounted the strongest challenge to Hill's hegemony in the middle years of the century. A previous generation gave grudging acknowledgement to Hill's role in the evolution of modern organ-building, usually depicting him as a primitive harbinger of Willis (a not inconsiderable accolade in the eyes of those who wrote about the organ in the earlier part of the present century). In recent years, much has been done to restore Hill to his proper place as the central figure in nineteenth-century organ-building, but Gray & Davison's contribution remains largely unrecognised. Yet in the 1850s, their work matched Hill's in importance, and set the pace of change for that decade much as Hill's had for the 1840s. The remainder of the present chapter must therefore be devoted to a consideration of their work.

GRAY & DAVISON, 1840 – 51

When Frederick Davison quit his partnership with William Hill to join Hill's chief rival, John Gray (1838), he took with him the experience of designing the first large organ on the German plan to be built in England (above, p. 183). He and Gray might reasonably have expected this to place them in a strong position to compete with Hill for business, should the new mode become established. It is therefore a disappointment to discover that, with a single exception, it was not until the end of the 1840s that Gray & Davison found themselves with opportunities to build C-compass organs on the scale of Hill's grandest instruments. No doubt this was partly due to Hill's determination to secure contracts by submitting low tenders and partly to Gauntlett's vigorous advocacy; being, by these means, first in the field, Hill gained a formidable advantage. But it may also be that the boldness of Hill's schemes, with their colourful nomenclature and vast expressive divisions, had a greater appeal for a generation that prized innovation than had the more staid offerings of Gray & Davison. The distinction is detectable in the tonal character of the instruments built by the two firms. Gray & Davison's diapason choruses are blander than Hill's, the flutes are less varied, the mixtures less forthright. Only when it comes to the reedwork can these organs compete with Hill's for sheer excitement. John Gray was widely acknowledged to be 'the best reed-voicer in the country' (*MP*, 18 July 1840) and his chorus reeds were direct descendants of 'that brilliant, *clangy*, description of reeds which Byfield made so deservedly famous' (below, p. 290); his trumpets and clarions imparted a vitality and colour to the choruses which distinguished them from the weightier, more massive effect of Hill's posaunes. The tradition established by John Gray outlived him (he died in 1849), and the firm was well placed to respond to the French fashion of the 1850s with its inevitable interest in reed tone.

Throughout the 1840s Davison remained largely content with the principles laid down in the Chester scheme of 1838. The 3-manual organ for St Saviour's, Liverpool (1840) was an unambiguous development of it; the double was on the Great, rather than divided between Choir and Swell, and the 4-stop Pedal had pretensions to being a chorus and not simply a bass (though, as in several of Hill's early C-compass organs, each rank had only a single octave of pipes), but in other respects, the Liverpool organ was very similar to Chester, only smaller. Excepting the C-compasses, the Pedal and the sub-unison, the stop list was conventional. In the following year (1841), the organ for Christ Church, St George's-in-the-East, was more enterprising, with doubles on both manuals, a complete Swell chorus and a 4-stop Pedal Organ with a reed. Even so, there are conservative features: the clarabella, double dulciana and divided sesquialtera & cornet in the Great convey an unmistakable whiff of the 1830s, and the absence of tonal novelties is in marked contrast to Hill's German System organs of the same year.[4]

Frustrated, perhaps, by the lack of orders for C-compass organs, Davison seized the opportunity presented by a commission to build an organ for the new church of St Paul's, Wilton Place, Knightsbridge, to create a 'Model Organ on the German Plan'. This was offered to the musical public 'for future imitation and preference' (*MW* xviii, 1843: 140) and was completed in 1843 (Plate 37). The scheme is a comprehensive statement of Gray & Davison's policy (Appendix 1, pp. 472–4). In planning it, Davison aimed 'to restore the vigour and sublimity of the giant-instrument, to combine with these the delicate refinements and brilliancy of the best modern organs, and by mechanical invention, to facilitate the hitherto surpassing difficulties of execution' (*MW* xviii, 1843: 140). His erstwhile partner could hardly have dissented from any of these objectives, but though there are strong affinities between the Model Organ and contemporary Hill schemes, the Knights-

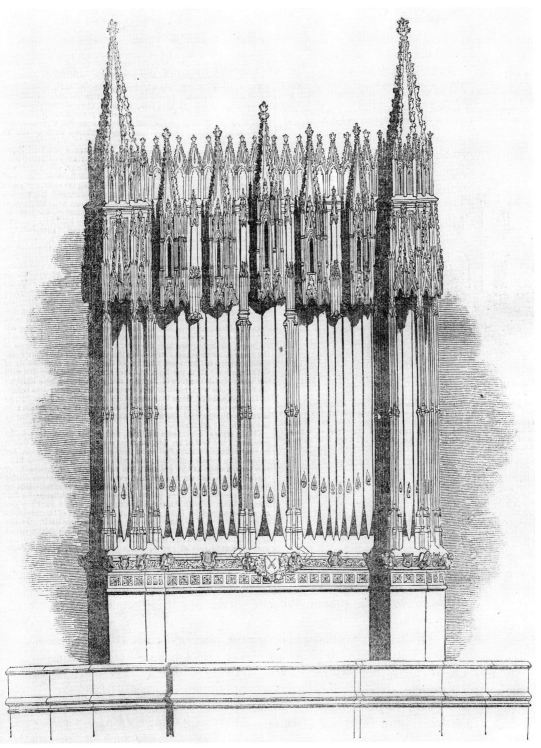

37 St Paul, Wilton Place, Knightsbridge. Gray & Davison's 'Model Organ' of 1843, with case by Thomas Cundy. (*ILN* 11, 3 June 1843: 392)

bridge specification differs in several important respects. First, with forty stops, Hill might have chosen to spread his resources over two, rather than three manual divisions, in order to ensure that the expressive department was as comprehensive as the unenclosed division (he did not do this at Worcester, but in a cathedral organ, a Choir was *de rigueur*). Secondly, Davison's full choruses are more obviously dependent upon reeds (at 8' and 4' on both Great and Swell), and those reeds are trumpets rather than posaunes. Thirdly, although there are tonal novelties, they are comparatively few in number and are not permitted seriously to affect the classic proportions of the English 3-manual scheme (in contrast to some of Hill's frankly unwieldy creations). Fourthly, the specification retains strong links with the earlier English tradition: by excluding a 4' flute from the Great and failing to include a representative of the 16' mutation series, it is at once more conventional and less flexible than a Hill organ of the period.

The Model Organ was evidently much admired. Compliments were passed on the diapasons ('bright and flowing') and the Swell ('grand and imposing'), and the builders were congratulated on being responsible for the most extensive Pedal Organ in the country. Much was made, too, of the introduction of a new stop, the keraulophon (*Gk.* 'horn-flute'). It was said to resemble 'a reed stop blended with the mellower sounds of the flute, and is, at the same time, extremely brilliant and delicate' (*MW* xviii, 1843: 140). The pipes were cylindrical, of metal, and the peculiar quality of the register was achieved by the scale and the presence of a small round hole near the top of the pipe.[5] Hill's corno-flute may have been the inspiration, and, if so, he later returned the compliment in the form of his so-called hohl-flute. Little is known of any original 'mechanical invention' included in the construction of the instrument. The Pedal was playable from a fourth keyboard at the bass end of the Choir keys, and this may have necessitated the provision of relief pallets; otherwise, it appears likely that the construction of the Model Organ was not distinguished by mechanical novelties so much as by a refinement of existing techniques.

It seems that the Model Organ served its purpose. For the remainder of the 1840s, Gray & Davison received a steady flow of orders for C-compass organs, and this, together with the continuing trade in long-compass instruments, made them probably the most productive builders of the decade (not excepting Hill).

A typical design during these years was a C-compass organ of two manuals and pedal with 20–5 stops.[6] The Great included a sub-unison, two 4's, two mixtures (with a separately drawing tierce in the earlier examples), a trumpet and a clarionet. The Swell was still short-compass (the bass octave being coupled permanently to the Great), but was otherwise complete, with double, mixture and two or three reeds. The Pedal usually consisted of a single 16' register (commonly designated 'Grand Open Diapason' after

38 Halifax Place Wesleyan Chapel, Nottingham, Gray & Davison, 1847. (1907)

1844) but occasionally ran to a (Grand) principal 8′; the Pedal compass was
C–e¹. Halifax Place Wesleyan Chapel, Nottingham (1847), was one of the
largest of the series (which explains the presence of the quint) and cost £425,
exclusive of the case (Appendix 1, pp. 474–5; Plate 38).

There were many smaller organs built during these years, and a few larger
ones. Among the latter were Trinidad Cathedral (1845), the Blind School

(1846), and St Mark's Church, St John's Wood (1847). Most of these C-compass schemes were unremarkable. There were, however, exceptions. In 1849, Gray & Davison added a 10-stop Pedal Organ to George Cooper's instrument at St Sepulchre, Holborn; with its 30-note compass, three reeds, metal violon and flue chorus capped by a 5-rank mixture, it threw into the shade Hill's still incomplete organ next door at Christ Church, Newgate Street – much to Davison and Cooper's satisfaction, no doubt.[7] Totally enclosed organs were probably too closely identified with Gauntlett and Hill to find much favour, but Davison built at least one; it had a single manual, a complete flue chorus and a cornopean (Bedford Chapel, 1844). The building of organs with the old compasses continued throughout the 1840s (Table 25). It finally came to an end in 1852 with the completion of a large new organ for Eton College Chapel. The reward of Gray & Davison's labours in this instance was a public rebuke from Henry Smart for having lent the sanction of their name to 'the old-fashioned, expensive, and ineffective GG compass' (*MW* xxx, 1852: 497); there was no subsequent backsliding.

Table 25 *Gray & Davison: long- and C-compass organs, 1841–52*

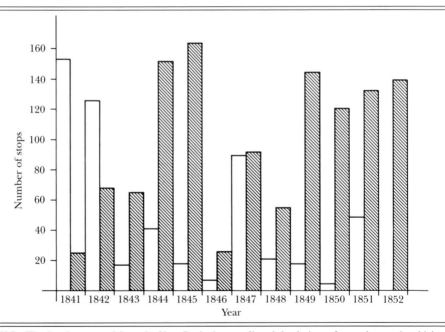

N.B. The data is extracted from the Shop Books (MSS 3–6) and the dating refers to the year in which the order was placed.

long-compass organs   C-compass organs

The successes of the 1850s were heralded by commissions for three large new organs on a similar scale to the Model Organ of 1843. St Francis Xavier, Liverpool (1849), had thirty-one stops, among which the most disappointing feature was the solitary grand open diapason on the Pedal. The organ for Boston Centenary Chapel, completed in 1850, was the most ambitious of the three. Like the Liverpool organ, it had a 16' reed chorus on the Swell, and, like it, was marred by the curtailing of the Swell registers at tenor c. The Great chorus included two mixtures and a quint, and there was a (wood) flageolet in addition to the fifteenth. The Choir had 11 stops: a gamba (the firm's first) in addition to the keraulophon, a gemshorn (another first) as well as the flute, and two 2's; a sesquialtera III and a corno di bassetto completed an unusually versatile department. The 6-stop Pedal included a 'Grand Violon 16' (this commenced life in the Shop Book as a metal open diapason) but there was no mixture. The provision of a tremulant and a sforzando pedal emphasised the progressive nature of the scheme. The fact that this instrument only cost £750 suggests that Davison may have learnt something from Hill about the advantages of keeping prices low (MS 2: 208). The third organ in the series, built for St Anne, Limehouse, but first put on display in the Great Exhibition,[8] had a similar scheme to the Liverpool instrument but with the infinite advantage of a 4-stop Pedal division (Appendix I, pp. 475–6). There was no 16' reed in the Swell (which was still only c-compass), but otherwise, the two stop lists are virtually identical.

The Limehouse organ survives, decrepit but still magnificent, and addresses both player and listener in the authentic tones of the mid-nineteenth century (Plate 39). The reeds (for all their irregularities) substantiate Gray & Davison's alleged eminence in the field of reed-voicing, and are instantly distinguishable from the plummy posaunes favoured by Hill; where Hill is looking to Northern Europe for inspiration, Gray & Davison are already looking to France (or back to eighteenth-century England?). The mildness of the diapason choruses (which the next generation would regard as under-powered) makes for excellent blend, and the effect of the mixture-work gives meaning to that favoured adjective of mid-Victorian critics, 'silvery'. Similarly, anyone listening to these flutes will come away with a better impression of what contemporaries meant by 'liquid' tone. The console (Plate 40), with its handsome fittings and elegantly engraved stop faces, is one of the few in this country to communicate unambiguously the aura of the mid-nineteenth century in the way that the best surviving consoles of Cavaillé-Coll do.

Mechanically, the organ reveals certain refinements. There are two bellows, placed in a frame behind the organ; one winds the manual divisions, one the Pedal. The Swell box originally possessed a double set of shutters, but these have long been disconnected, as has the sforzando pedal (Great to Swell) which may have been intended as an attention-catching novelty for

39 St Anne, Limehouse, Gray & Davison, 1851. The print shows the organ as it appeared in the Great Exhibition. The tops of the four 'towers' are now surmounted by curious fretwork caps, presumably added when the organ was installed at Limehouse.

the Exhibition. The Pedal stands on divided chests to either side of the Great and Choir; the two halves of the slides are connected by long wooden traces which run laterally across the organ; the chests supplying wind to the Pedal pipework are on top of the grooves, and the action is arranged to draw the pallets up rather than down. The layout of the manual divisions is conven-

40 St Anne, Limehouse. Console detail.

tional, lack of height for the Swell dictating that the Choir Organ should be placed (much to its musical advantage) between it and the Great. The primary key actions are constructed using squares, not backfalls.

The Limehouse organ was built on the eve of a significant development in

Gray & Davison's work and its survival is all the more valuable for that reason. The development was the result of the twin influences of Henry Smart and the concert organ. Smart's role will be examined in considering some of the organs over which he and Davison collaborated during the 1850s; the concert organ, however, was to have so fundamental an influence upon the evolution of English organ-building throughout the remainder of the century, that it requires separate treatment.

THE RISE OF THE CONCERT ORGAN

In architectural, cultural and social terms the Victorian town hall was a distinct phenomenon, wholly characteristic of the age and an uncompromising expression of some of its most cherished ideals. For our purposes, the term 'town hall' embraces a variety of buildings and functions. The most famous of the early town halls (Birmingham) was a large concert room; although it was built by the town commissioners and was to be widely used for public meetings, in settling the internal arrangements of the building priority was accorded to the needs of the triennial musical festivals. This singleness of function was unusual. In most of the later town halls the concert room was but one of a complex of facilities housed under the same roof. At Liverpool and Leeds it was the law courts, at Manchester the civic offices, which had to be accommodated in the same building as the public hall, and the size, cost and architectural elaboration of these buildings proclaimed (as was intended) the dignity, prosperity and taste of the governing classes. But although many of the grandest halls of the Victorian era were constructed at the behest of a corporation or commission, others (including most of the more modest halls) were the result of private subscription or commercial enterprise. Social mores were changing, and as the balls and routs of an earlier generation became increasingly unacceptable, the assembly rooms of the Georgian era gave way to 'music halls' intended principally to encourage choral, instrumental and vocal performances of an unexceptionable kind. Most of the early music halls were architecturally unpretentious, but later in the century they became more ambitious: Sheffield's Albert Hall, with its Cavaillé-Coll organ costing £5,500 (1873), is an example. In London, none of the leading concert halls were 'town halls' in the strict sense, but they merit consideration in this category because their function was in part analogous to the town halls of the northern cities. The Crystal Palace (removed to Sydenham when the Great Exhibition ended), the Alexandra Palace (1868) and the Royal Albert Hall (1871) were among the largest public halls of the nineteenth century and each contained a noteworthy organ. Finally, the category must be extended to include premises belonging to institutions with halls used for public musical performances. Mechanics'

Halls, Philharmonic Halls and London's Exeter Hall (the principal venue for metropolitan choral performances until the 1850s) are among these; their commitment to educational advancement and moral improvement draw them into that range of sympathies which motivated the building of the genuine town halls.

In an age that promoted general infirmaries to improve the health of the people, sewers and waterworks to improve their hygiene, chapels to improve their religion and temperance movements to improve their personal habits, it was only to be expected that 'improvement' would be among the principal motives of those who initiated the building of the town halls. By the 1850s, the provision of a grand organ had become an important plank in this particular platform. To demonstrate the utter seriousness of purpose which, for some, lay behind the commissioning of town hall organs, it is illuminating to turn to some reflections inspired by the inauguration of Gray & Davison's organ in Glasgow City Hall.

We rejoice that the organ, may be the means, along with other things, of aiding the cause of social improvement. Music in itself cannot do anything to elevate the people any more than it can demoralize them. In itself it is neither good nor bad, but, by association, it may be made to subserve the cause of truth, it may be made to awaken the imagination – to inspire great and heroic deeds – to advance the cause of virtue and morality, and in this way we hope the organ will become a powerful agent in helping to rescue numbers of the debased and vile from their habits of wretchedness and immorality . . . At present we fear there is too much work and too little play. There is too much hewing of wood and drawing of water, and the finer and more generous spiritual promptings of our nature are little cared for. Man is not all mud. He is more than stomach and cuticle. He has moments of inspiration when he thinks and feels like a god; and it is the duty of all who are in authority, or who, by their position and circumstances, have it in their power to infuse more of the poetical and the imaginative into the routine of the daily life of the people by every available means. And what means is so suitable, so pleasing, and so little alloyed with anything material and selfish as music . . .   (*MW* 1853, xxxi: 691)

Possibly such a view of the inherent innocence of music was still sustainable in the years preceding Wagner's mature outpourings. Certainly it was widely held. Hullah's Singing Classes and Curwen's Tonic Sol-Fa Association were conducted on the principle that morality could be stimulated by healthy musical activity, and Sir Arthur Sullivan hinted at an order of priorities for paternalistic local councillors when he maintained that 'Music can suggest no improper thought, and herein may be claimed its superiority over painting and sculpture' (Mackerness 1964: 154–8; 189). At the very least, music might keep the lower classes off the streets: away from 'the dangers of the theatre, the snares of the drinking saloons, and the dissipations of the drinking shops', as Curwen put it (*Tonic Sol-Fa Reporter*, May 1857). An organ had obvious advantages in the provision of wholesome musical entertainment. Its mechanical ingenuity and visual splendour made it an object of interest in its own right; a single organist could perform an entire concert; it was (increasingly) adapted to the performance of a wide range of music, popular and classical, sacred and secular. So a Grand Organ became an important weapon in the armoury of moral improvement.

In order to attract those who were to be improved, concessions were available to the working classes. At Birmingham, the weekly programme of two recitals was augmented to three in 1844 when 1,600 'working people' memorialised the trustees requesting lower prices and the provision of a recital outside working hours; as a result, an evening recital was instituted, admission to which cost a penny; the audiences were said regularly to number between 1,000 and 2,000 (*MW* xix, 1844: 396). Leeds was rather more expensive. In the 1860s, a seat in the balcony was sixpence, or one could pay threepence for the stalls. This was evidently felt to be excessive, and in 1862 it was agreed that 'working men in Institutions and large workshops [shall] be admitted to the Organ Performances at 7/- per hundred' (MS 42: 20 June 1862).

Moral improvement, then, was one of the objectives of those who commissioned the town hall organs. Education (the cultivation of taste) was another. The writer on the Glasgow organ is again informative:

Those who used to take delight in hearing or in practising the current popular music, whether sacred or secular, will, now that the organ has been erected, have an opportunity of listening to the sublime choral harmonies of Handel, Haydn, and Mendelssohn, accompanied by the only single instrument which can give them proper effect, and they will learn to appreciate the solemn and severe grandeur of the world-renowned fugues of John Sebastian Bach. Such music will create a new taste . . .   (*MW* xxxi, 1853: 691)

The didactic note is unmistakable. In the days before the establishment of orchestras and opera companies in the provinces, the role of the town hall organ in instructing musicians and the general public alike in musical repertoire was an honourable one. W. T. Best at Liverpool, William Spark at Leeds, William Rea at Newcastle, Edmund Chipp at Belfast and Kendrick Pyne at Manchester had the advantage of the most sophisticated modern organs complemented (in varying degrees) by a refined technique which together enabled them to give convincing performances of an enormous range of orchestral, instrumental, vocal and choral music. Programmes were carefully constructed to appeal to a wide variety of tastes, with light operatic transcriptions juxtaposed with Bach fugues, and melodic confections contrived to display the solo stops jostling for position with Handelian choruses.

There is an informative parallel here with one of the more notorious musical figures of the 1840s and 1850s. Louis Jullien was a virtuoso showman who delighted audiences up and down the country by displays of personal eccentricity and orchestral bravura. Wearing white gloves and wielding a bejewelled baton (brought to him at the commencement of each concert by a liveried footman) he gave theatrical direction to an orchestra, the attractions of which included (at various times) a 15' double bass, a giant saxophone and a drum which was so large that it had to be conveyed through the streets on a special truck drawn by two ponies. Not surprisingly, some pronounced him a charlatan. Yet his importance in the history of English music was not inconsiderable. He introduced Promenade Concerts, included extracts from symphonies and grand opera among the light music that comprised the greater part of his programmes, and enabled working people to attend his concerts by having tickets available at low prices (Carse 1951: *passim*). There is common ground here with the town hall organists, a point that is underlined by a comparison of Jullien's programmes with those given by W. T. Best at St George's Hall, Liverpool, during his tenure of the Organistship (Carse 1951: *passim*; *MW* xxxiv, 1856: 570–1). Best's concerts frequently began with an orchestral overture, and almost invariably, a Jullien programme would do likewise; each had a similar repertoire drawn from the works of Weber, Mozart, Rossini, Auber, Meyerbeer, Loder, Hérold and Wallace, and which was adapted to take account of the appearance of new works. Marches figured prominently in both sets of programmes: Mendelssohn's *Wedding March* and *War March of the Priests*, and *Grand Marches* by Beethoven (*Egmont*) and Spohr (*Jessonda*) were especially popular. When selecting odd movements from symphonies, Best seems to have preferred the *andantes* and *adagios* of Haydn, Beethoven, Mendelssohn and Mozart, whilst Jullien (characteristically) preferred *allegros*, but they were at one again in their taste for compiling 'reminiscences' of operatic scores: Bellini, Donizetti, Meyerbeer, Mozart, Weber and Balfe provided rich quarries. All Jullien's programmes included a quadrille of his own composition. It was an opportunity for grandiose display: the monster instruments could be shown off and the regular orchestral forces might be augmented with brass bands. Best's equivalent was one of a series of his own fantasias: *Fantasia on old English airs, Military Fantasia (commemorative of the 5th November), Fantasia upon Scotch airs, Fantasia upon English national melodies*; each gave ample opportunity to show off the resources of both player and instrument. The only point at which Best and Jullien parted company was Sacred Music. Best's Sunday programmes and Lenten recitals consisted largely of vaguely sacred material, and all his concerts would include at least one monumental chorus from an oratorio. And then, of course, there was Bach. But the similarities of approach emphasise a common purpose: to entertain and to instruct.

The town hall organs and organists of the second half of the nineteenth century exercised the greatest influence upon organ-building and organ-playing. The mechanical and tonal refinements of the instruments, and the technical accomplishments of the players set novel standards for emulation in other spheres; the grandest of the town hall organs overshadowed nearly all the larger species of English church organ, and the status (and remuneration) enjoyed by the élite corps of civic organists must have been the envy of many an undervalued cathedral musician. It was the 1850s and 1860s that saw the rise of the concert organ and its player. Hill's Birmingham organ was the prototype, hampered by primitive mechanical arrangements and limited powers of orchestral development. Gauntlett's concerto organ proved to be an aberration in the evolution of the genre. Willis's Liverpool organ was compromised by an anachronistic scheme (though the partnership of organ and player was to be of immense significance). It was, in fact, Gray & Davison who built the first modern English concert organs, and it is to their work in the 1850s that we must now turn.

SMART AND DAVISON: THE 1850s

By the early-1850s informed English organists increasingly cited the best modern French organs as models of mechanical ingenuity and artistic integrity. The stipulation in Willis's contract for St George's Hall (1851) that his work should be completed 'in the highly finished style of the best French instruments' has already been mentioned (above, p. 147). William Spark, comparing modern French and English organs in 1852, commented:

I may observe that the former are distinguished for the superiority of their material and workmanship, both in wood and metal – for their reeds, which are beautifully finished – and for their clever application of the pneumatic power; whilst the latter are equally superior to the French in the extent and effectiveness of the swelling organs – for the combination of their *mixtures*, or the chorus – and for the general weight of the whole instrument.   (Spark 1892: 266)

Other English organists were less charitably disposed towards the native product. Hopkins's visits to Paris (1844, 1853) soon convinced him of the superiority of the modern French organ. Amongst other encomiums upon the tonal finish and mechanical refinement of Cavaillé-Coll and Ducroquet, there is a reference to the organ in La Madeleine:

I do not think I ever heard anything so ethereal in its effect. Nor did I ever feel so convinced, by contrast, of the coarse, boisterous, and irreligious effect of the ponderous sound of large English pedal pipes.   (Pearce [1910]: 66)

Hopkins was not alone in his response. Some years later (1864) another writer exhorted anyone who doubted the superiority of French organs to make the journey to Paris:

Let him go the round with Cavaillé-Coll – the ever courteous man as well as great artist – from his first noble work at St. Denis to his last and best at St. Sulpice; and let him not omit Ducroquet's grand instrument at St. Eustache . . . Let him observe the scrupulous and wonderful care bestowed on every little part, and the perfect success of the whole. Let him rejoice, for once in his life, at sitting down to a key-board where everything combines to treat him like a gentleman; while every tone he evokes is as pure, as noble, and as refined, as is the exquisitely finished mechanism through which it is produced.   (*MW* XLII, 1864: 136–7)

Such enthusiasm might well have brought about an influential trade between Paris and London had it not been for one factor. Bemoaning the fact that Ducroquet's Exhibition organ ('no English builder ever did make such an organ') had found no purchaser in this country, the anonymous writer admitted that cost was the deterrent. For twenty-five stops, £1,200 had been asked – twice the price of an organ of similar size from one of the better London builders (*MW* XLII, 1864: 137). Not all were deterred by financial considerations; Cavaillé-Coll was to build a number of large organs for British customers during the 1870s, and these influenced some native builders, in Lancashire especially.[9] But during the 1850s and 1860s, the best Francophile organists could hope for was to persuade English builders to adopt particular tonal and mechanical features of admired Parisian instruments. The collaboration of Henry Smart (Plate 41) and Frederick Davison is the most conspicuous example of this. It offers an informative parallel to the German influences of the 1840s, and was carried to its furthest extent in the series of concert organs built by Gray & Davison during the 1850s.

Henry Smart (1813–79) was peculiarly fitted to play a part in the development of the concert organ. Besides being one of the most accomplished English organists of his generation, he had a detailed knowledge of both organ-building and engineering and this enabled him to propose mechanical solutions to various problems of console management and tonal effect which were being thrown up by changing musical taste. Mechanics had always fascinated him. As a small child he had often accompanied his father to the Theatre Royal, Drury Lane (Henry Smart, senior, was leader of the theatre's band) where the stage machinery inspired all manner of domestic experiments (*MT* XLIII, 1902: 297), and this interest took a more serious turn when, in adolescence, Smart secured admission to the drawing offices of Maudsley's, a famous engineering firm (Spark 1881: 4). There, he began to acquire that skill as a draughtsman which later excited the admiration of Cavaillé-Coll, who pronounced Smart's working drawings for the Leeds Town Hall organ to be 'equal if not superior' to anything of the sort he had seen (Spark 1881: 176). In view of this interest in mechanics, he was fortunate in his earliest experiences of organ-building. Through an acquaintance with the Robsons, he was given the freedom of Flight & Robson's workshops in St Martin's Lane (Spark 1881: 3). Flight & Robson were the leading manufacturers of mechanical organs in the metropolis, and, as well as a wide selection of barrel and machine organs, their premises housed the mighty Apolloni-

41 Henry Smart (1813–79).

con. Thus a connection between mechanical ingenuity and orchestral effect was forged in Smart's mind at an early age, stimulating his inventive curiosity and eventually fathering such devices as the adjustable composition pedals and the crescendo and diminuendo pedals at Leeds. Smart's sharp ear for orchestral effect had much to do with a third childhood influence: his uncle, Sir George Smart. Young Smart had no formal musical education (*MT* XLIII, 1902: 298) but it seems likely that he benefited from his uncle's interest, being invited to accompany him on various occasions when theatrical or orchestral performances were in preparation. Apparently he was allowed to sit in the orchestra pit at Covent Garden whilst Sir George was rehearsing Weber's *Oberon*, and he later (1831) was constant in his attendance at the theatre when Spohr's *Zemire und Azor* was in hand (*MT* XLIII, 1902: 298). The knowledge Smart acquired of orchestration and instrumental timbre through such experiences inspired his later attempts to make the organ a more adequate representation of the orchestra.

Smart's career as an improver of organs reputedly began at the age of eighteen, when he persuaded the Mayor and Corporation of Great Yarmouth (his mother had friends in the town) to permit the addition of composition pedals to the organ in St Nicholas's. He executed the work himself, and is said to have celebrated its successful accomplishment with a public performance on the instrument (Spark 1881: 9). His career as a professional organist began in 1831, when he was appointed to Blackburn Parish Church, but the metropolis had irresistible attractions and he returned there as organist of St Philip's, Regent Street, in 1836. Eight years later (1844) he was elected organist of St Luke's, Old Street, remaining there until 1865 when he moved to St Pancras Parish Church, a post he retained until his death in 1879. Smart was widely respected as composer, critic and performer (his reputation as a player seems not to have suffered following the onset of blindness in 1864) and each of these activities in some measure influenced his views on organ design.

Gray & Davison were engaged upon a major reconstruction of the organ in St Luke's, Old Street, at the time of Smart's appointment (*MW* XIX, 1844: 67). According to Spark (a devoted friend and uncritical biographer) Smart 'was always busying himself with improvements in the organ, many of which were not previously known in England' (1881: 17), but, unfortunately, the chronology is not clear. The specification as it appeared by 1855 (HRI: 461) had idiosyncratic features ('Principal' for open diapason, 'Sub-octave' for double diapason, and a concert flute rather than a stopped diapason on the Swell) but is otherwise recognisable as the work of Gray & Davison. More distinctive was the inclusion of sub- and super-octave couplers to connect Swell to Great: a novelty imported from across the Channel by Smart, and used here for the first time in an English organ (*MW* XXXIII, 1855: 130). The presence of a tremulant was a further indication of French influence; it had fallen into desuetude in England during the eighteenth century, and was reintroduced at St Luke's in a form adapted from contemporary French models (HR2: 94). These innovations were made 'about the year 1852'; it was then that a friend recalled having met Smart, who 'had just returned from Paris, where the newest improvements introduced into organ building by Cavaillé-Coll were eagerly examined by him, and brought over to England to be used in his own organ at St Luke's Church, Old Street, London' (Spark 1881: 288).

Smart's trip to Paris almost certainly had a particular object. In 1852 Gray & Davison began work on an organ for Glasgow City Hall, 'constructed on the plans, and, in some parts, from the drawings of Mr. Henry Smart' (*MW* xxxi, 1853: 539). It proved to be something of a landmark, both in the work of the firm and in the evolution of English organ-building during the third quarter of the century (Appendix 1, pp. 476–7). According to Spark, 'it was the first concert instrument erected in Great Britain in which appeared the sub and superoctave couplers, harmonic flutes, and other improvements, which Smart had seen the value of in Paris, and lost no time in applying to our own manufacture' (1881: 162). The original scheme had several progressive features. The keyboards had a 61-note compass: 'affording facility for the just execution of any known orchestral music without the distortion, inversion, and consequently frequent mutilation of its passages' (*MW* xxxi, 1853: 525); octave couplers were provided, the Swell exceeded the Great in the number of its registers and the Choir included a voix celeste. By these means, Smart and Davison set out to increase the flexibility of the concert organ. Then, probably following Smart's trip to Paris, significant alterations were made. The Great gained two harmonic flutes which, with the reeds, were placed on their own soundboard and supplied with wind at two different pressures. A coupler was provided to detach these four stops from the Great keys and unite them to the Swell, thus providing 'in many respects, the effect and advantage of a *fourth* key-board' (*MW* xxxi, 1853: 526). A gamba displaced the second open diapason on the Great, the Choir voix celeste acquired a second rank of pipes and the Pedal trombone was renamed 'Bombarde' (MS 6: ff. 23–6). Though small in number the changes are important in as much as they demonstrate the direct influence of contemporary French organ-building. Together they indicate the direction that Gray & Davison's work was to take in the 1850s and 1860s (especially in concert instruments) and, as such, deserve to be considered in more detail.

The treatment of the Great reeds and harmonic flutes represents the first application in this country of Cavaillé-Coll's 'increasing pressure' system. Smart expounded its virtues in the following terms:

This *increasing* pressure is adopted in deference to well-known acoustic laws, and will be found to greatly augment the volume and quality of the reed stops, besides entirely obviating that tendency to *thinness* and irregularity in the upper portions of their compass, which has been otherwise found irremediable.

(*MW* xxxi, 1853: 526)

There are two distinct principles here. First, it was recognised that both the power and the quality of the reeds could be improved by placing them on a higher pressure than was generally advisable for fluework. Hill had demonstrated this (sensationally) with the Birmingham tuba. Now, Davison adopted a more modest increase of pressure to extend the principle to the chorus reeds. Word of Cavaillé's experiments had reached England before this, and Wesley (or Davison?) had as early as 1846 proposed the use of distinct wind pressures for both chorus and orchestral reeds at Liverpool (MS 45: 1 May 1846) but the Glasgow organ was the first in which it was actually carried out. (The Great reeds in the Panopticon organ, which was being built at about the same time as the Glasgow instrument, were also on a higher pressure than the fluework.) The principle was, however, capable of further extension. The power of a reed voiced on a single wind pressure tends to fall off in the treble. By placing the treble on a higher pressure than the bass the problem is, to some extent, ameliorated. This was especially important to the concert organ at this stage in its development. The increasing refinement of orchestral instruments (brass and woodwind in particular) emphasised the shortcomings of the older imitative stops, and at a time when the concert organ was widely perceived as an orchestral substitute, this was a grave disadvantage. By enabling the voicer to capture at least something of the power and purity of tone characteristic of modern orchestral instruments, the increasing pressure system made a vital contribution to fulfilling the ambitions of Smart and other concert organists of his generation.

The original wind pressures at Glasgow are not known, but details have survived of those in the next concert organ in the series, the Birmingham Music Hall organ, completed in 1856. In the previous year, Davison had applied increasing pressure to the Great fluework as well as reeds in the organ for Magdalen College, Oxford (*MW* xxxiii, 1855: 130), and he adopted the same policy in the Birmingham organ. According to the Shop Book (MS 7: ff. 24–5) the Birmingham pressures were as follows; it will be noted that the whole of the Swell was on divided pressures and that, as at Glasgow, the Pedal flues and reeds were on different pressures.

Great   flues: bass 2¾″ treble 3¾″
            reeds & harmonic flutes: bass 3¾″ treble 5″
Swell   bass 2¾″ treble 3¾″
Choir   2¾″ throughout
Pedal   flues: 2¾″ reeds: 3¾″

The variations in pressure are modest by comparison with later work but they evidently satisfied Smart who referred approvingly to the 'grandeur, force, and brilliancy' imparted to the Great Organ through their agency (*MW* xxxiv, 1856: 569). By intensifying the tone, improving regularity of speech, sustaining the power of the *ensemble* and enhancing the prominence of the treble, the adoption of the increasing pressure system paved the way for important developments later in the century.

The introduction of harmonic flutes was another notable feature of the Glasgow organ. Harmonic flutes are double-length, and have a hole in the body midway between the mouth and the top of the pipe; they sound a pure, full note, reminiscent of an orchestral flute. Cavaillé-Coll has been credited with their invention (HR2: 137) and he was certainly the first to make them in their characteristic nineteenth-century form, but over-blowing flutes had been known in various parts of Europe for centuries (Williams 1966: 286). Smart commented approvingly on the 'surprising force, brilliance, and liquidity of tone' of which they were capable (*MW* xxxiv, 1856: 570), and it was assured that the same taste that had led to the popularity of Bishop's clarabella, Hill's wald-flute and Gray & Davison's own clarionet flute, would find a place for the harmonic flute in the concert organ. Later, it would establish itself as the characteristic 4′ flute of the Victorian church organ, but for the moment builders preferred to treat it as a solo stop, and to place it on a higher wind pressure than the remainder of the fluework. It is thus that it appears in Gray & Davison's work during the 1850s.

Other features of the Glasgow scheme represent borrowings from French usage. The touch was improved by the application of the pneumatic lever (probably to the Great and its couplers), and the tremulant and octave couplers appeared here for the first time in an English concert organ. These couplers, it should be noted, were inter-manual couplers; it was not until later in the century that octave couplers acting on the same manual became common. Describing their function, Smart wrote:

> By these means, on the one hand, the power of the instrument may be nearly doubled; and, on the other, such a number of varied, delicate, and exquisite combinations – such close mimicries of the most fanciful effects of the modern orchestra – may be attained, as can in no other conceivable way be placed under the will of a single performer.   (*MW* xxxi, 1853: 526)

The nomenclature of the voix humaine (Swell) and voix celeste (Choir) attests their origins, and the re-naming of the Pedal reed as 'Bombarde' is almost certainly a further indication of French aspirations.

The Glasgow organ demonstrates the extent of the debt which Smart and Davison owed to contemporary French practice. It should be compared with Hill's organ for the Panopticon (1854) and Willis's for Liverpool (1855); both instruments incorporated French features, but the Glasgow organ pre-dated them, and in its mechanical sophistication and tonal novelty can justly claim to be the prototype of the mid-Victorian concert organ. Just as Hill

and Gauntlett had refashioned the church organ in the 1840s, so Davison
and Smart in the 1850s set about turning the concert organ into an efficient
musical instrument. Smart's definition of a concert organ is therefore of
interest. It was, he wrote, 'an instrument . . . not only capable of efficiently
accompanying and supporting a large band of voices in the choruses of an
oratorio, but equally adapted to every species of solo performance, from the
severest fugue of Sebastian Bach, to the lightest modern French overture'.
His own 'selection of pieces' on the occasion of the Glasgow organ's unveil-
ing in Gray & Davison's Exhibition Room amply illustrates his contention
(*MW* xxxi, 1853: 525):

PART I

    1. Extempore
    2. Air, 'O thou that tellest'   Handel
    3. Overture, 'Der Freyschutz'   Weber
    4. Adagio, from Sinfonia in A Minor   Mendelssohn
    5. Air, 'Cujus animum' (*Stabat Mater*)   Rossini
    6. Chorus, 'The Lord shall reign'   Handel

PART II

    1. Overture, 'Midsummer Night's Dream'   Mendelssohn
    2. Airs, from 'Robert le Diable'   Meyerbeer
    3. Grand Fugue   S. Bach
    4. Air, 'He layeth the beams'   Handel
    5. Extempore
    6. March, Athalie   Mendelssohn

Both organ and performance were judged to be highly successful. According
to one writer, 'No instrument we remember to have heard lends itself so
equally to the execution of all styles of music, but most especially must all
musical auditors have remarked its singular capability of imitating many of
the most fanciful effects of the modern orchestra' (*MW* xxxi, 1853: 539).

    The completion of the Glasgow organ signalled a new departure in Gray
& Davison's work, and soon progressive features that had first appeared in
the concert organs began to find their way into the larger church instruments. A 2-manual for an Independent Chapel in Blackburn (1854) had a
10-stop full-compass Swell, and was recorded in the Shop Book as being 'the
first organ tuned [to] equal temp[eramen]t in the Factory' (MS 6: f.63).[10] At
Magdalen College, Oxford (1855), Davison managed to include many of the
Glasgow innovations (octave couplers, the pneumatic lever, increasing
pressure, a tremulant) in a small 4-manual scheme which also incorporated
the firm's first high-pressure reed – a tromba – speaking on a modest 6″ of
wind and projecting horizontally from the top of the excessively crowded
main case.[11] The presence of a concert flute, flute d'amour, piccolo and
corno di bassetto in the Choir, and a flute harmonique in the Solo, was clear

evidence of the influence which the concert hall was beginning to exert over the church. The organ for Sherborne (1856) was more conventional, and Smart took the church authorities to task for spending '£350 or £400' on 'a richly carved doll's house' (the case) when the tonal scheme was incomplete (*MW* xxxiv, 1856: 183),[12] but Davison managed to include a good number of the tonal and mechanical novelties found in the other organs, among them, the use of different pressures for the bass and treble of the Great. Only the experiment of using zinc resonators for the Pedal reed was judged to be a failure; the tone, Smart reported, was 'sharp and meagre to a degree that must convince even the most sceptical person of the influence exercised on the sound of a pipe by the material of which it is formed' (*MW* xxxiv, 1856: 182).

The series of concert organs resumed with that for Birmingham Music Hall (1856). It was smaller than Glasgow (thirty-seven stops rather than forty-seven) but incorporated all its mechanical innovations, improving on some. The increasing pressure system was more extensively applied than in any other English organ of the day, slide-valves replaced circular drop-valves in the design of the pneumatic levers, and the action of the composition pedals was pneumatically assisted (*MW* xxxiv, 1856: 569). The use of equal temperament (which Davison had been the first to apply in a large concert organ, at Glasgow) led to an interesting departure in the design of the Great chorus. In deference 'to the supposed antagonism of equal temperament to perfect thirds in compound stops' (*MW* xxxiv, 1856: 570) tierces were omitted from the two mixtures. The compositions are not recorded, but they may have been similar to those of the organ for Hope Street Chapel, Liverpool, which Gray & Davison were building at about the same time (MS 6: ff. 34–5):

	Sesquialtera		*Mixture*
C	15.19.22	C	26.29
c^1	8.12.15	c^1	19.22
c^2	1. 8.15	f♯	15.19
		c^2	12.15

Increasingly, Gray & Davison would omit tierces from their mixtures, a development paralleled in the work of other builders as the use of equal temperament became all but universal. The tonal finish of the Birmingham organ elicited a stream of praise from Smart: the Great was characterised by 'a grand and striking volume of tone', mixtures of 'extraordinary breadth and sonorous brilliancy', and 'superb' reeds; the Choir was 'replete with beauties', among them a corno di bassetto and a viol da gamba 'of the true Schulze–Töpfer school', whilst the usual effect of an English Pedal Organ was here vastly improved by the adoption of smaller scales for the 16' fluework (*MW* xxxiv, 1856: 569–70). In due course, Smart had an opportunity to match actions to words when the Music Hall closed its doors and the organ was up for sale. It was purchased for his own church of St Pancras, where it was erected (1865) with little alteration to the tonal scheme – an interesting reflection on the thin dividing line between church and concert hall in Smart's estimation.

On a wholly different scale was the third concert organ of the 1850s; it was commissioned for the Handel Festival of 1857, and stood in the transept of the Crystal Palace. It had sixty-six registers and four manuals, including a 20-stop Great Organ, and a 12-stop Pedal division with a 32′ reed (Appendix 1, pp. 477–9). Both tonally and mechanically this instrument represented the apogee of French influence in Davison's work. In place of composition pedals Cavaillé-Coll's 'combination pedals' were employed. These were ventils controlling the supply of wind to the two or more soundboards appropriated to each department of the instrument; the stops were grouped so that some sort of progression from *piano* to *forte* was possible, and the player set up his registration knowing which stops were winded through the agency of particular pedals; when a pedal was depressed, a preset registration could thus be brought into play. The increasing pressure system was as a matter of course adopted, but, bearing in mind that the organ would be required during the 1857 Festival to assist in supporting a choir of 2,000 voices and an orchestra of 500, it was deemed advisable 'to supply the pipes with air at a pressure considerably higher than that ordinarily employed' (*MW* xxxv, 1857: 392); unfortunately, details have not survived. It was remarked that with the same consideration in view, 'some of the more powerful stops of recent French origin have been introduced' (*MW* xxxv, 1857: 392). As well as seven harmonic flutes throughout the organ, there was a flute à pavillon 8′ on the Great and some of the trumpets were harmonic; the 32′ was a free reed, the first made in England, and, again, an import from France; the trombas in Solo and Swell were horizontally disposed. The scheme was impressively comprehensive and the French flavour is inescapable: the two 16′ flues, the variety of 8′ fluework, harmonic flutes at 8′, 4′ and 2′ pitch, ample mixturework and a battery of reeds bear testimony to the influence of contemporary French practice on the design of the Great Organ, for example, and individual features of each of the other departments make reference to it.

Three other concert organs were built during the 1850s. When St James's Hall opened in April 1858 (*ILN*, April 10 1858) it contained a huge one-manual organ supplied by Gray & Davison; the 18-stop manual division was pronouncedly French in character, with sub-bourdon, flute à pavillon, harmonic flutes and three reeds, and the 4-stop Pedal included a bombarde. The composition actions were pneumatic, and distinct (increasing) pressures were applied to the fluework and reeds (MS 8: job 10086). Not inappropriately, this was the organ later used in the première of Saint-Saëns's Third ('Organ') Symphony (1886).[13] The organ for Newcastle-upon-Tyne Town Hall (1859) was essentially a smaller version of the Crystal Palace instrument, but using conventional composition pedals rather than ventils. The manual 16′ reed was placed on the Great, not the Swell, and there was a *sforzando* pedal in the form of a Great-to-Swell coupler. But the most important of these three instruments – and Davison's *magnum opus* – was the organ for Leeds Town Hall.

William Spark has given an account of the circumstances in which he and Henry Smart won a public competition for plans and drawings for an organ for the new Leeds Town Hall (Spark 1881: 186–7). Tenders were invited, and the contract was awarded to Gray & Davison (MS 42: 28 October 1857).[14] The instrument was to be completed by 1 August 1858 (MS 41) but as late as November 1858 Davison had to apply for a further month in which to finish the work and the certificate of completion was not submitted until May 1859 (MS 42: 12 November 1858; 18 May 1859).

In the Leeds organ (Plate 42) Smart and Davison applied more extensively than in any previous instrument the various innovations that had appeared in the earlier concert organs (Appendix 1, pp. 480–2). Chorus reeds were placed on higher pressures than the fluework, and three distinct pressures of wind were applied to different parts of the Great compass. Solo, Choir and Swell could be connected to the Great by means of octave couplers, and both the Swell and the Echo (added in 1865, but part of the original scheme) had tremulants. It was at first intended to apply the pneumatic lever only to the Great, Swell and Solo Organs, and to the stop action, but before the instrument was complete Davison and Smart persuaded the Leeds committee to agree to its application to Choir and Pedal as well (MS 42: 17 July 1858; 4 December 1858); only Willis's Liverpool organ could boast so extensive an application of pneumatics at the time. The keyboard compasses exceeded those of the Crystal Palace in running to five complete octaves, C–c⁴. In all these respects, the Leeds organ revealed marked resemblances to other Gray & Davison organs of the 1850s. However, other features of the design went a good deal further than anything previously attempted under Smart's influence, or by Davison.

The experiment of using Cavaillé-Coll's combination pedals (ventils) was not repeated. Instead, Smart designed an adjustable composition pedal, acting by pneumatic agency, and specified the inclusion of four of these pedals at Leeds:

These . . . by an instantaneous adjustment [ventils to the pneumatic apparatus] act, as the player requires, on the Swell organ alone, or on the Swell, Great and Pedal organ simultaneously, or on the two latter only. Furthermore, each of these four composition pedals is capable of effecting *three* different combinations . . . the *modus operandi*, so far as the performer is concerned, being simply the setting of an index . . . one of which appertains to each of the composition pedals, to the number indicating the required combination.   (HR2: 520–1).

42 Leeds Town Hall, Gray & Davison, 1859. (*Building News*, 1858)

The action was reversible, and the availability of either Swell alone or Swell, Great and Pedal together must have had its uses, but it is surprising that a player of Smart's sophistication should have been satisfied with these limited and (surely) cumbersome means of controlling an instrument of ninety-three stops. The dials and ventils must have been a nightmare to visiting recitalists

who would otherwise be restricted to the use of four mechanical combinations for each piece. The flexibility of the organ was a little increased by
the provision of a ventil (controlled by a drawstop) to shut off wind to all the
Pedal registers apart from the bourdon and violon, and by the inclusion of
crescendo and *diminuendo* pedals (also designed by Smart); another ventil
admitted wind to the Back Great. But by comparison with Willis's combination pistons, or even, perhaps, Cavaillé-Coll's combination pedals, the
accessories must still have left Leeds a difficult instrument to control for
the purposes of the orchestral transcription. Smart's drawings show overhanging keys and terraced jambs after the modern French pattern (though
the jambs were splayed, not curved):[15] these would have made control a little
easier (Plates 43 and 44). So, too, would the grouping together of the coupler
drawstops over the upper keyboard: a feature which other builders later
favoured as a means of reducing the size of concert organ consoles.

Tonally, the scheme represented a development of ideas already tried at
Glasgow, Birmingham and the Crystal Palace. Both Solo and Great had
choruses of harmonic flutes, there were three free reeds, and the presence of
an harmonic trumpet and flute à pavillon on the Great, a vox humana on the
Swell and extensive reed choruses in all departments emphasised the continuing debt to France. Only a celeste was wanting (a curious omission) to
complete the picture. But in other respects, the scheme was innovative, and
particularly so in regard to two features.

There was, first, the 'Orchestral Solo Organ'. This, Spark was at pains to
point out, was simply what it claimed to be; it had no reference 'to those
massive or *full* effects, which properly are the province of other portions of
the instrument', but consisted simply of solo registers, each 'having the
nearest attainable relation to its orchestral prototype' (HR2: 518). Smart's
drawing (Plate 45) shows that all but one of these registers were disposed
horizontally ('a position which, by careful experiment, has been found to
add between twenty and thirty per cent to their ordinary intensity of tone')
and enclosed in two swell boxes 'having Venetian shutters above, below, and
in front' (HR2: 518). Neither Hill's organ at the Panopticon nor Willis's at
Liverpool had an enclosed Solo division, and the Leeds novelty was one that
would be widely imitated in the future. The ophicleide was unenclosed; it
had a wind pressure of 10″, whilst the remaining registers were on the
unusually high pressure of 6″ (bass) and 7″ (treble). As a further aid to
orchestral authenticity, seven 'mechanical combinations' permitted the
organist to play specified registers in octaves to one another, whilst only
depressing a single key:

Thus, for example, on drawing the stop . . . labelled 'flute, clarinet, and bassoon, in
double octaves', and pressing down the middle C of the solo clavier, the result will
be, the Tenor C of the *Cor Anglais*, the middle C of the *Clarinet*, and C above of the
8-ft. *Flute Harmonique*, sounding simultaneously.   (HR2: 518)

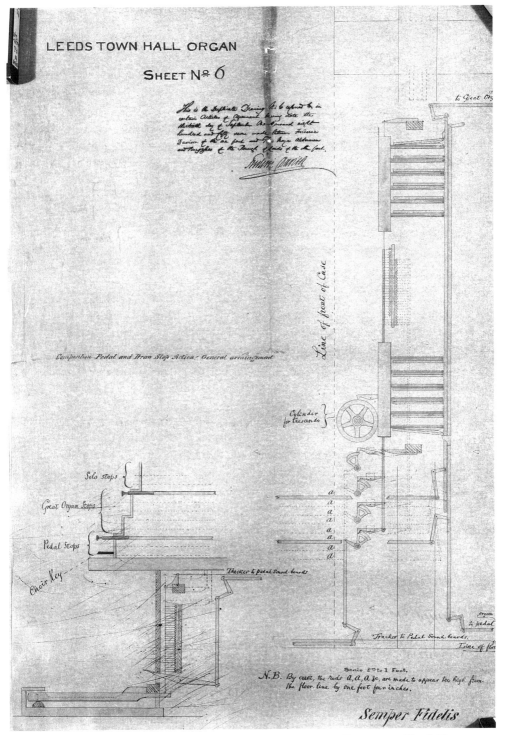

43 Leeds Town Hall, original drawings: console and stop action. (By courtesy of Leeds City Libraries, Archives Department)

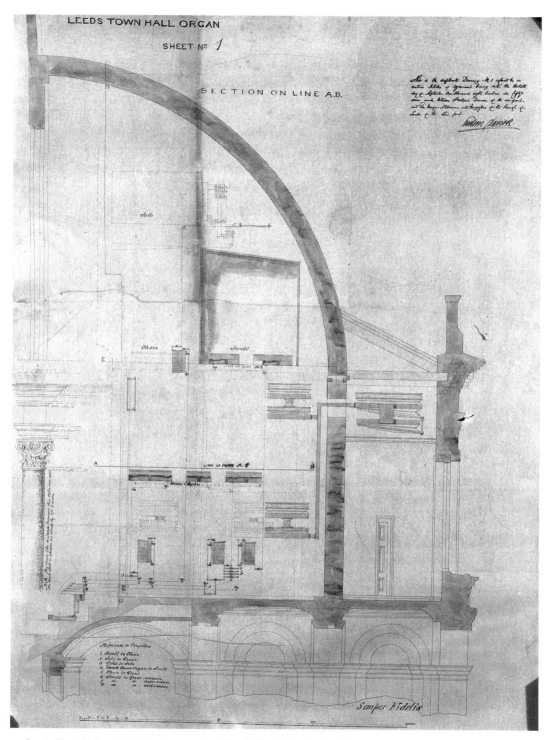

44 Leeds Town Hall, original drawings: section. (Leeds City Libraries, Archives Department)

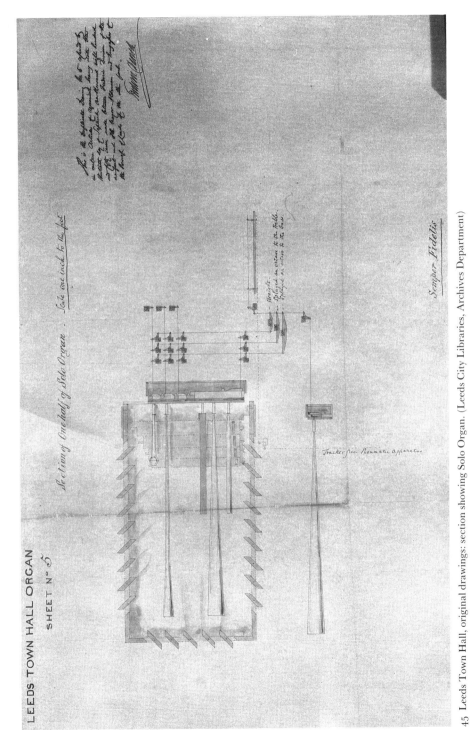

LEEDS TOWN HALL ORGAN

SHEET Nᵒ 5

Section of One half of Solo Organ. Scale one inch to the foot

Tracker for Pneumatic apparatus

Semper Fidelis

45 Leeds Town Hall, original drawings: section showing Solo Organ. (Leeds City Libraries, Archives Department)

Spark continued,

> By these contrivances . . . a very accurate imitation of almost all the ordinary wind combinations of an orchestra is placed easily within the grasp of *one* of the performer's hands, leaving the other free for any of those purposes of florid accompaniment in which the modern race of players are [*sic*] so proficient.   (HR2: 518)

All told, there was some justice in the claim that 'this Solo organ more nearly fulfils the objects implied in its title than any yet constructed' (HR2: 518).

The second innovation was the design of the Great Organ. It was conceived as two divisions, complete in themselves and each possessing a distinct character. Camidge had adopted the basic idea of dividing the Great into 'two distinct masses', and 'two or three continental examples' had attempted to take matters further and distinguish more effectively between the two divisions, but Leeds was novel in its thoroughgoing application of the principle. Smart and Spark planned the Front Great to be 'a comparatively *light*, though powerful and brilliant organ', whilst the Back Great included 'some of the strongest members of the flue-work' and composed 'a "band" entirely different to the foregoing in amount and quality of force'. They illustrated the point in more detail:

> Throughout all this, there are no 'vain repetitions' of similar scales and qualities. For example, the six stops which compose the 8 feet pitch of the flue-work, are an *open diapason* (of the Old English class), a *gamba* (of the conical description), a *bourdon*, a *flute à pavillon* . . . a *viola* (the largest and most powerful of the German kind known as 'string-toned stops'), and a *flute harmonique* . . . In the reed work, also . . . a similar variety is observed. The *trumpet* and *clarion* of the 'front' Great organ are intended to follow as nearly as possible the model of that brilliant, *clangy*, description of reeds which Byfield made so deservedly famous – a quality, by the way, far too much neglected of late years in this country; while in the 'back' Great organ, the modern English style of reed-work has been adopted for the *contra trombone*, *trombone*, and *tenor trombone*; and the most successful achievement of the French school has its representative in the *harmonic trumpet*.   (HR2: 519–20)

Broadly speaking, the Front Great followed the pattern of the German System instruments of the 1840s with a glance over its shoulder at the eighteenth century (the 'Byfield' reeds, the tierce mixture) whilst the Back Great derived from contemporary French models (harmonic flutes, bourdon, the mixtures, the reeds). The Front Great was permanently connected to the Great keyboard, but the ventil enabled the player to have the Back division on or off, and this division could also be coupled to the Swell keys and played against the Front Great.

The Leeds organ was the grandest of Gray & Davison's concert organs. Though Spark referred to the instrument as 'unrivalled' and claimed that the reeds were 'universally admitted to be the finest and most perfect specimens *sui generis* to be heard anywhere' (1892: 225), and although an impartial critic spoke of the *ensemble* as 'superb' and the variety of effect achieved by the mechanical accessories as 'astonishing' (*MW* xxxviii, 1860: 168), the instrument was dogged by ill-fortune. The original decision to employ Smart and Spark's plans aroused considerable controversy,[16] and Davison was not allowed sufficient time to install the organ. Various alterations had to be made on site, and it seems that the committee was not wholly satisfied with the completed instrument, for they called in Hopkins, and later Cooper, to report on it (MS 42: 23 November 1859; 21 December 1859). Eventually, in 1869, Gray & Davison's services were dispensed with (7 October 1869), and in 1898, most of the original fluework was ejected when Abbott & Smith reconstructed the instrument (Snow 1926: 85–6).

The concert organs of the 1850s had a formative influence on the evolution of Gray & Davison's style, as is evident in the larger church organs of the period. The instruments for Louth (1857), Stoke Newington (1858), Ludlow (1860), Llandaff Cathedral (1861), West Derby (1862) and Hereford Cathedral (1862) had octave couplers, tremulants, large full-compass Swells, quint mixtures, harmonic flutes and orchestral stops; some employed pneumatic assistance, and in a number of instances, the chorus reeds were winded on a higher pressure than the fluework. Around 1870, the firm's stylistic development slowed down. The moderate power of the choruses and the smoothness of the reeds which were hallmarks of Gray & Davison's work in the 1850s and 1860s merged imperceptibly with the growing taste for dense choruses and well-mannered reeds, and by the 1880s and 1890s, the firm's organs (which were perhaps always a little lacking in vigour) had become rather dull. Under the circumstances, it is all the more important to recognise their achievement (in collaboration with Smart) in building the first mature examples of the English concert organ.

PART III

10

The emergence of the Victorian organ, 1850–70

The Great Exhibition of 1851 was a triumphant celebration of human achievement and divine beneficence. It was a moment of supreme confidence, sustained by the failure of the revolutions of 1848 to shake the foundations of international peace, and by the inability of other nations as yet seriously to threaten Britain's claim to be the 'workshop of the world'. Never again would Victorian England be able to face the rest of the world with such composure. But for the moment, in a spirit of magnanimity, she invited her competitors to bring their wares to Joseph Paxton's Palace of Industry in Hyde Park, 'to present a true test and a living picture of the point of development at which the whole of mankind has arrived . . . and [to provide] a new starting point, from which all nations will be able to direct their future exertions' (cited, Briggs 1959: 398). In an age in which the inevitability of progress had assumed the status of an article of faith, a great exhibition of commerce and industry offered compelling attractions. The previous half century had witnessed unprecedented advances in both spheres, and now the fruits of technological innovation and commercial enterprise were to be displayed under a single roof. Although the emphasis was upon manufactures and the mechanical sciences, the fine arts were not excluded. Ecclesiastical furnishings, jewellery, pottery, furniture and sculpture found a place alongside steam-hammers, telescopes, plate-glass, knitting-machines, aniline dyes and artificial fertilisers. Yet not all exhibits could be neatly categorised as fruits of, on the one hand, scientific or, on the other, artistic endeavour. This was not perceived as a disadvantage: the Victorians took particular delight in artefacts which combined mechanical with artistic innovation. Among the objects on display at Hyde Park, few satisfied this characteristic enthusiasm so well as the large class of musical instruments, and within it, the organ was inevitably prominent: the most complex, most mechanical and (by virtue of the ambitious scale of some of its representatives) most visible instrument of all.

295

There were fourteen organs in the Exhibition, eleven by English builders, and one each from Germany, France and Italy. They varied in size from Willis's 70-stop instrument, placed in a gallery at the west end of the 'nave', to a curious 4-pipe instrument by Ducci of Florence designed to reinforce the low notes of an orchestra; it had received 'high praise' from Rossini (Pole 1851: 81). William Pole, Gauntlett's brother-in-law and later Professor of Engineering at the University of London, compiled a catalogue of the musical instruments in the Exhibition, and it must have been a cause of satisfaction to many who worshipped at the shrine of Progress that he could preface his remarks on the organs with an account of the considerable improvements that had taken place in recent years in both organ-building and organ-playing (1851: 59–62). The instruments themselves continued the story, and Pole took great pains to describe the innovations incorporated in each. With approval, he recorded improvements in the design of swell shutters (Gray & Davison; Willis), the application of varying wind pressures (Hill; Gray & Davison; Willis), the introduction of novel pallets and valves (Hill; Willis), and the employment of pneumatics in the construction of stop action (Hill) or key and combination action (Willis): all are carefully noted, together with a list of tonal improvements. In a spirit which the 1851 Commissioners would have applauded, Pole showed how the design of the English organs in the Exhibition exploited the progress of recent years and pointed the way to developments of even greater significance in the future.

The Great Exhibition has been characterised as a watershed in the history of the nineteenth century. It marked the transition to the mid-Victorian years, and the roots of much that we now regard as 'Victorian' can be traced back to it. It has always been regarded as an influential episode in the evolution of the English organ (Clutton & Niland 1963: 97–100), chiefly on account of the instruments by Willis and Schulze, but were one simply looking for a convenient date to flag the emergence of new trends in organ design destined to play a major part in the development of the instrument during the second half of the century, the claims of 1855 (the publication of Hopkins & Rimbault; the opening of the St George's Hall organ) or even 1862 (Schulze's organ for Doncaster) might be canvassed. In fact, the real consequences of the 1851 Exhibition were not immediately apparent. Willis's grand organ won him the contract for Liverpool, and was itself eventually purchased by the Dean and Chapter of Winchester for their cathedral (Matthews 1975: 11). For Willis, therefore, the Exhibition was momentous. But these organs were not completed until 1855 and 1854 respectively, and their true significance, as the foundation stones of Willis's later reputation in its two principal spheres, was not evident even then. The influence of two other Exhibition organs was also delayed. Ducroquet's instrument was in the modern French style, with *Grand Orgue*, *Recit* and *Pedale*, and its tally of twenty stops included no fewer than seven reeds. It was widely admired but, because of its price, found no purchaser. Yet it is clear that in some minds the quality and finish of its voicing and mechanism suggested comparisons with English work which were not to the advantage of the latter (above, p. 275). It may be that this helped to fuel a growing body of complaint in the musical press of the 1850s and 1860s concerning the poor materials and indifferent workmanship all too often encountered in English organs (below, pp. 374–6). Ducroquet's instrument may also have stimulated an interest in contemporary French organ-building: the use of the pneumatic lever and octave couplers, the application of a distinct pressure to the reeds of the *Grand Orgue*, and the inclusion of a harmonic flute and a free reed all represent features which were shortly to appear in the work of leading English builders (above, pp. 274–91). Though the Parisian outings of English organists undoubtedly played their part in this, the influence of Ducroquet's instrument should not be overlooked. As a portent of future developments, however, the French organ was easily eclipsed by the rather smaller instrument (sixteen stops) exhibited by Edmund Schulze of Paulinzelle. Whereas Ducroquet's organ was admired for its mechanical refinements, it was above all the tone of Schulze's organ that impressed; by making pipes with unusually wide flues, he was able to create particularly powerful choruses characterised by a remarkable fullness of tone, whilst, at the same time, producing softer registers (gedacts, geigens, gambas) of a delicacy and finesse to excite approval and imitation (Pole 1851: 79). The reception of Schulze's work in England merits separate treatment (below, pp. 383–8); probably no single builder had so considerable an influence upon the stylistic development of the English organ in the second half of the nineteenth century. But in 1851 this lay in the future. Although it seems that a number of players had been impressed by Schulze's Exhibition organ (Burn 1930: 101–2), and that others sought out the instrument after it had been re-erected in the Corn Exchange, Northampton (Shaw 1933: 84), it was not until the completion of the immense instrument for Doncaster in 1862 that Schulze's fame became widely established in England. Even so, the significance of 1851 in bringing Edmund Schulze to this country and providing opportunities for contact with English organists (Burn 1930: 101) should not be underestimated in view of later developments.

The 1850s have been described as a period of transition. The organs in the 1851 Exhibition substantiate this: in various important respects they are to be distinguished from the organs being made ten years earlier, yet tonally and mechanically, there is still some way to go before all the most characteristic features of the Victorian organ are in place. Quite soon, an irresistible stimulus for change would bring this about. In part, innovation was self-generating; organ-builders had a genuine curiosity about ways in which mechanisms might be improved, and the Great Exhibition itself, in which organs stood alongside manufacturing machines, may have fired their enthusiasm for experiment. But in addition to stimuli from within, organ-builders were obliged to take account of other, external changes that were bound to have implications for the design and construction of organs. The Ecclesiological Movement, for instance, was beginning to have a profound effect upon the appearance and layout of churches. As (usually) the largest single structure in the building, the organ could not expect to be exempt from scrutiny as to its credentials and purpose. The revival of congregational singing and the widespread fostering of parish choirs had further implications. And when the music provided for those choirs took an increasingly orchestral turn in the character of the accompaniments, this, too, required a positive response from the builders.

In what follows, we shall consider the ways in which the builders reacted to changing circumstances in the years following the Great Exhibition. Before doing so, it is necessary to discuss how organ-building itself was changing in the mid-Victorian years, and this can best be attempted by a survey of the businesses that flourished during those years.

ORGANS AND ORGAN-BUILDING, 1850–70

Few factors connected with English organ-building during the third quarter of the nineteenth century were of greater significance than the rise of provincial firms equipped to compete on equal terms with the metropolitan builders. By 1870, in the West Riding of Yorkshire alone, upwards of twenty businesses were listed in trade directories (White 1870; *West Riding* 1867), and among them were several that maintained workforces, timber yards, machinery and pipe-making shops able to compete with many London builders. Throughout Yorkshire, between two and three hundred men must by this date have been employed in making and tuning organs. Lancashire, with its densely populated industrial towns, presented a similar picture, with demand being stimulated by the multiplication of churches and chapels, and a growing willingness on the part of most denominations to tolerate the use of an organ. Less hampered by restrictive trade practices than their metropolitan counterparts and accustomed by the surrounding industrial environment to mechanical innovation and business efficiency, the northern builders were able to offer more favourable prices than their London rivals. By the 1870s, they had in consequence secured the lion's share of business in the north, though the largest and most prestigious contracts still tended to be awarded to the Londoners. There were other factors. By being generally less conservative than the London builders and more energetic in promoting mechanical and tonal improvements (console gadgetry, novel valves, combination actions, German flutes, French reeds) the northerners succeeded in appealing to the captains of industry who managed the affairs of many a church, chapel and corporation. But it was not only finance or the sort of window-dressing provided by patent devices that sold organs. Musical preference undoubtedly played its part. It is a mark of maturity that the northern builders evolved a style of organ able both to satisfy their clients and to be clearly distinguished from the work of the London builders. So, in Yorkshire the forthright tones of Schulze's organs provided the inspiration for Forster & Andrews, Charles Brindley and (later) Abbott & Smith; across the Pennines, the more sensuous and colourful tones of the modern French organ met with approval, and had a direct influence upon the work of Kirtland & Jardine, Wadsworth, and Whiteley Brothers.

Though the proliferation of builders in the north of England is especially notable, the period saw the establishment of new businesses and the expansion of old ones in most parts of the country. Bristol had a long-established tradition of independence in organ-building matters (above, pp. 49, 50). In 1858, W. G. Vowles inherited John Smith's business from his father-in-law (and Smith's step-son) Joseph Monday; Vowles soon moved to more spacious premises in St James's Square, and by the 1880s, was employing fifty workmen (*Work in Bristol* 1883: 165–6). From his Bristol base, he commanded much of the trade of south Wales and the west of England. Nicholson & Co. of Worcester (founded 1841) had a similar advantage in the west midlands and the Welsh border counties. Birmingham attracted E. J. Bossward who had worked with Hill on the Town Hall organ and stayed to set up his own business in 1847. John Banfield had already established himself there (1833), but there must have been ample trade, for a third builder, Halmshaw, had appeared by the mid-1850s ((*MG* I, 1856: 7). The east midlands were served by Charles Lloyd (Lloyd & Dudgeon of Nottingham, 1859), S. Taylor of Leicester (1860s) and T. H. Nicholson of Lincoln (*c.* 1860). A. T. Miller of Cambridge (1856) worked in Cambridgeshire and the surrounding counties building many excellent small organs for newly-restored churches, but the appearance of 'E. W. Norman, Organ Builder, Diss' in *c.* 1868, and the establishment of 'Norman Bros' a year or two later, heralded the advent of a business which, following its migration to Norwich, would increasingly dominate organ-building in East Anglia.[1]

The success of Norman Brothers must have been founded on a rising demand from churches in the small towns and villages of eastern England for unpretentious, well-constructed organs; in time, they built the most advanced organ workshops of the day (1898), employed 300 men and supplied organs to all parts of the country including the metropolis (Norman 1986: 54–7). But in the earlier phase of expansion, most provincial firms chose to establish themselves in, or in close proximity to, a large urban conurbation. In part this was due to ease of communication by road and rail, but it had at least as much to do with the fact that, whereas many country congregations were still content to do without organs, a town church or chapel without an organ was becoming the exception. In the south, this meant that places such as Bristol, Birmingham, Nottingham and Leicester were obvious bases for an aspiring organ-builder of the 1850s and 1860s; but it was in the north of England, where the Industrial Revolution had brought about massive concentrations of population in the manufacturing districts, that the true rivals to the London builders established themselves. Forster & Andrews (Hull; 1843), Peter Conacher (Huddersfield; 1849),[2] Kirtland & Jardine (Manchester; 1850),[3] Charles Brindley (Sheffield; 1854),[4] Wadsworth (Manchester; 1861), T. H. Harrison (Rochdale; 1861),[5] Wordsworth & Maskell (Leeds; 1866), Whiteley Bros (Chester; 1869), Abbott & Smith (Leeds; 1869), W. E. Richardson (Manchester; 1870)[6] and Alexander Young (Manchester; 1870) all established businesses during this period which, either from the start or after a short time, were equipped to manufacture the pipework and components required in the building of new organs. Although some of the London builders maintained branch offices in the provinces (for example in Liverpool, where Gray & Davison cornered much of the better trade when they took over Bewsher & Fleetwood's former connection) they were increasingly at a disadvantage in competing for contracts in the midlands and north.

Two recent studies cast valuable light upon the evolution of two particular provincial firms during the 1850s and 1860s. Laurence Elvin's monograph on Forster & Andrews (1968) recounts the rapid progress of a firm whose work was described by Edmund Schulze in 1864 as being 'quite as good . . . as the best London organ builders' (Elvin 1968: 17). No doubt Schulze's endorsement reflected the fact that Forster & Andrews were, at the time, his leading English disciples (below, p. 390), but the fact that they were already 'exporting' organs to the south of England and to Scotland indicates that Schulze was not alone in his opinion. They had attained this prominence over a relatively short period. The business was founded in 1843 when James Forster, apprentice and then journeyman with J. C. Bishop, returned to his native Hull, taking with him another of Bishop's men, Joseph Andrews. They acquired extensive premises (a disused Mechanics' Institute) and by 1846 were claiming to have 'the largest and most completely fitted up manufactory in the United Kingdom' – a claim which is difficult to reconcile with the statement in the same advertisement that the pipes in their organs were supplied from London. In their early years they built barrel organs, cabinet organs, piccolo, flute and flageolet organs, as well as church (finger) organs, but by 1851, with the care of Elliot & Hill's York Minster organ in their hands, the establishment of a branch office in York, and the inauguration of their own pipe-making shop, it is clear that the business was getting into its stride. Like all the northern builders they were zealous in making innovations: overhanging keys (Kirkstall Church, 1850), angled jambs (Honington Church, 1853), the pneumatic lever (Honington again), a radiating and concave pedal board (Independent Chapel, Keighley, 1856), adjustable composition pedals (All Souls, Halifax, 1858).[7] More significant, however, was the evolving tonal character of the firm's instruments. The partners visited the continent during the 1850s, travelling to France, Germany, Switzerland and Holland, and making contact there with a number of organ-builders (Elvin 1968: 14). It was, though, their association with Edmund Schulze that was to prove decisive in determining the musical identity of their instruments during the productive years of the 1860s and beyond. According to Schulze, Forster and Andrews 'often' visited him at Doncaster whilst he was erecting the organ in the Parish Church (17) and his opinion of their work has already been quoted. It was given in a letter to Dundee, in which Schulze, having himself declined to build an organ for the Kinnaird Hall, recommended Forster & Andrews for the work. They got the contract (1864) and built the 48-stop organ to a specification said to have been drawn up by Schulze (Appendix 1, pp. 482–4). Its German character is immediately apparent to anyone making a comparison with the smaller organ for Greenock Town Hall, built in 1862 (Elvin 1968: 16–17). German flutes and strings, a twelfth and fifteenth drawing on one slide, the large Pedal division with its concentration of 16′ basses, the use of mechanical extension, all attest Schulze's influence, distinguishing the scheme from that of Greenock which is much more in the style of a small concert organ of the 1840s or early-1850s. Thereafter, Forster & Andrews' work bore the unmistakable stamp of Schulze's influence, with strong Pedal basses, powerful but not dull diapasons, big quint mixtures, small-scale flutes and quiet strings.

By the 1860s, Forster & Andrews's business was thriving. This is evident from the fact that in the busiest year of that decade (1867) thirty organs were built (Elvin 1968: 20); in London, Gray & Davison made nineteen new organs in the same year (MS 10: *passim*), and Hill's tally may have been as low as thirteen (below, p. 397). The number of Forster & Andrews's workmen is uncertain. There were 'between 20 and 30' in 1859, and 120 by the late-1880s (Elvin 1968: 14, 25); we might guess that there would have been about fifty in 1870, and, if so, the firm had the resources to compete with any of the London builders. A contemporary account of the Charlotte Street works conveys the impression of an efficient and flourishing business.

The exterior of the establishment has a very commanding architectural appearance. Passing through the entrance hall . . . we enter first the offices where are the clerks, the designers and others. Here are also long rows of labelled duplicate keys of organs in various parts of the country which the firm keep in tune and in order. There are also blackboards with hooks and numbered brass tickets, each number representing one of the workmen and the whole so manipulated as to assist in keeping a record of the men's time and where they are employed. Here also are displayed numerous designs for organ cases and plans for the building of large instruments. Passing through a side door the visitor finds himself in the building room, where organs are put together. This room is some fifty feet square and about forty feet high and at the time of our visit three large organs were being put together within its walls. At the back of this hall a glass door gives entrance to a workshop about one hundred feet long and twenty feet wide. Above it are two others of similar size, with an underground shop of the same length. In this cellar is conducted one of the preliminary processes in organ building: the preparation of metal for pipes. At the extreme end of the underground shop there are appliances for forging those portions of the mechanism of an organ required to be of iron or brass, such as rods, rollers and a variety of connections. In this room is also found the steam machinery that drives the lathes, circular saws etc. in the upper workshops.   (Shepherdson 1873: 11–12)

Though incomplete, this is a fascinating glimpse of a manufacturing process in transition: the small workshop has given place to the factory; a craft has become a trade; modern factory methods are adopted to regulate the workforce and power the machinery. Were we told more, we would probably discover that pipes, soundboards and components were being manufactured to standard scales and dimensions, then stock-piled until required. All in all, the description neatly illuminates the changes that had taken place in the building of organs since John Gray compiled his workshop inventories in the 1820s (above, pp. 60, 62–4).

The point concerning innovations in business organisation and design methods is well made in a brief article by Michael Sayer (1976b) on the Manchester firm of Kirtland & Jardine. As early as the 1820s, Kirtland & Jardine's predecessor, Samuel Renn, had standardised the manufacture of organ parts (above, pp. 50, 61), but in contrast to this enterprise in mechanical matters, his tonal schemes varied little over the course of more than twenty years (Sayer 1976a: *passim*). In his article, Sayer demonstrates how Frederick Jardine continued to manufacture standard soundboards, action components and consoles, but adapted Renn's methods to take account of the considerable changes that had taken place since the 1820s. A crucial decision was to adopt Vogler's so-called 'Simplification System'. By laying out the soundboard with all but the lowest eighteen notes in due chromatic sequence large roller-boards could be dispensed with in favour of splayed backfalls or trackers connected directly to the pallet wire, and by providing common basses for stops of similar character, congestion and the size of soundboards could be reduced whilst permitting each pipe to stand directly over its groove without resort to conveyancing. This enabled the builder to produce cheaper organs, and the cost could be further reduced by placing two divisions on the same soundboard and allowing a single set of bass pipes to serve appropriate registers in two departments. Sayer cites Emmanuel Church, Barlow Moor, Manchester (1851) as an early example of this. There, Jardine provided the open diapasons of Great and Choir, and the Choir viola di gamba, with a common open bass; a single stopped bass served the stopped diapasons in each division and the Choir dulciana (172). Kirtland & Jardine were the first English builders to adopt the simplification system (they appear first to have used it at Yeovil Parish Church in 1850) and this is further evidence of the progressive spirit of the leading provincial builders; though it was open to musical objections (the use of common basses was widely criticised) the system had the undoubted merit in the circumstances of the north of England of allowing the builders to provide simple organs cheaply.

With the same object in mind, Kirtland & Jardine standardised their stop lists and pipe scales. A style was rapidly established and varied little during the years that Jardine presided over the firm (until 1874). More interesting were schemes for a small number of exceptional instruments, usually (as Sayer points out) the fruits of private benefaction. Holy Trinity, Hulme, was the first of these (1852). It was commissioned by Benjamin Joule,[8] a musical enthusiast and son of a wealthy Salford brewer. The organ was notable for its size (forty-five stops) and for its unusually complete specification, but its most striking feature was its Solo Organ. With a vox angelica, flauto traverso and flute harmonique it anticipated innovations which Gray & Davison and Hill would make in the following year in their concert instruments for Glasgow and the Panopticon.[9] The console stood 25′ in front of the organ (Renn had established the taste for detached consoles in Manchester) and the specification, whilst impressive enough, possessed no features other than the Solo Organ to distinguish it from the work of the leading London builders of the day. Only the Solo and the provision of four ventil pedals (their application is unknown) hinted at the model which was to provide the inspiration for Joule's next collaboration with Jardine: the organ for St Peter's, Manchester, completed in 1865 (Appendix 1, pp. 484–5). Sayer describes this as 'a French romantic organ' (173), but the original specification[10] suggests an eclectic approach, Joule and the builders drawing with equal freedom on the French and the German schools. A contemporary advertisement expounds this philosophy, claiming that

Messrs. *Kirtland & Jardine* have made personal examinations of some of the finest specimens of the German and French Schools of Organ Building . . . and they have adopted those Stops from the Continental Organs which are of new and beautiful tone, among which may be mentioned the *Viola* and *Cone Gambas*, the *Flute Harmonique*, the *Flauto Traverso*; the *Hohl*, *Doppel*, and *Suabe Flutes*; the *Salicional*, the *Vox Angelica*, the *Posaune*, *Cor Anglais*, &c.   (HRI: 599)

Thus, at St Peter's, the Great Organ was broadly French in inspiration, with harmonic flutes at 8′ and 4′, a (tin) gamba, a 16′ free reed and a harmonic trumpet. Turning to the Choir (and despite the presence of a celeste) German influence was in the ascendancy with gedact, spitzflöte and viol di gamba at 8′, and gemshorn, flauto traverso and rohrflöte at 4′. The Swell was a combination of English, French and German nomenclature, and so was the Pedal. There, a grosse quint, violoncello and posaune (all of wood) struck a German note alongside a montre and (tin) violon of French extraction. Among the accessories, the tremulant and octave couplers derive from Paris, but the absence of a Swell to Choir coupler, and the inclusion of neither ventils nor the pneumatic lever[11] underline the selective nature of the

influences from that quarter. All told, Joule's instrument was less consciously French in character than, say, Gray & Davison's Crystal Palace
organ (1857).

Kirtland & Jardine's other large organs of the 1850s and 1860s reflected a
similar synthesis of English, French and German influences. The organ for
the Free Trade Hall, Manchester (1857) had a huge Swell division of twenty
stops, with celeste, voix humaine, euphone (free reed) and octave clarion 2',
but the adoption of Töpfer's principles for calculating pipe scales taken with
the nomenclature of flutes and strings in each division attest German
influence, and the builders were careful to include the high-pressure reeds
and weighty Pedal stops that the English expected to find in their concert
organs. Church organs were more modestly eclectic, and there was the
occasional incongruity, as when Jardine, as late as 1868, was obliged by the
donor to tune a large new organ (St Thomas, Bury) to unequal temperament
(*MW* XLVI, 1868: 249). In all essentials, however, Kirtland & Jardine's style
was established by the mid-1850s. Founded upon the simplification system,
with additional mechanical refinements in the form of overhanging keys, an
improved tumbler coupler and the use of a distinctive relief pallet,[12] the
character of the firm's instruments did not alter radically during the years of
Frederick Jardine's control (he sold the business in 1874), though towards
the end of his career he experimented a little with mechanical extension for
Pedal registers (St Thomas, Werneth, Oldham; 1869), possibly drawing
upon Forster & Andrews's experience, under Schulze's ultimate direction,
in the organ for Dundee.[13]

For much of the 1850s and 1860s, Kirtland & Jardine's output averaged
seven or eight organs a year (Sayer 1976b: 172). A number of other provincial builders probably exceeded this total (Conacher, Brindley) and it could
not compare with Forster & Andrews's conspicuous productivity. But there
were many other firms in the provinces of modest achievement and limited
resources, who made a living out of tunings, repairs, small rebuilds and the
occasional new organ. Unable to maintain their own manufactory, they
relied upon a growing number of trade suppliers: pipe-makers such as John
Fincham (1837), Alfred Hunter (1841), John Courcelle (1853) and Edward
Violette (*c.* 1855); parts suppliers such as Thomas Harrison (1830) and
Solomon Wise (*c.* 1842); key-makers, leather merchants, reed-makers,
engravers and case-makers. Elvin has compiled a comprehensive list of these
tradesmen (1986: 159–67) revealing a network of (chiefly) small workshops
in both London and the provinces which supplied pipes and components to
organ-builders who lacked a full-scale manufactory. No doubt it was a
steady trade: in their early days, both Henry Willis and Thomas Lewis were
obliged to supplement the uncertain profits derived from an irregular flow of
orders for new organs by supplying pipes to other builders (Elvin 1984: 77;
1986: 165).

Although the 1850s and 1860s saw the rise of provincial firms able to contest the virtual monopoly of the metropolitan builders, this must not be taken to mean that London organ-building was devoid of significant developments. An older generation of builder was passing from the scene (Charles Allen, J. C. Bishop, John Gray, H. C. Lincoln, Timothy Russell), new businesses were being established, new names coming to the fore. Among them, Henry Jones (c. 1848),[14] William Hedgeland (1854), Hunter & Webb (1856),[15] Henry Wedlake (1858),[16] Henry Speechley (1860),[17] Alfred Monk (1862) and Eustace Ingram[18] founded firms which rapidly exploited the escalating demand for new organs in and around London, and were soon supporting workshops and wage lists to compare with the bigger northern firms. There was also August Gern, who came to erect Cavaillé-Coll's organ for the Carmelite Church, Kensington, and stayed to found his own business (1866); he built a substantial number of organs (generally of modest dimensions) in the French style for churches and private houses, without having any apparent influence upon his English contemporaries. There are, though, two other London builders whose work was to be extremely influential in the later Victorian years and who first received widespread notice during this period. They deserve more extended treatment.

T. C. Lewis's origins are obscure. He practised as an architect before embarking upon organ-building, and also claimed to be a bell-founder and pianoforte-maker,[19] but nothing is known of the circumstances surrounding this progression. He first appears as an organ-builder in 1863,[20] working from an address in Westminster (the same that he had occupied as an architect) and with a workshop in a disused church in Clapham. Later, he moved to Brixton. It seems that Lewis was no newcomer to organ-building. In a letter of 1863, he claimed that 'for many years past the proper effect of a grand organ, complete and in detail, has been almost my constant thought' (*MSt* I, 1863: 354), and a review of Lewis's new organ for St Mary, Birnam, near Dunkeld, repeats the claim, adding testimony to the high regard in which his work was held: 'What Mr Lewis has already done has given him a position among the first organ builders of the time, and he is known to have studied with success the science of organ building, to which, for some years, he has applied himself' (*MSt* I, 1863: 309). Lewis's quest for 'the proper effect of a grand organ' took him to Doncaster, where he was overwhelmed by the effect of Schulze's fluework ('anything finer it is, I believe, impossible to imagine') and the general quality and finish of the organ ('by far the grandest instrument I have ever heard') (*MSt* I, 1863: 354–5); thereafter, Schulze's work powerfully influenced his own. More will be said of this below (pp. 392–4). A further important contribution to his evolving style came from Cavaillé-Coll. Alongside the lieblich gedacts, hohlflötes, geigen principals and rohrflötes that he adopted from Schulze's use, Lewis set harmonic flutes, celestes, gambas and orchestral reeds derived from French practice. Unlike Willis, and some of the other English builders, Lewis commonly employed the same pressure throughout the organ (reeds as well as flues); when this was associated with generous winding, big quint mixtures and free-toned reeds, Lewis achieved a grandeur of effect which not all could admire (though many did) but which possessed a musical integrity all of its own. His most important work falls outside the period covered in the present volume. The series of ambitious instruments that began with St Mary's Roman Catholic Cathedral, Newcastle-upon-Tyne (1869), and continued in the following decade with organs for St Peter, Eaton Square (1874), Glasgow Public Hall (1877) and Ripon Cathedral (1878), led eventually to his *chef d'oeuvre*, the organ for Southwark Cathedral (1897), an instrument which in important respects anticipated developments in the first half of the present century. During the 1860s, Lewis's work was more modest, including a useful family of 'lieblich' organs, priced from £25 upwards, and intended 'to supersede the Harmonium for small Churches, Schools, and for private use' (*MSt* II, 1864: 406), but he was already laying the foundations of a reputation for excellence of workmanship and materials, and creating that synthesis of modern German and French tonalities within an English framework which was to make his a distinctive and influential voice in English organ-building for the remainder of the century.

Lewis's practice was diametrically opposed to that of the other great individualist of the later-nineteenth century, Henry Willis, and there was a conscious rivalry between the two with neither able to see much merit in the other's approach. The depth of their disagreement is revealed in Lewis's pamphlet, *A protest against the modern development of unmusical tone* (1897) in which (without naming his rival) he takes issue with many of the distinguishing features of Willis's practice: high pressures, high cut-ups, slotting, 'insipidly smooth' reeds, diminution of mixtures and eradication of mutations (*passim*). To be fair to Willis, some of these developments, pioneered in the 1860s and 1870s, had by the 1890s been taken by others to extremes of which he would not approve, but there is no denying the fundamental rift between his approach and Lewis's. Lewis's organs were dominated by big Schulze-inspired flue choruses, to which the chorus reeds, though adding colour and intensity, took second place. Willis's approach was utterly different. In his instruments, powerful (and, in the early years, bright) chorus reeds dominated the full organ; a tierce mixture formed a bridge between these reeds and a flue chorus characterised by impeccable blend, an even tone tending to closeness, and a distinct melodic bias in the voicing of individual registers. Each approach offered a different answer to the musical demands made by the nineteenth century, and (for all their differences) both Lewis and Willis would bequeath an important legacy to the twentieth century.

In turning to consider Henry Willis, we find ourselves confronted with one of the most remarkable figures in nineteenth-century organ-building. His influence upon the building and playing of organs in England (and to a lesser extent America) was of fundamental importance in the hundred years succeeding the Exhibition of 1851, and if a modern view of the development which this promoted is less favourable than one of forty or fifty years ago, nothing should be allowed to detract from the man's extraordinary inventive capacity and the confidence with which he forged an original but wholly legitimate interpretation of the romantic organ. His achievement will be considered at greater length in its proper place (below, pp. 412–41); for the moment, an outline sketch of his career must suffice.

Willis was born in London on 27 April 1821.[21] His father was a carpenter[22] who sang in the choir of the Surrey Chapel, Blackfriars, and was kettle-drummer to the Cecilian Society. These early musical associations were reinforced when the young Willis formed an acquaintance with George Cooper, junior; Willis later recalled how the two of them had competed in mastering the pedal board attached to an old harpsichord belonging to Cooper, senior. This, together with exercises in score-reading and improvisation, laid the foundations of an organ technique which in later years sustained Willis's reputation as a fine player; he was well able to demonstrate his own instruments and held organist's posts for much of his life.[23]

In 1835 he was apprenticed to John Gray. It was a fortunate beginning, for Gray's was the busiest organ manufactory in the metropolis, and his organs were noted for the refinement of their mechanisms and the excellence of their reeds (both areas in which Willis was later to distinguish himself). It seems that he did not complete his apprenticeship with Gray (*MG* II, 1857: 443) but by the early-1840s was working with W. E. Evans in Cheltenham. Wardle Evans kept a music shop, and was in business as an organ-builder, but he is chiefly remembered today as a pioneer of the harmonium (Ord-Hume 1986: 141). He was already experimenting with free reeds before Willis joined him and had produced a soprano voice guide, consisting of two octaves of reeds. Willis later claimed to have assisted Evans in developing this prototype ('I went into the matter with him') ending in the production of 'a perfect model of a two-manual free-reed instrument, with two octaves and a half of pedals' (*MT* xxxix, 1898: 298). Although Willis's chronology is confused, this was probably Evans's 'Organo Harmonica' of 1841, which according to Ord-Hume 'largely rendered obsolete' earlier attempts to manufacture reed organs (1986: 26). Whatever Willis's true contribution to the evolution of the harmonium his association with Evans was not without importance for his future career. Like Cavaillé-Coll, who scored an early success with his 'Poïkilorgue' (1834), Willis's experience with free reeds stood him in good stead when he was developing a distinctive approach to the voicing of reeds in pipe organs. And then, it was indirectly through Evans that he made a useful acquaintance. The Organo Harmonica was sent up to

London to be displayed at Novello's, in Dean Street, and Willis went with it. There, he was introduced ('as the constructor of this model organ') to Dr Wesley. Wesley's views on the Organo Harmonica are unrecorded, but his patronage (at Liverpool and Winchester) was later to be crucial in bringing Willis's work to notice.

Willis may have undertaken work on his own account during the three years that he was in Cheltenham[24] but by the beginning of 1845 (possibly earlier) he was back in London with his own business. We know this because in February of that year he supplied some wooden pipes to J. C. Bishop (Elvin 1984: 77). But the West Country connection was still valuable and secured him two of his earliest important contracts: Gloucester Cathedral (1847) and Tewkesbury Abbey (1848). Each entailed an extensive reconstruction of an existing instrument, and at Gloucester Willis's alterations included the creation of a C-compass, 12-stop Swell with a double venetian front. Little more is heard of him until 1851, with the appearance of the Exhibition organ, the award of the Liverpool contract and the taking out of the first in a long series of patents for improvements in organs.

The Exhibition organ was an extraordinarily bold speculation. At seventy stops it was twice the size of most cathedral organs, and its construction must have monopolised the resources of Willis's workshop (men, materials and machinery) for four or five months. Yet, with characteristic self-assurance, Willis went out, secured financial sponsorship, and provided himself with a magnificent advertisement for his work generally and his patented mechanical improvements in particular. The gamble paid off and the Exhibition organ proved to be the foundation-stone of Willis's later achievements. Never one to hide his light under a bushel, Willis wrote of his instrument in a descriptive brochure that 'it is presumed by its builder to be the first successful large organ yet constructed in England' (Sumner 1955: 20) and whilst such confident assertions did nothing to endear him to other practitioners, it is undoubtedly true that Willis's great achievement was to overcome the mechanical problems connected with the construction of large organs and satisfy the players' demands for ease of control.

The construction of the Exhibition organ had caused Willis to quit his original premises in Gray's Inn Road and move to Manchester Street.[25] There, he commenced building the organ for St George's Hall and reconstructing the Exhibition organ for Winchester Cathedral. Other large organs followed, for cathedrals (Carlisle, 1856; Wells, 1857), churches (St Matthias, Stoke Newington, 1853; Cranbrook Parish Church, 1854; St Hilary, Wallasey, 1861; St John, Taunton, 1864; St George, Preston, 1865) and concert halls (Agricultural Hall, Islington, 1862; Reading Town Hall, 1864). By the mid-1860s, Willis's business had grown to such an extent that he again needed larger premises. He acquired a circular building in Camden Town which had once been the studio of Robert Burford, a well-known artist, whose enormous panoramas of battles, landscapes and seascapes had provided popular entertainment for an earlier generation. Fitted up with galleries and offices, and with the addition of a number of out-buildings to house a metal shop, engineering department and mill, Burford's studio became 'The Rotunda Organ Works', the most commodious organ manufactory in London, and one in which the largest instruments could be assembled before being despatched to their destinations. By the end of the 1860s, Willis needed all the space he could find. As his reputation grew so did the demand for new organs. Large numbers of church organs of all sizes left the Camden Town manufactory, but alongside this regular trade, Willis's order book included a number of instruments in which monumental scale, mechanical complexity and tonal ambition combined in a novel way to mark a new departure in English organ-building. The organs for the Royal Albert Hall (1871), St Paul's Cathedral (1872), the Alexandra Palace (1873, 1875), Durham Cathedral (1876) and Salisbury Cathedral (1877) were pioneering instruments in this genre and were arguably the outstanding achievements of Willis's career.

   Willis held strong opinions and showed few inhibitions in expressing them. The award of the Liverpool contract did little to secure him friends in the organ-building establishment, and Willis did nothing to improve matters by trumpeting the '"curious" or "ingenious" or "patent" or "unique"' features of his scheme in advance of the organ's completion (*MW* xxxii, 1854: 566); he left himself open to a humiliating snub from the hostile musical press, and duly received it from the *Musical World* (xxxii, 1854: 617). ('Mr. Willis is . . . a very young man, and not yet entitled – whatever he may think to the contrary – to rank with the great organ builders of the world.') His behaviour a few years later over the Leeds Town Hall organ again reflected an immoderate opinion of his own abilities. Having failed to win the competition for plans and a specification, he wrote a peevish letter to the *Musical Gazette* hinting darkly at underhand dealings on the part of Smart and Spark, accusing the Corporation of a lack of good faith, questioning the honesty and the competence of the committee which had preferred the successful scheme to his own, and ending with a petulant squib to the effect that he alone held a patent for *crescendo* and *diminuendo* pedals and Spark and Smart's proposal to include them in their organ was therefore 'not legally possible' (*MG* i, 1856: 429–31). Henry Smart's dignified response (*MG* i, 1856: 464–5) merely served to make Willis look faintly ridiculous. These incidents came early in Willis's career, at a time when he was striving to make his mark, and whilst there is no doubt that he remained throughout his career a man of decided opinions who could in certain circumstances prove difficult and unyielding, the same qualities ('obstinate perseverance', as F. G. Edwards tactfully put it) provide the key to his technical and artistic success. In an article composed shortly before his death in 1901, Willis was described as 'the greatest organ builder of the Victorian Era' (*MT* xxxix, 1898: 303) and the writer suggested that he should share, with John Howe and Bernard Smith, the accolade 'Father'. Though we might now question the implied relegation of all other builders to a lesser division, the title has persisted, and is an appropriate testimony to Willis's pre-eminent ability to satisfy the most characteristic aspirations of the Victorian organist.

Willis's mechanical ingenuity, and his readiness to explore new techniques, meant that he was peculiarly well equipped to meet the challenges posed by changing architectural tastes and liturgical fashions. It is to these that we must now turn.

ECCLESIOLOGY

Few manifestations of English church life in the third quarter of the nineteenth century offer more persuasive evidence of the Anglican revival then taking place than the movement to promote the restoration of ancient churches and the building of new ones in a 'correct' Gothic style. Its origins are complex: the antiquarianism of the eighteenth century, the rise of the romantic movement and the Evangelical revival each played their part. But it was the Tractarian movement, and its Cambridge off-shoot, the Ecclesiological Movement, which finally provided the dynamic for a sustained assault on the dreariness and decay of so many of England's surviving mediaeval churches and cathedrals, and offered a justification for attempts to re-create in them, and in new churches built to meet the demands of a rapidly expanding population, a romantic ideal of Christian worship as it had been in the 'Age of Faith'. The adumbration and application of ecclesiological principles had implications for organs. On the one hand, they became more common. As a means of supplanting the despised gallery bands, providing accompaniment for a chancel choir and encouraging the congregation to join in hymns and whatever other musical portions of the service were allowed them, organs proved indispensable to the reformers (to the regret of the purists). On the other hand, and less favourably, restoration led to the sweeping away of west galleries and central screens. These had for many years housed the organs, and their disappearance left ecclesiologists with the problem of finding an alternative site elsewhere in the building. They seldom solved the difficulty to their (or the organ-builder's) complete satisfaction, the organ usually being awkwardly placed on the ground near the choir or in a specially constructed chamber. Added to this, the evolving pattern of worship in Anglican churches, with its enhanced rôle for choir and congregational music, the spreading practice of chanting the psalms, and the importance generally attached to dignity and seemliness in the execution of the liturgy, made demands upon the organ which could only be met by an extension of its powers. Organs had to become more flexible tonally and (an inevitable consequence) physically larger at just the moment when their accommodation was proving a major difficulty.

Objections to the existing location of organs had surfaced first in cathedrals. As early as 1789, the Earl of Radnor, writing of Salisbury Cathedral, claimed that 'the length of the great Isle including the Choir & morning chapel is of itself so beautiful as that any Interruption of the View not arising from Necessity is illjudged [sic], & misplaced, & consequently the Removal of the Organ . . . would be advantageous in point of Beauty'. Radnor's proposal was to have the organ 'divided into two parts placed against the two pillars at the entrance of the Choir . . . the Organist sitting in the middle' (Matthews 1972: 11) but in the event more cautious counsels prevailed, Green's new instrument (1792) duly providing ample grounds for criticism by those who regarded a large organ as an intolerable intrusion. Following the fire of 1829, Smirke contemplated dividing the York Minster organ, either by concealing it within the stone pulpitum or placing it in two departments on either side of the choir (Gray 1837: 17–18), but Camidge's ambitions and the inveterate conservatism of the gentlemen of Yorkshire defeated him, and it was not until 1848, when Edward Blore brought about the removal of the organ case in Westminster Abbey, and Hill was commissioned to divide the instrument locating Great and Swell at opposite ends of the screen, that the division of an organ on a central screen was finally carried out.[26] Soon, however, not only the organs, but the screens on which they stood were threatened. In 1851, George Gilbert Scott brought about the removal of the first in a series of cathedral choir screens (and, of necessity, their organs) when he redesigned the choir at Ely so as to reveal the vista (Cobb 1980: 80–1).

By then, the aesthetic considerations which had motivated Radnor and Smirke were being reinforced by distinct, and increasingly influential arguments originating in the study of the architectural principles and liturgical practice of the Middle Ages. The Cambridge Camden Society (founded by J. M. Neale, Edward Boyle and Benjamin Webb in 1839) promoted the 'science' of ecclesiology through publication and example, and by the mid-1840s it was no longer sufficient to view church architecure in purely aesthetic terms (White 1962: 25–115). The question of central screens in cathedrals illustrates this. The ecclesiologists' obsession with attaching some profound symbolism to every feature of a Gothic building led them to describe the choir arch (under which screen and organ usually stood) as symbolising 'that death . . . by which the Church Militant is divided from the Church Triumphant', and to regard this location for the organ as 'unseemly' (*Eccl* III, 1843–4: 1). But there was a yet more emotive issue at stake. To those who were seeking to undo what they more and more thought of as the worst effects of the English Reformation, the central screen, surmounted by its organ, was a physical barrier which had contributed to the 'degradation' and 'total uselessness' of the mediaeval nave (Baron 1858: 45; Rainbow 1970: 321). The ecclesiologists' philosophy led them to envisage the use, once again, of the entire cathedral for Divine Service. In tune with their partial understanding of mediaeval practice, they urged that only the clergy and the singers should occupy the choir; the proper place for the laity was the nave. They agreed that the intervention of the 'organ-loft' would make it 'impossible' for those in the nave to see or hear what was going on: 'but all that it proves is the necessity of removing the organ to some other part; and of replacing the cumbrous erection of the seventeenth century by a suitable Rood-screen' (*Eccl* II, 1842–3: 35). In the context of the 1840s, the ecclesiologists' desire to provide for massive congregations in the English cathedrals was definitely in anticipation of demand, but as the century progressed, and cathedrals gradually became the settings for large diocesan services and festivals, many Chapters were persuaded to remove a central screen so that nave and choir might serve as two halves of a single, vast room, flowing into one another. The introduction of 'Special Sunday Evening Services' at St Paul's in 1858 highlighted the difficulties presented by a central screen; the large congregations, seated in the nave and beneath the dome, could not hear the choir, and the screen organ was quite unable to give an adequate lead to congregational singing. The screen was therefore removed (in 1860), and Hill's redundant Panopticon organ was purchased to stand in the south transept. The old organ was placed under one of the arches on the north side of the choir (Sumner 1931: 18–19; Matthews & Atkins 1957: 264–5). But it was only some years later, when the singers were moved westwards to be nearer the space beneath the dome, and the application of pneumatics enabled Willis to build a new organ in two halves on either side of the choir, that a permanent solution was achieved (*MT* XXXIX, 1898: 301; Sumner 1931: 20–2). Despite the liturgical advantages of the arrangement, the remark of a later historian of St Paul's, that the effect of this re-ordering was to reduce the cathedral 'to something of the aspect of an overgrown parish church' (Matthews & Atkins 1957: 270) stands as a reasonable criticism of this, and many other similar schemes.

Objections to the conventional siting of the parish church organ were, if anything, more forcibly expressed. All the indignation which the conscientious ecclesiologist felt towards the west gallery position and its accompanying evils is summed up in a single sentence from an article on 'Organs' in the *Ecclesiologist* (the journal of the Cambridge Camden Society):

The west end is the most usual place for the organ in parish churches: and who does not recollect a hundred instances in which a fine window is blocked by a hideous organ-case, surmounted by indecent angels blowing trumpets between crowns and mitres, and resting on a flaunting western gallery with prominent seats for the singers?
                                                                    (III, 1843–4: 1).

The architectural impropriety of obscuring Gothic features by an arrangement lacking mediaeval precedent was a fault compounded by the abuses attendant upon the placing of singers alongside the organ in the gallery. J. M. Neale wrote that

> In country churches, the singing loft, during the performance of the Psalm or Hymn, becomes the cynosure of all eyes: the worshippers, or they who should be such, generally turn to it as to the centre of attention . . . where women-singers are allowed, and part-anthems sung, the notice which they attract from their station in front of the gallery might well enough befit a theatre, but is highly ludicrous in the House of God.   (Neale 1843: 15–16)

Apart from aesthetic and moral objections to the west end position, the ecclesiologists had a positive liturgical reason for wishing to abolish the galleries. This was their belief that the chancel was the proper location for the singers; they were 'ministers of divine worship' with 'a sacred office' to perform, and although laymen ('laicks'), should be robed and positioned in close proximity to the priestly ministers of the Divine Service (Jebb 1843: 188). Though initially opposed altogether to the use of organs in worship – 'church musick is almost exclusively *vocal*' (*Eccl* III, 1843–4: 2) – most ecclesiologists came to accept the inevitability – if not the desirability – of organs, and declared that the organ should accompany the singers eastwards.

Having condemned choir screens and west galleries the reformers felt obliged to suggest new locations for the displaced organs. Influenced by continental precedents, the ecclesiologists toyed with the provision of two organs in cathedrals – a grand west end organ for use upon 'great occasions', when it might accompany a large congregation singing antiphonally with the choir and generally adorn the worship, and a more modest choir organ, to accompany the daily service (*Eccl* IV, 1844–5: 6; XVII, 1856: 14). Nowhere, however, did they discuss how a west end organ was to be accommodated without detriment to the architecture of the English cathedral. The experiment was tried in a modified form at St Paul's (1861–72), York Minster (1863–1903) and Worcester Cathedral (1874–96), but in none of these instances was the problem of siting satisfactorily resolved, with the result that, once technical and tonal developments seemed to make the retention of two instruments unnecessary, the experiment was terminated. The most common solution to the problem of siting the cathedral organ in the third quarter of the century was to place it on the north side of the choir. In part, the ecclesiologists were influenced by foreign examples of small organs placed near the singers;[27] in part, they were inspired by mediaeval precedent. Jebb was quite clear that 'one side of the choir, generally the north, and towards the east end' was the conventional location for the organ in mediaeval times (1843: 197), and Rimbault stated unequivocally that, 'in the mediaeval ages', the organ 'was placed on one side of the choir; a position which seems to have been almost universal throughout Europe' (HR3: 79).

Hence, when central screens were removed at Durham (1847), Ely (1851),

St Paul's (1860), Bristol (1860), Chichester and Lichfield (1861), Hereford (1862) and Worcester,[28] in each case the organ was re-erected (or a new one provided) on one side of the choir. At Hereford, the organ stood on the south side of the choir, but in every other instance the north was chosen, the organ usually standing beneath the choir arcade and projecting back into the choir aisle. At Lichfield a curious arrangement was adopted. Holdich's organ was sited in the eastern chapels of the north transept (in a 'side-street', as an organist later observed) with the action passing through an aperture in the wall to the console standing in the adjacent choir aisle; there, it was remote from the singers, posing formidable difficulties for an accompanist who can have heard neither choir nor organ distinctly (Greening 1974: 8, 11–12). Lofts at Durham, St Paul's, Bristol, Chichester and Hereford raised the organs above the pavement of the aisle and at least ensured that the organist had some contact with the singers. At Ely, Scott attempted a more adventurous solution, providing a 'hanging' case after the model of Strasburg Cathedral; into this Hill inserted the Great and Choir of the reconstructed organ, leaving Swell and Pedal to stand in the triforium behind (*Handbook* 1855: 66).

The confidence with which ecclesiologists recommended these rearrangements was not echoed in the attitude of the organ-builders. Before 1870, their resources for coping with this radical reordering were extremely limited. J. C. Bishop, never the most progressive of spirits, was one of the first to be confronted with the problem when he was commissioned to re-site the Durham organ in 1847. In replying to a series of eight questions from the Dean and Chapter about the implications of this move, he gave it as his opinion that 'the tone of the Cathedral Organ will not be injured in quality by the removal [it] will [be injured] in quantity about one Fourth' (MS 62: 42–4). As the scheme involved burying the organ behind the 'Canopy work in the Side Aisle', Bishop was clearly speaking from the depths of his inexperience. He vaguely thought that 'the power might be increased to compensate for the situation by enlarging the scale of the pipes', but it was many years before he, or other English organ-builders, came to terms with the implications of the ecclesiological movement for cathedral organs. The instruments mentioned in the preceding paragraph were predominantly conservative in character, at best reflecting some of the innovations made by Hill and Davison in the 1840s, at worst mutilated survivals from the seventeenth or eighteenth centuries. Neither in tonal design nor physical disposition did these early victims of re-ordering attempt to overcome the disadvantages of the sites to which the ecclesiologists condemned them. In only two instances was a serious attempt made to alleviate difficulties by drawing upon techniques more usually employed at this date in the concert-organ field. At Hereford (1862) Gray & Davison divided the large Great Organ into 'front' and 'back' divisions. The former consisted of a powerful diapason chorus with a quint mixture and a trumpet; the pressure was on the high side for a church organ (3¼″) and, in an attempt to eliminate possible mechanical problems, the pneumatic lever was applied to the Great and its couplers. At St Paul's, Willis was called in only three years after Hill had moved the organ to the north side of the choir. He reconstructed the old organ, raising the console so that it was on a level with the top of the choir stalls,[29] and applying the pneumatic lever to the Great and to the Great and Choir couplers. He also provided pneumatic thumb pistons, introduced octave couplers and increased the wind pressure of the Great and Swell reeds to 5″.

It was Willis who first successfully addressed the challenge of ecclesiology. By applying a pneumatic connection to the divided parts of a single instrument, he made it possible to dispense with the central screen and yet find space for a large organ: the vista could then be appreciated. By raising wind pressures and developing brilliant fluework and powerful reeds, he transformed the character of the organ and evolved an idiosyncratic style: it became possible to provide reasonably adequate accompaniment for vast congregations dispersed throughout the building. The arrangement was not without its drawbacks, and many cathedral organists would continue to prefer the traditional position, where they were allowed to retain it, but there is no denying that Willis had found a brilliant solution to the apparently irreconcilable demands of ecclesiologist and organist.

When the ecclesiologists turned their attention to the parish churches, they found that the problems arising from the siting of the organ were, if anything, more perplexing than in the cathedrals. The difficulties were heightened by an ideological split within the ranks of the reformers. It was agreed that the chancel was the correct place for the singers; what was not agreed was whether the vocal part of the service should be congregational in character (a revival of plainsong) or choral (the introduction of the cathedral service into the parish church). The emergence of these two schools of thought has been ably described by Dr Rainbow (1970) and had important implications for the organ. If the service was to be congregational the architect was required to find space for a modest instrument near the singers, to whom it was duly subservient; if it was to be choral an organ capable of providing the increasingly ambitious accompaniments envisaged by contemporary choral composers and able also to lead the singing of hymns by a large congregation had somehow to be accommodated.

In mediaeval churches the housing of either type of instrument posed considerable difficulties. Smart's complaint that the organ 'is usually thrust about into any hole or corner of the building suggested by the vanity or ignorance of the architect' (*MW* xxxiii, 1855: 131) is a reflection of a genuine problem: how to site a large, post-mediaeval object in a mediaeval church. Smart, who, as a good Protestant Englishman had little time for 'piscina, sedilia, credence-tables, rood-screens, and other trumpery, of which neither the names nor uses find mention in the prayer-book, and which cannot be of the slightest service to any one [*sic*] either here or hereafter' (*MW* XXXIII, 1855: 131) had scant sympathy for the ecclesiologists and their dilemma, and saw no reason why the organ (and singers) should not remain in a gallery, but in an age when the Gothic Revival was beginning to affect the architecture and arrangement even of nonconformist chapels, he and his kind were clearly in a minority. The galleries were coming down and the organs had to go somewhere. The ecclesiologists themselves preferred the floor (having an inveterate dislike of galleries) and suggested 'a Chancel-Aisle or Chapel' as a suitable location, adding that if the organ were small, it might stand beneath the chancel arcade (*Eccl* III, 1843–4: 164). On another occasion, a position on the floor at the west end of the nave was commended; the distance from the singers in the chancel was not felt to be an insurmountable difficulty, and the writer noted with approval that it would have the advantage of restricting the amount of 'figured musick' which the choir could perform. Grudgingly, the same writer added that, 'if a proximity to the Choir be judged essential . . . a special building to contain the organ' could, in the case of new churches, be considered, always provided that the solecism of making it look like 'a sacristy, or porch, or chapel, or transept: in short, like any thing [*sic*] else than what it is' was scrupulously avoided (*Eccl* IV, 1844–5: 6–7).

In this context, it is interesting that the *Ecclesiologist* gave an extended review to Hopkins & Rimbault's *The organ: its history and construction* when it appeared in 1855 (XVII, 1856: 7–19). The review was largely concerned with Hopkins's views on the position and appearance of the organ: matters of great moment to ecclesiologists. Hopkins accepted that a west end location could have grave architectural disadvantages (HRI: 223) and that it was far from ideal where performance with a chancel choir was contemplated (226). When considering alternatives, he suggested that 'some elevated position, having space above, and both sides free' should be sought (226) and cited approvingly an organ by Gray & Davison in St Mary Magdalene, Munster Square (a Tractarian church, with a moderate choral tradition) which was supported on stone corbels against the wall of the south aisle, some eight feet above the pavement of the church. However, the solution to which Hopkins devoted most attention was the provision of an organ chamber. He admitted that this had 'natural disadvantages', but maintained that, with suitable precautions, these could be 'considerably modified' and a satisfactory result attained (226). These precautions included provision of a hollow wooden floor, lining the walls of the chamber with wooden boards, allowing a generous space between the top of the case (or pipe display) and the apex of the arch, and the construction of an arch into the nave aisle (in addition to that giving onto the chancel) (226, 229). In view of the influence which Hopkins's book was to have on Victorian organ design, there seems to be a strong case for describing him as the father of the organ chamber, but, having awarded this dubious title, it is only fair to Hopkins to point out that he drew a clear distinction between an 'organ-chamber' (of which he approved) and a 'recess' (of which he did not). The recess described a chamber with three solid walls, the display pipes of the organ being arranged 'so as to form an ornamental filling up of the arch' (227). Commenting on this 'most unfavourable plan', Hopkins stated:

With walls on three sides, and a tier of large pipes entirely occupying the fourth, the tone can only force its way through the interstices between the pipes, as water escapes through the fissures of a flood-gate. The contrivance is, in fact, more calculated to keep the tone back, than to let it out.   (227)

Despite these strictures, Hopkins must bear much of the responsibility for legitimising the consignment of organs to organ chambers. His own instrument at the Temple Church was (from 1843) housed in an unsightly chamber, created by removing the glass from one of the aisle windows and building the chamber ('a mean projection', the *Ecclesiologist* thought it) on to the exterior of the building. It was, in fact, a recess.

Hopkins belonged to that school of thought which approved both the use of a modified cathedral service in parish churches and the introduction of substantial modern organs to support it. Others were keen to instigate congregational singing but denied the need for large organs. A particular case was that of the village church. In the climate of the 1850s and 1860s, many a zealous parish clergyman recognised the raising and training of a chancel choir as a crucial plank in his campaign to elevate the standard of worship. Though there were those who continued to maintain a rigid ecclesiological orthodoxy by disputing the need for any accompanimental instrument, most now admitted the desirability of providing support for the voices. The difficulties were architectural and financial. On the one hand, many village churches were small and the creation of an organ chamber was out of the question; on the other, congregations were frequently struggling to raise considerable sums of money in order to put the fabric to rights and large expenditure on an organ was out of the question. This was the problem to which the Reverend John Baron addressed himself in a little book called *Scudamore organs, or practical hints respecting organs for village churches and small chancels, on improved principles* (1858, 1862). Wishing to provide an organ for his own church of Upton Scudamore in Wiltshire, which was then undergoing restoration, and finding himself constrained both by finance and a conviction that village churches had no need of large organs, he determined to return to first principles. In the best ecclesiological spirit he seized upon Pugin's maxim that 'Truth is an essential principle of Christian Architecture' ('a proposition which only needs to be enunciated in order to be approved') and applied it to the question of organs, concluding that 'Of all pieces of church furniture the organ seems to be that which is as yet least penetrated by the truthfulness which has been attempted, with more or less success, in every other part of the sacred edifice' (1858: 7). He went on to ask a fundamental question. What are the essential parts of an organ? His answer was straightforward. An organ consisted of 'a set of keys, with the requisite action to carry onward the touch of the player; a bellows; a wind-trunk; a windchest; and the pipes; with sufficient framework to hold these parts together, or at least connect them in working order' (1858: 23). In view of contemporary developments in organ design, characterised by Baron as 'the present epidemic tendency to multitudinous and agglomerative extravagance in organs' (39) it was a remarkable answer to give, and it anticipated the approach of those in the present century who have sought to rescue the organ from precisely the 'extravagance' against which Baron had protested. Baron's first endeavour, at Upton Scudamore, perfectly reflected the principles he had adumbrated. The organ stood against the north wall of the chancel, to the east of the stalls, projecting a mere 1'3″ (Plate 46). The keyboard (c–c³ only) was reversed and placed below the bookboard of the stalls 'so that the player can see and controul [sic] the whole choir'. The bellows were sited beneath the organist's seat, from whence the wind was conveyed by way of a trunk to the soundboard on which the single stop, an open diapason, stood. There was no case. The pipes were exposed to view, supported by an oak frame finished with a little chaste Gothic detail. The organ was built by one Hall, a local organ-builder, and cost £40 (1858: 15–16).

Baron's principal contentions – that organs need not be large and costly, and might yet satisfy ecclesiological scruples and provide adequate accompaniment for the reformed Anglican liturgy – were enthusiastically endorsed. He and Hall seem to have been responsible for a number of instruments (1858: 63), but, following the publication of *Scudamore organs* in 1858, others took up his ideas and applied them. Among these was Henry Willis, who built some two hundred 'Scudamore' organs between 1858 and 1862, and whose prospectus for these instruments was attached to the second edition of Baron's book (1862). All Baron's theories rested upon an unimpeachable ecclesiological standard, that 'the office of the organ, in ordinary parish churches, is to direct and support the singing; and that fulness, variety, and beauty, must mainly be supplied by the well-trained voices of the choir and congregation' (1858: 27). It was therefore of the greatest relevance to point out that 'one stop of forty-nine pipes may be made sufficient to direct and support the singing of a large village congregation' (1858: 35), though in certain circumstances, Baron was ready to tolerate up to four stops.[30] The least satisfactory aspect of his influence had to do with casework. He misunderstood its acoustical function (1858: 9–11) and could find no mediaeval precedent for it. In his anxiety to secure 'freedom of

46 Upton Scudamore Parish Church. The first Scudamore organ.
(Baron, 1858: frontispiece)

speech', he believed that the pipes should be in an exposed position, on an elevated soundboard, and without any enclosing casework (1858: 11).

Baron was not alone in his desire to secure 'a simple, reverent, truthful, and satisfactory organ at a moderate expense, suited to the humblest village church' (1858: 23). During the 1850s and 1860s, the influence of the ecclesiological movement was widely felt, and a number of builders responded with simple accompanimental instruments, sited with due attention to the ecclesiological proprieties. One such was A. T. Miller of Cambridge. He seems to have had a connection with the Sutton family, and his organs sometimes pay greater attention to casework and adornment than was common at the period, but otherwise these are solid, reliable instruments for country churches, many of which still do stalwart service. Eagles of Hackney experimented with a small organ for Preston in Kent (1858); the manual divisions were Great and Choir ('Swells are not at all suited to rural churches, on account of the reed stops, which are almost essential to them, requiring very frequent tuning'), each of which had a complete chorus up to 2', and there was a 4-stop Pedal division, of which the 8' and 4' registers were borrowed from the Great (*Eccl* XIX, 1858: 219–21). Lewis's 'Lieblich' organs, and the standardised chancel organs manufactured by many other builders, represented similar attempts to match ingenuity to the needs of country churches in the face of growing competition from harmonium manufacturers.

In summarising the influence of the ecclesiological movement upon organ design, three main points should be made. First, the insistence upon removing organs from galleries and the necessity therefore of siting them elsewhere in the building (and preferably close to the singers) imposed novel and unwelcome constraints upon the disposition of the instrument and the treatment of the voicing. Secondly, the style of worship promoted by the ecclesiologists, in which a surpliced choir played a prominent part, demanded a development of the organ's tonal resources. Thirdly, the views of the ecclesiologists radically affected the visual appearance of the organ. This last matter will be dealt with in due course (below, pp. 323–32); the other two deserve further consideration here.

The consequences of placing organs in organ chambers were highlighted by Hopkins, who cited the example of St Mark, Old Street Road. There, the organ-builder (Bevington) had estimated that 'only *one-fourth* of the tone of the instrument found its way into the church', and according to Hopkins the melody of a chorale 'played out on the Great Diapasons, Principal, and Trumpet of this organ, sounded no stronger than it would have done on the Stopped Diapason and Clarionet of most instruments that are favourably situated'. This was not, however, the experience of the unfortunate organist, for the organ 'produced a din around him like that heard from a peal of bells in a belfry' (HRI: 228). Yet this did not deter Hopkins from advocating chambers. Recognising the disadvantages, he offered the dangerous advice that an organ sited in a recess or chamber should be 'judiciously *enlarged*, in proportion to its *loss of power*', even suggesting that a recess

> frequently imparts to the tone of an organ a certain chasteness and kindliness of character, as well as a slight haziness – as though a fine veil were drawn over it – that is exceedingly pleasing, and even beneficial, if the volume and fulness of tone at the same time remain unreduced.   (HRI: 227)

Enlargement was one approach to the problem, and Hopkins sowed seeds which would bear fruit in the frequently pretentious, often ineffective organs provided for chambers of one sort or another over the course of the next hundred years.

A second approach was to attempt a stronger voicing. An example was described in the *Musical Gazette* in 1857. The new organ in St Stephen, Regent's Park (by Bevington) was located under one of the arches in the chancel arcade. As a result of a 'bold experiment in strong voicing' to overcome this bad siting, the organ was 'almost unpleasantly loud to the organist', but, in the body of the church, 'the effect of an organ of ordinary power, in a *good* position, is produced'. This was, the writer concluded, 'an instance of the necessity for employing additional strength of voicing, or heavier wind, in order to produce even an ordinary effect in the body of the church' (II, 1857: 442). A similar case was described in the following year; this time it was an organ by Forster & Andrews, at Lymm:

> the only position that could be found . . . was within the tower arch; and here, many musical as well as mechanical difficulties present themselves, the acoustical proper- ties of the tower absorbing at least one third of the tone, and the sill of the west window being under ten feet in height, necessarily involved keeping the centre portion of the instrument exceedingly low . . . the builders have, by adopting a heavy wind, and voicing the pipes strong, succeeded in distributing the musical powers of the various stops throughout the edifice.   (*MW* xxxvi, 1858: 45)

The need to adopt such expedients brought about a fundamental change in the character of the English organ: the mild, unassertive tone of the 1840s gave way to a brasher, more strident style of voicing, thus paving the way for the reception of Schulze's influence (on the one hand) and the acceptance, at least in some quarters, of the typical Willis product, with its relatively high pressures and reed-dominated choruses (on the other).

Professor Temperley has argued that 'the advance of choralism was in no sense a victory for the Oxford movement, or, indeed, for any idealistic group of churchmen' (1979a: 286) and it would therefore follow that the evolution of the Victorian organ as a choir accompanimental instrument is equally not to be attributed to the influence of any single party within the Church. As Temperley rightly maintains, the establishment of the parochial choral service was (in part) 'an expression of secular middle-class values and tastes' (286). In the nineteenth, as in the eighteenth century, many respectable congregations were happy to delegate the musical portions of the services to a choir of trained singers. For all this, it remains true that the most influential 'musical' churches were those of a Tractarian, or moderate High Church, persuasion, and that it was these churches that pioneered many of the arrangements respecting choirs which were later adopted (though select-ively, and in a modified form) by a broad cross-section of churchmen. An account from the 1860s of visits to two London churches in the vanguard of ritualism underlines this conclusion. At All Saints, Margaret Street, 'the organ sounded its first chord, all the people rose up as one man, and the choir and clergy began to stream in, arrayed in white'. The plainsong psalms were accompanied 'modestly and devoutly'. Following the Offertory Sentence, a voluntary was played whilst the collection was taken, and then, during the Communion itself, 'soft, low music, streamed from the organ'. The service concluded with the organ playing as choir and clergy processed from the church (*CMR* I, 1863–4: 146–8). The pattern was similar at St Matthias, Stoke Newington. The *Veni Creator* was sung in procession (it is not clear if it was accompanied); a voluntary was played between the conclusion of Mattins and the commencement of the Communion Service (more 'soft low strains'); and the Nicene Creed was sung by all to Merbecke's setting, accompanied by the organ (*CMR* II, 1864–5: 113–14). We recognise here features that remained a familiar part of Anglican worship for a century or more in churches with any musical pretensions, and which are still not uncommon today, despite the changes wrought by the liturgical reforms of the 1960s and 1970s. Organ and choir were used to instil a sense of decorum and create an atmosphere of reverent devotion in the minds of worshippers. The resources of a modern organ and a trained body of singers were employed to provide a commentary upon the movement of the liturgy, more and more taking advantage of the dramatic possibilities offered by contem-porary art music (though some adhered steadfastly to the more austere associations of plainsong). With the appearance of *Hymns ancient and modern* in 1861 (Temperley 1979a: 298) and the falling into desuetude of the old middle voluntary and interludes between verses of (metrical) psalms,[31] the charac-teristic musical features of what Temperley calls the 'Victorian Settlement' of Anglican worship were in place.

The design of the organs provided to accompany choirs inevitably re-flected the increasing tendency to support or heighten the emotional inten-sity of the music by rapid changes of dynamics or colourful choices of registration. Arrangements of continental masses were favoured at some of the 'advanced' London churches,[32] and anthems selected from oratorios were generally popular so that an orchestral approach to registration was unavoidable and came in turn to influence the style of church composers like Barnby, Stainer and Sullivan (below, pp. 348–9). A further important consideration was the provision of a sufficient variety of quiet registers. Spark urged that the Choir Organ should be developed exclusively as an accompaniment for the singers, and advised that the organ as a whole should offer 'those soft and sweet stops, which will be at once a sufficient support for the singing – and a means of giving that variety of expression to the music, which the ever varying sentiment of the words seems to require' (1852: 256). It was significant that Hill installed one of his totally enclosed organs in St Andrew's, Wells Street, a leading Tractarian church and one prominent in the choral revival; such an instrument supplied that flexibility and variety of effect more and more deemed to be essential in choral accompaniment. But the organ most consciously designed to meet the requirements of the more liberal school of ecclesiologists was (appropriately enough) the remarkable instrument built by Hill for William Butterfield's church of All Saints, Margaret Street (1859). The instrument was divided, and stood in the chapels to the north and south of the chancel. The 'north' organ consisted of Great, Choir and Pedal; the 'south' organ of Swell, Choir and Pedal (Appendix 1, pp. 485–6); trackers running beneath the chancel floor connected the south organ to the 4-manual console standing a little to the fore of the north organ. According to a report in the *Ecclesiologist*,

The main object of the plan of the organ . . . has been the attainment of the greatest possible variety and beauty of tone, together with sufficient depth and power fully to sustain (without overpowering it) the entire chorus of choir and congregation . . . while at the same time the antiphonal character of the singing might be aided and brought out, with more than ordinary prominence, by the unusual advantage of a local arrangement, and a consequent effect, equally antiphonal in the organ itself.

(xx, 1859: 301)

A review in the *Musical World* spoke approvingly of the distinct character possessed by each of the two Choir Organs, and commended Hill for the variety of tone which he had obtained from registers of similar construction in these departments. The Great trombone was disposed horizontally and projected from the front of the north case: 'and we doubt whether, for grandeur of effect, and character of tone, it has ever had its superior' (xxxvii, 1859: 364). The reversed console enabled the organist to command both choir and sanctuary, and the stop knobs were arranged in horizontal tiers, for ease of manipulation. Altogether, the All Saints' organ, with its unusual physical arrangements, its design for a particular liturgical function, and its careful provision of a wide selection of registers suitable for the accompaniment of a trained choir, is an appropriate monument to the influence of the ecclesiologists upon English organ design.

CASEWORK

. . . in these days Organs are a common luxury, even in the smallest and most remote places. Still, with all this anxiety to obtain the best possible Instruments (which undoubtedly prevails), it is quite extraordinary how little attention is paid to their appearance; or to the position they ought to occupy.

Churches, in other respects the most gorgeous, are frequently choked up by machines, which are little more than great stacks of pipes; often arranged in such a manner, that no possible ingenuity or expense can ever make them worthy of their position.

. . . there is no reason whatever, why an Organ should not sound well, and be made to look very beautiful too.   (Sutton 1872: 1–2)

Frederick Heathcote Sutton's protest, in his book *Church organs: their position and construction* (1872), against the prevailing treatment by architects and organ-builders of the organ's outward appearance, brought into the light of day a conflict which had rumbled beneath the surface of ecclesiology from the beginning. It was inevitable that a movement so immediately congenial to those of an antiquarian cast of mind would attract support from some who were less willing than the original Camdenians to reject all that was not Gothic. And so the anonymous contributor of the *Ecclesiologist*'s 1843 diatribe against organs, with his scathing dismissal of 'hideous' organ cases, bedecked with trumpeting angels, crowns and mitres (III, 1843: 1), was answered thirty years later by Sutton, who found it 'almost impossible not to look back with a sort of half regret upon the stately cases, with their rich towers and pilasters, which have succumbed to modern improvements' (1872: 4). Sutton's view is characteristically antiquarian: the only way to improve case design is to study 'ancient examples', and his book incorporates drawings showing how a consideration of surviving Gothic cases on the continent might bear fruit in the construction of new cases and the transformation of existing, but (in Sutton's view) unsatisfactory ones (Plates 47 and 48). It was a lesson that a number of architects, J. L. Pearson (1817–97) and G. F. Bodley (1827–1907) among them, were ready to learn, and their work marks a revival of the organ case following its eclipse during the third quarter of the century.[33] Yet it was not only to Gothic models that Sutton appealed. Deserting the narrow confines of ecclesiological orthodoxy, he urged architects in search of inspiration to turn their attention to English cases of a later era, 'which seem particularly worthy of study, on account of their form and construction' (1883: 20). Sutton had recently (1872) supervised the restoration of the early-sixteenth-century (?) case at Old Radnor, and his book included a short appendix in which the case is described and illustrated.[34] Old Radnor just about passes muster as a 'Gothic' case (though with a decided admixture of Renaissance detail), but the other case illustrated by Sutton (Framlingham), and a further eleven survivors listed as being 'useful to any one anxious to study the subject', date largely from the seventeenth century and would be regarded as hopelessly debased by an ecclesiologist of the 1840s or 1850s.[35]

Frederick Sutton (1833–88) was one of a small band of ecclesiologists who

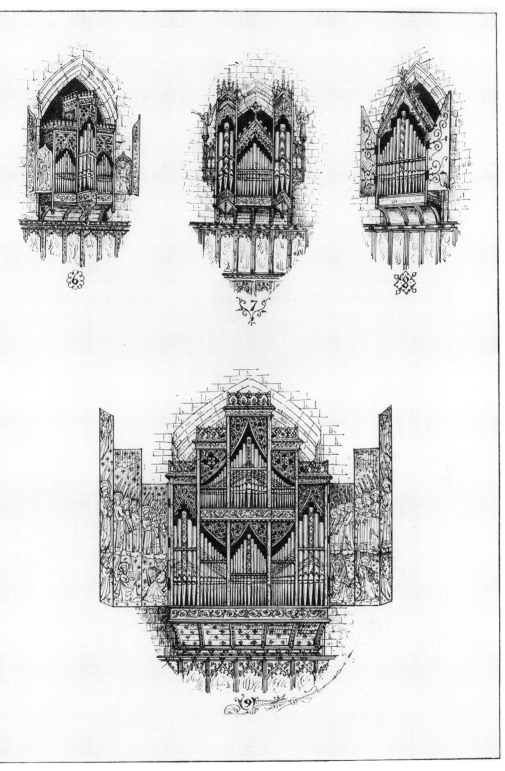

47 Designs for Gothic cases, from F. H. Sutton's *Church organs* (1872).

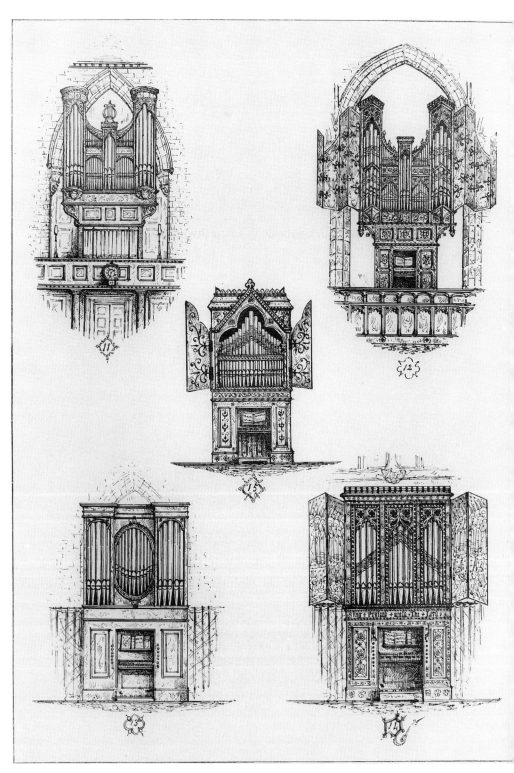

48 Proposals for the Gothicising of existing cases, from F. H. Sutton's *Church organs* (1872).

sought to prevent the wanton destruction of old cases and to encourage architects and church restorers to design new cases with due regard for the principles exemplified in the best old work, be it Gothic or Renaissance in inspiration. Sir John Sutton (Frederick's elder brother) made his protest in the *Short account*, and the Gothic cases he provided at Jesus College, Cambridge (1849; by Pugin), West Tofts (1857) and possibly St Andrew the Less, Cambridge (1854?), are early and exquisite examples, but neither his retiring disposition nor his conversion to Rome placed him in a strong position to be a decisive influence.[36] J. H. Sperling (1825–94) carefully preserved drawings of old organ cases and recorded the specifications of the instruments which they contained, but this antiquarian preoccupation perhaps sapped his energy for giving practical expression to his convictions; he too ultimately became a Roman Catholic (Thistlethwaite 1977: 88–92; Berrow 1983: 103). Canon W. E. Dickson (1823–1910) in his little work, *Practical organ-building* (1882) made an eloquent plea for the preservation of old organs (178–80) and earlier established his credentials as a preservationist by salvaging one of Smith's cornets when the University Organ in Cambridge was reconstructed (*MO* xvi, 1893: 398), but his sphere of influence seems not to have been extensive. Frederick Sutton, on the other hand, had forged plentiful connections through his activities as patron, church restorer, architect and artist, and both his book (which ran to three editions) and his association with particular instruments,[37] ensured that his influence was disseminated. The revival of the organ case owed a great deal to him.

Why was a revival needed? In order to answer this question it is necessary to return to an earlier phase in the history of the ecclesiological movement and to the emergence of what Clutton & Niland call 'the only really characteristic contribution of the Victorian age to the external appearance of the British organ' – the 'caseless' organ (1982: 232).

The ecclesiologists neither liked the organ nor understood it. That much is clear from the irritation with which they greeted the unregenerate insistence of (most) clergy and congregations that provision must be made for the accommodation of one of these cumbersome objects. But having grudgingly accepted its inclusion, they had then to determine its appearance. Here they were at a disadvantage. In seeking to rediscover the principles of Gothic architecture they were aided by the survival, admittedly in various stages of decrepitude, of numerous mediaeval buildings, up and down the country, and these provided ample precedents for study and emulation. Much church woodwork survived, too, and offered specimens of most of the principal items of church furniture for imitation. Except, that is, for the organ. With no survivals to guide them, the ecclesiologists were thrown upon their own resources.

Their solution rapidly established itself as a characteristic feature of the Victorian (new or restored) chancel. Simple panelling round the base;

exposed front pipes, sometimes coloured, sometimes plain; a little decorative ironwork; perhaps a painted scroll with a text or an inscription recording the name of the donor: the caseless organ commended itself to organ-builders because it was simple to construct, and to ecclesiologists because they believed it to be 'mediaeval'.

The origins of this misconception are described by Sutton.

> In the earlier days of the Gothic revival, small Organs were often designed, with scarcely any attempt at a case; the pipes being arranged, so as to form the front of the instrument, as we see in the pictures of Organs in the MSS., and stained glass, of the Middle Ages. In small Organs this plan answered very well; but the attempt to carry out this principle into very large Organs, was by no means so successful; and the consequence often was, an instrument which turned out a complete failure in an architectural point of view.   (1883: 2)

This was, of course, the principle expounded by Baron, whose book, *Scudamore organs*, contained a number of illustrations taken from frescos and engravings of 'antient organs'; all were portative or positive organs, and all showed a functional arrangement of pipes, supported by a simple wooden frame (1858: Plates 2 & 3). Sutton had no quarrel with Scudamores: they were 'often designed with great taste, and form a very elegant addition to the furniture of a small Church' (1872: 2); but he pointed out the absurdity of enlarging this model to provide a front for the typical Victorian 2- or 3-manual instrument. Unfortunately, by the time he wrote, the damage was done. As early as 1847, Butterfield included a design for a village church organ in *Instrumenta Ecclesiastica*, published by the Ecclesiological Society. This was intended to be a handbook of church furnishings for clergy and patrons anxious to forward 'true' principles, and its influence must have been widespread (Thompson 1971: 347). Butterfield's proposal showed a front of six buttressed panels (the keyboard was to be at the back) with the tops of the bass pipes projecting above it (I, 1847: plate LXIX). A second volume followed in the 1850s, and for this Butterfield prepared a further design (Plate 49). Here is the caseless organ in all its essentials. The construction is a simple frame, panelled below, open above, ornamented with a little architectural detail: weak buttresses at the corners of the base, quatrefoils and crenellations at impost level, tops of posts made to resemble pinnacles. The pipes are arranged symmetrically, but the obscuring of the mouths is a fatal solecism and leads one to wonder whether Butterfield really had much knowledge of practical organ design. Certainly, he seems to have subscribed to the strict school of ecclesiology, regarding organs as a nuisance (Thompson 1971: 389–90). His case for St Cross, Winchester (1867) follows the same principles as the 1856 design in *Instrumenta Ecclesiastica*; here, the pipe mouths are visible, but this 'spare structuralism' has a stern, unpleasing quality about it, which is all too typical of many larger caseless organs of the period (Thompson 1971: 476–7).

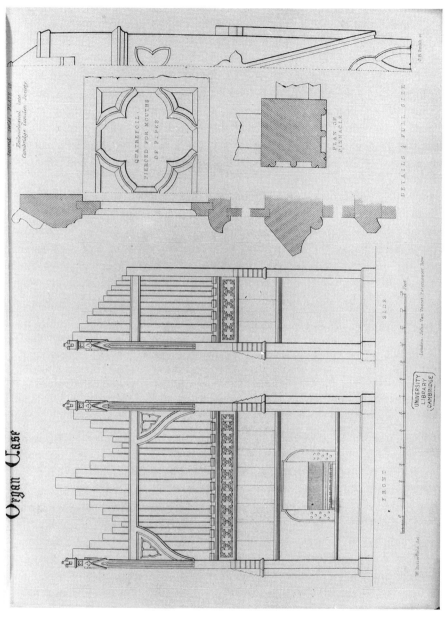

49 Design for an organ case by William Butterfield, from *Instrumenta Ecclesiastica* (1856).

Yet Victorian architects had at least one weapon in their armoury which could be used to relieve the monotony of wide expanses of pipes. This was the application of polychrome decoration. There were precedents for this in English organs of the seventeenth and early-eighteenth centuries, as J. H. Sperling pointed out in a letter to the *Ecclesiologist* (x, 1849: 375–8), but in any case the study of Gothic art and architecture was encouraging church builders to be much bolder in the use of colour. Sperling set out some principles. The colours employed 'should be few and brilliant – vermilion, blue, and green, being amply sufficient; white must be freely used in every pattern. The ground will of course be gold, – as the pipes have to be gilded before the diaper can be laid on'. Variety, he observed, was indispensable: 'no two pipes of the same pattern should be together, though each pipe will have its fellow on the opposite side to correspond with it – half a dozen well chosen patterns will be amply sufficient for any one organ case'. In selecting patterns, architectural devices should be avoided, and realism (perhaps employing shading to lend verisimilitude) must be eschewed. Bold and simple drawing was the most effective. Having said this, Sperling found some difficulty in suggesting suitable schemes ('it being much easier to find fault with existing ones, than to point out those which are more correct') but he had the following hints to offer:

For smaller pipes, floriation and running patterns of foliage seem desirable; this must of course be represented conventionally, as in architecture – e.g. roses (red), and lilies (white), with leaves, form an excellent design. Fleurs-de-lys, and scrolls with inscriptions, may occasionally appear . . . For large pipes, single figures of saints under canopies, or of angels playing upon musical instruments, are desirable . . . Excellent examples may be taken from the orphreys of copes in Ecclesiastical Brasses . . .

(377)

Architects were soon alive to the possibilities of this sort of embellishment, and where funds existed to do the job properly, the effect was frequently magnificent. A fine example survives at Turvey. Scott reconstructed the chancel in the early-1850s, and Hill's organ stands behind a stone screen on its north side; the front pipes are supported by decorative ironwork and arranged beneath three arches; they are gilded and richly diapered, the pattern varying from pipe to pipe. The fronts at St Michael's College, Tenbury,[38] Durham Cathedral (1876) and Eton College Chapel (1885) are of similar excellence (Plate 50). The most successful examples of the genre are undoubtedly those that follow Sperling's prescriptions. Where financial constraints dictated that simple colouring should be employed for the base rather than gilding, and where a dense, intricate and varied pattern was obliged to give way to rudimentary decoration around the pipe mouth or repetitive stencilling on the pipe bodies, the effect was usually altogether flatter and more prosaic. Polychromatic decoration could also easily create a false emphasis. Scott's front at Hereford (1862) exemplifies Sutton's warn-

50 St Michael's College, Tenbury. It is not clear whether the present arrangement and decoration of the front pipes survives from Flight's organ of 1854 or Willis's reconstruction of 1874.

ing that designs appropriate to smaller organs should not be scaled up for larger ones, and matters are not improved by the visual tensions set up between inverted v's in the outer flats and the regular v in the centre flat. Similarly, dozens of country churches house Victorian organs in which the excessive use of bands of colour or gilding circling the pipes gives a horizontal emphasis where a vertical one is needed. Yet despite its shortcomings, and the absence of subtlety in a good many schemes, it can be argued that the adoption of polychrome decoration did something to save the caseless organ from its intrinsic banality; the best examples have an integrity and a worth which can claim for them a small place in any discussion of Victorian ecclesiastical art.

With the rise of the caseless organ, and the committal of so many church organs to chambers or corners of buildings, it is hard to escape the conclusion that the third quarter of the nineteenth century represents the nadir of case design in England. R. C. Carpenter's case for Sherborne Abbey (1856) hints at what might have been possible, and in spite of Henry Smart's strictures ('a richly carved doll's house faced with a row of bedizened barbers' poles in lieu of front pipes') is extremely satisfying in the building (Plate 51). There was, though, a class of organ still sometimes suffered to remain in prominent positions, and so needing more orthodox architectural treatment. This was the cathedral organ. During the period under consideration, its chief practitioner was Sir George Gilbert Scott (1811–78).

Scott's first cathedral case was also his most successful. The Ely case of 1851, whilst altogether of its period, was inspired by the fifteenth-century case in Strasburg Cathedral (Scott 1879: 282). The result is a triumphant success, displaying a degree of assurance and invention that its author never managed to repeat (Plate 52). Although there are certain infelicities (principally, the overlength pipes) this case is always impressive when viewed from the pavement of the church: an effect for which the rich diapering of the pipes is in part responsible. (Ely is one of the earliest examples of its revived use.) Even apparent offences against the grammer of good case design (pipes in the sides of the case; pipes protruding above the woodwork) seem not to matter. This wonderful composition is topped out with 'an army of rejoicing angels' (Berrow 1983: 95) and forms an integral part of Scott's adornment and re-ordering of choir and sanctuary.

It is hard to find the same enthusiasm for any other of Scott's cases. St Mary, Nottingham (1871) had obvious affinities with Ely, but the scale was out of all proportion to the available space, and much was lost when the deep pipe shades shown in Scott's original drawing were modified before the organ's completion (Sumner 1937: opp. 31; cf. Freeman 1921b: plate 88). The Manchester Cathedral case (1871) saw a return to rejoicing angels and had a certain charm, attributable in part to its modest scale, but the overhang of the main case was clumsily handled, as was the little 'Choir' case on the east side of the screen. The same elements were re-worked for the Chester case of 1876 (a sumptuous composition, yet lacking the spontaneity and liveliness of Ely) and for Ripon in 1878, the latter being surely Scott's least happy cathedral work. The truth is that Scott never improved on his earliest essay, and continued to make extensive use of the same model throughout his career: the west front of the Ripon case is a direct crib from Strasburg.[39]

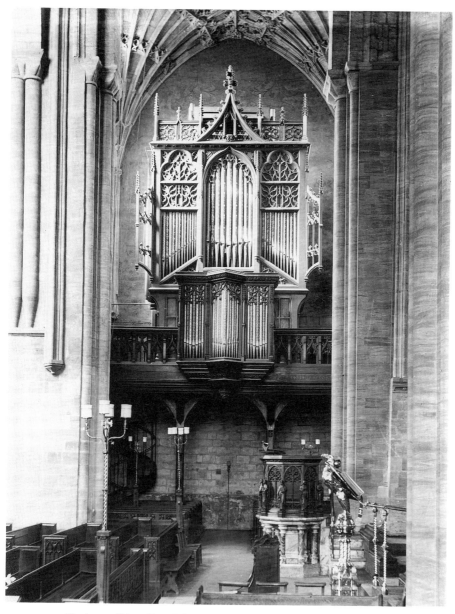

51 Sherborne Abbey, Gray & Davison, 1856. (1934)

Scott deserves praise for his attempt to design Gothic cases at a time when most architects, influenced by the rising tide of ecclesiology, were not only content with the 'great stacks of pipes' of which F. H. Sutton complained, but believed them to be licensed by mediaeval precedent. The 1850s and 1860s were the decades in which the caseless organ seemed to be carrying all before it. St Anne, Limehouse (Plate 39) retains the vestiges of a wooden

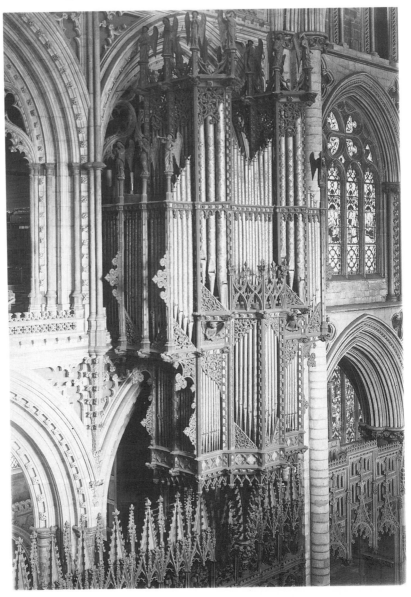

52 Ely Cathedral, Hill, 1851. Case by G. G. Scott.

case, with bizarre fretwork mitres surmounting the towers and a steeply
rising toe-board, but such links with the past were soon discarded and the
majority of church organs were furnished with the minimum of woodwork
above impost level. And not only the church organs. Glasgow City Hall
(1853), the Handel Festival Organ in the Crystal Palace (1857), St James's
Hall (1858) and Newcastle Town Hall (1859) were all effectively caseless,
though the tops of the pipes might be fitted with ornamental caps (New-

castle) or grouped in a 'tower' surmounted by woodwork (Crystal Palace). These were probably all organ-builders' cases, modest in their ambitions and modest in their effect. In the hands of an architect, such opportunities might yield more sensational results. Released from the constraints of the case, with its conventional vocabulary of pipe shades, towers and flats, and its inherited assumptions about the relative proportions of the exposed pipes, architects found themselves at liberty to redeploy the basic elements of the organ front. One of the first to take advantage of this was C. R. Cockerell (1788–1863) in his case for St George's Hall, Liverpool (Plate 24). This has a monumental, almost sculptural quality, with pipes standing free of any enclosing woodwork, and the dark finish of the casework splendidly contrasts with the opulence of the diapered pipes. Only the usual wretched caps (some of which have been removed in the present century) mar what is otherwise one of the finest cases of the Victorian era. Cuthbert Broderick's case for Leeds Town Hall (1859) is less innovative (there are clear affinities with Birmingham); its most striking feature, the huge 'cart-wheel' medallion above the central flat, is either an ingenious way of distracting attention from the excessive width of the flat beneath or a slightly clumsy way of disguising the Swell and Solo departments behind (Plate 42). The inevitable pipe caps are here in neo-classical guise. Hill & Woodhouse's case for Bolton Town Hall (1874) is in the same tradition, and draws directly on both Liverpool and Leeds.

Yet it was not the town halls of the north, but two metropolitan concert halls that inspired the most radical treatment of the organ's appearance. Henry Willis was a pioneer of the caseless organ in cathedrals (Carlisle, 1856; Wells, 1857), churches (King's College, London, 1854[?]; Lambourn, 1858; Foxearth, 1863; St John, Taunton, 1864; St George, Preston, 1865) and concert halls (Aberdeen Music Hall, 1859). In due course he would be responsible for giving ultimate expression to the principles of the caseless organ in his instrument for Salisbury Cathedral (1877); there, naked front pipes, unadorned and with no visible means of support, are ranged symmetrically on opposite sides of the choir, the only visual interest being contributed by the use of two styles of mouthing (bay-leaf for the flats, French for the 'towers') and the slightest movement in the alignment of the mouths. Depending upon one's point of view, it was either a fearless gesture of the Victorian imagination or a *reductio ad absurdum* of the ecclesiologists' argument, and certainly there were those who felt it inappropriate to strike so incongruously contemporary a note in one of England's greatest mediaeval cathedrals. But a concert hall – that temple of popular entertainment – was another matter. There, the taste for monumentality, modernity and mechanical novelty could properly be indulged. It was to this sentiment that Willis responded in his grand organs for the Royal Albert Hall (1871) and the Alexandra Palace (1873). The scheme for the Alexandra Palace seems to have been the earlier of the two in conception, though the organ in the Royal Albert Hall was the first to be completed. The designs for the fronts are similar. The tendency characteristic of mid-Victorian cases to intricacy of detail and complexity of structure is banished. There are no prudish caps for exposed pipe tops nor fussy applications of polychrome to bare surfaces. Huge pipes are mounted on a massive wooden base. At the Alexandra Palace the contours are sharply defined, and the decoration, though admirably bold, is applied selectively (Plate 53). But the most noteworthy innovation is a large open arch in the middle of the case giving an unrestricted view of the Great pipework assembled on its soundboards. Here, Willis was taking the

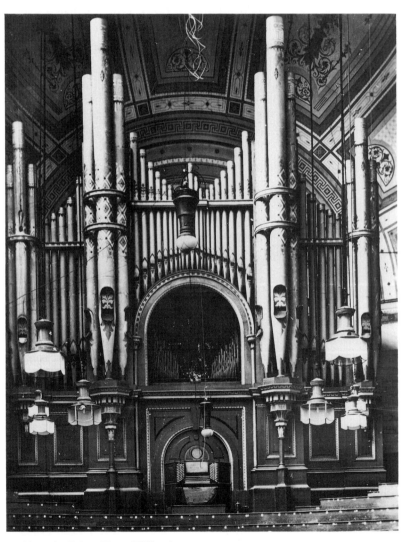

53 Alexandra Palace, Henry Willis, 1875.

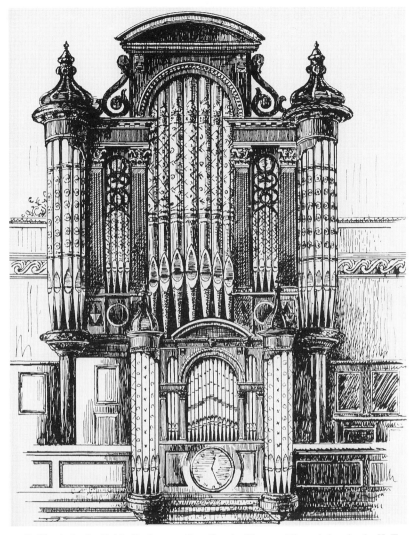

54 St Martin-in-the-Fields, Bevington, 1854. Case by Thomas Allom. A drawing by H. T. Lilley.

principle of the caseless organ to its logical conclusion and making a feature of the working parts of the instrument in a manner that anticipated the unencased organs of the mid-twentieth century. The same feature appeared in the Royal Albert Hall organ, with three similar openings (nicely mirroring the arches of the boxes behind the organ) allowing audiences glimpses of the organ's cavernous interior. In their blatant functional simplicity, their delight in revealing the instrument's internal mysteries, and their sheer size, these two organs express the zest and self-confidence which characterised the heyday of the Victorian concert organ. They also testify to Henry Willis's ability to deploy his skills as engineer, mechanic and artist to capture the public imagination and steal a march on his rivals.

In a consideration of case design during the third quarter of the nineteenth century, an account of the persistence of architectural cases in a classical style inevitably bears the character of a footnote to more significant developments elsewhere. Few classical cases were installed in major churches of the

55 St Pancras Parish Church, Gray & Davison, 1865. The instrument came from Birmingham Music Hall (1856) and the case was probably an adaptation of that made for John Gray's St Pancras organ of 1822.

Anglican Establishment during this period, and the exceptions are invariably conservative in conception. Thomas Allom's case for St Martin-in-the-Fields (1854) has a certain solidity about it, placing it firmly in the Victorian era, but in other respects, its eclectic classicism shows little advance on the technique of the Thaxted case (Plate 54). The inspiration was evidently the east window of Gibbs' church. The St Pancras case (1865), containing the former Birmingham Music Hall organ, seems to have been an adaptation of the existing case (Plate 55).[40] In a neo-classical building this was eminently appropriate; it is informative, though, to observe how pipe shades, polychrome, and some extra cresting have transformed what must have been an elegant and restrained composition in the Grecian style into an ornate, typically fussy example of mid-Victorian taste. But if classicism was frowned upon in Anglican circles, this was not so in two other spheres. In many quarters it was still felt to be the most suitable style for public buildings and certainly for buildings intended for public entertainment. The Kidderminster Music Hall case has already been mentioned (above, pp. 251–2). Two years earlier (1853) Holt had installed an organ in a simple classical case in St George's Hall, Bradford. 'Caseless' organs in town halls usually employed classical detail for woodwork and decoration (Liverpool, Leeds, Bolton and Huddersfield), and throughout the period complete cases with classical fronts continued to be made occasionally for small music rooms (Wednesbury Town Hall, 1872). The other sphere in which classicism was still often preferred was the nonconformist chapel. Though some nonconformists sought to challenge the Establishment on its own ground by building in the Gothic style (Dixon & Muthesius 1985: 229–33) many resisted the unwelcome ecclesiastical associations and continued to opt for classicism. Yet the same dissenters might, by the 1850s, be keen to acquire an organ for their chapel. Organ-builders (especially firms like Forster & Andrews, and Brindley & Foster, working in districts where nonconformity was strong) were therefore called upon to supply organs in simple classical cases to harmonise with their surroundings, and this they did throughout the period. Tending always to be a little behind the Church of England in their tastes, nonconformists only later abandoned these plain yet dignified cases for the ubiquitous pipe-rack, which, of course, had no unhappy doctrinal overtones.

11

Music and mechanics

COMPOSERS, PERFORMERS AND THE ORGAN

The nineteenth century witnessed activity on an unprecedented scale in the design, improvement and manufacture of musical instruments. Delight taken in novelties, admiration for innovations justifying the epoch's view of itself as an age of improvement, desire to extend the range of musical possibilities by increasing the power and proficiency of individual instruments: all these characteristic preoccupations of the mid-nineteenth century fuelled this activity. It contributed to the organisation of musical instrument manufacture along factory lines; also to the emergence of orchestral and keyboard instruments in something closely resembling their modern form. In time, there came a reaction, and the 1890s saw the birth of the early music movement, with its questioning of the assumptions that lay behind the concept of musical progress propagated during the previous hundred years, but such critical attitudes were relatively rare in the middle of the century. Then (and for long after) composer and performer alike relished the opportunities offered by technical innovation, sometimes proposing changes themselves, sometimes gratefully exploiting improvements introduced independently by enterprising instrument-makers. It is a distinction that is often hard to draw: change inspired by the imagination of a performer who can envisage possibilities perhaps obscured from the practical man; or change brought about by a craftsman or mechanic who discovers how to make something work better. Each had a part to play in the history of musical instrument-making in the nineteenth century.

It has been shown already that the organ was particularly susceptible to innovation. In an age fascinated by acoustics, mechanics and engineering it offered more scope than any other single instrument for experiment and investigation. At the same time, the musicians were pressing for improvements. They wished the organ to become more expressive, less inflexible, better able to imitate other instruments. The organ-builder found himself surrounded with powerful inducements to make innovations, both tonal and mechanical.

340

The prevailing sentiment is neatly presented in a paragraph taken from a description of Gray & Davison's organ for Glasgow City Hall (1853). The writer (possibly Smart) acknowledges the achievements of the previous generation, but insists that much remains to be accomplished.

Great as have been the improvements in its [sc. the organ's] construction in this country within the last twenty years, there yet remains much ground for the complaint, often urged, of its insufficient adaptability to *variety* of style in music. While indisputedly suited to the grand, severe, and massive, it yet but cumbrously lends itself to the tender, expressive, and passionate. Its tones, admitted to be majestic and striking, are yet often too reviled as cold and unsympathetic. Its mechanism, while efficient in strength and certainty of action, is frequently clumsy and unscientific in detail, and invariably more or less distressing in its operation on the performer.   (*MW* xxxi, 1853: 526)

It was to be the business of organ-builders and organists over the course of the next two decades to meet these criticisms. The huge organs of the 1830s (York, Birmingham) had given a hint of what was possible, but they were crippled by primitive mechanisms and repetitious tonal schemes. The German System instruments of the 1840s were infinitely more varied tonally, and the best of them undoubtedly met the demand for 'Bach' organs, but neither the restraint of their choruses nor the discretion of their solo stops (with the exception of the high-pressure reed) satisfied the rising generation, and the multiplication of organs with 12- or 14-slider soundboards and extended columns of stops only underlined the deficiencies of the conventional mechanical arrangements.

The background to the change in musical taste has already been sketched (above, pp. 88–93). The present chapter is principally concerned to consider in some detail the mechanical innovations promoted by players and composers who were influenced by this. But in order to establish the context more precisely, it will be helpful first to look briefly at the demands of the players and the achievements of the builders as they are reflected in the use of the organ during the 1850s and 1860s.

According to William Spark, it was Samuel Sebastian Wesley who 'was the first to suggest a greatly varied style and expression, and to infuse orchestral combinations and colouring into organ playing' (1888: 97). The evidence for this is scattered. Wesley was sparing in the use of registration markings in his published music, largely restricting himself to indications of manual and dynamics. When he was more explicit (for example, in the *Andante in G*, written in 1863 for the opening of Willis's instrument in the Agricultural Hall) the results are disappointing, suggesting that Wesley's approach to registration remained much the same as it had been in the 1830s, when the accompaniments to *The Wilderness* and *Blessed be the God and Father* were registered in a manner that was both unprecedentedly detailed and strikingly original. Wesley was never so consistently meticulous again.

Although the *Anthems* of 1853 (a collected edition of twelve, some written specially, others of earlier date) includes some arresting effects – for example, the opening of *Wash me throughly*, with the plaintive treble solo accompanied by a Swell reed, high in its range – it is a matter for regret that the composer who contrived such a suitably sombre registration for 'The grass withereth, and the flower thereof falleth away' (*Blessed be the God and Father*) failed to rise to the challenge of 'Their idols are silver and gold' (*Ascribe unto the Lord*), at least in print. This last point should not be overlooked. Wesley committed comparatively few of his musical thoughts to paper, and his reputation during his lifetime depended at least as much upon his performance (in which extemporisation was especially admired) as upon his published works. The following report of his playing at Birmingham Town Hall during the 1849 Festival, when his reputation and powers were at their height, underlines this, and is typical of many other accounts of similar occasions throughout Wesley's career.

Dr. Wesley, the most justly celebrated performer of the present day, played a solo on the great organ of the Hall. Dr. Wesley began with a very long *fantasia*, the plan of which we cannot pretend to define after a single hearing. In the course of the *fantasia* almost every effect of which the resources of this enormous instrument are capable was developed by the learned musician with masterly skill. But by far the most interesting part of his performance was the extemporaneous *fugue* with which it terminated. A more ingenious and extraordinary improvisation we never listened to. Dr. Wesley chose an unusually short theme, as though resolved to show how easily he could set contrapuntal difficulties at defiance. After working this with remarkable clearness, he introduced a second subject which he soon brought in conjunction with the first, and subsequently a third; ultimately combining the three, in the *stretto* of the *fugue*, with the facility of a profound and accomplished master. Dr. Wesley's performance was greeted with uproarious applause, and, while he was playing, it was interesting to observe the members of the orchestra and chorus crowding round the organ, anxious to obtain a view of his fingers or his feet, with which he manages the ponderous pedals with such wonderful dexterity.   (*MW* xxiv, 1849: 567)

Wesley's skill as a contrapuntalist seems not to have declined as the years went by, but, equally, it seems not to have progressed. The admiration is not diminished, but it is the admiration born of respect rather than of novelty. Hubert Parry heard him improvise a fugue at Gloucester in 1865:

He began the accompaniment in crotchets alone, and then gradually worked into quavers, then triplets and lastly semiquavers. It was quite marvellous. The powerful old subject came stalking in right and left with the running accompaniment wonderfully entwined with it – all in the style of old Bach.   (Graves 1926, 1: 56–7)

Parry's testimony is valuable; so, too, is Elgar's. He heard Wesley improvise in Worcester Cathedral, probably in 1874, and later recalled that he had 'built up a wonderful climax of sound before crashing into the subject of the "Wedge" Fugue' of Bach (Moore 1987: 66). The reports of these two eminent musicians confirm Wesley's stature, and suggest that what survives on the printed page offers only limited insight into his genius, both as composer and performer, but, at the same time, Wesley must by the 1860s and 1870s have appeared in the character of a survivor from a former age. Stylistically, his roots lay in the first half of the century, his 'unique amalgam' (Temperley 1981: 199) powerfully influenced by his father and Bach, and to a lesser extent, Purcell and Spohr, and yet wholly individual. As a player, his withdrawal from the competition for the organistship of St George's Hall in 1855 marked his eclipse; despite his reputation as a 'pedallist' in the 1840s, he could not compete with Best's fluency, and Statham recalled that he (Wesley) evidently found it advisable to watch his feet when playing demanding pedal passages; he also commented shrewdly that, had Wesley's Liverpool application been successful, his programmes would have made 'no sort of concession to popular taste', and so he would have deprived himself of the key to success so securely grasped by Best (Statham 1909: 217–18).

Wesley's career marks the end of a chapter in the history of organ composition and performance in England, and it is entirely appropriate that the concluding volume of Robin Langley's recent anthology, *English Organ Music*, is devoted exclusively to his works. Despite his pioneering performances of Bach, and the extensive use made of the pedals in his writing, he is an essentially conservative figure, whose vision was to some extent restricted throughout his life by the limitations (mechanical and tonal) of the organs of the 1830s and 1840s even when (as at Winchester) he had an ambitious modern instrument at his disposal. The controversies over compass and temperament at St George's Hall are evidence of this, quite as much as the modest registrational demands of his 1853 collection of anthems. Though (as Spark testifies) he was not averse to orchestral colourings in organ performance, earning himself the reputation of a progressive during the 1830s and 1840s, his use of the instrument probably changed little in essentials after this; his practice remained unaffected by the more thoroughgoing orchestralisms of the rising generation of players.

Wesley's compositions were conceived for instruments with few registrational aids. The same could not be said of the works of the only other English composer of the period whose contribution to the repertoire continues to be heard at all frequently: Henry Smart. Prefacing a new edition of Smart's *Compositions for the Organ* (*c.* 1933), Purcell J. Mansfield suggested that they had retained their appeal '[by] virtue of their dignified diatonic style, their wide diversity of form and content – ranging from the simple church voluntary to the most brilliant concert piece for the organ recital – together with the remarkable ease and fluency of melodic and harmonic progressions which are their invariable characteristics'. Fluency (which Smart undoubtedly possessed) is a mixed blessing for a composer, and those melodic and harmonic progressions to which Mansfield referred have a certain predictability about them which the listener may find unrewarding after a time, but there is no denying that Smart made an important contribution by writing organ music at a time when, *faute de mieux*, most English organists existed on a diet of vocal and orchestral arrangements. Unlike Wesley (who, for all his protestations, did little to assist the average organist in his weekly tasks) Smart sought to exploit the resources of the contemporary organ, with its orchestral registers, registration aids and assisted actions. The concert organs of the 1850s, culminating in Leeds with its ambitious mechanical innovations (above, pp. 284–91), show that Smart was in the vanguard of the movement to orchestralise this type of instrument, and the fact that he had the Birmingham Music Hall organ installed in St Pancras with minimal alteration suggests that he believed the mechanical and orchestral novelties pioneered in these secular instruments to have a use in church organs, too.

Smart's endorsement of these progressive features is reflected in his compositions.[1] The provision of pistons or combination pedals (ventils) seems, for example, to be assumed in the *allegro* of the *Postlude in E♭* (1879) where the player is required, first, to make a gradual *crescendo* by adding specified stops, and then to reverse the process. The *Con moto moderato (en forme d'ouverture)* of 1867 (?), makes more extensive demands of the same sort, requiring accessories to draw solo stops or alter combinations. Some of the registrations are novel. A short passage on the Swell voix humaine (or oboe) with the tremulant is found in the *Andante in A major* (1863); no. 3 (*andante con moto*) of *Six Easy Pieces* (*c.* 1870) specifies Choir bourdon and flute (16.8, or 16.4?) as accompaniment to a Swell solo; in no. 6 (*Quasi Pastorale*) of *Twelve Short and Easy Pieces* (*c.* 1870) Smart suggests that a solo might be played on the Choir flute 4′ an octave lower, in order, one presumes, to obtain a brighter tone than the stopped diapason would yield. Mixtures are seldom mentioned (being understood to be part of the full chorus), but registrations with a sub-unison (16.8.4 or 16.8) are common. In one piece (*Grand Solemn March in E♭*, *c.* 1870) Smart even requires the use of the Swell-to-Great sub-octave coupler.

Smart's brisk *postludes* and tender *andantes* were to set a fashion in composition for the organ which would find favour until the 1950s, and is still not altogether extinguished. Much the same could be said of his approach to registration, though here he was not unique. His *mezzo-piano* movements, often in triple time, and usually exploiting imitative solo registers (oboe, clarinet, claribel, harmonic flute) and encouraging the use of the Swell pedal, are reminiscent in mood of Mendelssohn's quieter moments. Long after Smart's compositions had disappeared from concert programmes, his influence upon the use of the church organ lingered, mediated by the continuing popularity with parish organists of his own pieces and those of a host of imitators.

The influence of a third figure was of a different order. Both as practitioner and apologist William Thomas Best (1826–97) was in the forefront of the controversy concerning the orchestral use of the organ. Though he held church posts (Levien 1942: 16, 41, 48) it was as a concert organist that he secured a remarkable reputation, first, briefly, at the Panopticon in Leicester Square (1854–5) and then, for thirty-nine years, at St George's Hall, Liverpool (1855–94). Best's technique, associated with Willis's grand organ, brought the orchestral transcription to a degree of sophistication beyond which that questionable *genre* could not advance. It was to involve him in controversy (something Best never minded) with, among others, Sir Walter Parratt, who described Best's organ arrangements as 'examples of misapplied skill' (*M O* xv, 1892: 355), but his *Arrangements from the Scores of the Great Masters* (1862–74), his edition of Handel's organ concertos (*c.* 1860, 1879), and numerous lesser arrangements of vocal and orchestral pieces had a considerable influence upon organ-playing, as had his *Modern School for Organ Playing* (1853), *The Art of Organ Playing* (1869) and *First Organ Book* (1883), all of which elucidated Best's own approach to the instrument.

Willis's contribution to Best's success was crucial. First, he provided him with an instrument in which the natural resistance of key and pedal actions when associated with large soundboards was overcome by pneumatic agency, and then he applied the same means to increasing vastly the registrational possibilities of his 100-stop instrument by providing six thumb pistons to each department and six general pistons to act on the whole organ. Pneumatics to assist the motion of the Swell shutters, together with various forms of relief pallet, further eased the organist's task. Finally, Willis paid attention to the console arrangements: the keyboards were brought as close together as possible, the stop jambs were angled, and the pedal board was made (at Wesley's suggestion) concave and radiating.

Best's performance of orchestral transcriptions depended for its effect upon technical fluency and a minute control of every detail of his performance (expression, registration, timing of stop changes). He declined to have an assistant to turn pages or change stops. One observer later recalled that Best

would turn over half a page beforehand or delay till well into the next page, just when he could spare a hand. To see him turn over and re-arrange the stops while he was playing a terrific solo on the pedals was to witness a most elegant and deliberate piece of detachment. The audience could hardly believe that the same person was doing with his hands what they could see, and at the same time performing the prodigies of pedalling they could hear.   (Levien 1942: 28–9)

Whereas the previous generation of players had carefully observed a distinction between the touch and fingering appropriate respectively to the organ and the piano,[2] Best inaugurated a most significant change of direction by developing a technique based on that of the best contemporary pianists. It is said that Thalberg (1812–71) was his model. According to Levien, 'Best's manual work was that of a pianist of the first rank', and he further claimed that it was Best's practice 'to apply the best pianoforte fingering to the organ, subject only to such modifications as that instrument demanded' (1942: 13, 24–5). Again, Willis's contribution was vital: without the ease of control permitted by the use of pneumatics, Best would never have been able fully to exploit the possibilities of a pianistic technique on the St George's Hall organ. Under his direct influence (through his tutors, through his organ performances) English organists came to demand lighter actions adapted to the ready performance of scores characterised by piano figurations and demanding the use of piano fingerings for their successful accomplishment.

Best had a clear notion of the effects he sought to achieve. Precise registrations are given in his *Arrangements*, and as a testimony to the fidelity of his intentions, it is notable that the scores include indications of the orchestration employed by the original composer. These transcriptions assume the availability of a large modern organ (indeed, they reflect accurately the resources of the Liverpool instrument). A Choir voix celeste is frequently demanded, and a Pedal violon is often indicated where definition in the Pedal line is of special importance. The Swell reeds are regularly coupled through to the Great, and Full Swell occurs repeatedly. Changes of manual require considerable dexterity, and Best carefully specifies dynamic levels and the use of the Swell pedal. It would be impossible to be faithful to Best's intentions without the assistance of those accessories which were gradually establishing themselves as standard features of the concert organ during the 1860s.

Best's preoccupation with the concert organ is accurately reflected in the various schemes for new organs for which he was responsible. An early example occurs in his *Modern School for the Organ* (1853). This 3-manual instrument with forty-three stops is very much in the manner of Hill (and perhaps influenced by Hill's scheme for the Panopticon), with seven ranks of mixtures (II.III.II) and four reeds (16.8.8.4) on the Great, an echo cornet and five reeds (16.8.8.8.4) on the Swell, and an 8-stop Pedal; the only curiosity is the provision of a 'Corno-Inglese' as the sole Choir reed (11). The Carlisle Cathedral specification (1856) in which Best had a hand is in the same tradition, though smaller; the Swell vox humana and Choir clarionette hint at the concert hall, and the little Choir Organ has already degenerated into a Solo division, but, in other respects, the scheme offers few surprises (Appendix 1, pp. 487–8). More unusual is Wallasey Parish Church (1861), of which Best was organist. The organ was built by Willis, and had two manuals and twenty-six stops. The Great was unremarkable (though this is an early example of a 4′ harmonic flute appearing on the Great of a church organ) but the Swell is eye-catching on account of its truncated flue chorus (8.8.4.4.III) and Best's preference for a 16′ reed over a flue double. This is made more curious by the absence of a 4′ reed (though a vox humana is included). The Pedal, too, is notable. There are two flues (16.16) and two reeds (16.8). Perhaps the bassoon 8′ was meant to improve the definition of the Pedal, but, if so, this almost certainly had more to do with the demands of the solo (orchestral) repertoire than congregational accompaniment.

Best's scheme for Bolton Town Hall (1874) is particularly informative. His description of the effects he sought from individual registers has survived, and we have to thank Cecil Clutton for publishing the complete document (1984). It is, first, worth noticing the instructions concerning the placing of the keyboards. They were 'to be brought as near each other as possible, without in anyway [sic] interfering with the length of the black keys, so that passages can readily be played on any two keyboards by the same hand' (29). Best goes on to give precise measurements for the keys themselves (white keys to be 5″ long, black keys 3″) and for the pedal board. All stop knobs were to be 'within immediate reach of either hand', and certain of the coupler knobs were to be placed directly in front of the player, below the music desk. The position of the Swell and Solo keyboards was reversed so that Solo and Great could be played by the same hand. Ventils were to be provided, rather than the more usual composition pedals. These highly specific and sometimes idiosyncratic directions reveal the desire of the concert organist to have keyboards, stop knobs and accessories under his immediate control; thanks to the increasingly sophisticated nature of the mechanical arrangements, the organ-builder was equipped to oblige him.

The Bolton stop list is singular and repays careful study (Appendix 1, pp. 488–9). The orchestral character of the instrument is indicated by the fact that only the Great Organ retains a complete diapason chorus, and even there, the twelfth and fifteenth draw on the same slide. The strings, flutes and reeds are treated orchestrally; five of the flutes were harmonic, and Best was keen that the strings should possess a very reedy tone and speak promptly. On the Solo Organ, the cor anglais and clarionet & bassoon were to be enclosed in a swell box and equipped with a tremulant; the tone was 'to be imitative of the orchestral instruments so named' (31). He was even more precise about the tuba mirabilis. This stop

must have two distinctive qualities of tone. From C.C. to middle e′ . . . the tone must resemble an 'Ophicleide' of extraordinary power, and from the next note to the top, that of a Concert 'Trumpet'.												(31)

Similarly, the Swell hautbois must recall its orchestral prototype, and not be ('as is usually the case') 'a mere combination-stop, destitute of any individuality of tone' (31). Altogether, the Bolton scheme accurately reflects both the strengths and the weaknesses of the course which the concert organ was taking in the third quarter of the nineteenth century. Infinitely more versatile tonally and flexible mechanically than the concert organs of an earlier era, it allowed the skilful executant to perform transcriptions in such a way as to give a fair impression of the original orchestration, but this was at the cost of sacrificing some of the organ's unique characteristics. In the Bolton scheme, Best was in danger of turning all the manual divisions apart from the Great into solo departments, and an 8-stop Pedal Organ (which, in the 1840s, would have provided scope for a fully developed chorus) does little more than offer basses and imitative registers. This is obviously what Best intended, and such a scheme was doubtless a wonderful vehicle for virtuosic display, but it was less commendable as a model for imitation, and undeniably contained the seeds of future decadence.

Although mechanical and tonal innovations tended to be pioneered in concert instruments, it was not long before change in that sphere began to affect the church organ. Of course, most church organs were smaller than those in concert halls, and the need for accessories to control the stops or lighten the touch was not usually so pressing. Even the largest church organs seemed, to some more conservative spirits, to require few mechanical contrivances to assist the player: Hill reconstructed the York Minster organ in 1859, leaving it with sixty-nine stops and just eight (fixed) composition pedals. There was also less scope for performing full-blooded orchestral transcriptions in the church service, though, as noted above, choruses and arias from oratorios and other sacred compositions were felt to be highly appropriate fare, and these could be rendered in a highly orchestral manner. However, some organists and organ-builders were anxious to take advantage of developments, tonal and mechanical, in the concert organ in order to improve the church instrument, and in this they found allies among the rising generation of composers.

Following Wesley's lead, composers were beginning to explore the possibilities for dramatic effect offered by independent organ accompaniments. At first, the demands they made were relatively modest. Walmisley's *Evening Canticles in D minor* (1855) use the organ to excellent effect, and Gatens has pointed out the novel orchestral character of the accompaniments to two earlier anthems, both dating from around 1840, *If the Lord Himself* and *The Lord shall comfort Zion* (1986: 109–11), but there is nothing very subtle about the registrations specified in these works and they could have been accomplished without the necessity of mechanical accessories. The same cannot be said of John Stainer's *I saw the Lord* (1858). Though ridiculed when the reaction against Victorian culture was at its height, this piece achieves striking effects by setting the organ accompaniment against the voices (as in the opening bars, in which reiterated chords on Full Organ alternate with unison phrases employing all voices) and, later, using a restless pedal figure to build up tension through 'And the posts of the door mov'd' until the climax of the anthem is reached at 'and the house was filled with smoke', in which the organ again plays a crucial part. Such colourful organ accompaniments were to become the norm for large-scale anthems and canticle settings, and as they became more elaborate, they provided an incentive to organ-builders to borrow from the concert organ in order to enhance the scope of the church instrument. In the face of such irredeemably operatic pieces as Joseph Barnby's *King all glorious* (1868) or Arthur Sullivan's *Sing, O heavens* (1869), there was little else to be done.

The careers of Wesley, Smart and Best illustrate the gradual adoption of orchestral effects and textures as legitimate goals for the organist. We must now consider the mechanical innovations which made these developments possible, and first and foremost, the various attempts to lighten the touch of the keys.

ACTIONS

Relief pallets

The nineteenth century saw an endless succession of experiments with the design and construction of pallets.[3] The earliest attempts concentrated, necessarily, upon the problem of supplying large pedal pipes with wind; Hill's box pallet (1828) and Willis's cylindrical pedal valve (1851) have already been described (above, pp. 125, 148) and Gray & Davison developed a novel pallet for the same purpose (1855).[4] By the end of the 1840s, builders were equally concerned to find ways of overcoming the resistance of large pallets in manual soundboards. The means commonly adopted in devising these 'relief' pallets was to cause the force exerted by the player to act initially on a small portion of the pallet which, because of its smaller surface area, required less force to overcome the wind; the theory (upon which modern research has cast doubts) was that the air pressure above and below the pallet would thus be equalised rapidly and the greater portion of the pallet would descend readily, restrained only by the spring. This is the principle exemplified by William Holt's 'Jointed Pallet' (1849),[5] George Jardine's 'Valve Pallet',[6] and Hill's 'Relief Pallet' (1868)[7] (Figures 18–20).

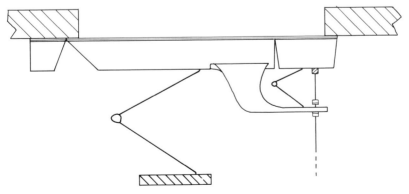

18 Holt's jointed pallet. (*RAM* xvi, N.S., 1850: 29–30)

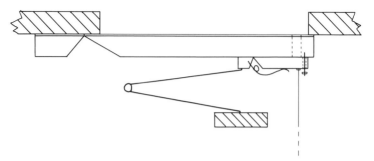

19 Jardine's valve pallet. (HRI: 32)

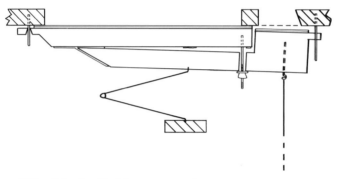

20 Hill's relief pallet. (Audsley 1905, II: 232)

The same principle was exploited and refined in Barker's relief pallet (1850s?) and Willis's 'Hollow Valve' (1861) (Figures 21 and 22). Barker's pallet was conceived as a double pallet, the lower of which moved first before drawing down the larger upper pallet to which it was attached; in order to reduce the mass of the latter, it was hollowed out. Willis adopted the notion of a hollow pallet, but took it further (*PA* 1861: 53). He bored holes through the sides of the pallet to admit compressed air into the cavity formed by the leather covering across the top of the pallet, so that virtually the only resistance to be overcome by the player was that created by the air pressing

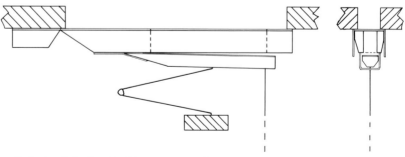

21 Barker's relief pallet. (Audsley 1905, II: 234)

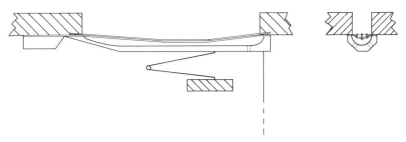

22 Willis's hollow valve. (Audsley 1905, II: 234; *PA* 1861: 53)

23 Willis's diaphragm-aided pallet. (Audsley 1905, II: 236)

against the leather. A different version, intended primarily for pedal chests and for the bass grooves of manual soundboards, was also patented (Audsley 1905, II: 235) and both were extensively employed in Willis's organ for the Exhibition of 1862; significantly, the hollow valve was commended for its facility 'to inject wind at a high pressure into the pipes' (*Guardian* 26 November 1862). At the same time Willis patented a simple device whereby a flexible diaphragm, placed in the base of the chest and supported by a convex disc attached to the pallet wire, assisted the descent of the pallet (Figure 23).

Most of these pallets found wide application, both in the work of their original inventors and (where patents permitted) others, and there were many other less enduring attempts to relieve the action of pallets.[8] They had this in common: that they preserved a purely mechanical connection between key and pallet. Other developments, however, were making for the supplementing, and ultimately, the replacement, of mechanical linkage, and to these we must now turn our attention.

The pneumatic lever

The earliest record of an attempt to employ pneumatic assistance to overcome the resistance of large pallets dates from 1827. In that year, Joseph Booth built an organ for the church at Attercliffe, near Sheffield, and

placed the lower pipes (wood) of the open diapason of the GG manual on a small separate sound-board, and to the pull-down of every separate pallet he attached a small circular bellows below. A conveyance from the great organ sound-board groove conducted wind into this bellows, which, opening downwards, drew with it the pallet. These small bellows Mr. Booth used to call *puffs*.   (HR2: 59)

The church records of Attercliffe contain no mention of Booth's work, and nor are further applications known (though, in the nature of things, it is probable that Booth and his successors made occasional use of these puffs without bothering to announce the fact).[9] By dispensing with the mechanical connection between key and pallet, providing a separate pallet for each note, and introducing a pneumatic agency, Booth actually anticipated the second stage in the application of pneumatics to organs: tubular-pneumatic action. For the moment, however, others concentrated not on replacing, but on assisting the mechanical system. In this preoccupation we find the origins of the pneumatic lever.

The history of the pneumatic lever is obscure and poorly documented. Two men claimed its invention and early application – Charles Spackman Barker (1806–79)[10] and David Hamilton (*fl.* 1822–64)[11] – and in each case, the only real evidence in support of the claims that are advanced is provided by personal testimony compiled years after the events in question.

Hamilton's account is comparatively straightforward. Writing in 1851, he claimed (impersonally) that

Many years ago he discovered a new principle in mechanism, which he applied for relieving the weight of the touch of large instruments. This invention he added to the organ in St John's Episcopal Church, Edinburgh, in 1835, and a paper was read at a meeting of the British Association at Birmingham in 1839, explanatory of a model of it which he then exhibited. He afterwards found this identical invention (in all its details the same as his model) applied in that of the Madeleine Church in Paris, under the name of the 'Pneumatic Lever', and which he has reason to believe was taken from his model, as its first introduction in Paris was subsequent to the date of the exhibition at Birmingham.   (Hamilton 1851)

Two observations can be made. The first is that – whilst it is unlikely that Hamilton would have fabricated a story so susceptible to investigation – the official reports of the Birmingham meeting of the British Association contain no reference to Hamilton or his invention, and appear in other respects to be a comprehensive record of the business transacted on that occasion. The second point is, that if Hamilton's model (Figure 24) is compared with an early diagram of Barker's lever (Figure 25) there are clear differences in construction. The exhaust valve is internal in Barker's design, external in Hamilton's; the mode of connecting the wind channel to the bellows differs; the bellows in Barker's version is designed to draw up a tracker, presumably connected to a square or backfall to convey the action horizontally, whilst Hamilton's bellows draws down a tracker connected directly to the pallet wire; in Barker's plan, the bellows was inflated with air compressed more densely than that employed to wind the organ generally (Thompson 1851: 352) and this is unlikely to have been the case in Hamilton's model. Unless,

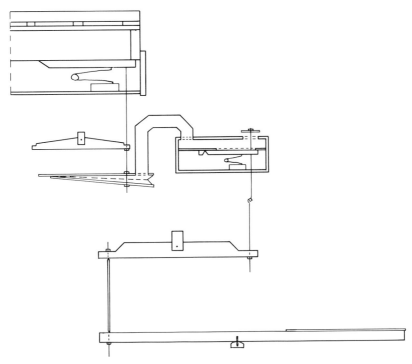

24 Hamilton's pneumatic lever, *c.* 1839. Drawn from Hamilton's model now in the Royal Scottish Museum, Edinburgh.

therefore, an earlier version of Barker's lever more closely resembled Hamilton's, the latter's statement that the rival lever was 'in all its details the same as his model' must be questioned. Perhaps, like Booth, Hamilton failed to grasp the implications of his discovery (the use of the lever in the St John's organ is its only recorded application) and was understandably aggrieved when he discovered that someone else had been more prescient.

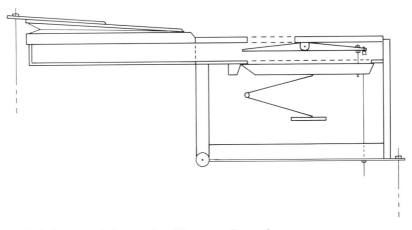

25 Barker's pneumatic lever, *c.* 1851. (Thompson 1851: 351)

Barker's account of the invention of the pneumatic lever is as unsatisfactory as it is self-congratulatory (Bryceson 1869: 16). From it, he excluded all mention of the various modifications to the original design that had taken place during the 1830s, and likewise, all reference to the assistance that he had received from others in developing the lever. According to Bryceson, who had an account of the business from Barker himself, 'it was in 1832 that Mr. Barker . . . was led to reflect on the serious inconveniences arising from the extreme heaviness of touch in all large organs'. As a result of 'persevering studies' he discovered 'an efficacious remedy for this defect, by the invention of what has since been called the pneumatic lever'. In 1833, the account goes on, Barker wrote to Camidge, asking to be allowed to prove the efficiency of this lever by applying it to one of the heaviest keys of the York organ. Camidge replied that 'to such an instrument as ours it would most certainly be very important, where four organs have to be played occasionally by ONE set of keys, and I should be happy to recommend its adoption' (16). Camidge's qualified enthusiasm, Barker's selective quotation from his letter, and his silence respecting an actual experiment with the lever at York make it unlikely that anything came of Barker's proposal – certainly, 'financial difficulties' precluded its permanent adoption. The account then mentions that Barker was no more successful in urging the application of his invention to the Birmingham organ, and moves on rapidly to Barker's correspondence with Cavaillé-Coll (1837), his journey to France at the latter's invitation 'to examine the possibility of applying his invention to the magnificent organ' for St Denis, the decision to employ the lever 'under his [sc. Barker's] immediate superintendence', the sealing of a French patent (1839) and the triumphant success of St Denis (16).

Barker's account implies that both the principles and essential details of the pneumatic lever were to be found in the model offered to Camidge in 1833, and that it was mere obscurantism that prevented its application in England during the 1830s. Other sources show this to have been far from the truth. According to Pole,

In his first attempts he [sc. Barker] adapted to each note of the instrument a piston, working in a small cylinder, and the rod of which communicated with the machinery to be moved. The key opened a small valve and admitted into the cylinder air compressed to a high pressure, which lifted the piston, and thereby opened the valves of the sound-board. This arrangement of the apparatus, however, was expensive and unusual, and required the air to be considerably compressed . . .

(1851: 76)

It seems likely that this piston and cylinder device was the one offered to Camidge, and, later, to Hill for the Birmingham organ. The date when Barker abandoned this machine and turned to bellows for his motor remains uncertain. Pole claimed that it was 'soon' after the initial trials of the piston and cylinder design (76); another source, that it was about the time the

Birmingham organ was completed in 1834 (*MSt* xiv, 1871: 4). Péschard
(who was, with Barker, an early pioneer in the application of electricity to
organ actions) stated that Barker first experimented with the use of small
puffs between key and pallet *c.*1836 (cited, Wedgwood 1934: 50). He
understood from Barker himself that the idea had arisen from experiments to
neutralise the wind pressure on the pallet by attaching it to a small compensating bellows, inside the wind-chest (Figure 26). Barker told Péschard that
he once got this compensating bellows so big that the pallet remained open,
and that it was this which inspired the development of the pneumatic lever
(50). If this sequence of events is correct, it may be that Barker united the
principal feature of each experiment – the compressed air of the one, and the
bellows of the other – to produce an auxiliary agency to aid the descent of the
pallet.

   Barker made no allusion to assistance from others in developing his lever,
yet it appears that credit is due to at least two organ-builders. Despite
Barker's implication that no English organ-builder had the foresight to
understand the potential of his invention,[12] it seems that William Hill gave
him useful advice. Writing of the completion of the Birmingham organ,
Hill's obituarist notes,

it was almost at this time that Mr. Barker called upon Mr. Hill with a rough model of
his pneumatic bellows, which it is no detriment to that ingenious mechanist to say
was an extremely crude one. Mr. Hill saw where this imperfection lay, and invited
the designer to stay at his works and improve it, which he did; and it was, we believe,
at his suggestion that the exhaust valve was devised, which brought the machine to a
workable shape.   (*MSt* xiv, 1871: 4)

If this is correct, it goes a long way to explaining the curious fact that Barker
never patented his invention in England. It is also reasonable to assume that

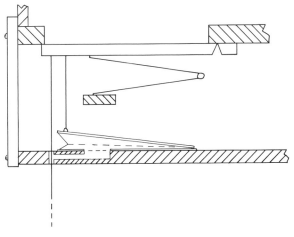

26 Barker's compensating bellows.

Cavaillé-Coll played some part in perfecting the lever. Although the French patent was in Barker's name, he had an arrangement with Cavaillé-Coll whereby the latter was at liberty to use the lever in his organs subject to a payment of 2,000 francs on each occasion; it proved to be a worthless privilege, but may initially have been an acknowledgement of Cavaillé's contribution to the lever's development.[13] Barker left Cavaillé-Coll in the early-1840s, and undertook the direction of, first, the firm of Dublaine & Callinet, and then, the same firm under the title and ownership of M. Ducroquet. In this capacity, he was responsible for Ducroquet's organ at the Great Exhibition (1851). The pneumatic apparatus was a much-admired feature of this instrument, and its description (Pole 1851: 76) tallies with the illustration in *Thompson's Cyclopaedia of Useful Arts*, issued in the same year (Figure 25). Barker would refine his invention further,[14] but by this time, the English builders were beginning to show more interest, and, unhampered by a Barker patent, to make their own experiments.

There was apparently no attempt to apply the pneumatic principle in an English organ before 1847.[15] In that year, Hill submitted a report to the committee overseeing the construction of St George's Hall, Liverpool, concerning the provision of an organ, in which he specified the introduction of the pneumatic lever to the key action, and the use of pneumatics for the combination actions. He added that pneumatic action had 'never yet been used in this country, the expense alone prevented its general adoption' (MS 45: 28 September 1847). Hill's hopes of the Liverpool contract were fated to be disappointed, but in 1849 he introduced the pneumatic lever at Birmingham Town Hall, applying it to the Great keys (Thistlethwaite 1984: 18). Earlier in the same year, Walker had added the pneumatic lever to some part (which, is not specified) of his instrument in Exeter Hall, London, and this, according to Hopkins, was 'the first instance of its employment by any of the London builders' (HR1: 468). Two years later, Hill pioneered the application of the lever to stop action. The stops of his Exhibition organ were controlled by keys, 'something like those of the manual claviers', placed on either side of the keyboards. Each stop had two keys, one to bring the register on, one to cancel it. The action of the keys affected a series of pneumatic levers communicating with the sliders (Pole 1851: 64).

In the twenty years that followed, the leading builders gradually adopted the pneumatic lever, improving its design and experimenting with its application. Examples from Gray & Davison's work have already been discussed (above, pp. 274–91), and it will be evident that the pneumatic apparatus was of particular importance to that firm during the 1850s on account of their preoccupation with concert organs. Similarly, Hill employed pneumatic assistance in the Panopticon organ (1853) for the key actions of the Great and Pedal (and for the Great couplers?), for the combination pedals and the stop action (*MW* xxxii, 1854: 476–7). Thereafter, Hill & Son regularly used the pneumatic lever in concert organs of the largest class, but, at least during

William Hill's lifetime, its use in church instruments was restricted to those whose layout was complicated by difficult locations (All Saints, Margaret Street, 1859) or in which the size of the soundboards foretold an unusual degree of resistance from the key actions (York Minster, 1859).

It was, however, Henry Willis who made the most extensive use of the pneumatic lever in his organs during this period. In 1851, he patented a lever which, he claimed, incorporated three improvements on earlier designs. First, it dispensed with the higher pressure of wind, and drew compressed air from the organ's general supply; secondly, a more reliable exhaust valve was devised; thirdly, a vertical arrangement of the bellows in two or more tiers was proposed (*LJA* xl, 1851: 1–8; Pole 1851: 70). In this form, the lever required a check to arrest the motion of the inflating bellows, and was consequently noisy in action. Willis addressed himself to the problem, and in 1853 patented a modified design featuring the internal throttle valve (*LJA* xlv, 1854: 249–51). With this, the design of the pneumatic lever which Willis applied extensively in his larger organs over the next three decades was essentially complete.[16] In the Exhibition organ of 1851, the lever had been applied to the keys of Great and Swell, but not to their couplers (Pole 1851: 70; *MW* xxxii, 1854: 616); four years later, at Liverpool, the lever was applied to all four keyboards and their couplers, and a double set of levers was provided for the Pedal; thereafter, it invariably appeared in Willis's largest organs, and by 1870, it was not unusual to find it applied to the Great keys and associated couplers in church organs of more modest dimensions.[17]

Tubular-pneumatic action

Although there had been earlier experiments in France,[18] the history of tubular-pneumatic action in England begins during the 1850s, when Henry Willis first dispensed with the mechanical linkage between key and pallet, employing, in place of the customary tracker work, small trunks to convey compressed air to levers directly beneath the chest. A sticker connected the tail of the pedal to a square or backfall, attached to a pallet wire. This operated a valve inside what was effectively a large touch box. As the valve opened, wind was released into a trunk or groove, passing, at the other end, into large-diameter lead tubing which conveyed it to a small bellows below the chest. The bellows inflated, causing the pallet to descend in the usual manner. The grooves were parallel, and were usually constructed in the form of a grid, which was then sealed on both sides with boards; the channel containing the valves and compressed air communicated either directly with the grooves or by way of individual lengths of lead tubing. The grid might be laid horizontally (beneath the main bellows, for example) or placed vertically, in the position of an enormous roller-board; the latter was more usual when the action had to be conveyed to one side of the organ.

Willis made extensive use of this action. Early examples were found at

Harberton (1857) and Totnes (1861), in both instances applied to the pedals, but he later used it occasionally for manual divisions, as at the Union Chapel, Islington (1877) where the Swell Organ stands on one side of the chamber and the Pedal on the opposite side (below, pp. 429–30).

It is said that Willis saw an organ erected on the Barker lever system and operated by compressed air in tubes at the Paris Exhibition of 1867, and this experience led him to think of replacing the wooden grooves with runs of lead tubing (Whitworth 1948: 10). He was not, however, alone in thinking along these lines. In 1869, Edwin Horsell Pulbrook, of Tooting, who is otherwise unknown to history, patented a form of transmission embracing all the essential features of tubular-pneumatic action (Audsley 1905, II: 283–6). He described his improvements in the following terms:

Heretofore in Organs, where the keys are placed at some distance from the instrument, motion has been communicated to the pallets from the keys by means of levers or rods known as trackers, or by electricity; now, according to my Invention, I connect the pneumatic apparatus at or near the keys with the pneumatic apparatus in the instrument, and in connection with the pallets, by means of a tube or tubes. By these means it is almost immaterial how far the keys may be distant from the instrument, for whether the keys are but a few feet therefrom, or say fifty feet therefrom, in both cases an equally light touch is obtained.   (283)

Pulbrook's 'invention' was really a development of the pneumatic lever, as he himself made clear when describing its principal feature; this was, he claimed,

The dividing of the pneumatic apparatus into two parts or portions, one part or portion containing the valves to be placed near the keys, and the other or movable part at or near the sound-board, and in connection with the pallets thereof, the two portions or parts being connected by tubes or tubing through which air is conveyed as required . . .   (286)

Bearing promise of detached consoles for the architects and lightness of touch for the organists, it is scarcely surprising that tubular-pneumatic action was widely taken up by the builders, most of whom developed their own version, and applied it extensively. The period 1880–1910 might be described as its heyday, and thus falls outside the scope of this volume, but a word should be said in conclusion about Willis's earliest use of this mechanism.

By using tubular-pneumatic action Willis was able to divide the organs in St Paul's (1872), Durham (1876) and Salisbury (1877) Cathedrals. He had patented a form of tubular-pneumatic stop action in 1868 (PA 1868: 9) and the scheme for the Alexandra Palace organ, drawn up that same year, announced that 'the whole draw stop movement' would be upon this principle (MW XLVI, 1868: 406). Though highly convenient in a vast concert organ, it was essential to the scheme contemplated by Willis for St Paul's, and there, it had also to be applied to the key actions of those departments

(Swell, Choir) sited in the south case, and the Pedal Organ, most of which was awkwardly placed in a cramped position behind the stalls. No description of the mechanical arrangements at St Paul's has survived, but Henry Willis III recorded what he found at Salisbury before the reconstruction of 1934. He wrote that his grandfather's original action

> consisted of touch-boxes placed at the base of the north side, operated by trackers from the keys [the 1877 console was on the north side], the depression of which opened a pressure-valve and closed an exhaust, so charging a tube of ⅞ inch diameter with wind at the main pressure of 17½ inches. These tubes ran under the chancel to the base of the south side, where circular membranes were inflated, pulling down and opening the manual pallets by means of long trackers . . . The Pedal mechanism was on similar lines, generally speaking . . . but the pneumatic tubes ran direct to the chests.   (*Rotunda* v, 3, 1934: 6)

Clearly, at this stage, Willis felt tubular-pneumatic actions to have limited application. In the same year that Salisbury was completed, he built the Union Chapel organ using the earlier system of wooden trunks where tubes would have taken up less space and been more flexible. Even so, the advent of tubular-pneumatics meant that the days of expensive Barker lever actions were numbered, and that the mechanical connection between key and pallet would eventually be dispensed with by many as an unnecessary constraint upon architects and organ-builders.

Electric action

Like tubular-pneumatic actions, electric actions hardly figured in English organ-building during the period under discussion. However, the first successful attempts to replace mechanical or pneumatic transmission between key and pallet with electrical wires had been made by 1870 and deserve brief notice.

The earliest investigations were conducted by William Wilkinson in the 1820s. This was before Wilkinson established his own business in Kendal (1829), when he may have been working with the Greenwoods (Sumner 1977: 26–7). He was acquainted with William Sturgeon, the inventor of the electromagnet, and it is recorded that Wilkinson experimented with using electromagnets to control the pallets of an organ he had built (Hinton 1909: 25n; Sumner 1977: 26–7). Rather as with Booth's tentative use of pneumatics, little seems to have come of this.

Gauntlett's fertile brain conceived the notion of uniting all the organs in the Great Exhibition by means of an electrical action, so that they might be played at once and from a single console. When it was announced that Paxton's Palace of Industry was to be re-established as a permanent exhibition in Sydenham, Gauntlett approached the Crystal Palace Company 'and proposed the erection of *facsimiles* of the eight most celebrated organs in

Europe, and playing them altogether or separately in the centre of the building' (HR2: 74). The committee declined the proposition. Gauntlett's mechanism was defective. He envisaged the armatures of the electromagnets being connected directly to the ends of the pallets, thus demanding much space and a considerable electrical current (HR2: 74), but his patent for the system (1852) makes reference, almost casually, to the principle which was to be crucial in developing a workable model, namely, that pneumatic levers might be worked with magnets and armatures (*LJA* xlii, 1853: 172). John Goundry took out patents in 1863 and 1864 for a system which included the application of electromagnetism to the action of a pneumatic lever, but his proposals were complex and impracticable (Hinton 1909: 25–27; HR2: 74–5).

The development of a workable electric action commenced with the collaboration of Dr Albert Péschard (1836–1903) and C. S. Barker. This is described by Hinton (1909: 28–44) whose conclusion is that Barker sought to take much of the credit due to Péschard. They began their experiments in 1861. Péschard took out patents in 1863 and 1864, which 'set forth for the first time . . . the principle upon which all subsequent electro-pneumatic actions are founded' (Audsley 1905, ii: 707–8), and in 1866 Barker completed the first successful electric-action organ, at Salon (Hinton 1909: 56–7). Two years later, in 1868, he applied electricity to the action of a new 3-manual organ for St-Augustin, Paris, and it was this (then incomplete) instrument which was brought to the attention of Henry Bryceson during the Paris Exposition Universelle of 1867. According to Bryceson's own account, 'we at once recognised the impending revolution in large instruments', and Bryceson Bros & Co. negotiated the grant of a sole concession to employ the system in England once Barker had taken out an English patent, which he did in January 1868 (Bryceson 1869: 17).[19]

The first electric organ in England was built for Her Majesty's Opera, then housed in the Theatre Royal, Drury Lane; it was placed in the wings on one side of the stage and the console was positioned in the orchestra pit, fifty feet away.[20] Keys and pipes were connected by a cable of insulated wires, and the drawstop action was controlled by the same means (Hinton 1909: 53). Both these features made their first appearance on this occasion.

William Spark saw the Drury Lane instrument, and approved. The organist, he wrote, 'sits in the orchestra near the conductor at a great distance from the organ, and is enabled to produce effects which he himself can hear, and obtain such unanimity in performance with the band and chorus as to stamp the invention at once with the verdict of success'. He praised the touch as being 'as light as a grand piano', and, in an ominous prophecy of future developments, described the advantages of the detached console as 'inestimable'. It would, he thought, be of the greatest utility in churches: 'the organist can sit near the choir, the organ being anywhere – in the vault or roof if necessary – and hear the music as the listeners hear it' (*MSt* IX, 1868: 40).

Spark's view of the electric organ's possibilities was borne out by immediate events. The organ built by Bryceson for Christ Church, Camberwell (1868) was placed in a chamber over the vestry with the console fifty-five feet away among the choir-stalls. (It had previously been used at the Three Choirs Festival, at Gloucester, where the advantages of the detached console were doubtless appreciated.) According to Hopkins, exhaust was used for the key pneumatics, and exhaust and pressure for the stop action. Next, Bryceson applied an electric action to the organ in St Michael's, Cornhill. Here, again, there was a detached console, on the opposite side of the church, with the choir intervening between player and pipes (HR2: 87). A different arrangement was attempted at St George, Tufnell Park (1869) where the organ was placed over the west door (HR2: 87).

Bryceson pioneered various improvements in Barker's system, including a new form of pallet which permitted the pneumatic lever to be dispensed with (1868) and a system for operating stop action electrically (1868, 1869) (*MSt* VIII: 137; IX: 140), but the need to employ large, powerful and therefore costly electromagnets, associated with expensive batteries which, in those days, were difficult to maintain in working order probably militated against a widespread adoption of electric actions, and, following the construction of the organs mentioned and one or two others around 1870, interest waned. It was not until Robert Hope-Jones appeared on the scene in the early-1890s that the matter was again taken up energetically in England.[21]

Other innovations

By the end of the century, it was apparent that the introduction of pneumatics and then electrics had paved the way for a phase of unprecedented innovative activity among the builders, promoting a wide range of developments in the design of actions and their component parts, and releasing a flood of console gadgetry, some of it more ingenious than useful. Most of this came in the years after 1870. However, the demands of the players together with the inherent problems of managing large organs encouraged builders of the 1850s and 1860s to explore ways of refining the construction of their instruments, and the principal innovations of this period are summarised below.

WINDING

(i) Distribution of wind

Earlier in the century builders had rejected the construction of a single large bellows with a number of feeders in favour of the provision of two or more bellows of smaller capacity where the unusual scale of the organ demanded a prodigious supply of wind. This system was extended when space and funds permitted, by the introduction of a primary reservoir, feeding a series of individual reservoirs located near the chests they were to supply. At Lincoln's Inn Chapel (1856) Hill provided a primary reservoir under the organ gallery measuring sixteen feet by three feet, and this supplied wind to the individual reservoirs. An important consequence of this arrangement was that the stability of the supply was improved; the blower exerted his strength in supplying the primary reservoir rather than those directly winding the chests, 'so that it is out of the power of that important, but not always too intelligent, functionary, to disturb the steady pressure of air allotted to the pipes' (*MW* xxxiv, 1856: 788). Willis may have been the first to make extensive use of this arrangement of primary and secondary reservoirs. At Birmingham, Hill had separated feeders and reservoirs but provided no primary reservoir, probably leading to considerable unsteadiness when the demand was great (*PMEM* November 1846: 26). At Liverpool, however, the feeders in the blowing chamber below the Hall communicated directly with primary reservoirs which then distributed the wind to twelve secondary reservoirs inside the organ (ms 46: 25 October 1851). Gray & Davison adopted a similar arrangement at Leeds (1859), where there were no fewer than twenty-one internal reservoirs (ms 41).

The distribution of wind in large organs was accomplished by means of wind trunks, which consumed valuable space. A refinement pioneered by Hill was to make the main timbers of the building frame hollow (though still strong enough to support the soundboards) and employ them as conduits for the wind. This was a feature of his 1851 Exhibition organ (Pole 1851; 64), and its use at the Panopticon was commended by Smart (*MW* xxxii, 1854: 476). Gray & Davison dispensed with wind trunks to the Great Organ at Leeds by the same means (ms 41).

(ii) Mechanical blowing

The introduction of mechanical blowers has been thoroughly chronicled by Laurence Elvin, in his *Organ blowing, its history and development* (1971). Although expanded stop lists, the occasional use of high pressures, and the gradual appearance of pneumatics made growing demands on wind supply, manual blowing was regarded as adequate for all but the largest organs during the period under discussion. Steam power was apparently first employed in connection with an organ in Flight & Robson's Apollonicon, though it is not clear if this was so from the instrument's inception (1817) nor if steam power was used to blow the organ as well as to rotate the barrels. It proved unreliable and soon gave way to more conventional means (Ord-

Hume 1978: 115). In 1845, Wesley (of all people) proposed the application of steam power to the blowing arrangements at St George's Hall. He reported that John Gray had given his opinion that

There can be no difficulty whatsoever in making steam power available for blowing the bellows. I wish I could always use it.   (MS 45: 23 October 1845)

Hill, on the other hand, commented that

The adoption of Steam power to blow the bellows is totally unnecessary – I would ensure their being worked efficiently by two or three men even when the full organ is used. The inconvenience attending the introduction of steam power must be manifest to every practical man.   (28 September 1847)

Ironically, Hill was the first builder to construct an organ blown by steam power (Panopticon, 1853) but the plant was not of his manufacture, and its performance and design proved less than satisfactory (MW xxxii, 1854: 477).[22] In 1855, Willis's organ for St George's Hall was opened, and it incorporated what was presumably the first successful steam-powered blowing plant, with an 8 h.p. engine (HR2: 502).[23] David Joy and William Holt patented an early form of hydraulic engine in 1856; in the following year, two of their engines were supplied to the organ in the Free Trade Hall, Manchester (Elvin 1971: 38; HR2: 508), and five were later employed at Leeds Town Hall (1859). Willis patented his own hydraulic engine in 1857. In 1859, Hill added hydraulic engines to the organ of King's College, Cambridge, this being one of the earliest uses of mechanical blowing for a church organ.[24]

To place these exceptional cases in context, it is worth noting that Hill's reconstruction of the York Minster organ in 1859 did not include the introduction of mechanical blowing and that the Birmingham Town Hall instrument was hand blown until 1890 (Perkins 1905: 19). Chichester Cathedral retained manual blowing into the 1920s (Clutton 1931: 71). Throughout the period under consideration mechanical blowing was sufficiently rare to have little bearing on the design of the vast majority of organs.

SWELL BOXES

Hill's pioneering efforts with large swell boxes have already been mentioned (above, p. 236). Builders adopted various expedients to improve the effectiveness of the expressive powers of the box, some concentrating on the construction of the box itself, others on the action of the shutters. As early as 1824, Hodges had inspired a swell box constructed with double panels, the intervening space being packed with shavings and sawdust (above, p. 158) and Gray & Davison made a similar box for the organ in the Music Hall, Windsor Castle, in 1841 (Warren 1842: 92). Wesley stipulated a double-panelled box for St George's Hall in his earliest (1846) scheme (MS 45: 1 May

1846). This mode of construction became usual for the largest swell boxes. Willis used 3″ pine planks for the box in his Exhibition organ (Sumner 1955: 20), but at Liverpool he worked to Wesley's specification, building a box with some 4″ of packed sawdust between the panels (MS 46: 25 October 1851). Gray & Davison's swell box at Leeds Town Hall was made of yellow deal; according to the contract, the 1″ gap between the double panels was to be 'closely packed with felt wadding or some other non-conducting substance of a like nature' (MS 41). To make for a proper reflection of the sound when the shutters were open, builders experimented with various linings for the inside of the box; brown paper, 'well coated with glue', eventually established itself as the most popular (HRI: 67). Opinion was divided between the merits of felt and leather as the most suitable material for covering the bevelled edges of the shutters so as to silence their action and improve the *pianissimo*: Willis's Exhibition organ used leather (Sumner 1955: 20).

Throughout the period, swell pedals were of the simplest design – short, projecting levers of wood (later, of iron), more or less accessible to the player's right foot. An elementary system of levers made the connection with the shutters, and had a weight attached at some suitable point to assist their closing (cf. Figures 3, 13 and 27). Before 1850, it was unusual for any means to be provided of fixing the shutters at an intermediary point between open and closed. Hill's Exhibition organ was commended for an improvement in this respect:

Each of the two pedals working the two sets of shutters is furnished with a rack and self-acting catch, which cause it to remain stationary at any point it is set to by the player; by placing, however, the foot on a particular part of the pedal, the catch is thrown out of gear, and the pedal follows the foot up or down in the ordinary way.

(Pole 1851: 65)

The development of some such device was crucial in the age of the orchestral transcription; quite apart from its intrinsic powers of subtle expression, it was unthinkable that the right foot of such a pedallist as W. T. Best should be constantly engaged in managing an ungovernable swell pedal. Presumably, ratchets to fix the position of the pedal became common, but there is a surprising lack of evidence about this. The control of shutters might also be assisted by the application of pneumatic levers. Willis was probably the first builder to attempt this, at Liverpool, but a few years later (1861) he patented an apparatus which illustrates to the point of absurdity just how far the Victorian fascination with mechanical innovation could go. The player had within his reach a mouthpiece ('something like that of a cigar holder') attached to a flexible tube. This led to a small bellows which, when the player breathed into the mouthpiece, expanded, ultimately setting the shutters in motion (*Guardian* 26 November 1862). This contrivance was applied (in addition to the conventional swell pedal) to the organs for the

Industrial Exhibition (1862), Newark Parish Church (1866) and the Royal Albert Hall (1871). It seems not to have met with widespread approval.

COMPOSITION ACCESSORIES

Bishop's failure to patent his composition action (above, p. 54) left the field open for other builders to develop their own versions; composition pedals were widely accepted as an improvement and little is heard of shifting movements after the 1820s. Elliot & Hill were using composition pedals by 1830, when the large organ for Oldham was provided with three, and in 1832, a 14-stop instrument for Keswick (a house organ) was provided with five – an unusually generous provision (Buckingham LIV, 41). Unfortunately, contemporary sources fail to throw light on the original provision of composition pedals in Hill's two largest organs of the 1830s; all that can be said is that by 1844 York had ten, and Birmingham seven (Allerston & Pickwell: *passim*). By 1840, when the Gray & Davison Shop Books commence, it was common practice for 3-manual, and more substantial 2-manual organs to have three composition pedals to the Great; the very largest instruments had additional pedals to the Swell, and, occasionally, the Pedal.[25] By the mid-1850s, 2-manual organs were usually provided with two or three pedals to the Swell. Hill's largest organs might have eight (York, 1859) or nine (Panopticon, 1853) composition pedals, though less ample provision had been made in some of his biggest organs of the previous decade (Great George Street, Liverpool, had three to the Great and two to the Swell; St Mary-at-Hill had three to the Great).

   Hill was the first to apply pneumatic assistance to conventional composition actions, at the Panopticon, in 1853 (*MW* XXXII, 1854: 476–7). Gray & Davison followed, at St George's Chapel, Windsor, in 1855 (XXXIII, 1855: 798). The same system was employed in the Birmingham Music Hall organ (1856), of which Smart commented,

The performer will at once appreciate the application of the Pneumatic Lever. In place of the violent and disagreeable exertion often necessary on the old system, he finds the stops springing in or out by groups with all possible promptness, in obedience to a pressure on the pedal not exceeding a few ounces, and, therefore, wholly insignificant.   (XXXIV, 1856: 569)

Smart's words convey something of the unqualified enthusiasm with which the concert organist welcomed all mechanical improvements calculated to render their cumbersome machines more manageable and less inflexible.

   Yet the most important development in pneumatically assisted composition actions pre-dated Hill's Panopticon organ, and was to have a far-reaching effect upon performance and technique. From the key slips of Willis's 1851 Exhibition organ projected a number of small studs, each of which corresponds to, and is labelled with, a certain combination of stops belonging to the clavier adjoining; when the hands are upon the keys, these studs, lying directly below, can be touched easily with the thumbs, and when any one of them is slightly pushed in, in this manner, it draws the combination of stops to which it corresponds, in the same manner as the composition pedals. This is effected by the aid of a pneumatic apparatus. (Pole 1851: 70)

Simple in conception, elegant in execution, Willis's invention represented a perfect meeting of musical need and mechanical insight, and, as the means of promoting a legitimate development in the use of the organ, it has a strong claim to be considered his most important contribution to the evolution of the console. He took out a patent in February, 1851 (*LJA* xl: 4–8). Willis seems originally to have regarded his thumb pistons as superseding composition pedals, none of which were provided in the Exhibition organ, and in that instrument he also duplicated each set of pistons so that they were available to either the left or the right thumb (Pole 1851: 71). In the organs for Carlisle and Wells Cathedrals, thumb pistons were provided, but no composition pedals.[26] The contract for St George's Hall specified six thumb pistons to each department. Those for the Pedal were to act through the medium of the pistons in the Great key slip, though they would also be able to act '*ad libitum* by means of a pedal' (ms 46: 25 October 1851); there were, in addition, six general pistons, set in the tops of the key cheeks at the bass and treble ends of the Great and Choir keyboards, and the contract stated that the couplers were to be brought into action by means of pedals.[27] The latter was a feature of Willis's organs for the 1862 Exhibition (*Guardian* 26 November 1862) and King's College, London (Sumner 1955: 32). He also eschewed composition pedals in the first Alexandra Palace organ. According to the scheme published in 1868 (*MW* xlvi: 406) there were to be six pistons to each department, and 'numerous pedals, commanding the various organs on the French system'. Whether these pedals controlled ventils or couplers is not clear. However, by the time this instrument went up in flames (1873), the 'French system' seems to have fallen out of fashion; Willis's second organ for the Palace (1875) had six pneumatic composition pedals to the Pedal Organ (hr3: 469).

Henry Smart's adjustable composition pedal has already been mentioned (above, pp. 284–6). Rather similar (and a little earlier in date) was Forster & Andrews's pneumatic combination pedal, said to have been patented in 1855 (above, p. 301). It was employed in a number of the firm's large organs, in addition to the conventional composition pedals. In the first organ for All Souls, Halifax (1858), one of these combination pedals was attached to both Great and Swell, the first having eight predetermined combinations available, the second six:

The combination movement in connection with the pedals is arranged immediately over each set of keys, an index plate showing the particular combination arranged for the pedal, which arrangement is made by the organist whilst playing, by simply moving the pointer on the index plate, a little to the right or left, according to the combination desired.   (*MW* xxxvii, 1859: 757)

No further description has survived.

SFORZANDO AND CRESCENDO PEDALS

The sforzando pedal enjoyed a brief vogue during the 1850s and 1860s. It was first employed by Lincoln, presumably under Gauntlett's direction, in the organ for St Olave, Southwark (1844–6); like most later examples, it took the form of a Great to Swell coupler. The organist played on the Swell, and by depressing the sforzando pedal brought the Great into action; as soon as the pedal was released, the connection was broken (HRI: 54–5). At about the same time, Hill included a sforzando pedal in the Ashton-under-Lyne organ. Thereafter, Gray & Davison appear to have used it most extensively,[28] though Kirtland & Jardine made at least two examples,[29] and Willis provided one at the Royal Albert Hall (1871) and the Alexandra Palace (1875). Forster & Andrews's organ in the 1862 Exhibition boasted two sforzando pedals, one coupling Great to Swell, and the other Pedal to Great (Elvin 1968: 15). Schulze's Doncaster organ had a 'Thunder Stop', probably a type of sforzando effect.

A contemporary source states that Hill was the first English builder to introduce the crescendo pedal: his instrument for the Panopticon had two pedals, one for the *crescendo*, one for the *diminuendo* (*MG* ii, 1857: 444). For some reason, the pedal never acquired great popularity in England, possibly because of the already ample provision of accessories for manipulating the stops. It reappeared in two of the schemes for Leeds Town Hall, and Hill's contract for York Minster (1859) specified the provision of 'a crescendo action for Great Organ Stops' (MS 89), though as this appears in no known specification of the organ, it is unlikely that it was ever installed. Willis's scheme for Leeds included crescendo and diminuendo pedals, to be made according to the model he patented in 1857 (*LJA* vi, n.s., 1857: 353–5), and Smart and Spark sent in drawings for a similar device with their scheme. Though Willis waxed indignant about this in the press (*MG* ii, 1857: 429, 443, 464, 478) he declined Smart's challenge to take them to court over the authorship of the mechanism, and the completed organ included the pedals.

CONSOLES

(i) Angled jambs

It was during the years succeeding 1851 that improvements in the layout of stop actions first permitted organ-builders to place the stop jambs at an angle to the keyboards. Although this proved to be one of the more enduring innovations of the period its origins are obscure. Forster & Andrews claimed to have used angled jambs as early as 1850 (Elvin 1968: 15); evidence for this is lacking, but angled jambs were certainly a feature of their instruments for the Industrial Exhibition and Greenock Town Hall (both 1862). The earliest example which can be dated with confidence comes in an account of the organ built in 1853 for Whitchurch, Shropshire, by Jackson of Liverpool. In that instrument (and in one completed early the following year for the Public Hall, Clayton Street, Liverpool) the jambs were placed at 45 degrees to the keyboards (*MW* xxxii, 1854: 61). Whether Jackson had got wind of plans for St George's Hall is not known, but Willis's instrument there had 30 degree jambs: a decided advantage to the player in an organ of 100 stops. For the same reason, the jambs at Leeds Town Hall were splayed, but there, the horizontal arrangement of the drawstops (and possibly their terracing in the French manner) rendered the console unusual. Hill introduced angled jambs at York in 1859 (ms 89), and they appeared three years later in Willis's Exhibition organ (*Guardian* 26 November 1862). By the end of the 1860s, angled jambs had become a regular feature of the largest concert organs, but their use in church organs remained rare. Willis probably first used them in cathedral organs (Salisbury for certain; perhaps St Paul's) and the practice then spread gradually to smaller church instruments; St Stephen, Hampstead (1871), had straight jambs: Union Chapel, Islington (1877) has angled ones.

Terraced jambs (usually straight) are occasionally found at this period, inspired no doubt by contemporary French work. Leeds Town Hall has already been mentioned; three known examples by Hill are Lincoln's Inn Chapel (1856), All Saints, Margaret Street (1859) and St Stephen, South Lambeth (1861). A further variation was the use of sloping jambs. Hill employed them (unusually) in Dr Monk's house organ (1866) but it was Forster & Andrews who made the most regular use of them during the 1860s and 1870s (Elvin 1968: plates 6 and 19).

Most builders used stop knobs with wooden heads and inset ivory shields engraved with the name of the stop or coupler. The knobs varied in virtually all details from builder to builder, and a comparison makes an interesting study. Willis favoured Gothic lettering and Roman numerals; Hill preferred plain upper case; Brindley adopted (appropriately) a distinctive Germanic script. Department labels were still rare. Some builders distinguished the knobs belonging to different divisions by varying the colour of the initial capital letter of the stop name; Hill sometimes stained the surfaces of the shields with the same purpose. Willis's later consoles are graced with columns of solid ivory stop knobs, plainly engraved in upper case lettering; they combine with angled jambs and overhanging keys to impart a sense of decent luxury and concern for the organist's comfort (Plate 56). It is not

56 Union Chapel, Islington, Henry Willis, 1877. The console. The department labels are not original. These, and other alterations (the balanced swell pedals, the Choir piccolo, the panels to reinforce the stop jambs), were made earlier in the present century.

certain when Willis first used these ivory knobs, though the organs for the Royal Albert Hall (1871), the Alexandra Palace (1875), and Salisbury Cathedral (1877) had them (Plate 57). Other builders eventually followed his example.

The arrangement of the stop knobs also varied. As specifications were extended and the taste for frequent changes of registration grew, the long vertical columns of knobs found in earlier consoles, including many of the 1840s, fell from favour. Builders experimented with horizontal displays of drawstops, either arranging departments in double columns side by side (Preston, St George, 1865) or in rows one above the other (St Mary the Great, Cambridge, 1870). Like the terraced jambs, this had the additional advantage of enabling consoles no longer enclosed by casework to be kept comparatively low.

(ii) Overhanging keys

Kirtland & Jardine may have been the first to make the upper keyboard(s) overhang the lower (above, p. 304). As 3- and 4-manual consoles became more common, and a more pianistic approach to technique came into

57 The Royal Albert Hall, Henry Willis, 1871. The console. (*c.* 1900)

fashion, the relative position of the keyboards was a matter of some import-ance. By bringing the upper keys forward builders afforded the player a greater degree of control over his performance. Overhanging keys were a feature of the Leeds Town Hall console, and also of Willis's 1862 Exhibition organ. By the mid-1860s, most builders seem to have adopted the practice in 3-manual consoles.

(iii) Pedal boards

Hopkins noted in 1855 that there was no fixed width in England for a pedal board, 'which is a circumstance much to be regretted' (HR1: 262). He had no occasion to alter his text when the third edition of his book appeared, twenty-two years later (1877), though shortly after, in 1882, the College of Organists attempted to establish standard dimensions. Throughout the period under discussion, practice varied from one builder to another, doubtless to the frustration of the organists. The German System organs of the 1840s seem to have had flat pedal boards with parallel keys. Hill's (or Camidge's) experi-ment of a radiating pedal board in the York Minster organ (HR1: 263) was not repeated until Willis adopted Wesley's suggestion that the concave design of board used in Schulze's Exhibition organ might be usefully com-bined with the radiating principle (MT xxxix, 1898: 300). The result was the Wesley–Willis pedal board, which appeared in the Winchester Cathed-ral and St George's Hall organs, and was thereafter regularly used by Willis. Hill used a radiating and concave pedal board at York in 1859 (MS 84: f. 3), but seems to have continued to make parallel and concave, as well as parallel and flat boards. Probably most builders left the choice to the client.

THE INTRODUCTION OF EQUAL TEMPERAMENT

Writing in 1870, Dr E. J. Hopkins sought to lend further authority to his arguments in favour of equal temperament by listing a number of dis-tinguished instruments in which that system had, by then, been adopted. The list includes various prestigious London organs (St Paul's, Westminster Abbey, Temple Church) before concluding with 'all the Town Hall organs in the Kingdom' (HR2: 182). This confirms what might, in any case, have been surmised: that the requirements of the concert organ played a major part in the growing preference for equal temperament.

A form of unequal temperament remained the normal tuning for English organs until the late-1850s. Some attempts have been made in recent years to recover this tuning (Padgham 1986: 86–93 gives examples) but reliable information is hard to come by. A writer of the 1850s described the English organ temperament of his day as being 'unlike any system used for this, or any other instrument, in any other country', and characterised it thus:

The ordinary keys – C, G, F, and D, were kept very good; while from these points of departure every successive advance brought an increase of disagreeables, until the climax of horror was reached in the keys of A flat, D flat, and G flat, which were absolutely unuseable except in cases of the greatest emergency.

(*MW* XXXII, 1854: 699)

At a period when the English organ was used largely for accompaniment, and when the standard repertoire of church music was 'particularly guiltless of modulation' (699) the desire for change had evidently been slight. By the middle years of the century, however, the situation had altered.

The greatly increased use of the organ as a concert instrument and as a substitute for the orchestra in the accompaniment of oratorio highlighted the deficiencies of tuning to the old mode. A writer of 1857, commenting on the old temperament, observed: 'The organ is often rendered useless in an orchestra for the same reason [sc. the temperament], or entire movements must be transposed into another key' (*MG* II, 1857: 89). The performance of orchestral transcriptions similarly exposed the shortcomings of unequal temperament. The chromaticisms and modulations of much orchestral writing adapted ill to unequal-tempered organs. Such characteristics were also creeping into ecclesiastical music, and Dr Wesley (a redoubtable defender of the old mode of tuning) left himself open to ridicule when he sought to defend the adoption of unequal temperament at St George's Hall. As one critic put it:

I think Dr. Wesley's accuracy of ear may not only be doubted but denied, after writing such passages as constantly occur in his service and anthems, knowing and advocating the ordinary mode of tuning organs in England; for the sake of rendering his own compositions endurable, one would have supposed the Doctor would have been the first to advocate the equal temperament.   (*MG* II, 1857: 114)

Wesley maintained his views with typical acerbity,[30] but in this, as in many other things, the tide was running against him; by the end of his life, he must have known that the battle was lost, but he at least had the satisfaction of putting Hill's Panopticon organ (one of the first tuned to equal temperament) into his preferred tuning when it was installed in the Victoria Rooms, Clifton (*c.* 1873).[31]

It was Wesley's opinion that the only reason equal temperament had made 'any head at all' in England was 'owing to the works of Seidel and Messrs. Rimbault and Hopkins' (*MSt* I, 1862–3: 338). Whilst these works undoubtedly made their contribution (Hopkins's lengthy summary of the arguments, complete with extensive musical examples, for the rejection of unequal temperament is especially impressive) Wesley's natural aversion to equal temperament blinded him to its virtues. Although he, and others, deplored the '*grating, nasal* twang' which they claimed to detect in the newer system (*MSt* I, 1862–3: 338), many organists welcomed it as greatly increasing the scope of the instrument. It was both stimulated by, and itself encouraged, the performance of music of an orchestral character on the organ.

The introduction of equal temperament is poorly documented. Perkins claimed that the Birmingham Town Hall organ was tuned to equal temperament in 1843 (1905: 18); this seems improbable.[32] Hill's organ in All Saints, Northampton, had been put into equal temperament by the mid-1850s (MS 80: 196), most likely under the influence of Charles McKorkell, but the precise date of the conversion is not known. By 1854, it could be recorded that Hill's organs at Christ's Hospital, Farm Street Jesuit Church, the Panopticon and St Walburgh, Preston, were tuned to equal temperament (*MW* XXXII, 1854: 699). Davison's instruments for Glasgow City Hall and Magdalen College, Oxford, had the same tuning by this date; the Shop Book usefully records that an instrument for the Independent Chapel, Blackburn, was 'the first organ tuned equal temp. in the Factory' (MS 6: f.62). Other firms were less forward-looking. The first reference to equal temperament in Walker's Shop Book is found at the beginning of 1856, and, if Wesley is to be believed, Willis was so persuaded of the virtues of unequal temperament that he continued to use it for some time after the completion of the Liverpool instrument unless expressly instructed to adopt the new system, as he was at Carlisle (*MG* II, 1857: 77).

Although equal temperament seems to have become established as normal practice in new organs by the 1860s,[33] the conversion of existing instruments was a slower business. Willis's organ for Wells Cathedral, for example, remained in unequal temperament until 1895 (Pearce 1912: 42), presumably retaining this tuning even after the reconstruction of 1893. A survey by Mackenzie of a small sample of tuning records identifies 1875 as the 'peak year' for conversions to equal temperament (1979: 59–60). From this it is clear that it must have been well on towards the end of the century before equal temperament was thoroughly established in fact, as well as in theory.

12

German influences, 1855–70

DISSATISFACTION WITH ENGLISH BUILDERS

In 1864, an article appeared in the *Musical World* entitled 'Good reasons for bad organs' (XLII: 136–8). The second paragraph set the tone of the discussion:

We well remember that, not more than thirty years since, it was the settled habit of organ-builders, professors, and amateurs to think and speak of the merit of foreign organs as a complete delusion. Not that they had any proper means of forming an opinion on the matter. They were at no pains to see and hear for themselves what the continental artists were doing at the time. They were simply content to believe that their own performances were the best in the world, – that no German could equal them – especially, that no Frenchman could make an organ at all, – and to put down all accounts to the contrary as the result of travellers' ignorance. This was in the days when one heard of nothing but fine diapasons and monstrous pedal pipes; and, beyond these, not the faintest notion existed as to what truly constituted the plan and characteristics of a *large* organ. Within the last few years, however, English opinion on this subject, as on many others, has undergone a vast change. A flying speed by land and sea, cheap fares, and all manner of voyaging facilities, have sent Englishmen by shoals to the Continent . . . Our organ-builders, unfortunately, have not generally availed themselves of these privileges; but our organ-players *have*, and it is interesting to watch the effect of experience as reflected in their totally changed habit of thought. From the more enthusiastic of these, indeed, it is now very common to hear the avowal that an organ-hunting expedition to the continent has satisfied them that there is not an English organ worth playing on! Now, allowing for the dazzle of novelty and some trifle of exaggeration, there must be a little truth in all this.   (136)

One need not look far to find similar complaints and the same conclusions elsewhere. A protracted correspondence in the *Ecclesiologist* during 1864–5, for example, argued the relative merits of Willis and Schulze, and offered useful insights into the shortcomings of contemporary English organ-building (XXV, 1864: 20, to XXVI, 1865: 117, *passim*). No doubt changing taste, fickle as ever, played its part in shaping opinion; the fact that an influential band of organists and critics came, during the 1860s, to prefer a German organ to an English one did not mean that the latter was *ipso facto* a bad instrument. It is impossible, though, reading the musical journals of the period and scrutinising some of the organs, to believe that the complaints were altogether groundless.

Dissatisfaction fell into two main categories. First, the prevailing tonal character of the instruments was criticised, and it was objected that they lacked the 'necessary power to fill a large church or music-hall' (*Eccl* xxv, 1864: 22). It was this that sparked off the correspondence in the *Ecclesiologist*. The *pleno* of the 'immense organ' in York Minster was condemned as 'small and poor' (23); the diapasons in Willis's organ in St George's Hall, Liverpool, were, it was said, 'universally admitted to be the weak point of the instrument' (xxvi, 1865: 113); the 'thin, piercing, reedy tone of the diapasons' in Hill's organ for the Ulster Hall, Belfast, was criticised as 'proof of anything but power' (114). It was maintained that English organ-builders were concentrating their efforts in the wrong quarter. The 'present low state of the art', suggested one writer, was 'caused in great measure by the attempt to supersede the orchestra by the organ'. The same writer deplored the obsession with mechanical innovation and all the 'modern trickery' needed to facilitate an orchestral style of performance, and he denied the desirability of resorting to high pressures when 'abundance of power' could be supplied by '3 or 3½ inch pressure when the pipe is properly voiced' (xxv, 1864: 130–2). In contrast to contemporary trends towards intricacy and elaboration, the writer pleaded for church organs to be built 'strong and plain', and for the tone to be 'firm and powerful, with a preponderance of diapason' (132). It is interesting that lack of power is still (by implication) a concern, forty years after the inauguration of the Insular Movement, and it was Schulze's ability to supply this desideratum that ensured his success in England.

The second area of complaint concerned standards of workmanship. The root of the problem was 'that detestable practice of competition' (*Eccl* xxv, 1864: 134), denounced by one contemporary as having so debased the craft of organ-building that it had become 'all but as distinctly a *trade* as a butterman's or a butcher's' (*MW* xli, 1863: 733). 'One of the Craft' described a typical example of this widespread practice. When an organ was required, a committee ('who know nothing of the duties they are called upon to perform') was set up and circularised builders requesting estimates for an organ at a price not to exceed a given sum. The estimates were then compared, 'to see who offers the largest number of *pipes* and *registers* for the smallest sum'. In order to give the best impression, builders resorted to a variety of expedients: 'single stops will have two registers, several will be deficient of the lower octave, inexpensive stops with fancy names and plenty of mixtures to swell up the number of pipes [will be included]'. The consequences were only to be expected:

I have seen organs without a particle of tin in the pipes, with the exception of what is contained in the solder, wood composition pedals, deal upperboards, spruce used for fitting up, many parts of the internal work finished with a jack plane, but with a showy key board and fine draw stop knobs, names given to stops quite foreign to the pipes in the organ, either from the ignorance of the builder, not knowing the nature of the stops represented, or for cheapness.   (*MW* XLII, 1864: 311)

This view of contemporary standards of workmanship among English builders was by no means unique; another commentator remarked that it would be easy 'to point out hundreds of modern English instruments which will not last fifty years' (*Eccl* xxv, 1864: 359). Specifications of the period reveal many examples of the short-selling to which 'One of the Craft' referred, and the speedy passing of many instruments supplied by builders of the second and third rank fulfils the prediction of the other writer concerning their longevity. At the same time, some allowance must be made for sheer conservatism. Despite some remarkable innovations in the construction and design of organs, William Hill's practice throughout the 1850s retained many significant affinities with an earlier style of organ-building: the quality and thickness of the pipe metal, the voicing and scaling of the pipes, the construction of soundboards and actions, and the general layout of his instruments reflect continuity rather than cheapjack workmanship. Tourists acquainted with the organs of Cavaillé-Coll or Schulze were impatient with such conservatism. However justified, it is apparent that there was, by the mid-1850s, significant dissatisfaction with English organ-building, and this prepared the ground for the reception and enthusiastic endorsement of a model which seemed to have precisely those qualities of simplicity of construction and strength of tone that detractors complained were conspicuously lacking in the native product.

PREPARING THE GROUND

Although the work of Cavaillé-Coll was an important influence on English organ-building generally and the design of certain instruments in particular during the 1850s, this proved to be a comparatively short-lived phase. Willis's work continued, until the 1870s, to draw in a characteristically selective way upon contemporary French practice, and the arrival of Cavaillé's large organs for Sheffield (1873), Blackburn (1875) and Manchester (1877) undoubtedly administered a fillip to French taste in their immediate vicinities, but in the long run, the model which was to have the greatest influence upon the tonal evolution of the English organ was not French but German. The inauguration, in September 1862, of Edmund Schulze's 94-stop instrument for Doncaster Parish Church was a landmark, and its impact upon some of the northern builders was direct and immediate, but the ground had been prepared for a favourable reception of German ideas in the previous decade.

The foreign tours of English organists and organ-builders during the first half of the nineteenth century were discussed above (pp. 175–80). The paragraph from 'Good Reasons for Bad Organs' quoted at the beginning of the present chapter makes it clear that this foreign travel continued, and accelerated, in the years after 1850 as an expanding railway network and improved roads put continental tourism within the reach of more and more members of the professional and commercial classes. The same picture is presented in a Dickensian tale from *Household Words* concerning the appointment of a new parish organist and the reconstruction of the church organ. In it is depicted 'Mr. Twirk', the local well-to-do musical amateur, who 'had just returned from the Continent, bringing with him several scores of Corelli, most beautifully transcribed by an Italian *maestro*, two violins of fabulous ages, and a plan and programme of the contents of about half the continental organ cases' (*MG* I, 1856: 165). Then there is 'Mr. Sebastian Bach Schulze, sub-organist to St. Doncaster', who contests the vacant organistship and, against all odds, is elected. Twirk organises a subscription for the reconstruction of the elderly organ (contributing handsomely to it himself), the work is put in hand and completed, and all ends happily – a situation perhaps seldom encountered in reality. Fiction though it is, this delightful story is rooted in fact. Mr Twirk denotes a type rather than an individual, though (apart from his more modest social standing) he recalls Sir Frederick Gore Ouseley who, during an extended tour of the continent in the early-1850s, 'played on almost every celebrated organ in Western Europe' (Lahee 1909: 195). Mr Sebastian Bach Schulze can hardly be other than Jeremiah Rogers, organist of Doncaster Parish Church.

Although English musical tourists continued to visit the great organs of the eighteenth century, there is, after 1850, a growing interest in contemporary organ-building. Far from being an aberration, this is much more in keeping with the spirit of mid-Victorian England, expressed in the cult of progress and enthusiasm for improvement, than the earlier concern with older instruments. It may have been stimulated by an expansion in the amount of material available in print concerning modern continental organs, and, within this category, by two works in particular that appeared during the 1850s.

Before 1850, for those unable to travel, information about foreign organs was restricted to a limited selection of stop lists regularly reprinted in a variety of musical journals and handbooks. *Hamilton's catechism of the organ*, a pocket-book of which the first edition appeared *c.* 1838 and which maintained its popularity for quarter of a century (a fourth edition appeared in 1865) included a chapter of foreign organ specifications; the second edition (1842) has stop lists of Haarlem (Müller), Fribourg (Moser), Gersau

(Moser), Weingarten (Gabler), the Michaeliskirche in Hamburg (Hilde-brandt) and Silbermann's Dresden organs (Warren 1842: 103–16).[1] There was also an extended bibliography listing thirty-six foreign works on the construction of the organ, and a further ten dealing with the instrument's history (9–10). Most were German. Very probably, the list was extracted from a foreign encyclopaedia;[2] there is no evidence that any of these publications were available in England and their influence must have been negligible. The same cannot be said of another German publication, *Die Orgel und ihr Bau* (1843), by J. J. Seidel, of Breslau. This was translated into English in 1852 as *The organ and its construction: a systematic hand-book for organists, organ-builders, &c*, and hence the English musical public had placed before it an 'unusually important' (Williams 1966: 324) modern work on the theory and practice of organ-building from a tradition very different from its own. Until the publication of Hopkins & Rimbault three years later, it was the most comprehensive treatise available in English.[3]

It is unfortunate that Seidel's translator is not identified. It would have been intriguing to know who lay behind the publication of this work in England. Occasionally he adds a footnote to the text, occasionally interjects to say that he has omitted material which he deems to be of no interest to English readers, but in general he is faithful to Seidel's original and so initiates his public into a distinctively German view of contemporary organ-building questions.

There are, for instance, discussions of Vogler's simplification system (26), the use of free reeds (25–6), means for making the organ more expressive (26–8) and a description of mechanical extension (29). Though all these were features of German practice which had either already made an appearance in English organ-building, or were to do so in the near future, arguably the most influential sections of Seidel's translated work were the glossary of registers and the stop lists of celebrated organs. The former, observed the anonymous translator, incorporated 'a number of very fine registers, which are hardly known in England', the consequence of this neglect being that English organ-builders 'can never obtain . . . that beautiful variety which we so frequently meet with in German organs' (89). The ensuing list includes a goodly number of registers which were indeed scarcely known in England when Seidel's work appeared, but which, either in name or construction, were introduced during the 1850s and 1860s; it is likely that Seidel (and later Hopkins) was important in popularising novel registers and nomenclature. The following may be cited as examples: Aeoline, Block Flute, Dolcan, Dolce, Doppel-flöte, Flauta amabilis, Flautino, Fugara, Nacht-horn, Phys-harmonica, Portunal, Quintatön, Rohr-flute, Spitz-flute, Unda Maris, Viola, Viola d'amour, Violone and Vox Angelica (89–110). The model specifications which appear towards the end of the book exhibit the same generous provision of flutes and novelties which came to typify the Victorian organ, and Seidel's appendix of specifications introduced English readers not to the monuments of the past (though a few were included) but to the work of contemporary German builders: Walcker of Ludwigsburg, Müller of Breslau, Buchholz of Berlin, Buckow of Hirschberg, Schulze of Paulinzelle and others (179–205). All in all, the Seidel translation gave a first airing to principles which were shortly to be taken up enthusiastically in England through the advocacy of the most influential book on organ-building to be published in England during the nineteenth century: *The organ, its history and construction*, by E. J. Hopkins and E. F. Rimbault.

Edward John Hopkins was born in Westminster in 1818. Following a spell as a chorister at the Chapel Royal and several organistships in and around London, he was appointed organist of the Temple Church in 1843, a post he retained until 1898. He died in 1901 (Pearce [1910]: *passim*). In matters of organ-building, Hopkins was as much a convert to the modern German school as his contemporary, Henry Smart, was to the French. He made occasional tours of the continent in the company of friends (including Jeremiah Rogers, the Doncaster organist), and extracts from the journal in which he recorded these excursions testify to the impression made by the work of Schulze. For instance, writing in 1852 of Schulze's organ in Bremen Cathedral, Hopkins confessed

The effect of the Organ . . . was exceedingly solemn, grand, or soothing, according to whether I used the 16 and 8 ft. diapasons, the full organ, or the Flutes and Gedackts. In fact, I never at any organ, in the whole course of my life, felt myself under such a species of enchantment. Indeed the excitement was so great that I had two or three times to leave the church in the most urgent state.   (Pearce [1910]: 66)

Hopkins's conversion (the term is scarcely too strong) was to have considerable implications for the future of English organ-building. Not only the tone of the Schulze organs, but the scrupulously high quality of the materials, the painstaking attention to the finish of the instruments, and Edmund Schulze's personal modesty and openness contrasted favourably with English organs and organ-builders. At the end of the 1852 trip he ordered six ranks of pipes from Schulze,[4] but more significant commissions were to follow, principally Doncaster Parish Church (Hopkins was associated with Rogers in the decision to employ Schulze)[5] and the addition of several ranks of pipes to the Temple Church organ in 1859 (HR2: 454). Of equal importance was the effect that these German experiences had upon the text of Hopkins & Rimbault.

The book falls into two parts. Dr Rimbault's 'Historical account of the organ' is a valuable work in its own right; though it draws upon a common currency of anecdotage from various musical publications of the eighteenth and nineteenth centuries, it was the most comprehensive attempt to date to compile a chronological account of organ-building in England (Rimbault's coverage of foreign builders is much thinner).[6] But it is inevitably overshadowed by Hopkins's magisterial treatise on the construction, design and use of the organ. Expounding various principles which were to become articles of faith for Victorian organists and organ-builders (equal temperament, organ chambers, mixture compositions, deployment of registers) Hopkins discusses, often in considerable detail, everything from creaking bellows to the scaling of hohl-flutes, from the pricing of organs to the optimum length of keys. In the present context, however, it is his espousal of certain principles and practices derived from contemporary German usage which is most significant. In the section dealing with 'the interior arrangement of the organ', for instance, he comments with approval on the 'roominess' of the modern German organ, largely arising, he maintains, from 'the ample size of the sound-boards', which itself has the advantage of allowing every pipe to be placed directly over its wind channel (HRI: 272). He then discusses the ways in which the German builders lay out their soundboards and the dimensions of the grooves. Lest it be thought that 'roominess' is waste of space, Hopkins points out that 'free air is the most important element in the production of a buoyant and sweet quality of tone'; resonance is the quality achieved by the roominess of German organs, whereas England is 'by no means destitute of organs that are nearly as crowded, and almost as destitute of resonance, as a broker's shop' (274). Commending the 'very simple, yet orderly and systematic, distribution of the several parts of which the [German] organ is composed' (272), Hopkins moves on to a consideration of Vogler's simplification system (274–6). Significantly (in view of ecclesiological pressures) he declares the direct action layout to be particularly appropriate for an organ required to speak in two directions, for example, one placed in a side chapel or at the end of an aisle (276). Turning next to a further aspect of the space problem, he conducts a short excursus into the history of the scaling of bass pipes, giving instances of the comparatively modest scales employed by the continental builders (again, chiefly German) and the excessive scales found in English organs (281–3). The latter invariably produce registers 'too powerful and predominating' whereas the former 'speak with a promptness and fulness that is highly satisfactory' (281).

German influences continue to assert themselves in Hopkins's consideration of tonal matters. In discussing the formation of the diapason chorus, he argues at length for the inclusion of manual doubles to correct the 'misproportion' found in the earlier English organs (130–9). The first double to be included in any manual division should be stopped, because it is of prompter speech and not so weighty as an open register (316). To assist builders, Hopkins includes outline scales of a manual bourdon based on the stop in Schulze's Exhibition organ, by then at Northampton, which, he says, will ensure 'a perfectly firm, plump, and pure tone' (283). He also has ideas about reforming the English mode of composing mixtures, and gives various plans, several of which show the direct influence of German practice (251–

8). They are all, for example, quint mixtures; Hopkins excludes the tierce from chorus mixtures and instead proposes that it should be incorporated in a German-type sesquialtera of two ranks with a starting composition of 12.17 (258). Chorus mixturework in larger organs should comprise one mixture characterised by 'fulness of tone' and one yielding 'a sharp and clear tone', respectively named ('after the German manner') 'Full Mixture' and 'Sharp Mixture' (251). The nomenclature was not merely whimsical. According to Hopkins, the adjective 'Full' served a didactic purpose, 'inasmuch as fulness of tone is by no means a common attribute of an English Mixture, although it is one of the leading characteristics of a German one in the Treble' (257–8). The adoption by a number of English builders during the 1860s of bold quint mixtures, breaking at the c♯s, and usually acquiring a unison in the treble was probably a direct result of Hopkins's influence. Like Seidel, Hopkins included a glossary of stop names in his book. Though not as wide-ranging as the former, it includes various registers then little known in England and corrects misunderstandings about others of which the names, if not the forms, had been introduced in the 1840s. Among the former are the voix celeste, dolcan, geigen principal (or violin diapason), and spitz-flute; among the latter, the wald-flute and hohl-flute (112–25). Elsewhere, Hopkins describes the lieblich gedackt ('frequently introduced by Schulze'), commends its economy of space and delicacy of tone, and gives outline scales (284). Free reeds are briefly discussed (283–4). Details are given of the construction of blocks for wooden flutes in Germany, and of the treatment of languids (90).

Hopkins's 'Plans for organs of various sizes' are fascinating, because, with the possible exception of the generosity of mixturework on the Great (another borrowing from German practice), they offer a *coup d'oeil* of the Victorian organ. That this proves to be the case is convincing testimony to the pervasive influence of Hopkins & Rimbault. Successive editions of the book incorporated revised versions of these plans, at once summarising developments since the previous edition and providing a demonstration of Hopkins's influence. Take, for example, the plan for an organ of two manuals and thirteen or fourteen stops. In the 1855 edition it is a highly conventional, even slightly conservative scheme, with a short-compass Swell and no tonal novelties beyond a gamba (HRI: 294–5):

Great Organ (C to g³)		*Swell Organ (c to g³)*	
Open Diapason	8	Open Diapason	8
Gamba *or* Dulciana (c)	8	Stopped Diapason	8
Stopped Diapason	8	Principal	4
Principal	4	Hautboy	8
Stopped Flute	4		
Twelfth	2⅔	*Pedal Organ (C to f¹)*	
Fifteenth	2	Open Bass	16
Mixture	III	Octave Bass (coupler)	8

By 1870, when the second edition appeared, the scheme has been transformed (HR2: 312). The upperwork has been consolidated into two 2-rank mixtures, the Swell now has a complete compass, German flutes and strings have displaced several of the English registers, and, taking his own advice, Hopkins has substituted a German-style bourdon for the (over-scaled?) open bass provided on the Pedal in the earlier plan. Hopkins had proposed all these improvements in the first edition of his treatise; that they could now appear as part of a standard scheme for a new organ in his second edition is evidence that his proposed reforms had been understood and widely adopted. The specification appears there (and, unaltered, in the third edition of 1877) as follows.

Great Organ (C to g³)		*Lieblich Gedact*	8
Open Diapason	8	Violino, Principal or	
Stopped Diapason	8	Gemshorn	4
Dulciana (grooved bass)	8	Mixture (12.15)	II
Principal	4	Trumpet or Horn or	
Flute (Stopped, Open or		Cornopean	8
Harmonic)	4		
Mixture (12.15)	II	*Pedal Organ (C to f¹)*	
		Stopped Bass (1877: Bourdon)	16
Swell Organ (C to g³)		Bass Flute (by coupler)	8
Violin Diapason, Open			
Diapason or Spitzflöte (c)	8		

These plans (there are twenty of them in the second edition, including, significantly, eleven for 'positif' organs and chancel organs which had not featured in 1855 at all) are a valuable illustration of the evolution of the Victorian church organ, and, especially, of the manner in which the German influences of the 1850s and 1860s were absorbed. This is perhaps most obvious in the smaller schemes, with the prominence given to flutes, strings and upperwork derived from German usage, but in the more ambitious schemes, the extensive provision of mixtures in the manual divisions and the importance evidently attached to Pedal basses tell a similar story.

Hopkins's concluding contribution to the dissemination of knowledge respecting the contemporary German organ was to commend to English organists what was 'not only a very interesting, but also a very instructive employment' – the study of foreign organ specifications (HR1: 313). To this end, an appendix was attached to his treatise containing some 300 stop lists. Rather fewer than half were of foreign organs, and of these, the majority were instruments that had been constructed or reconstructed during the nineteenth century. Cavaillé-Coll was represented (three organs), but among the contemporary builders Germans predominated: there were schemes for organs by Buchholz, Müller, Buckow and Walcker, among others. By far the best represented, however, was the Schulze family, with no fewer than ten specifications.

EDMUND SCHULZE

It was the Prince Consort who invited the Thuringian organ-builder Johann Friedrich Schulze (1793–1858) to send a sample of his work to the Great Exhibition of 1851 (Burn 1930: 101). Though working within a tradition broadly descended from Gottfried Silbermann, Schulze had, as a young man, been influenced by theorists such as J. C. Wolfram, J. Wilke and J. G. Töpfer, and his close association with the latter over the reconstruction of the organ in Weimar Cathedral (1824) was to have a profound effect upon his outlook (Sumner 1957a: 9). He made extensive use of Töpfer's ratio for pipe measurements (the so-called Normal Scale),[7] and made various mechanical improvements in his organs. In other respects, he was a conservative, continuing to build complete choruses with mixtures and mutations; these powerful choruses, complemented by strong pedal basses, and contrasting with the soft and gentle voicing of the secondary divisions (delicate gedacts and stringy gambas) are the hallmarks of Schulze's style, perpetuated in the work of his sons (Williams 1966: 166–7).

There were six of these. Heinrich Edmund (1824–78) was the eldest, and took over the business upon his father's death whilst working on the new organ for the Marienkirche, Lübeck. Two other brothers seem to have been involved in the business: Eduard (1830–80), who completed work outstanding at Edmund's death before himself being carried off by the family pulmonary complaint, and Herwart (1830–1908), who later settled in England as a wood-carver (Sumner 1957a: 11; Johnstone 1978: 6).

Edmund Schulze (Plate 58) was despatched to London in 1851 with the organ for the Exhibition. The reputation that the instrument earned, and the contacts that Schulze established, laid the foundations for the firm's future success in England. Throughout the summer the organ (Appendix 1, pp. 489–90) attracted considerable attention. It impressed the auditors for a number of reasons. Foremost among them was its power. One contemporary observed that it 'emitted the greatest volume of tone, for the number of stops employed, that we ever heard' (*MW* XLII, 1864: 136). This was due to a number of factors; wide mouths, generous winding and straight-line scaling each played a part. An organ-builder who saw the Exhibition organ after its removal to Northampton (Plate 59)[8] commented on Schulze's distinctive approach:

The method of voicing and regulating was novel then. The Open Diapason had no tips, the pipes were cut off and *inserted* in the upperboards, not resting in a

58 Edmund Schulze (1824–78).

countersunk hole as we placed them and still do. (Schulze adopted our plan later.)
The strength of tone &c. was adjusted at the flue which was very narrow. The wood
pipes were also regulated in the same way and the bore of the foot was not stopped.

(MS 35)

To a generation constantly disappointed by the lack of power manifested in
English organs, the sheer volume of the Schulze organ was a revelation. But
it was also admired for the quality of its softer registers. A reviewer who
heard the instrument in Northampton remarked that 'the sweetness of the

59 The Exchange Rooms, Northampton. The Schulze organ from the Great Exhibition.
(*Building News*, 1863)

tone reminded us strongly of the one [sc. organ] used at the Temple Church'
(*MW* xxx, 1852: 13). The allusion to 'Father' Smith's organ is interesting.
Contemporaries detected a mellowness in Schulze's work which they had
previously assumed could only be acquired as an organ matured over the

course of many years. This is borne out by an anecdote telling how Jeremiah Rogers first encountered Schulze.

The story is perhaps well known of Mr. Jeremiah Rogers of Doncaster: how one day he betook himself to the Exhibition; how, on touching the keys of a certain small instrument [i.e. Schulze's organ] he sprang up, exclaiming, 'The man has got some old pipes in his organ'; how he then dragged up a stool and, thrusting his body into the frame, declared, 'Nay, they are not old pipes, but new ones'; and how thus he discovered Edmund Schulze.   (Burn 1930: 101)

Another writer told how, 'with a skill all his own', Schulze was able to obtain tone from wooden pipes 'which formerly were only approached by fine metal pipes or reeds' (MS 33). One is reminded of the approval with which the wooden diapasons of another German (?), Bernard Smith, were greeted in England.

It was therefore Schulze's gifts as a voicer, together with a meticulous attention to regulation and a refusal to use any but the finest materials, that led to the award of the Doncaster contract. Though the Exhibition organ had undoubtedly made its mark, the Doncaster organ was on a wholly different scale and was, moreover, a permanent fixture (Appendix 1, pp. 490–2). It proved to be one of the two most influential organs built in England during the second half of the century. Writing shortly after its opening (September 1862), a correspondent in the *Musical World* underlined the significance of the Doncaster organ:

The arrival of this great German instrument among us has administered such a sharp stimulant to the well-nigh defunct *corpus* of English organ-building art that, already, the patient gives signs of at least exerting itself towards the recovering of a hearty life. Our builders have taken to bestirring themselves in all manner of ways: and full time they did. There is no longer any question of how much faith should be given to travellers' tales about Haarlem and Rotterdam, and the like. Here, within a four-hours' ride of London, is a great big German fact to say for itself what a fine German organ is reputed to say.   (XLI, 1863: 733)

Schulze's lack of reserve, and his readiness to welcome other builders at Doncaster to inspect the work as it proceeded (Spark 1892: 184) contributed materially to the influence of the instrument and its builder. Such openness apparently contrasted with the obscurities practised in English organ-building circles, a point not lost on one Doncaster enthusiast: 'There is no quackery or impudent pretence about the matter, no trick to conceal, no unheard-of-invention to parade' (*MW* XLI, 1863: 733). Another writer reported Schulze's willingness to give the scales of his pipes 'to all who ask him' (*Eccl* xxv, 1864: 22), whilst yet another was glad to observe 'a disposition among our builders to avail themselves of the lessons they may learn from [Doncaster]' (Spark 1892: 184). Although the English builders generally would scarcely have endorsed the judgement of one zealot, who proclaimed the Doncaster organ to be 'the noblest work of organ-building art that England has ever heard or seen' (*Eccl* xxv, 1864: 22), it brought them into direct contact with an established, and legitimate, tradition of organ-building very different from their own, and one that throughout the remainder of the century was to have an important influence upon their own work. The solidity and massiveness of construction, the prodigious supply of wind to the chests,[9] the care taken in the selection and maturing of timbers,[10] the substance and quality of the metal pipes,[11] and the time taken in finishing[12] – all contrasted with contemporary English practice. The mechanics, however, were widely regarded as 'old-fashioned' (*Eccl* xxv, 1864: 80); 'the weight and resistance of the draw-stop action', 'the great noise created by the movement generally', and 'the very primitive construction of bellows' were criticised even by those who admired the tone of Schulze's organ (284). Certainly, the blowing arrangements were unusual by English standards. Three tiers of four diagonal bellows, each 10′ long by 5′ broad, were placed at the back of the organ.

Each bellows was connected by a rope and pulley to a panel sliding perpendicularly in its frame, a foot-hole being provided in the panel in which the blower placed his feet, his weight bringing down the panel and thus raising the bellows. As the blower brought down one slide, he stepped on to the next, and so on.

(Whitworth 1929: 46)

An illustration of the blowing apparatus (in use) will be found in Elvin's *Organ blowing* (1971: plate 4). Four blowers were required when the full resources of the organ were to be employed (*Doncaster Chronicle*, 27 September 1895). Progressive organists and organ-builders also criticised the simple console; as the means of controlling an instrument of ninety-four stops, it was felt to compare unfavourably with contemporary English concert organ consoles. But in tonal matters, Schulze succeeded in satisfying the current fashions in an exemplary manner. William Spark's assessment is fairly typical and all the more valuable coming from one who, under the influence of Henry Smart, was something of a Francophile. He commended the 'sublime foundation tone-power' of Doncaster, continuing,

The flue-work of the great and choir organs, as far as the 4-feet tone, is truly superb, and I have never heard – not even from the finest of Silbermann's famous instruments in Germany – a finer variety, beauty, and rich, distinctive character [of] tone – pure, unattenuated, unadulterated tone. The player, especially if he can extemporise fairly well, sits with a flood of sound ready to the touch of his fingers, and a store of thunder lying harmless at his feet. The thickness, depth, and independence of the pedal organ here vindicate supremely the ascendancy of this important section; where, especially in slow subjects, when the bass rolls in its ponderousness – there is no disputing it – it is like the *fiat* of the Omnipotent. The swell, solo, and echo organs have also their gems, especially the harmonic flutes, and many other delicately voiced stops. I am bound, however, to admit that the reeds and mixtures, particu-

larly of the great organ, are not, so far as my own individual opinion goes, equal to
the other parts of the instrument. But Schulze did not affect reeds much . . .

(Spark 1892: 187)

Spark was writing in the 1880s, and his comments perhaps reflect that
growing disaffection with mixturework which characterised both that and
succeeding decades. Others were less concerned about the shortcomings of
Schulze's reeds, and the comments made on this subject by one observer
illuminate one of the reasons why the Schulze type of instrument had a
particular attraction in certain quarters at a time when English builders
were devoting much of their effort to the development of the concert organ.

Here is purity combined with grand solemnity of tone, exquisite delicacy in the
smaller flue stops, and a prodigious power of diapason and chorus, *unassisted by reeds*;
in short, here we find that religious quality which makes the organ pre-eminently the
Church's instrument.   (*Eccl* xxv, 1864: 22)

Reformers of the 1830s were using precisely the same phrases to describe
what they sought from a church organ (with the exception of the exclusion of
reeds). The significant change is that it is not an English, but a German
organ-builder who is meeting their expectations. Under the circumstances,
it is scarcely surprising that Schulze's influence was so great. For those who
were unhappy about the orchestral tendencies of Willis's work, and who
were still disappointed by the old-fashioned cut of the instruments made by
the more conservative builders, Schulze's work, and especially his monumental organ at Doncaster, established a new ideal. His later English work[13]
was to be received with equal respect, but it was Doncaster that showed the
way.

THE RECEPTION OF GERMAN INFLUENCES

During the 1850s, English organ-builders absorbed the German influences
mediated by Seidel, Hopkins, contacts with Schulze and foreign travel in a
fitful and largely unsystematic way. An early example of the direct influence
of Hopkins & Rimbault is to be found in the composition of the Great
mixtures in Walker's organ for St Barnabas, Kensington, built in 1856.
There, the Full Mixture (15.19.22) and Sharp Mixture (22.26.29) probably[14] had the same composition as proposed by Hopkins in one of his plans
(HRI: 255), the only difference being that they broke back a semitone earlier,
on the c's. According to the *Musical Gazette*, this gave the mixtures 'an
amount of firmness, fulness, and power [in] the treble that is most satisfactory' (I, 1856: 274). In other respects, too, the scheme is much in the spirit of
the 1855 edition of Hopkins & Rimbault; it may be that Hopkins had a hand

in it. Though his influence was generally welcomed, and causes for which he campaigned such as equal temperament, full-compass Swells and moderately-scaled Pedal registers steadily won acceptance, there were dangers. A correspondent, writing to the *Musical Standard* in 1863, praised Hopkins's book, saying it had 'done good service if it has only caused persons to think about the subject', but he added that, at the same time, it had supplied ignorant organ-builders with a new vocabulary of stop-names with which to mystify their customers: 'there are not three Organ Builders in London who know how to make and voice properly either the "German Gamba" or the "Lieblich Gedact", yet these are stops one sees constantly figuring in specifications' (II, 1863: 92). We may detect a whiff of the purist here, but it is undeniable that many stop lists of the period are curious affairs, with English sesquialteras, early-Victorian clarabellas, stops drawing in halves, short-compass Swells, over-scaled Pedal divisions, and the odd flute or string with a German name, all jostling for position. Joseph Walker is not to be reckoned among the class of builder responsible for such pretentious incoherence, but his Shop Book demonstrates what could happen. Innate conservatism did not prevent him from feeling under some obligation to make concessions to the current taste, and so his organ for St Audeon, Dublin (1861) included a 'Lieblick Gedact', 'Gemshorn', 'Spitzflote' and 'Rohrflote' in its stop list. But all was not as it seemed. Not wishing to dismay his pipe-maker, Walker indicated in brackets the pipe constructions that he had in mind: they were, respectively, 'Stop Diap', 'Principal', 'Open Diap' and 'metal flute' (MS 20: 15). It alerts us to the superficial nature of German influences in the work of many English builders at this period.

Others were more serious. Among the London builders, the character of Hill's work changed radically at this time under the direct, or indirect, influence of German organ-building (below, pp. 395–6). Gray & Davison were evidently too content with their synthesis of English and French idioms to be so thoroughgoing, but they had experimented way back in 1850 with pyramidal basses in wood for the metal conical gamba and gemshorn in their organ for Boston Centenary Chapel (HR2: 105), and in 1856 they included a gamba 'of the true Schulze–Töpfer school' in the Birmingham Musical Hall organ (*MW* xxxiv, 1856: 570). It was not difficult to embrace registers of 'the small scale and delicate tone brought into fashion by Schulze' (*MW* xlii, 1864: 613) within the tonal framework of Gray & Davison's refined, slightly understated instruments, and their organs of the 1860s and 1870s often included a few registers of German derivation: gambas (cylindrical and conical), gemshorns, spitzflötes, rohrflötes, lieblich gedacts, hohlflötes, lieblich bourdons. Willis was less enthusiastic. Only a solitary lieblich gedackt gave any hint of German influence in the stop list of his organ for the International Exhibition of 1862, and although gedacts at 16, 8 or 4 foot pitch had become common in his instruments by the mid-1860s, he showed little interest in other German pipe constructions. His approach to the scaling, winding and voicing of chorus registers was utterly different from Schulze's, and the external influences on his work continued to be predominantly French rather than German (below, pp. 416–17).

The piecemeal adoption by the London builders of features of German organ design underlines the courage of Kirtland & Jardine in undertaking Joule's massive scheme for St Peter's, Manchester as early as 1856, and their adventurousness in adopting Töpfer's scales for the Free Trade Hall the following year (above, pp. 303–4). The synthesis of English, French and German idioms discernible in the schemes for these ambitious instruments was consistently reflected in the firm's smaller organs of the late-1850s and 1860s. The German influence was most apparent in the development of the Swell flue chorus which might consist of a bourdon (16'), spitzflöte and gedact (8'), gemshorn (4'), fifteenth (2') and mixture (II) – as at St Michael (RC), Clithero (1858), Bethsaida Chapel, Hanley (1864) and Henshaw's Blind Asylum, Manchester (1866). St Thomas, Bury (1868), shows how the same principles might be adopted in a larger instrument; there, the Swell consisted of: lieblich bourdon (16'); spitzflöte, lieblich gedact and hohlflöte (8'); gemshorn and gedact flöte (4'); fifteenth (2'); twenty-second (1'); and three reeds. Another Manchester builder, Edward Wadsworth, retained the lessons that he had learnt with Jardine and adopted a similar approach; though in his organs, the German influence extended to the Great flutes which were usually a rohr gedact and lieblich flöte (Edgeley, 1865; Runcorn, 1866).

Forster & Andrews's connection with Schulze has already been mentioned (above, p. 301). The firm's instruments built during the late-1850s remained conservative in tonal design, but regular trips to Doncaster whilst Schulze was at work bore fruit in the 37-stop organ for the 1862 Exhibition. Töpfer's scaling was adopted, and the stop list included a hohlflöte and waldflöte (Great), flauto traverso (Swell), lieblich gedact, spitzflöte and gemshorn (Choir). Later in the same year, however, caution was thrown to the winds, and a Choir Organ emerged for Beverley Road Wesleyan Chapel, Hull, with the following remarkable specification: Lieblich Bordun 16', Flute d'Amour 8', Still Gedact 8', Zartflöte 4', Spitzflöte 4' and Krummhorn 8'. Thereafter, the firm's work continued in the same vein: big, bright choruses capped with strong quint mixtures; weighty pedal basses; ample provision of flutes and strings, most of them with German names. Their credentials as disciples of Schulze were impeccable. Hopkins retained them to undertake a reconstruction of the Temple Church organ in 1878, and as late as 1908, the firm was employing as head-voicer a man who had trained with Schulze and had been responsible for making the resonators of the 32' reed for Doncaster (MS 34).

A number of other English organ-builders claimed to work in the style of

Schulze. The Leeds firm of Abbott & Smith (founded 1869) stated that, in tonal matters, they followed 'almost exclusively, in the steps of the late Edmund Schulze, of Paulinzelle, Germany, whom many competent judges consider to have been the greatest master of the voicer's art that the present century has produced' (Abbott & Smith 1896: *passim*). Other builders who had either worked with them or been influenced by them (James Jepson Binns, for example) were inclined to imitate Schulze's work with varying degrees of commitment and (inevitably) success. There are, though, two builders whose work justifies more extended treatment in this context.

Various stories associate the names of Charles Brindley and Edmund Schulze. It has been claimed that Brindley studied organ-building in Germany; that he worked at Paulinzelle; that he worked with Schulze on the Doncaster organ; that he employed German workmen and, specifically, one of Schulze's brothers during his early years in Sheffield (Knott 1973: 4). All this may be true (though the report of Schulze's brother working with Brindley sounds far-fetched) but it is at least as likely that these tales are apocryphal and arose because of Brindley's early conversion to German ways.

This seems to date from 1858, when Brindley was commissioned to supply a temporary organ for Doncaster; it stood first in the Grammar School and later in the new Parish Church, waiting for Schulze's instrument to be completed. It is said that Schulze himself supplied Brindley with several ranks of pipes for the organ; also, that he was in the habit of practising on it (*O O D*: 11). With lieblich gedacts (16', 8'), geigen principal (8'), violoncello (8'), rohrflute (8'), viol d'amour (8') and gemshorn (4') this instrument indicated clearly the direction in which Brindley's work would develop. The style was consolidated rapidly. A report in the *Musical Standard* described Brindley's new organ for St Andrew, Halstead, which was completed about the same time that Schulze's Doncaster organ was opened.

The instrument is built on the German plan. In the English plan, we have but duplicates of the various stops on each manual, merely differing in power, while in the German we have the same kind, but different in quality. Thus in the organ under notice, we have, in the Great Organ, the Hohlflöte; in the Swell, the Rohr Gedact; and in the Choir, the Lieblich Gedact. In an English organ these would all have been Stop Diapasons of different qualities. The Principal is also similarly treated. In an English organ, we should have had four principals, viz., one on each manual, and the pedal. Here there are Great Organ, Principal; Swell, Spitzflöte; Choir, Gemshorn; and Pedal, Violoncello . . .
(1, 1862: 26–7)

The distinction between English and German organs is one with which Hill and Gauntlett had been familiar twenty years before. They had, however, retained the framework of the English organ (scaling, voicing, mixture compositions, power levels) and few of their borrowings from German practice had been literal. The generation of the 1860s had both the opportunity and the will to emulate contemporary German builders more closely, and in the work of Brindley (among others) we see the consequences. Take, for example, two surviving instruments: the Albert Hall, Launceston, Tasmania (1861) and Gainford Church, Co. Durham (1865). The Launceston scheme (Appendix 1, pp. 492–3) is remarkably complete. The Great chorus is scaled according to Töpfer's principles (Stiller 1984: 24) and incorporates a 5-rank quint mixture retaining the 1′ rank until c² (as does the 4-rank mixture on the Swell). The fluework of Choir and Swell consists of lightly voiced flutes and strings: there is no attempt in either division to develop a diapason chorus, and the big mixture in the Swell is surely intended to be used with the reeds. Wooden pipes are used solely for basses in the manual divisions; the metal gedacts have wooden stoppers, and, like much of the pipework, are made of spotted metal. The chests are chromatic (Spiller 1984: *passim*). Similar features are to be observed in the slightly smaller instrument at Gainford. Of this organ, as of Brindley's instrument for St John, Chapeltown, Sheffield (1863), it could be said: 'The full organ is remarkably brilliant and cheerful, and without mixtures the tone is round, full and vigorous' (*MSt* 1, 1863: 271). No organ of the 1840s (and certainly none of the 1820s or 1830s) would have been described as 'cheerful', and the voicing techniques which remained popular among English builders into the 1850s were not calculated to develop 'vigorous' choruses. Brilliance, cheerfulness and vigour were Schulze's gifts to those builders who chose to follow his example. Brindley was among them, and until changing fashion dictated a reduction in the power of the upperwork, and the adoption of factory methods of organ-building led to a decline in individuality, his organs demonstrated as well as any the decisive influence of Edmund Schulze.

We may turn finally to T. C. Lewis. A technical study of his work is outside the scope of the present volume (and would more properly be included in an account of English organ-building after 1870) but it will be appropriate to indicate something of the nature of the debt owed by Lewis to Schulze. A little has already been said about this (above, pp. 305–6). That Lewis admired Schulze's work is plain enough from his remarks on the Doncaster organ (*MSt* 1, 1863: 354–5). His principal criticism concerned the reeds ('I must say the great organ reeds do seem to me to cast a dullness over the flue work'), and he expressed the view that 'the great organ being a mass of body, tone, and brilliance, requires to my mind reeds of great power and vivacity to blend with it' (354). Whilst he was only too ready to imitate Schulze's approach to fluework in his own instruments, Lewis attempted to improve on the German's reeds: so, for example, at St Peter, Eaton Square (1874) the Great reeds (16.8.4) were placed on a separate soundboard with a higher pressure than the fluework. Against Schulze's fluework, however, Lewis had few criticisms to make. Some had characterised it as 'gamba-ish'. Lewis agreed that the pipes came onto speech in a manner not unlike that of a gamba ('but a great deal quicker'), adding that all Schulze's fluework was voiced along these lines, 'and this to a certain extent accounts for the magnificence of his mixtures' (354). He explained,

Mr. Schulze's peculiarity of voicing, as compared with the English mode is, that in all cases of open metal flue work not being flutes, the wind is thrown more out of the pipe at the mouth, causing the tone to be less fluty and far more powerful, taking a much greater quantity of wind without over-blowing.   (354)

Lewis would strive in his own instruments for a similar effect using similar means (Lewis 1897: 4–7). Further correspondences with Schulze's work emerge the closer one studies a Lewis organ. The lieblich gedacts ('among the most charming stops of the organ') which appear in virtually all Lewis's instruments, the strings, and the flauto traversos found in some of his larger organs: all derive from Schulze's practice, based doubtless on technical information that 'he willingly gave away' (12). All in all, Lewis was Schulze's most consistent, and most successful, English disciple, due in part to the frequent communication which he had with the master (Lewis 1897: 11–13).

In conclusion, we might consider two large organs by Lewis from this period. The metal pipework of St Mary's Roman Catholic Cathedral, Newcastle-upon-Tyne (1869) was made of spotted metal, as was that of Doncaster. Particular attention was paid to an adequate and steady provision of wind, and to this end, Lewis had adopted a novel arrangement to prevent demands on the winding system by the Pedal division adversely affecting the manual departments (HR3: 561–2). The tonal scheme attests its inspiration. The Swell chorus consists of geigen principals (8′, 4′) and a consolidated mixture (12.15); there are two further strings (including a celeste) and a lieblich gedact. The reeds introduce a French note, with bassoon (16′), oboe & bassoon (8′), voix humaine (8′), trumpet (8′) and clarion (4′). The Great consists of a straightforward chorus, concluding with a 3-rank mixture and a trumpet. The Choir is a 7-stop department of delicately voiced registers: a lieblich gedact 16′ (but no 2′), a vox angelica (8′) and a flute harmonique (4′) among them. The Pedal consists of four 16′ basses, a quint and an octave coupler. All the essentials of the Schulze style are present: only the reeds, the undulating stops and the harmonic flute introduce a slightly different note.

The organ for St Peter, Eaton Square (1874), was both larger and more ambitious (Appendix 1, pp. 493–5). Lewis's application of higher pressures to the reeds than to the fluework of the Great has already been mentioned: this was something that Schulze hardly ever did.[15] But the extent of his debt to Schulze immediately becomes apparent when the fluework of the Swell and Choir Organs at Eaton Square is compared with the same divisions in the Doncaster organ (Appendix 1, pp. 490–1). Though the latter is, in each instance, several stops larger, the parallels are striking. In the Great Organ, too, it is apparent that the same objectives are being pursued, and by similar means. The characteristic influences of Schulze upon English builders have been too frequently rehearsed to bear further repetition, but in Lewis's organ for Eaton Square, we see the extent to which one particular native builder had absorbed the lessons he had received and had succeeded in creating a style which, whilst heavily dependent upon his mentor, had nonetheless an individuality and maturity of its own.

13

Hill & Son, 1856–70

William Hill died at the age of eighty-one in December 1870. He was still very much in harness: within a fortnight of his death he had been working on a 66-stop organ for Melbourne Town Hall, 'for which he drew all the plans, an extraordinary feat for a man of his advanced age' (*MSt* xiv, 1871: 5). Earlier in the year he had superintended the reconstruction of the organ in Trinity College, Cambridge (Cobb 1895: 15). These facts, together with Hill's regular appearance throughout the 1860s as correspondent and signatory are evidence that he continued to be closely involved in the direction of the firm until the end of his life. It is likely, therefore, that it was he who was responsible for the marked change in the character of the firm's organs during the late-1850s. Having pioneered the construction of large ojgans in the 1830s and been instrumental in carrying out the reforms of the 1840s, Hill now, in the 1850s, adapted his style to take account of contemporary taste. Choruses were bolder, basses spoke their notes more promptly, big quint mixtures lent brilliance to the Full Organ; chorus reeds were full-toned and more regular than earlier examples; delicate solo registers proliferated. The construction of the organs changed, too. Spotted metal was occasionally employed; generally, the pipe metal was of better quality and thicker than in the past. Soundboards were more spacious, winding more generous, and the structure of even quite modest instruments acquired a massiveness which was novel. Though Hill's eldest son, Thomas (1822–93), undoubtedly played a part in these developments, and especially so after he became a partner in 1856 or 1857, there is every reason to think that William Hill was himself responsible for initiating this final phase in his career.

Contemporaries noted the changed character of the firm's instruments. When Hill built a 3-manual Nave Organ for York Minster in 1863, a review had this to say:

Taking into account the comparatively limited number of stops . . . it is remarkable that an instrument which is far from being of immense size, should be capable of

395

producing such a powerful body of sound . . . The secret is that the Messrs. Hill have taken advantage of what has been learned in Germany relative to making organs of moderate dimensions loud voiced and powerful, and they have also gained a knowledge as to the best means of furnishing a more abundant supply of wind than has been usual amongst other organ builders in England. The great organ portion of the new instrument is nearly as loud and equally as fine in tone as the same department of the splendid organ belonging to the choir . . .

(*YG* 17 October 1863: 4)

Anyone who hears the same instrument today, standing in the church of St Thomas, Radcliffe, Manchester, cannot doubt that Hill was striving for an exceptional effect to fill the vast nave at York; yet, although the power levels may have been greater, the approach to voicing, scaling and balance is typical of Hill's organs of the 1860s. An account of the St Albans Abbey organ, built in 1861, implies that the new style was established by then:

The great soundboards measure about twelve feet in length, and those of the other departments are constructed on a proportionate and similarly admirable scale, so that nearly all the pipes in the instrument stand immediately over their wind . . . There is a firmness, nervousness, and resonant ring about the whole organ that is eminently satisfactory; and this character extends even to the Choir Organ, the part that in nearly all new English organs is so weak and insignificant, but which in this example, is as lively and spirited as the best specimens to be met with occasionally in old organs.   (*CMR* 1, 1863: 33)

The reference to 'English organs' is significant: the spacious soundboards, generous winding and adoption of quint mixtures, together with the appearance of gedacts, lieblich flötes, lieblich bourdons, violones and violoncellos in Hill's organs all imply that modern German organ-building provided the inspiration for the change of direction.[1]

Following several thin years on either side of 1860, Hill & Son's business picked up, and by the end of the decade output was averaging around 500 stops a year. Hill & Son's *List of principal organs* (1881) is not a complete record and some of the dates it gives are inaccurate, but the impression it conveys of a significant growth in output during the second half of the 1860s is undoubtedly correct (Table 26). The business was still conducted from Elliot's old premises in Tottenham Court, redesignated 261 Euston Road in 1857. Hill may have retained ancillary workshops elsewhere, but the severe constraints imposed by the relatively small site must have become intolerable as business expanded and it comes as no surprise that Thomas Hill moved to a purpose-built factory (York Road, Camden Town) within a year or two of his father's death. No evidence survives of the number of men employed at this time, but, even allowing for a degree of mechanisation, the volume of work would have required perhaps double the numbers employed during the prosperous years of the 1840s.

Frederick Davison's success in winning contracts for many of the most prestigious new instruments of the 1850s, together with the emergence of

Table 26 *Hill & Son, 1856–72: organs built*

Year	Number of organs	Total number of stops
1856	9	173
1857	15	298
1858	7	134
1859	15	238
1860	6	130
1861	10	199
1862	10	179
1863	5	104
1864	12	178
1865	13	220
1866	15	285
1867	13	266
1868	24	499
1869	24	435
1870	22	562
1871	34	615
1872	30	511

Source: Principal Organs built by Messrs. Wm. Hill & Son (1881)

Note The list is not comprehensive. York Minster (1859) was unaccountably omitted but has been included in the calculations recorded in the table. No other major omissions have been identified and the table therefore offers a fairly reliable indication of Hill & Son's output. It includes some reconstructions, but only those sufficiently extensive to be reckoned the equivalent of new organs.

Willis, on the one hand, and the northern builders on the other, meant that Hill was unable to dominate the progressive movement in English organ-building as he had during the years of collaboration with Gauntlett. Nevertheless, his achievements and experience gave him claim to a pre-eminence that few disputed, and the years after 1855 saw a steady flow of large contracts and a number of important ones. The organs for York Minster (1859), King's College, Cambridge (1860), St Albans Abbey (1861), Edinburgh University (1861), Ulster Hall, Belfast (1862), Bath Abbey (1868), St John's College, Cambridge (1869) and Peterborough Cathedral (1870) all date from this era in the firm's stylistic development. Following William Hill's death, his son made some modifications, but he seems to have been a more conservative figure than his father and the characteristics first established in the 1860s persisted throughout his direction of the firm, attaining their fullest expression in the 126-stop scheme for Sydney Town Hall (1890).

A consideration of Hill's work at this period will follow, but first it will be useful to describe two instruments in some detail.

The earliest reference to the 'Music Hall', Belfast, in Hill's Letter Book is dated 5 March 1859, when it was recorded that an estimate had been prepared for the removal of the Panopticon organ (then up for sale) to Belfast (MS 12: 378). Nothing came of this, and in May 1860 Hill drew up a scheme for a new organ of three manuals and forty-eight stops (389). This was to cost £2,000. An enlarged (undated) proposal followed (407), and then in October 1861 a specification closely approximating to that of the organ as it was built appears (402). Subsequent alterations included changes of nomenclature ('Rohr Flute' became 'Lieblich Flote', 'Cremorne' became 'Clarinet') and the addition of three further registers to the Solo (the original scheme provided for tubas 8' and 4', and a harmonic flute 4'). Edmund Chipp, who had been appointed organist, opened the new organ at the end of 1862, and the *Musical World* gave the final specification as follows (XLI, 1863: 5).

Great Organ (C to g³)

Double Open Diapason	16
Open Diapason I	8
Open Diapason II	8
Stopped Diapason (wd)	8
Gamba	8
Quint	5⅓
Principal	4
Harmonic Flute	4
Twelfth	2⅔
Fifteenth	2
Full Mixture	IV
Sharp Mixture	III
Double Trumpet	16
Posaune	8
Trumpet	8
Clarion	4

Swell Organ (C to g³)

Bourdon & Double Diapason (wd & m)	16
Open Diapason	8
Stopped Diapason (wd)	8
Salicional	8
Principal	4
Suabe Flute (wd)	4
Twelfth	2⅔
Fifteenth	2
Full Mixture	IV
Double Trumpet	16
Horn	8

Trumpet	8
Oboe	8
Clarion	4

Choir Organ (C to g³)

Gedact (wd)	16
Cone Gamba	8
Keraulophon (c)	8
Stopped Diapason (wd)	8
Octave	4
Lieblich Flöte	4
Gemshorn Twelfth	2⅔
Flautina	2
Dulciana Mixture	II
Bassoon (c)	16
Clarinet	8

Solo Organ (C to g³)

Lieblich Gedact (wd & m)	8
Harmonic Flute	4
Piccolo	2
Vox Humana (enclosed)	8
Tuba	8

Pedal Organ (C to f¹)

Double Open Diapason (wd)	32
Open Diapason (wd)	16
Violon (wd)	16
Bourdon (wd)	16
Octave	8
Violon (wd)	8
Twelfth	5⅓
Fifteenth	4
Trombone (wd)	16
Clarion	8

Swell to Great
Choir to Great[2]
Solo to Great
Great to Pedal
Swell to Pedal
Choir to Pedal
Solo to Pedal

4 composition pedals to Great & Pedal
3 composition pedals to Swell
Tremulant to Solo
Pneumatic lever to Great and couplers

The organ cost £3,300, which included diapering (since overlaid) on the front pipes. The case is an unprepossessing affair, barely saved from being dubbed a civic pipe-rack by the retention of moulded tower caps reminiscent of Birmingham (Plate 60).

The internal layout is straightforward. The Pedal registers stand on two large slider soundboards behind the outermost flats with the pipes arranged chromatically (basses at the back, trebles at the front). The 32′ is ranged across the back of the organ. The Great is placed centrally, at impost level, on two soundboards: reeds to the rear, flues to the fore. The Choir stands behind the Great and beneath the Swell. The (now) dummy reed resonators which project from the front of the organ are probably relics of 1862 when there is every reason to believe that the tuba was disposed horizontally; the remainder of the Solo Organ would have stood just behind on its own soundboard.

60 The Ulster Hall, Belfast, Hill & Son, 1862. (1978)

Hill & Son rebuilt the organ in 1903. New actions (pneumatic) and a new console were provided and the manual key compasses were extended. The tonal alterations were significant, but not drastic: William Hill's scheme survived largely intact.[3] Following conversion to electro-pneumatic action *c*. 1930, and, as a consequence, years of unreliability, a further reconstruction took place in 1978 by N. P. Mander Ltd.[4]

ST JOHN, HYDE PARK CRESCENT (1865)

Hill's estimate for a new organ for St John's Church, Paddington,[5] was submitted during the first half of 1865. The instrument was to have three manuals and twenty-six stops, and was to stand in the gallery, on either side of the west window (MS 13: 12). He later persuaded the church authorities against dividing the organ (thus saving £30), and obtained approval for certain additions to the specification: a salicional and vox humana on the Swell; violons 16′ and 8′, and a fifteenth on the Pedal; a tremulant and a Swell to Choir coupler. With these alterations, the organ was to cost £830, less £100 allowed for the old organ (12). The stop list published in *The Choir and Musical Record* (IV, 1866: 128) agrees with Hill's records.

Great Organ (C to g³)
Bourdon & Double Diapason	16
Open Diapason	8
Stopped Diapason (wd)	8
Cone Gamba	8
Principal	4
Wald Flute (wd)	4
Twelfth	2⅔
Fifteenth	2
Mixture	IV
Posaune	8

Swell Organ (C to g³)
Bourdon (wd)	16
Open Diapason	8
Stopped Diapason (wd)	8
Salicional (c)	8
Principal	4
Fifteenth	2
Mixture	II
Cornopean	8
Oboe	8
Vox Humana	8

Choir Organ (C to g³)
Dulciana	8

Stopped Diapason (wd)	8
Gemshorn	4
Suabe Flute (wd)	4
Flautina	2
Clarionet	8

Pedal Organ (C to e^1)

Open Diapason (wd)	16
Violone (wd)	16
Bourdon (wd)	16
Violone (wd)	8
Fifteenth	4

Swell to Great
Swell to Choir
Great to Pedal
Swell to Pedal
Choir to Pedal

3 composition pedals to Great
2 composition pedals to Swell
Tremulant [Swell?]

In 1880, Thomas Hill moved the organ to the east end of the north aisle (Plate 61). The Pedal was provided with a new soundboard, the violone 8' being replaced with a metal principal and the fifteenth with a trombone. Other structural alterations were made to adapt the instrument to its new site but there were no further tonal changes (MS 14: 105). Tubular-pneumatic action was introduced in 1925 by Rushworth & Dreaper. Fortunately, lack of funds prevented any wholesale revision of the tonal scheme; although the reeds were revoiced, it would seem that the intention was to restore the original character rather than change it, and the instrument today sounds much as it did in 1865.[6]

STOP LISTS

A comparison of typical stop lists from the 1860s with others from the 1840s speedily illuminates some of the changes that had taken place. Gone are the huge 2-manual schemes, like Cornhill and St Mary-at-Hill; gone, too, are the small mixtures, 16' mutations and other novelties (oboe-flutes, corno-flutes, cromorne-flutes) which had either failed to catch on or had already fallen from favour. In 3-manual schemes the Great was relatively smaller, and the Swell larger than in the 1840s. It (the Swell) was usually full-compass and might – especially in a church organ – have as many stops, or even more stops, than the Great (St Albans is an example of the former,

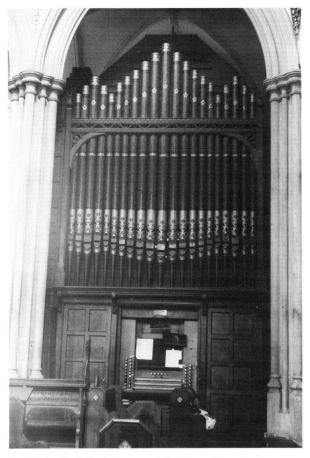

61 St John, Hyde Park Crescent, Hill & Son, 1865 and 1880.

Peterborough Cathedral of the latter). Pedal upperwork would usually be sacrificed to make way for another 16′ stop (a violone or bourdon), though the largest organs still had complete Pedal choruses with mixtures and mutations (York, Melbourne). Posaunes and trumpets, cornopeans and horns continued to fill the ranks of the chorus reeds, but hautboys had become oboes and cremonas clarinets. Alongside the familiar names, others, of more recent importation, assumed a new importance.

There was, for example, the vox humana. Hill had made one for the Panopticon where it was placed in the Solo Organ. Despite Smart's criticisms of this first attempt (*MW* XXXII, 1854: 534–5) the stop appeared shortly afterwards in the organs for Lincoln's Inn Chapel (1856) and All Saints, Margaret Street (1859), and thereafter became a regular feature of Hill's larger 3-manual organs. Its popularity declined after the 1860s and it was frequently ejected to make way for an additional string, usually a celeste. The latter was not unknown in Hill's practice before 1870, but remained rare. There was an unenclosed vox angelica of two ranks in the Solo Organ at the Panopticon, and an early proposal for its use in a church organ is found in an estimate of 1854 for Lancaster Priory. There, it was to have been on the Choir. Although no place was found for it in the 69-stop scheme for York Minster (1859), future developments were remarkably anticipated by the inclusion of a vox angelica in the Swell Organ for St Asaph Cathedral in the same year. The Swell at St John's College, Cambridge (1869) also had one, but undulating registers were not common in William Hill's time, and, when provided, were usually to be found on the Choir Organ (Nottingham, Mechanics Hall, 1869; Church of the Holy Name, Manchester, 1871) or, in 4-manual schemes, the Solo (Trinity College, Cambridge; Melbourne Town Hall).

Both the vox humana and vox angelica were of French inspiration. Harmonic flutes came out of the same stable and slowly established themselves during the 1850s and 1860s. Hill used them most extensively in concert organs (Panopticon, Belfast, Melbourne) but they also appeared in large church organs: on the Great at Montreal Cathedral (1858), York Minster and St Albans, and in the Solo Organs at York and Trinity College, Cambridge. By the end of the 1860s, Hill's characteristic Great wald-flute was often obliged to give place to a harmonic flute.

Having adopted gemshorns and conical gambas, and introduced various other registers of (apparently) German origin during the 1840s, Hill may possibly have been responsible for stimulating the interest in contemporary German organ-building that now, in the 1850s, forced English builders to consider going further in their imitation of the German example. At Lincoln's Inn Chapel, in 1856, he provided his Choir Organ with a stopped diapason 'scaled according to the extremely small dimensions generally used in Germany' (*MW* xxxiv, 1856: 787), and although English nomenclature was retained on this occasion, this early gedact was soon followed by others, correctly named. York Minster and King's College, Cambridge, both had gedacts on the Choir, and by the mid-1860s a gedact frequently displaced the stopped diapason as the conventional Choir 8′ flute.[7] To accompany it, Hill adopted the lieblich flöte. This was a soft 4′ flute which sometimes (though by no means always) took the place of a suabe-flute. One of its earliest appearances was in the York Minster Nave Organ (1863). The surviving example in Dr Monk's organ (1866), now at Washington, is a stopped metal register, but it may also have been made of wood.

Another German importation, the rohr flute, was less common at this period. It first appears in an estimate of 1855, then in the Swell at St Albans. It is seldom found after this until the 1870s. Similarly, the spitz-flute put in an occasional appearance. Dr Monk seems to have favoured it: one was included in the Great of the scheme he prepared for Sydney Cathedral, and his own house organ had a spitz-flöte on the Swell (both 1866).

Hill continued to use 3-rank tierce mixtures for organs of average size and smaller during the 1860s. Like other builders, he may have questioned the wisdom of retaining tierces in an instrument tuned to equal temperament, and by the end of his life, the firm had begun to eliminate them above the middle of the tenor octave. The composition of the Great Mixture in the organ for Holy Trinity, Sydenham (1866) may be compared with the Kidderminster and Hulme composition of the previous decade (above, p. 243).

C	17.19.22
g	15.19.22
b¹	8.12.15

However, the most important departure from Hill's earlier practice was the introduction of big quint mixtures of four or five ranks, designed to complement the massive flue chorus for which he strove with his weighty 16′ and 8′ diapasons. In the largest organs, two were provided, usually designated 'Full Mixture' and 'Sharp Mixture', as Hopkins had proposed. York offered one of the earliest examples (Appendix 1, pp. 495–7) with, in addition to quint mixtures of four and three ranks respectively, a tierce mixture, a glockenspiel[8] and a (solo) cornet. This array of mixturework was exceptional. More typical was the Ulster Hall (below, p. 410). Melbourne Town Hall may have been similar (Appendix 1, pp. 497–9), and also, with slight variations to take account of a different disposition of ranks, St Albans, Bath Abbey and St John's College, Cambridge. In smaller organs a single mixture had to serve both functions. This was less flexible. In the organ for Sydney Cathedral, for example, the 5-rank mixture on the Great encompassed the same range of pitches as the two Belfast mixtures combined (15.19.22.26.29). Five ranks was unusual; four ranks, as at Hyde Park Crescent (below, p. 409), was more common, and the composition there is probably typical.

The treatment of the Swell mixture varied. In the Hyde Park Crescent and Sydenham organs the mixtures consist of two ranks commencing at 19.22 and breaking back to 12.15 in the treble octave. In larger organs, however, the Swell mixture was designed along similar lines to the main Great mixture: that in the Ulster Hall organ has a starting composition of higher pitch than the Full Mixture on the Great, but in the treble, the two mixtures are virtually identical (below, p. 410). A further variation is to be seen in the Sydney Cathedral scheme, where Monk specified an echo dulciana cornet of five ranks[9] but provided no conventional chorus mixture. Small mixtures were still included in the Choir Organs of the largest instruments; the dulciana mixture in the Belfast organ probably had a starting composition of 19.22,[10] and there were similar registers in the York and Melbourne organs.

It is possible to see how these various innovations affected the design of Hill's organs by studying specifications of the period. The reconstruction of the York organ in 1859 was a significant moment for William Hill, offering an opportunity to apply the lessons learnt during the 1840s to the remodelling of one of his earliest and most ambitious instruments. The establishment of orthodox compasses, the modification of the scales and the elimination of most of the duplication were essential features of the scheme, and Hill revised the main choruses to include adequate sub-unison tone, mutations and mixtures (Appendix 1, pp. 495–7). Outstanding features include the huge Great and Pedal divisions (the latter, with nineteen stops, was the most comprehensive of Hill's career), the extensive provision of reeds in the Swell and the placing of the tubas in a horizontal position, pointing down the nave, where they achieved an effect that was both musically and visually dramatic. Inevitably, the York scheme was influenced by the need to retain much of the existing pipework. There were no such constraints at St Albans (though a single register survived from an earlier organ). The stop-list (Appendix 1, pp. 499–500) gives a good indication of the way things were going. The Swell is as large as the Great and includes a 16' reed chorus. Each division has a string register (a feature which had appeared earlier in concert organs, like Kidderminster) and where, ten years before, Hill might have been expected to provide a complete Pedal chorus with a mixture, there are now four 16' registers and a solitary 8'. The manual compass of C–g³ would by the mid-1860s become established as standard for all but the smallest church organs, though the pedal compass of C–f¹ continued to be reserved for instruments in which there was an attempt to give some degree of independence to the division. This was the case at the Ulster Hall, though the absence of a mixture in this 10-stop Pedal Organ is a sign of changing priorities, at least for concert organs, and the provision of violones at 16' and 8' pitch establishes a characteristic feature of Hill schemes of the 1860s.[11] The secular calling of this particular instrument is most apparent in the stop lists of the Choir and Solo Organs. Hill provided a complete chorus on the Choir, from sub-unison to mixture, incorporating several registers of German inspiration and two imitative reeds. The Solo had flutes at 8', 4' and 2', with an enclosed vox humana and a tuba. The modest dimensions of this department may be interestingly compared with the same division in the Melbourne Town Hall organ (Appendix 1, pp. 497–9); this 13-stop Solo Organ was of similar proportions to those found in Willis's concert instruments and would have satisfied the most ambitious player of the period. Returning, finally, to church organs: Hyde Park Crescent is fairly typical of 3-manual schemes from the mid-1860s. The retention of a wald-flute on the Great, and the use of 1840's nomenclature for the 8' and 4' flutes on the Choir is a conservative feature, but the proportions and intentions of the stop list are altogether characteristic, with Swell and Great of similar size, an accompanimental Choir division and a Pedal conceived primarily as a bass. In larger church organs, the dividing line between the ecclesiastical and the secular was becoming more difficult to draw. The stop list for the Church of the Holy Name, Manchester, drawn up in March 1870, could serve as the basis for a concert instrument (Appendix 1, pp. 500–1); with the addition of a small Solo Organ, the resemblance to Belfast or Melbourne would be irresistible.

PIPEWORK

The character of Hill's metal pipework changed in the years succeeding 1855. In part this was due to the employment of pipe metal containing a higher proportion of tin than had been usual in the 1840s (above, p. 237), but there was an alteration in the appearance of the pipes, too, with the scored mouths with pressed-in upper lips, looking a little like French mouths, giving way to a less distinct formation of the upper lip. (Paradoxically, front pipes with French mouths became increasingly common in Hill's work at about this time.) As well as improving the quality of his plain metal, Hill began to cast it in thicker sheets; this had tonal implications, and also ensured that the pipes were better able to withstand the rigours of cone-tuning. Most of the pipework in the Belfast and Hyde Park Crescent instruments is of this sort. It has not been possible to analyse a sample: the proportion of tin to lead is probably around 1:3.

Spotted metal was sometimes used, either for reed resonators (York Minster, Ulster Hall) or entire instruments (Edinburgh University, Sydney Cathedral), though in the latter case, zinc might be used for pipes below 4' and for the largest reeds (Melbourne Town Hall).

There was little variation in wind pressures. Most organs remained on a single pressure, usually 3" (All Saints, Margaret Street; Hyde Park Crescent; Sydenham). The Pedal might be given a slightly increased pressure of wind (as at Belfast, if the pressures are original), and, of course, the occasional tuba would be on 10" or 12". The only significant innovation was the provision of a distinct pressure of wind for the chorus reeds of the Great, and sometimes the Swell, in the largest instruments. Hill did this first in the Panopticon organ, then at St George's Hall, Bradford, and then at York, in each instance applying the higher pressure to the Great reeds.[12] If the application of a higher pressure to the Swell reeds at Belfast is an original feature it may qualify as the earliest example, though no doubt Hill increasingly took advantage of the possibilities offered by a separate reed sound-board in his largest organs.

The voicing of Hill pipework from the 1860s differs significantly from his earlier practice. Languids are thicker (2 to 2.5 mm for the 1′ pipes at Belfast) with a bevel of between 30° and 45° out of the vertical, though tending to the former. The flues are notably wide by comparison with the 1840s: part, no doubt, of Hill's attempt to get more wind to his pipes. The lower lip is slightly dubbed in the bigger pipes. Nicking is not consistent from one instrument to another. That found in the Belfast organ is a development from Hill's earlier usage: frequent light nicks (around twenty in the 1′ pipes of the 16′, 8′ and 4′ registers) taking the form of small v-shaped incisions in the languids of the larger pipes. A different approach appears in the Radcliffe and Hyde Park Crescent organs. Here, Hill was striving for monumental flue choruses able to fill (in the first case) the nave of York Minster and (in the second) a large galleried church accommodating an extensive congregation. The quint mixtures would provide the necessary brilliance. Beneath them, Hill wanted a massive foundation, and the nicking (frequent and deep v-shaped incisions) was calculated to assist this. It is curious that Hill did not use the same technique in the Belfast organ, where the same considerations must have applied, though the slightly earlier date may be the explanation. There are differences, too, in the mouthing of these instruments. At Belfast, the mouths are quarter mouths, cut up a quarter (rather more for the open diapason 1 and principal). The mouths at Hyde Park Crescent, however, are consistently closer to two-ninths of the circumference than to a quarter, and, with the exception of the open diapason, are cut up around one third.

Details of scalings at Belfast and Hyde Park Crescent will be found in Tables 27 to 29. The usual caveat must be entered against drawing firm conclusions from highly selective data, but one or two points may be tentatively made. In both instruments the scaling pattern is similar to that observed in Hill's organs of the 1840s. The upperwork (principals, twelfths, fifteenths and mixtures) is all of the same scale, with no distinction being made in the treatment of the mutations. In the Belfast organ the first open diapason is two pipes larger in scale than the upperwork (and the double open diapason is much the same). At Hyde Park Crescent, however, the open diapason is at least five pipes larger than the rest of the chorus, with the exception of the 16′ (which is halfway between the two). This is further evidence for Hill's wish to provide a substantial foundation for his chorus in this particular instrument. In the Ulster Hall organ, the Swell chorus registers are one, or possibly two pipes smaller than the corresponding stops on the Great; unfortunately, the Swell at Hyde Park Crescent is inaccessible, but the contemporary instrument built for Holy Trinity, Sydenham, suggests that Hill adopted a similar policy for scaling the Swell in his church organs.

Table 27 *St John, Hyde Park Crescent,*
1865: pipe scales

GREAT ORGAN: DIAPASON CHORUS

	c	c¹	c²	c³
Double Open Diapason	n.a.	82*	48.5	29.5
Open Diapason	102*	55	34	20.5
Principal	45	27	16.5	11
Twelfth	32.5	20.5	13	8.5
Fifteenth	27	16	10.5	7.5
Mixture I	20.5	16.5	13	16.5
II	17	12.5	10.5	10.5
III	14	10.5	8	9
IV	10.5	7	7	8

	Composition:		
	C	19.22.26.29
	C♯	15.19.22.26
	C♯¹	12.15.19.22
	C♯²	1. 8.12.15

WOOD FLUTES

Gt Stopped Diapason (a)

		Internal		*Sides*
	c	52	× 65*	10
	c¹	30	× 38	8
	c²	20	× 25	5
	c³	10	× 14	4

Gt Wald Flute (b)

	c	35	× 47*	7
	c¹	22	× 27	5
	c²	15	× 18	5
	c³	9.5	× 12.5	3.5

Ch Stopped Diapason (c)

	c	47	× 59*	8
	c¹	28	× 36	6
	c²	18	× 22	5
	c³	10	× 13	4

Ch Suabe Flute (d)

	c	27.5	× 35	6
	c¹	18	× 24	4.5
	c²	12	× 17	4
	c³	8.5	× 12	3.5

(a) The stoppers are pierced from g.
(b) The bottom octave is stopped and pierced.
(c) The stoppers are pierced from g.
(d) The bottom octave is stopped and pierced.

The scales of the wooden flutes at Hyde Park Crescent are given (Table 27) and these may be compared with earlier examples. Conical registers in this instrument (cone gamba) and the Sydenham organ (cone gamba,

Table 28 *Ulster Hall, Belfast, 1862: scales of Great and Swell flue choruses*

GREAT ORGAN

	C	c	c¹	c²	c³
Double Open Diapason	n.a.	n.a.	94	53	30.5
Open Diapason I	n.a.	93*	54.5	30	21
Open Diapason II	n.a.	80	47.5	28	18
Principal	86	50	29.5	19	12
Twelfth	62	37	22	13.5	9.5
Fifteenth	51	30	19	12	9
Full Mixture I	50	29.5	22.5	18.5	18
II	37.5	22.5	19	14	11.5
III	30	18.5	14	12	9.5
IV	22	14	12	10	8.5
Sharp Mixture I	29.5	18	14	11.5	12
II	22	14	12	9.5	9.5
III	18.5	12	9.5	8	8.5

	Compositions:	C	15.19.22.26	22.26.29
		c♯	12.15.19.22	19.22.26
		c♯¹	8.12.15.19	15.19.22
		c♯²	1. 8.12.15	8.12.15

SWELL ORGAN

	c	c¹	c²	c³
Double Diapason	n.a.	80*	47.5	27
Open Diapason	n.a.	52	30.5	19
Principal	47.5	28	18	11.5
Fifteenth	28	18.5	12	8.5
Full Mixture I	21	18	18	18.5
II	18	13	13	11.5
III	13	12	11.5	9.5
IV	12	9.5	9.5	8

	Composition:	C	19.22.26.29
		c♯	15.19.22.26
		c♯¹	8.12.15.19
		c♯²	5. 8.12.15

Wind pressures (as before 1978 reconstruction)

Great and Swell fluework, Choir Organ	3″
Pedal fluework	3½″
Swell reeds, Solo Organ	4″
Great and Pedal reeds	4¾″
Solo Tuba	12″

Table 29 *Diameters of reed resonators: Ulster Hall, Belfast, and St John, Hyde Park Crescent*

	C	c	c¹	c²	c³
Ulster Hall					
Gt Double Trumpet	177	126	89	63	51
Posaune	177	126	89	63	n.o.
Trumpet	110	76	57	44	n.o
Clarion	89	63	51	n.o.	flue
Hyde Park Crescent					
Gt Posaune	146*	101	83	63	n.a.

gemshorn) are virtually identical in scaling and treatment to the Kidderminster registers of the same name (Table 23).

Little technical information can be offered concerning Hill's reeds during this period as no examples have been available for detailed measurements in recent years. The diameters of the Great resonators in the Belfast and Hyde Park Crescent organs are given in Table 29, but beyond indicating Hill's retention of a powerful posaune as his standard chorus reed in this department, they are unenlightening. In the Swell, horns became more common (perhaps a sign of the growing taste for opaque tone) though the cornopean was still often found. Open shallots were still usual for chorus reeds.

14

Henry Willis

Beside William Hill, Henry Willis (Plate 62) appears a thoroughly modern figure. He was a fearless innovator, untinged with that characteristic English retrospection, which at its best nurtures respect for inherited principles, and at worst degenerates into simple nostalgia. Not that Hill was a mindless conservative. But many of the battles that he fought were won before the younger man had established himself as an independent builder, and with the growing tendency during the 1850s and 1860s to introduce mechanical and tonal features of the most advanced concert organs into church instruments, Hill had only limited sympathy. He therefore appears something of a conservative by the standards of the rising generation of builders in these decades. Willis was no conservative. In the mechanism, voicing and use of the organ he was an unapologetic innovator who had scant patience with a more cautious approach. The string of patents that he took out between 1851 and 1893, together with the not infrequent complaints about his cavalier attitude to old pipework when reconstructing organs[1] serve to substantiate his title.

Despite the eminence that Willis enjoyed during his lifetime and subsequently, he awaits both a definitive biography and a detailed study of his work. Even a reliable job list is lacking. F. G. Edwards described him as 'tenaciously holding a strong belief in his own powers', and although he went on to add that 'Mr Willis is entirely free from a merely conceited opinion of himself' (1898: 302) it is clear that Willis's strong character did nothing to secure him sympathetic reporting in the musical press, at least during his earlier years. It is consequently difficult to be sure of the impression that Willis, and Willis's organs, made on his contemporaries in the 1850s and 1860s.

Some correspondence in the *Ecclesiologist* (xxv–xxvi, 1864–5) between partisans respectively of Schulze and Willis, with interventions by a third party, helps a little, though embattled positions and acknowledged preju-

62 Henry Willis (1821–1901). (1898)

dices scarcely promote an objective discussion. Much of the debate revolved around the legitimacy of what one correspondent termed the 'mechanical perfection' of the modern organ, and another 'the clever mechanical tricki-ness of the present day' (xxv: 80, 131). For the first writer, Willis's organs were exemplars of all that might be accomplished in the way of mechanical refinement, and despite his grumbles about mechanical 'trickery', the Schulze partisan was forced to admit that Willis was 'a very clever and ingenious mechanic with also an artistic ear for tone' (xxv: 130). None could deny, then or now, that Willis's achievements as an engineer were outstanding: in his application of pneumatic action in its various forms to the design of organ actions, he revolutionised the art of organ-building. The question upon which organists were divided (at least in the earlier part of Willis's career) was whether or not this was a legitimate development. Willis's critic feared that organ-builders were devoting their energies to mechanical innovation at the cost of proper attention to the tonal development of their instruments. For him, Schulze, with his disregard for mechanical novelties and his painstaking labours on the voicing and finishing of the organ at Doncaster was the ideal (xxv: 21–2). Using traditional methods he secured a quality and power of tone that easily eclipsed the St George's Hall organ (which obviously embodied all that this correspondent loathed in contemporary English organ-building). The third writer took up a different point. He had no time for a reactionary approach to mechanical improvement: 'It is generally found that good mechanism and good tone go together, as examples of which I need only refer to the instruments of Cavaillé and Willis' (xxv: 135). Far from accusing contemporary builders of neglecting the tonal development of the instrument, he was concerned that the current fashion for orchestral innovation in the design of concert organs was beginning to affect church instruments. Interestingly, he cites Willis's organs in this connection:

I must be excused for saying that the orchestral organs of [Willis] are more successful than his church instruments, all of which partake of this orchestral character from the excessive brilliancy of the chorus work and reeds. This may be allowable when we come to erect grand west-end organs in our cathedrals . . . but bright mixtures and powerful reeds do not support, but drown, voices . . .

(xxv: 135)

The writer was not hostile to Willis: indeed, he described him as his 'favourite English builder', so these comments are all the more valuable. The same may be said of his remarks (in the same vein) concerning Willis's earliest cathedral organs:

The Winchester is certainly the best of our cathedral organs, but there the proportion of reeds is less than usual in Mr. Willis's works, in one of which the reeds form more than *one third* of the sounding stops. The Wells (and still more the Carlisle) organ is wanting in delicate flue stops: when in S. Martin's Hall [being exhibited prior to erection at Carlisle] it was of course used for solo playing, not accompaniment; and I recommend J. C. J. [one of the other correspondents] to inquire whether the Dean and Chapter of Wells were satisfied to exchange the rich and mellow . . . diapasons of Schmidt and Green for the vigour of their new instrument.   (135)

The remarks concerning the lack of 'delicate' registers are illuminating. To twentieth-century ears, Willis's organs are not deficient in soft accompanimental stops, but it seems that his contemporaries, comparing his work with that of other mid-nineteenth-century builders, concluded that Willis was setting out on a new course. It is true that Willis's registers generally are scaled and voiced to speak directly and with a full tone (possibly this is what contemporaries meant by 'purity' of tone); this was a reflection of the demands of the concert organist for stops that could imitate the technical efficiency and tonal refinement of modern orchestral instruments. As a result, even the softer voices in a Willis Choir or Swell division stand in a different relationship to a choir of singers from that of the more discreet stops characteristic of the older generation of builders.

The correspondence in the *Ecclesiologist* makes it clear that Willis's organs were at the centre of the debate concerning the extent to which the concert organ should be permitted to influence the church instrument. The subject aroused strong passions. Hearing, in 1879, that Willis had submitted a scheme for a reconstruction of the organ in Westminster Abbey[2] Dr Monk felt compelled to protest.

Is it true (I hope and trust *not*) that the Abbey Organ is about to be given up to the same treatment which has befallen Wells, Salisbury, New Coll., Oxford, and a few other famous old – but most unfortunate – Organs?

I trust not: and hope, most devoutly, that, as against Noise, 'Music' may once more 'win the day'.

Being dead against the modern fashion of *forcing* tone, at cost of *Quality*; of changing the mellow, rich, and sober tones of our English Cathedral Organs of the best type, into the likeness of German and French Instruments of the most pronounced kind; and of producing a screaming, brawling Organ, neither suited for a reputable Street, or tolerable as a make-shift Military Band, – I most devoutly hope that the Abbey Organ – always renowned among its compeers – is not about to be sacrificed to the mad, and reckless, demand for more noise, that is so rife at the present (little) moment of time.

But I have another and deeper quarrel with this tendency.

Our Cathedral Organs are eminently, and chiefly, for accompanimental purposes; they should support, enfold, and dignify the voices of the Choir. All this our old, and best instruments of modern build, most perfectly accomplish. But not so the Willisean monster; which (not to speak of the Horror in the Albert Hall) has found entrance into several of our Cathedrals – alack the day!

This Machine, with its heavy wind-pressures and obstreperous style of voicing, is totally unfit to accompany an average Choir; or, generally, to do aught but stifle and drown it. Cathedral Choirs are notoriously small and miserably inadequate to the requirements of the noble spaces in which they are placed; were they usually formed of *hundreds* of voices . . . there then might be a shred of propriety in the present rage for Stentor-like Stops, and Brobdingnagian Organs; but – as things really are, the introduction of the noisy, blatant, coarse style which is now too much puffed off, and admired, is, to my feeling – and I venture to say in the judgement of many other musicians of far more weight than my poor self – a thing to be greatly – deeply – deplored.[3]

Monk's impassioned epistle is not quoted as a piece of objective criticism; its caustic tone is too sustained for it to be of much value in that respect. But it is incontrovertible evidence that Willis's contemporaries regarded his work as marking a new departure, and that, in the church sphere, at least, it was deeply controversial. Monk's criticisms pivot on the unsuitability of Willis's cathedral organs for choir accompaniment (though it is plain that he finds their whole aesthetic vulgar) and he – like the writer in the *Ecclesiologist* – complains particularly that they overpower the singers and lack the resources to 'support, enfold, and dignify' the choral singing. It is a criticism that is hard to refute. Increase of volume was undoubtedly one of Willis's objectives: he placed the 'diapasons' of the 1862 Exhibition organ on 5″ wind pressure, and claimed that it could be made 'the most powerful instrument in the world' (*Eccl* xxv: 136; xxvi: 114). In providing organs for vast auditoriums such as the Alexandra Palace and the Albert Hall, sheer volume was a necessary preoccupation, but it was less evidently so in the case of a cathedral such as St Paul's, where Willis applied similar techniques to the attainment of power and purity of tone (below, p. 436).

   In evolving a style Willis absorbed a variety of influences. He visited France in 1848 and 1849, meeting Cavaillé-Coll and Barker (Sumner 1955: 16). Thereafter, aspects of the contemporary French organ found expression in his own instruments, but seldom in their original form. The prominence of reeds in Willis's schemes is an example, but although his reeds, like Cavaillé's, dominate the full choruses the treatment is quite different, Willis preferring to use closed shallots, weighted tongues in the bass, and resonators of natural rather than harmonic length.[4] This produced a closer, more controlled, though no less powerful tone than Cavaillé's practice, and, like it, depended upon the application of relatively high pressures. More generally, the smooth, even tone of Willis's organs (flues and reeds alike) is surely a direct allusion to Cavaillé's style, and, in his flutes, Willis took full advantage of the harmonic system as a means of attaining 'purity' of tone. Mechanically, too, the debt was fundamental. Though invented by an Englishman, the pneumatic lever was first applied successfully in French organs, and it was in these instruments no doubt that Willis first saw its possibilities. Again, he made the invention his own, through his improvements to its design and his exploration of its potential uses, but Cavaillé's work was the starting point. Ventils he also used. Characteristically, he went one better by devising his own system for controlling the registers of the various divisions, but he continued to make use of ventils throughout the period under discussion, and evidently regarded them as a useful adjunct to his combination pistons. Indeed, the French influences were still powerful at the end of this period: the close resemblances between the Great of Willis's Albert Hall organ and the *Grand-Orgue* of Cavaillé-Coll's instrument in St-Sulpice, Paris (1863) cannot be explained as mere coincidence (Sumner 1955: 33–4).

Willis's work reveals other stylistic debts: to Schulze (gedacts, strings) and, of course, to the English tradition in which he was brought up by John Gray. But although this rightly implies that there was an element of eclecticism in Willis's approach, it should not be allowed to obscure his originality. William Hill had been responsible for innovations of the utmost importance in the evolution of the English organ, but tonally his instruments retained strong stylistic links with the builders of the eighteenth and early-nineteenth centuries; this was one reason why he was content to re-use old pipework when its condition merited such a course. Willis, though, created a new style, in which scaling, voicing, wind pressures and regulation conspired to create a different tonal ethos and to express a new concept of the relationship between the various parts of the whole. This in itself was highly significant, but in association with Willis's consummate skills as an engineer, it led to the emergence of a new type of instrument: the English romantic organ. This was Henry Willis's achievement. His great concert organs (Liverpool, Alexandra Palace, Albert Hall) were monumental accomplishments of a rare mechanical and musical imagination; they (and to a lesser extent, his church organs) establish his claim to be reckoned among the great artist-engineers of the Victorian era.

Before turning to a more detailed consideration of Willis's work it will be helpful to look at three instruments which cast light on the evolution of his style.

WINCHESTER CATHEDRAL, 1854

Following the Great Exhibition, Willis's organ was offered for sale and was eventually secured for Winchester Cathedral on the advice of Dr S. S. Wesley, the Organist. It cost the considerable sum of £2,500, which may be compared with £687 for Hill's Worcester Cathedral organ (1842) and £3,050 for the Panopticon organ (1853).

No doubt considerations of both cost and space precluded the possibility of re-erecting the Exhibition organ at Winchester without alteration and Willis was obliged to reduce the scheme from the original seventy stops (Appendix 1, pp. 453–5) to forty-eight. This probably necessitated new soundboards, and the interior of the organ would have been completely re-planned to fit into Blore's existing case. The excisions from the 1851 scheme are informative. Wesley was able to make some economies by eliminating most of the duplication in the specification, but he then chose to retain complete choruses in each division (apart from the Solo, which was anyway an addition) at the cost of strings, flutes and imitative reeds. The organ was opened on 3 June 1854 and finally completed in November of that year.

There is some doubt about details of the scheme. An account of the instrument as it stood in November 1854, apparently supplied by Willis himself, is entered into the Chapter Acts, but it does not altogether agree with the version in the 1855 edition of Hopkins & Rimbault.[5] The Winchester account is as follows (Matthews 1975: 11–13).

Specifications of the contents of the Organ now standing in the Cathedral at Winchester, November 28th, 1854.

The Instrument consists of four rows of Keys, each from C.C. to G in alt and two Octaves and a fifth of Pedals. The Great Organ contains Thirteen stops, viz.:

1.	Double Diapason (open, metal)	16 ft.
2.	Open Diapason (open, metal)	8 ft.
3.	Open Diapason (open, metal)	8 ft.
4.	Stopped Diapason (Claribella Treble)	8 ft.
5.	Principal	4 ft.
6.	Principal	4 ft.
7.	Twelfth	3 ft.
8.	Fifteenth	2 ft.
9.	Sesquialtera (3 ranks)	
10.	Mixture (3 ranks)	
11.	Trumpet	8 ft.
12.	Trombone	8 ft.
13.	Clarion	4 ft.

The Pedal Organ contains eight stops, viz.:

1.	Double Double Diapason (open, wood)	32 ft.
2.	Double Diapason (wood)	16 ft.
3.	Violone (open, metal)	16 ft.
4.	Octave	8 ft.
5.	Super Octave	4 ft.
6.	Sesquialtera or Mixture (3 ranks)	
7.	Trombone	16 ft.
8.	Tromba	8 ft.

The Swell Organ contains thirteen stops, viz.:

1.	Double Diapason (lower Octave closed)	16 ft.
2.	Open Diapason	8 ft.
3.	Stopped Diapason	8 ft.
4.	Flute (closed, wood)	4 ft.
5.	Principal	4 ft.
6.	Twelfth	3 ft.
7.	Fifteenth	2 ft.
8.	Sesquialtera (3 ranks)	
9.	Mixture (3 ranks)	
10.	Trombone	16 ft.
11.	Trumpet or Ophicleide	8 ft.
12.	Hautboy	8 ft.
13.	Clarion	4 ft.

The Choir Organ contains nine stops, viz.:

1.	Open Diapason	8 ft.
2.	Dulciana	8 ft.

3.	Stopped Diapason	8 ft.
4.	Principal	4 ft.
5.	Flute (open, wood)	4 ft.
6.	Fifteenth	2 ft.
7.	Mixture (3 ranks)	
8.	Cremona	8 ft.
9.	Oboe Orchestral (from Middle C)	8 ft.

The Solo Organ contains six stops, viz.:

1.	Double Dulciana	16 ft.
2.	Viol di Gamba	8 ft.
3.	Flute (Metal, Harmonic)	4 ft.
4.	Picolo [sic] (Metal, Harmonic)	2 ft.
5.	Corno de [sic] Bassetto	8 ft.
6.	Oboe (Orchestral from Middle C)	8 ft.

The Couplers or Mechanical stops are:

1. Choir to Pedals
2. Great to Pedals
3. Swell to Pedals
4. Swell to Great
5. Choir to Great

The Swell Organ is completely prepared for another Reed Stop of eight feet on the light pressure of Air and also by removing the plate of 4 ft. for either an open Diapason or Dulciana. The Solo Organ is also prepared for two other Stops, the draw stops of which, together with that for the Reed Stop of eight feet in the swell are left blank on the Ivory – The Pedal Organ sound boards are prepared for another Reed Stop of four feet complete, excepting the draw stop. The Pneumatic Lever is applied in its most perfect form to the Great Organ Manuals and to a portion of the Swell Organ in its original form.

The Couplers on the Manuals are brought into action by this machine without adding to the weight of touch.

The Wind is supplied by two large Bellows, one having four feeders, the other two; these are blown by three lever handles, there is also a third bellows or reservoir receiving its supply from either of two handles which propel the Wind to all portions of the Instrument. The Pneumatic Combination movement is applied in its elaborate form to the Great and Choir Organs each having six changes and there are besides these, three composition Pedals to the Pedal Organ, two of which act upon the Great Organ combination movement, producing by one effort, a Piano or Forte upon both Organs.   Henry Willis

The principal differences in the Hopkins & Rimbault specification (HRI: 547) concern the Solo Organ, which has harmonic flutes at 8′ and 4′, the piccolo, orchestral hautboy and corno di bassetto of the Chapter Acts scheme, and then a horn 8′. The Pedal has a double dulciana instead of the violone, and there is no orchestral oboe on the Choir (this may, in any case, be a copyist's error), but the remaining differences are minor ones of nomenclature. It is impossible to account for the revision of the Solo Organ stop list: Hopkins may have got hold of an earlier draft which was subsequently revised, or Willis may have made alterations shortly after the completion of the instrument.

The organ has been reconstructed on various occasions.[6] Some of the 1851 pipework has survived (though not without alteration) and when the most recent work was undertaken, it was possible, through the courtesy of Harrison & Harrison, to inspect it. The builders were also most helpful in supplying full details of the extant reeds. This information is summarised in Tables 30 and 31.

Table 30 *Winchester Cathedral: fluework*

Scales of some registers from the 1854 organ, formerly in Willis's organ for the Great Exhibition (1851)

Great Organ

	C	c	c^1	c^2	c^3
Double Open Diapason			86	48	28
Open Diapason I	168	90.5	50	29.75	18
Open Diapason II	143	82.5	46.5	27.5	n.o.
Principal I	86	48.5	28.5	17.25	11.5
Principal II	76	44	25.5	15.75	11.5

NB These registers bear the same stop names in the present organ following the reconstruction of 1988.

Table 31 *Winchester Cathedral: reeds*

Details of reeds surviving from the 1854 organ, formerly in Willis's organ for the Great Exhibition (1851)

Great Double Trumpet 16' (1854: Trombone 8')

	1	2	3	4	5	6	7	8
c	88.5	17.5	8	9.5	38	8	2248	89
c^1	54	14	8	6.25	25.5	6.25	1105	73
c^2	39.5	9.5	6.25	6.25	16	5	539	57
c^3	31.5	8	4	5.5	14	4	257	48

Great Trumpet 8'

	1	2	3	4	5	6	7	8
C	95	19	9.5	10	31.5	8.5	2133	95
c	57	12.5	6.25	8	20.5	6.25	1028	73
c^1	44	10	5.5	5.5	17.5	5.5	597	60
c^2	33	8	4	5.5	14	4	260	52.5
c^3	25.5	7	3	5	11	4	n.a.	n.a.

Great Clarion 4'

	1	2	3	4	5	6	7	8
C	55.5	12.5	7	7	22	5.5		
c	39.5	9.5	5.5	6.25	16	5		
c^1	31.5	8.5	4	5.5	12.5	4	n.o.	
c^2	25.5	7	4	5	11	2.5		
c^3	flues							

Swell Contra Posaune 16' (1854: Trombone 16')

	1	2	3	4	5	6	7	8
C	152	28.5	14	16	54	12.5	n.a.	120
c	92	16	8	8.5	35	7	2191	95
c¹	50.5	12.5	7	7	24	5.5	1079	73
c²	41	9.5	5	5.5	19	4	533	58
c³	31.5	7.75	4	5	14	4	254	51

Swell Cornopean (1854: 'Trumpet or Ophicleide')

	1	2	3	4	5	6	7	8
C	95	20.5	11	11	33.5	8.5	n.a.	102
c	55.5	14	7.75	7.75	22	6.25	1085	76
c¹	41	11	6.25	6.25	17.25	5.5	546	67
c²	31.5	8.5	5	5	12.5	3	n.o.	n.o.
c³	25.5	6.25	4	5	12.5	3	n.o.	n.o.

Swell Clarion 4'

	1	2	3	4	5	6	7	8
C	54	14	8	8	24	6.25	1114	79
c	41	11	6.25	6.25	24	5	533	70
c¹	31.5	9.5	5	6.25	12.5	4	552	54
c²	24	8	4	5	11	3	260	58
c³	flues							

Pedal Ophicleide 16' (1854: Trombone 16')

	1	2	3	4	5	6	7	8
C	152	27	14	16	50.5	12	n.a.	146
c	95	21	11	11	38	9.5	n.a.	102
c¹	63.5	14	8	8.5	25.5	7	n.a.	n.a.

Key
1 Length of shallot
2 Diameter of lower end of shallot
3 Diameter of top of shallot
4 Maximum width of shallot face
5 Length of shallot opening
6 Maximum width of shallot opening
7 Length of resonator
8 Diameter of resonator

ST GEORGE, PRESTON, 1865

An historian of Preston, writing in 1883, described St George's Church, and noted that

In the gallery, at the west end, there is a handsome, magnificently-toned organ. It was erected – supplanting a commoner one – in September, 1865. The cost of this instrument was about £1,000; the money being subscribed by the congregation.

(Hewitson 1883: 473)

This organ was built by Henry Willis, and is now one of the few survivors of the many that he supplied to churches and chapels in and around Liverpool, Blackburn and Preston.

A contemporary handbill[7] announced the organ's opening for 22 September 1865 and gave details of the programmes to be played at three o'clock in the afternoon and eight o'clock in the evening by W. T. Best:

AFTERNOON

Organ Sonata – No. 1 – (F minor)	Mendelssohn
Larghetto – from the Quintett for the Clarionet and Stringed Instruments	Mozart
Passacaglia (Variations and Fugue on a Ground Bass)	Bach
Pastorale and March	W. T. Best
Air, 'What though I trace each herb and flower'	
and	
Chorus, 'Your Harps and Cymbals sound' (*Solomon*)	Handel

EVENING

Organ Concerto – No. 2 – (B flat major)	Handel
Romance – (G major) – op. 40	Beethoven
Prelude and Fugue – (G minor)	Bach
Chopin's celebrated Funeral March	F. Chopin
Fantasia and Fugue	W. T. Best
Overture to the Oratorio, *The Last Judgment*	Spohr

The local press was uninformative about these recitals, beyond a general commendation of Best's performances and a reference to 'the beauty and richness of many of the solo stops' (*Preston Chronicle*, 30 September 1865).

The church was 'almost entirely rebuilt' in 1885 (*VCH, County of Lancaster*, VII: 103) and the organ was moved to a shallow transept on the north side of the chancel; the original front, complete with console doors, faces west (Plate 63), but the rest of the instrument was turned through ninety degrees, and the console (necessarily) resited, so that the player now sits in the conventional Victorian position with his back to the chancel (Plate 64). A tradition that the removal was carried out by Willis cannot be confirmed, but the conservative nature of the work (the only detectable alteration was to put the Pedal onto tubular-pneumatic action) might tend to support this.

Less laudably conservative was a 'restoration' undertaken in 1974. The original bellows were removed and compensator units installed. A balanced Swell pedal replaced the original lever.

The stop list (unaltered since 1865) follows.

Great Organ (C to g³)	
Double Diapason	16
Open Diapason	8
Gamba	8
Claribel Flute (wd)	8
Principal	4
Flute Harmonique	4

63 St George, Preston, Henry Willis, 1865. The present transept front, showing the original position of the console.

64 St George, Preston. Console detail.

Twelfth	$2\frac{2}{3}$
Fifteenth	2
Sesquialtra	III
Posaune	8
Clarion	4

Swell Organ (C to g³)

Contra Gamba (wd & m)	16
Open Diapason	8
Salicional	8
Lieblich Gedact (wd & m)	8
Principal	4
Flute Harmonique	4
Piccolo	2
Mixture	III
Cornopean	8
Hautboy	8
Clarion	4

Choir Organ (C to g³)

Claribel Flute (wd)	8
Dulciana	8
Viol d'Amour	8
Vox Angelica	8
Gemshorn	4
Flute Harmonique	4
Flageolet	2
Corno di Bassetto	8
Orchestral Oboe	8

Pedale (C to f¹)

Open Diapason (wd)	16
Bourdon (wd)	16
Violoncello	8
Viola	4
Fourniture	III
Ophicleide (wd)	16

Swell to Great
Swell to Choir
Swell to Pedals
Great to Pedals
Choir to Pedals

3 combination pedals each to Great and Swell
Swell pedal

Access to all divisions is difficult, and the scales given in Table 32 have therefore had to be restricted to the Great Organ. The layout of the organ is shown in Figures 27 and 28.

Table 32 *St George, Preston, 1865: scales of Great chorus*

	c	c¹	c²	c³
Double Diapason			40.4	25.6
Open Diapason		51.5	30.5	19
Gamba	70*	41	25	15.75
Principal	42	25.25	15	9.75
Twelfth	26.5	15.75	10.5	7.25
Fifteenth	23.75	14.5	9.25	7
Sesquialtra I	21	19	12.25	11
II	18.75	16.25	11	9
III	15.5	14	9.25	7
Composition:	C	17.19.22		
	c¹	12.15.17		
	f♯²	8.12.15		

UNION CHAPEL, ISLINGTON, 1877

Though falling outside the period under consideration, Willis's organ in the Union Chapel, Islington, so conspicuously demonstrates the outcome of various developments in tonal and mechanical design which have been (or will be) noted that it seems justifiable to include it in the present work.

Union Chapel is a remarkable building conceived to house a remarkable ministry. The Revd Henry Allon (1818–92), who ministered there from 1844 until his death, was a distinguished nonconformist divine who attracted vast congregations to the Chapel. In part, they came to hear Allon preach, but they were also attracted by the quality of the congregational psalmody. Allon had introduced a weekly psalmody class as a means of elevating the musical participation of the congregation in worship; it was attended with great success, and under the direction of successive organists (Dr Gauntlett, 1852–61; Ebenezer Prout, 1861–72) and the overall superintendance of Allon, the music at Union Chapel came to excite 'the admiration of Church-men and Nonconformists alike' (Curwen 1880: 173). The *Congregational Psalmist* (1858) was among various publications in which Allon was involved and which did much to improve the character of music in nonconformist worship generally.[8]

As one might expect, in view of Gauntlett's involvement, an organ found a place in Allon's scheme of reform. He found an organ in the old chapel in 1844; a new one was built by Gray & Davison in 1852, and then, following the enlargement of the chapel (1861) Holdich was commissioned to provide a new instrument in 1867. This had three manuals and thirty-seven stops,

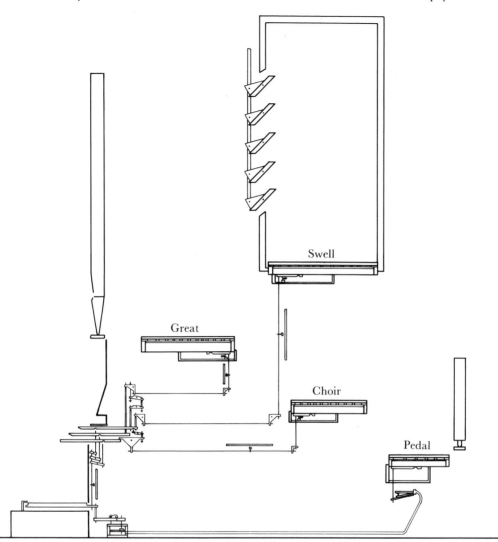

27 St George, Preston: key and pedal actions. The tubular-pneumatic action to the Pedal is not original.

and was designed by Gauntlett (*CMR* VI, 1867: 160; Curwen 1880: 175). It was planned to move it to the new Chapel, built between 1874 and 1877, but Holdich seems to have objected to the proposed site (Benham 1931: 233) and the expense of removal was not far short of the cost of a new instrument. Willis was thereupon commissioned to build a completely new organ.

The building is unusual, to say the least. 'It is circular in form, with three deep recesses, and a lofty and dome-shaped roof' (Benham 1931: 233). The capacity is considerable. The organ stands behind the massive pulpit in a

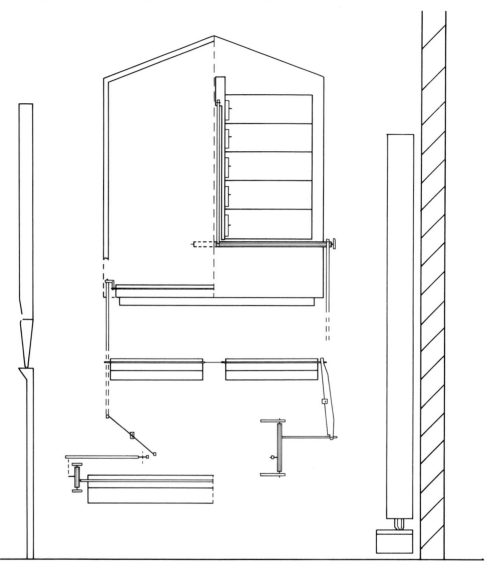

28 St George, Preston: stop action.

chamber, the floor of which is several feet below the level of the floor of the main building (Figures 29 and 30). Although a screen of stone arches and grilles conceals the pipework, there is little to impede the sound: the pipework speaks directly into the open space above it whence it is disseminated round the building with ease. Indeed, the resonant acoustic amplifies the brilliance of the mixturework and reeds, making for an effect which contrasts with Willis's later, more ponderous *plenos*.

The original stop list was as follows.

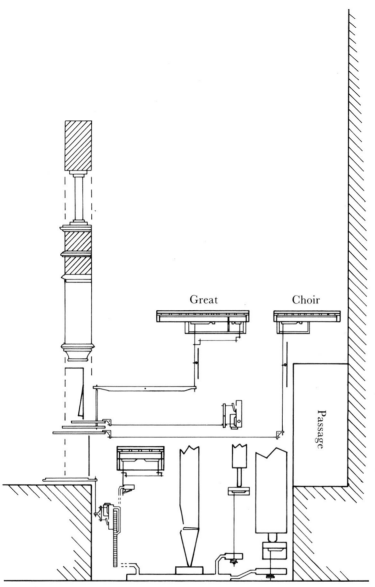

29 Union Chapel, Islington: Great, Choir and Pedal actions. This shows the valves with which the pedal action communicates and a cross-section of the grid carrying compressed air to the pneumatic levers under the Pedal chest; it also shows how pneumatic action is used to control the subsidiary pedal chests standing behind the main Pedal soundboard. The Swell action is designed along similar lines to that of the Pedal.

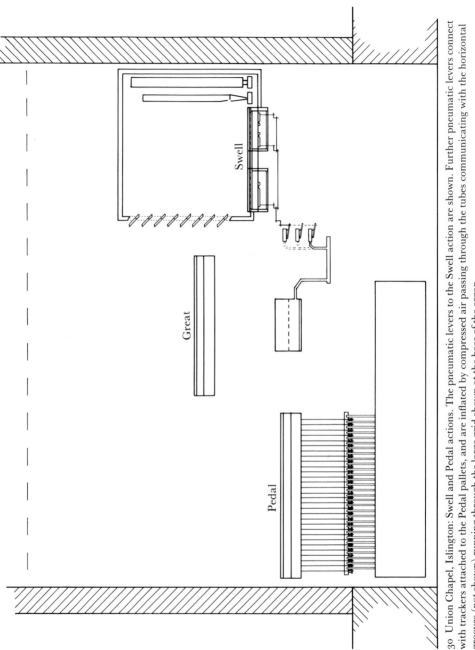

30 Union Chapel, Islington: Swell and Pedal actions. The pneumatic levers to the Swell action are shown. Further pneumatic levers connect with trackers attached to the Pedal pallets, and are inflated by compressed air passing through the tubes communicating with the horizontal grooves (not shown) running through the large grid shown at the base of the organ.

Great Organ (C to a³)

Double Open Diapason	16
Open Diapason	8
Flauto Dolce	8
Stopped Diapason (wd & m)	8
Claribel Flute (wd)	8
Principal	4
Harmonic Flute	4
Twelfth	2⅔
Fifteenth	2
Mixture	III
Trumpet	8
Clarion	4

Swell Organ (C to a³)

Contra Gamba	16
Open Diapason	8
Lieblich Gedackt	8
Salicional	8
Vox Angelica	8
Gemshorn	4
Lieblich Flöte	4
Mixture	III
Trumpet	8
Oboe	8
Vox Humana	8
Clarion	4

Choir Organ (C to a³)

Lieblich Gedackt	8
Dulciana	8
Viol d'Amore	8
Claribel Flute (wd)	8
Concert Flute	4
Lieblich Flute	4
Gemshorn	4
Corno di Bassetto	8

Pedal Organ (C to f¹)

Open Diapason (wd)	16
Open Diapason (m)	16
Bourdon (wd)	16
Principal	8
Ophicleide	16

Choir to Great
Great to Pedal
Swell to Pedal
Choir to Pedal

Composition pedals (no details)
Great to Pedal (double-acting   pedal)
Tremulant (Swell)

Wind pressures[9]
Great and Pedal reeds: 12″
Swell Cornopean and Clarion: 7″
Remainder: 3½″ or 4″

The organ has suffered comparatively little alteration over the years.[10] It survives to provide a convincing résumé of Henry Willis's style, when he was at the height of his powers in the mid-1870s. By employing pneumatics to overcome the difficulties of siting, and by applying higher pressures to the chorus reeds in order to meet the demands of an unusually spacious auditorium, Willis demonstrated the mature application of techniques that had been evolving during the preceding decades. The console, too, with its angled jambs, overhanging keys and solid ivory stop knobs represents a break with the mid-nineteenth century and marks a new concern for the player's comfort and convenience (Plate 56). All told, it is a fine example of Henry Willis's best work.

STOP LISTS

It is evident from contemporary reactions to Willis's instruments that he was identified at an early stage in his career as an innovator. That being so, it is particularly interesting to note that the stop lists of many of his organs of the 1850s are distinctly conservative in conception, including a number of features originated by the Insular Movement during the 1830s and 1840s. Despite its C-compass, the Gloucester Swell of 1847 is surprisingly unenterprising, with its duplication of the open diapason and its lack of a double. The small 3-manual for St Matthias, Stoke Newington (1853) could have been designed by John Gray in the 1830s, with the exception of the C-compass for Great and Choir, whilst the Hampstead organ of 1852 is a conservative 2-manual, with a claribella and dulciana on the Great, reminiscent of J. C. Bishop's work ten years before. This conservatism extended to the most ambitious instruments. The extensive duplication in the 1851 Exhibition organ has already been mentioned (above, p. 111). Its presence is as unexpected, after all that had gone on during the 1840s, as is the absence of any real novelties among the fluework: a solitary metal flute and three imitative strings hardly count for much in a 70-stop scheme. The reeds hold promise of better things, and we know, in any case, that Willis's organ made a great impression, but it remains curious that he staked all on an instrument that was so behind the times in the development of its tonal scheme. Exactly the same criticisms could be made of the Liverpool organ, but there, Wesley must carry much of the blame and the undoubted success of the instrument was despite the shortcomings of its specification.

Willis continued to build smaller organs in a conservative style well into the 1860s,[11] but the Cranbrook organ of 1854 inaugurated a new trend. It is a large 2-manual, of twenty-two stops, with doubles on both divisions, a string in the Swell and a harmonic flute on the Great. Importantly, the Swell has a 16' reed (no 4') and so represents one of Willis's earliest attempts to develop what was to become his characteristic Full Swell in which a double reed was a vital component. The organs for the cathedrals of Winchester, Carlisle and

Wells followed. Though Wesley's influence ensured that the Winchester scheme assumed a more conservative cast than might have been the case had Willis been left to his own devices, the complete Pedal Organ, the powerful reed chorus in the Swell, and the creation of a frankly orchestral division are all features presaging future developments. The Carlisle scheme – possibly under Best's influence – takes matters a stage further (Appendix 1, pp. 487– 8). A 16' reed chorus is again a prominent feature of the Swell, which also includes a vox humana. The flue chorus, on the other hand, is no longer complete: there is no fifteenth, but instead a wooden flageolet, and the chorus mixture has made way for an echo dulciana cornet. The Choir has become a little Solo division; in the Pedal, an 8' reed seems to have displaced the mixture. The Wells organ (Appendix 1, pp. 455–6) illustrates the genesis of Willis's standard Choir Organ. For some time, elements of the old English Choir Organ survived (notably the open diapason and the principal) but they were eventually swallowed up in a division consisting entirely of gedacts, strings, harmonic flutes and orchestral reeds. Willis's last cathedral organ, for Lincoln (1898), shows the eventual result of this line of develop- ment, but Wells is the starting point. In other respects, the scheme bore strong resemblances to Winchester and Carlisle. The absence of strings (apart from a metal violone on the Pedal) is noteworthy, as is the retention of duplication in the Great flue chorus, but it was otherwise a fine and versatile scheme, enhanced by a generous provision of combination pistons.

By the end of the 1850s, certain characteristic stylistic elements had established themselves: the preponderance of the reeds; the Full Swell based on a 16' reed; a tendency to dilute the flue choruses; the widespread use of claribel flutes, harmonic flutes and imitative reeds; the retention of bold tierce mixtures to complement the powerful chorus reeds. The Exhibition organ of 1862 provided a summary and suggested future developments. Particularly notable was the growing use of French nomenclature and registers drawn from French practice: Pedale (instead of Pedal Organ), flute à pavillon, flute traversière, fourniture, trompette harmonique, vox ange- lica. Compared with this, the appearance of a lieblich gedackt on the Choir might have been overlooked; it was, though, a register that would soon become a standard feature of Willis's Choir and Swell divisions. Alongside this interest in colourful accompanimental and solo voices, an observer might also have noted that only the Great Organ now had a complete diapason chorus.

The 1860s saw the consolidation of these stylistic trends. Wooden flutes (apart from claribels) were gradually replaced with metal ones, and har- monic flutes became standard in all manual departments (Preston has three). Slotting became more common. It was used for string stops to give them a more pronounced tone (the Choir gemshorn at Preston belies its name by having cylindrical pipes with slots) and for the basses of chorus registers to improve definition. Willis evidently found the technique particu- larly successful with Pedal stops; a metal violone was often included in his

Pedal divisions, sometimes displacing the bourdon, and at Preston and in other instruments of this period, the 8' and 4' registers are relatively narrowly scaled and slotted (violoncello, viola). A contra gamba begins regularly to displace the Swell double diapason at this time (Preston; Ewell; St Stephen, Hampstead) and also, occasionally, the Great double (Tiverton). Chorus reeds, meanwhile, became both smoother and more powerful, the result of increased sophistication of technique and freer application of high pressures. By the 1870s Willis's Pedal ophicleides are too big to be used with manual flue choruses alone; they take their scale from the Great reeds, which, equally, dominate the chorus. Occasionally, Willis would use harmonic trebles[12] but generally these trumpets, posaunes, trombones, trombas and bombardes had resonators of natural length. Where a complete Swell reed chorus was provided, the 16' might be a contra posaune (St Paul's) or contra fagotto (Wallasey), usually accompanied by a cornopean and clarion.

The French influence upon Willis's work attained its zenith in the organs for the Alexandra Palace and the Royal Albert Hall. The former incorporated parts of the 1862 Exhibition organ[13] worked up into an 87-stop scheme including no fewer than twenty-six reeds (Appendix 1, pp. 501–3). The use of ventils, in addition to combination pistons, underlined the source of the inspiration. The extensive use of imitative strings, orchestral reeds and harmonic flutes was carried a stage further in the 111-stop specification for the Royal Albert Hall. The Great had harmonic flutes at 16', 8', 4' and 2', and each department had a harmonic piccolo 2', Willis noting that 'the effect of wood is imparted by the harmonic construction, and the disadvantage of using wood for small pipes is therefore avoided' (HR3: 463). There were 32', 16' and 8' violones on the Pedal, a violone and contra gamba (both 16') on the Great, and strings in all departments. In order to augment the reed chorus of the Great, Willis included a trompette harmonique and a clarion harmonique each of two ranks (16' and 8', 8' and 4'); the Choir also had the former, but for the Swell, Willis deserted his French model for English high-pressure reeds, providing tubas at 8' and 4' as (probably) at Liverpool. The multi-ranked mixtures of Great, Swell and Pedal were reminiscent of Cavaillé-Coll's schemes, as was the limited use (for the Pedal Organ) of ventils.

With the Liverpool,[14] Alexandra Palace and Royal Albert Hall organs to his credit, Willis could claim pre-eminence among English builders as a constructor of concert organs. Another organ built at this period finally established his claim to recognition in the church sphere. Though small by comparison with secular instruments (fifty-one stops) the St Paul's organ of 1872 was to exercise a decisive influence over the conception of the English cathedral organ down to the present day. Having solved the mechanical problem of accommodating the organ to the satisfaction of musicians and ecclesiologists alike (above, p. 315) Willis prepared a stop list (Appendix 1, pp. 503–5) which expressed concisely all the principal features of his mature style: distinct pressures for chorus reeds; relatively high pressures for fluework; tierce mixtures; gedacts, strings, orchestral reeds; a 16′ reed chorus in the Swell; powerful tubas in the Solo; an undulating string in the Swell. With its refined voicing and mechanical sophistication, its power and its express-iveness, the St Paul's organ perfectly served the rising musical aesthetic represented by Dr John Stainer, who succeeded Goss as organist in 1872. It was a thoroughly contemporary instrument, and Willis was to reap his reward over the next thirty years in the form of an impressive list of contracts from churches and cathedrals for organs conceived along similar lines.

LAYOUT AND ACTION

Willis's surviving organs at Lambourn (1858) and Preston (1865) have essentially the same layout as Hill's Kidderminster organ (Figures 27 and 28): the Swell is behind the Great at a higher level with the Choir squeezed in beneath it; the Pedal soundboard is at the back of the organ with the bass of the wood open diapason standing on its own chest down the sides of the organ. Given the space, Willis's preference was for a horizontal arrangement of the manual soundboards with the Choir placed between Great and Swell. He was able to achieve this at Tiverton (1870) and St Stephen, Hampstead (1871). Usually, however, difficulties of siting prevented so satisfactory an outcome. It is therefore understandable that, by releasing builders from the constraints of a purely mechanical action, pneumatic action in its various forms offered builders a tempting prospect. Union Chapel is an early example of its application (Figures 29 and 30). The Great soundboard is in the middle with the Choir behind: a perfectly conventional arrangement. The Pedal soundboard stands on one side of the chamber. It would have been possible to use tracker action for this, accepting the risks inherent in the use of long rollers to convey the action to one side, but instead, Willis used his system of pneumatic levers and grooves (above, p. 357); by the standards of the day, it was altogether more reliable. The Swell presented even more of a problem. In order to accommodate it on the opposite side of the chamber to the Pedal, Willis had to turn the soundboard through ninety degrees. Again, tracker action was not impossible – simply undesirable – and Willis chose to use the same system as for the Pedal.

The Preston drawings (Figures 27 and 28) illustrate a typical Willis tracker layout of the 1860s. He dispensed with the old tumbler and sliding manual couplers (HRI: 52–3) and devised a system using squares and backfalls. As well as being easier to regulate, these had the advantage of permitting the introduction of a Swell to Choir coupler (as at Preston). A cruder version is found in the Lambourn instrument. Willis claimed to have invented this arrangement during his time with John Gray, and there is a similar coupling system in the Limehouse organ (1851). He also claimed to have invented the pedal couplers seen at Preston. They work through a series of backfalls and stickers operating on the underside of the key tails. Willis's claim should be treated with caution; Hopkins describes the system (HRI: 55) without any mention of Willis or Gray as its author. Concurrent invention is a recognised phenomenon.

PIPEWORK

Like other English builders Willis usually employed a compound of lead, tin and antimony for his metal pipework during the 1850s. He used this 'blue-looking lead metal' in the Wells Cathedral organ (*MG* II, 1857: 443) and also in the instrument for the 1862 Exhibition. In the latter case, it was alleged that he nearly lost his prize medal on account of the prevalence of antimony metal in the organ (*Eccl* xxv, 1864: 358–9). Although it was said that Willis claimed that 'the quality of the metal has nothing on earth to do with the quality of tone' (xxvi, 1865: 20) the experience at the Industrial Exhibition may have had an effect, and by the mid-1860s it could no longer be said that Willis used 'scarce anything but antimony' (xxv, 1864: 358). Most of the pipework in the organ for St John, Taunton (1864) is made of a compound of tin and lead in the proportions of approximately 2:3; this may have been one of the four large organs built by Willis in that year which 'almost entirely used spotted metal' (xxvi, 1865: 20). Preston and Tiverton use a decent plain metal; Hampstead had spotted metal fronts. When money was no object Willis was ready to use metal of a fine quality throughout.[15] Tin and lead in the proportions of 5:4 were employed for the internal pipes of the Royal Albert Hall organ, and the front pipes had 90 per cent tin, being 'burnished and polished in the same manner as those of the best Continental organs' (HR3: 465). Six years later all the pipework of the Salisbury Cathedral organ, with the exception of the fronts and the pipes stood in the transept, was made of spotted metal (MS 87).

Wind pressures have already been mentioned. For instruments of average size with no exceptional features Willis continued during this period to use much the same pressures as other builders; Preston is on 3¼″ throughout, and this is probably typical of the 1860s. It is said that the original pressures at St Paul's were these:

GREAT	fluework:	3½″ (old)	5″ (new)
	reeds:	6″	
SWELL	fluework:	3½″	
	reeds:	6″	
CHOIR	fluework:	2½″	
	reeds:	3½″	
SOLO	fluework:	4″	
	reeds:	3½″ (light reeds)	
		14″ & 17½″ (heavy reeds)	
PEDAL	fluework:	2½″ (violone) 3½″ (32′) 7″ (others)	
	reeds:	3½″ (32′) 18″ (others)	

These measurements must be treated with some caution[16] but if authentic they demonstrate clearly how Willis used differing wind pressures to create an instrument capable of considerable variations of intensity and volume. The Choir fluework is still on a modest low pressure, compatible with its gentle voicing and mild tone. The Swell and Great flue choruses use higher pressures, and the new fluework of the Great is on the exceptional (for a church instrument) pressure of 5″. Then come the chorus reeds on still higher pressures, and finally the Solo and Pedal reeds, whose winding reflects their role (new to the Pedal) of climax stops. The Union Chapel wind pressures (again, assuming them to be authentic) illustrate the same principles on a smaller scale (above, p. 431).

The fluework of Willis's organs does not exhibit the same variety of construction as that of Hill, Gray & Davison or the northern builders influenced by Schulze. In his earliest organs wooden flutes predominated; the flutes and piccolos of the 1851 Exhibition organ were all of open wood construction, with the single exception of a stopped metal flute on the Choir. The Liverpool organ was similarly lacking in metal flutes, and only the appearance of one and two harmonic flutes respectively in the Carlisle and Wells organs distinguished them in this respect from Willis's other organs of the 1850s. Sometimes the nomenclature was misleading: many of Willis's 'stopped diapasons' were actually clarabellas with an open wood treble; but, in general, Willis seems not to have striven for great tonal variety from his fluework at this period.

The picture began to change around 1860. The 1862 Exhibition organ made much more adventurous use of metal flutes, introducing the flute à pavillon, flute traversière, concert flute and (metal) lieblich gedact to Willis's practice. Another instrument built in that year was equally innovative. At Wadham College, Oxford (Appendix 1, p. 505) all the flutes with the exception of the Swell bourdon were of metal. The Great claribel had a metal harmonic treble. The rohr-flute and the Swell lieblich gedackt were of a pattern that was to become familiar in Willis's work: metal bodies with long bored wooden stoppers. There was even a rank of conical construction – the Great spitz-flute – a rarity in Willis's organs; however, Willis drew back from including two such novelties in a single instrument, and the gemshorn (like the example at Preston) was a cylindrical slotted register. Wadham is something of a curiosity in Willis's output; possibly its uncharacteristic specification is the fruit of some don's whims. Throughout the 1860s, Willis relied heavily on claribels (open wood), lieblich gedacts (stopped metal), harmonic flutes and harmonic piccolos (metal) to create the effect he sought. Larger instruments offered more scope: the Great of the Royal Albert Hall organ included a flute conique 16′ (a tapering harmonic register inspired by St-Sulpice) and it is interesting that Willis made a positive virtue of the fact that the only wooden pipes to be found in the manual divisions of that instrument were the basses to four flutes (HR3: 463–5).

Willis's strings may be divided into two categories: those that were slotted, and those that were not. By the 1860s, the salicional was the principal survivor in the latter group; it was scaled as a dulciana, with small toes and a narrow (one-fifth) mouth. Most strings, however, were slotted. The contra gambas, gambas, violones, violas and viols d'amore belong to this category; they were usually more generously winded than the salicionals but, like them, had narrow mouths.

There is little to be added concerning reeds (above, pp. 420–1). Willis relied heavily upon his brother, George, in this field, and it is probably he who was responsible for the evolution of the firm's distinctive style of reed-voicing.[17] His initials and the date (1851) appear on the blocks of the C pipes at Winchester that have survived from the Exhibition organ. Mr Peter Hopps of Messrs Harrison & Harrison has kindly furnished the details which appear in Table 31. The shallots are closed, and their design is easily distinguishable from that of the shallots in the reeds added by Willis in 1897. It will be noticed that the resonators have a much smaller diameter than Hill's chorus reeds, a point that is underlined by a comparison of the Reading Town Hall posaune with Hill's stop of the same name in the Belfast organ (Tables 33 and 29). In all respects, the treatment was as different as the intention.

Table 33 *Reading Town Hall: scales of the 1864 pipework*

(1) Metal fluework

GREAT ORGAN

	C	c	c^1	c^2	c^3
Double Diapason			78	42.5	26
Open Diapason [1]		85	50.5	31	19
Principal	80*	45	26.5	16	10
Flute Harmonique		46	41	25.5	15.5
Twelfth	48*	28.25	16.5	10.5	7
Fifteenth	42*	24.5	16	10.25	7
Sesquialtera I	34.5	20.5	18	12	11
II	30.5	18	15.5	8	6.5
III	23	14	13	8.25	6.5

Composition:	C	17.19.22
	c^1	12.15.17
	$f\sharp^2$	8.12.15

SWELL ORGAN

	C	c	c^1	c^2	c^3
Open Diapason		82*	49.5	28	17.25
Stopped Diapason (b)	wd	wd	43	28	19
Principal		45*	26.5	16	10
Piccolo (c)	48	41*	25	15	10
Sesquialtera I		21.5	17.5	11.5	10
II		19	15.5	10	8
III		16.5	13.5	9	7

Composition:	C	17.19.22
	c^1	12.15.17
	$f\sharp^2$	8.12.15

CHOIR ORGAN

	C	c	c^1	c^2	c^3
Salicional			35	21	12
Flute Harmonique (d)	62*	46*	41	24.5	15
Piccolo Harmonique (e)	44*	39*	23	13.5	8.5

(2) Wooden flutes

		Internal	Sides
GREAT CLARIBEL FLUTE 8′ (f)			
	c	46 × 60	9
	c^1	36 × 44	7
	c^2	25 × 31	5
	c^3	17 × 24	4
CHOIR LIEBLICH GEDACT 8′ (g)			
	c	50 × 62	10
	c^1	32 × 46	6
	c^2	21 × 27	6
	c^3	17 × 20	5.5
SWELL DOUBLE DIAPASON (h)			
	c^1	48 × 60	9
	c^2	30 × 35	6
	c^3	20 × 24	6

(3) Reed resonators: diameters

	C	c	c^1	c^2	c^3
Gt Posaune		85	67	60	50
Sw Cornopean		75	68	56	50
Hautboy		75	55	45	37.5
Ch Corno di Bassetto	45	35	30	27	25
Orchestral Oboe	50	35	26	22	20

Notes

(a) Harmonic from c^1; open metal bass.
(b) Stopped metal with bored stoppers from c^1; basses of stopped wood, the tenor octave bored.
(c) Harmonic from c; open metal bass.
(d) Harmonic from g♯; open metal bass.
(e) Harmonic from c; open metal bass.
(f) Open from c^1; stopped wood bass.
(g) Originally called Claribel Flute; open from g, with stopped wood bass.

Much the same could be said of the scaling and voicing of the flue choruses. From the start, Willis demonstrated a tendency to vary more widely the scaling of his chorus registers than (for example) Hill. Little can be gleaned from the surviving ranks of the 1851 Exhibition organ (Table 30) except that the double open diapason and principal 1 were of the same scale, with the two open diapasons respectively one pipe larger and one pipe smaller (the second principal was probably two pipes smaller). Liverpool is more informative (Table 14). Again, the 16′ and the first principal are of the same scale, joined here by the third open diapason. The other open diapasons are one and two pipes larger. The upperwork gets progressively smaller, with, at this relatively early date, Willis making his quints (quint and twelfth) four pipes smaller than the principal I and his tenth a full six pipes smaller. The Liverpool organ also shows early evidence of a narrowing of the mouths: the principal II, twelfth, quint, fifteenth and tenth all have mouths of between two-ninths and one-fifth of the circumference (the other ranks have quarter-mouths). It is of interest to observe that the scales of the Swell chorus registers are exactly the same as the corresponding ranks on the Great.

Preston, and the original (1864) pipework in the Reading Town Hall organ[18] offer evidence for the 1860s (Tables 32 and 33). Each has a Great open diapason of the same scale: the same scale that Willis used for the third open diapason at Liverpool. Thereafter, the scaling patterns are related but not the same. In both cases, the open diapason is substantially larger than the other ranks, three pipes larger than the double and two pipes larger than the principal at Reading, and four pipes larger than both in the Preston organ. The fifteenths are smaller again, and both twelfths are a good six pipes smaller than the 8'. At Reading, the Swell open diapason is a little smaller than that of the Great, but the principal has the same scale as the Great principal. In view of this gradual diminution in scales it is a surprise to discover that the mixtures are, if anything, of larger scale than the corresponding ranks in the chorus; this is particularly true of the quint and unison in the Preston organ, and the quint at Reading. Possibly Willis realised that he could not afford to reduce the scale of his mixturework if it was to act as an effective bridge between his powerful reeds and the remainder of the fluework. For the same reason, the tierce was a vital component in Willis's chorus mixtures. The Great and Swell mixtures at Reading, Preston and the Union Chapel have exactly the same composition:

C   17.19.22
c¹   12.15.17
f♯²   8.12.15

Here we have the old sesquialtera & cornet converted to a completely different role (one that the French would understand). Even so, it is an unexpected survivor in the work of the most progressive English builder of his generation, and suggests that Willis retained more of the lessons he learnt in John Gray's workshop than is sometimes allowed.

The mouths of the fluework in the Preston and Reading instruments consistently come out at two-ninths of the circumference except for the twelfths and nineteenths which narrow to one fifth. The mouths are cut up to one third of their width. Slotting is already a feature. At Preston, it is as follows:

Great	Double Diapason	C–e¹
	Open Diapason	C–a
	Principal	C–F♯
Swell	Open Diapason	C–a
	Principal	C–F♯
Pedal	Violoncello	throughout
	Viola	throughout

Table 34 *Union Chapel, Islington, 1877: scales of Great and Swell choruses*

GREAT ORGAN

	C	c	c¹	c²	c³
Double Open Diapason			75	44.5	26
Open Diapason		98*	56.5	33	22
Principal	82*	48	29	18	11
Twelfth	48*	29	18	11.5	8
Fifteenth	44	26	16	11	8
Mixture I	31	19.5	17	11	10.5
II	28	17.5	14	10	8
III	24.5	14.5	12	8	7.5

Composition:	C	17.19.22		
	c¹	12.15.17		
	f♯²	8.12.15		

SWELL ORGAN

	C	c	c¹	c²	c³
Contra Gamba			68	41	25
Open Diapason		85	48.5	29.5	18
Principal	72	44.5	27	17	10.5

The contra gambas on the Great at Tiverton and Swell at St Stephen, Hampstead, were slotted throughout the compass.

Languids of the 1860s were quite thick (2.5 to 3 mm at 1′) with a bevel 30 degrees out of the vertical. Flues were wide and the lower lip was increasingly dubbed (curved in towards the languid). Nicking altered as the period advanced. At St George's Hall, though the nicks are frequent (an average of twenty-five in the languid of a 2′ pipe) they are still small and light; by 1865 (Preston) the nicks are firmer, making a small v-shaped incision in the languid, and by 1871 (Hampstead) although the number of nicks has decreased they are again heavier and also appear in the lower lip. A few years later, at Salisbury (1877) the nicks have become deep notches in both languid and lip (an average of twenty in the 2′ pipe).

Like Salisbury, Union Chapel (Table 34) reveals Willis adopting larger scales for his open diapasons, gradually diminishing the already reduced scale of his upperwork, and making a clear distinction in the scaling of the Swell and Great choruses. These features, together with the proliferation of 8′ registers in the Union Chapel specification and the tendency more and more to tip the balance of the full choruses in favour of the reeds, point to the next stage in the evolution of Willis's style and are hence outside the scope of the present work.

15

Epilogue

The death of William Hill in 1870 was a symbolic moment for English organ-building. The present work has attempted to demonstrate that Hill's contribution to the transformation of the English organ was of central importance. In pursuing innovation and consolidating a new style he travelled further than any of his contemporaries and he laid foundations upon which the next generation (Willis among them) were glad to build. Starting at a time when the instruments of George Pike England and William Gray represented all that was best in English organ-building, and when an organ with twenty stops was regarded as large, he lived to witness the rise of Henry Willis, and the conception of monster organs such as St George's Hall, the Alexandra Palace and the Royal Albert Hall. In more general historical terms, his career spans the period between Waterloo (1815) and the Second Reform Act (1867). But temperamentally he belongs in the company of other unashamed innovators who straddle the years linking the Georgian and early-Victorian eras. Hill's work in the 1830s and 1840s exhibits a willingness to experiment, and a desire to take advantage of contemporary technical developments, which (albeit, on a much more modest scale) place it, historically, alongside Brunel's Clifton Suspension Bridge, Stephenson's London to Birmingham Railway and Paxton's Crystal Palace.

Yet it is necessary to recall that Hill was born in the eighteenth century, and that his master, Thomas Elliot, learnt his craft in the 1760s and 1770s. Various features of Hill's practice, some of which he bequeathed to the nascent Victorian organ, reflect this pedigree and stress the continuities which other developments might tend to obscure. The imitation of orchestral instruments engaged the energies of eighteenth-century builders, as did the possibilities of swell boxes and the provision of weighty basses. The nineteenth-century builders, led by Hill, achieved much more spectacular results, but the origins of these preoccupations lay in the previous century. In other respects, too, the organs built by Hill, and many of his contemporaries, possess clear affinities with English organs of the eighteenth century: tierce mixtures, the retention of the twelfth, the use of stopped diapasons,

442

and the balance between flues and reeds are examples of this, but further investigation would almost certainly reveal that it extended to matters of scaling and construction.

Hill's work can thus be characterised as an inspired union of conservatism and innovation, and it establishes a context for the study of the Victorian organ. Within this frame of reference, various movements or trends made particular contributions to the evolution of the typical organ of 1870. Weighty pedal registers (usually of wood) and large-scale open diapasons were legacies of the Insular Movement of the 1820s and 1830s. C-compass keyboards and full-compass pedal boards were the contribution of the German System, together with a repertoire of novel flutes, strings and reeds to swell the growing stock of such delights. The large swell boxes of the 1840s also set a standard for later emulation, and manual doubles soon became a regular feature of even quite small instruments. Mechanical and tonal refinements inspired by contemporary foreign builders were bequeathed by the 1850s and 1860s: harmonic flutes, celestes and the pneumatic lever from France; gedacts, wooden strings and quint mixtures from Germany. If to this list is added the impetus lent by orchestral transcriptions to the adoption of equal temperament and the development of mechanical playing aids, and the encouragement to explore new styles of voicing and disposition offered by the Ecclesiological Movement, then the origins of some, at least, of the most distinctive features of the Victorian organ have been described.

Change is a complex and fascinating business. This study has endeavoured to analyse the most eventful era in the history of the making of organs in England. Though the upheavals of the mid-century promoted a diversification of styles which stands in marked contrast to the (relative) uniformity of the days when William Hill began building organs in Tottenham Court, there is a good case for arguing that a new consensus had emerged by 1870. It is therefore at that point that the present study closes.

Appendix 1: Specifications

1 Ashridge, Hertfordshire THOMAS ELLIOT, 1818

Great Organ (GG, no GG♯, to f³)

Open Diapason	8
Open Diapason (G)	8
Stopped Diapason (wood)	8
Principal	4
Flute (stopped wood)	4
Twelfth	2⅔
Fifteenth	2
Sesquialtra	II
Mixture	II
Trumpet	8
Pedal Diapason (wood)	8 12 pipes

Swell Organ (f to f³)

Open Diapason	8
Stopped Diapason (wood)	8
Principal	4
Hautboy	8

Pedal [to] Great Organ
Swell to Great [added ?]

Pedals: GG to c, 17 notes

Source The organ; Buckingham LIII: 82.

2 Crick Parish Church, Northamptonshire, formerly in the Chapel Royal, St James's Palace THOMAS ELLIOT, 1819

Great Organ (GG, no GG♯, to f³)

Open Diapason	8
Stopped Diapason (wood)	8
Principal	4
Twelfth	2⅔
Fifteenth	2
Sesquialtra	II

444

Mixture	II
Trumpet, bass & treble	8

Choir Organ (G G, no G G♯, to f³)

Stopped Diapason (wood)	8
Dulciana	8
Principal	4
Flute (wood)	4
Cremona	8

Swell Organ (f to f³)

Open Diapason	8
Stopped Diapason (wood)	8
Principal	4
Trumpet	8
Hautboy	8

Pedal Coupler [Great to Pedal]

Pedals: G G to G [?]

Source CR xv: 552

3   St James, Bermondsey J. C. BISHOP, 1829

Great Organ (G G to f³)

Open Diapason	8
Open Diapason	8
Stopped Diapason	8
Principal	4
Twelfth	2⅔
Fifteenth	2
Sesquialtera	III
Mixture	II
Trumpet	8
Clarion	4

Choir Organ (G G to f³)

Open Diapason	8
Stopped Diapason	8
Dulciana (G)	8
Principal	4
Flute	4
Fifteenth	2
Cremona & Bassoon	8

Swell Organ (G to f³)

Open Diapason	8
Open Diapason	8
Stopped Diapason	8
Principal	4
Cornet	V
French Horn	8

Trumpet	8
Hautboy	8

Pedal Organ (GG to g)

Double Diapason (wood)	16
Unison Diapason (wood)	8
Trombone	8

Swell to Great
Swell to Choir
Choir to Great
Great to Pedals
Choir to Pedals

3 composition pedals to Great
1 shifting movement for reducing Swell to diapasons
1 pedal for coupling Swell to Great

Swell keyboard was full compass from GG with the bottom octave coupled permanently to the Choir.
A separate keyboard to the left of the Choir enabled the Pedal stops to be played manually.

Source MS 55; *CR* XVII, 1835: 501–2; HRI: 486

4   St Giles, Camberwell J. C. BISHOP, 1844

Great Organ (C to f³)

Open Diapason	8
Open Diapason (wood bass)	8
Claribella (wood; in halves)	8
Stopped Diapason (wood)	8
Principal	4
Principal	4
Twelfth	2⅔
Fifteenth	2
Sesquialtera	III
Furniture	III
Mixture	II
Doublette	II
Trumpet	8
Clarion	4

Swell Organ (C to f³)

Double Diapason (halves)	16
Open Diapason	8
Open Diapason (wood bass)	8
Stopped Diapason (wood)	8
Principal	4
Fifteenth	2
Sesquialtera	III
Mixture	II
Doublette	II
Trumpet	8
Horn	8

Hautboy	8
Clarion	4

Choir Organ (C to f³)

Open Diapason	8
Stopped Diapason (wood)	8
Dulciana	8
Claribella (wood)	8
Principal	4
Flute (open wood)	4
Fifteenth	2
Mixture	II
Cremona & Bassoon (in halves)	8

Pedal Organ (C to d¹)

Double Open Diapason (wood)	16
Open Diapason	8
Double Trumpet (wood)	16

Great to Pedals
Swell to Pedals
Choir to Pedals
Swell to Great
Wood open (bass of Great Claribella) to Pedals

8 composition pedals

Mixture compositions (1989):

Gt Sesquialtra	C	17.19.22
	c¹	12.15.17
	f♯²	8.12.15
Furniture	C	24.26.29
	c	15.19.22
	c¹	1. 8.15
Mixture	C	26.29
	c	22.29
	c¹	15.22
	c²	8.15
Sw Sesquialtera	C	17.19.22
	c¹	12.15.17
	f♯²	8.12.15
Ch Mixture	C	19.22
	c¹	8.15
	f♯²	1. 8

Source MS 61: 101–2, 114–15; HRI: 482–3

5   Blackburn Parish Church JOHN GRAY, 1828 AND 1832

Great Organ (GG to f³)

Large Open Diapason	8
Open Diapason	8
Stop Diapason	8

Principal	4
Twelfth	2⅔
Fifteenth	2
Sesquialtra & Cornet	IV
Mixture	II
Trumpet	8
Clarion	4
Pedal Double Diapason	16 18 notes

Swell Organ (c to f³)

Double Diapason	16
Open Diapason	8
Stop Diapason	8
Principal	4
Fifteenth	2
Trumpet	8
Hautboy	8

Choir Organ (GG to f³)

Stop Diapason	8
Dulciana	8
Principal	4
Flute	4
Fifteenth	2
Clarionet [*sic*]	8

Pedals to Great
Pedals to Choir
Swell to Great

The Choir Organ stood in its own case and was enclosed in a venetian swell.

Pedals: GG to c, 18 notes

Source MS 1: 168; Bertalot 1970: 2–4

6   Exeter Hall, Strand, London JOSEPH WALKER, 1839

Great Organ (FF to g³)

Open Diapason, large	8
Open Diapason, small (wood bass)	8
Stopped Diapason	8
Principal	4
Twelfth	2⅔
Fifteenth	2
Sesquialtra	III
Mixture	II
Furniture	II
Trumpet	8
Clarion	4

Swell Organ (F to g³)

Sub-bass & Double Diapason	16
Open Diapason	8

Stopped Diapason	8
Dulciana	8
Principal	4
Twelfth	$2\frac{2}{3}$
Fifteenth	2
Sesquialtra	III
French Horn	8
Hautboy	8
Clarion	4

Choir Organ (F F to g³)

Open Diapason	8
Stopped Diapason	8
Dulciana (F)	8
Principal	4
Flute	4
Fifteenth	2
Cremona & Bassoon	8

Pedal Organ (C to e¹) (a)

Double Diapason (wood)	16
Double Diapason	16
Principal	8
Fifteenth	4
Mixture	III
Posaune	16
Trumpet	8

Swell to Great
Choir to Great
Great to Pedals
Swell to Pedals
Choir to Pedals

3 composition pedals to Great

(a) The compass of the Pedal registers was seventeen notes, C to e, one octave less than the pedal board.

Source Musical Journal 1, 1840: 34, 59; Warren 1842: 57–8

7   Everingham, Catholic Chapel CHARLES ALLEN, *c.* 1837

Great Organ (G G, no G G♯, to f³)

Open Diapason	8	
Stop Diapason (metal from g)	8	chimneys
Dulciana	8	
Principal	4	
Twelfth	$2\frac{2}{3}$	
Fifteenth	2	
Sesquialtra & Cornet	IV	
Trumpet	8	
Pedal Pipes (wood)	8	17 notes

Swell Organ (f to f³)

Open Diapason	8
Stop Diapason (metal)	8
Principal	4
Fifteenth	2
Trumpet	8
Hautboy	8
Cremona	8

Pedal Chorus [Great to Pedal]
Coupler [Swell to Great]

Pedals: GG (no GG♯) to c, 17 notes

Composition of Sesquialtra & Cornet:

GG	17.19.22
f♯	12.15.17
c¹	8.12.15.[17]
f♯²	1. 8.12.[15]

Source The instrument

8   Chester Cathedral GRAY & DAVISON, 1843

Great Organ (C to f³)

Double Diapason, bass & treble	16
Open Diapason	8
Open Diapason	8
Stop Diapason, bass, and	
Clarabella Flute, treble	8
Fifth (stopped)	5⅓
Principal	4
Flute	4
Twelfth	2⅔
Fifteenth	2
Sesquialtra	III
Mixture	II
Furniture	II
Trumpet	8
Clarion	4

Swell Organ (F to f³)

Double Diapason, bass & treble	16
Open Diapason	8
Stopped Diapason	8
Principal	4
Flute (stopped)	4
Sesquialtra	III
Cornopean	8
Hautboy	8
Clarion	4

Choir Organ (GG to f³)

Open Diapason	8
Stopped Diapason, bass & treble	8
Dulciana (G)	8
Principal	4
Flute (wood)	4
Fifteenth	2
Clarionet (in a swell box)	8

Pedal Organ (C to d¹)

Open Diapason (wood)	16
Stopped Diapason (wood)	16
Principal	8
Fifteenth	4
Tierce	$3\frac{1}{5}$
Sesquialtra	II
Trombone	16

Swell to Great
Swell to Choir
Great to Pedals
Choir to Pedals
Swell to Pedals

4 composition pedals to Great & Pedal

According to the entry in Gray & Davison's Shop Book, the keys of each manual extended to GG. In the case of the Great the bottom five notes acted on the Pedal; in that of the Swell, the bottom ten notes acted on the Choir.

Source MS 3: f. 49; *MW* XVIII, 1843: 388

9   St Luke, Chelsea BEGUN BY NICHOLLS, INSTALLED AND FINISHED BY JOHN GRAY, 1824

Great Organ (GG to f³)

Open Diapason	8	
Open Diapason	8	
Open Diapason	8	
Stopped Diapason	8	
Stopped Diapason	8	
Principal	4	
Principal	4	
Twelfth	$2\frac{2}{3}$	
Fifteenth	2	
Fifteenth	2	
Tierce	$1\frac{3}{5}$	
Sesquialtra	IV	
Trumpet	8	
Clarion	4	
Pedal Pipes	16	17 notes (GG–B unisons)

Choir Organ (GG to f³)

Stopped Diapason	8
Dulciana	8
Principal	4
Flute	4
Fifteenth	2
Bassoon & Cremona	8

Swell Organ (f to f³)

Open Diapason	8
Open Diapason	8
Stopped Diapason	8
Dulciana	8
Dulciana	8
Principal	4
Principal	4
Flute	4
Cornet	III
Trumpet	8
Hautboy	8
Clarion	4

Couplers not recorded

Pedals: GG to c

Source CR XVII, 1835: 685; *MW* VIII, 1838: 280–1; Warren 1842: 77–8

10   St John's College, Cambridge WILLIAM HILL, 1839

Great Organ (FF to f³)

Double Stopped Diapason (FF to c)		
and Double Dulciana (c♯ to f³)	16	
Open Diapason, large scale	8	
Open Diapason	8	(a)
Stopped Diapason	8	
Claribella (c¹)	8	
Principal, large scale	4	
German Flute, 'voiced very softly' (F)	4	
Twelfth & Fifteenth	II	
Fifteenth, large scale	2	
Sesquialtra	III	
Pausanne	8	(a)

Choir Organ (FF to f³)

Stopped Diapason	8
Dulciana (F, then grooved)	8
Open Diapason, small scale	8
Principal	4
Flute	4
Cremona (c)	8

Swell Organ (F to f³)

Open Diapason	8	
Stopped Diapason	8	
Dulciana	8	
Principal	4	
Harmonica	4	
Sesquialtra	IV	(a)
French Horn	8	(a)
Hautboy	8	
Clarion	4	(a)

Pedal Organ (FF to c)

Double Stopped Diapason	16	(b)

Pedals on Great [Great to Pedal]
Pedals on Choir [Choir to Pedal]
Great and Swell [Swell to Great]
Great and Choir [Choir to Great]

4 composition pedals to Great
Pedal to take off Swell reeds

(a) The contract states that these were to be prepared for but not installed, though the 8′ reeds on Great and Swell seem to have been present by the time the installation was completed in 1839.
(b) Borrowed from the Great.

Source MS 25 (Covenant between Hill and the College, 29 September 1838).

The precise specification of the organ as built is difficult to establish. Further sources to consult are: 'Organs' in J. J. Smith, *Cambridge Portfolio* (*c.* 1839) [an incomplete account by Walmisley]; 'Church Organs in Cambridge – No. 1', in *Cambridge General Advertizer*, 6 March 1839; HRI: 541; W. E. Dickson, 'Old Times in Cambridge', in *MO* XVI, 1893: 398.

11   The Great Exhibition HENRY WILLIS, 1851

Great Organ (C to g³)

Double Diapason	16
Bourdon	16
Open Diapason	8
Open Diapason	8
Stopped Diapason	8
Principal	4
Principal	4
Wood-flute	4
Twelfth	2⅔
Fifteenth	2
Fifteenth	2
Piccolo (wd)	2
Doublette	1
Sesquialter	III
Fourniture	III
Mixture	III
Trumpet	16

Trumpet	8
Clarion	4
Octave Clarion	2

Choir Organ (C to g³)

Bourdon	16
Open Diapason	8
Dulceana	8
Viol di Gamba	8
Stopped Diapason	8
Viola	4
Flute – metal	4
Flute – wood	4
Principal	4
Piccolo (wd)	2
Fifteenth	2
Corno di Bassetto	8
Cremona	4
Oboe – orchestral	8

Swell Organ (C to g³)

Double Diapason	16
Double Dulceana	16
Open Diapason	8
Open Diapason	8
Dulceana	8
Viol di Gamba	8
Stopped Diapason	8
Flute (wd)	4
Principal	4
Principal (soft quality)	4
Twelfth	2⅔
Fifteenth	2
Fifteenth (soft quality)	2
Dulcimer (soft quality)	III
Sesquialter	III
Fourniture	III
Mixture	III
Trombone	8
Trumpet	8
Clarion	4
Hautboy	8
Cremona	8

Pedal Organ (C to g³)

Double-double Diapason (wd)	32
Double Diapason (wd)	16
Double Diapason	16
Violon (soft quality)	16
Bourdon (wd)	16
Octave (wd)	8
Octave	8

Quint	5⅓
Super Octave	4
Sesquialter	III
Mixture	III
Tromba	16
Trombone	8
Clarion	4

Great to Pedals
Choir to Pedals
Swell to Pedals
Swell to Great
Choir to Great
Great to Swell [*sic*]
Swell to Choir

Combination pistons (pneumatic) to each manual division

Source Pole 1851: 68–72; Sumner 1955: 18–20

12   Wells Cathedral HENRY WILLIS, 1857

Great Organ (C to g³)

Double Diapason	16
Open Diapason	8
Open Diapason	8
Stopped Diapason (wd)	8
Principal	4
Principal	4
Twelfth	2⅔
Fifteenth	2
Sesquialtera	III
Mixture	III
Posaune	16
Trombone	8
Clarion	4

Choir Organ (C to g³)

Double Diapason (wd)	16
Open Diapason	8
Dulciana	8
Stopped Diapason (wd)	8
Principal	4
Flute Harmonique	4
Piccolo Harmonique	2
Clarinet and Corno di Bassetto	8
Oboe, orchestral (g)	8

Swell Organ (C to g³)

Double Diapason and Dulciana	16
Open Diapason	8
Stopped Diapason (wd)	8
Principal	4

Fifteenth	2
Echo Cornet	III
Contra Fagotto (wd)	16
Trumpet	8
Hautboy	8
Clarion	4

Pedal Organ (C to f¹)

Double Diapason (wd)	16
Violone	16
Principal	8
Fifteenth	4
Mixture	III
Trombone (wd)	16
Posaune	8

Swell to Great
Choir to Great
Great to Pedals
Choir to Pedals
Swell to Pedals

6 combination pistons to Great
4 combination pistons to Swell
Pneumatic lever to the Great keys

Source MG II, 1857: 286; HR2: 554

13   Chapel Royal, St James's Palace HILL & DAVISON, 1837

Great Organ (GG to f³)

Open Diapason, No. 1	8
Open Diapason, No. 2	8
Stopped Diapason	8
Principal	4
Principal (wd)	4
Twelfth	2⅔
Fifteenth	2
Fifteenth (wd)	2
Sesquialtera	IV
Trumpet	8
Clarion	4
Pedal Pipes	8 17 notes

Choir Organ (GG to f³)

Open Diapason	8
Stopped Diapason	8
Dulciana	8
Principal	4
Flute	4
Fifteenth	2
Cremona and Bassoon	8

Swell Organ (G to f³)

Open Diapason	8
Stopped Diapason	8
Dulciana	8
Claribella	8
Principal	4
Fifteenth	2
French Horn	8
Trumpet	8
Oboe	8
Clarion	4

Great to Pedals
Choir to Pedals
Swell to Great
Choir to Great [?]

4 composition pedals

Source MW vi, 1837: 75n; HRI: 477

14   St James, Bristol JOHN SMITH, 1824

Great Organ (C to e³)

Open Diapason	8	
Open Diapason	8	
Stopped Diapason	8	
Principal	4	
Principal	4	
Twelfth	2⅔	
Fifteenth	2	
Fifteenth	2	
Tierce	1⅗	
Larigot	1⅓	
Twenty-second	1	
Sesquialtera	[III]	(a)
Mixture	II	
Trumpet	8	
Octave Bassoon	4	

Inside Choir (C to e³)
Chiefly borrowed, by communication, from Great Organ

Open Diapason	8
Stopped Diapason	8
Principal	4
Flute	4
Clarionet	8

Choir Organ (C to e³)

Stopped Diapason	8
Dulciana	8
Principal	4

Flute	4
Fifteenth	2

Swell Organ (c to c³ [*sic*])

Open Diapason	8
Stopped Diapason	8
Principal	4
Twelfth	2⅔
Fifteenth	2
Tierce	1⅗
Cornet	[III] (a)
Trumpet	8
Hautboy	8
Cremona	8

Pedal Organ (C to c¹)

Double Stopped Diapason	32
Open Diapason	16
Stopped Diapason	16
Principal	8
Bassoon	16

Swell to Great
Swell Octave to Great (b)
Swell to Choir
Choir to Great
Great to Pedal
Choir to Pedal

4 ventils for shutting off the wind to the various divisions
Manual keyboard for playing Pedal

(a) A connecting stop for drawing the preceding three registers.
(b) The Swell soundboard was provided with an extra octave of pipes for use with this coupler.

Source Harmonicon III, 1825: 28–9; HRI: 550–1

15   St Stephen, Bristol JOHN SMITH, JUNIOR, 1836

Great Organ (CC to f³) (a)
Enclosed in a swell box

Open Diapason	8
Stopped Diapason	8
Principal	4
Twelfth	2⅔
Fifteenth	2
Tierce	1⅗
Larigot	1⅓
Twenty-second	1
Trumpet	8

Choir Organ (CC to f³) (a)

Open Diapason	8

Stopped Diapason	8
Principal	4

Pedal Organ (C to b [?])
Open Pedal Pipes	16	24 notes

Choir to Great
Choir Octave to Great
'Pedals octave to Great' [Great Octave to Pedal ?]

(a) According to Sperling, the bottom octaves of both Great and Choir acted only on the Pedals.

Source *Bristol Mirror* 7 May 1836; MS 80: 114

16   St John, Chester HILL & DAVISON, 1838

Great Organ (C to f³)
Open Diapason, No. 1	8
Open Diapason, No. 2	8
Stopped Diapason	8
Principal	4
Twelfth	2⅔
Fifteenth	2
Sesquialtra and Cornet	IV
Trumpet	8

Choir Organ (C to f³)
Double Stopped Diapason, 'to meet same stop in the Swell'	16
Open Diapason (G)	8
Stopped Diapason and Clarabella	8
Dulciana (c)	8
Principal	4
Fifteenth	2
Cremona (c)	8

Swell Organ (C to f³) (a)
Double Stopped Diapason	16
Open Diapason	8
Stopped Diapason	8
Principal	4
Fifteenth	2
Mixture	III
Trumpet	8
Hautboy	8

Pedal Organ (C to c¹)
Double Open Diapason (zinc)	16
Double Stopped Diapason	16
Double Trumpet	16

Swell to Great
Choir to Great

Great to Pedal
Choir to Pedal
Pedal Octave

3 composition pedals to Great
2 composition pedals to Swell

(a) The Swell stops had a compass of c to f^3 and the lowest octave of the keyboard was permanently coupled to the Choir Organ.

Source MW x, 1838: 44; Warren 1842: 94

17   Worcester Cathedral WILLIAM HILL, 1842

Great Organ (C to f^3)
Bourdon and Tenoroon Diapason	16
Open Diapason	8
Open Diapason	8
Stopped Diapason	8
Quint	5$\frac{1}{3}$
Principal	4
Wald-flute	4
Twelfth	2$\frac{2}{3}$
Fifteenth	2
Sesquialtra	III
Mixture	II
Doublette	II
Posaune	8

Choir Organ (C to f^3)
Stopped bass and Clarabella	8
Dulciana	8
Principal	4
Stopped-flute	4
Oboe-flute	4
Fifteenth	2
Cremona	8

Swell Organ (c to f^3)
Double Dulciana	16
Open Diapason	8
Stopped Diapason	8
Dulciana	8
Principal	4
Suabe-flute	4
Flageolet	2
Doublette	II
Echo Cornet	V
Cornopean	8
Oboe	8

Pedal Organ (C to e^1)
Open Diapason	16

Stopped Diapason	16
Principal	8
Fifteenth	4
Sesquialtra	v
Trombone	16

Swell to Great
Swell to Choir
Pedals to Great
Pedals to Choir

5 composition pedals

Source MS 12: 115, 119–20; MS 81: 43

18   Edinburgh Music Hall WILLIAM HILL, 1843

Great Organ (C to f³)

Bourdon and Tenoroon	16
Unison, open	8
Unison, closed (halves)	8
Quint	5⅓
Octave	4
Wald-flute	4
Duodecima	2⅔
Super-octave	2
Sesquialtra	III
Mixture	II
Doublette	II
Posaune	8

Choir Organ (C to f³)

Unison, closed, and Clarabella	8	
Salicional	8	
Viol di Gamba	8	
Celestina	4	
Closed Flute	4	
Oboe-flute	4	
Piccolo (metal)	2	
Cremona	8	
Corno-flute	8	
Cornopean, bass	8	(a)

Swell Organ (c to f³)

Tenoroon Dulciana	16
Unison, open	8
Unison, closed	8
Octave	4
Suabe-flute	4
Flageolet	2
Doublette	II
Echo Cornet	IV

| Cornopean | 8 |
| Oboe | 8 |

Pedal Organ (C to d^1)

Contra Bass, open	16
Bourdon, stopped	16
Trombone (wood)	16

Swell to Great
Choir to Great
Great to Pedal
Choir to Pedal

3 composition pedals

(a) This cornopean bass of twelve notes was probably intended to complete the short-compass cornopean on the Swell. The Swell keyboard may have been of full compass, C to f^3, with the bottom octave permanently coupled to the Choir, though there is no explicit evidence for this.

Source MS 12: 116; HRI: 555–6

19   Nottingham, Mechanics' Hall BEVINGTON, 1849

Great Organ (C to g^3)

Bourdon and Tenoroon	16
Open Diapason	8
Stop Diapason	8
Hohl Flute	8
Quint	5$\frac{1}{3}$
Principal	4
Wald Flute	4
Decima	3$\frac{1}{5}$
Fifteenth	2
Triplet	III
Sesquialtra	III
Great Posaune	8
Trumpet	8
Octave Trumpet	4

Swell Organ (c to g^3)

Great Double Diapason	32
Double Diapason	16
Open Diapason	8
Stop Diapason	8
Quint	5$\frac{1}{3}$
Principal	4
Wald Flute	4
Fifteenth	2
Piccolo	2
Octave Fifteenth	1
Furniture	v
Trombone	16

Cornopean	8	
Clarion	4	
Octave Clarion	2	

Solo or Choir Organ (C to g^3)

Double Diapason	16	
Stop Diapason	8	
Dulciana	8	
Viol di Gamba	8	
Flute	4	
Flageolet	2	
Bassoon	16	[?]
Clarionet	8	
Oboe	8	

Pedal Organ (C to d^1)

Double Open	16	
Unison Open	8	
Trombone	16	

4 couplers
8 composition pedals

Source Nottingham Review 19 October 1849; cf. HRI: 534

20   Christ Church, Newgate Street RECONSTRUCTED BY WILLIAM HILL, 1838

Great Organ (C to f^3)

Double Open Diapason	16	
Open Diapason	8	
Open Diapason	8	
Stopped Diapason	8	
Principal	4	
Twelfth	2$\frac{2}{3}$	
Fifteenth	2	
Sesquialtra	V	
Mixture	V	
Trumpet	8	(a)
Posaune	8	
Clarion	4	

Swell Organ (C to f^3)

Double Diapason	16	
Open Diapason	8	
Stopped Diapason	8	
Principal	4	
Flageolet	4	
Fifteenth	2	
Sesquialtra	V	
Horn	8	
Trumpet	8	

Hautboy	8
Clarion	4

Choir Organ (C to f³)
Open Diapason (G)	8
Stopped Diapason	8
Principal	4
Stopped Flute	4
Fifteenth	2

Pedal Organ (C to g¹) (b)
Open Diapason (wood)	16
Open Diapason, small (wood)	16
Open Diapason (metal)	16
Principal	8
Twelfth	5⅓
Fifteenth	4
Sesquialtra	v
Mixture	v
Posaune	16
Clarion	8

8 couplers (unspecified)
1 shifting movement to the Swell
no composition pedals

(a) This was later transposed into a 16′ register (HRI: 450) though its compass may not have been completed until the rebuild of 1868.

(b) None of the Pedal stops had a complete compass. With the possible exception of the larger of the wooden open diapasons (the old double pedal pipes) which had seventeen notes, the flue registers had only a single octave of pipes. The reeds were even more deficient: they had only five notes derived from the old manual basses GG to BB.

Source MW VIII, 1838: 279–81; MS 79: 8; HRI: 449–50; MS 13: 26

21   Christ Church, Newgate Street UNEXECUTED SCHEME BY H. J. GAUNTLETT AND WILLIAM HILL (*c.* 1840)

Great Organ
Bourdon and Tenoroon Diapason	16
Open Diapason	8
Open Diapason	8
Viol di Gamba	8
Stopped Diapason	8
Quint	5⅓
Principal	4
Principal	4
Wald-flute	4
Fifteenth	2
Piccolo	2
Larigot	1⅓
Tierce	1⅗

Doublette	II
Larigot Mixture	V
Tierce Mixture	V
Cornet de Cinque	V
Furniture de Cinque	V
Contra-fagotto and Tenoroon Trumpet	16
Trombone	8
Clarion	4
Octave Clarion	2

Choir Organ

Sub-Bass	16	
Open Diapason	8	
Stopped Diapason	8	
Dulciana	8	
Claribel-flute	8	
Principal	4	
Oboe-flute	4	
Stopped-flute	4	
Twelfth	$2\frac{2}{3}$	
Fifteenth	2	
Sesquialtera	III	
Mixture	II	
Echo Dulciana Cornet	V	
Cornopean	8	
Cromorne	8	
Swiss Cromorne-flute	8	[?]

Swell Organ

Bourdon and Tenoroon Dulciana	16
Open Diapason	8
Stopped Diapason	8
Principal	4
Flageolet	4
Fifteenth	2
Mixture	V
Oboe	8
Tromba	8
Corno	8
Clarion	4

Pedal Organ

Open Diapason, large (wood)	16	
Open Diapason, small (wood)	16	
Open Diapason, Montre (metal)	16	
Bourdon	16	[?]
Principal	8	
Fifteenth	4	
Tierce Mixture	V	
Larigot Mixture	V	
Contra-posaune	16	
Posaune	8	

8 couplers

'And room left for the Grand Ophicleide and an Œolophon on a separate row of keys.'

Source Hill 1841

22   St Luke, Cheetham Hill, Manchester WILLIAM HILL, 1840

Great Organ (C to f³)

Bourdon and Tenoroon Diapason	16
Open Diapason	8
Stopped Diapason, bass and treble	8
Principal	4
Twelfth	2⅔
Fifteenth	2
Flageolet	1
Sesquialtra	III
Mixture	II
Trombone	8

Choir Organ (C to f³)

Open Diapason	8	
Stopped Diapason, bass and treble	8	
Principal	4	
Fifteenth	2	
Dulciana	8	(b)
Claribella	8	
Oboe-flute	4	
Wald-flute	4	
Flageolet	2	
Cremona	8	

Swell Organ (c to f³)

Double Diapason, bass and treble	16
Open Diapason	8
Stopped Diapason	8
Principal	4
Doublette	II
Horn	8
Oboe	8

Pedal (C to d¹) (b)

Open Diapason	16
Stopped Diapason	16
Trombone	16

Swell to Great
Choir to Great
Great to Pedals
Choir to Pedals
Swell to Pedals

3 composition pedals to Great
2 composition pedals to Swell

(a) The Choir stops are given here in the same order as they are recorded in Hill's Letter Book (MS 12: 74); the dulciana, and the following registers, are there designated 'Solo Stops'.
(b) The Pedal stops had a single octave of pipes. Hill originally proposed making them playable from the lowest octave of the Great keyboard (MS 12: 74) but it is not known if this was done.

Source MS 12: 42, 74, 80; Warren 1842: 101–2; HRI: 510–11

23   Great George Street Chapel, Liverpool WILLIAM HILL, 1841

Great Organ (C to f³)

Bourdon and Tenoroon Open Diapason	16	
Open Diapason	8	
Open Diapason	8	(a)
Stopped Diapason, bass and treble	8	
Quint	5⅓	
Principal	4	
Stopped-flute (metal)	4	
Twelfth	2⅔	
Fifteenth	2	
Tierce	1⅗	
Sesquialtera	III	
Mixture	II	(b)
Doublette	II	
Trombone	8	(c)
Clarion	4	
Octave Clarion	2	

Swell Organ (C to f³)

Bourdon and Tenoroon Dulciana	16
Open Diapason	8
Stopped Diapason, bass and treble	8
Dulciana (Echo)	8
Principal	4
Suabe-flute	4
Twelfth	2⅔
Fifteenth	2
Flageolet	2
Sesquialtera	III
Mixture	II
Echo Dulciana Cornet	V
Contra-fagotto	16
Cornopean	8
Trumpet	8
Oboe	8
Clarion	4
Swiss Cromorne-flute	8

Choir Organ (C to f³)

Stopped Diapason	8
Dulciana	8

Claribel-flute	8
Oboe-flute	4
Wald-flute	4
Piccolo	2
Corno-flute	8
Cromorne	8

Solo Organ (playable from the Swell keys)

Tuba Mirabilis	8	(d)

Pedal Organ (C to d¹)

Grand Open Diapason	16	
Bourdon	16	
Principal	8	(e)
Fifteenth	4	(e)
Sesquialtra	v	(e)
Trombone	16	

Swell to Great
Choir to Great
Great to Pedal
Swell to Pedal
Choir to Pedal
Pedal Octave [?] (f)

4 composition pedals

(a) Not included in Hill 1841 or Warren 1842: 85.
(b) HRI: 508 gives three ranks, but two is more likely.
(c) Hill 1841 (and, following him, Warren 1842) adds a 16′ reed to the Great ('Contra-fagotto and Tenoroon Trumpet') but there is no evidence of its existence elsewhere.
(d) Hill 1841 states that this stop had its own keyboard. Both *Gawthrop* and HRI imply that this was not the case, and *Gawthrop* specifically states that it was played from the Swell.
(e) If *Gawthrop*'s account of the organ in 1841 is correct, then these registers were added later (both Sperling and Hopkins record their existence). Hill 1841 implies that a 32′ contra bourdon was originally intended. Assuming it was never installed, there would have been room for additions to the Pedal Organ; but it may be, in any case, that the Pedal was radically reconstructed sometime during the 1840s (above, p. 204).
(f) *Gawthrop* and Hill 1841 claim that there were six couplers. Hopkins records the first five given above. Could a Pedal octave coupler, as proposed at an earlier stage by Hill (MS 12: 84) have been the sixth?

Source MS 12: 81–5, 92, 97, 98; *Gawthrop's Journal* 18 December 1841; Hill 1841; Warren 1842: 85–6; MS 80: 158; HRI: 508

24   Easton-on-the-Hill, Parish Church G. M. HOLDICH, 1849 (a)

Great Organ (C to f³)

Bourdon (C to B)	16
Open Diapason	8
Stop'd Diapason Bass (C to B)	8
Clarabella (c)	8
Principal	4

Flute	4
Twelfth	2⅔
Fifteenth	2
Tierce	1⅗
Sesquialtera	II
Trumpet	8 (b)
Pedal Pipes	16 (c)

Swell Organ (C to f³) (d)

Double Diapason	16
Dulciana	8
Stopped Diapason	8
Principal	4
Fifteenth	2
Hautboy	8

Coupler, Swell [Swell to Great]
Pedals, Great [Great to Pedal]
Pedals, Swell 4′ [Swell Octave to Pedal]

4 composition pedals to Great

(a) The date is that given by Sperling; no date is recorded at the console.
(b) Holdich prepared for the addition of a trumpet; the present one, which is said to be by Holdich, was installed in 1972.
(c) Sperling states that there were one-and-a-half octaves of stopped Pedal pipes, C to g. The original pedal board may have been restricted to the same compass.
(d) The Swell pipework commences at (tenor) c. The lowest octave of the keyboard sounds the bourdon and stop'd bass of the Great Organ when those registers are drawn, thus providing a 'choir bass'.

Source The organ; MS 80: 197

25   Lichfield Cathedral G. M. HOLDICH, 1861

Great Organ (C to f³)

Sub Bass (C to B)	16
Tenoroon (c)	16
Open Diapason	8
Open Diapason, bass (C to B)	8
Open Diapason (c)	8
Bell Gamba (c)	8
Clarabella	8
Stopped Diapason	8
Octave	4
Gamba Octave	4
Wald Flute	4
Super Quint	2⅔
Super Octave	2
Tierce	1⅗
Sesquialtera	II
Doublette	II
Mixture	II

Posaune	8
Clarion	4

Choir Organ (C to f³)

Stopped Diapason, bass and treble	8
Dulciana	8
Principal	4
Flute	4
Fifteenth	2
Cremona (c)	8

Swell Organ (C to f³)

Bourdon (C to B)	16
Double Diapason (c)	16
Open Diapason, bass (C to B)	8
Open Diapason (c)	8
Keraulophon (c)	8
Stopped Diapason	8
Principal	4
Fifteenth	2
Tierce	1⅗
Sesquialtera	II
Mixture	II
Tromba (c)	16
Cornopean, bass (C to B)	8
Cornopean, treble (c)	8
Trumpet	8
Hautboy (c)	8
Clarion	4

Pedal Organ (C to e¹)

Double Double Open Diapason (C to B)	32
Double Open Diapason	16
Montre	16
Grand Bourdon	16
Octave	8
Super Octave	4
Sesquialtera	II
Mixture	II
Grand Trombone	16
Grand Trumpet	8

Pedals to Great [Great to Pedal]
Pedals to Swell [Swell to Pedal]
Pedals to Choir [Choir to Pedal]
Swell to Great
Swell to Choir
Great to Choir [?]
Octave Coupler Pedals

8 composition pedals

Source HR2: 499–500

26   Worcester, Music Hall JOHN NICHOLSON, 1854

Great Organ (C to g³)

Great Diapason, metal throughout	16
Open Diapason	8
Open Diapason, small	8
Gamba	8
Bourdon	8
Quint	5⅓
Octave	4
Gemshorn	4
Wald Flute	4
Twelfth	2⅔
Fifteenth	2
Tierce	1⅗
Mixture	v
Posaune	8
Clarion	4
Spare slide	

Swell Organ (C to g³)

Great Diapason, open throughout	16
Open Diapason	8
Stopped Diapason	8
Gamba	8
Keraulophon	8
Octave	4
Gambette	4
Wald Flute	4
Super-octave	2
Mixture	v
Trombone	16
Cornopean	8
Hautboy	8
Clarionette	8
Clarion	4
Spare slide	

Choir Organ (C to g³)

Open Diapason	8
Viol di Gamba	8
Dulciana	8
Clarabella	8
Stopped Diapason	8
Harmonic Flute	4
Dulcet	4
Suabe Flute	4
Octave Flute	2
Echo Cornet	v
Trumpet	8
Spare slide	

Pedal Organ (C to f¹)

Great Diapason, open, wood	32
Open Diapason	16
Open Diapason, small, wood	16
Dulciana	16
Violon	16
Bourdon	16
Quint, Stopped	10⅔
Principal	8
Bass Flute	8
Fifteenth	4
Mixture	III
Posaune	16

Swell to Great
Swell to Choir
Choir to Great
Great to Pedal
Choir to Pedal
Swell to Pedal
Pedal Octave
Swell Octave

Ventil to Pedal Organ
Sforzando pedal
Tremulant (Swell)
10 composition pedals
Pneumatic lever attachment [assisting Pedal couplers?]

Source HRI: 498–9; Wickens 1974 cites another source (*Berrow's Worcester Journal*, 3 November 1854) and notes discrepancies between the two versions of the stop list; HRI is preferred here, but both should be consulted.

27   St Paul's, Wilton Place, Knightsbridge GRAY & DAVISON, 1843

Great Organ (C to f³)

Double Diapason, bass and treble	16
Open Diapason	8
Open Diapason	8
Stopped Diapason	8
Principal	4
Twelfth	2⅔
Fifteenth	2
Sesquialtra	IV
Mixture	II
Furniture	II
Trumpet	8
Clarion	4

Swell Organ (C to f³)

Double Diapason, bass and treble	16
Open Diapason	8
Stopped Diapason	8

Principal	4
Flute	4
Fifteenth	2
Sesquialtra	III
Mixture	II
Cornopean	8
Trumpet	8
Hautboy	8
Clarion	4

Choir Organ (C to f³)

Stopped Diapason, bass and treble	8
Dulciana	8
Keraulophon	8
Clarabella Flute	8
Principal	4
Flute	4
Fifteenth	2
Piccolo	2
Mixture	II
Clarionet	8

Pedal Organ (C to e¹)

Open Diapason	16
Stopped Diapason	16
Principal	8
Fifteenth	4
Sesquialtra	IV
Trombone	16

Swell to Great
Swell to Choir
Great to Pedals
Swell to Pedals
Choir to Pedals

4 composition pedals to Great
2 composition pedals to Swell
2 composition pedals to Pedal

A separate keyboard was provided to the left of the Choir keys from which the Pedal might be played.

Mixture compositions:
Some notes on proposed compositions survive in the Shop Book (MS 3: f.42). They are incomplete, and may not have been carried out, but are nonetheless worth recording here.

Gt Sesquialtra	C	15.17.19.22
		[break at c¹ ?]
	f²	12.15
Gt Mixture	C	[26].29
	f¹	19.22
	f²	15

Gt Furniture	C	22.29 [*sic*]
	f¹	22.22
	f²	15
Ch Mixture	C	19.22
	f²	15
Sw Mixture	C	15.22
		[no more given]

Source MS 3: f.42; *MW* XVIII, 1843: 140–1

28   Nottingham, Halifax Place Wesleyan Chapel GRAY & DAVISON, 1847

Great Organ (C to f³)

Double Diapason, bass, C to d¹	16
Double Dulciana, from d♯¹	16
Open Diapason	8
Stopped Diapason, bass, C to B	8
Clarabella Flute (c)	8
Dulciana	8
Quint	5⅓ (a)
Principal	4
Flute (c)	4
Twelfth	2⅔
Fifteenth	2
Sesquialtra	III
Mixture	II
Trumpet	8
Clarionet (g)	8

Swell Organ (C to f³) (b)

Double Diapason	16
Open Diapason	8
Stopped Diapason	8
Principal	4
Fifteenth	2
Sesquialtra	III
Cornopean	8
Hautboy	8
Clarion	4

Pedal Organ (C to d¹)

Grand Open Diapason	16	
'Grand Principal octave Pedal Coupler'	8	(c)

Great to Pedal
Swell to Great

6 composition pedals

(a) This was prepared for in 1847. Andrew Freeman found a keraulophon in its place in 1907.

(b) The compass of the Swell stops commenced at (tenor) c. The lowest octave was permanently coupled to the Great.
(c) Presumably a simple octave coupler; if so, the 16′ probably had an extra octave of pipes to accommodate it.

Source MS 5: ff.3–4

29   St Anne, Limehouse GRAY & DAVISON, 1851

Great Organ (C to f³)

Double Open Diapason	16
Open Diapason	8
Open Diapason	8
Stopped Diapason	8
Octave	4
Flute (stopped wood)	4
Twelfth	2⅔
Fifteenth	2
Flageolet (open wood)	2
Sesquialtra	III
Mixture	II
Posaune	8
Clarion	4

Choir Organ (C to f³)

Stopped Diapason, bass	8
Clarionet Flute (c)	8
Dulciana	8
Keraulophon	8
Octave	4
Flute (open wood)	4
Fifteenth	2
Clarionet	8

Swell Organ (C to f³) (a)

Bourdon	16
Open Diapason	8
Stopped Diapason	8
Octave	4
Fifteenth	2
Sesquialtra	III
Cornopean	8
Oboe	8
Clarion	4

Pedal Organ (C to e¹)

Grand Open Diapason	16
Grand Bourdon	16
Grand Octave	4
Grand Bombarde	16

Swell to Great
Swell to Choir

Great to Pedals
Choir to Pedals
Swell Octave to Pedals

Sforzando pedal [Great to Swell]
Composition pedals:
    1 Swell: Stopped Diapason, Cornopean
    2 Swell: Full Swell
    3 Great: Open Diapason [I], Stopped Diapason, Flute, Flageolet
    4 Great: Double Open Diapason, Open Diapasons, Stopped Diapason
    5 Great: Double Open Diapason, Open Diapasons, Stopped Diapason, Octave, Twelfth,
       Fifteenth, Sesquialtra
    6 Great: Full Great

Mixture compositions:

Gt & Sw Sesquialtras	C	17.19.22
	f♯²	12.15
Gt Mixture	C	26.29
	f♯	19.22
	f♯¹	12.15

(a) The pipework commences at (tenor) c and the lowest octave is permanently coupled to the Choir.

Source The organ; Pole 1851: 65–7

30   Glasgow City Hall GRAY & DAVISON, 1853

Great Organ (C to c⁴)

Bourdon	16
Open Diapason	8
Stopped Diapason	8
Gamba	8
Flute Harmonique	8
Octave	4
Piccolo	4
Flute Harmonique	4
Twelfth	2⅔
Fifteenth	2
Ottavina	2
Sesquialtra	III
Mixture	III
Posaune	8
Clarion	4

Swell Organ (C to c⁴)

Bourdon	16
Open Diapason	8
Keraulophon	8
Stopped Diapason, bass	8
Clarionet Flute	8
Octave	4
Flute	4
Fifteenth	2

Flageolet	2
Sesquialtra	III
Mixture	II
Contra-Fagotto	16
Cornopean	8
Oboe	8
Voix-Humaine	8
Clarion	4

Choir Organ (C to c⁴)

Open Diapason (tin)	8
Stopped Diapason, bass	8
Clarionet Flute	8
Salcional	8
Voix-Celeste	8
Octave	4
Flute	4
Fifteenth	2
Piccolo	2
Corno di Bassetto	8

Pedal Organ (C to f¹)

Contra Bourdon	32
Open Diapason	16
Bourdon	16
Octave	8
Fifteenth	4
Trombone	16

Swell to Great
Swell to Great, Super-Octave
Swell to Great, Sub-Octave
Choir to Great, Sub-Octave
Great to Pedals
Swell to Pedals
Choir to Pedals
Great reeds and harmonic flutes to Swell, by a pedal

6 composition pedals to Great
2 composition pedals to Swell
Tremulant (Swell)

Source MS 6: ff.23–6; *MW* XXXI, 1853: 525–6; HRI: 554–5

31   Crystal Palace, Handel Festival Organ GRAY & DAVISON, 1857

Great Organ (C to a³)

Double Open Diapason, metal	16
Double Dulciana	16
Flute à Pavillon	8
Viol de Gamba	8
Octave	4

Harmonic Flute	8
Clarabel Flute	8
Flute Octaviante	4
Super Octave	2
Flageolet Harmonic	2
Quint	5⅓
Twelfth	2⅔
Mixture	IV
Furniture	III
Cymbal	V
Bombarde	16
Posaune	8
Trumpet	8
Clarion	4
Octave Clarion	2

Choir Organ (C to a³)

Bourdon	16
Gamba	8
Salcional	8
Voix Celeste	8
Clarionet Flute	8
Gemshorn	4
Wald Flute	4
Spitz Flute	2
Piccolo	2
Mixture	II
Cor Anglais and Bassoon	8
Trumpet (small scale)	8

Swell Organ (C to a³)

Bourdon	16
Open Diapason	8
Keraulophon	8
Concert Flute	8
Octave	4
Flute	4
Vox Humana	8
Twelfth	2⅔
Super Octave	2
Piccolo	2
Mixture	IV
Scharf	III
Contra Fagotto	16
Cornopean	8
Oboe	8
Clarion	4
Echo Tromba	8

Solo Organ (C to a³)

Harmonic Flute	8
Flute Octaviante	4
Mixture	II
Corno di Bassetto	8
Grand Tromba	8

Pedal Organ (C to f¹)

Contra Bass	32
Open Diapason, wood	16
Violon	16
Open Diapason, metal	16
Octave	8
Twelfth	5⅓
Super Octave	4
Mixture	IV
Contra Bombarde, free reed	32
Bombarde	16
Trumpet	8
Clarion	4

NB The stops are grouped by soundboards, each subject to the control of a combination pedal, or ventil.

Swell to Great
Swell to Great, Sub Octave
Swell to Great, Super Octave
Swell to Pedals
Swell to Choir
Solo to Great
Solo to Choir
Great Super Octave
Solo to Pedals
Choir to Pedals
Great to Pedals
Choir to Great

Sforzando pedal [Great to Swell]
Tremulant (Swell)
3 combination pedals (ventils) to Great & Pedal
2 combination pedals (ventils) to Swell
1 combination pedal (ventil) to Choir
All couplers excepting those associated with the Solo Organ acted upon by individual pedals

Source MW xxxv, 1857: 391–3

32   Leeds Town Hall GRAY & DAVISON, 1859

Great Organ (C to c⁴)

FRONT GREAT

Double Diapason, metal	16
Open Diapason	8
Spitz Gamba	8
Stopped Diapason	8
Octave	4
Wald Flöte	4
Twelfth	2⅔
Fifteenth	2
Quint Mixture	IV
Tierce Mixture	V
Trumpet	8
Clarion	4

BACK GREAT

Bourdon	16
Flute à Pavillon	8
Viola	8
Flute Harmonic	8
Quint	5⅓
Octave	4
Flute Octaviante	4
Piccolo Harmonic	2
Cymbal	III
Furniture	IV
Contra Trombone	16
Trombone	8
Trumpet Harmonic	8
Tenor Trombone	4

Swell Organ (C to c⁴)

Bourdon	16
Open Diapason	8
Stopped Diapason, bass and treble	8
Keraulophon	8
Harmonic Flute	8
Octave	4
Gemshorn	4
Wood Flute	4
Twelfth	2⅔
Fifteenth	2
Piccolo	2
Sesquialtra	IV
Mixture	III
Contra Fagotto	16
Trumpet	8
Cornopean	8
Oboe	8

Vox Humana	8
Clarion	4

Choir Organ (C to c⁴)

Sub Dulciana	16
Open Diapason	8
Stopped Diapason, bass, C to B	8
Rohr Flute, metal (c)	8
Salcional	8
Viol de Gamba (c)	8
Octave	4
Suabe Flute	4
Flute Harmonic	4
Twelfth	2⅔
Fifteenth	2
Ottavino, wood	2
Dulciana Mixture	V
Euphone, free reed	16
Trumpet	8
Clarion	4

Orchestral Solo Organ (C to c⁴)

Bourdon	8
Concert Flute Harmonic	8
Piccolo Harmonic	4
Ottavino Harmonic	2
Clarinet	8
Oboe	8
Cor Anglais and Bassoon, free reed	8
Tromba	8
Ophicleide	8

By mechanical combination:
Clarinet and Flute, in octaves
Oboe and Flute, in octaves
Clarinet and Bassoon, in octaves
Clarinet and Oboe, in octaves
Oboe and Bassoon, in octaves
Flute, Clarinet and Bassoon, in double octaves
Flute, Oboe and Bassoon, in double octaves

Echo Organ (C to c⁴) (a)

Bourdon	16
Dulciana	8
Lieblich Gedact, wood	8
Flute Traverso, wood	4
Flute d'Amour	4
Dulciana Mixture	IV
Carillons (f to c⁴)	

Pedal Organ (C to f¹)

Sub-Bass, open metal	32
Contra Bourdon, wood	32

Open Diapason, wood	16
Open Diapason, metal	16
Violin, wood	16
Bourdon, wood	16
Quint, open wood	10⅔
Octave	8
Violoncello	8
Twelfth	5⅓
Fifteenth	4
Mixture	IV
Contra Bombard, free reed	32
Bombard	16
Fagotto	16
Clarion	8

Solo to Great
Great to Solo
Solo Super Octave
Solo Sub Octave
Swell to Great
Swell to Great, Super Octave
Swell to Great, Sub Octave
Swell to Choir
Choir to Great
Great to Pedal
Swell to Pedal
Choir to Pedal
Solo to Pedal
Echo to Solo
Echo to Choir
Full Pedal Organ

Swell pedals to Swell and Solo
Tremulant to Echo
Tremulant to Swell (by pedal)
Ventil to Back Great
Pedal to couple Back Great to Swell
Crescendo and diminuendo pedals
Wind couplers to composition pedals

4 adjustable composition pedals, each with an index for setting to desired combination of stops

(a)　The Echo Organ was part of the original scheme but was not added until 1865.

Source HR2: 515–21; Spark 1892: 218–31

33　Kinnaird Hall, Dundee FORSTER & ANDREWS, 1864

Great Organ (C to a³)

Double Diapason (wd & m)	16
Open Diapason	8
Violin Diapason	8

Hohlflöte (wd)	8
Stopped Diapason (wd)	8
Principal	4
Harmonic Flute	4
Twelfth	$2\frac{2}{3}$
Fifteenth	2
Full Mixture	V
Sharp Mixture	III
Double Trumpet	16
Trumpet	8
Posaune	8
Clarion	4

Choir Organ (C to a³)

Bourdon (wd & m)	16
Dulciana	8
Lieblich Gedact (wd & m)	8
Viol d'Amour	4
Gedact Flöte	4
Flautino	2
Krummhorn	8

Swell Organ (C to a³)

Double Stopped Diapason (wd)	16
Open Diapason	8
Viol di Gamba	8
Stopped Diapason (wd & m)	8
Principal	4
Flauto Traverso Harmonic	4
Mixture	IV
Contra Fagotto	16
Horn	8
Hautboy	8
Clarion	4

Solo Organ (C to a³)

Harmonic Flute	8
Flute Octaviante	4
Orchestral Clarionet	8
Orchestral Oboe	8
Tuba (unenclosed)	8

Pedal Organ (C to f¹)

Double Open Diapason (wd)	32	prepared
Large Open Diapason (wd)	16	
Open Diapason	16	
Violon (wd)	16	
Bourdon (wd)	16	
Quint (wd)	$10\frac{2}{3}$	
Principal	8	
Flute (wd)	8	
Violoncello (wd)	8	

Trombone	16
Trumpet	8

Solo to Great
Swell to Great
Choir to Great sub-octave
Great to Pedals
Swell to Pedals
Choir to Pedals
Great Organ reeds (?)

4 combination movements to Great & Pedal
3 combination movements to Swell
Tremulant (Swell)
Swell pedals to Swell and Solo

Source HR3: 608–9

34   St Peter, Manchester KIRTLAND & JARDINE, 1856

Great Organ (C to g³)

Double Open Diapason	16
Open Diapason	8
Stopped Diapason	8
Gamba	8
Flute Harmonique	8
Viola d'Amour	8
Quint	5⅓
Principal	4
Flute Harmonique	4
Clear Flute	4
Twelfth	2⅔
Fifteenth	2
Full Mixture	V
Sharp Mixture	IV
Euphone (free reed)	16
Trompette Harmonique	8
Clarion	4

Choir Organ (C to g³)

Bourdon	16
Spitzflöte	8
Dulciana	8
Viol di Gamba	8
Gedact	8
Voix Celeste	8
Gemshorn	4
Flauto Traverso	4
Rohr Flöte	4
Fifteenth	2
Mixture	IV
Contra Fagotto	16
Clarinet	8

Swell Organ (C to g³)

Bourdon	16
Open Diapason	8
Stopped Diapason	8
Hohl Flöte	8
Principal	4
Gedact Flöte	4
Twelfth	2⅔
Fifteenth	2
Clear Mixture	v
Cornopean	8
Hautboy	8
Cor Anglais	8
Voix Humaine	8
Clarion	4

Pedal Organ (C to f¹)

Sub-bass	32
Montre	16
Violin	16
Stopped Diapason [*sic*]	16
Grosse Quint	10⅔
Principal	8
Violoncello	8
Twelfth	5⅓
Fifteenth	4
Posaune (free reed)	16
Trumpet	8

Swell to Great
Swell to Great Super Octave
Swell to Great Sub Octave
Choir to Great
Great to Pedals
Swell to Pedals
Choir to Pedals
Pedal Organ to Pedals [ventil?]
Clochette

6 composition pedals
Sforzando pedal
Tremulant (Swell)

Source MG 1, 1856: 174

35   All Saints, Margaret Street, London HILL & SON, 1859

NORTH ORGAN

Great Organ (C to f³)

Double Diapason	16
Open Diapason	8
Stopped Diapason	8

Octave	4
Wald Flute	4
Twelfth	2⅔
Fifteenth	2
Mixture	III
Trombone	8 (a)

Choir Organ (C to f³)

Stopped Diapason	8
Cone Gamba	8
Octave	4
Nason Flute	4
Vox Humana	8

Pedal Organ (C to f¹)

Open Diapason (wd)	16

SOUTH ORGAN

Swell Organ (C to f³)

Bourdon	16
Open Diapason	8
Stopped Diapason	8
Octave	4
Twelfth	2⅔
Fifteenth	2
Mixture	II
Cornopean	8
Oboe	8

Choir Organ (C to f³)

Stopped Diapason	8
Dulciana	8
Gemshorn	4 (b)
Suabe Flute	4
Cormorne	8

Pedal Organ (C to f¹)

Open Diapason (m)	16

North to South Choir
Swell to Great
Great to Pedal
Swell to Pedal
North Choir to Pedal
South Choir to Pedal

3 composition pedals to Great
2 composition pedals to Swell

The four keyboards were arranged in the order: South Choir, North Choir, Great and Swell, the latter being the highest of the set.

(a) Called 'Posaune' in *Eccl*.
(b) Called 'Octave' in *Eccl*.

Source M W XXXVII, 1859: 363–4; *Eccl* XX, 1859: 303; MS 12: 373

36   Carlisle Cathedral HENRY WILLIS, 1856

Great Organ (C to g^3)

Double Open Diapason	16
Open Diapason	8
Stopped Diapason (wd)	8
Principal	4
Twelfth	2$\frac{2}{3}$
Fifteenth	2
Sesquialtera	v
Furniture	iii
Trombone	8
Trumpet	8
Clarion	4

Choir Organ (C to g^3)

Open Diapason	8
Clarabella (wd)	8
Dulciana	8
Gamba	8
Harmonic Flute	4
Clarionette	8

Swell Organ (C to g^3)

Double Dulciana	16
Open Diapason	8
Stopped Diapason (wd)	8
Principal	4
Flageolet (wd)	2
Echo Cornet	v
Contra Fagotto (wd)	16
Horn	8
Oboe	8
Vox Humana	8
Clarion	4

Pedal Organ (C to f^1)

Open Diapason (wd)	16
Violone	16
Bourdon (wd)	16
Principal	8
Fifteenth	4
Trombone	16
Trumpet	8

Swell to Great
Choir to Great
Pedals to Great [Great to Pedal]
Pedal to Swell [Swell to Pedal]
Pedal to Choir [Choir to Pedal]

6 combination pistons to Great & Pedal

6 combination pistons to Swell
Tremulant to Swell

Source HR2: 523; Nicholson 1907: 9–10

37   Bolton Town Hall GRAY & DAVISON, 1874

Great Organ (C to c³)

Double Open Diapason	16
Open Diapason	8
Viola	8
Claribel Flute (wd)	8
Principal	4
Flute Octaviante	4
Quint Mixture	II
Great Mixture	V
Double Trombone	16
Harmonic Trumpet	8
Clarion	4

Choir Organ (C to c⁴)

Bourdon (wd)	16
Violin Diapason	8
Vox Angelica	8
Lieblich Gedact (wd & m)	8
Flauto Traverso	4
Piccolo	2
Echo Dulciana Cornet	V
Trumpet	8

Solo Organ (C to c⁴)

Concert Open Diapason	8
Flute Harmonique	8
Flute Octaviante Harmonique	4
Cor Anglais	8
Clarionet and Bassoon	8
Tuba Mirabilis	8
Carillon (bells)	[4]

Swell Organ (C to c⁴)

Lieblich Bourdon (wd & m)	16
Open Diapason	8
Viol di Gamba	8
Voix Celestes	8
Lieblich Gedact (wd & m)	8
Salicet	4
Nazard	2⅔
Flautino	2
Mixture	III
Vox Humana	8
Corno di Bassetto	8
Hautbois	8

Trumpet	8
Clarion	4

Pedal Organ (C to g¹)

Double Open Diapason	32
Contra Bass	16
Bourdon (wd)	16
Violon	16
Clarabella Bass (wd)	8
Violoncello	8
Trombone	16
Trumpet	8

Swell to Great
Solo to Great
Swell to Choir
Solo to Choir
Swell sub-octave
Swell super-octave
Solo sub-octave
Solo super-octave
Choir to Pedals
Great to Pedals
Solo to Pedals
Swell to Pedals

4 ventils to Great & Pedal
3 ventils to Swell
Pedals to couplers: Swell to Great, Solo to Great, Great to Pedals, Solo to Pedals
Tremulant to Swell reeds
Tremulant to Solo Cor Anglais and Clarionet

The four keyboards were arranged in the order: Choir, Great, Solo and Swell, the latter being highest in the set.

Source HR3: 597–8; Clutton 1984: 27–8

38   Great Exhibition, Hyde Park J. F. SCHULZE, 1851

Hauptwerk (C to f³)

Bordun	16
Principal	8
Gambe	8
Hohlflöte	8
Gedackt	8
Octave	4
Mixtur	v
Trompete	8

Oberwerk (C to f³)

Lieblich Gedackt	16
Geigen Principal	8
Lieblich Gedackt	8

Flöttraverso	8
Flöttraverso	4
Principal	4

Pedal (C to d¹)

Subbass	16	[Hw. Bordun]
Octavbass	8	
Violon	8	[Hw. Principal]
Flötenbass	8	[Hw. Hohlflöte]
Posaune	16	

Oberwerk to Hauptwerk
Hauptwerk to Pedal
Oberwerk suboctave to Hauptwerk

Source Burn 1930: 102 (quoting a leaflet issued by Schulze); cf. Pole 1851: 78

39 Doncaster Parish Church EDMUND SCHULZE, 1862

Great Organ (C to a³)

Sub Bourdon (c)	32
Double Open Diapason	16
Bourdon	16
Open Diapason	8
Octave [*sic*]	8
Hohl Flöte	8
Stopped Diapason	8
Great Quint	5⅓
Principal	4
Gemshorn	4
Stopped Flute	4
Twelfth	2⅔
Fifteenth	2
Mixture	V
Cymbal	III–V
Cornet (c)	IV
Double Trumpet	16
Trumpet	8
Posaune	8
Horn	8
Clarion	4

Choir Organ (C to a³)

Lieblich Gedact	16
Geigen Principal	8
Viol di Gamba	8
Flauto Traverso	8
Salcional	8
Lieblich Gedact	8
Geigen Principal	4
Lieblich Flute	4
Flauto Traverso	4

Quintaton	4
Flautino	2
Mixture	III
Clarionet	8

Swell Organ (C to a^3)

Bourdon	16
Open Diapason	8
Gemshorn	8
Terpodion	8
Harmonic Flute	8
Rohr Flute	8
Principal	4
Harmonic Flute	4
Stopped Flute	4
Viol d'Amour	4
Mixture	V
Scharf	III
Cornet (c)	IV
Double Bassoon	16
Trumpet	8
Hautboy	8
Horn	8
Clarion	4

Solo Organ (C to a^3) [largely borrowed from Swell]

Gemshorn	8
Harmonic Flute	8
Rohr Flute	8
Harmonic Flute	4
Stopped Flute	4
Double Bassoon	16
Hautboy	8
Horn	8
Vox Humana	8

Echo Organ (C to a^3)

Tibia Major	16
Vox Angelica	8
Harmonica	8
Flauto Traverso	8
Flauto Amabile	8
Celestina	4
Flauto Dolcissimo	4
Harmonica Ætheria	II

Pedal Organ (C to e^1)

Sub Principal	32
Major Bass	16
Principal, bass	16
Sub-bass	16

Open Diapason, bass	16
Violone	16
Great Quint	$10\frac{2}{3}$
Minor Bass	8
Octave Bass	8
Violoncello	8
Flute, bass	8
Great Tierce	$6\frac{2}{5}$
Quint, bass	$5\frac{1}{3}$
Fifteenth, bass	4
Tierce	$3\frac{1}{5}$
Mixture	II
Cymbal	II
Contra Posaune	32
Posaune	16
Bombarde	16
Contra Fagotto	16
Trumpet	8
Horn	8
Fagotto	8
Clarion	4

Great to Pedals
Swell to Great
Choir to Great

2 combination stops for the Great
2 combination stops for the Swell
1 combination stop for the Pedal
1 combination stop for the Choir
Thunder pedal
Tremulant to Swell

Source HR2: 530–1

40   Albert Hall, Launceston, Tasmania CHARLES BRINDLEY, 1861

Great Organ (C to g³)

Double Stop Diapason	16
Open Diapason	8
Rohrflöte	8
Gamba	8
Principal	4
Flöte	4
Twelfth	$2\frac{2}{3}$
Fifteenth	2
Mixture	V
Trumpet	8

Swell Organ (C to g³)

Double Diapason	16
Gemshorn	8

Flaut d'Amour	8
Gemshorn	4
Mixture	IV
Horn	8
Oboe	8
Clarion	4

Choir Organ (C to g³)

Spitzflöte	8
Lieblich Gedact	8
Dulciana	8
Spitzflöte	4
Lieblich Flöte	4
Piccolo	2
Clarinette	8

Pedal Organ (C to f¹)

Major Bass	16
Bourdon	16
Flute Bass	8
Trombone	16

Swell to Great
Great to Pedal
Swell to Pedal
Choir to Pedal

No details of accessories

Mixture compositions:

Gt Mixture	C	15.19.22.26.29
	f♯	12.15.19.22.26
	c♯ ¹	8.12.15.19.22
	c♯ ²	1. 8.12.15.19
Sw Mixture	C	15.19.22.26
	c	12.15.19.22
	c♯ ²	8.12.15.19
	f♯ ²	1. 8.12.15

Source Stiller 1984: 18–19

41   St Peter, Eaton Square, London T. C. LEWIS, 1874

Great Organ (C to a³)

Open Diapason	16
Bourdon	16
Open Diapason, no. 1	8
Open Diapason, no. 2	8
Stopped Diapason	8
Viola	8
Hohlflöte	8
Viol di Gamba	8
Octave	4

Gemshorn	4
Hohlflöte	4
Quint	2⅔
Great Mixture	v
Full Mixture	ii
Mixture	iv
Trumpet	16
Trumpet	8
Clarion	4

Swell Organ (C to a³)

Bourdon	16
Geigen Principal	8
Rohrflöte	8
Flute Harmonique	8
Gamba	8
Voix Célestes	8
Geigen Principal	4
Flute Harmonique	4
Mixture	v
Trumpet	16
Trumpet	8
Oboe and Bassoon	8
Voix Humaine	8
Clarion	4

Choir Organ (C to a³)

Lieblich Gedact	16
Lieblich Gedact	8
Salicional	8
Vox Angelica	8
Flauto Traverso	8
Salicet	4
Lieblich Gedact	4
Flauto Traverso	4
Lieblich Gedact	2
Mixture	iii
Orchestral Oboe	8
Clarionet	8

Pedal Organ (C to g¹)

Great Bass	16
Sub-Bass	16
Violon	16
Quint Bass	10⅔
Octave Bass	8
Flute Bass	8
Violoncello	8
Posaune	16
Trumpet	8

Great to Pedals
Swell to Pedals

Choir to Pedals
Swell to Great
Choir to Great

Ventil to Great reeds
Ventil to Front Great soundboard
Ventil to Pedal Great Bass, Quint Bass and Octave Bass
Ventil to Pedal reeds
Ventil to Pedal Violon and Violoncello
Reversible pedal, Choir to Pedals
Reversible pedal, Swell to Pedals
Reversible pedal, Great and Pedal reeds
4 composition pedals to Great
3 composition pedals to Swell
Pedal to bring out all ventil stops and Great to Pedal
Pedal to take in all ventil stops and Great to Pedal
Swell pedals to Choir, Swell and Voix Humaine
Tremulant

Source HR3: 481–2

42   York Minster HILL & SON, 1859

Great Organ (C to g³)

Double Open Diapason	16
Bourdon (wd)	16
Open Diapason, east	8
Open Diapason, west	8
Open Diapason	8
Gamba	8
Stopped Diapason (wd)	8
Quint	5⅓
Octave	4
Octave	4
Gemshorn	4
Harmonic Flute	4
Twelfth	2⅔
Fifteenth	2
Octave Flute (wd)	2
Full Mixture	IV
Sharp Mixture	III
Tierce Mixture	III
Cornet	IV
Glockenspiel	II
Double Trumpet	16
Posaune	8
Trumpet	8
Clarion	4

Choir Organ (C to g³)

Gedact (wd)	16
Open Diapason	8

Dulciana	8
Stopped Diapason (wd)	8
Octave	4
Wald Flute (wd)	4
Fifteenth	2
Mixture	II
Clarionet	8

Swell Organ (C to g³)

Bourdon (wd)	16
Open Diapason	8
Dulciana	8
Stopped Diapason	8
Octave	4
Fifteenth	2
Full Mixture	III
Dulciana Mixture	III
Double Bassoon	16
Horn	8
Trumpet	8
Oboe	8
Vox Humana	8
Clarion	4

Solo Organ (C to g³)

Harmonic Flute	4
Tuba	8
Tuba	4

Pedal Organ (C to f¹)

Double Open Diapason (wd)	32
Double Open Diapason (m)	32
Open Diapason (wd)	16
Sub Bass (wd)	16
Open Diapason (m)	16
Violone (wd)	16
Bourdon (wd)	16
Quint (stopped)	10⅔
Octave	8
Octave Bass (wd)	8
Flute Bass (wd)	8
Twelfth	5⅓
Fifteenth	4
Mixture	V
Sackbut (wd)	32
Trombone	16
Bassoon	16
Clarion	8
Octave Clarion	4

Great to Pedals
Swell to Pedals

Choir to Pedals
Swell to Choir
Swell to Great
Solo to Swell
Swell to Great (duplicated?)

4 composition pedals to Great
2 composition pedals to Swell
2 composition pedals to Pedal
Tremulant

Source HR2: 527–8

43   Melbourne Town Hall HILL & SON, 1872

Great Organ (C to c⁴)

Double Open Diapason	16
Bourdon	16
Open Diapason	8
Open Diapason	8
Gamba	8
Stopped Diapason	8
Principal	4
Principal	4
Harmonic Flute	4
Twelfth	2⅔
Fifteenth	2
Mixture	IV
Mixture	III
Double Trumpet	16
Posaune	8
Trumpet	8
Clarion	4

Choir Organ (C to c⁴)

Bourdon	16
Gedact (metal treble)	8
Salicional	8
Dulciana	8
Principal	4
Gamba	4
Gemshorn Twelfth	2⅔
Gemshorn Harmonic	2
Dulciana Mixture	II
Clarionet	8

Swell Organ (C to c⁴)

Bourdon	16
Open Diapason	8
Stopped Diapason (metal treble)	8
Cone Gamba	8
Pierced Gamba	8

Principal	4
Suabe Flute	4
Twelfth	2⅔
Fifteenth	2
Mixture	IV
Double Trumpet	16
Cornopean	8
Oboe	8
Clarion	4

Solo Organ (C to c⁴)

Lieblich Bourdon (c)	16
Harmonic Flute	8
Vox Angelica (2 ranks)	8
Flute Octaviante	4
Piccolo	2
Glockenspiel	II
Bassoon (c)	16
Clarionet	8
Orchestral Oboe (c)	8
Vox Humana	8
Oboe Clarion	4
Tuba Mirabilis	8
Tuba Mirabilis	4

Pedal Organ (C to f¹)

Double Open Diapason (m)	32
Open Diapason (m)	16
Open Diapason (wd)	16
Bourdon	16
Quint	10⅔
Principal	8
Violon	8
Twelfth	5⅓
Fifteenth	4
Mixture	III
Trombone	16
Clarion	8

Swell to Great
Swell to Great sub-octave
Swell to Choir
Choir to Great sub-octave
Solo to Great
Solo to Pedal
Choir to Pedal
Swell to Pedal
Great to Pedal

4 composition pedals to Great
3 composition pedals to Swell
2 composition pedals to Choir

4 combination stops (by hand) to Solo
Tremulant to Solo

Source HR3: 455

44   St Albans Abbey HILL & SON, 1861

Great Organ (C to g³)
Double Open Diapason	16
Open Diapason	8
Open Diapason	8
Stopped Diapason	8
Gamba	8
Principal	4
Harmonic Flute	4
Twelfth	2⅔
Fifteenth	2
Full Mixture	III
Sharp Mixture	II
Posaune	8
Clarion	4

Choir Organ (C to g³)
Stopped Diapason	8
Cone Gamba	8
Dulciana	8
Gemshorn	4
Wald Flöte	4
Flautino [*sic*]	2
Clarionet	8

Swell Organ (C to g³)
Double Diapason	16
Open Diapason	8
Stopped Diapason	8
Keraulophon	8
Principal	4
Rohr Flöte	4
Twelfth	2⅔
Fifteenth	2
Mixture	III
Double Trumpet	16
Horn	8
Oboe	8
Clarion	4

Pedal Organ (C to f¹)
Open Diapason (wd)	16
Bourdon (wd)	16
Violone (wd)	16
Principal	8
Trombone	16

5 couplers (no details)
5 composition pedals (no details)
Tremulant

Source CMR 1, 1863: 33; MS 12: 396

45   The Church of the Holy Name (RC), Manchester HILL & SON, 1871

Great Organ (C to g³)

Double Open Diapason	16
Open Diapason	8
Open Diapason	8
Stopped Diapason	8
Gamba	8
Principal	4
Harmonic Flute	4
Twelfth	2⅔
Fifteenth	2
Full Mixture	IV
Sharp Mixture	III
Posaune	8
Clarion	4

Choir Organ (C to g³)

Lieblich Bourdon	16	
Gedact	8	
Dulciana	8	
Salicional	8	
Voix Celeste (c)	8	
Gemshorn	4	
Lieblich Flute	4	
Flautina	2	
Corno di Bassetto (c)	16	[?]
Cremona	8	

Swell Organ (C to g³)

Bourdon	16
Open Diapason	8
Stopped Diapason	8
Pierced Gamba	8
Principal	4
Suabe Flute	4
Twelfth	2⅔
Fifteenth	2
Mixture	III
Double Trumpet	16
Horn	8
Oboe	8
Vox Humana	8
Clarion	4

Pedal Organ (C to f¹)

Sub Bass	32
Open Diapason (wd)	16
Violone	16
Bourdon	16
Principal	8
Bass Flute	8
Fifteenth	4
Mixture	III
Trombone	16

Great to Pedal
Swell to Pedal
Choir to Pedal
Swell to Great
Swell to Choir

4 composition pedals to Great
3 composition pedals to Swell

Source MS 13: 83

46   Alexandra Palace, London HENRY WILLIS, 1868–73

Great Organ (C to a³)

Double Diapason	16
Bourdon	16
Open Diapason	8
Open Diapason	8
Open Diapason	8
Viol di Gamba	8
Claribel	8
Quint	5⅓
Principal	4
Flute Traversière	4
Quinte Octaviante	2⅔
Super Octave	2
Piccolo	2
Sesquialtera	V
Mixture	III
Trombone	16
Bombard	8
Trumpet	8
Posaune	8
Clarion	4

Swell Organ (C to a³)

Double Diapason	16
Bourdon	16
Open Diapason	8
Open Diapason	8
Salcional	8

Lieblich Gedact	8
Flute Harmonique	8
Principal	4
Flute Octaviante	4
Flauto Traverso	4
Twelfth	2⅔
Fifteenth	2
Sesquialtera	v
Mixture	iii
Contra Posaune	16
Contra Fagotto	16
Cornopean	8
Trumpet	8
Hautboy	8
Voix Humaine	8
Clarion	4

Choir Organ (C to a³)

Contra Gamba	16
Viol di Gamba	8
Salcional	8
Claribel	8
Flute Harmonique	8
Lieblich Gedact	8
Vox Angelica	8
Flute Octaviante	4
Gemshorn	4
Viola	4
Lieblich Flöte	4
Flageolet	2
Mixture	iii
Corno di Bassetto	8
Trompette Harmonique	8
Clarion Harmonique	4

Solo Organ (C to a³)

Violoncello (imitative)	8
Viola (imitative)	4
Flute Harmonique	8
Flute Octaviante	4
Concert Flute (imitative)	4
Piccolo (imitative)	2
Claribel	8
Bombardon	16
Trumpet (harmonic)	8
Ophicleide	8
Bassoon	8
Oboe (orchestral)	8
Clarionette (orchestral)	8
Clarion	4

Pedal Organ (C to f^1)

Double Diapason (wd)	32
Double Diapason (m)	32
Sub Bourdon	32
Open Diapason (wd)	16
Violin (m)	16
Bourdon	16
Contra Basso (open wood)	16
Octave	8
Principal	8
Super Octave	4
Sesquialtera	III
Mixture	II
Bombard	32
Trombone	16
Ophicleide	16
Clarion	8

Solo to Great
Solo sub-octave
Solo super-octave
Solo to Choir
Swell to Great
Swell to Great sub-octave
Swell to Great super-octave
Choir to Great
Pedal in octaves (acting on 16′ and 8′ reeds)
Pedal in octaves (acting on 4′ and mixtures)
Solo to Pedals
Swell to Pedals
Choir to Pedals
Great to Pedals

6 combination pistons to each manual
Ventils to all divisions (no details)

Source MW XLVI, 1868: 406

47   St Paul's Cathedral, London HENRY WILLIS, 1872

Great Organ (C to a^3)

Double Diapason	16
Open Diapason	8
Open Diapason	8
Claribel Flute	8
Quint	5$\frac{1}{3}$
Principal	4
Flute Harmonique	4
Octave Quint	2$\frac{2}{3}$
Super Octave	2
Fourniture	III
Mixture	III

Trombone	16
Tromba	8
Clarion	4

Swell Organ (C to a³)

Contra Gamba	16
Open Diapason	8
Lieblich Gedact	8
Salicional	8
Vox Angelica	8
Principal	4
Fifteenth	2
Echo Cornet	III
Contra Posaune	16
Cornopean	8
Hautboy	8
Clarion	4

Choir Organ (C to a³)

Bourdon	16
Open Diapason	8
Dulciana	8
Violoncello	8
Claribel Flute	8
Lieblich Gedact	8
Flute Harmonique	4
Principal	4
Flageolet	2
Corno di Bassetto	8
Cor Anglais	8

Solo Organ (C to a³)

Flute Harmonique	8
Concert Flute	4
Corno di Bassetto	8
Oboe	8
Tuba Major	8
Clarion	4

Pedale (C to f¹)

Double Open Diapason (wd)	32
Open Diapason (wd)	16
Violone	16
Octave	8
Violoncello	8
Mixture	III
Contra Posaune	32
Grand Bombard	16
Clarion	8

Solo to Great
Choir to Great
Swell to Great
Swell to Great sub-octave

Swell to Great super-octave
Great to Pedals
Choir to Pedals
Swell to Pedals
Solo to Pedals
Ventil Pedale

4 combination pistons to each manual
4 combination pedals to the Pedale, acting on the Great pistons
1 pedal, Great to Pedal (double-acting)
1 pedal, Swell to Great

Source HR3: 457

48   Wadham College, Oxford HENRY WILLIS, 1862

Great Organ (C to g³)

Open Diapason	8
Claribel Flute	8
Rohr Flute	8
Salcional	8
Octave	4
Flute Harmonique	4
Spitz Flute	2
Trumpet	8

Swell Organ (C to g³)

Bourdon	16
Violin Diapason	8
Lieblich Gedackt	8
Gemshorn	4
Mixture	III
Cornopean	8
Oboe	8

Pedal Organ (C to f¹)

Open Bass	16
Sub Bass	16
Flute Bass	8

Great to Pedal
Swell to Pedal
Swell to Great
Swell to Great super-octave
Swell to Great sub-octave

No details of accessories

Source The organ

49   Reading Town Hall HENRY WILLIS, 1864

Great Organ (C to a³)

| Double Diapason | 16 |
| Open Diapason | 8 |

Stopped Diapason and Claribel Flute	8	
Gamba	8	(a)
Principal	4	
Flute Harmonique	4	
Twelfth	2⅔	
Fifteenth	2	
Sesquialtera	III	
Posaune	8	
Clarion	4	(a)

Swell Organ (C to a³)

Double Diapason (wd)	16	
Open Diapason	8	
Lieblich Gedackt (wd & m)	8	
Principal	4	
Piccolo Harmonique	2	
Mixture	III	
Cornopean	8	
Hautboy	8	
Vox Humana	8	(a)
Clarion	4	(a)

Solo Organ (C to a³)

Salcional	8	
Claribel Flute	8	
Viol d'Amore	8	(a)
Flute Harmonique	4	
Piccolo Harmonique	2	
Oboe (orchestral) and Bassoon	8	
Corno di Bassetto	8	

Pedal Organ (C to f¹)

Open Diapason	16	
Bourdon	16	
Violoncello	16	[?] (a)
Octave	8	
Ophicleide	16	(a)

Swell to Great
Swell to Great, sub-octave
Swell to Great, super-octave
Swell to Pedal
Great to Pedal
Solo to Pedal

Combination pistons (no details)
1 pedal, Great to Pedal (double-acting)

(a) Prepared for only in 1864.

Source Marr 1982: 7–9

Appendix 2: Documents

A   Recitals by Elizabeth Stirling (1837, 1838).

St Katherine's, Regent's Park (August 1837) and St Sepulchre's, Holborn (October 1837)

1   Fantasia and fugue in C minor. – John Schneider.

2   Trio in G for two rows of keys and pedal, on the chorale 'Allein Gott in der hoh' from the 'Exercises pour le clavecin.' – Seb. Bach.

3   Prelude in E flat from the Exercises. – Seb. Bach.

4   Trio in G for two rows of keys and pedal, from the Exercises, on the chorale 'Dies sind die heiligen.' – Seb. Bach.

5   Prelude and fugue in C major, No. 3 of the first set of pedal fugues. – Seb. Bach.

6   Trio in E minor, from the Exercises on the chorale (in canon) 'Vater unser imm [*sic*] himmel-reich.' – Seb. Bach.

7   Prelude and fugue in E minor, No. 6 of the first set. – Seb. Bach.

8   Canonic variations in C on the Christmas hymn 'Vom himmel hoch' (Haslinger's edition). – Seb. Bach.

9   Prelude and fugue in A minor, No. 1 of the first set. – Seb. Bach.

10   Trio in D minor, from the Exercises on the chorale (in the pedal) 'Jesus Christus unser Heiland.' – Seb. Bach.

11   Prelude and fugue in C minor, No. 4 of the first set. – Seb. Bach.

12   Prelude and fugue in A major. – E. Webbe.

St Sepulchre's Holborn (July 1838)

1   Fugue in C minor from the Exercises on the chorale 'Kyrie Gott Vater.' – Seb. Bach.

2   Fugue in C minor from the Exercises on the chorale 'Gott heiliger Geist.' – Seb. Bach.

3   Adagio from the 4th sonata in E flat, with violin obligato. – Seb. Bach.

4   Prelude and fugue in G minor. (Lonsdale's Ed. and Coventry and Hollier). – Seb. Bach.

5   Second trio in C minor from the Six. (Wesley's Ed. Lonsdale). – Seb. Bach.

6   Prelude and fugue in D major. (Coventry and Hollier). – Seb. Bach.

7   Andante from a quartet. – Mozart.

8   Toccata in D minor. (Breitkopf and Hartel). – Seb. Bach.

9   Trio in G major, No. 6 of the Six. – Seb. Bach.

10   Prelude and fugue in C minor. (No. 1. Novello). – Mendelssohn.

11   Trio in C, No. 5 of the Six. – Seb. Bach.

12   Fantasia and fugue in G major. (Coventry and Hollier). – Seb. Bach.
13   Adagio from a quartet. – Haydn.
14   Prelude and fugue in E flat on St Ann's tune (Lonsdale and the Exercises). – Seb. Bach.

Source MW IX, 1838: 209

B   A Description of the New Organ erected in the Church of St Olave, London Bridge, Southwark. Designed by Dr. Gauntlett.

The new great organ in St Olave's church, Southwark, has been erected by the liberality and munificence of the parishioners. The specification was designed by Dr. Gauntlett, the originator of many of the improvements in organ building recently introduced in this Country. The work was commenced in March, 1844, by Mr. Lincoln, one of Her Majesty's organ builders, and was completed in April, 1846, by Messrs. Hill & Co., organ builders to the Queen, and builders of the great organs in York Minster, and Worcester Cathedral, and of those in the town hall, Birmingham, and music hall, Edinburgh. The new St Olave's organ differs in its foundation from the 16-feet gamut instruments designed by Dr. Gauntlett, and built by Messrs. Hill & Co., for London, Liverpool, Manchester, Ashton-under-Lyne, Stratford-upon-Avon, &c. &c., and as it is an extension of the novelties displayed in these instruments, a more detailed notice than ordinary may not be considered uninteresting or unnecessary. For a long period the parish church organ in England was a mere copy of the light accompaniment organ found in the English cathedrals, and so long as congregational singing was confined to the children of the parochial schools, such an instrument might be considered sufficient to support the body of soprani voice emanating from such a quire. But the general attention now paid to congregational psalmody, has led, and is still leading, to a great change in the character of this interesting part of divine service; and it is manifest, that where is heard the voice of 'the great congregation', there must be also heard what Maister Mace has styled 'the great congregational chorus' of the organ to lead and support it. Although this 'congregational chorus' has long existed in the large organs of Germany, it has been confined in England until recently, to the dissenting chapels in the north. The old organ of Christ Church, Newgate Street was quite inadequate to the support of 1,000 children's voices, and would have been comparatively useless had 500 men assisted in upraising the metrical hymn. The male voice is a greater absorbent of organ tone than that of the woman or boy; and where men sing, an English cathedral organ becomes inefficient, and the great psalmodic organ of Germany will be found the only genuine auxillary to a noble and heart-stirring hymnology.

The St Olave's organ has been constructed on the principle of the congregational organ. The grant appropriated for the musical portion of the instrument did not exceed £500. This sum included also the erection of the organ: the case, the painting, and the gilding were extras. In order to make the instrument a feature, its strength was thrown into the great, or chorus organ. To have made a small great organ, a small quire organ, and a small swell organ, such as are found in the churches of St. Saviour, Southwark, and St. James Bermondsey, would have been no novelty; and considering the requirements of a large school, and numerous congregation, of little or no use in St Olave's church. It is a generally received opinion that the erection in England of the congregational organ of Holland and Germany was impossible, owing to its great cost, and Dr. Gauntlett was anxious to demonstrate that by confining the attention of the builders to one prominent detail of the great German organs, its more important features might be developed in this country at comparatively a small expense. The new organ of St Olave's will cost considerably less than the new instruments in St James' church, Bermondsey, and St Giles', Camberwell, whilst its powers are fully equal to leading double the quantity of voice either of those instruments could support. In breadth and grandeur of tone there is no parochial organ in England to equal it, and perhaps but few even on the continent. To have attempted an imitation of the general details of a grand organ like Christ church, would have been out of the question; a great swell organ, like that of All Saints, Gordon Square, coupled with a small chorus organ, would have been unsymmetrical; the union of the equally-sized swell and grand organs had been accomplished at St. Peter's, Cornhill. Great efforts were being made at the Temple Church, at St. Giles' Camberwell, at St. Mary's Lambeth, at St. Saviour's Southwark, and at St Paul's Wilton Place; but Dr. Gauntlett pledged his word to the parishioners of St. Olave, that the great manual organ of their Instrument should excel anything that had yet been attempted in the metropolis. He believes he has kept his word, and faithfully performed his duty in this respect, for a more magnificent chorus organ does not exist in any metropolitan or suburban church.

The weight and solidity of the diapasons are unexampled, and the liquid singing quality of the open unison he thinks unrivalled. The corno-par-premier-force although not of the full scale of the grand posaune provided for larger churches, is yet a magnificent reed and of extraordinary breadth and equal quality. The octave reeds run throughout the clavier. The solo reeds, musette, chalmeau, and corno flute, are severally beautiful and new in respect of body of tone. The mutation or harmonic stops have the novelties of the diapente or quint, the decima, the fourniture, the octave settima (the note Col. Thompson designated as the anomalous harmonic) and the doublette, or sedecima and its octave. The foundation stops have amongst them a 16 gamut flute of metal and wood, and a 32 gamut untersatz of open metal and closed wood.

The Swell organ ranges from tenor c to f in alt, and consists of 10 stops, the pedal organ ranges from CCCC to DD a compass of 27 notes, and one 32 and two 16 independent gamuts. The pedal trombones are such as only Messrs. Hill can create.

The superb organ of St Olave's will be found a delightful companion to the beautiful instrument in St. Peter's, Cornhill, designed by Dr. Gauntlett, and built by Mr. Hill in 1841. And when the great metropolitan organ of Christ church shall be completed in all its noble variety of seventy-one stops, London may challenge any capital in Europe to excel, or indeed equal three such splendid specimens of musical beauty, and rare artistical skill.

Great Organ [C to f³]
1.   Manual Untersatz or Sub Bourdon
2.   Manual Bourdon, and
3.   Manual Tenoroon
4.   Open Unison
5.   Viol di Gamba, unison
6.   Salicional, unison
7.   Claribel-flute, unison (wood)
8.   Closed flute, unison (wood)
9.   Unison Bass, closed (wood)
10. Musete [*sic*] and Chalmeau, solo reed
11. Cornoflute, a reed with wood cylinder
12. Corno-par-premier-force
13. Diapente
14. Octave
15. Wald-flute, octave (wood)
16. Clarion, octave reed
17. Decima
18. Duodecima
19. Quinta-decima
20. Piffero (wood)
21. Decima-septima
22. Sesqui-altera
23. Quinta-decima
24. Larigot and Sedecima
25. Fourniture

26. Octave-septima and Glockenspiel
27. Octave-clarion

Swell Organ [c to f³]
1. Tenoroon (wood closed and metal open)
2. Open Unison
3. Closed Flute, unison (wood)
4. Octave
5. Suabe Flute (wood)
6. Quinta-decima
7. Sedecima
8. Flageolet
9. Corno du Chant*
10. Hautbois

Pedal Organ [C to d¹]
1. Pedal Untersatz (closed wood)
2. Contra Bass or Principal 16 feet (open wood)
3. Grand Trombone 16 feet

* Messrs Hill & Co. are now engaged in adding a Corno par premier force of a 16 feet gamut to the swell of the great unison organ in York-minster. It will be blown with the same weight of wind as is the ophicleide (or tuba mirabilis) in the hall organ at Birmingham, but what its effect will be against a mere unison organ remains to be tested. There is a fine Corno du chant upon a weight of six inches in the noble organ of the mechanics' institute Liverpool, which in beauty and purity of tone is a powerful rival to the celebrated corno anglais of those clever artists, the Messrs. Cavaille Coll of Paris.

The only omission in this grand manual is that of the sackbut, or 16-feet gamut trumpet. As there was no room for both the untersatz and the double 16-feet gamut trumpet, and as Christ church organ is designed for the latter, and Dr. Gauntlett had already put it into the two great organs in Ashton-under-Lyne and Liverpool, he preferred selecting the novelty of the 32 feet diapason on the keys, nothing of the sort having yet been attempted even at York or Birmingham.

The grand organs [*sic*] are divided into four sound boards, all upon one weight of wind; there are no foundation harmonic pipes, owing to this circumstance, otherwise this great invention of modern times would have been attempted. To those interested in the improvement of organs, a visit to the celebrated organ in the Chapel Royal of St. Denis, near Paris, would well repay the exertion and in this organ are some beautiful examples of harmonic tones from diversified pressure of wind. Dr. Gauntlett proposed to put the swell organ upon a strong weight of wind, and to have a large wooden tube to convey the sound into the belfry. The swell when open would cause a very distant effect, and when closed bring an extraordinary column [*sic*] of sound into the church; but as this formed no part of the original contract, its execution has been left for future consideration. Many of the new swell organs on the continent are blown with a heavier weight of wind than their great manuals, and the crescendo and diminuendo thus obtained is more striking. Messrs. Hill & Co. are now trying the experiment in the great organ building for Turvey Church, Bedfordshire.

C   Extract from William Hill's Circular, 1841.

For some years past Mr. Hill has been engaged in erecting Organs on a scale of grandeur and magnificence altogether new, and before unattempted in this country: during, however, the last two years, by the kindness of his patrons, he has been enabled to eclipse in these points the most celebrated builders on the continent: as in the Organ in St Peter's, Cornhill, London, erected last year, and the Organ in the New Chapel, Great George Street, Liverpool, erected this year, he has built the most comprehensive and varied Swell Organs which have yet been attempted; and in the Great Metropolitan Organ of Christ Church Newgate Street, re-erected during the last year, he has prepared a Grand Manual Organ, which will, when completed, exceed in weight and brilliancy of tone any single Manual of any Organ in Europe. In these efforts Mr. Hill has been assisted by the advice and suggestions of some of the most eminent professors and amateurs for which he desires to express his grateful acknowledgements, being assured that it is only by the union of musical with mechanical skill, that this most noble and commanding of instruments can be brought to perfection.

In his recently-built instruments, Mr. Hill has followed the principles adopted by the celebrated Organ Builders of Germany, in the compass of the manuals, and the mode of the blending of the stops; but in purity, power, and grandeur of tone, he conceives that he has rivalled the efforts of his predecessors. He has imitated them in the plan of confining the manual to 54 notes (from CC to F in alt), because it condenses within a compass of four octaves and a half every pipe from the CCCC (32 feet) to the smallest that can be made to speak – a compass of upwards of seven octaves; – it secures the greatest weight of tone to the manual that can possibly be given to it; – it brings every combination of pipe within the grasp of the performer; and it enables the performer to play as written, and with ease to himself, the compositions of the most celebrated Organ composers. He has however increased the extent of the pedal board, which now embraces two octaves and two notes (from CCC to D), a compass which is required in the execution of the music of Sebastian Bach.

Mr. Hill has secured the weight of tone necessary to form the foundation of a Grand Organ, by the introduction of the Contra-Bourdon and Bourdon stops; – the first places the CCC pipe on the tenor C of the manual, and in the immediate reach and constant use of the player; – the second, which places the CC pipe on the tenor C of the manual he has made an entirely new stop, by an alteration of the scale hitherto in use. The weight of tone given by these stops has enabled him to introduce the novelties of the Quint or Double Twelfth, and the Tenth or Double Tierce; it has also induced him to complete a new combination of the compound stops called Sesqui-alteras, Mixtures, Fournitures, Doublettes, &c. &c., whereby are produced those brilliant and silvery qualities of tone which give life and animation to the ensemble. In all these alterations from the mode of blending the stops hitherto adopted in this country, he has acted in the spirit of the old and most celebrated builders of Holland and Germany. But in *variety* of tone, he has made improvements, which he ventures to suppose have not been surpassed by any builder of ancient or modern times. In the Reed stops, he has invented seven new forms, as exemplified in the Grand Ophicleide, the Contra-Fagotto, the Trombone, the Clarion, the Corno-flute, the Cromorne-flute, and the Clarionet or Chalemeau. In the Flute stops, he has adopted the Wald-flute, Oboe-flute, Suabe-flute, Flageolet, and two kinds of Piccolo; he has enriched the Swell Organ by the introduction of the new stop called the Echo Dulciana Cornet, a stop of five ranks of pipes, of the delicate scale and voicing in use for the Organ of the drawing-room, and which has proved a most valuable addition to the resources of the performer.

D   Extract from William Pole, *Musical Instruments in the Great Industrial Exhibition of 1851* (pp. 63–5).

Messrs. Hill & Co. exhibit a small but effective organ, of 16 stops, and containing several novelties. It has two rows of keys, and the contents are as follows:–

Great Organ (lower clavier)

1.	Double Diapason	Open 16 feet.
2.	Open Diapason	Open 8 feet.
3.	Stopped Diapason	Stopped 8 feet.
4.	Octave	Open 4 feet.

5.	Twelfth	Open 2⅔ feet.
6.	Fifteenth	Open 2 feet.
7.	Sesquialter	Compound 3 ranks.
8.	Cornopean	Reed 8 feet.
9.	Krum-horn	Solo reed 8 feet.
10.	Wald-flute	Open wood 4 feet.

Swell Organ (upper clavier)

1.	Claribel	Open wood 8 feet.
2.	Gems-horn	Open 8 feet.
3.	Hohl-flute	Open 8 feet.
4.	Hautboy	Soft reed 8 feet.
5.	Tuba Mirabilis	Loud reed 8 feet.

Pedal Clavier

| 1. | Double Diapason | Open wood 16 feet. |

The compass of both the manual claviers is 4½ octaves, from C to F; that of the pedals is 2¼ octaves, from C to E.

The stop called *cornopean*, in the great organ, is a reed giving a round full tone; the *krum-horn* has a cylindrical pipe, and the tone is of a thinner and softer quality; the *wald-flute* is an open wood solo stop, voiced in a peculiar manner.

In the swell, the *claribel* is an open wood stop, now often substituted in the treble for the stopped diapason, as giving a better quality of tone, and being more useful for solo playing. The *gems-horn* is an open metal pipe, with a tube tapering upwards above the mouth in the form of a frustum of a cone: the stop is taken from the Germans. The *hohl-flute* is an open metal pipe, giving a clear reedy tone.

The *tuba mirabilis* is a new kind of reed stop, invented by Mr. Hill, and first introduced by him into the organ in the Town Hall, Birmingham. It is on a large scale, and blown by a very high pressure of wind, equal to that of a column of water about 11 inches high. It gives a fine round tone, and is of itself nearly equal in power to all the rest of the organ put together.

There are four composition pedals to change the stops in the great organ; – the first brings on Nos. 1, 2, and 3; the second, Nos. 1, 2, 3, 4, and 6; the third, Nos. 1 to 7; and the fourth the full organ. There are also couplers to unite the two claviers, and to cause the pedal-keys to act on either the great organ or the swell.

The stops are not worked by draw-stops, on the customary plan, but by keys, something like those of the manual claviers, placed on each side, within reach of the performer's hands. One row of these keys serves to open the several stops, and another to shut them. As, however, the mere pushing down of a key with the finger would not, of itself, give power or motion enough to move the slider – the aid of an intermediate apparatus, on the principle of the 'pneumatic lever' . . . is called in. The pressing down of the key admits, by a small valve, compressed air into a bellows, the motion of which is communicated to the slider.

In the bass half of the instrument, Mr. Hill has adopted a new kind of valve or pallet, with the object of lightening the touch. It is on the principle of what is called the *double-beat* valve, used in steam-engines. The valve hangs vertically, and shuts upon two vertical faces; and it is only the pressure of wind acting on the surface contained between these two faces, which has to be overcome in opening the valve.

Another novelty in this organ is the arrangement of the trunks or passages conveying the compressed air from the bellows to the wind-chests of the sound-boards. These are, in large organs, of considerable size, and, as usually placed, come very inconveniently in the way of the various movements and machinery connected with the keys, stops, composition pedals, &c. Mr. Hill dispenses with them altogether, by making the framing and main standards which support the sound-board, *hollow*, and using them as wind passages. This ingenious contrivance leaves the space under the sound-boards completely free and open, and gives increased facilities for the beneficial arrangement of the action.

There are two bellows, one for ordinary pressure, and one for the highly compressed air required for the 'tuba mirabilis.' They are both worked by the same handle, and are so connected that any escape, by over-blowing the high-pressure bellows, is not lost, but passes into that of the lower pressure.

The whole of the pipes are enclosed in a box, having moveable Venetian shutters in front; so that the entire organ forms one large swell: within this is also contained another box, with a similar Venetian front, enclosing the organ of the upper clavier: this latter, therefore, forms a swell within a swell, and its sound, when both are shut, is very subdued.

Each of the two pedals working the two sets of shutters is furnished with a rack and self-acting catch, which cause it to remain stationary at any point it is set to by the player; by placing, however, the foot on a particular part of the pedal, the catch is thrown out of gear, and the pedal follows the foot up or down, in the ordinary way.

This organ has no case – the whole of the machinery being exposed to view. The wind-chest is provided with a glass front, by which the peculiar construction of the valves may be seen.

Notes

1 The English organ in 1820

1 Some late examples of compasses terminating at e^3 are: York Minster, 1803 (Blyth); All Saints, Derby, 1808 (Elliot); St Michael's, Bristol, 1817 (Smith).

2 The Thaxted specification agrees with that given by Sperling (except that the number of ranks in the second mixture is said to be three, rather than two), and as local tradition asserts that the organ came from St John's Chapel, there seems little reason to question the attribution. Sperling gives a date of 1836, but the unreliability of his dating of instruments, coupled with the fact that the casework has a distinctly Regency flavour about it, tends to support the view that the organ standing at Thaxted is the one mentioned in the 1824 circular.

3 The Chapel was discovered to be unsafe in November 1856 (Bateman 1860: 172) and no further services were held there. *The London diocesan calendar* (1863), under the entry for St Andrew, Holborn, records that the chapel was then 'being taken down'.

4 An anonymous folio commonplace book kept by a Thaxted inhabitant (1854–87) records the opening of the organ and its provenance in June 1858. It was quoted in the Thaxted Bulletin (Autumn 1988). I am most grateful to Mr Julian Litten for this information.

5 George Cooper (a hostile witness) wrote that this organ was 'from its erection to its final condemnation in 1834 . . . a source of *unceasing annoyance* to the choir and organists' (*MW* IV, 1837: 68). Another writer (or possibly Cooper again: the article is unattributed) spoke of it as 'the worst instrument of this maker: the tone being extremely harsh and unmusical' (*CR*, xv, 1833: 551).

6 3-manual organs at St John's, Hackney (1797), Sheffield Parish Church (1805) and St Mary Magdalene, Holloway Road, Islington (1814) all had two open diapasons on the Great, as did at least two 2-manual instruments – the parish churches of Bradford, Wiltshire (1800) and Richmond, Yorkshire (1811). Smaller 3-manual organs for Bishops Cannings (1809) and Westbury (1814) had only a single open diapason, as did the rather larger organ for Lancaster Parish Church (1811).

7 Examples include: Hanover Square concert rooms (1804); Bromsgrove Church (1808); Stockport Sunday School (1811); St John's, Hull (1815); Tottenham Church (1817).

8 There are one or two exceptions: for example, small 3-manual organs by England at Bishops Cannings (1809) and Westbury (1814).

9 Stephen Bicknell tells me that the Russell organ in St Paul's, Canonbury (Islington) had a mounted cornet. The church was built in 1826–8.

10 Even then there were exceptions – for example, Avery's organ for Carlisle Cathedral (1806) which had three manuals, seventeen stops and no pedals.

11 According to Rees (1819: xxv: 'Organ') the Great Yarmouth organ had *two* stop knobs for

the Double Diapason following G. P. England's work in 1812; there are ambiguous references to the organs in St Patrick's, Soho, and Sheffield Parish Church which can be interpreted to support the view that pedal pipes were sometimes available on the manual.

12 Among them, St Mary, Bathwick (1820), the Philanthropic Chapel (1825), and Blackburn Parish Church (1828), all built by the Grays.

13 The organ which Samuel Green erected in Westminster Abbey for the Handel Commemoration of 1784 possessed a long movement allowing the keys to be placed 23' in front of the case and 19' lower than conventional key frames in the front of the organ (Rees 1819, xxv: 'Organ').

14 In smaller organs the pedal sometimes acted directly on the (single) slider, or it might move an additional slider acting as a ventil to shut off the wind supply to a group of stops (cf. Wilson 1968: 21). In larger church organs duplicate sliders were usually provided so that the pedal did not affect the slider directly connected to the drawstop.

15 The Donaldson organ (1790) now in the Holywell Music Room, Oxford, has a 'choir' pedal, as had Donaldson's organ for Mansfield Parish Church (1794).

16 The originator of the venetian swell is not known with any certainty. Hopkins claimed that it was Samuel Green, and that he adapted the venetian swell from 'the better class of harpsichord' (HR3: 91); Pearce (paradoxically naming the authority of Hopkins, though without citing a source) stated that the device was not found 'amongst Green's latest work' but was 'constantly met with' in the organs of England and Avery (1912: 6); a writer in the *Edinburgh Encyclopaedia* (1830) attributed the innovation to Flight & Robson – possibly because it was employed in their Apollonicon organ (1817) (*EE* xv: 678). Though clear evidence is lacking, Green's known character as an innovator together with his construction of large swell boxes which must have been too large to be made with the conventional sliding front (St Katherine-by-the-Tower, 1778; St George's Chapel, Windsor, 1789) lend some support to the claim made for him by Hopkins. See also, Wickens 1987: 35–9.

2 Organs and organ-building, 1820–40

1 See, for example, the intemperate letter from Cooper to the editor of the *Musical World* (IV, 1837: 68–9) respecting the Elliot organ in St James's Chapel Royal; some of the more colourful passages were clearly omitted upon publication, but Cooper's animosity towards Elliot, and the claims of Elliot & Hill to have a business connection with Snetzler, are evident enough. As is stated elsewhere, Cooper may have been the author of the article in the *Christian Remembrancer* (xv, 1833: 551–2) about the Chapel Royal organ; it, and an article concerning the Westminster Abbey organ in a previous issue (xv, 1833: 498–9), are scathing on the subject of Elliot's work. Cooper appeared for the defence (as did John Gray) when Hill took the Dean & Chapter of York to court over the costs of the new Minster organ, which, again, does not argue for any great intimacy between the two (Gray 1837: 31–4). There was at least a suspicion that Cooper was responsible for Hill's failure to secure the contract for the reconstruction of the organ in Trinity College, Cambridge, in 1836 (Gray 1837: 33); and it is not impossible that, if this thesis is correct, Cooper was in part responsible for Elliot & Hill's failure to secure much business in London in the 1820s and 1830s.

2 This claim has been thoroughly explored by B. B. Edmonds (Edmonds and Plumley 1988: 56–9), to whom I am indebted for much useful information on the subject. John Snetzler (1710–85) is said to have taken James Jones as a partner towards the end of his career; Snetzler himself retired in 1781, and when he died four years later, Jones was named as an executor in his will. Jones may have continued the business under the name of 'Snetzler and Jones' from premises in Stephen Street (later occupied by G. P. England) and, if so, he

may have retained the services of Snetzler's foreman, one Ohrmann (a Swede). At some stage, Ohrmann established his own business (or bought up Jones's?), and by 1799, Ohrmann & Co. is recorded at 13 Tottenham Court. He was for a time in partnership with John Nutt, who was named as his 'late partner' in Ohrmann's will (their only known work of any importance was a new organ for Macclesfield Parish Church, and a major overhaul and lowering of pitch at St Paul's Cathedral, both in 1803) (HRI: 445; Sumner 1931: 17). Ohrmann died in 1803, Nutt in 1804. By September 1804 Elliot was paying rates on *12* Tottenham Court (may there have been some confusion over the numbering, and *were* Elliot's premises those of Ohrmann & Nutt?). Elliot can claim a further (if unsubstantiated) connection with the partnership, in the form of a tradition that he was himself in partnership with Nutt at some point. Some of the 'evidence' is circumstantial and some rests on no more than longstanding tradition. Clearly, Elliot laid claim to descent from Snetzler, and equally clearly there was some dispute about this (witness George Cooper's animadversions in *MW* IV (1837): 68–9). At best, the connection was somewhat tenuous. The earlier part of the story receives some support from a statement in 1810 that 'Messrs Ohrmann and Nutt . . . formerly worked for Messrs Snetzler and Jones, organ builders, in Stephen-street, Tottenham-court-road' (*Monthly Magazine*, XXIX, 1810: 205).

3   The date (1815) given in Hill's obituary for the inauguration of his association with Elliot could well be imprecise. However, the Ashridge tale would scarcely have come into being had Hill not been actively involved in the business by the time that organ was built (1817–18). The marriage with Elliot's daughter must have taken place by 1822, which is the latest possible date for the birth of Thomas Hill (*c.* 1821–93), though it could have been somewhat earlier.

4   1825 is often quoted as the date for the commencement of the partnership, though authority seems to be lacking. According to Maxwell, Elliot's executor and brother-in-law (1837: 4), the true date was 1828. Although, by his own admission, Maxwell had not been closely associated with Thomas Elliot during his lifetime, and may not, therefore, be deemed an irrefutable witness, his careful investigation of the circumstances surrounding the contract for the York Minster organ, together with the fact that the surviving account book of the partnership (MS 11) has only a handful of entries pre-dating 1829, tend to add a little weight to his claim.

5   This excludes tuning contracts, of which Gray had thirty-six in 1830; all but four of these were in London, and whilst most were for a quarterly tuning, it is interesting to discover that a number of the larger metropolitan organs were tuned monthly (MS 1: *passim*).

6   Years later, it was alleged that Elliot & Hill had been the first of the leading builders deliberately to cut prices, and it was implied that this had had a deflationary effect upon the price of organs, at the inevitable cost of quality (*MW* XLII, 1864: 137).

7   Langwill and Boston 1970: 79; Clutton and Niland 1982: 273–4; *Littlebury's Directory & Gazetteer of Herefordshire*, London, 1876–7.

8   John Wesley's own attitude to the use of organs in Methodist worship was somewhat ambivalent, though he seems generally to have opposed it. It is said that three chapels acquired organs during his lifetime (at Bath, Keighley, and Newark) but for three decades following his death (1791) the Conference took a consistently firm stand against the introduction of organs (in some chapels, including those of Leeds, instrumental music in the form of a band was permitted, and provided accompaniment for the singers). In 1820, the Conference finally agreed that 'in some of the larger chapels, where some instrumental music may be deemed expedient in order to guide the congregational singing, organs may be allowed'. It was still, though, necessary to obtain the permission of the Conference for the installation of an organ, and proposals to seek this frequently caused controversy and even schism. City Road Chapel, London (the founder's own chapel) had no organ before the 1880s; before 1850, the singing had been led by a band of flute, clarinet, double-bass

and bass viol, but, following a secession, the music was left in the hands of a precentor without instrumental support (Scholes 1944: 570–2).

9 The history of the Brunswick Chapel case is tainted with the uncertainty which obscures the history of the instrument as a whole. The case as shown in an illustration to Snow's article (1935: opp. 173) almost certainly represents an expansion of the original case of 1828 (of which no drawing seems to have survived).

10 Michael Gillingham has kindly drawn my attention to an unexecuted design by Wyatt for an organ case for Durham Cathedral. It is more conventional in its treatment, and represents a marked improvement on his realised schemes.

3   The Insular Movement

1 There are countless examples throughout the organ compositions of Samuel Wesley's taste for intricate, often whimsical melody, but see, for instance, the first eight bars of the opening movement of the *Voluntary in B flat* (1829), which Wesley dedicated to Thomas Attwood. For Adams, see Voluntary 5 (A minor) of the *Six Voluntaries* (1820); the opening movement has a dramatic passage over a pedal point, with contrasting sections of 4-part harmony and chromatically flavoured passages on the Choir. As for S. S. Wesley, his earliest major anthems – *The Wilderness* (1832) and *Blessed be the God and Father* (1834) – already reveal the interest in using registration to heighten the emotional character of a passage, the awareness of the dramatic possibilities of setting contrasting movements alongside one another, and the taste for punctuating the musical text with chords of a striking harmonic construction or dynamic level which were to characterise his cathedral music.

2 See, for instance, Rees's *Cyclopaedia* (1819: n.p.): 'And it had been well if the trumpet had never been used as any other than a chorus-stop; for its use, as an imitation of a real trumpet, has given rise to the introduction of a variety of imitation-stops; most of them a disgrace to the noble instrument in which they are suffered to intrude; and its consequence, a trifling and vitiated style of performance, equally disgraceful to the taste of this country, where only it is cultivated.'

3 Gray & Davison regularly used the term 'Clarionet' for a short-compass Choir reed after 1842, but preferred 'Hautboy' to 'Oboe' until the 1850s (MSS 3–6: *passim*). Hill usually specified an 'Oboe' after 1841, rather than a 'Hautboy', but seems throughout the 1850s to have reserved 'Clarinet' for his concert organs (MS 12: *passim*). Other builders, similarly, reflected their conservatism or otherwise by their choice of nomenclature.

4 Vincent Novello's *Select organ pieces, from the masses, motetts, and other sacred works of . . . the German and Italian schools* was particularly widely disseminated; the earliest numbers appeared *c.* 1830 and reflect the limited scope of the contemporary English organ (and organist). Significantly, this collection was still available at the end of the century (*MT* xxxvii, 1896: 724). The musical journals of the period record the publication of numerous transcriptions of oratorio pieces, and all the major series (James Stimpson's *Organist's Standard Library*, and W. T. Best's *Arrangements from the scores of the great masters*, for instance) included them.

5 For example: St John's Chapel, Bedford Row (Lincoln, 1821); St Pancras Parish Church (Gray, 1822); York Minster (Ward, 1823); St Mary Abchurch, London (Bishop, 1825); St Mary Magdalen, Taunton (Smith, 1824); All Saints, Hereford (Lincoln, 1826); St Mary Moorfields, London (Bevington, 1830?); Christ Church, Bristol (Smith, 1837); St John's College Chapel, Cambridge (Hill, 1838); Exeter Hall, London (Walker, 1839); Armagh Cathedral (Walker, 1840); Walthamstow Church (Allen 1845); Cashel Cathedral (Bevington, 1846); Jamaica Cathedral (Walker, 1847); St Paul, Brighton (Holdich, 1851).

6 Trinity Church, Ryde (Bevington/Holdich, 1835?); St George, Everton (Bewsher, 1845).

7 For example, *Hamilton's catechism of the organ* (1st edition *c*. 1838) and Joshua Done, *A complete treatise on the organ* (1839?).

8 The organ was built by Nicholls (successor to G. P. England) for Nuneaton Church. Both Nicholls and the benefactor who had commissioned the organ became insolvent, and the instrument was purchased in an unfinished state by John Gray for £300 (MS 86: f2). Gray sold it to St Luke's for £840 and it was erected in 1824. It seems that there was at first a temporary case: Savage's case was added in 1825 (MS 1: 39).

9 Hill seems to have treated 'Posaune' and 'Trombone' as interchangeable at this period. His Letter Book (MS 12: 9) records 'Posaune or Trombone' in the stop-list for St John's College, Cambridge (1838), and there is a trombone in the scheme for St Luke's, Cheetham Hill, Manchester (1839) (MS 12: 74) which appeared as a posaune in the finished organ. St Peter's, Cornhill, offers further variations. The 1839 contract had 'Large Horn' (and 'Octave Horn') but the stop knobs were labelled 'Corno-trombone' and 'Corno-clarion' (above, p. 221).

10 Christ's Hospital, 1830 (according to Hamilton); Birmingham Town Hall, 1834; King's College, Cambridge, 1834; various schemes in the Letter Book between 1838 and 1840.

11 There was almost certainly a connection. The French horn specified for St John's College, Cambridge, was later referred to simply as 'Horn' (cf. MS 25 and *Cambridge General Advertizer*, 6 March 1839), and the French horn and horn specified respectively for St Peter's, Cornhill, and St Luke's, Cheetham Hill (both 1839) had become cornopeans by the time the organs were built.

12 The cornopean in the Cornhill organ was probably the first made by Hill, followed closely by a similar stop in the organ for St Luke's, Cheetham Hill (also 1840). Thereafter, it rapidly established itself as the standard Swell reed in Hill's instruments. The claim made in Sperling (MS 79: 84) that Hill built an organ for Christ Church, Maida Hill, in 1834, and that this contained the first cornopean is based upon inaccurate dating: an estimate for the organ appears in the Letter Book (MS 12: 105) dated 28 July 1841.

13 Other examples are: St Mary, Bryanston Square, 1824 (Bishop); All Souls, St Marylebone, 1824 (Bishop); St Peter, Walworth, 1825 (Lincoln); Holy Trinity, St Marylebone, 1827 (Bishop); St Mark, Pentonville, 1828 (Gray); Oldham Parish Church, 1830 (Elliot & Hill); Blackburn Parish Church, 1832 (Gray); Hereford Cathedral, 1832 (Bishop); Liverpool Parish Church, 1833 (Gray). Bishop made some use of e-compass for larger organs during the 1820s and 1830s. Examples include: St John, Waterloo Road, 1824; St Mark, North Audley Street, 1825; St Peter, Pimlico, 1837.

14 Newark Parish Church, 1835 (Bishop); St John's College, Cambridge, 1839 (Hill); Exeter Hall, 1839 (Walker); Chester Cathedral, 1843 (Gray & Davison); Jamaica Cathedral, 1847 (Walker); St Paul's Cathedral, 1849 (Bishop).

15 It must have been provided at St Sepulchre, Holborn, in 1826. Bishop undertakes to provide it in his estimates for St Peter's, Pimlico (1827) and St James, Bermondsey (1829), though in both instances, it seems that a simple coupling of Swell to Choir is involved.

4   Three case studies

1 This is the specification as given in the *York Gazette*, 5 July 1823, the organ having been completed a few days before. One or two corrections are made by reference to Camidge's own account of the 1821–4 work (Gray 1837: 49–50).

2 According to *YG*, 5 July 1823, the scales of the wooden registers at FF were as follows: Double Stop Diapason, 16″ wide; Double Open Diapason, 16″ wide; Sackbut, 14″ square at the top of the resonator; Trombone, 10″ square; Shawm, 8″ square.

3 In March 1834, the *Mechanics' Magazine* (xx: 404–5) reproduced a stop list which had appeared 'some months ago', in the *York Courant*; a search has failed to locate it. Other

sources consulted are: *MW* IV, 1837: 118–19; *YG*, 28 October 1837; Maxwell 1837: 28–30; Allerston & Pickwell 1844.

4 Camidge refers to a Choir trumpet in a letter to Hill (Maxwell 1837: 30). Allerston & Pickwell (1844) include a bassoon [8] and clarionet [4] in the Choir Organ, and it may be that this bassoon was really a small-scale trumpet. The 1834 version has cremona [8] and clarionet [4]. The cremona (if it existed) would have had a bassoon bass, and Camidge may at an early stage have had the treble replaced to make a bassoon of full compass.

5 This only appears in the 1834 stop list. Later specifications have four 8′ reeds in the Swell, rather than three, and it seems likely that the celestina soon made way for an extra reed. It is just possible that the celestina was an incorrectly-named reed (cremona?).

6 Peculiar difficulties attend any attempt to establish the precise nature of the Pedal specification at any point in its development. The 1834 stop list includes two 16′ reeds not given here: fagotto, and bass horn. These do not appear elsewhere, though it is possible that they are related to the '2 large Shawm Basses' which Camidge (?) included in the *YG* (1837) version (though these were stated to be of 8′ [i.e. 4′] pitch, and were associated with the Great stop list). If *MW* (1837) is correct, one of the 16′ flues and the 16′ reed each had only a single octave of pipes; there may be a grain of truth in this (the double-bass diapason is the most likely identification for the 16′ flue), but as the *MW* version of the specification is generally unreliable, it is impossible to know what to make of this.

7 Zinc was used for the large Pedal pipes at Birmingham (1834), and was regularly used for 32′ and 16′ basses by Hill for the remainder of his career. He occasionally employed it for Pedal reed resonators, as in 1840 at St Luke's, Cheetham Hill, Manchester (HR2: 144).

8 Hill received the Silver Medal of the Society of Arts for the invention in 1841 (*Transactions of the Society for the Encouragement of Arts, Manufactures, and Commerce*, LIV, 1841–2: 98–101). Box pallets were used at Birmingham Town Hall (where they still control the supply of wind to the largest pipes in the case front) and Stratford-upon-Avon (1841), and were regularly used by Hill throughout his career to supply the largest pipes with wind.

9 The sources are: *YG*, 28 October 1837; MS 12: 110, 114, 121, 174; Stimpson 1845: *passim*; Hamel 1849: I, CXXII–CXXVI.

10 According to Camidge (*YG*, 28 October 1837) this was to meet the Pedal 32′, though it is difficult to understand the usefulness of such an arrangement.

11 Omitted in *YG*, 28 October 1837.

12 'Mr Drury has been engaged to supply a set of his justly celebrated musical bells, which will form one of the novel and important additions to the varied powers of this instrument' (*Mechanics' Magazine* XX, 1834: 403).

13 At some stage (1837 or 1843?) most of the borrowed registers acquired two octaves (more or less) of independent pipes which could only be played from the fourth keyboard; three wholly independent stops (vox humana, harmonica and claribella) also appeared (Stimpson 1845: 13–14).

14 This comes from an unidentified newspaper cutting of the nineteenth century in a scrapbook belonging to Mr Lawrence Firth (information supplied by the Revd B. B. Edmonds). Cf. Edmonds & Thistlethwaite 1976: 79 for a further connection between railway signalling and high-pressure reeds.

15 Hill made his second 'Grand Ophicleide' for the new organ in the Great George Street Chapel, Liverpool, in 1841 (Warren 1842: 85). He supplied (even if he did not install) 16′ and 8′ reeds for the York Minster organ in 1846 (*YG*, 27 June 1846), and made other examples in the course of the next few years. The only other builder who is known to have made (installed?) a high-pressure reed during the 1840s is Postill of York, who added a 'Posaune Trumpet' to the organ of Howden Parish Church in 1846 (unidentified newspaper cutting in scrapbook belonging to Mr Lawrence Firth). By the mid-1850s, other builders had begun to make high-pressure reeds. Gray & Davison's first was a horizontal

'Tromba' on 6″ at Magdalen College, Oxford, in 1855 (*MW* xxxiii, 1855: 130), and in the same year, Willis completed his Liverpool organ with four (?) high-pressure reeds (above, pp. 148–9).

16 There was an exception: Willis had been obliged to adopt equal temperament in his new organ for Carlisle Cathedral (1856) at the behest of the Organist (*MG* ii, 1857: 77).

17 This is according to a pencilled note inside the front cover of the copy of Perronet Thompson's *The theory and practice of just intonation* (London, 1850) in the Organ Club Library, Royal College of Organists.

18 The scheme which Hill submitted in February 1851 is recorded in his Letter Book (ms 12: 267–70). It was to have eighty-one stops, and was essentially a larger version of the organ for the Royal Panopticon (1854).

19 They were revoiced on 15″ to 20″ in 1867 (hr2: 503).

5   The Bristol reformation

1 The letters appeared under the signature 'Minimus', but there can be little doubt from their tone and content that Hodges was the author.

2 Hooper (1948: 76) gives no source for the suspiciously large Swell Organ that he claims the organ possessed as early as 1725; the claim must be treated with considerable scepticism.

3 It should be recorded that, although Smith's octave coupler of 1824 may have been the first example of a *manual* octave coupler in England, the Harris & Byfield organ in St Mary Redcliffe, Bristol, had possessed a type of *pedal* octave coupler, acting on the manual, since its inception in 1729, and this may have been the origin of Smith's interest in octave couplers (Morgan 1912: 7–8; Pearce 1912: 132).

6   Bach, Mendelssohn and the English organ, 1810–45

1 The reference is found in an article describing four metropolitan organs: Christ Church, Newgate Street; Christ Church, Spitalfields; St Luke, Chelsea; St Sepulchre, Holborn. 'The choir organs in each of these fine instruments are contemptible, and nearly useless. The great advantage of a good choir organ is, that it affords the facility of playing a trio on two manuals and pedal obligato. Not one of these instruments present [*sic*] this opportunity, as there are no open diapasons, principals, &c. in the lower manuals, to match in body and quality of tone the middle manuals. It was the opinion of M. Mendelssohn that this was a fault which universally prevailed in our English organs, and one which could not be too speedily rectified. The swell organ should be the soft accompanying organ; the choir to contain the solo stops and large diapasons, principals, sesqui-altra, &c.' (*MW* viii, 1838: 281). It is not clear whether the final sentence quoted represents Mendelssohn's prescription, or is a deduction from it.

2 English organists might be forgiven for harbouring misconceptions about the appropriate *tempi* for Bach's organ works. The Haslinger edition of the *Sechs Präludien und Fugen* (Vienna, *c.* 1830) proposes wholly impractical *tempi*: e.g. quaver = 100 for the *Prelude in B minor* (bwv 544) and crotchet = 116 for the *Prelude in C minor* (bwv 546). These were probably intended for application when the pieces were played on the pianoforte, but their publication may well have misled organists.

3 Recalling hearing Mendelssohn play at St Peter's, Cornhill, Miss Mounsey commented: 'I remember how – according to my experience – he played Bach *slower* than I expected; but instead of rattling off the semiquavers he made them flow impressively and seriously . . .' (ms 68: f.85). I am indebted to Dr Christopher Kent for drawing my attention to this ms.

4 Details of appointments from: *BMB*, Pearce 1909, Dawe 1983: *passim*.

5 No. 1 in this edition was the *Toccata and Fugue in D major/minor* (BWV 913), not now regarded as being an organ piece.

6 Dragonetti (1763–1846) was the leading virtuoso bass player of the day, and greatly in demand at festivals and in the London theatres. Edwards (1896: 725) records a report that the Coventry & Hollier *Grand Studies* were issued 'at the expense and risk of Signor Dragonetti', but there appears to be no way of substantiating this claim. The double bass parts supplied by Dragonetti frequently depart radically from Bach's original.

7 *Prelude in A minor* (BWV 569); *Prelude and Fugue in E major* (BWV 566); *Prelude and Fugue in D minor* (BWV 539); *Fantasia in G minor* (BWV 542i); *Prelude and Fugue in G major* (BWV 550); *Prelude and Fugue in D major* (BWV 532); *Prelude and Fugue in E minor* (BWV 533); *Fugue in G minor* (BWV 542ii); *Toccata and Fugue in D minor* (BWV 565).

8 *Prelude and Fugue in A minor* (BWV 543); *Prelude and Fugue in B minor* (BWV 544); *Prelude and Fugue in C major* (BWV 545); *Prelude and Fugue in C minor* (BWV 546); *Prelude and Fugue in C major* (BWV 547); *Prelude and Fugue in E minor* (BWV 548).

9 *Toccata and Fugue in F major* (BWV 540); *Toccata and Fugue in D minor (Dorian)* (BWV 538).

10 It may be that the *Prelude and Fugue in G major*, added to the existing *Grand Studies* about this time, was included in the fifth category.

11 Redlich has shown that two of the three continental editions of the *Well-tempered Clavier* (1800–1) were already available in English reprints (1952: 292–5). Wesley seems to have worked from the Zurich (Naegeli) edition (Edwards 1896: 656), but he may have had access to MS sources (Burney, Horn?) in addition.

12 In a letter to Novello from Great Yarmouth (18 July 1815), Wesley refers to playing 'the triple fugues [*sic*] in E♭' on 'the most magnificent organ I have yet heard' [sc. St Nicholas, Great Yarmouth] (MS 64). Cf. Jacob's 1827 edition of BWV 552ii: *A Grand Fugue . . . in three movements and on three subjects* . . . The Yarmouth organ at this time had double pedal pipes (but a pedal board of only seventeen notes).

13 Information from an unidentified newspaper cutting in the collection of the Revd B. B. Edmonds.

14 These diaries seem to have passed from the Hopkins family into the possession of C. W. Pearce; attempts to trace them through Pearce's descendants have proved fruitless.

7 The German System

1 Writing to Chester on 11 May, Davison added a postscript to the effect that a long movement could be added 'without further preparation in the interior of the organ' (MS 12: 8). This was evidently not part of the original scheme. The Coronation Organ, however, had to be fitted with a long movement, and this is probably the explanation.

2 It would be interesting to know whether Gauntlett's dismissal had anything to do with a change of proprietorship in 1838, when Frederick Davison (the organ-builder) bought the *Musical World* (Davison 1912: 46). Gauntlett's editorship came to end in October 1838, about the time that the partnership between William Hill and Frederick Davison was terminated (*MW* x, 1838: 77, 234). Is it possible that Gauntlett was somehow implicated in the circumstances surrounding the dissolution of the partnership? Did he and Davison fall out over the authorship of the German System, perhaps? That the *Musical World*'s animosity had to do with a difference of opinion between Gauntlett and Davison seems to have been widely rumoured at the time; in 1844, a paragraph in the journal attempted a reply to accusations in the *Morning Post* that its abuse of Gauntlett arose from the fact that it was in the proprietorship 'of organ builders not employed by Dr. Gauntlett to carry out his great improvements in organ building' (XIX, 1844: 51). The fact that the 'reply' consisted only of further abuse seems to lend some support to the claim.

3 To be fair, these are taken from Gauntlett's own description of the organ (Appendix 2, pp. 508–10) and may not have appeared on the console. The nearest Hill came to falling in with Gauntlett's complete scheme of nomenclature was in the organ for the Mechanics' Institute, Liverpool, where the Great is a smaller version of St Olave's. The specification of a proposed organ for the Surrey Chapel which appears in *Hamilton's Catechism* (Warren 1842: 82–3) reveals an extensive application of Gauntlett's nomenclature.

4 Upon William Hill's death in 1870, the direction of the firm passed to his eldest son, Thomas (*c.* 1821–1893), who had worked with his father since at least 1840 (MS 12: 95). He was, in turn, succeeded by his son, Arthur George Hill (1857–1923), under whom the firm amalgamated with Norman & Beard Ltd (1916).

5 It seems that provision was made (possibly in 1838) for a 16' reed in the Great at Newgate Street. Hill provided for its addition (by transposing one of the 8's and adding a bass) in an estimate of 1843 (MS 12: 137). The work seems not to have been undertaken then, though it had probably been done by the time the organ was rebuilt in 1867. The Liverpool organ (1841) was also designed to take the addition of a double reed in the Great (98), and in his reconstruction of the Westminster Abbey instrument (1848) Hill transposed an existing trumpet of 8' pitch to make a short-compass 16' register (207).

6 The original estimate provided for a 'Small Bassoon to Tenor C' (MS 12: 83). The scheme was amended while the organ was under construction and this stop became a 'double Bassoon' (98). It seems probable that it was a comparatively mild register, and, if so, can only have represented a modest step in the direction of the later Victorian 'Full Swell'. Similarly, in an early estimate for Ashton-under-Lyne (April 1843), the Swell double reed was to be a 'Corno di bassetto (a double Bassoon to Tenor C)' (138).

7 According to Hopkins, Hill's early cone gambas were surmounted by a bell (HR2: 103; 137–8) but this is not the case in St Mary-at-Hill or in other early survivors known to the present writer.

8 With the exception of the pre-1838 doubles, all the flue registers of the Pedal had only a single octave of pipes, and the two reeds had only five pipes each (G–B), made up of discarded manual basses (MS 13: 26).

9 It is unlikely that the extended keyboard was, in fact, made. Its provision may, of course, have been part of the earlier scheme, which Gauntlett felt he could not drop.

10 Marshall was a founding member of the Handel Society (1843), and was the local secretary for Leamington (*MW* XVIII, 1843: 346).

11 The evolution of the scheme is discussed in more detail in Renshaw 1968: *passim*. See also: Clayton & Renshaw 1968; Renshaw 1970. These three articles represent an invaluable record of the Great George Street organ on the eve of the disgraceful sequence of events which led to its destruction.

12 As evidence of this, the organ was successfully transferred to St Paul's Cathedral in 1861 (*MW* XXXIX, 1861: 40). There it stood in the South Transept and was used principally to accompany the Special Sunday Evening Services begun in 1858, for which large congregations gathered under the Dome and in the Nave. (Upon the removal of the organ screen, the existing cathedral organ had been re-sited on the north side of the Choir, in a position from which it was impossible for it to provide support for congregational singing in other parts of the building.) It was removed in 1873, following Willis's reconstruction of the main organ, and went to the Victoria Rooms, Clifton, Bristol; little survived a drastic rebuilding by Robert Hope-Jones at the end of the century.

13 Thus the pipework of the Stalybridge organ survives in a later instrument by Hill (Wickens 1978: 14–15).

14 The source of the specification as printed by Hill in the *Circular* has not been traced. It differs from Burney (1775, II: 306–9) and Hamilton (Warren 1842: 104–6), in, for example, omitting the 4' and 2' reeds on the Pedal, and some of the pitches are given

inaccurately. It is valuable, however, not as a reliable account of the Haarlem organ (which it clearly is not) but as an indication of what Hill *thought* the Haarlem organ was like and took as a model for his own work. The pitches of the Grand and Pedal Organs are as given by Hill, except in the case of stopped registers, where actual pitch has been substituted for the length of the longest pipe; those of the 'Solo' and Choir (not given by Hill) are surmised from other contemporary accounts.

8   The work of William Hill, 1839–55

1   A copy of this leaflet is pasted inside the cover of MS 72.

2   There are minor discrepancies between the testimony of the *Circular* and that of the 1840 console, now preserved in the vestry at Cornhill. The name-plates (which, for the manuals, are probably original) describe both open diapasons as 'Principal Diapason', nomenclature which HR also employs (e.g. HR2: 459). The two dulcianas are called 'Dulcian' (possibly an engraver's slip), and the couplers refer to 'Grand' rather than 'Great'. More puzzling is the fact that there are three stop knobs which appear to have controlled Pedal registers: 'Bourdon, CCC', 'Grand Diapason, CCC 16'' and 'Grand Trombone, CCC 16''. The most likely explanation is that the Bourdon was added in 1867 or 1882 when, according to Pearce (1909: 71), Hill & Son made alterations and additions, and that the existing two Pedal registers were re-named at the same time.

3   These may be detected by reference to HR2: 462. The 16' registers on each manual are called 'Bourdon and Open Diapason'; the Viol di Gamba is simply 'Gamba'; 'Flageolet' is substituted for Piccolo. The Pedal stops are respectively 'Open Diapason 16', 'Octave 8' and 'Trombone 16'.

4   The details are found in MS 14: 86, dated May 1879. New split pallets were provided for the Great and a Harmonic Flute 8' took the place of the Krum Horn, which migrated to the new Choir Organ. The new Pedal stops were a Contra Bourdon 32' and Bourdon 16', and the compass of the three existing registers was extended to f¹. New bellows were provided to supply the expanded Pedal division, necessitating the reconstruction of the blowing plant in the tower. Four new couplers (Swell to Choir; Choir to Pedal; Swell Octave; Swell Sub-octave) were added, and a reversible pedal for the Great to Pedal coupler. Though not mentioned in the Shop Book, the Swell Contra Trombone 16' was probably added at this time and it is likely that the mixture compositions were adjusted to eliminate the tierces, except in the bottom octave.

5   The 1848 pipework was carefully preserved, though the mixture compositions were again altered. The Harmonic Flute of 1880 was removed and a Krum Horn inserted in its place; this is not, however, the original rank, but a relatively modern register. Not the least unfortunate consequence of the 1971 work was the painting of much of the interior woodwork, making it impossible to distinguish the original from more recent work.

6   The earliest reference to the wooden Violon (it was more usually known as 'Violone') seems to be in an estimate for Coventry Music Hall dated 13 September 1854 (MS 12: 321). One was ordered for Trinity College, Cambridge, in July 1855 (333) but it is not known whether this, or the Kidderminster register, appeared first.

7   The pallets were refelted and some split pallets were introduced; new squares and new wires were provided, and the whole action was rebushed; the coupler actions were renewed and three composition pedals were provided for the Swell. New keyboards and a new pedal board to RCO standards were provided. The Swell Gamba, the Pedal Principal, the Choir Salicional and the Great Gamba were revoiced (MS 15: 13).

8   When the 15-note compass of 1840 was eventually extended a new 4-slide soundboard was introduced behind the Great; this is shown in Figure 12. The compass then became twenty-seven notes (1867?), being finally extended to thirty notes (1882 or 1891).

9 Holy Trinity, Taunton (1845) preserves the same arrangement of divisions as Kidder-minster, and internal evidence suggests that Eastbrook Hall, Bradford (also 1845) was essentially the same, though there, greater height was available and the Choir was consequently not so buried. The Choir Organ at Great George Street Chapel, Liverpool (1841) was 'crammed in' under the Swell (Clayton and Renshaw 1968: 105) but the fact that it was something of an afterthought may account for its particularly obscure position.

10 The organ in the Roman Catholic Cathedral at Arundel was installed by Hill & Son in 1873. It is clear, however, from the construction of the pipework, that it was based on an earlier organ by the firm; most of the flue pipes have the indented French mouths used by the firm between 1847 and 1859 (above, pp. 237–8) and the thinness of the metal suggests a date in the earlier part of that period.

11 The Tuba Mirabilis knob from the 1849 console is illustrated ('Actual Size') in Perkins (1905: opp. p. 26). This survived, and was incorporated in a walking stick for the use of the Organist to the Corporation; it was seen by the writer in 1974, but has since disappeared.

9   The transition

1 A brass plate on the console of the organ recorded that 'This organ, of a 32 feet Manual Gamut, was designed by Mr. [sic] H. J. Gauntlett, commenced by Mr. Lincoln, 1844, and perfected by Mr. William Hill, 1846' (HR2: 485). Elsewhere, Gauntlett stated that the instrument was 'completed' by Hill (Gauntlett: 1846). The circumstances leading to this collaboration can only be conjectured. Hill may have supplied some of the pipework, for Gauntlett reports that the Pedal reed was such 'as only Messrs. Hill can create' (1846).

2 There is some uncertainty about the compasses. Hopkins (HR1: 495–6) states that Great and Swell were C–g^3 but that the Choir was GG–g^3. It is not impossible that this is correct (a long compass was still found useful for accompanying singers) but Sperling (MS 80: 112) states that all three keyboards began at C.

3 The confused history of this instrument has been disentangled by David Wickens (1974). He notes that there is some uncertainty about the original specification (8). As Wickens has shown, Hopkins (HR2: 496) gives both the location and the date of the organ incorrectly.

4 The stop list of this organ appears in Hamilton (Warren 1842: 76–7) but there appears to be no mention of it in the Gray records. The earliest surviving Shop Book was begun in 1840, and so it is possible that the entry was made in the previous (lost) volume; however, the Account Books are complete from 1821, and there seems to be no mention of the instrument there, either. Sperling's specification (MS 79: 88) probably comes directly from Hamilton.

5 In many mid-Victorian examples of the keraulophon, the hole appears in a sliding cap at the top of the pipe; it is not known whether this was a feature from the start.

6 E.g. Tenbury Parish Church; St Patrick, Manchester; Mosley Street Chapel, Manchester (all 1843); St James, Bradford; 'Oldham' (both 1844); Wesleyan Chapel, Burnley; 'Stretford' (both 1845); Cross Street Chapel, Manchester (1846); 'West Bromwich'; Halifax Place Chapel, Nottingham (both 1847).

7 A mystery surrounds the addition of this Pedal Organ. In June 1849, Cooper wrote to the Vestry informing the members that he had been offered 'by a Gentleman, a Pupil of mine, a complete Pedal Organ including Sound-Board, Mechanism Bellows and handsome draw stops which formed part of a magnificent instrument, built, I may almost say, under my own superintendance, but which on completion was found to be too large for the purpose he required'. This Pedal Organ was to be had for £200, and its addition would make the St Sepulchre's organ 'the finest of its size in the world'. The 'Gentleman' was anxious to settle the matter, as he was paying warehousing on the pipes and parts of the

Pedal Organ and had another customer who would certainly purchase it if St Sepulchre's declined this advantageous offer (MS 74: 516). The Vestry voted the necessary funds, and 'George Jones Esq' was duly reimbursed for his Pedal Organ (MS 73: 357). The mystery is compounded by the fact that the Pedal Organ appears in Gray & Davison's Shop Book simply as an order for St Sepulchre's dated 7 August 1849 (MS 5: f.40). Was there a Mr Jones? Or was the whole business an elaborate ploy to ensure that Cooper had 'the finest organ of its size in the world' at his command?

8 The order (MS 5: f.53) is dated August 1850 and entered as 'Limehouse'. It would seem that the organ was always intended for Limehouse, but that arrangements were made for it to be put on display in the Exhibition before being erected there.

9 Huyben's chronological list of Cavaillé-Coll's organs (1983: 5–10) includes ten instruments for the British Isles. They are: Carmelite Church, Kensington (1866); Convent of the Good Shepherd, London [?] (1867); London [unidentified] (1873); Albert Hall, Sheffield (1873); Paisley Abbey (1874); Bellahouston Church (1874); Bracewell Castle (1870) [removed in 1875 to Ketton Hall and enlarged, and later rebuilt in the Parr Hall, Warrington]; Blackburn Parish Church (1875); Manchester Town Hall (1877); Sheffield (unidentified, undated). Cf. Cavaillé-Coll 1929: 159; Sumner 1954: 80–1.

10 This would have been in the first half of 1854. A new organ for the Hanover Square Rooms, installed in 1853, was altered to equal temperament in April 1854 (MS 6: f.47).

11 Hill was the first English builder to make a horizontal reed: the Solo tubas at the Panopticon (1854) were placed thus. The inspiration was ultimately the Spanish organ, but it is probable that the direct influence was Cavaillé-Coll (again). Hill usually reserved this disposition for solo reeds (York Minster, 1860), but occasionally used it for a stop intended to have a chorus function (All Saints, Margaret Street, 1859). Gray & Davison's practice was similarly varied. At Ludlow (1860) the horizontal reed was, like the Magdalen stop, a Solo register, but in the Llandaff Cathedral organ (1861) now at Usk the Trumpet on the Great is disposed horizontally.

12 The actual cost of the case was £170 (MS 2: 183).

13 I owe this information to Mr Kent Stalker.

14 Spark has given an account of the controversy surrounding the selection of both plans and builder (Spark 1892: 218–21). Some of this must have been due to the fact that Spark and Smart's competitors were professional organ-builders who doubtless resented the pretensions of mere 'professors' in preparing detailed technical drawings, but the fact that five reputable firms (including Hill and Gray & Davison) were prepared to tender indicates that Smart's plans were perfectly workable. In view of Smart's involvement the selection of Gray & Davison to build the organ has a certain inevitability about it; Willis evidently thought so, and this probably explains why he declined to tender formally but wrote privately to the chairman of the Organ Committee, offering to build the instrument for a certain sum (Spark 1892: 220).

15 In the original drawings the jambs are straight, set at right-angles to the key cheeks, with the stops of each department grouped together in a single terrace. On 1 May 1858 the committee agreed to Davison's proposal to make them splayed (MS 42).

16 See, for example, Henry Willis's vindictive letter in the *Musical Gazette* and ensuing correspondence (*M G* II, 1857: 429–31; 443–4; 464–5; 478–9).

10   The emergence of the Victorian organ, 1850–70

1 Datings for the establishment of individual firms are drawn either from advertisements in periodicals (e.g. *M O*) or from MS note-books compiled by J. T. Lightwood and now in the possession of the Revd B. B. Edmonds. On the origins of Norman & Beard, see Norman 1986: 58–9.

2 Conacher took Brown, one of his workmen, into partnership in 1854, and the business was known as Conacher & Brown until the partnership was dissolved in 1857 (*MG* III, 1858: 387). Conacher's brother, James, was a partner during the 1860s and 1870s, when the firm was known as Conacher & Co. This partnership was dissolved in 1879, and James Conacher set up on his own account in Huddersfield.

3 1850 is the date of the partnership between James Kirtland and Frederick Jardine, but the business was a continuation of that of Samuel Renn, Kirtland's uncle by marriage (Sayer 1976b: 169–70; but on date of the commencement of the partnership, cf. Sayer 1974: 111).

4 Brindley was joined by A. Healey Foster (who may have been in business briefly on his own) in about 1871, and the firm was subsequently known as Brindley & Foster (White 1871, 1872: *passim*).

5 Thomas Harrison removed to Durham in 1872 where he was joined by his brother, James; from that point, the firm was known as Harrison & Harrison (Elvin 1973: 52–9).

6 William Richardson was partner in the business of Bishop, Starr & Richardson from 1857–61. He was then in business on his own account in London for nine years, moving to Manchester in 1870 (Elvin 1984: 68, 342–3).

7 This is said to have been patented in 1855 (Elvin 1968: 14; also, the builders' own account of the 1862 Exhibition organ, transcribed Elvin: 15) but the present writer can find no record of it. The 1862 Exhibition organ had a single combination pedal (in addition to six composition pedals with fixed selections of stops) capable of producing eight different combinations and acting simultaneously on the different departments of the instrument. The required combination was set by means of an index, by either the player or an assistant (*MSt* I, 1862: 24).

8 Joule had earlier (1851) commissioned an organ from Kirtland & Jardine for St Margaret's Church, Whalley Range (*MWL*, 1872: 391).

9 Unfortunately, even Joule's finances did not run to the installation of the planned Solo Organ at the same time as the rest of the instrument, but the design was complete and prepared for in 1852.

10 The stop list was extensively revised, both before and after the opening of the organ. *Musical Gazette* (I, 1856: 43) gave a version with fifty stops. By the time the organ was opened, later in the year, this had been extended to include fifty-five stops (*MG* I, 1856: 174). Subsequent alterations and additions tended to reinforce the French character of the instrument (e.g. the Solo Organ, with three harmonic registers at 8′, 4′ and 2′, and the rearrangement of the Choir reeds); HR2 lists sixty-one stops, and a later version (*MWL*, 1872: 506–7) has sixty-five.

11 The simplification system was, of course, used for the action layout. According to a contemporary report, by this method 'the touch is more prompt and certain; while, at the same time, more elastic and flexible. Indeed, when used without the coupler stops, the several manuals are as easy to the touch as the most highly finished grand pianoforte' (*MG* I, 1856: 173–4). The qualification concerning the couplers may be significant, though, according to Sayer (1976: 174) Kirtland & Jardine never during this period resorted to pneumatic assistance, even in the largest instruments.

12 The two upper keyboards are shown as overhanging in the earliest Jardine drawing (3-manual organ for Maer Hall, Staffordshire; 1850), and this established itself as a standard feature of the firm's instruments. The tumbler coupler (HR2: 55) seems first to have been used in 1851 in an organ for Mytholmroyd Church (Sayer 1976b: 171). The Jardine relief pallet (HR2: 34) was invented by Frederick Jardine's uncle, George Jardine, who had settled as an organ-builder in New York in 1837, after working with Flight & Robson and Joseph Walker in England (Ochse 1975: 161). Frederick Jardine served an apprenticeship with Bishop, and then worked with his uncle in America; upon his return to England he joined James Kirkland to become manager of Renn's old business whilst Sarah Renn was

still alive; the formal partnership seems to date from 1850, when Mrs Renn died (Sayer 1974: 111; 1976b: 170).

13 According to Hopkins (HR2: 315) Wadsworth and Robson had also built Pedal Organs using mechanical extension by 1870. The basic principle involved using a 42-note chest with two sets of pallets for the eighteen notes common to the 16′ register and its 8′ extension (or the 8′ register and its 4′ extension). Each pedal key had two trackers, connected to pallets controlling notes an octave apart. Thus, when C was depressed, the pallets controlling both the C- and the c-pipes were drawn down, and, subject to the control of the usual sliders, the notes sounded.

14 Henry Jones was born in 1822 and died in 1890. Before setting up on his own he was with Walker.

15 Alfred Hunter (1827–1911) was apprenticed to Holdich; he later worked for Bevington and Bishop. He went into partnership with Webb (another of Bishop's men), but Webb left to become a publican during the 1860s and Hunter carried on the business under his own name. It is not known whether he was related to another Alfred Hunter (fl. 1835–55), a pipe-maker who supplied the trade (Elvin 1984: 340–1).

16 Wedlake was Henry Willis's first apprentice.

17 Henry Speechly was nephew to J. C. Bishop. He worked with his uncle for some years during the 1840s before leaving to join Henry Willis. He became Willis's foreman, specialising in the construction of soundboards, and then, in 1860, left to establish his own business (Elvin 1984: 334–5).

18 Ingram was born in 1839. He was apprenticed to an organ-builder named Snell and at the age of twenty-one was articled to Willis to learn reed-voicing. After having established his own business he was briefly in partnership with Speechly (from 1873). His sons established businesses in Hereford and Edinburgh. Ingram (senior) acquired Holdich's business in 1894, but the firm of Holdich & Ingram was shortly afterwards taken over by Gray & Davison (*BIOSR* 4/4: 11).

19 The claim is found in Lewis 1897: 2–3. He seems to have been in business as a bell-founder, for he states elsewhere in the same work that he had been responsible for casting, amongst others, the set of eight bells for St Andrew's, Wells Street (27).

20 The earliest reference that the present writer has found to Lewis as an organ-builder is an advertisement dated February 1863 (*MSt*1, 1863: 184). Other sources claim that he was in business by 1861 (*NG* x: 708).

21 Unless otherwise indicated, the biographical details in this section are drawn from F. G. Edwards's article, 'Henry Willis', based on an interview with its subject (Edwards 1898) and W. L. Sumner's short study, *Father Henry Willis* (1955).

22 I am indebted to Mr John Sinclair Willis for this information. Henry Willis's father is usually described as a builder (cf. Sumner 1955: 11) but it seems that his trade is given as 'carpenter' in the register recording Henry Willis's marriage.

23 During his youth, he was organist of Christ Church, Hoxton; he was later appointed to Hampstead Parish Church (about the time he installed the new organ in 1852) and was then organist for almost thirty years of Islington Chapel of Ease, now St Mary Magdalene, Holloway Road, until the mid-1890s (*MT* xxxix, 1898: 297–8).

24 According to Sperling, he undertook minor work at St James, Cheltenham, and Winchcombe Parish Church in 1843 and 1844 respectively (MS 80: 116; 113). Even if these dates are correct, Willis may only have been acting as agent for Evans.

25 Sumner (1955: 20n) gives a list of Willis's business addresses extracted from the St Pancras rate books. They were: 2½ Foundling Terrace, Gray's Inn Road (1848–50); 18 Manchester Street (1851–9); 119 Albany Street (1859–65); Rotunda Works, Rochester Place (1866–1905).

26 Divided organs were not wholly unknown before this date. James Wyatt designed a

divided case for Green's reconstruction of the organ in New College, Oxford, in 1794, so as to expose the west window (Wickens 1987: 152–3). In 1844 the organ in St Mary Magdalen, Taunton, was divided on either side of the west window by James Ling (*MW* XIX, 1844: 311).

27 See, for example, *Eccl* IV, 1844–5: 6, where Notre Dame, Paris, is cited as an example of this arrangement.

28 Most of the dates given refer to the inauguration of the new (or rebuilt) organ; it is seldom easy to discover at what stage in a wholesale restoration perhaps lasting many years the screen was actually taken down. An exception is the date given for Chichester (1861) which is when the screen was demolished, precipitating the fall of the central tower; the organ seems to have been reinstated in 1867 (Plumley & Lees, 1988: 7–8). At St Paul's, Wren's screen was removed in 1859 (Matthews & Atkins, 1957: 264), the organ was resited on the north side of the choir during 1860 (MS 12: 387), and by the beginning of 1861 the former Panopticon organ was installed in the transept (Matthews & Atkins, 1957: 265).

29 It seems that Hill had left the organ in 1860 with the keyboards 'in the stalls' (HR2: 450). Probably the organ itself stood on a loft behind the stalls, but Hill carried the action down so that the organist might sit near the singers. If so, considerable alterations to the rear stalls would have been necessary.

30 He lists the open diapason, stopped diapason, principal and fifteenth as being the 'foundation stops' of the organ, and seems to think that these are the registers best adapted to the accompaniment of singers and congregation. He adds, however, that the dulciana, dulciana principal and flute may be found serviceable in particular situations (1858: 34–5).

31 On the abandonment of interludes, see: *MW* XXXII, 1854: 257; *CMR* II, 1864–5: 113. Also, Temperley 1979a: 311.

32 For example, at St Andrew's, Wells Street, where masses by Beethoven, Cherubini, Schubert, Haydn, Mozart and Hummel were frequently performed, and where Gounod attended services when staying in London (Temperley 1979a: 284).

33 Pearson's case for St James, Weybridge, which probably dates from the enlargements of 1864–70 (Quiney 1979: 282) seems to be an early and surprisingly mature example of the direct inspiration of a continental model, presumably, in this instance, the organ front of 1474–83 in S. Petronio, Bologna (though Freeman 1921b: 25 suggests that the outline of the case of *c.* 1380 in Salamanca Cathedral may have been an additional source). Pearson went on to design a number of excellent cases (Freeman 1921b: 69–70; Clutton & Niland 1982: 243–6). Bodley knew F. H. Sutton and was much influenced by him (Clutton & Niland 1982: 243; Gillingham 1987: 33). The case at Hoar Cross (*c.* 1876), once attributed to Bodley, is now known to be by Sutton, and the similarities between one of Bodley's earlier cases, for St John the Baptist, Tue Brook, Liverpool (*c.* 1870?), and Figure 9 in Sutton's *Church Organs* can scarcely be a coincidence. Bodley's work (most of which, as concerns organ cases, falls outside the period covered here) represents an admirable response to the ideals propagated and illustrated by Sutton, with whom quite clearly he was closely associated, and there seems no reason to dissent from Freeman's judgement that he was 'the most uniformly successful of all modern architects in this special branch of their craft' (1921b: 69). See also, Clutton & Niland 1982: 243–9; Adcock 1950.

34 It was Sir Henry Dryden, the antiquary, who drew Sutton's attention to the remains of an ancient organ case in the remote church of St Stephen, Old Radnor. Sutton described what he found in a monograph (*Some account of the mediaeval organ case still existing at Old Radnor*, 1866) and was then responsible for the restoration of 1872, including no doubt, its conjectural features and the design of the organ placed by Walker inside the restored case (Clutton & Niland 1982: 153–7).

35 The list consists of: Framlingham, Suffolk; King's College, Cambridge; Tewkesbury Abbey; St John's College, Cambridge (by then in Old Bilton, near Rugby); Stanford-on-Avon, Northamptonshire; Worcester Cathedral; Gloucester Cathedral; Little Bardfield, Essex; St Paul's Cathedral; Southwell Minster; Finedon, Northamptonshire; Norwich Cathedral (Sutton 1883: 28).

36 The cases at Great Bardfield (c. 1860) and Harlton (1869) have also been attributed to the influence of Sir John Sutton (Clutton & Niland 1982: 240, 238). In view of his conversion, and extended absences from England, it seems more likely that the 'Sutton' influence was mediated by Frederick Heathcote, his younger brother.

37 The case at Theddingworth (Sutton 1872: Figure 14) and that at Stockcross (clearly influenced by the fourteenth-century case at Sion, Switzerland) were evidently designed by Sutton, and according to Sir Ninian Comper he had a hand in many others, importantly through his informal association with Bodley & Garner (Gillingham 1987: 33).

38 The dating of the pipe decoration is elusive. It probably dates from the original installation of the instrument in 1854, but could conceivably be later: 1869, when the instrument was reconstructed by Harrison of Rochdale, or 1874, when Willis effected an extensive rebuilding.

39 It is informative to note that when Scott set aside the Strasburg model, as in the transept case for Worcester Cathedral (1874) the result was dull and lacking in confidence.

40 Evidence for this is offered by the contract drawings, dated 13 August 186., now in the possession of Mr Michael Gillingham. They show the case as it emerged from the reconstruction, but without the pipe shades or horizontal reed. The upper cresting is also different. A pencilled note implies that woodwork and 'embellishments' from the existing case were to be retained. Supporting evidence that the 1865 case was not part of the original Birmingham organ comes from the fact that the Music Hall was in the Gothic Revival style (*MW* xxxiv, 1856: 556); a Grecian case would hardly have been placed in an otherwise Gothic interior.

11   Music and mechanics

1 For a general study of Smart's organ compositions, the reader should refer to Hill 1988. The datings for individual pieces in the main text are drawn from this.

2 For example, Joseph Warren, in his *Instructions and observations on the art of performing on the organ* (3rd edn, c. 1855) comments on the distinction between pianoforte and organ that 'although the fingering of both instruments is in the main the same, yet the mode of performing on the organ differs so materially from the mode of performing on the piano, that the style of playing a piano will not do for the organ; nor that of the organ for the piano'.

3 Some of these are described in Hopkins (HR3: 32–4) and Audsley (1905: II: 229–42).

4 This seems to have been first applied at St George's Chapel, Windsor, in 1855. Henry Smart reported,

> The pallets of the pedal organ are of a novel construction, are very light and noiseless, present a large sectional area of opening with a small amount of motion, and, though not positively equilibrated, offer but slight resistance to the opposing air-pressure. They have the advantage, also, of opening two grooves of the sound-board at once . . .
>
> (*MW* xxxiii, 1855: 798)

5 Patent granted 10 December 1849 (*RAM* xvi, 1850: 29–31). The pallet could be made in two forms, both of which are illustrated in *RAM*. The wooden arm connecting the main portion of the pallet to the pallet wire was replaced with a metal bar in later versions (Audsley 1905, II: 232).

6 It was used by George Jardine of New York, and was introduced into the organs of Kirtland & Jardine of Manchester, probably during the 1850s (HR2: 34). Audsley describes it (1905, II: 230–1) but does not mention Jardine; his sole authorship must therefore be questioned.

7 Hopkins describes Hill's relief pallet as 'unsurpassable for simplicity in construction, and lightness and elasticity in touch' (HR2: 34). It is also illustrated and described by Audsley (1905, II: 231–2).

8 For example, Hill's 'Double-Beat' valve (Pole 1851: 64), Willis's brass pallet (*LJA* XL, 1851: 3), and Willis's 'Floating Valve' (*LJA* XVI [NS], 1862: 348–50).

9 It would, for instance, be curious (assuming the Attercliffe experiment to have been successful) if the Booths had not employed the puffs in the Brunswick Chapel organ of 1828. A rather colourful account in the *Leeds Mercury*, 18 April 1911, implies that he did, and *en passant* dates his use of pneumatics to an accidental discovery made in 1825.

10 On Barker, see: Hinton 1900: 89–90; 1909: 34–44. Barker was born in Bath. He was apprenticed to an apothecary, but being repelled by the drawing of teeth (an essential part of an apothecary's trade in those days) turned to organ-building. He was briefly in business in Bath (*c.* 1830). Following his collaboration with Cavaillé-Coll, he became manager to Dublaine & Callinet, and then to their successor, Ducroquet (above, p. 356). Although he exhibited an instrument on his own account at the Paris Exhibition of 1855, he remained with the Ducroquet business after it passed into the hands of Merklin. In 1860 he entered into a partnership with Verschneider. In 1870 he migrated to Dublin, where he built a few organs (disastrously). He was living in reduced circumstances by 1876, when a subscription was opened to furnish him with an annuity (*MT* XVII, 1876: 607). He died in 1879.

11 Hamilton studied organ-building in Germany 'where he resided for a number of years'. He first appears in the Edinburgh directories in 1822–3, as 'Hamilton, David and Company, piano-forte makers, 63 North bridge'. By 1824–5, he has become 'musical instrument maker', and, in 1825–6, 'piano forte and organ builder'. By 1838–9, the business had been renamed 'Hamilton & Müller, organ builders' (the German name of Hamilton's partner may be significant). It is said that David Hamilton was succeeded by his son, Thomas, in 1864 (information from Mr Colin Menzies). Hamilton is an unusual figure who deserves closer study. His *Remarks on organ building* (1851), as well as describing his background, include various claims to have introduced German and other continental features into British organ design which ought to be investigated.

12 An example of Barker's version of the reception of his invention in England is found in the remarks of C. M. Philibert in *L'Orgue du Palais de l'Industrie d'Amsterdam* (Amsterdam, 1876: pp. 34ff), cited in: Douglass 1980, I: 32. He tells how the English builders

utterly scorned the work of a bold novice who dared interfere with the arcana of their routines . . . This simplest of devices was condemned as very complicated; although sturdy, it was called fragile; and its responsiveness was pronounced sluggish. It was even claimed that the lightness of its key action would encourage organists to play too fast.

This is not the only instance of Barker failing to give due credit to his collaborators (Hinton 1909: 28–33).

13 It seems that Barker was not the most scrupulous of men, and Cavaillé-Coll wrote to him in 1842, complaining that he (Barker) licensed others to use the lever at a quarter of the price he charged him. He added that although he had had several opportunities to propose the application of Barker's lever, 'at such a high price I will avoid doing so whenever possible' (Douglass 1980, I: 197).

14 There is, for example, what is claimed to be a 'facsimile' of an original drawing by Barker of an improved version of the lever, dating from 1850: see, Hinton 1900: Plate IX.

15 A possible exception concerns the Birmingham Town Hall organ. According to an account of the instrument, apparently dating from before the reconstruction begun in 1842, the largest hammers of the Carillon (bells) were operated by pneumatic means (Hamel 1849: cxxv; cf. Thistlethwaite 1984: 18). If this is correct, it remains uncertain when the pneumatics were added (1837?), or whether conceivably they date from the original installation of 1834, i.e. when Barker tried to interest Hill in his invention.

16 Vincent Willis, Henry Willis's son, was responsible for the next significant modifications in the firm's design of pneumatic lever; these were the subject of a patent issued in 1884 (Audsley 1905, II: 252).

17 Amongst the church organs of this period which incorporated pneumatic assistance were: Winchester Cathedral, 1854 (Great, Swell, couplers); Wells Cathedral, 1857 (Great); St Paul's Cathedral, 1862 (Great, couplers); St John, Taunton, 1862 (Great); St Stephen, Hampstead, 1871 (Great). It is likely that in those instances where the Great alone appears, from contemporary accounts, to have received the application of the lever, the associated couplers were also assisted.

18 According to Meyrick-Roberts, a French organ-builder, Moitessier of Montpellier, patented a system of pneumatic transmission in 1835, later exhibiting in Toulouse an organ of two manuals and fourteen stops built on this principle (1850); at about the same time he applied a tubular-pneumatic action to a 42-stop organ at La Dalbade, Toulouse (1922: 77).

19 Barker promptly regretted granting Bryceson the sole concession, because he realised that it would delay a widespread adoption of his system, and thus deprive him of profits. Bryceson was persuaded to relinquish the sole concession, but retained the right to make full use of the patent (Bryceson 1869: 17). In fact, few English builders sought to use Barker's patent.

20 This organ was first used on 25 May 1868. It consisted of a Swell Organ and single Pedal stop, there being insufficient time to complete the second manual division (Hinton 1909: 53, 59–60). It was later removed to the Polytechnic Institution, Regent Street.

21 For descriptions and discussions of these early actions, see: Bryceson 1869: *passim*; HR2: 69–87; Audsley 1905, II: 705–19; Hinton 1909: *passim*.

22 Steam power was retained when the Panopticon organ was moved to St Paul's Cathedral (HR2: 449).

23 Curiously, the high-pressure bellows was still operated manually, and placed inside the organ, near the appropriate chest (Elvin 1971: 34).

24 Elvin claims that Willis applied one of his hydraulic engines to the organ in Carlisle Cathedral (1971: 47). I can, though, find no evidence for this.

25 For example: St Paul, Wilton Place (1842) had an exceptional provision, with four pedals to the Great and two each to Swell and Pedal; Chester Cathedral (1844) had four to the Great and two to the Pedal.

26 At Carlisle, Willis provided six thumb pistons to Great and Pedal, and six to the Swell. At Wells, there were six to the Great (and Pedal?) and four to the Swell. An account of the Winchester organ, apparently coming from Willis himself (above, p. 419) states that Great and Choir each had six pistons (but the Swell had none), with, in addition, three composition pedals to the Pedal, 'two of which act upon the Great Organ combination movement, producing by one effort, a Piano or Forte upon both Organs' (Matthews 1975: 13).

27 A diagram of the console (*Supplement to the Musical Standard*, 25 April 1896) shows that the general pistons were duplicated, i.e. there were six to the right and six to the left, and that each united the action of the pistons in the other four divisions bearing the same number as itself. So, in pressing general piston 1, the Great (and Pedal), Swell, Choir and Solo pistons numbered 1 were brought into play. It is not clear if the intention of controlling the

couplers by pedals was carried out. The diagram of 1896 (which, of course, shows the console after the alterations of 1867) has six pedals duplicating the action of the six general pistons, and reversible pedals for the Great to Pedal and Solo to Great couplers, but the other couplers appear to be served solely by drawstops. I am most grateful to Mr Douglas Carrington for drawing my attention to this diagram.

28 E.g. Boston, Centenary Chapel, 1850; St Sepulchre, Holborn, *c.* 1850; Christ Church, Spitalfields, 1852; Crystal Palace, 1857; Newcastle Town Hall, 1859.

29 The specimen in Stockport Sunday School (1853) achieved its effect by bringing all three Swell to Great couplers (unison, octave and sub-octave) into action at once (HR2: 511).

30 See, for example: *MG* II, 1857: 76–7, 89, 114–15; *MSt* I, 1862–3: 337–8; II, 1863–4: 138–40, 220–3.

31 The copy of Perronet Thompson's *The theory and practice of just intonation* (1850) in the Organ Club Library (RCO) has a note inside the cover to this effect.

32 1848 is a more likely date, if indeed the Birmingham organ was tuned equal at any early stage.

33 Though there were doubtless many exceptions, including Willis's instrument for Broom-hall Chapel, Sheffield, 1864 (*MSt* II, 1863–4: 316) and Jardine's for St Thomas, Bury, 1868 (*MW* XLVI, 1868: 249).

12   German influences, 1855–70

1 Brief details are also included of: Seville Cathedral; Görlitz, SS Peter & Paul; Merseburg Cathedral; Amsterdam, Nieuwe Kerk and Oude Kerk; Lisle, S. Pierre; Tours Cathedral; Alost, St Martin; Groningen, Maartenskerk; Berlin, Garnisonkirche and Cathedral; Ulm Cathedral; Vienna, Michaeliskirche; Rome, St John Lateran; Strasburg Cathedral; Rotterdam, St Laurens; Baltimore Cathedral (Warren 1842: 116–19).

2 The bibliography seems to have been added by Joseph Warren, who was responsible for the second edition (1842) of *Hamilton's catechism*. In a footnote (10), he refers his readers to three works from which presumably he drew his material: Forkel's *Allgemeine Literatur der Musik* (Leipzig, 1792), Lichtenthal's *Dizionario e Bibliografia della Musica* (Milan, 1826), and *Systematisch-Chronologische Darstellung der Musikalischen Literatur* (Leipzig, 1836).

3 It may be an accurate reflection of the reception that Seidel's work received that it went into a second edition on the eve of the publication of Hopkins & Rimbault (1855).

4 This is recorded in Hopkins's journal in a continuation of the extract about the Bremen visit quoted above. It survives in some notes made by the Revd J. H. Burn from the journal before the latter disappeared. (These notes are in the collection of the Revd B. B. Edmonds, to whom I am grateful for permission to cite them.) The destination of these six registers is not apparent, though some other references imply that it might be Manchester (Jardine? Joule?).

5 See: *Doncaster Chronicle*, 27 September 1895. This is an account of the organ, and of its reconstruction in 1895 by Abbott & Smith, for which Hopkins was consultant.

6 Edward Francis Rimbault (1816–76) was son of Stephen Francis Rimbault (1773–1837), organist of St Giles-in-the-Fields and a member of Samuel Wesley's circle. E. F. Rimbault had lessons with Wesley and, during the course of his life, occupied various London organistships. He was the foremost English musical antiquarian of the mid-Victorian years, active in the formation of the Musical Antiquarian Society and the Percy Society, editor of musical publications for the Motett Society and of several volumes for the Handel Society. He was offered the Professorship of Music at Harvard, but declined it. His vast music library was auctioned off after his death. According to *NG* (XVI: 25–6) his importance was an educational one: 'his work first gave the ordinary musician some awareness of the riches of England's musical past' (26).

7 Töpfer believed that there should be a uniform scaling for each flue chorus, with the area of a cross-section of a diapason pipe being in the proportion of $\sqrt{8}:1$ to the pipe an octave above. This yielded a convenient scaling pattern (convenient, later, for factory organ-building) with the scale halving regularly at the seventeenth pipe. Different scales were, of course, to be adopted for different types of register, but the principle remained the same: a uniform scaling throughout the rank, halving regularly.

8 Through the influence of a local musician, Charles McKorkell, the Exhibition organ was purchased for the Northampton Corn Exchange and erected there at the end of 1851. It was moved to the new Town Hall in 1868, and a large Swell Organ, supplied with pipework by Cavaillé-Coll, was added in the following year. It was dismantled in 1890 to make way for some structural alterations to the building and was never re-erected. Some mystery surrounds the disposal of the surviving parts, but it seems that whatever remained was acquired by Conacher in 1905 and used up in various other instruments (Shaw 1933: *passim*; I am most grateful to Mr Bryan Hughes for drawing my attention to this article).

9 'Schulze was perhaps the first to point out the need of, or at any rate fully to provide for, large volumes of wind [for] soundboards of great capacity rather than for heavy pressures; for a gale of moderate velocity but large in quantity. By thus providing abundant wind for liberally scaled pipes, Schulze got a free, full, and round bell-like tone which carried further than that of smaller scaled pipes under higher wind pressure' (Allbutt 1925: 83).

10 J. H. Burn recorded the following extract from Hopkins's journal, relating to his visit to Schulze's workshop at Paulinzelle on 28 July 1858. 'Schulze has a seasoning room. The wood for the pallets, after being well-seasoned, is split with a hatchet to prove the straightness of the grain, & only such wood is used as exhibits the right grain. The pallets are then cut out, and boiled in water for 3 hours, to subject them to the extremes of heat and humidity combined, and then placed in a hot air stove for a week to subject them to extremes of heat and dryness combined. It is only after the wood has successfully passed through this test that it is allowed to be worked up into pallets. The oak for the sides, and the oak for the upper boards, is likewise kept in the same hot dry room for 6 or 8 weeks. The deals for the soundboard bars are also kept for about the same time in the same place' (MS 32). Schulze declined to use 'raw' wood anywhere in his organs, and soon found a timber merchant in England (in West Hartlepool, for some reason) where ten-year-old oak could be obtained (Allbutt 1925: 85).

11 See: *Eccl* xxv, 1864: 358. Forster & Andrews told J. H. Burn in 1908 that all the metal pipework for Doncaster, with the exception of the 32′ reed, was made to Schulze's specifications by Violette, a London pipe-maker. The zinc pipes were made by Kitsell. The wood pipes, however, came directly from Paulinzelle. The reason for having the metal pipework made in England was apparently the relative cheapness of tin here at the time (MS 34).

12 See: *Eccl* xxv, 1864: 22. The contract for the Doncaster organ was placed in 1857. Work seems to have begun in 1859 at Paulinzelle, and then transferred to Doncaster, where Schulze required eighteen months to erect and finish the instrument (Spark 1892: 183–4).

13 Schulze's major projects in England can be summarised as follows.

> 1851 Great Exhibition (removed the same year to the Corn Exchange, Northampton)
> 1859 Temple Church, London (additions)
> 1862 Leeds Parish Church (additions and revoicing)
> 1862 St Mary, Tyne Dock (temporary organ, removed in 1864 to St Thomas, Sunderland)
> 1862 Doncaster Parish Church
> 1863 Christ Church, Doncaster
> 1864 St Mary, Tyne Dock (removed to Ellesmere College, *c.* 1980)
> 1869 Meanwood Towers, near Leeds (re-erected in St Bartholomew, Armley, in 1879)
> 1873 St Peter, Hindley

1878 Charterhouse School Chapel
1879 St Peter, Harrogate

Abbott & Smith's 1896 brochure has a list of Schulze organs, which includes two undated commissions in addition to those mentioned above: 'Staincliffe', Seaton Carew (house organ?); Wesleyan Chapel, Ashbrolee, Sunderland (is this connected with the first Tyne Dock instrument?). Further details of most of these instruments can be found in the files of the *Organ* and *Musical Opinion*. There is an excellent booklet on the Armley organ by Dr K. I. Johnstone (1978).

14 The doubt arises from what may very well be a misprint in the account of these mixtures in the *Musical Gazette* (I, 1856: 274). There, the composition is given as:

	Full Mixture	Sharp Mixture
C	15.19.22	22.26.29
c^1	8.12.15	15.19.22
c^2	1. 8.15	12.15.19
f^2	1. 8.15	12.15.19
c^3	1. 8.15	8.12.15

There is no break in either mixture at f^2, which must be a mistake. It seems therefore likely that the second break of the Sharp Mixture, at c^2, should actually be 12.19.22, as suggested in Hopkins (HRI: 255).

15 It is said that Schulze was inspired to use a higher pressure for the reeds in an organ for Cologne by hearing the effect of Willis's reeds.

13   Hill & Son, 1856–70

1 It would be interesting to know if Hill's collaboration with Schulze over the reconstruction of the Leeds Parish Church organ in 1862 is of any significance here. Unfortunately, it is not clear whether they worked in association or independently (Burn 1934: 19).

2 This does not appear in the *Musical World* specification; it is present, though, in the scheme as recorded in the Hill Letter Book (MS 12: 402).

3 The principal changes were as follows (displaced 1862 register given in brackets). Great: Clarabella (Quint). Swell: Voix Celeste (Twelfth). Choir: Geigen Principal (Cone Gamba); Lieblich Gedact (Keraulophon); Octave Gamba (Octave); String Gamba (Gemshorn Twelfth). Solo: Piccolo made harmonic, and Harmonic Flute 8′ and Orchestral Oboe 8′ added. Pedal: Bass Flute (Twelfth); Contra Fagotto (Fifteenth). Details from: MS 15: 24.

4 Whilst welcoming the resuscitation of this grand instrument, and acknowledging that most (not all) of the 1862 material was retained, it is a matter for regret that a more conservative approach was not adopted in developing the programme for the 1978 work. The Choir, Solo and Pedal Organs have been transformed in such a way as to destroy the relationship between different departments intended by the original builder.

5 Some confusion arises from the conflicting designations of this church. St John, Paddington, was used at the time Hill built his organ. Later, it was known as St John, Southwick Crescent, and today, more usually, as St John, Hyde Park Crescent.

6 At some date (possibly 1925) the Swell vox humana gave way to a voix celeste, the salicional being then renamed 'Echo Gamba'. The 1865 gemshorn on the Choir also disappeared at some stage: the slide is now occupied by a singularly pointless Corno Flute 8′.

7 There were other possibilities. The Ulster Hall had a gedact 16′ on the Choir, and a lieblich gedact 8′ on the Solo; Edinburgh University had a 'Gedact Flute' of 4′ pitch on the Swell.

8 The Glockenspiel consisted of a twelfth and tierce, to be used with the stopped diapason. Its compass began at tenor c (MS 84: f.2).

9 This was of full compass, apparently with a composition of 1.8.12.15.17 throughout the range (MS 13: 17).

10 The present stop breaks back to 12.15 at c¹ but it seems not to be original.

11 The typical Hill violone is a wooden register, but it should be recorded that metal ones were made for Edinburgh University and Sydney Cathedral.

12 At York, the Great Harmonic Flute and Cornet were also on the high-pressure soundboard.

14   Henry Willis

1 The most notorious case was his failure to heed Ouseley's instructions to retain thirteen stops from the organ by Samuel Green and others in Wells Cathedral when commissioned to rebuild the instrument (Colchester 1979: 8–9). It is notable that very few of Willis's major organs retained more than a handful of pipes from an earlier instrument. In view of his idiosyncratic approach to voicing and scaling, Willis no doubt felt unduly compromised by the need to use older material.

2 Willis's proposal is transcribed in: Sumner 1955: 44.

3 This letter is quoted by B. B. Edmonds in 'A sack of shakings', *Organ* XXXVII, 1957–8: 141. I am grateful to him for permission to quote it.

4 These were preferences rather than absolute rules of practice. Willis sometimes used open shallots (Bonavia-Hunt 1920: 76) and made harmonic reeds when seeking a special effect or catering for a large building; some of the chorus reeds on the Great at the Albert Hall were harmonic or had harmonic trebles.

5 I am most grateful to Miss Betty Matthews for permission to cite this document which was first transcribed in her *Organs and organists of Winchester Cathedral*.

6 By Willis in 1897; Hele, 1905; Harrison & Harrison, 1937; Harrison & Harrison, 1988 (Matthews 1975: *passim*).

7 A copy is gummed inside the cover of the St George's Churchwardens' Accounts, vol. 3, in the Lancashire County Record Office in Preston.

8 On Allon see: Curwen 1880: 173–8; *DNB*, Supplement, I: 41–2.

9 As given in: Benham 1931: 234.

10 In 1909, Messrs Walker replaced the Choir gemshorn with a piccolo. Monk & Gunther undertook work in the 1940s. The most significant change was the enclosure of the Choir Organ. At the same time, a Choir tremulant was added; it, and the existing Swell tremulant, which had originally been controlled by a pedal, were provided with drawstops. Balanced swell pedals were introduced, and the stop jambs were reinforced by the addition of new panels on top of the old ones (this has not improved the appearance of the console).

11 For example, All Saints, Stonebridge Common (1857), or Foxearth, Essex (1862?). The former organ (*MG* II, 1857: 222) had a stopped diapason drawing in halves on the Great and a 5-stop short-compass Swell, completed by a Choir bass. Only the appearance of a harmonic flute on the Great, and the (consequent?) absence of a twelfth identifies it as a product of the 1850s rather than the previous decade.

12 The Great bombarde 8' at St Stephen, Hampstead, had two octaves of harmonic resonators: probably a response to the low-roofed chamber in which the organ stood, and the lack of an accompanying 4' reed.

13 The Exhibition organ went first to the Agricultural Hall, Islington, where it was opened by Wesley at the end of 1863. When it later became available for disposal, it was decided to

use it as the basis for the first Alexandra Palace organ (Sumner 1955: 33n). This instrument was totally destroyed by fire within a few days of its opening in 1873.

14 Willis made modifications to the Liverpool organ in 1867. The work was extensive, Willis no doubt welcoming an opportunity to remove some of the archaisms in the original scheme. Each manual division gained a lieblich gedact; the Great acquired a flute à pavillon, violoncello, octave viola and flauto traverso, accommodated by eliminating some of the duplication and two of the mixtures. The Choir gained a voix celeste, as did the Swell (also a gemshorn and a vox humana). Four reeds, on a pressure of 15″ to 20″ were added to the Solo. See: *MSt* vii, 1867: 257; HR2: 502–3.

15 As he had done at St George's Hall, in accordance with the contract (above, p. 146).

16 They are recorded by Freeman (1922a: 10) who unfortunately does not name his source. He implies that they were fixed when a gas engine was installed to blow the organ in 1880. This is not recognised as a year when other alterations were made to the instrument, but it is not impossible that Willis took the opportunity to make some modifications (e.g. to the pressures applied to the Solo and Pedal reeds). On the other hand, Freeman also records the wind pressures following the reconstruction of 1897–1900 (13) and these are significantly higher than those attributed to 1880, which must therefore certainly predate them.

17 George Willis was born in 1826. He worked with J. C. Bishop between 1844 and 1850, when he left to join his brother. According to Audsley (1921: 132) he also trained with John Courcelle, a celebrated reed-voicer. He was described by Bonavia-Hunt as the 'great pioneer of the modern scientific school of reed-voicing' (1920: 76) and by Henry Wedlake as 'the greatest artist in reed voicing in this or any other country' (*Organist & Choirmaster*, 1903: 227). He introduced the practice of weighting the tongues of the reed basses, though the precise date of this innovation is unknown.

18 Willis built an organ for the old town hall at Reading in 1864 (Appendix 1, pp. 505–6). He completed and enlarged this instrument in 1882, when it was moved into the new Large Hall. The 1864 pipework was little altered and is valid evidence for Willis's work during the early-1860s. I have discussed this instrument elsewhere (Marr 1982: 25–37). The scales accompanying this earlier article were taken using a different method from that adopted in the present volume and in order to be consistent were taken again for inclusion in Table 33 above.

List of references

1 Manuscript sources

These are arranged alphabetically by location. The number refers to citations in the text (e.g. MS 34). Shelf marks are given whenever possible.

BIRMINGHAM: *CENTRAL LIBRARY, BRITISH ORGAN ARCHIVE*

 1 Gray & Davison archive: Accounts, vol. 1 (1821–38)
 2 Gray & Davison archive: Accounts, vol. 5 (1849–57)
 3 Gray & Davison archive: Shop Books, vol. 1 (1840–2)
 4 Gray & Davison archive: Shop Books, vol. 2 (1843–6)
 5 Gray & Davison archive: Shop Books, vol. 3 (1847–51)
 6 Gray & Davison archive: Shop Books, vol. 4 (1851–4)
 7 Gray & Davison archive: Shop Books, vol. 5 (1854–7)
 8 Gray & Davison archive: Shop Books, vol. 6 (1857–60)
 9 Gray & Davison archive: Shop Books, vol. 7 (1861–5)
10 Gray & Davison archive: Shop Books, vol. 8 (1865–8)
11 Hill, Norman & Beard archive: Elliot & Hill Partnership Account (1827–32)
12 Hill, Norman & Beard archive: William Hill's Letter Book (1838–61)
13 Hill, Norman & Beard archive: Hill & Son, Estimate Books, vol. 2 (1861–77)
14 Hill, Norman & Beard archive: Hill & Son, Shop Books, vol. 2 (1875–83)
15 Hill, Norman & Beard archive: Hill & Son, Shop Books, vol. 5 (1901–15)

BIRMINGHAM: *CENTRAL LIBRARY, LOCAL STUDIES DEPARTMENT*

16 Papers relating to the Triennial Musical Festivals, Part One (6): J. F. Schwenke to Chevalier Neukomm, August 1832

BRANDON: *J. W. WALKER & SONS, LTD, BUSINESS ARCHIVES*

17 Shop Books, vol. 1 (1840–61)
18 Ledger, vol. A (1836–52)
19 Order and Memorandum Book (1837–1840)
20 Shop Books, vol. 2 (1861–5)

BRISTOL: *BRISTOL RECORD OFFICE*

21 St James, Bristol: Vestry Minutes (1802–24) [P/stJ/v/6]
22 St James, Bristol: letter of John Smith to churchwardens and vestry, 10 June 1820 [P/stJ/v/20/47]
23 St James, Bristol: letter of Edward Hodges to vestry, 5 December 1821 [P/stJ/v/20/48]
24 St Nicholas, Bristol: Vestry Minutes (1777–1829) [P/stN/v/1]

CAMBRIDGE: *ST JOHN'S COLLEGE, ARCHIVES*

25 Covenant between William Hill and the Master, Fellows and Scholars for building a new organ, dated 29 September 1838
26 Agreement between W. Hill & Son and the Master, Fellows and Scholars for the reconstruction of the Chapel organ, dated 10 December 1867

CAMBRIDGE: *TRINITY COLLEGE, ARCHIVES*

27 John Gray's estimate for the reconstruction of the Chapel organ, dated 25 May 1835

CAMBRIDGE: *UNIVERSITY LIBRARY, ARCHIVES OF THE DEAN AND CHAPTER OF ELY*

28 Letter concerning the reconstruction of the cathedral organ from James Ambrose, dated 18 November 1808 [4/5/20]

CAMBRIDGE: *UNIVERSITY LIBRARY, UNIVERSITY ARCHIVES*

29 Audit Book, vol. IV (1787–1822)

CHELMSFORD: *ESSEX COUNTY RECORD OFFICE*

30 Thaxted, St John the Baptist: faculty application and grant for rearrangement of pews and re-paving, dated September 1879 [D/CF 18/7]
31 Thaxted, St John the Baptist: volume of churchwardens' accounts and vestry minutes (1840–93) [D/F 16/5/10]

CLARE, SUFFOLK: *COLLECTION OF THE REVD B. B. EDMONDS*

32 Extracts from E. J. Hopkins's Journal, compiled by J. H. Burn, c. 1900
33 Undated letter (c. 1900) from John Rogers to J. H. Burn
34 Letter from Forster & Andrews to J. H. Burn, dated 2 November 1908
35 Undated letter (1930s) from E. H. Suggate to B. B. Edmonds concerning Schulze's Great Exhibition organ

EXETER: *EXETER CATHEDRAL LIBRARY, ARCHIVES OF THE DEAN AND CHAPTER*

36 Estimate for the reconstruction of the York Minster [*sic*] organ by Benjamin Blyth, 1802 [7062/1818]
37 Estimate for repair of the Exeter Cathedral organ from G. P. England, 1814 [7062/1815]

HEREFORD: *HEREFORD CATHEDRAL LIBRARY*

38   Chapter Acts, 1796–1814

39   Chapter Acts, 1814–1834

40   S. S. Wesley: autograph score of *The Wilderness*, dated 1834, in organ book. [C.9.xii: 52–73]

LEEDS: *CITY LIBRARIES, ARCHIVE DEPARTMENT, LEEDS CORPORATION ARCHIVE*

41   Contract and drawings for Leeds Town Hall organ, dated 13 September 1857 [Town Clerk's Dept, Committee Clerk's Records, Shelf 91]

42   Sub Town Hall (Organ) Committee Minutes (1856–69) [Town Clerk's Dept, Committee Clerk's Records, Shelf 91]

LINCOLN: *COLLECTION OF LAURENCE ELVIN, ESQ.*

43   Forster & Andrews business archive: Ledger, 1844–57

LINCOLN: *LINCOLNSHIRE RECORD OFFICE, RECORDS OF THE DEAN AND CHAPTER OF LINCOLN*

44   Volume labelled 'Bells: Clock: Organ' [A/4/14]

LIVERPOOL: *LIVERPOOL RECORD OFFICE, LIVERPOOL CORPORATION ARCHIVES*

45   Law Courts Committee Minutes. Vol. 3 (2), May 1840 to July 1849

46   Law Courts Committee Minutes. Vol. 3 (3), July 1849 to January 1856

LONDON: *BISHOP & SON, BUSINESS ARCHIVES*

47   Miscellaneous papers: estimate for 'Collonell Chichester', dated 7 November 1820 [I:D.18]

48   Miscellaneous papers: estimate for St Mary Abchurch, *c.* 1822 [I:H.40]

49   Miscellaneous papers: estimate for St George's, Camberwell, 1824 (?) [I:D.16)

50   Miscellaneous papers: memorandum of agreement for new organ at St Mary's, Leicester, *c.* 1824 [I:G.34]

51   Miscellaneous papers: estimate for the new church [St John's] in Waterloo Road [1824] [I:H.42]

52   Miscellaneous papers: estimate for organ for 'the New Church Wyndham place' [St Mary, Bryanston Square], 1824 [II:J.16]

53   Miscellaneous papers: submission to Marylebone Vestry for the building of new organs for All Souls [Langham Place] and Christchurch [Cosway Street], [1824] [II:H(A).15]

54   Miscellaneous papers: estimate for organ, St Peter, Pimlico, 1837 [I:H.41]

55   Miscellaneous papers: specification of organ, St James, Bermondsey [1829] [mislaid?]

56   Miscellaneous papers: estimate for new organ, Crosby Hall, 1834 [I:G.35]

57   Miscellaneous papers: estimate for alterations to Norwich Cathedral organ, *c.* 1834 [II:L.19]

58   Miscellaneous papers: estimate for reconstruction of Newark Parish Church organ, 20 August 1835 [I:J.44]

59   Miscellaneous papers: estimate for Kenilworth Church, 15 November 1839 [I:F.31]

60 Miscellaneous papers: estimate for Millichope Hall (Revd Mr Pemberton), July 1840. [Organ now at Kinlet.] [1:J.47]
61 Estimate Book, vol. I (1840–3)
62 Estimate Book, vol. III (1845–51)
63 Ledger, vol. I (1846–54)

LONDON: *BRITISH LIBRARY, DEPARTMENT OF MANUSCRIPTS*

64 Letter of Samuel Wesley to Vincent Novello, 18 July 1815 [Add 11, 729]
65 Letter of J. W. Fraser to Vincent Novello, 31 December 1830 [Add 11, 730]
66 Samuel Wesley's *Reminiscences* [Add 27, 593]
67 Samuel Wesley's *Lectures* [Add 35,015]
68 Letters of Elizabeth Mounsey to F. G. Edwards, 20 and 21 February 1892 [ff.10–11] and 3 December 1894 [f.85] [Add 41,572]

LONDON: *GREATER LONDON RECORD OFFICE, 40 NORTHAMPTON ROAD*

69 Minutes of the Committee of St Peter's Church, Saffron Hill [P82/PET/16]

LONDON: *GUILDHALL LIBRARY, ARCHIVES DEPARTMENT*

70 St Katherine Coleman, Vestry Minutes, vol. 2 (1802–43) [MS 1123]
71 St Mary-at-Hill, Eastcheap, Vestry Minutes, vol. 4 (1843–80) [MS 1240]
72 St Peter-upon-Cornhill, Vestry Minutes, vol. 5 (1831–41) [MS 4165]
73 St Sepulchre Holborn, Vestry Minutes, vol. 8 (1831–50) [MS 3149]
74 St Sepulchre Holborn, Churchwardens Accounts, vol. 10 (1849–50) [MS 3146]

LONDON: *HOLBORN BOROUGH LIBRARY, REFERENCE DIVISION*

75 St Andrew Holborn, rate books. Church rate (second division), Theobalds Road

LONDON: *N. P. MANDER LTD, ST PETER'S ORGAN WORKS*

76 Transcript (*c.* 1900?) of (now destroyed) 'G. P. England' notebook

LONDON: *MARYLEBONE LIBRARY, ARCHIVES DEPARTMENT*

77 St Marylebone Parish Church, Proceedings for building a new church, vol. IV (1817–20)

LONDON: *ROYAL COLLEGE OF MUSIC, LIBRARY*

78 *Organographia* [RCM MS 1161]

LONDON: *ROYAL COLLEGE OF ORGANISTS, LIBRARY*

79 Sperling Notebooks, vol. 1
80 Sperling Notebooks, vol. 2
81 Sperling Notebooks, vol. 3

LONDON: *ROYAL COLLEGE OF ORGANISTS, ORGAN CLUB LIBRARY*

82   S. W. Harvey papers

NORWICH: *NORFOLK COUNTY RECORD OFFICE*

83   Letters of Dr A. H. Mann, vol. II [MS 4224]

OXFORD: *NEW COLLEGE, ARCHIVES*

84   Account of York Minster organ (*c.* 1860) by C. Mayo

PRESTON: *LANCASHIRE COUNTY RECORD OFFICE*

85   St George's, Preston, churchwardens' accounts, vol. 3 [PR 2317/3]

RAMSEY, ISLE OF MAN: *COLLECTION OF CECIL CLUTTON, ESQ.*

86   Scrap-book, possibly compiled by Thomas Bennett (1799–1848) containing manuscript
     and printed material relating to organs

SALISBURY: *CATHEDRAL LIBRARY, ARCHIVES OF THE DEAN AND CHAPTER*

87   Chapter Lease Book (1863–77). Includes transcript of Henry Willis's contract for the
     building of a new organ, dated 6 October 1876 (pp. 304–7)

SOUTHREPPS, NORFOLK: *PRIVATE COLLECTION*

88   'An Account of Organs & Organ Builders – collected by Henry Leffler. 1800.'

YORK: *MINSTER LIBRARY, ARCHIVES OF THE DEAN AND CHAPTER*

89   Contract between Hill & Son and the Dean and Chapter for the reconstruction of the
     Minster organ, 1859

2   Other sources

Unless otherwise indicated the edition cited is always the first; when reference is made in the
text to subsequent editions details of these are given, though the place of publication is not
repeated if it is the same as for the first edition.

Abbott & Smith. 1896. *Abbott & Smith, Organ Builders, Leeds*. Trade brochure. Leeds.
Adcock, E. 1950. 'Bodley organ cases', *Organ*, XXIX, 103–11.
Alden, J. H. 1944. 'Organs of St Peter's College, Radley, Berks.', *Organ*, XXIII, 97–106.
Allbutt, C. 1925. 'Edmund Schulze and the Armley Organ', *Organ*, V, 78–86.
Allerston & Pickwell (publishers). 1844. *An historical and descriptive account of the York Cathedral
     organ. Together with an analytical and comparative view of the Birmingham and Haarlem organs*. York.
Aris's Birmingham Gazette. 1824–88. Birmingham.
The Athenaeum. 1828–1921. London.
Audsley, G. A. 1905 (repr. 1965). *The art of organ-building*. 2 vols. New York.
     1921. *Organ stops and their artistic registration*. New York.

Baines, A. 1976 (repr. 1978). *Brass instruments, their history and development*. London.

Banfield, S. 1981. 'Aesthetics and criticism' in N. Temperley (ed.), *The romantic age, 1800–1914* (*Athlone History of Music in Britain*, vol. 5), 455–73. London.

Barnard, L. S. 1954. 'Two Sussex organs', *Organ*, xxxiv, 12–18.

Baron, J. 1858. (2nd edn 1862). *Scudamore organs, or practical hints respecting organs for village churches and small chancels, on improved principles*. London.

Bateman, J. 1860. *The life of the Right Rev. Daniel Wilson, D.D., late Lord Bishop of Calcutta and Metropolitan of India*. London.

Belcher, J. 1970. *The organs of Chester Cathedral*. Chester.

Benham, G. 1931. 'Interesting London organs: xxv Union Chapel, Islington; xxvi King's College, Strand', *Organ*, x, 233–6.

Berrow, J. B. J. 1983. 'Some aspects of mid-nineteenth century organ-case design', *BIOSJ*, vii, 90–107.

Bertalot, J. 1970. *The organs of Blackburn Cathedral*. Blackburn.

Bicknell, S. 1981. 'English organ-building 1642–85', *BIOSJ*, v, 5–22.

BIOS Journal. 1977–. *Annual journal of the British Institute of Organ Studies*.

BIOS Reporter. 1976–. *Quarterly newsletter of the British Institute of Organ Studies*.

Bishop, J. 1968. *Henry John Gauntlett: an estimate of his work with particular reference to organ design*. Unpublished D.Mus. preparatory thesis, University of Edinburgh.

    1971. *A frustrated revolutionary: H. J. Gauntlett and the Victorian organ*. Lecture delivered at the RCO.

Blake, S. T. 1979. *Cheltenham's churches and chapels, A.D. 773 to 1883*. Cheltenham.

Blewitt, J. [*c.* 1790]. *A complete treatise on the organ to which is added a set of explanatory voluntaries*. London.

Boeringer, J. 1977. 'The organs of the Lincolns', *BIOSJ*, i, 11–17.

Bonavia-Hunt, N. 1920. *The church organ: an introduction to the study of modern organ-building*. London.

Booth, P. F. 1911. 'Organ-building romance', *Leeds Mercury*, 18 April.

Briggs, A. 1959. *The Age of Improvement*. London.

Bristol Mirror. 1819–64.

Brown, J. D. and Stratton, S. S. 1897. *British musical biography*. Birmingham.

Bryceson, H. 1869. 'The electric organ', *MSt* x, 16–21.

Buckingham, A. 1972–5. 'Buckingham's travels' (Buckingham's journal, ed. L. S. Barnard), *Organ*, lii (1972–3): 6–14, 50–7, 99–106, 175–83; liii (1973–4), 30–7, 17–24 [*sic*], 78–85, 119–26; liv (1974–5), 41–8.

Burn, J. H. 1930. 'Edmund Schulze's Exhibition organ', *Organ*, x, 100–3.

    1934. 'Edmund Schulze's English organs', *Rotunda*, v, 18–23.

Burney, C. 1775. *The present state of music in Germany, the Netherlands, and United Provinces*. 2 vols. London.

Byard, H. 1967. 'Two old organs: Ramsbury and Lambourn', *Organ*, xlvi, 173–80.

Cardwell, J. H., Freeman, H. B., and Wilton, G. C. 1898. *Two centuries of Soho, its institutions, firms, and amusements*. London.

Carse, A. 1951. *The life of Jullien*. Cambridge.

Cavaillé-Coll, C. and E. 1929. *Aristide Cavaillé-Coll, ses origines, sa vie, ses oeuvres*. Paris.

Chadwick, W. O. 1966 & 1970. *The Victorian Church*. 2 vols. London. 2nd edn, Part i, 1970.

The Christian Remembrancer. 1819–68. London.

Clarke, B. F. L. 1938 (2nd edn 1969). *Church builders of the nineteenth century*. London.

    Parish churches of London. 1966. London.

Clayton, A. and Renshaw, M. 1968. 'Anatomy of an organ – Great George Street Chapel, Liverpool', *Organ*, xlvii, 97–106. (*See also*: Renshaw, M.)

The Clergy List. 1841–1917. London.

Clutton, C. 1931. 'The organ at Chichester Cathedral', *Organ*, XI, 71–8.
    1948. 'The organ in St Michael's College, Tenbury', *Organ*, XXVII, 108–14.
    1984. 'W. T. Best as consultant', *BIOSJ*, VIII, 26–35.
Clutton, C. and Niland, A. 1963 (2nd edn 1982). *The British Organ*. London.
Cobb, G. 1980. *English cathedrals, the forgotten centuries*. London.
Cobb, G. F. 1895. *A brief history of the organ in the chapel of Trinity College, Cambridge*. Cambridge. 2nd edn (ed. A. Gray) 1913.
Cocheril, M. 1982. 'The Dallams in Brittany', *BIOSJ*, VI, 63–77.
Colchester, L. 1951 (7th edn 1979). *The organs and organists of Wells Cathedral*. Wells.
Colvin, H. 1954 (2nd edn 1978). *A biographical dictionary of British architects, 1600–1840*. London.
Crosse, J. 1825. *An account of the grand musical festival held in September 1823 in the cathedral church of York*. York.
Crotch, W. 1812. *The elements of musical composition*. London.
    1831. *Substance of several courses of lectures on music*. London.
Cunningham, C. 1981. *Victorian and Edwardian Town Halls*. London.
Curwen, J. S. 1880. *Studies in worship-music, chiefly as regards congregational singing*. London.
    1885. *Studies in worship music, second series*. London.
Davison, H. 1912. *From Mendelssohn to Wagner*. London.
Dawe, D. 1987. *Organists of the City of London, 1666–1850*. London.
Dickson, W. E. 1881 (2nd edn 1882). *Practical organ-building*. London. Repr. Oxford, 1981.
The Dictionary of National Biography. 1885–1900. London. 1st Supplement 1901; 2nd Supplement 1912.
Dixon, R. and Muthesius, S. 1985. *Victorian architecture*. London.
Doncaster. *The organs and organists of Doncaster*. Doncaster, *c.* 1970.
Done, J. [1839]. *A complete treatise on the organ*. London.
Douglass, F. 1980. *Cavaillé-Coll and the musicians*. 2 vols. Sunbury.
The Ecclesiologist. Journal of the Cambridge Camden Society (1841–5), later the Ecclesiological Society (1846–68).
Edinburgh Encyclopaedia. 1830. Edinburgh.
Edinburgh Gazetteer. [Edinburgh, *c.* 1825.]
Edmonds, B. B. 1957–8. 'A sack of shakings', *Organ*, XXXVII, 140–7.
    1960. 'Once upon a time', *Organ Club Handbook*, VI, 42–57.
Edmonds, B. B. and Plumley, N. M. 1988. 'Thomas Elliot, organ-builder', *BIOSJ*, XII, 56–71.
Edmonds, B. B. and Thistlethwaite, N. J. 1976. '"An effect probably never before obtained . . ."', *Organ*, LV, 74–84.
Edwards, F. G. 1896. 'Bach's Music in England', *MT*, XXXVII: 585–7, 652–7, 722–6, 797–800.
    1898. 'Henry Willis', *MT*, XXXIX, 297–303.
Elvin, L. 1932. 'The organ of St Botolph's church at Boston in Lincolnshire', *Organ*, XII, 72–7.
    1962. 'The organs at the International Exhibition, 1862', *Organ*, XLII, 16–27.
    1968. *Forster and Andrews, organ builders*. Lincoln.
    1971. *Organ blowing, its history and development*. Lincoln.
    1973. *The Harrison story. Harrison and Harrison, organ builders, Durham*. Lincoln.
    1984. *Bishop and Son, organ builders*. Lincoln.
    1986. *Family enterprise: the story of some North Country organ builders*. Lincoln.
The English Musical Gazette. 1819. London.
The Examiner. 1808–81. London.
Frampton, H. A. 1960. 'The organ in the Music Hall, Kidderminster', *MO*, LXXXIV, 39–43.
Freeman, A. 1921a. 'An interesting survival: St Katharine Coleman', *Organ*, I, 31–5.
    1921b. *English organ-cases*. London.

1922a. 'The organs of St Paul's Cathedral', *Organ*, II, 1–15.

1922b. 'The organs of Bristol Cathedral', *Organ*, II, 65–73.

1924. 'The organ at the Foundling Hospital, London', *Organ*, III, 193–200.

1925. 'The organs of St James's Palace', *Organ*, IV, 193–202.

1926. *Father Smith, otherwise Bernard Schmidt, being an account of a seventeenth century organ maker*. London. (*See also*: Freeman, A. and Rowntree, J.)

1927. 'The organs of Bath Abbey', *Organ*, VI, 197–206.

1939. 'Organ cases of the Gothic Renaissance', *Organ*, XVIII, 140–9.

1944. 'Samuel Green', *Organ*, XXIII, 153–62.

1945. 'The Earl of Bute's machine organ', *Organ*, XXIV, 109–15.

Freeman, A. and Rowntree, J. 1977. *Father Smith*. Oxford. (New edn of Freeman 1926, with additions).

Gatens, W. J. 1986. *Victorian cathedral music in theory and practice*. Cambridge.

Gauntlett, H. J. 1846. *A description of the new organ erected in the church of St Olave, London Bridge, Southwark*. London.

Gawthrop's Journal. c. 1841. Liverpool.

The Gentleman's Magazine. 1731–1907. London.

Gill, C. 1952. *A history of Birmingham*. 2 vols. Oxford.

Gillingham, M. 1971. 'The organs and organ-cases of Gloucester Cathedral' in S. Evans (ed.), *Gloucester Cathedral Organ*, Gloucester, pp. 1–25.

1987. 'Rebuilding the Chichester organ', *The Organbuilder*, V, 32–7.

Grace, H. 1934. 'The organ' in H. Grace (ed.), *The new musical educator*. Second edn, vol. III, pp. 195–201. London.

Graves, C. L. 1926. *Hubert Parry, his life and works*. 2 vols. London.

Gray, J. 1837. *Letters to the editor of the 'Musical World' relative to the York organ*. London.

Greening, R. G. 1971. 'The organs at Armitage', *Organ*, L, 119–23.

1974. *The organs of Lichfield Cathedral*. Lichfield.

Grove, G. 1879–89. *A dictionary of music and musicians*. 4 vols. London. 6th edn (*The New Grove dictionary of music and musicians*) London, 1979.

Haggard, J. 1829–32. *Reports of cases argued and determined in the ecclesiastical courts at Doctors' Commons and in the High Court of Delegates*. 4 vols, vol. III, 1832. London.

Hamel, P. M. 1849. *Nouveau manuel complet du facteur d'orgues, ou traité théorique et pratique de l'art de construire les orgues*. 3 vols. Paris.

Hamilton, D. 1851. *Remarks on organ building and the causes of defective instruments*. Edinburgh.

Hand-book of the cathedral church of Ely; with some account of the conventual building. 1855. 3rd edn. Ely.

The Harmonicon. 1823–33. London.

Harvey, S. 1923. 'The organs of Canterbury Cathedral', *Organ*, III, 1–19.

Hawkins, J. 1776. *A general history of the science and practice of music*. 5 vols. London.

Heaton, J. 1835. *Walks through Leeds*. Leeds.

Henthorne, R. 1970. *Some matters musical in St Mary's parish church, St Neots*. St Neots.

Herefordshire. 1876. *Littlebury's directory and gazetteer of Herefordshire*. Hereford.

Hewitson, A. 1883. *History of Preston in the county of Lancashire*. Preston.

Hicklin, J. 1846. *The history of Chester Cathedral*. Chester.

Hill, D. G. 1988. *Henry Smart*. Schagen.

Hill, W. 1841. *Circular*. London.

Hill & Son. 1881. *List of principal organs built by Messrs. Wm. Hill & Son*. London.

Hinton, J. W. 1900. *Organ construction*. London.

1909. *Story of the electric organ*. London.

Hodges, F. H. 1896. *Edward Hodges*. New York and London.

Hooper, J. G. 1948. 'The organs and organists of St James's, Bristol', *Organ*, XXVIII, 75–82.

Hopkins, E. J. and Rimbault, E. F. 1855. *The organ, its history and construction.* 2nd edn 1870. 3rd edn 1877. London.

Hughes, R. 1955. *A Mozart pilgrimage.* London.

Humphries, C. and Smith, W. C. 1970. *Music publishing in the British Isles.* 2nd edn. Oxford.

Hunt, H. 1907. *Bristol Cathedral Organ.* Bristol.

Hurd, M. 1981. *Vincent Novello – and Company.* London.

Huybens, G. 1983. 'Liste des travaux exécutés par Aristide Cavaillé-Coll', *ISO Information,* no. 23, 43–55.

Instrumenta Ecclesiastica 1st series 1847; 2nd series. 1856. Published by the Ecclesiological late Cambridge Camden Society. London.

ISO Information. 1969–. Published by the International Society of Organbuilders. Lauffen/Neckar.

Jebb, J. 1843. *The choral service of the united Church of England and Ireland.* London.

Johnstone, K. I. 1978. *The Armley Schulze organ.* Leeds.

Kent, C. 1984. 'Sir Frederick Ouseley (1825–89)', *BIOSJ,* VIII, 36–50.

Kollman, A. F. C. 1799. *An essay on practical musical composition.* London.

Knott, J. 1973. *Brindley and Foster, organ builders, Sheffield, 1854–1939.* Bognor Regis.

Lahee, H. C. 1909. *The organ and its masters.* London.

Lampadius, W. A. 1876. (transl. W. A. Gage). *A life of Felix Mendelssohn Bartholdy.* London.

Langwill, L. G. and Boston, J. N. T. 1970. *Church and chamber barrel organs.* 2nd edn. Edinburgh.

Lascelles and Co's directory and gazetteer of Herefordshire. 1851. Hereford.

Latrobe, J. A. 1831. *The music of the church considered in its various branches, congregational and choral: an historical treatise for the general reader.* London.

Leeds. 1817–34. *General and commercial directory of the borough of Leeds.* Leeds.

Levien, J. M. 1942. *Impressions of W. T. Best (1826–1897).* London.

Lewis, T. C. 1897. *A protest against the modern development of unmusical tone.* London.

Lincoln, H. C. 1843. *Mr. H. C. Lincoln's new organ circular for 1843.* London.

London. 1820–. *Post Office London directory.* London.

The London diocesan calendar. 1863. London.

The London journal of arts and sciences. 1820–66. From 1855 known as *Newton's London Journal of arts and sciences.* London.

Mackenzie of Ord, A. C. N. 1979. 'The well-tuned organ. An introduction to keyboard temperaments in eighteenth and nineteenth century England', *BIOSJ,* III, 56–72.

Mackerness, E. D. 1964. *A social history of English music.* London.

Macrory, E. 1911. *Notes on the Temple organ.* 3rd edn. London.

Marr, P. (ed.) 1982. *The organ in Reading Town Hall: a symposium.* Reading.

Marsh, J. 1791. *Eighteen voluntaries.* London.

Mathew, A. G. 1952. 'A coronation organ', *Organ,* XXXI, 173–9.

Mathew's annual Bristol directory. 1815. Bristol.

Matthews, B. 1972. *The organs and organists of Salisbury Cathedral.* 2nd edn. Salisbury.
      1975. *The organs and organists of Winchester Cathedral.* 2nd edn. Winchester.

Matthews, W. R. and Atkins, W. M. 1957 (2nd edn 1964). *A history of St Paul's Cathedral* London.

Maxwell, A. 1837. *A letter to Jonathan Gray . . . concerning the York Minster organ.* London.

The Mechanics' Magazine. 1823–59. London.

Menzies, C. 1986. 'Not all tartan and haggis', *Organ Club Handbook,* 81–9.

Meyrick-Roberts, R. 1922. 'The founders of modern organ-building', *Organ,* II, 73–80.

The Monthly Magazine. 1796–1843. London.

Moore, J. N. 1987. *Edward Elgar, a creative life.* Oxford.

Morgan, R. T. 1912. *St Mary Redcliffe, Bristol, a short account of its organs.* Bristol.

The Morning Post. 1773–1902. London.

The Musical Gazette. 1856–9. London.

The Musical Journal. 1840. London.

The Musical News. 1891–1927. London.

Musical Opinion. 1878–. London.

The Musical Standard. 1862–1933. London.

The Musical Times. 1844–. London.

The Musical World. 1836–91. London.

Neale, J. M. 1843. *Church enlargement and church arrangement.* Cambridge.

Nettel, R. 1946. *The orchestra in England: a social history.* London.

New Grove dictionary of music and musicians. See: Grove, G.

Nicholson, S. H. 1907. *Carlisle Cathedral, its organs and organists.* Carlisle.

Norman, H. 1986. 'The Normans, 1860–1920', *BIOSJ*, x, 53–61.

Ochse, O. 1975. *The history of the organ in the United States.* Bloomington.

Oliver, D. J. 1966. 'The organ in the church of St John the Evangelist, Taunton', *Organ*, XLV, 163–70.

Ord-Hume, A. W. J. G. 1978. *Barrel Organ.* London.

1986. *Harmonium: the history of the reed organ and its makers.* London.

The Organ. 1921–. London.

The Organbuilder. 1983–. Oxford.

The Organ Yearbook. 1970–. Amsterdam.

Ouseley, F. A. G., Willis, R. and Donaldson, J. 1853. *Crystal Palace Company, grand organ, preliminary report to the directors.* London.

Padgham, C. A. 1986. *The well-tempered organ.* Oxford.

Parson, W. 1826. *General and commercial directory of the borough of Leeds.* Leeds.

Patents for inventions: abridgement of specifications, class 88, music and musical instruments. 1855–1930. London.

Pearce, C. W. 1909. *Notes on old London city churches, their organs, organists, and musical associations.* London.

[1910]. *The life and works of Edward John Hopkins.* London.

1912. *Notes on English organs of the period 1800–1810 . . . taken chiefly from the MS. of Henry Leffler.* London.

1926. 'A few reminiscences of organ enthusiasts of the past', *Organ*, v, 138–49.

1927. *The evolution of the pedal organ.* London.

The Penny Magazine. 1832–45. London.

Perkins, C. W. 1905. *A short account of the organ in the Town Hall, Birmingham.* Birmingham.

Pevsner, N. 1977. *The buildings of England: Herefordshire.* 2nd edn. London.

Plumley, N. M. 1981. *The organs and music masters of Christ's Hospital, Horsham.* Horsham.

Plumley, N. M. and Lees, J. 1988. *The organs and organists of Chichester Cathedral.* Chichester.

Pole, W. 1851. *Musical instruments in the Great Industrial Exhibition of 1851.* London.

Polko, E. 1869. (transl. Lady Wallace). *Reminiscences of Felix Mendelssohn-Bartholdy – a social and artistic biography.* London.

Port, M. H. 1961. *Six hundred new churches.* London.

The Practical Mechanic and Engineer's Magazine. 1841–7. Glasgow.

Proceedings of the Musical Association. 1874–. London.

Purey-Cust, A. P. 1899. *Organs and organists of York Minster.* York.

The Quarterly Musical Magazine and Review. 1818–28. London.

Quiney, A. 1979. *John Loughborough Pearson.* London.

Radcliffe, P. 1967. *Mendelssohn.* 2nd edn. London.

Rainbow, B. 1970. *The choral revival in the Anglican Church, 1839–1872.* London.

Redlich, H. F. 1952. 'The Bach revival in England: a neglected aspect of J. S. Bach', *Hinrichsen music book, year book 1952*, 287–300.

Rees, A. 1819. *The Cyclopaedia, or universal dictionary of arts, sciences, and literature*. London.

Renshaw, M. 1968. 'Anatomy of an organ', *Organ*, XLVIII, 81–94. (See also: Clayton and Renshaw)

    1970. 'Great George Street Chapel, Liverpool – and some other matters', *MO*, XCIII, 317–19.

The Rotunda. 1926–34. London.

Rowntree, J. 1978. 'Bernard Smith, organist and organ builder, his origins', *BIOSJ*, II, 10–20.

    1987. 'Lulworth Chapel and a missing Arne mass', *MT*, CXXVIII, 347–9.

Russell, R. 1939. 'The organ of Christ Church, Spitalfields', *Organ*, XIX, 113–20.

Sayer, M. 1974. *Samuel Renn, English organ builder*. Chichester.

    1976a. 'Industrialised organ building: a pioneer', *Organ Yearbook*, VII, 90–100.

    1976b. 'Kirtland and Jardine of Manchester', *Organ*, LIV, 169–76.

    1980. 'English organ design in the Industrial Revolution', *BIOSJ*, IV, 90–9.

Scholes, P. A. 1944. *The Oxford companion to music*. 5th edn. London.

Scott, G. G. 1879. *Personal and professional recollections*. London.

Seidel, J. J. 1852. *The organ and its construction: a systematic hand-book for organists, organ-builders, etc.* London. [Eng. transl. of *Die Orgel und ihr Bau*. Breslau, 1843.]

Shaw, F. W. 1933. 'The story of a Northampton organ', *The Northampton County Magazine*, VI, 83–4, 106–8.

Shaw, W. 1976. *The organists and organs of Hereford Cathedral*. Hereford.

Shepherdson, W. 1873. *The organ: hints on its construction, purchase, and preservation*. London.

Smith, T. 1833. *A topographical and historical account of the parish of St. Mary-le-bone*. London.

Snow, H. 1931. 'The organs of Chesterfield Parish Church', *Organ*, X, 237–41.

    1926. 'Leeds Town Hall organ', *Organ*, VI, 81–9.

    1935. 'The organ in Brunswick Chapel, Leeds', *Organ*, XIV, 172–6.

Spark, W. 1852. 'Choirs and organs: their proper position in churches' in W. Spark, *Musical reminiscences*, London, 1892, 251–66.

    1881. *Life of Henry Smart*. London.

    1888. *Musical memories*. London.

    1892. *Musical reminiscences, past and present*. London.

Statham, H. H. 1909. *The organ and its position in musical art*. London.

Stiller, J. 1984. 'A Victorian export to Australia: the Brindley organ in the Albert Hall, Launceston, Tasmania', *BIOSJ*, VIII, 18–25.

Stimpson, J. 1845 (2nd edn 1846). *A short description of the Great Organ in the Town Hall, Birmingham*. Birmingham.

    [1880]. *A concise history of the Town Hall organ, Birmingham*. Birmingham.

Sumner, G. 1977. 'Thomas Wilkinson of Kendal and the organ in Preston Public Hall', *BIOSJ*, I, 26–47.

Sumner, W. L. 1931. *The organs of St Paul's Cathedral*. London.

    1937. 'The organs of St Mary's Parish Church, Nottingham', *Organ*, XVII, 30–7.

    1952 (3rd edn 1962). *The organ, its evolution, principles of construction, and use*. London.

    1954. 'The Cavaillé-Coll organ in the Parr Hall, Warrington', *Organ*, XXXIV, 80–4.

    1955. *Father Henry Willis, organ builder, and his successors*. London.

    1957a and b. 'The Schulze family', *Organ*, XXXVII, 8–14, 96–100.

Sutton, F. H. 1866. *Some account of the mediaeval organ case still existing at Old Radnor*. London.

    1872 (3rd edn 1883). *Church organs: their position and construction*. [Sutton 1866 incorporated as an appendix, hence 1872 is reckoned to be the 2nd edn]. London.

[Sutton, J.] 1847 (repr. Oxford, 1979). *A short account of organs built in England from the reign of King Charles the Second to the present time*. London.

Temperley, N. 1977. *Jonathan Gray and church music in York, 1770–1840*. York.

1979a. *The music of the English parish church*. 2 vols. Cambridge.

1979b. 'Organs in English parish churches', *Organ Yearbook*, x, 83–100.

1979c. 'The Bach revival', *NG*, I, 883–6.

1981. 'Cathedral music' in N. Temperley (ed.), *The romantic age, 1800–1914 (Athlone History of Music in Britain*, vol. v), 171–213. London.

Thistlethwaite, N. J. 1976. '"E pur si muove" – English organ-building 1820–1851', *Organ Yearbook*, VII, 101–15.

1977. 'Source materials from the early 19th century', *BIOSJ*, I, 75–100.

1983. *The organs of Cambridge*. Oxford.

1984. *Birmingham Town Hall organ*. Birmingham.

Thompson's Cyclopaedia of Useful Arts. 1851. London.

Thompson, P. 1850. *The theory and practice of just intonation illustrated by the description of the enharmonic organ*. London.

Thompson, P. 1971. *William Butterfield*. London.

Tonic Sol-fa Reporter. London.

Wallace, Lady (transl.) 1863. *Letters of Felix Mendelssohn Bartholdy*. London.

Warren, J. *c.* 1838 (2nd edn 1842). *Hamilton's catechism of the organ*. London.

Wedgwood, J. I. 1935. 'Was Barker the inventor of the pneumatic lever?', *Organ*, XIV, 49–52.

Wesley, E. 1875 (repr. 1957). *Letters of Samuel Wesley to Mr. Jacobs, organist of Surrey Chapel, relating to the introduction into this country of the works of John Sebastian Bach*. London.

West Riding. 1867. *Post Office trades directory, West Riding of Yorkshire*. Sheffield.

White, J. F. 1962. *The Cambridge Movement*. Cambridge.

White, W. 1838, 1870. *History, gazetteer, and directory of the West-Riding of Yorkshire*. 2 vols. Sheffield.

1851. *General directory of Kingston upon Hull, and the City of York*. York.

1871, 1872. *General and commercial directory . . . of Sheffield*. Sheffield.

Whitworth, R. 1929. 'The organs of Doncaster parish church', *Organ*, IX, 42–9.

1945. 'The organ in Wallasey Parish Church', *Organ*, XXV, 54–9.

1930 (3rd edn 1948). *The electric organ*. London.

Wickens, D. C. 1974. 'A remarkable Worcester organ', *Organ*, LIII, 5–12.

1975. 'Dating', *Organ*, LIV, 32–40.

1977. 'Second enclosure', *Organ*, LV, 160–5.

1978. 'The organs of Stalybridge', *Organ*, LVII, 13–16.

1987. *The instruments of Samuel Green*. London.

Willemant, T. 1844. *An account of the restoration of the collegiate chapel of St George, Windsor*. London.

Williams, P. F. 1962. *English organ music and the English organ under the first four Georges*. Unpubl. D.Mus. dissertation, University of Cambridge.

1963. 'J. S. Bach and English organ music', *Music and Letters*, XLIV, 140–51.

1966. *The European organ, 1450–1850*. London.

Wilson, M. 1968. *The English chamber organ*. Oxford.

Work in Bristol: a series of sketches of the chief manufactories in the city. 1883. Bristol.

York Gazette. 1823–1954. York.

3 Organ references

The references are intended to direct the reader to contemporary (or more recent) sources from which an accurate account of an organ's specifications may be derived. No attempt has been made to provide a comprehensive bibliography for the instruments listed and anyone wishing to embark on a detailed study would need to consult a wider range of material than is covered here. Where known, the name of the builder (see abbreviations below) and the date of his work is given. The references are arranged in three divisions: London (City), Greater London and Outside London.

ABBREVIATIONS

AV	Avery		HDV	Hill and Davison
BAN	Banfield		HO	Holland
BEV	Bevington		HR	Hugh Russell
BEW	Bewsher and Fleetwood		HT	Holt
BLY	Blyth		HW	Henry Willis
BOO	Booth		JCB	J. C. Bishop
BRI	Brindley		J	Jardine
BRY	Bryceson		JD	James Davis
BUC	Buckingham		JN	Nicholson of Worcester
CA	Charles Allen		JO	Jones of Sheffield
CC	Cavaillé-Coll		JS	John Smith
CH	Crang and Hancock		JSJ	John Smith, junior
D	Dobson		JW	Walker
E	Elliot		KJ	Kirtland and Jardine
EAG	Eagles		NI	Nicholls
EH	Elliot and Hill		NR	Nicholson of Rochdale
ES	Schulze		PC	Conacher
EW	Wadsworth		PIL	Pilcher
F	Flight		R	Robson
FA	Forster and Andrews		RB	Richard Bridge
FR	Flight and Robson		REN	Renn (and Boston)
G	Gray		SG	Samuel Green
GD	Gray and Davison		SNE	Snetzler
GE	George England		TCL	T. C. Lewis
GPE	George Pike England		TEL	Telford of Dublin
H	Hill		TP	Thomas Parker
HAR	Harrison of Rochdale		TR	Timothy Russell
HCL	H. C. Lincoln		WA	William Allen
HD	Holdich		WS	Wood and Small of Edinburgh

A   LONDON (CITY)

Christchurch, Newgate Street

EH 1827, 1831, 1834. *MW* VIII, 1838: 279–81; Plumley 1981: 48–52.
H 1838. MS 79: 8.

Christ's Hospital

EH 1830. Warren 1842: 56; MS 79: 198.

Crosby Hall, Bishopsgate

JCB 1834 (proposal). MS 56.
HCL 1842. Lincoln 1843.

St Andrew-by-the-Wardrobe

G 1805. Pearce 1909: 164–5.

St Dunstan-in-the-East

G 1820. MS 79: 10.

St Dunstan-in-the-West

R 1834. MS 79: 37; Pearce 1909: 185.

St Edmund, Lombard Street

JCB 1833. Warren 1842: 80; HRI: 455–6.

St Katherine by the Tower

SG 1778. MS 76: 35; Warren 1842: 65.

St Mary Abchurch

JCB 1822. MS 48.

St Mary Woolnoth

Butler 1835. *MSt* v, 1866: 99–100.

St Mary-at-Hill

H 1848. Above, pp. 222–5.

St Matthew, Friday Street

GE 1762. Pearce 1909: 213.

St Michael Cornhill

R 1849. HRI: 453–4.

St Olave Jewry

JW 1846. MS 79: 3.

St Paul's Cathedral

To 1855. *EMG* I January 1819: 5–8; *Times* 10 November 1828; *CR* xv, 1833: 430–1; Warren 1842: 53–4; MS 62: 203–4; HRI: 445–6; Elvin 1984: 162–6.
HW 1863. HR2: 450–1.
HW 1872. Above, pp. 503–5.

St Peter-upon-Cornhill

H 1840. Above, pp. 215–22.

St Sepulchre, Holborn

G 1817. *CR* xv, 1833: 625; Pearce 1909: 13 (incorrect attribution).
G 1826, 1828, 1834. MS I: 5, 49; MS 74: 4 February 1834; *MW* vIII, 1838: 279–81.
GD 1849. MS 5: f.40.

St Stephen Walbrook

G 1826. MS I: 50; *CR* xvi, 1834: 111.

St Swithun, London Stone

G 1809. MS 79: 25.

St Vedast, Foster Lane

JW 1853. MS 79: 26.

B　GREATER LONDON

Acre Lane, Clapham: new church

JCB *c*. 1828. *CR* xv, 1833: 743.

Agricultural Hall, Islington

HW 1863. *See*: Crystal Palace, International Exhibition 1862.

Alexandra Palace

HW 1873, 1875. *MW* xLVI, 1868: 406; HR3: 468–70.

All Hallows, Tottenham

E 1817. MS 79: 73.

All Saints, Gordon Square

H 1846. MS 79: 113.

All Saints, Margaret Street

H 1859. Above, pp. 485–6.

All Souls, [Langham Place] St Marylebone

JCB 1824. MS 53; MS 79: 81.

Apollonicon, St Martin's Lane

FR 1817. Ord-Hume 1978: 100–27.

Bedford Chapel

GD 1844. MS 4: f.23; MS 79: 93.

Chapel Royal, St James's Palace

E 1819. Above, pp. 444–5 (Crick).
HDV 1837. Above, pp. 456–7.

Chapel Royal, Whitehall

E 1814. Buckingham LIII: 81.

Christ Church, St George's-in-the-East

GD 1841. Warren 1842: 76.

Christ Church, Spitalfields

RB 1735. *CR* XV, 1833: 681–2.
HCL 1837. *MW* VIII, 1838: 279–81.
GD 1852. HRI: 459–60.

Crystal Palace

Great Exhibition 1851. Pole 1851: 43–81.
Handel Festival 1857. Above, pp. 477–9.
International Exhibition 1862. Elvin 1962.

Exeter Hall, Strand

JW 1839. *Musical Journal* I, 1840: 35, 62;
    Warren 1842: 57–8; MS 79: 197.

Foundling Hospital

TP 1768. Freeman 1924: 195.
BEV 1855. *MW* XXXIII, 1855: 677.

Hanover Square, concert room

E 1804. Pearce 1912: 161.
GD 1853. MS 6: f.47.

Holy Trinity, Brompton

JW 1848. MS 17: 29.

Holy Trinity, Gray's Inn Road

H 1840. MS 79: 93.

Holy Trinity, Newington [Southwark]

TR 1824. MS 79: 176.

Holy Trinity, Paddington

JCB 1846. MS 63: 30 July 1846.

Holy Trinity, St Marylebone

JCB 1827. MS 79: 80.

Holy Trinity, Sydenham

H 1866. MS 13: 20.

King's College, Strand

HW 1854 (?). Benham 1931: 236.

Lincoln's Inn Chapel

H 1856. MS 12: 339, 342; *MW* XXXIV, 1856:
    787–8.

Opera House, Covent Garden

SG 1794. Pearce 1912: 160.

Philanthropic Society Chapel, Southwark

G 1825. MS 78: 326.

Portland Chapel

H 1847. MS 12: 181; MS 79: 87.

Portuguese Chapel, South Street

GPE 1808. Pearce 1912: 104.

Royal Albert Hall, Kensington Gore

HW 1871. HR3: 463–5.

*Royal Panopticon of Science and Art, Leicester
    Square*

H 1853. Above, pp. 212–14.

St Andrew, Wells Street

H 1847 and 1849. MS 12: 206, 225, 241; MS 79: 83.

St Anne, Limehouse

HR 1811. *CR* XVI, 1834: 568–9; Pearce 1912: 102.
GD 1851. Above, pp. 475–6.

St Barnabas, Kensington

JW 1856. *MG* I, 1856: 273.

St Barnabas, Pimlico

F 1849. MS 79: 35.

St Barnabas, Stockwell

H 1850. MS 12: 252.

St Dunstan, Stepney

HR 1808. Pearce 1912: 114.

St George, Bloomsbury

HO 1788. Pearce 1912: 92.

St George, Camberwell

HCL 1824. *CR* XVIII, 1836: 108.
JCB 1824 (proposal). MS 49.

St George, Southwark

? 1808. MS 76: 41.

St George's Cathedral (RC), Southwark

JCB 1848. MS 62: 125–6.

St Giles, Camberwell

JCB 1844. MS 61: 101–2, 114–15; HRI: 482–3.

St James, Bermondsey

JCB 1829. MS 55; *CR* XVII, 1835: 501–2; HRI: 486; *MT* L, 1909: 517–20.

St James, Clapham

JCB 1832. MS 79: 165.

St James, Clerkenwell

GPE 1792. Pearce 1912: 93.

St James, Piccadilly

JCB 1852. MS 79: 112; HRI: 473.

St James's Hall

GD 1858. MS 8: job 10086.

St John, Hackney

GPE 1797, G 1828. Pearce 1912: 99; *CR* XV, 1833: 743.

St John, Hampstead

HW 1852. MS 79: 78.

St John, Hyde Park Crescent (Paddington)

H 1865. Above, pp. 401–2.

St John, Waterloo Road (Lambeth)

JCB 1824. MS 51; *CR* XVIII, 1836: 41; HRI: 481.

St John's Wood Chapel

GD 1842. MS 3: f.36; MS 79: 82.

St Luke, Chelsea

NI/G 1824. MS I: 39; MS 86: 2; *MW* VIII, 1838: 279–81.

St Luke, Old Street

GD 1844, 1852. HRI: 461.

St Margaret, Westminster

AV 1804. MS 76: 46; Pearce 1912: 119.

St Mark, Clerkenwell
G 1828. MS 1: 65; Warren 1842: 69.

St Mark, Kennington
G 1831. MS 1: 89; MS 79: 159.

St Mark, North Audley Street
JCB 1825. MS 79: 106.

St Mark, Pentonville
See: St Mark, Clerkenwell.

St Mark, St John's Wood
GD 1847. MS 5: ff.5–6; MS 79: 82.

St Martin-in-the-Fields
G 1800. Pearce 1912: 107.
BEV 1854. *MW* XXXII, 1854: 803, 835–6.

St Mary, Bryanston Square (St Marylebone)
JCB 1824. MS 52.

St Mary, Moorfields (RC)
BEV *c*. 1830. Warren 1842: 74.

St Mary, Stoke Newington
GD 1858. MS 8: job 10088; HR3: 504.

St Mary, Walthamstow
CA 1845. MS 80: 97.

St Mary, Wanstead
H 1847. MS 12: 214, 215.

St Mary, Whitechapel
D 1817, 1820. MS 76: 53.

St Marylebone Parish Church
G 1818. MS 77: 11; MS 79: 80.

St Mary Magdalene, Holloway Road, Islington
GPE 1814. MS 79: 62.

St Mary Magdalene, Peckham
GD 1841. MS 3: f.34.

St Matthias, Stoke Newington
HW 1853. MS 79: 127.

St Michael, Chester Square
R 1845. MS 79: 33; HRI: 478–9.

St Michael, Highgate
GD 1842. MS 3: f.41.

St Olave, Southwark
HCL/H 1844–6. Above, pp. 508–10.

St Pancras Parish Church
G 1822, 1832, 1835. MS 1: 26; MS 79: 85.
GD 1865. *See*: Birmingham, Music Hall.

St Patrick, Soho
G *c*. 1810. MS 79: 208; Pearce 1912: 108.

St Paul, Covent Garden
G 1798. Pearce 1912: 95.
BEV 1862. *MW* XL, 1862: 501.

St Paul, Wilton Place, Knightsbridge
GD 1843. Above, pp. 472–4.

St Peter, Eaton Square
TCL 1874. Above, pp. 493–5.

St Peter, Saffron Hill
H 1836. MS 69; MS 79: 108.

St Peter, Walworth
HCL 1825. *CR* XVIII, 1836: 175.

St Philip, Waterloo Place

JD 1820 (?) and JCB 1832. *CR* XVIII, 1836: 434.

St Saviour, Southwark

HR 1800. Pearce 1912: 59.
JD 1818. *CR* XV, 1833: 683; MS 79: 151.
TCL 1897. *Organ* XII, 1932: 96–7.

St Stephen, Hampstead

HW 1871. No printed source known (organ now lost).

St Stephen, Islington

H 1854. MS 12: 318.

St Stephen, Lambeth

H 1861. MS 12: 399.

St Thomas the Rolls Chapel

HCL 1842. Lincoln 1843.

Surrey Chapel, Blackfriars Road, Southwark

E (no date). Pearce 1912: 105.

Temple Church

JCB 1843. Macrory 1911: 39; Elvin 1984: 179.
ES 1859. HR2: 454–5.
FA 1878. Macrory 1911: 46–7.

Union Chapel, Islington

HW 1877. Above, pp. 426–32.

Wesleyan Chapel, Poplar

H 1848. MS 12: 229; MS 79: 133; HRI: 459.

Westminster Abbey

E, EH, H 1820–42. *Times* 10 November 1828; *CR* XV, 1833: 498–9; Warren 1842: 54.
H 1848. MS 12: 207, 211; MS 79: 44.

C OUTSIDE LONDON

Amersham, St Mary

BRY 1852. MS 80: 20.

Armagh Cathedral

JW 1840. MS 81: 133.

Armitage, St Luke's Mission Church

H 1847. Greening 1971: 121.

Arundel Cathedral (R C)

H 1873. *West Sussex Gazette* 3 July 1873; Barnard 1954: *passim*; above, p. 524, n. 10.

Arundel, St Nicholas

G 1820. MS 81: 8.

Ashridge, Hertfordshire

E 1818. Above, p. 444.

Ashton-under-Lyne, St Michael and All Angels

H 1845. MS 12: 132, 137, 144, 149, 151, 153; MS 80: 163; HRI: 513.

Bath Abbey

JS 1836. Freeman 1927: 200.
H 1868. *CMR* VII, 1868: 103.

Bath, St Mary, Bathwick

G 1820. No source known (organ now in the Staatliches Institut für Musikforschung in Berlin).

Battle Abbey

BEV 1846. MS 81: 9.

Belfast, St Patrick

G 1840. MS 81: 135.

Belfast, Ulster Hall

H 1862. Above, pp. 398–401.

Belfast, Victoria Hall

R 1855. *MW* XXXIII, 1855: 84.

Birmingham, Christ Church

E 1815. Buckingham LIII: 80–1.

Birmingham, Music Hall

GD 1856. MS 7: job 10047; *MW* XXXIV, 1856:
556–7, 569–70.

Birmingham, St Gregory, Small Heath

H 1846. MS 80: 264.

Birmingham, St Martin

E 1822. MS 81: 21.

Birmingham, Town Hall

H 1834, 1837, 1840. Above, pp. 127–35.
H 1843, 1845, 1849. Thistlethwaite 1984:
13–19.

Bishop's Cannings, St Mary

GPE 1809. MS 81: 104.

Blackburn, Independent Chapel, Chapel Street

GD 1854. MS 6: ff.62–3.

Blackburn, St Mary

G 1828, 1832. MS 1: 63; MS 80: 168; Bertalot
1970: 2–4.

Bolton Town Hall

GD 1874. Above, pp. 488–9.

Boston, Centenary Chapel

GD 1850. MS 5: ff.47–9; HRI: 531–2.

Boston, St Botolph

NI 1820. Elvin 1932: 73.

Bradford, Eastbrook Chapel

H 1845. MS 12: 162; HRI: 520.

Bradford, St George's Hall

HT 1853, H 1856. *MG* I, 1856: 345.

Bradford, St James

GD 1844. MS 4: f.21.

Bradford-on-Avon, Holy Trinity

GPE 1800. MS 81: 105.

Brighton, St Paul

HD 1851. MS 81: 6.

Brighton, St Peter

NI 1818. MS 81: 3.

Bristol Cathedral

JS 1821. Hunt 1907: 9.

Bristol, Christ Church

JSJ (?) 1837. MS 80: 114.

Bristol, Lord Mayor's Chapel

JS 1830. MS 80: 106.

Bristol, St James

JS 1824. Above, pp. 457–8.

Bristol, St Michael

JS 1817. MS 80: 109.

Bristol, St Nicholas

JS 1821. MS 80: 106.

Bristol, St Stephen

JSJ 1836. Above, pp. 458–9.

Bromsgrove, St John the Baptist

E 1808. Buckingham LIII: 82.

Burnley, Wesleyan Chapel

GD 1845. MS 4: f.49.

Bury, St Thomas

KJ 1868. *MW* XLVI, 1868: 249.

Calcutta, St John (?)

H 1844. MS 12: 136, 158.

Cambridge, Jesus College

JCB 1849. MS 62: 7–8; MS 80: 30.

Cambridge, King's College

AV 1803, H 1834. *Cambridge General Advertizer*
    22 May 1839; MS 80: 28; Pearce 1912: 78.
H 1860. MS 12: 364, 382.

Cambridge, St Andrew the Less

? 1854 (?). Freeman 1939: 148;
    Thistlethwaite 1983: 70.

Cambridge, St John's College

HDV 1839. Above, pp. 452–3.
H 1869. MS 26.

Cambridge, St Luke

H 1855 (St Mary, Whitechapel). MS 12: 316,
    320, 330.

Cambridge, St Mary the Great (University Organ)

AV 1805. *Cambridge General Advertizer* 10
    April 1839; MS 80: 24.
H 1870. MS 13: 70, 74.

Cambridge, Trinity College

AV 1801. MS 76: 74; MS 80: 23; *Cambridge
    General Advertizer*, 22 May 1839; Cobb
    1913: 23–4.
FR 1819, G 1836. MS 27; Cobb: 24–5, 26–8.
H 1855. MS 12: 333.
H 1871. HR3: 568–9.

Canterbury Cathedral

H 1849. Harvey 1923: 12–14.

Carlisle Cathedral

AV 1806. Buckingham LII: 13–14.
HW 1856. Above, pp. 487–8.

Cashel Cathedral

BEV 1846. MS 81: 133.

Cheadle, St Giles

H 1850. MS 12: 252; MS 80: 261.

Chelmsford, St Mary

HR 1811. Pearce 1912: 133.

Chester Cathedral

GD 1844. *MW* XVIII, 1843: 388.

Chester, St John

HDV 1838. Warren 1842: 93–4.

Chesterfield, St Mary and All Saints

JO 1851. MS 80: 73.

Chichester Cathedral

PIL 1829, GD 1844. MS 2: f.17; MS 81: 1.

Clifton, Christ Church

JW 1849. MS 17: 57; MS 80: 110.

Clifton, Holy Trinity

G 1838. *MW* IX, 1838: 264; MS 80: 110.

Clifton, St Andrew

JS 1822. MS 80: 110.

Clithero, St Michael (RC)

KJ 1858. *MG* III, 1858: 269.

Cork, – ? –

GD 1841. MS 3: f.32.

Cottenham, All Saints

H 1847. MS 80: 35.

Cranbrook, St Dunstan

HW 1854. HR1: 545.

Croydon, St John the Baptist

AV 1794. Pearce 1912: 135.
E 1819. Buckingham LIII: 84–5.

Demerara, St George's Cathedral

GD 1841. MS 3: f.40.

Derby, All Saints

E 1808. Buckingham LIII: 31.

Doncaster, St George

BUC 1823. Buckingham LII: 51.
ES 1862. Above, pp. 490–2.

Dorchester, St Peter

JCB 1823. Buckingham LIII: 22.

Dorking, St Martin

EH 1831. MS 11: f.18; MS 79: 171.

Dublin, St Audeon

JW 1861. MS 20: 15.

Dublin, Trinity College

TEL 1838. *MW* VIII, 1838: 268; MS 81: 128.

Dundee, Kinnaird Hall

FA 1864. Above, pp. 482–4.

Durham Cathedral

GPE 1815. Buckingham LII: 7; MS 80: 87.
HW 1876. HR3: 552.

Easton-on-the-Hill Parish Church

HD 1849. Above, pp. 468–9.

Edgeley, St Matthew

EW 1865. *MW* XLIII, 1865: 40.

Edinburgh, Music Hall

H 1843. Above, pp. 461–2.

Edinburgh University, Music Room

H 1861. *MW* XXXIX, 1861: 174–7; HR2:
   560–1.

Ely Cathedral

EH 1831. MS 11: f.21.
H 1851. MS 12: 248, 277; HR1: 539.

Epsom, St Martin and St John

JW 1856. *MG* I, 1856: 7.

Eton College, Chapel

G 1841. MS 3: f.3.
GD 1852. *MW* XXX, 1852: 497–8.

Everingham, Catholic Chapel

CA 1837 (?). Above, pp. 449–50.

Everton, St George

BEW 1845. MS 80: 170.

Ewell, St Mary the Virgin

HW 1867. *CMR* VI, 1867: 50.

Ewelme, St Mary

H 1840. MS 12: 87, 103.

Exeter, St David

FR 1820. MS 80: 60.

Gateshead, St Mary

WS 1825. MS 80: 89.

Glasgow City Hall

GD 1853. Above, pp. 476–7.

Glasgow Public Hall

TCL 1877. HR3: 605–6.

Gloucester Cathedral

JCB 1831. Gillingham 1971: 12.
HW 1847. MS 80: 101.

Gloucester, Shire Hall

JN 1849. HR1: 495–6.

Great Yarmouth, St Nicholas

GPE 1812. Pearce 1912: 88.

Halifax, St John Baptist

H 1838 (proposal). MS 12: 36.

Halstead, St Andrew

BRI 1862. *MSt* I, 1862: 26–7.

Harberton, St Andrew

HW 1857. *MG* II, 1857: 503.

Henley-on-Thames, St Mary the Virgin

HD 1855. *MW* XXXII, 1854: 756.

Hereford, All Saints

HCL 1826. MS 80: 127.

Hereford Cathedral

E 1806. MS 38: 163; MS 39: 107.
JCB 1832. MS 39: 372–3; *MT* XLI, 1900: 300.
GD 1862. MS 9: job 10167; HR2: 494–5.

Huddersfield, Buxton Road Chapel

R *c.* 1850. HR1: 516–17.

Huddersfield, Highfield Chapel

JW 1854. HR1: 517–18.

Hull, Beverley Road Wesleyan Chapel

FA 1862. Elvin 1968: 43.

Hull, St John

E 1815. Buckingham LII: 13.

Hull, St Stephen

H 1847. MS 12: 212; MS 81: 74.

Jamaica Cathedral

JW 1847. MS 17: job no. 366.

Kidderminster, St George

EH 1828. MS 11: f.2.

Kidderminster Town Hall

H 1855. Above, pp. 227–9.

Kinlet, St John Baptist

JCB 1840. MS 60.

Lambourn, St Michael and All Angels

HW 1858. Byard 1967: 177–80.

Lancaster, St Mary

GPE 1811. MS 81: 153.

Launceston, Tasmania, Albert Hall

BRI 1861. Above, pp. 492–3.

Leeds, Brunswick Chapel

BOO 1828, *c.* 1850. *Leeds Mercury* 6
   September 1828; MS 81: 66; HRI: 521.

Leeds, Oxford Place Wesleyan Chapel

H 1837. Warren 1842: 89.

Leeds, St Peter's Chapel

BOO 1838. Warren 1842: 89–90; MS 81: 65.

Leeds Town Hall

GD 1859. Above, pp. 480–2.

Leicester, St Margaret

CH 1773. Buckingham LIII: 119.

Leicester, St Mary

JCB 1824. MS 50.

Lichfield Cathedral

SG 1790. Pearce 1912: 67.
HD 1861. Above, pp. 469–70.

Lincoln Cathedral

WA 1826, CA 1851. MS 44; HR2: 531–2.

Liverpool, Great George Street Chapel

H 1841. Above, pp. 467–8.

Liverpool, Hope Street Chapel

GD 1856. MS 6: ff.34–5.

Liverpool, Mechanics' Institute

H 1843. MS 12: 132, 134, 142.

Liverpool, St Francis Xavier

GD 1849. MS 5: ff.41–2; MS 80: 162.

Liverpool, St George's Hall

HW 1855. Above, pp. 135–49.

Liverpool, St Nicholas

G 1833. MS 1: 112; MS 80: 166.

Liverpool, St Paul, Toxteth Park

BEW 1847. MS 80: 169.
BAN 1853. *MW* XXXI, 1853: 540–1.

Liverpool, St Saviour

GD 1840. MS 3: f.11.

Llandaff Cathedral

GD 1861. MS 8: job 10119; HR3: 581 (date
   incorrect).

Louth, St James

GD 1857. MS 7: 10078; *MG* II, 1857: 571.

Lowther Castle

SNE (?) *c.* 1780. Buckingham LIII: 120.

Ludlow, St Laurence

GD 1860. MS 8: job 10113; HR3: 563.

Macclesfield, St George

REN 1824. MS 80: 48; Sayer 1974: 7, 72.

Manchester Cathedral

H 1871. HR3: 603–4.

Manchester, Church of the Holy Name

H 1871. Above, pp. 500–1.

Manchester, Cross Street Chapel

GD 1846. MS 4: f.51.

Manchester, Free Trade Hall

KJ 1857. HR2: 508–9.

Manchester, Henshaw's Blind Asylum

KJ 1866. *MW* XLIV, 1866: 763.

Manchester, Holy Trinity, Hulme

KJ 1852. HRI: 511.

Manchester, Moseley Street Chapel

GD 1843. MS 4: f.7.

Manchester, Radnor Street Chapel

H 1850. MS 12: 254.

Manchester, St Luke, Cheetham Hill

H 1839. Above, pp. 466–7.

Manchester, St Mary, Hulme

H 1858. MS 12: 362.

Manchester, St Patrick

GD 1843. MS 4: f.5.

Manchester, St Paul, Withington

HCL 1843. Lincoln 1843.

Manchester, St Peter

KJ 1856. Above, pp. 484–5.

Manchester, Zion Chapel, Hulme

H 1847. MS 12: 216, 217.

Melbourne, Australia, Town Hall

H 1872. Above, pp. 497–9.

Monk, Dr

H 1866. MS 13: 23.

Montreal Cathedral, Canada

E 1816. Buckingham LIII: 79–80.
H 1858. MS 12: 372.

Newark, St Mary Magdalene

GPE 1804. Buckingham LII: 50; Pearce 1912: 144; MS 80: 208.
JCB 1835. MS 58.
HW 1866. *MSt* V, 1866: 7.

Newcastle-upon-Tyne, St Mary's Cathedral (RC)

TCL 1869. HR3: 560–2.

Newcastle-upon-Tyne, St Thomas

EH 1831. MS 11: f.25; MS 80: 282.

Newcastle-upon-Tyne, Town Hall

GD 1859. HR3: 562.

Newfoundland, Canada, St John's Cathedral

R 1853. HRI: 565.

Northampton, All Saints

H *c*. 1845. MS 12: 156, 157; MS 80: 196; HRI: 542.

Norwich Cathedral

JCB 1834. MS 57.

Nottingham, Halifax Place Wesleyan Chapel

GD 1847. Above, pp. 474–5.

Nottingham, Holy Trinity

JW 1845. *Nottingham Journal* 27 June 1845.

Nottingham, Mechanics' Hall

BEV 1849. Above, pp. 462–3.
H 1869. HR3: 557.

Nottingham, St James

E 1816. Buckingham LII: 53.

Nottingham, St Mary

BUC 1839. Buckingham LII: 52.
JCB 1871. HR3: 555–6.

Nottingham, St Peter
BUC 1826. Buckingham LII: 53.

Oldham, – ? –
GD 1844. MS 4: f.14.

Oldham Parish Church
EH 1830. MS 11: f.20; MS 80: 164; HRI: 515–16.

Oldham, St Thomas Werneth
J 1869. *MW* XLVII, 1869: 495.

Oxford, Christ Church Cathedral
GD 1847. MS 5: f.15.

Oxford, Magdalen College
GD 1855. MS 6: ff.64–6; *MW* XXXIII, 1855: 130–1; HRI: 493.

Oxford, Wadham College
HW 1862. Above, p. 505.

Pershore Abbey
HR 1826. MS 81: 47.

Peterborough Cathedral
WA 1809. MS 80: 195. Pearce 1912: 71.
H 1870. MS 13: 50.

Plymouth, St Andrew
HCL 1827. Buckingham LIII: 120.

Preston, St George
HW 1865. Above, pp. 421–6.

Preston, St Walburgh
H 1853. MS 12: 297, 299.

Preston, (Kent) St Mildred
EAG 1858. *Eccl* XIX, 1858: 219–20.

Reading Town Hall
HW 1864, 1882. Above, pp. 505–6.

Redhill, St John
TR 1850. MS 79: 174.

Richmond (Yorks), St Mary
GPE 1811. Pearce 1912: 148.

Ripon Cathedral
TCL 1878. HR3: 575–6.

Runcorn, St Paul's Wesleyan Chapel
EW 1866. *CMR* V, 1866: 164.

Ryde, Holy Trinity
BEV/HD 1835. MS 80: 124.

St Albans Abbey
G 1820. MS 80: 129; *Hants Advertizer* 26 December 1868 [*sic*]; Freeman and Rowntree 1977: 50.
H 1861. Above, pp. 499–500.

St Asaph Cathedral
H 1859. MS 12: 379.

St David's Cathedral
HCL 1843. Lincoln 1843; MS 81: 111; HRI: 554.

St Neots, St Mary
HD 1855. Henthorne 1970: 7–8.

St Petersburg, British Embassy Chapel
H 1843. MS 12: 108, 110 (?), 120, 124; *MP* 2 May 1843.

Salisbury Cathedral

SG 1792. Pearce 1912: 72.
BLY 1823. Buckingham LIV: 42; Matthews
    1972: 15.
HW 1877. MS 87; HR3: 534.

Scone Palace, Long Gallery

E 1813. Buckingham LIII: 37; LIV 44–5.

Selby Abbey

REN 1825. MS 81: 72; Sayer 1974: 73.

Sevenoaks, St Nicholas

AV 1798. Pearce 1912: 151.

Sheffield, Albert Hall

CC 1873. Spark 1892: 193–8.

Sheffield, St John, Chapeltown

BRI 1863. *MSt* I, 1863: 271.

Sheffield, St Peter

GPE 1805. Buckingham LII: 50.

Sheffield, St Philip

H 1840. Warren 1842: 98–9.

Sherborne Abbey

GD 1856. MS 6: ff.59–61; *MW* XXXIV, 1856:
    182–3.

Southwell Minster

BUC 1821. Buckingham LII: 55.

Stalybridge, St Paul

H 1844. MS 12: 146.

Stanwix, St Michael and All Angels

H 1841. MS 12: 102, 105.

Stockport Parish Church

E *c.* 1808. MS 80: 43.
JD 1823. Buckingham LII: 178.

Stockport, St Thomas

REN 1834. MS 80: 48.

Stockport, Sunday School

E 1811. Buckingham LIII: 84.
KJ 1853. HR2: 511–12.

Stratford-upon-Avon, Holy Trinity

H 1841. MS 12: 43, 80; Warren 1842: 97;
    HRI: 499.

Stretford, – ? –

GD 1845. MS 4: f.43.

Sydney, Australia, St Andrew's Cathedral

H 1866. MS 13: 17; *CMR* VII, 1866: 242.

Sydney, Australia, Town Hall

H 1890. Audsley 1905, II: 721–4.

Taunton, Holy Trinity

H 1845. MS 12: 170; MS 80: 246.

Taunton, St John

HW 1864. Oliver 1966: 164.

Taunton, St Mary Magdalen

JS 1824. MS 80: 246.

Tenbury, St Mary

GD 1843. MS 4: f.3.

Tenbury, St Michael's College

F 1854. *MG* I, 1856: 308; Kent 1984: 49–50.
HAR 1869. Elvin 1973: 39–40.
HW 1874. Clutton 1948: 110.

Tewkesbury Abbey

HW 1848. MS 80: 103; HRI: 496.

Tiverton, St Peter

HW 1870. No printed source known.

Trinidad Cathedral

GD 1845. MS 4: ff.30–1.

Truro, St Mary

BUC 1836. Buckingham LII: 99–100.

Turvey, All Saints

HD 1838. *MW* VIII, 1838: 185.
H 1855. HRI: 541–2.

Walsall, St Matthew

SG 1773. Pearce 1912: 153–5.

Warwick, St Mary

BAN 1842. *MW* XVII, 1842: 150.

Waterford Cathedral

E 1817. Buckingham LIII: 80.
H 1858. MS 12: 366, 369; *MW* XXXVI, 1858: 604.

Wells Cathedral

HW 1857. Above, pp. 455–6.

West Bromwich Parish Church

H 1846. *See*: Birmingham, St Gregory, Small Heath.

West Bromwich, – ? –

GD 1847. MS 5: f.1.

Westbury, All Saints

GPE 1814. MS 81: 103.

West Derby, St Mary

GD 1862. MS 8: job 10124.

West Tofts, St Mary

JCB 1857. Freeman 1939: 148; Clutton and Niland 1982: 235–8.

Winchester Cathedral

AV 1799. Pearce 1912: 75.
BLY 1825, 1838. MS 80: 117; Matthews 1975: 10.
HW 1854. Above, pp. 417–21.

Windsor Castle, Music Room

GD 1841. Warren 1842: 91–2.

Windsor Castle, St George's Chapel

TO 1843. *CR* XVII, 1835: 109.
GD 1843. Willemant 1844: 50–2; MS 80: 9.
GD 1855. *MW* XXXIII, 1855: 798–9.

Windsor Castle, St George's Hall

H 1852. MS 12: 288; HRI: 491.

Wivenhoe, St Mary

F 1842. Lincoln 1843; MS 80: 97.

Woburn Church

TR 1836, 1848. MS 80: 3.

Woodbridge, St Mary

G 1818. Pearce 1912: 159.

Worcester Cathedral

H 1842. Above, pp. 460–1.

Worcester, Music Hall

JN 1854. Above, pp. 471–2.

Wrexham, St Giles

BEW 1827 (?). MS 81: 113; Freeman 1944: 161.

Yeovil, St John Baptist

JS 1840. MS 80: 248.

York Minster

To 1859: above, pp. 118–27.
H 1859. Above, pp. 495–7.

York Minster, nave organ

H 1863. HR3: 541–2.

Index